T0317712

A DICTIONARY OF TRANSPORT ANALYSIS

A Dictionary of Transport Analysis

Edited by

Kenneth Button

University Professor, School of Public Policy, George Mason University, USA

Henry Vega

George Mason University, USA

Peter Nijkamp

Professor of Regional, Urban and Environmental Economics, VU University Amsterdam, The Netherlands

Edward Elgar
Cheltenham, UK • Northampton, MA, USA

Published by
Edward Elgar Publishing Limited
The Lypiatts
15 Lansdown Road
Cheltenham
Glos GL50 2JA
UK

Edward Elgar Publishing, Inc.
William Pratt House
9 Dewey Court
Northampton
Massachusetts 01060
USA

A catalogue record for this book
is available from the British Library

Library of Congress Control Number: 2010925937

ISBN 978 1 84376 375 8 (cased)

Typeset by Servis Filmsetting Ltd, Stockport, Cheshire
Printed and bound by MPG Books Group, UK

CONTENTS

CONTRIBUTORS

William P. **Anderson**, University of Windsor, Canada
Jean **Andrey**, University of Waterloo, Canada
Erel **Avineri**, University of the West of England, UK
Kay W. **Axhausen**, ETH Zurich, Switzerland
Peter **Baker**, Cranfield University, UK
Athanasios **Ballis**, National Technical University of Athens, Greece
Brien **Benson**, George Mason University, USA
David **Bernstein**, Pennsylvania State University, USA
Michel **Beuthe**, Facultés Universitaires Catholiques de Mons, Belgium
Chandra **Bhat**, University of Texas, Austin, USA
William **Black**, Indiana University, USA
Patrick **Bonnel**, Laboratoire d'Economie des Transports, Lyon, France
Mary R. **Brooks**, Dalhousie University, Canada
Kenneth **Button**, George Mason University, USA
Roberta **Capello**, Politecnico di Milano, Italy
Mashrur (Ronnie) **Chowdhury**, Clemson University, USA
Louis F. **Cohn**, University of Louisville, USA
Michael **Corbett**, HDR Inc., USA
Álvaro **Costa**, University of Porto, Portugal
Graham **Currie**, Monash University, Australia
Patrick **DeCorla-Souza**, United States Federal Highway Administration, USA
Marco **Diana**, Politecnico di Torino, Italy
Martin **Dijst**, Utrecht University, The Netherlands
Kieran P. **Donaghy**, Cornell University, USA
Robert S. **Done**, University of Arizona, USA
Kieran **Feighan**, Pavement Management Services Ltd, Australia
Manfred **Fischer**, University of Economics and Business Administration, Vienna, Austria
Heike **Flämig**, Technical University of Hamburg, Germany
Peter **Forsyth**, Monash University, Australia
Ryan N. **Fries**, Southern Illinois University Edwardsville, USA
Terry L. **Friesz**, Pennsylvania State University, USA
Philine **Gaffron**, Hamburg University of Technology, Germany
Oliver H. **Gao**, Cornell University, USA
Jonathan L. **Gifford**, George Mason University, USA
Moshe **Givoni**, University College London, UK
Andrew **Goetz**, Denver University, USA

Aaron **Golub**, Arizona State University, USA
Margaret **Grieco**, Napier University, UK
Gene **Griffin**, North Dakota State University, USA
Richard **Gritta**, University of Portland, USA
Bernhard **Hachleitner**, Endlos Production, Austria
Susan **Handy**, University of California, Davis, USA
Matthew **Hardy**, Noblis, USA
David A. **Hensher**, University of Sydney, Australia
Markus **Hesse**, University of Luxembourg, Luxembourg
Veli **Himanen**, JP-Transplan Ltd and Relate Partership, Finland
Mike **Hirst**, Loughborough University, UK
Christian **Holz-Rau**, University of Dortmund, Germany
Michael **Iacono**, University of Minnesota, USA
Lutz **Ickert**, ProgTrans AG, Basel, Switzerland
Stephen **Ison**, Loughborough University, UK
Milan **Janic**, Technical University of Delft, The Netherlands
Tae Il **Kim**, Pennsylvania State University, USA
Tschangho John **Kim**, University of Illinois at Urbana-Champaign, USA
Andrew **Koh**, University of Leeds, UK
Tomasz **Komornicki**, Institute of Geography and Spatial Organization, Polish Academy of Sciences, Poland
Changhyun **Kwon**, Pennsylvania State University, USA
Andrew **Lee**, University of California, Davis, USA
Il Soo **Lee**, Pennsylvania State University, USA
David **Levinson**, University of Minnesota, USA
Todd Alexander **Litman**, Victoria Transport Policy Institute, Canada
Becky P.Y. **Loo**, University of Hong Kong, Hong Kong
Berendien **Lubbe**, University of Pretoria, South Africa
Yongchang (Max) **Ma**, IEM, Inc.
Tim **Martin**, ARRB Group Ltd, Australia
Andreas **Matthes**, University of Technology Dresden, Germany
Mike **McDonald**, University of Southampton, UK
B. Starr **McMullen**, Oregon State University, USA
Ronald W. **McQuaid**, Napier University, UK
Francesca **Medda**, University College, London, UK
Paul **Metaxatos**, University of Illinois at Chicago, USA
Michael D. **Meyer**, Georgia Institute of Technology, USA
Olaf **Meyer-Rühle**, ProgTrans AG, Basel, Switzerland
Patricia L. **Mokhtarian**, University of California, Davis, USA
Heidrun **Mollenkopf**, German National Association of Senior Citizens Organisations, Germany
Kai **Nagel**, ETH Zurich, Switzerland

Anna **Nagurney**, University of Massachusetts, USA
Christopher **Nash**, University of Leeds, UK
Debbie A. **Niemeier**, University of California, Davis, USA
Paul **Nieuwenhuis**, Cardiff University, UK
Peter **Nijkamp**, Free University of Amsterdam, The Netherlands
Morton E. **O'Kelly**, Ohio State University, USA
Eric **Pels**, Free University of Amsterdam, The Netherlands
Marco **Percoco**, Bocconi University, Italy
Melvyn J. **Peters**, Old Dominion University, USA
Paul C. **Pfaffenbichler**, Vienna University of Technology, Austria
David **Pitfield**, Loughborough University, UK
Stefan **Poppelreuter**, mpuls GmbH, Germany
Andrew **Potter**, Cardiff University, UK
Emile **Quinet**, Ecole Nationale des Ponts et Chaussées, France
Amelia **Regan**, University of California, Irvine, USA
Aura **Reggiani**, University of Bologna, Italy
Aisling **Reynolds-Feighan**, University College Dublin, Ireland
Andy **Richards**, University of Southampton, UK
Piet **Rietveld**, Free University of Amsterdam, The Netherlands
Matthew A. **Rigdon**, Pennsylvania State University, USA
Amanda **Root**, University of Oxford, UK
Roberto **Roson**, Ca'Foscari University, Italy
Georg **Rudinger**, University of Bonn, Germany
Sara E. **Russell**, Old Dominion University, USA
Ilan **Salomon**, Hebrew University, Jerusalem, Israel
Deborah **Salon**, Columbia University, USA
Georgina **Santos**, University of Cambridge, UK
Ian **Savage**, Northwestern University, USA
Jens **Schade**, Dresden University of Technology, Germany
K. Warner **Schaie**, Pennsylvania State University, USA
Joachim **Scheiner**, University of Dortmund, Germany
Laurie **Schintler**, George Mason University, USA
Bernhard **Schlag**, Dresden University of Technology, Germany
Darren M. **Scott**, McMaster University, Canada
Derek **Scrafton**, University of South Australia, Australia
Ashish **Sen**, University of Illinois at Chicago, USA
Yoram **Shiftan**, Technion, Israel Institute of Technology, Israel
Brian **Slack**, Concordia University, Canada
Raghavan **Srinivasan**, UNC Highway Safety Research Center, Chapel Hill, USA
Sivaramakrishnan **Srinivasan**, University of Florida, Gainesville, USA
Dominic **Stead**, Delft University of Technology, The Netherlands

Seiji S.C. **Steimetz**, California State University at Long Beach, USA
Eliahu **Stern**, Ben-Gurion University of the Negev, Israel
Karl **Storchmann**, Whitman College, USA
Roger R. **Stough**, George Mason University, USA
Yusak O. **Susilo**, University of the West of England, UK
Wayne K. **Talley**, Old Dominion University, USA
Isabelle **Thomas**, University College London, UK
Thorolf **Thoresen**, Asset Management, ARRB Group Ltd, Australia
Lourdes **Trujillo**, University of Las Palmas, Gran Canaria
Dimitrios A. **Tsamboulas**, National Technical University of Athens, Greece
William **Tuttle**, Independent author and consultant
Barry **Ubbels**, Free University of Amsterdam, The Netherlands
Satish **Ukkusuri**, Rensselaer Polytechnic Institute, USA
Eddy **Van de Voorde**, University of Antwerp, Belgium
Marianne **Vanderschuren**, University of Cape Town, South Africa
Thierry **Vanelslander**, University of Antwerp, Belgium
Wijnand W. **Veeneman**, Delft University of Technology, The Netherlands
Henry **Vega**, George Mason University, USA
Alain **Verbeke**, University of Calgary, Canada
Erik **Verhoef**, Free University of Amsterdam, The Netherlands
Roger **Vickerman**, University of Kent, UK
William G. **Waters** II, University of British Columbia, Canada
David **Watling**, University of Leeds, UK
Bart **Wiegmans**, Technical University of Delft, The Netherlands
George **Williams**, Cranfield University, UK
Frank **Witlox**, Ghent University, Belgium
Guang **Yang**, George Mason University, USA
William **Young**, Monash University, Australia
Luca **Zamparini**, University of Lecce, Italy
Yan **Zhou**, Clemson University, USA

PREFACE

Bringing this body of work together has taken nearly five years. People are busy and good contributors have many other things on their hands. We hope that the final product is useful as a reference source and complements the vast amount of material that is now available on the World Wide Web. The advantage we think the product has is that the entries are by named authorities which allows readers to have some guarantee of their quality and there is extensive cross-referencing that allows for important linkages to be chased up. We also hope that the quality of the drafting makes the various items accessible to the widest possible audience.

In putting this volume together we are very grateful for the time and effort contributed by the contributors – without them there would be no *Dictionary*.

Kenneth Button, Henry Vega and Peter Nijkamp

INTRODUCTION

Transport analysis is an area of study rather than an academic discipline such as physics, linguistics or economics. To understand how transport systems work, and how transport institutions develop and function, and to appreciate the way individuals and companies view transport services, requires the application of a multiplicity of disciplines. Transport is a complex activity involving numerous interactions between actors both those interested in their own movements but also those affected by the actions of other. It entails the provision of a diverse range of technologies and infrastructures, and functions within a labyrinth of legal boundaries. It is also an emotional topic, taking up far more hours and column inches in the media than can be conceivably justified by its economic or social importance. In sum, it is complex and emotional.

This *Dictionary* seeks to help those less familiar with transport analysis to gain a foothold in the subject, and to offer information on particular topics to those already versed in some aspects of the field who wish to widen their knowledge. It sets out to pick out the main concepts and ideas of transport analysis, together with some particular institutions and technologies that are relevant, and to offer short explanations of their meaning and relevance to the study of transport. It is certainly not all-embracing, either in the range of subject covered or in the depth of coverage of these items. It focuses on the social science side of the subject; there is little, for example, on civil or mechanical engineering.

But what is a dictionary, and how does this volume fit with the generally held view of what a dictionary should do? Following Sandro Nielsen, a dictionary may be regarded as a lexicographical product that is characterized by three significant features: it has been prepared for one or more functions; it contains data that have been selected for the purpose of fulfilling those functions; and its lexicographic structures link and establish relationships between the data so that they can meet the needs of users and fulfil the functions of the dictionary. Perhaps the key point here relates to the idea that a dictionary should be useful and meet the needs of readers.

Unlike the dictionaries of the Akkadian Empire, written on cuneiform tablets that contain bilingual Sumerian–Akkadian wordlists, the *Dictionary of Transport Analysis* contains no translations from English, and gives rather more time to explaining and discussing some basic concepts. Further unlike its Akkadian counterparts, the *Dictionary* arranges material alphabetically along the lines of Samuel Johnson's famed *A Dictionary of the English Language* of 1755, rather than by subject grouping. It is also not a glossary, an alphabetical list of defined terms in a specialized field; and it goes beyond a defining dictionary, which provides a core glossary of the simplest meanings of more complex concepts. The contributors often include examples and illustrations, look at differing perspectives, and frequently discuss empirical findings pertinent to their topics.

Putting together a dictionary of any kind is not an easy task. In this case where there are multiple contributors, there are particular problems of coordination and timing. It is claimed that it took 120 years to type the 59 million words of the second edition of the *Oxford English Dictionary*, 60 years to proofread it, and 540 megabytes to store it electronically. The *Dictionary of Transport Analysis* took fewer years to complete, less time to proofread, and requires fewer megabytes of storage. Advances in technology clearly helped in the organization and production as well. Nevertheless, it has taken time to complete and one must be amazed at the patience of those who contributed the earliest.

The editors owe a massive debt to the various contributors, some of whom have had to endure a long wait before the product appeared. They have produced more than 200 original contributions that differ in style and approach but retain high-quality scholarship and analysis. The contributors were limited both in terms of their contributions and in the amount of additional reading they could suggest. To help with the flow of entries, there are no citations in them in the traditional sense but the further reading captures the concepts of those mentioned in the text of each entry and provides additional material for those wishing to know more about the subject of a contribution. There is extensive cross-referencing of contributions in **bold** to reflect the 'relationships between the data', as suggested by Nielsen when discussing the functions of a dictionary.

The cross-referencing has, we hope, been done in a helpful way. Where there is frequent use of a term in close proximity, it is not put into bold in every case. Also, there has been a sensitivity to meaning; for example the term 'packaging' is referred to with regard to the materials used to protect a shipment and to packages of policy measures, but the cross-referencing is limited to the former. Also, similar terms are cross-referenced; for example there is an entry on 'taxicabs' but this is cross-referenced as 'taxi' as well. Equally, terms used in very nearly all contributions such as 'roads' or 'buses' are not always highlighted; it is not thought to be that helpful in a product of this kind. Finally, some terms that are set in bold may be prefixed by something like 'transport' or 'traffic and' as an entry in the *Dictionary*. We hope an element of common sense has prevailed in the way this is done.

As for subject coverage, this is inevitably subjective, and another set of editors may well have included material that we have missed, or excluded items we felt fit to include. That is inevitable: we all have our biases and range of interests. There is also some overlap in material. All we can say in our defence is that we feel that the topics covered, while far from complete, should provide considerable insights into transport analysis for those interested in the field. The balance of entries and the space devoted to each was largely an editorial decision, with suggestions coming in from contributors for additional material as the project progressed. The authors were asked to draft their contributions as either 800- or 1500-word pieces with very few, but readily accessible references. Exposition was seen as the key rather than utter completeness. This weighting in term of size vaguely, but not completely, reflects the broadness of a topic rather than its intrinsic importance. The longer entries, for example, cover more general subjects such as transport economics.

A

accessibility

Accessibility (or just 'access') is the ability to reach desired goods, services, activities and destinations (together called opportunities). A stepladder provides access to the top shelf in your kitchen. A local store is an accessible place to shop. A highway or transit improvement can increase the services and jobs accessible from a neighbourhood.

Access is the ultimate goal of most transportation, excepting the small portion of travel in which movement is an end in itself (for example cruising, historic train rides, horseback riding, jogging). Even recreational travel usually has a destination, such as a resort or a campsite.

Three general factors affect physical accessibility:

- **Mobility**, that is, physical movement. Mobility can be provided by walking, cycling, public transit, ride-sharing, **taxis**, automobiles, trucks and other modes. All else being equal, increased speed, service quality or affordability of a mode improves access by that mode.
- Mobility substitutes, such as **telecommunications** and delivery services. These can provide access to some types of goods and activities, particularly those involving information.
- Land use, that is, the geographic distribution of activities and destinations. The dispersion of common destinations increases the amount of **mobility** needed to access goods, services and activities, reducing accessibility. When real estate experts say 'location, location, location' they mean 'accessibility, accessibility, accessibility'.

Accessibility reflects the **generalized cost** (time, money, discomfort and risk) needed to reach activities. Where the marginal financial cost of travel is relatively low (for example, for automobile owners in areas where roads and **parking** are unpriced), travel time tends to be the dominant component of accessibility. Individuals often evaluate accessibility in terms of convenience, that is, the ease with which they can reach what they want. A shop that is relatively accessible to consumers is called a convenience store, and a home near common destinations is said to have a convenient location.

Given enough time and money nearly every location on earth is accessible, but the degree of accessibility varies widely, depending on the location, time and person. The relative degree of accessibility affects where you go, what you do, who you know, your household costs, and your opportunities for education, employment and recreation. Accessibility can affect the types of economic activity that occur in an area, and therefore property values.

Accessibility can be viewed from different perspectives, including a particular location, a particular group or a particular activity. It is therefore important to specify the perspective being considered when describing and evaluating accessibility. For example, an older apartment building with stairs and narrow hallways may be accessible for physically able young people, but not for **elderly** residents or people with physical disabilities. A particular location may be easily accessible by automobile but not by walking and transit, and so is unsuited to non-drivers. A building may have adequate automobile access but poor access for large trucks, and so is suitable for some types of commercial activity but not others.

How transportation is measured affects how accessibility is evaluated and the range of solutions to transportation problems that are considered. Standard transport modelling and evaluation techniques tend to be traffic-based, that is, they can predict how transport and land use changes affect motor vehicle movement, and so favour automobile-oriented transport improvements. In recent years, **mobility**-based evaluation techniques, which measure the movement of people and goods, have become more common. This tends to give greater consideration to transit and ride-sharing, but still treats movement as an end in itself. Measuring transport in terms of accessibility expands the range of impacts and solutions further, to include mobility substitutes and land use factors.

Accessibility is a well-recognized concept in the disciplines of geography and urban economics, which have developed various methods of measuring the accessibility of different locations. Some regions have integrated transportation and land use models that can quantify how various combinations of land use and transportation system changes affect accessibility. For example, such models might be able to predict how a new transit route with a major portion of jobs and public services located near its stations would affect access to employment and services by various demographic groups (lower income, women, **elderly**, people with disabilities). However, such models tend to be expensive to build and are generally applied on a regional scale.

The words 'accessibility' and 'access' have many meanings and implications. From a transport perspective, the focus is primarily on physical access to goods, services and destinations. There are other factors that affect access. For example, access to medical services requires not only physical access to medical facilities, but also that services be affordable and understandable to potential users.

The word 'access' has several specific meanings in transportation planning. In pedestrian planning it often refers to accessible design, meaning facilities designed to accommodate people with disabilities and other special needs. For example, a pathway designed to accommodate people in wheelchairs may be called 'accessible'. In roadway engineering 'access' refers to connections to adjacent properties. A 'limited access' highway has minimal connections to adjacent properties, while a local road provides direct access. Access management refers to programmes to limit the number of driveways and intersections on highways to improve traffic flow and **safety**.

Further reading
Bureau of Transportation Statistics (2001). *Special Issue on Methodological Issues in Accessibility: Journal of Transportation and Statistics* **4** (2–3).
Kockelman, K. (1997). Travel behavior as a function of accessibility, land use mixing, and land use balance: evidence from the San Francisco Bay Area. *Transportation Research Record* **1607**, 116–25.
Litman, T. (2001). Measuring transportation: traffic, mobility and accessibility. *ITE Journal* **73**, 28–32.

Todd Alexander Litman

accountancy data and airline finances

There has been an epidemic of bankruptcies in transportation, particular in the airline sector of the industry. Methods that could predict insolvency, or at least gauge relative financial condition, would be very useful to a wide group of interested parties such as stockholders, lessors, bondholders and other creditors, the flying public and governmental agencies that oversee the carriers. Traditional financial analysts have used various income statement and balance sheet items to compute ratios that are gauges of financial performance. Financial ratios are generally grouped into four important categories, each of which measures an aspect of financial health. These ratio groups are liquidity, leverage, activity or efficiency, and profitability. They measure, respectively: the ability of the firm to pay off its current debts (current liabilities) with short-term funds (current assets); the extent to which a company uses debt to finance its assets; the **productivity** or turnover of assets; and the firm's profitability relative to sales, assets or equity.

Newer statistical and mathematical techniques have vastly increased the power of traditional financial analysis, especially in the area of forecasting insolvency several years in advance. Undoubtedly, the most famous of these models is the Altman Z Score. Edward Altman of NYU, the 'father of financial bankruptcy forecasting', designed what is the most famous bankruptcy-forecasting model, the Z Score. Specified using a database of 33 failed and 33 non-failed manufacturing companies, Altman used a stepwise multiple discriminant regression, or MDA approach, to specify the following model using a set of 23 different financial ratios, five of which appear in the final equation:

$$Z = 0.012X_1 + 0.014X_2 + 0.033X_3 + 0.006X_4 + 0.999X_5$$

where $X_1 - X_5$ are ratios that measured each of the aspects of strength. X_1 = net working capital to total assets (a liquidity ratio); X_2 = retained earnings to total assets (a profitability ratio); X_3 = operating profit to total assets (a profitability ratio); X_4 = market value of equity to book value of debt (a leverage ratio); and X_5 = operating revenues to total assets (an efficiency ratio).

High ratios increase the Z Score and thus lessen the danger of failure, and vice versa. These ratios were weighted by the intercept terms to produce the Z Score. Altman found that the critical values of the Z were 1.81 and 2.99. Firms with scores of < 1.81 fit a bankruptcy profile, while firms with Zs > 2.99 fit the solvency profile. Scores between the two values lie in what Altman called the 'grey zone' where profiling is more difficult. Altman argued for a 2.67 cut-off, if one barrier was desired. The model's overall success rate in forecasting insolvency was 76 percent. It has been used in air transport to predict carrier failures successfully as early as the 1980s where it correctly presaged the bankruptcy filings of both Braniff and Continental. It should be noted that the model can also be used to assess overall relative financial strength for comparative purposes.

It could be argued, however, that a model derived from a sample of the same industry would be even more accurate than a generalized model such as the Altman Z Score. With that in mind, several analysts developed an industry-specific model, AIRSCORE, which was specified using a sample restricted to the airline industry. It included a significant sample of the large and smaller carriers. Using the MDA approach utilized by Altman, the model derived was:

$$AIRSCORE = -0.34140X_1 + 0.00003X_2 + 0.36134X_3 \qquad (1)$$

The three ratios that were predictive of insolvency or stress were: X_1 = interest / total liabilities (a leverage ratio); X_2 = operating revenues per air mile (an efficiency ratio); and X_3 = shareholders' equity / total liabilities (a debt ratio).

Because the distribution of the scores made the application of a single cut-off point difficult and inappropriate, several 'gray zones' were defined and the model yielded results similar to the Altman Z Score. It was able to achieve accuracy rates of between 76 percent and 83 percent, depending on the zone used. AIRSCORE has been used by researchers at Massachusetts Institute of Technology (MIT) to track carrier performance.

Logistic regression analysis has also been used to forecast financial stress and has become widely accepted. Logit models estimate the probability of bankruptcy and are also useful in ranking firms in terms of financial strength. A logit model has been developed by Pilarski and Dinh to gauge airline financial stress. Called P-Score, the model takes the form:

$$W = -1.98X_1 - 4.95X_2 - 1.96X_3 - 0.14X_4 - 2.38X_5 \qquad (2)$$

where: X_1 is operating revenues / total assets (an efficiency ratio); X_2 is retained earnings / total assets (a profitability ratio); X_3 is equity / debt obligations (a leverage ratio); X_4 is liquid assets / current maturities – debt obligations (a leverage ratio); and X_5 is earnings before interest and taxes/ operating revenues (a leverage ratio).

P is determined by: $P = 1/[1 + e^{-w}]$. Several input ratios (X_1, X_2 and X_3) are borrowed from the Altman Z Score model. Rather than producing a score that must be compared to a scale, as is the case with the previous models, this model produces the probability of bankruptcy. P is that probability. The higher the P value, the greater is the financial stress and the more likely is the chance of failure. P-Score is used by the United States Department of Transportation to track financial strength.

While financial variables are obviously important to the prediction process, Gudmundsson argued that other non-financial variables may also play a role, especially when forecasting multicountry failure. Like Pilarski, he also felt that logistic regression analysis (LRA) provides a better forecast than MDA. Gudmundsson specified the following model:

$$Z = B_o + B_1X_1 + B_2X_2 + B_3X_3 + B_4X_4 + \ldots\ldots\ldots B_nX_n \qquad (3)$$

and:

$$P = 1/[1+e^{-z}] \qquad (4)$$

As in the case of the Pilarski Model, P is the probability of bankruptcy. The independent variables in the regression are: X_1 is load factor (that is, the percentage of the aircraft filled); X_2 is number of passengers per departure; X_3 is hours flown per pilot; X_4 departures per aircraft; X_5 is pilots per aircraft; X_6 is employees per aircraft; X_7 is average age of aircraft fleet; X_8 is annual inflation rate in the carrier's home economy; X_9 is different brands of aircraft operated; and X_{10} is political influence (a dummy variable: yes = 1; no = 0).

The data set used by Gudmundsson consisted of ratios, as well as continuous and nominal variables, collected over the period 1996 to 1998 for 41 commercial airlines. (Data were collected from the Air Transport World's *Airline Report*, IATA *World Airline Statistics* and ICAO *Annual Digest of Statistics*.) While not all the variables allowed to enter the model were statistically significant, the overall accuracy rate of his model was 90.2 percent.

Subsequent research efforts have employed even more powerful techniques such as neural **networks** (artificial intelligence), genetic algorithms and fuzzy logic.

Further reading
Altman, E. (1983). *Corporate Financial Distress: A Complete Guide to Predicting, Avoiding and Dealing with Bankruptcy*. New York: John Wiley & Sons.
Gritta, R. (2005). Air carrier financial condition: a review of discriminant, logit and neural network models for measuring the financial fitness of the US airline industry. In K.J. Button and D.A. Hensher (eds), *Handbook of Transport Strategy, Policy and Institutions*. Amsterdam: Elsevier.

Richard Gritta

activity-based models

Activity-based models belong to the activity-based approach to travel demand analysis in which individual travel behaviours are studied in a multidisciplinary framework emphasizing the importance of time and space constraints. In general, three basic comprehensive modelling approaches can be distinguished within the activity-based approach: the constraints-based models and two types of choice-based models, that is utility-maximizing and computational process models.

Constraints-based models examine whether particular activity patterns can be realized within a specified time–space environment. These models require activity programmes which describe a set of activities planned to be conducted during a period of a day. A combinatorial algorithm is typically used to reduce the set of all possible activity sequences by checking for their feasibility in terms of a set of predefined constraints.

One of the first constraints-based models developed is Lenntorp's PESASP model. This model evaluates all possible activity sequences for a priori defined activity programmes. PESASP generates spatial choice sets in light of a set of predefined constraints: that is, activity duration, location of bases (for example residential and fixed work places), length of time windows, travel speed and opening hours of facilities. In contrast to Lenntorp's model, in MASTIC the combinatorial algorithm is extended with the travel–time ratio (ratio between travel time and activity duration). Additionally, it is based on a shortest-route algorithm between concentrations of destinations. Finally, MASTIC is primarily used to test the feasibility of observed individual activity programmes.

Other constraints-based models are CARLA and BSP. CARLA applies a branch-and-bound-based combinatorial algorithm which selects only feasible activity programmes and subsequently generates feasible schedules of activities in time and space. In contrast to CARLA and similarly to PESASP, BSP evaluates all possible sequences of activity–destination combinations.

Utility-maximizing models are based on utility-maximizing theory in which it is assumed that individuals combine utilities from the attributed values of each choice alternative into some overall measure of utility according to a simple algebraic rule.

A well-known model is STARCHILD. This is a modelling system consisting of modules that represent successive stages in the activity pattern choice process. Interdependencies among members of the household, and the interrelationship between individual activity scheduling decisions and with the transportation and land use system are explicitly modelled. The multinomial logit model is applied to assign utility values to each feasible activity pattern as a function of travel time, waiting time and participation time.

In contrast to STARCHILD a day activity schedule approach breaks the activity scheduling process down into a number of hierarchical nested partial decisions, like primary daily activity pattern as a multidimensional choice, the primary tour of a day (including. times, destinations and modes) and the secondary tour of a day. It assumes a nested logit model in which the choice made at one level is also influenced by the expected maximum utility derived from any alternative at the levels below comprising it.

Other utility-maximizing models are an applied activity-based travel **demand model**, a stop generation and tour formation model, PETRA, COBRA, and PCATS and PCATS-RUM.

The computational process model modelling approach does not apply utility-maximizing principles but choice heuristics. These rules of thumb are used to yield acceptable suboptimal solutions without requiring extensive data manipulations. These heuristics often take the form of 'if. . .

then. . . else' rules that specify which decision will be made as a function of a set of conditions.

SCHEDULER is a model of activity scheduling applying heuristics. It is composed of a long-term and a short-term calendar. An individual selects a set of high-priority activities from the long-term calendar. On the basis of temporal constraints these activities are partially sequenced, then activity locations are determined based on a distance-minimizing heuristic. Based on more detailed information, a more detailed schedule is 'mentally executed' in a next stage in which mode decisions are also made and conflicts between activities are solved. Finally, less prioritized activities are tried to be fitted into open time slots in the schedule.

AMOS simulates the scheduling and adaptation of schedules and the resulting travel behaviour of individuals and households. Adaptation behaviour is treated as a learning process in which individuals gain knowledge about aspects of the new travel environment as they attempt to adapt to it. Caused by changes in the environment, an individual tries out a preferred set of responses until a satisfactory pattern is established. The simulation procedure is repeated until stability is reached.

Other computational process models are the cognitive model of planning of Hayes-Roth and Hayes-Roth, the rule-based model of Vause, SMASH and CHASE.

Further reading

Dijst, M., T. de Jong and J. Ritsema van Eck (2002). Opportunities for transport mode change: an exploration of a disaggregated approach. *Environment and Planning B* **29**, 413–30.

Timmermans, H. (2000). Theories and models of activity patterns. In T. Arentze and H. Timmermans (eds), *Albatross: A Learning Based Transportation Oriented Simulation System*. Eindhoven: EIRASS, Eindhoven University of Technology.

Martin Dijst

advanced driver assistance systems

Advanced driver assistance systems (ADAS) involve assisting with – and automating – various basic driving tasks: vehicle following, lane keeping, lane changing, and proper speed keeping. The systems are based on modern technology for sensing, data processing, data transmission, operational decision-making and task actuation. ADAS are a specific category of **intelligent transport systems** (ITS). In the United States, the term 'advanced vehicle **safety** systems' (AVSS) is more commonly used. A distinction can be made among lateral control, longitudinal control, direct driver control and integrated systems.

In the area of lateral control, systems are available to help with lane keeping and warning, as well as monitoring blind spots. The ADA System for lane keeping provides driver assistance for anti-collision purposes along the lateral axis of the vehicle. Moreover, it assists the driver in situations of tiredness and distraction, because it warns the driver in cases of swerving off the lane. The blind spot monitoring relies on an opto-electronic takeover sensor checking the lateral blind areas of the vehicle. The driver is warned when an overtaking vehicle is detected.

In the area of longitudinal control, the following are included: adaptive cruise control (ACC), stop-and-go, collision warning and avoidance system (CAS), intelligent speed adaptation (ISA) and pedestrian detection. ACC is a vehicle system that will automatically control vehicle cruising speed and, when necessary, will operate the throttle and brakes to maintain a safe distance to the vehicle in front. Stop-and-go systems are a special case of ACC systems. They permit the vehicle to adjust automatically in terms of 'speed and stop' according to the behaviour or position of the vehicle in front. The CAS aims to reduce the risk of collisions with obstacles ahead. A sensor, usually in the form of laser or microwave radars, measures the distance, angular position and relative speed of the obstacles in front of the vehicle. ISA is an automatic control system that determines the maximum vehicle speed, based on the prevailing **speed limits** and a variety of traffic characteristics. The pedestrian detection system warns the driver when **pedestrians** penetrate the predicted path of the vehicle. Such systems rely on the interaction between on-vehicle sensors and road users using appropriate equipment.

As regards direct driver control, vision enhancement systems augment the driver's vision under conditions of reduced visibility and hazardous conditions such as fog, rain, snow or darkness. Driver monitoring systems monitor the driver and provide a warning if their ability to control the vehicle is impaired (for example, in cases of drowsiness due to fatigue, or alcohol abuse).

Integrated systems, which make full use of the different technologies described above, appear the most promising in terms of enhancing road **safety** and driver comfort. Such ADAS are also expected to increase road infrastructure capacity, and to reduce the negative **externalities** of road transport in general.

Further reading
Macharis, C., A. Verbeke and K. De Brucker (2004). The strategic evaluation of new technologies through multi-criteria analysis: the Advisors case. In E.

Bekiaris and Y.J. Nakanishi (eds), *Economic Impacts of Intelligent Transportation Systems. Innovations and Case Studies*. Amsterdam: Elsevier/JAI Press.

Panou, M. and, E. Bekiaris (2004). ITS clustering and terminology: one concept with many meanings. In E. Bekiaris and Y.J. Nakanishi (eds), *Economic Impacts of Intelligent Transportation Systems. Innovations and Case Studies*. Amsterdam: Elsevier/JAI Press,

Alain Verbeke

ageing road users

Road users age, as all human beings do. Consequently, as the process of ageing is accompanied by the increased probability of physical deficiencies in walking, visual acuity, hearing, memory, and so on, the risk of losing physical competencies and sensory abilities may increase as well. Hence, traffic participation and moving about will become more strenuous with advancing years. At the same time, the importance of **mobility** has increased in modern industrial societies. It has become a major condition for ensuring the ability to lead an autonomous life and participate actively in society.

Maintaining mobility demands at least minimal functional capacities and, when physical mobility declines, suitable means of transportation. That is why older road users' state of health and the transport options available to them are their most important resources. Concerning transport modes, older people in Europe are far less 'auto-mobile' than in the United States. Their most usual transport mode – at least currently – is simply walking. Almost half of all trips made by the people who participated in a European study were on foot. The car, used as a driver or as a passenger, was the second most important mode. **Public transport** seems to play a role when no other alternatives are available or when the system is well organized, with a high frequency of traffic service and a dense **network** of stops. The **bicycle** can be an alternative where no public transportation is available, as long as geographical or topographical circumstances are favourable.

The older Europeans in this study also make fewer trips per day and travel shorter distances than comparable American elders. On average, the spatial range of their **mobility** (in terms of everyday trips) is limited to 1–3 km. A gap exists between older people who do not have a car and those who are actively able to drive or to use a car as a passenger: car drivers are more often on the go. At present, the share of pensioner households that own a car still varies greatly. Older people in Italy most frequently have a car available, followed by older adults in Finland and Germany. Overall access to cars is consistently higher in **rural** compared to urban regions. A far lower share of Eastern European elders own a car compared to their Western European contemporaries, particularly in **rural areas** where access to a car is even lower than in the urban areas of these countries.

With regard to age and **gender**, similar structural patterns can be observed throughout countries, albeit on different levels: households of younger age groups (55–74 years old) more often have access to cars than households of the older groups (aged 75 or older). Older women of the present generation have less education, a lower income, more rarely possess a driving licence, and therefore own a car less frequently than men of the same age. This relation will change, however, in the coming years. In rural areas of western Germany and Italy, for instance, the gender gap has already levelled off among younger men and women.

The various options for outdoor mobility find expression in the older persons' subjective evaluations of their possibilities to get where they want or need to go. As expected, people are more satisfied in urban areas, and younger persons (55–74 years) are more satisfied than older (75+) road users. In regression analyses, though, it was found that biological age is not the critical factor determining the extent of satisfaction with one's mobility options. By contrast, being physically able to move about, being satisfied with the public transport system, and being able to drive a car (and not just to have a car available) were the most important variables in almost all regions studied.

The question arises as to the consequences the increasing number of older car owners will have on the possibilities and preferences of ageing adults to be on the go. The problems of older drivers, especially those that are caused by sensory and **mobility** impairments or Alzheimer's disease, have become an issue of general concern. **Elderly** drivers do not have a disproportionately greater frequency of involvement in accidents compared to younger drivers. As a person ages, though, the risk of them having an accident grows in relation to driving performance (and hence in relation to the exposure to danger). Walking or biking are not good alternatives either: elderly people are very vulnerable as unprotected road users.

The mobility needs of older road users can be supported by technological advances at various levels. Automobiles and buses can be redesigned to fit older drivers' capabilities better by using a variety of cutting-edge technologies. These devices still need further improvement, though, because they might also overload older drivers due to decreasing information processing capacity. The application of acoustic warning methods is limited because the ability to understand speech information at a low signal-to-noise ratio declines as well.

As a result, two parallel but opposing tendencies can be observed. On the one hand, the greater availability of private cars and technological advances may expand the older road users' options for being on the go. On the other hand, the growing volume and density of traffic that results also increases the potential hazards of such travel. Traffic **congestion**, particularly in urban centres, has reached an extent that may unsettle elderly people and keep them from venturing out. Older road users whose physical strength and sensory abilities are waning are often in particular need of a car in order to deal with daily demands and to join in social or cultural activities. Ensuring them opportunities for moving about despite the physical handicaps and possible spatial barriers that exist in their world would thus greatly contribute to their quality of life. Therefore, the question of whether and how external conditions and demands of the environment can be harmonized with individual needs and resources will be a societal and political topic in the years to come.

Further reading
European Conference of Ministers of Transport (2000). *Transport and Aging of the Population* (Report of the 112th Round Table on Transport Economics). Paris: OECD Publications.
Ketcham, C.J. and G.E. Stelmach (2001). Age-related declines in motor control. In J.E. Birren and K.W. Schaie (eds), *Handbook of the Psychology of Aging* (5th edn). San Diego, CA: Academic Press.
Mollenkopf, H., F. Marcellini, I. Ruoppila, Z. Széman and M. Tacken (eds) (2005). *Enhancing Mobility in Later Life – Personal Coping, Environmental Resources, and Technical Tupport. The Out-of-home Mobility of Older Adults in Urban and Rural Regions of Five European Countries*. Amsterdam: IOS Press.

Heidrun Mollenkopf

agriculture and transport

A convergence of domestic and international prices for agriculture markets has not occurred despite advances in information technology that have made it much easier for information on demand and supply conditions to be disseminated across markets, for centralization of commodity markets, and a global economic liberalization resulting in lower tariffs. More strikingly, since 2000 (and especially during the 2008 food prices crisis) the prices of agricultural commodities showed more volatility than prices in other sectors of the economy. An important factor seems to be the costs associated with transportation of agricultural and food products. Empirical evidence seems to support the claim that volatility in freight rates can affect not only the domestic price of corn in the United States, but also its price in neighbouring Canada. Similarly, studies have further contributed to the understanding of how price volatility is transmitted and to the extent freight prices can have a significant role in determining international food prices. Although the research interest in the economics of agricultural transport is relatively new, throughout history agriculture transportation has been crucial to the undertaking of efficient and profitable production. The importance of transportation to agriculture derives mainly from the impact that the costs associated with moving agricultural, food products and fertiliizers have on agricultural prices. These costs can be grouped in four broad categories: financial, time costs, environmental and access.

Estimating the financial costs associated with agricultural transport from an aggregated perspective is difficult. Macroeconomists' estimations in developed countries claim that they are high, that significant resources are wasted, and that financial gains can be achieved by improving transportation infrastructure. From a firm's perspective, these costs are financially important because commodity traders make purchasing decisions based not only on the price of the agricultural commodity, but also on the transportation costs of moving it. Purchasing of agricultural goods involves two separate decisions: the buying of the commodity at the farm gate and the negotiation of the cost to transport it.

In the **international trade** in grains, the first concern of the trader is the negotiation of transportation services; that is, the availability of the service and the cost of transportation services from the farm gate to the exporting domestic port and then to the foreign port of entry. The decision on when and what price to pay for the grain itself is usually made at a later time once transportation services have been contracted. These two decisions are interdependent and are affected by external conditions out of the control of the trader. Weather, for instance, can affect the time of harvest. Also, good weather in a producing region can determine that most of the production will be harvested in a short period of time increasing the immediate demand for transportation and raising transportation prices. Changes in fuel prices often result in changes to freight rates. Distance between origin and destination, however, may not necessarily result in changes in the freight rate. In the United States, barge price volatility used to have a greater impact on grain prices and margins than that arising from ocean price volatility. Consequently, efforts are undertaken to provide information on grain transportation costs and to assist farmers' cooperatives with the negotiation of a futures contract for barge rates to reduce volatility in the underlying spot market. A similar situation occurs in the international trade of wheat where there is evidence that domestic prices are more relevant to the domestic price of wheat flour than long-distance ocean travel. For example, domestic road transportation costs of imported wheat into Ecuador from Canada, or wheat imported from the United States into Nicaragua or Honduras, are greater than the ocean transportation costs from North American ports to the destination countries. Agricultural transportation often requires switching modes necessitating multimodal port facilities. A shipment of grains, very often, would travel by road, rail, barge and ocean vessel.

Time costs are associated with the perishability characteristic of agricultural and food products. Although they vary depending on the shelf life of each commodity, they can be prohibitive in that the excessive length of the journey can make the good worthless. New technologies for handling and extending shelf life have, however, resulted in perishable products becoming an emerging component of trade in food and agricultural products. Advances in refrigerated cargo, including refrigerated containers and trucks, as well as fast air transport delivery, have made possible long-distance movements of agricultural products such as bananas and other food products, and flowers. The use of air transportation has become critical in the transportation of live animals over long distances, and food aid during emergencies. For ocean transport, containerization and **intermodal** technology have radically increased the speed and reliability of ocean service.

Regarding the environmental cost of transporting food products, there has been an increase in the desire of consumers, mainly in developed countries, to know where the food they purchase is being grown. Environmental groups have suggested the concept of the 'food mile' in an effort to quantify in a simple way the environmental footprint of moving agricultural production to the consumer. Developing such measures has been challenging as they not only need to incorporate distance elements but also the transportation mode used, **fuel efficiency** of engines, and the efficiency of individual food **supply-chains**, which include not only the food product itself but also **packaging**.

Three of the most important social costs associated with transporting food are: the cost of the disappearance of family farming due to large-scale production and long-distance shipping of food production; the impact of heavy trucks on the integrity of road infrastructure and motorist **safety**, and **accessibility**. In the context of agriculture and transportation, accessibility refers to cases where residents of low-income areas and transit-dependent individuals, in urban and rural areas, are poorly served by food retailers.

Although evidence suggests that a large part of the famines that affected the world in the nineteenth and twentieth centuries were exacerbated in places in which road and railway networks were inadequate, controversy persists today surrounding the relevance of transportation to agriculture. In developed Western countries efforts have been carried out to increase the overall efficiency of their transportation networks and to expand access, while at the same time the debate on abating the environmental footprint of agricultural production and trade has intensified. On the other hand, in developing countries, with the exception of China, little has been done to achieve efficiency gains or to offset the negative **externalities** associated with transportation. Only in the last few years, have international development organizations such as the **World Bank** and regional development financial institutions included as part of their research portfolio the assessment of transportation costs of food products, and they are in the process of developing policy guideless to better assist countries in reducing these costs.

Further reading
Haigh, M.S. and H. Bryant (2001). The effect of barge and ocean freight price volatility in international grain markets. *Agricultural Economics* **25**, 41–58.
Yu, T.H., D.A. Bessler and S.W. Fuller (2007). Price dynamics in US grain and freight markets. *Canadian Journal of Agricultural Economics* **55**, 381–97.

Henry Vega

air quality

In addition to its targeted primary effects, transportation also has unwanted side-effects, negative externalities. One of the major side-effects is caused by exhaust emissions produced by the motors of vehicles. Transportation produces a number of emissions with varying degrees of adverse impact. These include global pollutants (such as carbon dioxide that contributes to climate change), national or regional pollutants (nitrogen oxides which produce acidification or acid rain) and local pollutants (such as particulate matter which contributes to respiratory health problems). Transportation's contribution to environmental pollution is particularly large in urban areas, where transportation is by far the most significant contributor of most atmospheric emissions.

Concerns regarding the influence of motor vehicle traffic on air quality, and therefore on human health, has a long history starting early in the twentieth century when General Motors developed combustion engines which needed leaded gasoline. Lead was already known to be a poison. The next phase started in the 1950s when it was realized that emissions produced smog in California. This led to intense – still continuing – discussions about the direction of transport policy.

Even though all transportation modes produce exhaust emissions, there are great differences between modes. In the local and regional contexts, it is road traffic – cars, vans, trucks, **buses** and, in some countries,

motorcycles – that have the major impact on air quality. Air quality in any area is decreased in relation to the amount of motor vehicle traffic and to the exhaust emission rates of vehicles. The exhaust emission rates of vehicles depend mainly on the size, age and maintenance of vehicles.

Air quality is influenced by exhaust emissions, which mix with air. The resulting air quality in any area largely depends on – in addition to the volume of exhaust emissions – local geographical and climate conditions. If the area is well ventilated, for example from ocean or sea winds, air quality remains much better than in an area situated in a closed valley. It is possible also for the wind to blow emissions from one area to another. Weather may have various influences: sunshine activates ozone and smog production from emissions, and windless weather with special temperature conditions may restrict air movements in a way that progressively concentrates pollutants in the air. Air quality is influenced also by emissions from other sources, for example factories, power plants, fires and heating. Natural windblown dust or dust from construction and maintenance activities, such as de-icing sand and resuspension, also have to be considered.

Local air quality can be gauged by measuring the amount of pollutants in the air. In most big cities are measurement stations which continuously measure the amount of some pollutants. It is also possible to estimate air quality with dispersion models. These consider the spatial and temporal dispersion of emissions, including the formation of secondary pollutants. As inputs the models need, in addition to emission data, data on background air quality, weather conditions and geography. The accuracy of the models is often quite poor but, if calibrated with the aid of up-to-date data on air quality, short-term forecasts can be reliable.

Exhaust emissions from combustion engines include almost 200 different components. In respect to their impact on air quality, most concerning are the primary pollutants: carbon monoxide (CO), nitrogen oxides (NOx), volatile organic compounds (VOCs), particulate matter (PM) and lead (Pb). In addition, mobile sources emit five gaseous air pollutants – acetaldehyde, acrolein, benzene, 1,3-butadiene and formaldehyde – which all present a threat for public health in urban areas.

Some emissions stay in the air as they are, but some transmogrify into secondary pollutants. The most important of the latter is ground-level ozone (O_3). It is formed from VOCs combining in the atmosphere with nitrogen oxides in the presence of sunlight.

Carbon monoxide (CO) is a poisonous gas produced by the incomplete burning of carbon in fuel. Carbon monoxide is not a permanent component in the air and after some hours it is transformed to carbon dioxide. Nitrogen oxides (NOx) contribute to the acidification of natural ecosystems and to the formation of ground-level ozone. NOx is formed when fuel is burned at high temperatures. Nitrogen dioxide (NO_2) is a brownish gas mainly formed in the atmosphere through the oxidation of the primary air pollutant nitric oxide (NO), which is one component in nitrogen oxides emissions.

Volatile organic compounds (VOCs) also contribute to the formation of ozone. VOCs emissions are caused not only from tailpipe exhaust, but also by evaporation of gasoline during vehicle refuelling, operation and **parking**. Small particles, with an aerodynamic diameter less than 10 micrometres, are likely responsible for most of the adverse effects of particulate matter because of their ability to enter the human respiratory system during inhalation. That is why air quality standards use their concentrations as indicators for particulate matter. Actually, a subfraction of the PM10 particulate matter – the particles less than 2.5 micrometers in diameter – are the most dangerous, since particles of this size are transported deep into the lungs.

Carbon monoxides, VOCs and lead are mainly produced by gasoline-engined cars, which also contribute to the emissions of nitrogen oxides. Diesel vehicles – cars, trucks and buses – contribute mainly to the emissions of nitrogen oxides and particulate matter.

Since the early 1990s NOx and VOCs emissions per capita have clearly decreased in the European Union (see Table). In the United States the emissions per capita are much higher and the reduction in VOCs has been quite modest, and NOx emissions have actually increased. It should be noted that in the European Union a greater share of NOx and VOCs emissions originate from road transport compared to the United States; that is, total emissions (transport and other sources) in the United States are then much higher.

	NOx per capita (kg) during a year		VOCs per capita (kg) during a year	
	Mid-1990s	Late 1990s	Mid-1990s	Late 1990s
EU	16	12	14	9
US	29	30	21	19

Other transportation modes – rail, waterborne and air – have less impact on air quality than road transportation. Locally they may produce significant amounts of emissions, but usually there are a few people in the vicinity to suffer from them. If **railways** are electrified, emissions are related to electricity production. Diesel locomotives can be compared to trucks when considering the production of emissions; that is, the major concern is in respect to nitrogen oxides and particulate matter. Waterborne transport may influence air quality not only in harbour areas, but also through acidification impacts in larger areas. Ships often use oil with a high sulphur content resulting in emissions of sulphur dioxide (SO_2). When nitrogen oxides produced by ships are also taken into account, it has been calculated that international shipping traffic accounts for 10–15 per cent of total deposition over Western Europe. The influence of aviation on air quality around **airports** includes emissions of CO, NOx, and hydrocarbons.

Reductions in transportation-related emissions have been obtained with the introduction of catalytic converters in new gasoline-engined cars, stricter regulations on emissions for diesel vehicles, improved reformulation of gasoline and tighter limits on vapour leakage from cars fuel systems. Modest reductions in the United States in the 1990s were partly due to the introduction of catalytic converters in the mid-1970s.

The decrease of emissions in Europe since 2000 has consequently improved air quality. Clear improvements have occurred in the concentrations of CO, NO_2 and lead. However, the air quality situation in European cities is still a concern with nearly all urban citizens experiencing pollutants in excess of accepted standards. Of special concern are concentrations of PM10, benzene and ozone, and in spite of clear improvements there still exist many cities with NO_2 concentrations exceeding the standards.

Air quality monitoring sites in the United States show a 94 per cent decline in the concentrations of lead, a 54 per cent decline for CO, and a 30 per cent decline for both PM10 and ozone from 1975 to 1995. Correspondingly, violations of federal air pollution standards have dramatically decreased. However, it has been estimated that some 90 million Americans still live in areas with at least one pollutant exceeding accepted standards.

Poor air quality is a serious issue in most big cities in developing countries. For example in the autumn of 1998 the mean ambient PM10 concentration in Cairo was as high as 211 $\mu g/m^3$, even in residential areas. The corresponding figure for lead was 1 $\mu g/m^3$ in residential and 11 $\mu g/m^3$ in industrial areas. The World Health Organization has estimated that in the early 2000s high levels of lead were in the blood of 15–18 million children in developing countries.

Further reading

European Environment Agency (2000). *Are we Moving in the Right Direction? Indicators on Transport and Environment Integration in the EU.* Copenhagen: European Environment Agency.
Pickrell, D. (1999). Cars and clean air: a reappraisal. *Transportation Research, A* **33**, 527–47.

Veli Himanen

air traffic control

Air traffic control (ATC) seeks to ensure safe and efficient air traffic movements from the time an aircraft start its engines at the departing airport until it parks at the destination airport. ATC deals with these requirements by dividing the airspace into airport zones, terminal, and low- and high-altitude en route areas, each sub-divided into the smaller parts – ATC sectors.

The airport zone is an airspace surrounding an airport about 8 miles wide and up to 3000 feet. Terminal area is the airspace surrounding one or few closed busy airports, 40–50 miles wide and 3000–10 000 feet. Tower and approach-terminal control, respectively, provide the approaching and departing aircraft guidance through these areas along the prescribed fixed and/or flexible – radar-supported – trajectories (Graves, 1998).

The low-altitude en route area is the airspace between the terminal areas/airport zones with the relative height of 10 000–25 000 ft. Usually, the short-haul flights cruise while the long-haul flights climb and descend in this area.

The high-altitude en route area is the airspace above the low-altitude area, which spread over the whole country or wider with the relative height above 25 000 ft. There, the long-haul flights cruise along the airways at constant altitudes – flight levels, which are vertically separated for at least 1000 ft.

The ATC consists of the ground and air, avionics components. Communication facilities and equipment constitute a **telecommunication network** – data link system – for transmission of the air–ground, air–air and ground–ground information about the aircraft position, surrounding traffic and weather. In the ATC of many countries, the information is transmitted by voice, however, the recent upgrading of the Data Link System allows digital transmission of the routine information without voice communications, which will generally increase the ATC capacity.

Navigational facilities and equipment include the ground aids for the aircraft primary navigation and global satellite system as a supplement. These are: the external overall and over-water en route aids – VOR, DME, VOR/DME, OMEGA, LORAN-C; the internal overland and over-water en route and terminal aids – Doppler Navigation System, Inertial Navigation System (INS), RNAV systems; the external overland airport and terminal area aids – instrumental landing systems (ILS) and microwave landing systems (MLS); and the airport external equipment – the approach lighting systems, slope indicators, surface detection equipment and so on.

Surveillance facilities and equipment include the integrated primary and secondary (SSR) beacon radar system, the latter with the most recent complement called the automatic dependent surveillance (ADS) system. The primary radar only detects the presence of aircraft. The secondary radar provides the more precise information on the aircraft code, altitude and speed. Both radar systems allow monitoring and controlling the separation between aircraft while airborne and on the ground (at airports) by ATC.

ATC personnel consist of teams of the air traffic controllers (one to three per team) and the aircraft crews (pilot and co-pilot and, rarely, the flight engineer per crew). The air traffic controllers are responsible for the safe traffic in the ATC sectors. The aircraft crew navigates the aircraft by using avionics.

The ATC separates the aircraft most frequently by the horizontal and vertical minimal distances of 5 nautical miles and 1000 feet, respectively. The aircraft may have either instrumental flight rule (IFR) or visual flight rule (VFR) status. Under the IFR status, the pilots perform a primary navigation while the ATC cares about the safe separation. The VFR status is allocated mainly to smaller planes, which care about both navigation and safe separation.

Air traffic management consists of the functions such as the airspace management, air traffic services and traffic flow management. The first function provides the airspace for the optimal flight profiles. The second function supports the safe, efficient and regular movement of air traffic. The last function optimizes the costs of flight delays and prevents the system overloading with the **safety** implications.

The ATC performs almost all the primal control functions, which appears convenient in terms of monitoring and controlling of air traffic, but also inconvenient due to the ATC's inability to provide the fuel-optimal routes for many aircraft and an increased ATC workload due to the complexity and concentration of tasks. This initiated the concept of moving the control-separation tasks from the ATC to the aircraft, which will try to optimize their routes. The concept called Free Flight allows monitoring of the surrounding traffic by the pilots instead of by the ATC on the ground, by using the convenient cockpit display supported by the automatic dependent surveillance broadcast.

Further reading
Graves, D. (1998). *UK Air Traffic Control: A Layman's Guide* (3rd edn). Shrewsbury: Airlife Publishing.
Janic, M. (2001). *Air Transport Systems Analysis and Modeling*. London: Taylor & Francis.

Milan Janic

aircraft and high-speed train substitution

Since the development of the high-speed train (HST) it became apparent that rail services can offer some of the services provided hitherto by aircraft. This is not only due to the speeds at which trains can now travel, but also because train journeys usually start and end in the city centre while airports are usually located on the outskirts of cities, hence rail provides shorter city centre to city centre journey time.

The rapid growth of the air transport industry has resulted in increasing capacity shortages at many major airports and in the **air traffic control** (ATC) system. This leads to increased travel time and increasing delays to air passengers, mainly for those who travel through hub airports. At the same time, increased recognition of the environmental damage caused by aircraft operation, mainly in terms of the impact on **climate change** and air pollution, makes the HST an ideal substitute to the aircraft on some short-haul routes, to relieve **congestion** and reduce the environmental damage from aircraft operation.

Short-haul aircraft routes that are suitable to be served by HST are normally routes of around one hour's flight or around three hours' HST journey between major cities where demand is high. Below that the car will usually be preferred and above that the plane will dominate regardless of whether HST services are provided or not. Furthermore, if demand between the cities is not high, HST will not be a viable alternative. Those short-haul aircraft routes are usually high-frequency routes served by relatively small planes (usually single-aisle Boeing 737 or Airbus 320 family aircraft with capacity of less than 150 seats), and therefore consume valuable runway and ATC capacity.

From an environmental aspect HST is a better option than the plane because it has less impact on **climate change**. The operation of HST is also believed to result in less air pollution than the operation of aircraft, but this depends on the sources of **energy** used to power the HST. The less that these sources are coal (main source of SOx gases) and other non-renewable sources, the greater the advantage of using HST as a substitute for aircraft. Regarding **noise** pollution, it is hard to confirm whether shifting services from aircraft to the HST will result in reducing the number of people exposed to high noise levels. However, it is easier to block the noise from running trains than from flying aircraft albeit at a cost.

For passengers, other than the benefits of shorter journey times and possibly more reliable journey times when travelling from city centre to city centre, the HST journey offers the advantage of one continuous journey compared with an interrupted journey when using the aircraft;

for example the journey to the airport, check-in time, flight, check-out, and journey from the airport. Therefore, the HST also offers considerably more opportunities to work and use travel time effectively.

The ability of the train to provide services that traditionally were supplied by airlines often results in competition between the modes. Evidence show that even when the HST captures considerable market share, for example between London and Paris, airlines still provide a high level of service on HST routes, and even increase their service frequency, using smaller aircraft (if traffic is lost to the HST), preventing any real environmental benefits from mode substitution. Yet, when HST services take the place of the aircraft but not the airline, the airline offers some of its services using HST, as is done by several airlines, notably Lufthansa on the Frankfurt–Stuttgart route. Such substitution can free-up runway capacity and create environmental benefits, as long as the freed runway capacity is not used to serve other, longer routes. Such cooperation between air and rail modes requires that the airport will have a station on the HST **network** and that there will be integration between the air and the rail services (mainly fast and smooth interchange between the plane and the train, of both passengers and baggage). This kind of mode substitution, which leads to 'airline and railway integration', is mainly of interest to airlines adopting **hub-and-spoke operation**. In the 'integrated hub', airline services from the hub are served by either aircraft or HST.

Although the number of routes where mode substitution can take place is relatively limited, the nature of these routes suggests that the impact of mode substitution can be large. To increase the potential for mode substitution, development of the HST **network** must be made with the locations of the large hub airports in mind, and likewise, decisions on where to build new runways or airports must properly account for the spatial configuration of the high-speed rail network.

Further reading

Givoni, M. (2007). Environmental benefits from mode substitution – comparison of the environmental impact from aircraft and high-speed train operation. *International Journal of Sustainable Transport* **1**, 209–30.

Givoni, M. and D. Banister (2006). Airline and railway integration. *Transport Policy* **13**, 386–97.

Intergovernmental Panel on Climate Change (1999). *Aviation and the Global Atmosphere*. Cambridge: Cambridge University Press, published for the Intergovernmental Panel on Climate Change.

Moshe Givoni

airlines

An airline is a company or an organization operating aircraft on a commercial basis carrying passengers, freight and mail. Flights can be operated on a scheduled or non-scheduled, charter basis. To function as an airline it is necessary to hold an operating licence issued by the relevant regulatory authority where the airline is based. In regulated markets airlines also require route licences to operate in specific city-pair markets. Bilateral agreements specify the terms of trade in respect of the provision of air services between countries. Airlines designated to operate an international route must usually be majority owned and managed by nationals of the designating state.

Determining the total number of airlines operating in the world is a far from straightforward task. According to the International Civil Aviation Organization (ICAO), in 2005 a little over 800 airlines were operating scheduled passenger services on domestic and/or international routings. *Flight International* magazine, which provides an annual listing of the world's airlines, estimated that there were over 1400 commercial airlines in existence in 2006. This figure however excludes many airlines operating aircraft equipped with fewer than 20 seats. The most comprehensive listing is provided by JP Airline-Fleets International, which in 2007 had over 6000 entries, but this includes some non-commercial operators of aircraft.

Several types of airline exist, the most common of which include **network** (sometimes referred to as legacy) carriers, **low-cost airlines**, regional carriers, charter carriers and express parcel carriers. Network carriers operate predominantly scheduled services on route networks that are focused on one or more traffic hubs. In 2008, American Airlines was the largest network carrier in the world when measured in terms of passenger traffic. The airline operated a fleet of 650 aircraft from four traffic hubs (Chicago, Dallas, Miami and San Juan) to 160 destinations worldwide. American Airlines' regional affiliate, American Eagle, with a fleet of 259 regional jet and turbo-prop aircraft, extended the company's overall **network** coverage to a further 117 destinations. In 2009, Delta's merger with Northwest Airlines saw the combined company overtake American Airlines in size.

Emirates, based in the Middle East at Dubai, is one of the world's fastest-growing network carriers serving over 100 destinations. It operates a fleet of 108 aircraft and in 2009 had no fewer than 196 large aircraft on order, of which 58 are the double-deck A380. Emirates, like most network airlines, configures its aircraft with a mix of two and three seating classes (first, business and economy). There are, however, several network carriers, including British Airways, Japan Airlines and Qantas that now offer a fourth class of service on their long-haul flights (premium economy).

Low-cost (sometimes referred to as no-frills) carriers (LCC) are a feature of deregulated markets and have become a worldwide phenomenon. They operate predominantly short- and medium-haul scheduled passenger services, typically using jet aircraft seating around 150 economy class passengers. Regional carriers typically operate smaller capacity aircraft (over 90 seats) on less dense routes than are operated by network carriers. Besides operating services on their own behalf, they can be involved in operating franchised services for network carriers providing necessary feeder traffic. There is considerable variation in terms of both the size of aircraft operated by regional airlines and the types of routes flown. For example, the Spanish regional carrier Air Nostrum operates services on behalf of Iberia, a mixed fleet of jets (with 50–89 seats) and turbo-prop aircraft (with 52 to 70 seats). At the other end of the size and route density range, Sun Air, for example, provides interisland services from its base at Nadi in Fiji using a mixed fleet of turbo-prop (with 18 seats) and piston-engined (with nine seats) aircraft. Scheduled services to remoter communities are often subsidized by central or regional governments.

Non-scheduled, charter passenger traffic accounts for around 10 per cent of world demand. Of this, Europe accounts for 90 per cent, the majority made up of holiday travellers carried by airline subsidiaries of the large tour operating companies. In 2006, the average seating capacity of the UK's largest charter airlines was 230. By comparison, most scheduled **network** carriers in Europe use Airbus 319/320 or Boeing 737 aircraft seating no more 150 passengers for their short-haul services. On both short- and long-haul flights charter airlines instal many more seats than network carriers. For example, on long-haul flights British Airways configures its three-class Boeing 767–300 aircraft with 181 seats, in sharp contrast to the 328 seats that are fitted to the same aircraft type used by Thomsonfly. Europe's charter airlines typically fly average sectors of 2000–3000 km in marked contrast to the 1000 kms average flown by LCC.

Express parcel carriers, such as FedEx and DHL, are just one example of a large group of airlines that specialize in the movement of freight. While some cargo airlines operate scheduled services, the majority of such carriers operate on an ad hoc charter basis.

Further reading
International Civil Aviation Organization (2006). Annual Review of Civil Aviation 2005. *ICAO Journal* **61** (5).
JP Airline-Fleets International (41st edn) (2007). New York: Bucher & Co. Publications.

George Williams

airport design

The airport design process requires considerable knowledge of local terrain and local weather conditions. Knowledge of local weather phenomena, such as persistent fog or excessive turbulence, might rule out certain locations. Wind data are also taken into account to determine runway orientation, because aircraft prefer to take off and land into the wind. Runway length requirements arise from knowledge of aircraft performance, and this can reflect local conditions too, such as airfield elevation. The volume of expected traffic can influence the number of runways, as multiple runways can be essential to achieve necessary levels of capacity. Thus the airport runway layout can be drawn, and assessed, to determine where it fits in overall. The remaining operational aspect is to ensure that the site selected, when statutory imaginary surfaces are constructed around it, does not invite risk because of terrain and other obstacles.

The above considerations can lead to the identification of a site, or indicate several possible sites. The most important and as yet unconsidered aspect is to take into account the local population. The approach and landing paths have to meet noise criteria and the access to and from the airport has to be convenient for users. The latter might determine where on the overall site plan one will prefer to have the passenger terminals, and in addition there will be need for consideration of freight terminals, maintenance hangars and other facilities. Only when these aspects are determined, and apron sizes and configurations have been settled in strict numerical terms can the taxiway system that will link the runways and the terminal facilities be designed. When specific issues such as taxiway runway and approach lighting, and navigation aid facilities, have been incorporated then the 'air-side' design is complete.

Land-side design focuses on factors that affect access and terminal facility characteristics. Terminals are where architectural flair can be dominant, but the reconciliation of service needs and aesthetically delightful solutions is not an easy proposition. An airport will be designed to cope with a particular service demand, which will logically be some way into the future, so that review of facilities does not lead to the airport becoming a continuously active building site. But overscaling facilities invites excessive costs, which detracts from commercial viability.

The latest terminal concepts to win favour, because they help to combine long-term visions with the practical issue of cost, are 'flexible'. They might be based on a building-block approach, so that central facilities can be expanded, and internal walls reconfigured with ease. There is a move towards 'satellite' terminals, with the realization that the sheer size of a single central terminal can make it unusable. Having provided adequate space for necessary functions, the distances that passengers travel have to be monitored in design. Long distances are ideally avoided, or alleviated with assistance like moving walkways. Sometimes it is helpful to use a multi-storey terminal, but reconfiguration is more difficult, and the exchange of baggage and passengers between floors requires more ingenuity. This usually increases cost, and leaves operations vulnerable to equipment failures – but the designer might choose this because the building is more compact, and they will use redundancy to alleviate the impact of critical item failures. In recent years, having more shops has lightened the internal journey load within airports, and the concession revenue in terminals has become a high proportion of overall revenue from operations. In small airports the biggest revenue earnings will be aircraft movement fees, and perhaps car **parking**, but the big airports have the potential to serve millions of customers every year. They can do well from a terminal design that incorporates concessions.

Further reading
de Neufville, R. and A.R. Odoni (2003). *Airport Systems; Planning, Design and Management*. New York: McGraw-Hill.
Horonjeff, R. and F.X. McKelvey (1994). *Planning and Design of Airports*. New York: McGraw-Hill.
Kazda, A. and R.E. Caves (2000). *Airport Design and Operation*. Pergamon-Elsevier: Oxford.

Mike Hirst and *David Pitfield*

airports

Although the role of an airport in an aviation **network** may be obvious, it is difficult to give a precise definition. Various activities take place at airports, some of which may not even be the responsibility of the airport operator. Air-side activities, land-side activities and air traffic control are all relevant activities that take place at an airport. Some airport operators may choose to offer certain services themselves, while other airports license third parties to offer these services. The bundle of services offered by different airports may therefore be rather different, which explains the difficulty in providing a precise definition of what an airport is. In the discussion of airport functions and their implications for operations and policy-making, a crucial point in the discussion is the objective of the airport operator. Many airports are still owned and operated publicly, but increasingly airports are being privatized. Prices charged by public airports often do not reflect demand conditions. For instance, landing fees are usually weight-based, while at congested airports they should reflect the fact that demand is too high in relation to the capacity.

The nodal function is arguably the most important function of an airport. Although aeronautical revenues may be swamped by commercial revenues at some airports, the core business is still the aviation side. The underlying idea is simple: without aircraft, there are no passengers. The airport is the place where various links meet, and is the starting or end point for the trip along a link. An airport is thus the place where supply and demand in passenger and freight aviation markets meet. The airport has no other function in this 'limited' concept. But even in such a limited concept, various types of airports can be identified. The status of an airport in an aviation **network** is decided upon by the airlines. An airline chooses what markets, and thus airports, to serve and how to structure its network. In **hub-and-spoke networks**, all traffic is routed via one or a few hub airports. All passengers travelling between airports that are not hub airports must necessarily make a transfer at a hub airport. In other network types, radial or linear, transfers are not necessary.

Flights at hub airports are usually organized in banks. A bank of arriving aircraft is followed by a bank of departing aircraft. In the time in between the banks, transferring passengers move to their connecting flights. Since hub airports generally have more traffic than 'spoke' airports, a hub position may be desirable. For instance, airports with a hub position may be an important stimulant to the regional economy. To obtain such a desirable position, airports can offer hubbing airlines favourable operating conditions, such as low airport charges, sufficient capacity, and so on. But it is important to realize that airlines operate hub-and-spoke networks to exploit density economies. By maximizing load factors, airlines are able to operate with relatively low average costs per passenger. Airlines will thus locate hubs at airports which given them ample opportunity to exploit density economies. Typically these will be airports with large home markets. Good **accessibility** may have a positive impact on the size of an airport's home market, but investments in accessibility are usually beyond the control of an airport operator. The airport can, however, not be sure that it will obtain or keep a hub position. The aviation market is highly volatile, and large **network** carriers (operating hub-and-spoke networks) face financial difficulties. Low-cost carriers, operating point-to-point or radial networks, show better economic performance. Such airlines do not use hubs.

The airport thus has only a limited role when only the nodal function is considered. In more complicated models, the airport combines the nodal function with commercial objectives. The simple fact that transfer passengers need to come to the airport to 'consume' their purchased airline seat gives the airport operator the opportunity to operate or license all kinds of commercial activities. **Parking**, shopping, catering, casinos, hotels, and so on may all be found at airports. As already mentioned, the revenues from these commercial activities may be quite substantial compared to aeronautical revenues. Commercial activities do not include aircraft handling, luggage handling and all other activities that are necessary for the air-side to function smoothly and safely, although the airport may outsource such activities to commercial agents. When these aspects are included in the definition of an airport or an airport's output bundle, one can think of a supermarket concept.

In the supermarket concept, a wide range of products is offered at the airport. In this concept, a commercial function is complementary to the nodal function. The core product is still the aviation activity, but once the passengers, and those seeing passengers off, are at the airport there is time for shopping, eating, gambling, and so on. The airport operator exploits the opportunities by offering such activities directly to the passengers or through licensees. Because the commercial function is complementary to the nodal function, demand for both activities is interdependent. For instance, when the aviation charges are too high, this will impact on the number of passengers, and thus the potential clients for commercial activities.

An extended range of commercial activities may be considered as an indication of the high quality of an airport, and may attract more transfer passengers, so that aeronautical revenues increase. There are also complementarities on the cost side: think of, for instance, joint assets such as terminal buildings. In practice, it may be difficult to disentangle the operational costs for commercial and aeronautical use. In theory, a private operator will assign the cost of joint assets to the activity that has the lowest demand sensitivity. Most likely this concerns the aeronautical activities, although there exists hardly any empirical evidence on this. A common conjecture is that airports engage in cross-subsidization: aeronautical activities are financed by commercial activities. It is thus questionable whether this holds true for privatized airports, but for public airports it may certainly be true, for instance when landing fees are below the market price and cost.

In the two concepts considered, airports can both be public and private, but it has already been mentioned that strategies are different for public and private airports. In the past, airports were usually seen as public entities of national importance, maybe even a public nuisance of national importance. Airports were important because of the economic impact and strategic value. But when the political trend of **privatization** set in, airport privatization also became an issue in many countries. The common rationale for airport privatization is increased efficiency.

But with the privatization of an airport one likely creates a monopoly. In multiple airport regions, passengers may choose between different departure airports, but this choice is highly dependent on airline strategy. The question thus arises whether airports have an incentive to abuse any market power that they may have. Airports have market power vis-à-vis airlines simply because airlines may have no other alternative in a specific city or region. When an airport sets its landing fees too high, airlines may choose not to operate from it. When the airport has a hub function in an aviation network, this strategy may have severe consequences. Now that alliances dominate the intercontinental markets, hub airports may lose a lot of traffic when an alliance moves its main base of operations to another airport which has more favourable operating conditions.

It is thus not clear whether airports will abuse market power when only the **network** function is considered. David Starkie gives another reason why airports may not abuse market power. Because the network and commercial functions are complementary, abuse of market power in the network function limits the demand and thus revenues in the commercial function. But still the authorities should be aware of the possibility that private airports may abuse market power, and hence of the possible need to regulate airports. Airports are usually regulated by means of price caps or rate-of-return regulation. Access to airports, by airlines, either incumbent or new entrants, is then left unregulated, and could be the source of formidable inefficiencies. At many slot-constrained airports where demand exceeds capacity, slots (the right to land or take off during a specific time interval) are usually allocated according to 'grandfather rights'; an airline that used a slot in the previous period may also operate it in the current period. This means that slots are not necessarily used by the airlines that value them the most; another allocation might lead to higher welfare. Welfare levels at airports following the first-come, first-served principle also do not reach optimal welfare levels because of **congestion** costs. **Privatization** is thus not enough to ensure efficient operation of the airport system. A system in which each airport is at its optimal capacity in relation to demand and its complementary airports, and in which the capacity is optimally distributed over the airlines, is necessary to exploit the maximum benefits airports can offer.

Further reading
Doganis, R. (1992). *The Airport Business*. London: Routledge.
Starkie, D. (2001). Reforming UK airport regulation. *Journal of Transport Economics and Policy* **35**, 119–35.

Eric Pels

alternative fuels

Petrol has been the dominant transportation fuel since the invention of the automobile, although other fuels have been tried, some – such as diesel oil and liquefied petroleum gas (LPG) or propane – with considerable success. Others have been experimented with primarily because of their lower or less harmful emissions. Other technologies to power cars abandon internal combustion altogether. During the latter years of the twentieth century many pinned their hopes on gaseous hydrocarbon fuels as a solution to the air pollution caused by vehicle emissions. In addition, known reserves of natural gas are larger than those for oil, while LPG is already produced as a by-product of the refining process.

LPG is a mixture of butane and propane. It is a by-product of the refining process and therefore widely available wherever oil refineries operate. Nevertheless its popularity has been limited to a few countries, notably the Netherlands, Italy and, more recently, Australia while in countries like Japan and South Korea, LPG has been popular for **taxi** use. The emissions advantage of LPG has been known for many years, yet it was not until the late 1980s that it began to be actively promoted as a cleaner alternative fuel. LPG is considered particularly attractive for commercial vehicles which operate in an urban environment. A number of buses and local authority vehicles have been converted. Heavy diesel engines are relatively easy to convert to run on LPG or compressed natural gas (CNG), although they have to be turned into spark-ignition engines.

Natural gas, or methane, has a lower **energy** density and therefore needs a larger additional tank, although it has a slight emissions advantage over LPG. It burns cleanly and is readily available in many parts of the world, with a more equal distribution than oil. It has proved popular with fleet users in countries such as Canada, Australia, Sweden, the United Kingdom and Germany. It comes in two forms: either as CNG in which case it is still gaseous; or alternatively as liquid natural gas (LNG) which requires storage at very low temperatures, although more can be carried in the same volume than with CNG. LNG availability is more limited as this technique is used mainly for storing longer-term reserves, while CNG is readily available in many countries from the domestic distribution infrastructure which supplies natural gas for heating and cooking.

Alcohol fuels, ethanol and methanol, have been used in automotive applications for a long time, particularly as high-octane fuels for racing cars. Their suitability in motor racing is because they burn more completely. They therefore also produce lower emissions, though they are still hydrocarbon fuels. Ethanol can be produced from the fermentation of a range of different crops. In the mid-1970s the Brazilian government launched the 'Proalcool' programme as an import substitution project. In the wake of the oil crisis of 1973–74 Brazil felt it spent too much on importing oil to run its cars and a means was devised to substitute this with ethanol produced from sugarcane. Although the programme suffered a decline in the 1990s, environmental concerns combined with the avail- ability of new flex-fuel vehicle technologies have prompted a revival in recent years with Brazil now exporting ethanol to many other countries. In the United States, a large-scale conversion of corn crops to ethanol started in the early twenty-first century, followed by growing interest in developing countries and Europe. In practical terms there are limitations to this approach as vast areas of dedicated crop cultivation would be required to run a significant proportion of the world's cars on this fuel, although where surpluses of crops rich in sugar exist it may be feasible locally. The biofuels industry is more optimistic about the potential of so-called second-generation biofuels, produced from non-food crops and waste biomass.

Methanol is more dangerous to handle than ethanol, or even petrol, and requires a completely different fuel delivery system as it corrodes most existing fuel system materials. Nevertheless it enjoys some popularity as an alternative fuel. In practice it is usually mixed with petrol in order to control its effects somewhat and make cold starting easier. M85 (85 per cent methanol, 15 per cent petrol) is produced this way. M85 became a popular alternative fuel in parts of the United States from the early 1990s. More recently, methanol has come to be regarded as a useful source of hydrogen for feeding fuel cells. In this application it may prove more useful than as a direct fuel for internal combustion engines.

There have also been several attempts at developing alternative fuels for diesel engines. Many heavy diesel engines have now been converted to run on gaseous fuels for use in urban areas to reduce emissions. These, however, need to be converted to spark ignition. By the late 1990s the most promising diesel alternative was dimethyl esther, or DME. This is derived from natural gas and an engine needs modifications to the injection system in order to use it, but emissions are much improved. Much of the develop- ment work on DME is being carried out in Scandinavia. Other alternatives to diesel oil are the so-called biodiesels. These are derived from biomass (plant-based materials), such as rapeseed oil or soya, and can be used with little or no modification. Volkswagen was one of the first car-makers to make all its diesel engines capable of running on biodiesel. The **European Union** has a legal requirement to make all vehicle fuels contain at least 5.75 per cent biodiesel or bioethanol by 2010.

Hydrogen appears to offer the ideal solution. It is not a fuel as such, but an **energy** carrier in that energy needs to be used to extract it from either water or hydrocarbon fuels, including biomass. However, it is suited for burning in internal combustion engines with relatively minor modifications, and its emissions are essentially water. In practice very low levels of hydrocarbons are also emitted because of the lubricating oil that is still required by the engine. Hydrogen can be burned in existing internal combustion engines, so a wholesale move away from existing engine technology and production facilities would not be required. Mazda has reported that its Wankel rotary engines are particularly suited to running on hydrogen. However there are some problems, mainly centring around hydrogen production. H_2 does not occur naturally in its pure form and is usually produced from water or some hydrocarbon fuel such as methanol. This process can be quite **energy**-intensive and therefore raises the question of what energy source to use to make hydrogen; a process that can itself be polluting.

Hydrogen also presents storage problems. Existing storage solutions such as compressed hydrogen tanks or metal hydride are quite bulky and hydrogen tends to escape through evaporation over a relatively short period of time. By the late 1990s thinking therefore moved more towards generating hydrogen on board the vehicle from a hydrocarbon fuel such as methanol or even petrol. However as most hydrogen is derived from fossil fuels, it does not solve the problem of over-reliance on scarce oil reserves, unless the hydrogen is derived from water using renewable energy, as is done in Iceland. Around 3 per cent of the world's hydrogen is currently produced this way. Where hydrogen may have a role to play is in fuel cells, although the hydrogen generation problem has yet to be solved.

Many other alternatives have been tried in the search for cleaner and more sustainable automotive fuels and in the foreseeable future the monopoly of gasoline and diesel is likely to be gradually eroded around the edges by such developments.

In addition to alternative fuels for internal combustion engines, alternatives have also extended to alternatives for the internal combustion engine itself. Although after the scope for massive sales of new vehicles, this is generally considered a less attractive option by the motor industry as it means scrapping the existing engine production facilities and losing the expertise in conventional internal combustion technology built up over more than a century. Among alternative powertrains, battery-electric vehicles have a long history, and recent advances in battery technology are making these increasingly viable. The petrol–electric **hybrid engine**, popularized by the Toyota Prius and Honda Insight, combines a conventional with an alternative powertrain, making it more appealing to car-makers. It has met with considerable success and diesel–electric hybrid powertrains are already in use for commercial vehicles, while they are under development for cars in Europe. Plug-in hybrids form a compromise between battery electrics and existing hybrids. They do not suffer the limited range of battery-electric vehicles, while their ability to be charged from the grid allows cleaner energy input where sustainable electric generation is used. Plug-in hybrids use smaller internal combustion engines only for electricity generation, and entered the market from 2008 onwards. In the longer term, many still see considerable promise from the hydrogen fuel cell. Around 1000 experimental fuel cell cars were in use by 2007 and Honda first offered its FCX Clarity fuel cell car for lease in 2008.

Further reading
Mondt, R. (2000). *Cleaner Cars: The History and Technology of Emission Control Since the 1960s.* Warrendale, PA: Society of Automotive Engineers.
Nieuwenhuis, P. and P. Wells (2003). *The Automotive Industry and the Environment: A Technical, Business and Social Future.* Cambridge: Woodhead.
Romm, J. (2004). *The Hype about Hydrogen: Fact and Fiction in the Race to Save the Climate.* Washington, DC: Island Press.

Paul Nieuwenhuis

attitudes of the public to transport policy

There are clear divergences in attitudes about the acceptability of different transport policies, and understanding these attitudes to policy is important to formulating policy. Numerous opinion surveys have shown that push measures (for example improving public transport or creating pedestrian zones) are generally considered much more acceptable than pull measures (for example road tolls or fuel prices). Measures to support public transport are generally seen as the most acceptable and effective of all pull measures, while fiscal measures such as road pricing, **parking** charges and fuel taxes are seen as the least acceptable of push measures. The cost of pull measures, however, are generally more expensive to implement than push measures: most requiring capital investment, often on an ongoing basis, while push measures are often low-cost or can even be used to raise revenue. Public support for all mechanisms for funding transport policies is limited, which means that while pull measures are seen as more acceptable, there is often little public enthusiasm for paying for them out of the public purse. Thus, it is not the case that the most publicly acceptable policies are the most widely implemented.

Public support for general measures that affect all travellers everywhere (for example increasing the cost of fuel or decreasing funding for road maintenance) is usually lower than for specific targeted measures that affect particular groups and/or particular areas (for example road pricing or **congestion** pricing). There is, nevertheless, still a clear majority opinion against measures to reduce car use, even in the age of high levels of congestion. In fact, over recent decades there appears to have been a hardening of public opinion against many measures that seek to tackle transport problems such as congestion, despite the fact that congestion has continued to grow in most locations. Measures that attempt to reduce car dependence seem more unpopular than ever. Interestingly, however, public support for these sorts of policy measures may increase after their introduction, as in the case of the introduction of congestion pricing in London and Stockholm in 2003 and 2006 respectively. Opinion surveys in these cities show that local public support for congestion pricing increased after introduction of the policy.

People in higher income groups, who use the car most, are often more supportive of measures to reduce congestion than those in lower social groups, who make less use of the car. Education and income levels appear to have a strong influence on attitudes towards these types of measures. While this might appear rather contradictory, it may well reflect little more than selfish enthusiasm for measures that reduce other people's car use and improve driving conditions for the remaining car users. Despite wider support for public transport and taxing private transport among people with higher levels of income and education, there is little support for measures that have implications for speed reduction or time loss (for example lower **speed limits** or traffic calming measures) among this group. Thus, support is mainly limited to measures that are considered to affect other people and improve the situation for the individual. Public opinion about policies is not always identical to the opinions of local politicians and civil servants. Policies to support public transport often have a lower level of support among local politicians and civil servants than among the general public. On the other hand, local politicians and civil servants may give more support to various regulatory and economic measures than the general public do.

The popularity of any measure is by no means an indication of its effectiveness. Indeed, the popularity of a measure may lie precisely in its ineffectiveness. For example, drivers often support better public transport not because they intend to use it but because they believe that others will do so and improve driving conditions for themselves. It is even suggested that there could be an inverse relationship between the acceptability of a policy and its effectiveness. It could be, for example, that people may choose to give strategic answers in opinion surveys or vote strategically in the hope that measures will not be implemented if public support for or opinion of policy effectiveness is low.

Although it is widely agreed that measures to improve public transport are the single most acceptable type of measure according to public opinion surveys, research suggests that these will really only be effective when combined with other restraint measures (using a push and pull approach) – the idea of policy packaging. By packaging policies, push measures can be made more publicly acceptable if they are part of a combination of both push and pull measures. Thus, policy packaging offers a potential way of introducing less popular, but more effective, policy measures while maintaining a reasonable level of public support. There may also be a substantial difference in opinion about the acceptability of push measures, depending on whether the revenues from them are hypothecated to pull measures, such as providing additional public transport services funded through **congestion** charging, which is how congestion pricing was 'packaged' in London. In general, hypothecation can help to improve the public acceptability of push measures.

Further reading
Exley, S. and I. Christie (2002). Off the buses? In A. Park, J. Curtice, K. Thomson, L. Jarvis and C. Bromley (eds), *British Social Attitudes: The 19th Report*. London: Sage Publications / National Centre for Social Research.
Jones, P. (1991). UK public attitudes to urban traffic problems and possible countermeasures: a poll of the polls. *Environment and Planning C* **9**, 246–56.

Dominic Stead

automobile history

The history of the automobile can be traced back to the age of steam. By the turn of the twentieth century, in the United States at least, there was still an even split in market share between steam, electric and gasoline cars, but it was the gasoline car that eventually won. The fast-running gasoline engine was developed in France by Lenoir and Germany by Otto and was first fitted to what are regarded as cars by Daimler and Maybach in Cannstatt, and Benz in Mannheim, both in Germany. Benz, in particular, drew on the new bent tube technology developed for the **bicycle** to build his chassis. The vehicle's viability was proven by the first motorist, Bertha Benz who drove her husband's new machine 100 km to her parents. The next move was made by the French who started to industrialize the gasoline car and started to supply components to allow many firms to build their own cars, prompting a proliferation of the number of car manufacturers.

After these early European developments, it took the United States to effectively start the mass production of cars. Ford took an Italian concept and adapted it to mass production, at least of the engine and chassis elements. These changes alone began to transform the industry into one capable of mass-producing cars to the designs of the period. What eluded Ford, however was the ability to mass-produce bodies and this became increasingly a bottleneck preventing the mass production of complete cars. Ford outsourced bodies from a range of firms and painted them in-house. This caused problems, as paint took days or even weeks to dry, leading to high levels of work in progress. The missing piece in the jigsaw was provided by Edward Budd, whose Philadelphia firm developed technologies enabling the mass production of all-steel bodies. This allowed bodies to be heated thereby speeding up the drying of paint from days to hours. This came at the cost of very high capital investment in presses and dies, but with the added benefit of lower unit cost, smaller inventories and an ability to reduce labour. Mass production of cars was now possible. In the next phase the chassis was eliminated to create the unibody, also pioneered by Budd with Citroën of France.

The final element was the development of mass car markets and marketing; this is largely attributable to General Motors (GM). GM introduced the idea of using styling and colour, employing new DuPont paints enabled by all-steel bodies, rather than technology, to sell cars. It also introduced the idea of a product range, allowing customers to progress up as their income grew from Chevrolet, via Oakland and Pontiac to Buick and Oldsmobile, and then on to La Salle and Cadillac. Regular model changes were introduced to create perceived obsolescence making people replace cars. Two more elements were also important in stimulating mass motorization, and these were the introduction of vehicle finance through the General Motors Acceptance Corporation (1919), and the introduction of the trade-in in the mid-1920s.

This paradigm defines the mass car industry to this day, although engines now have dedicated plants, many of the components Ford made in-house are outsourced, and car 'assembly' plants primarily make and paint steel bodies. GM's key principles are still used. These developments allowed the growth of mass motoring and a transformation of the infrastructure in many countries to accommodate the car. However, after having initially been welcomed as a cleaner alternative to the horse, the more highly motorized parts of the world began to suffer the first negative environmental consequences of mass motorization. This began in Southern California, leading to the first emissions regulation in the early

1960s. For the next 40 years, California would consistently lead the world in regulating vehicle emissions. **Safety** concerns highlighted by Ralph Nader in the 1960s led to more critical consumer attitudes and also to greater regulation of the car.

Further innovations in car manufacturing were led by Japan, and Toyota in particular, whose novel Toyota Production System improved on all aspects of the systems established by Ford, Budd and GM. Toyota's methods were gradually adopted by the older firms in Europe and North America in the 1980s and 1990s, leading to more efficient manufacturing and the making of higher-quality cars. The rise of the Japanese car industry also marked the beginning of Asia as a car-making and car-consuming continent, as Japan was followed by South Korea, Malaysia and, more recently, India and China as major and growing automobile manufacturing locations and markets. While many of the established car firms benefit from these new markets, their sheer size has raised concerns about the environmental implications of what could be a doubling of the number of vehicles in use between 2010 and 2050.

Further reading
Flink, J. (1988). *The Automobile Age*. Cambridge, MA: MIT Press.
Nieuwenhuis, P. and P. Wells (2003). *The Automotive Industry and the Environment: A Technical, Business and Social Future*. Cambridge: Woodhead.

Paul Nieuwenhuis

B

back-haul problem

The back-haul problem occurs when demand on the A–B market is different from demand on the B–A market. This situation of asymmetric demand poses efficiency problems, since the capacity supplied for transport in the busy direction may remain partly unused in the other direction. The back-haul problem is almost universal. It can be observed at the level of **international trade** – oil tankers approaching Kuwait tend to be empty; for interregional freight transport – barges on the Rhine tend to be fuller upstream than downstream; and also for passenger travel – trains entering the centres of metropolitan areas during the morning peak tend to be fuller than trains going in the opposite direction. The back-haul problem is one of the fundamental reasons why average load factors in transport are low. There are various strategies that firms may follow to overcome the back-haul problem: waiting, triangular routing, pricing and spatial strategies.

Waiting means that a vehicle after unloading at the destination waits until there is demand for a return trip. This strategy is promising when the asymmetry in demand has a temporal nature. For example in a transport market that is basically balanced there may nevertheless be temporary fluctuations in demand, so that it may pay for a transport company to wait until there is a return load. When there are structural imbalances waiting is not a viable strategy. A main difference between passenger transport and freight transport is that the former is by and large balanced during longer periods – commuting within ten hours, holiday traffic within one or two weeks. Public transport companies may therefore decide to keep a proportion of their vehicles near the destination of the morning trip to use it for the afternoon return trip.

Triangular routing means that transport companies do not only define their services in terms of A–B markets and vice versa, but they introduce additional services on B–C and C–A. This is one of the many examples of **network** economies.

Pricing is another strategy that carriers may use. In a free market, prices in the busy direction will be higher than in the opposite direction. Once the costs of the trip have been made in the busy direction, any fare higher than the additional costs of taking loads on the return trips will be attractive to the carriers concerned. This obviously leads to shifts of costs from shippers in one direction to shippers in the other direction, and in the past regulatory authorities have found reasons to correct for this by price regulation.

In passenger public transport such differences in prices according to distance are less common. In liberalized aviation markets travellers are used to price variations, but in most railway and transit markets direction-dependent prices have not been employed, even though imbalances in demand may be substantial. One reason is probably that differentiated prices are perceived to lead to equity problems, and that travellers may find it difficult to absorb information on fares that are differentiated according to too many dimensions. Nevertheless, it can be shown that from a welfare economic perspective the net welfare effect of the introduction of direction-dependent fares may well be positive. One conclusion of this line of argument is that the back-haul problem may manifest itself in unequal flows in both directions, but not necessarily so. Depending on price **elasticities** of demand, equal flows but different fares may also be a sign of the back-haul problem.

A final way to overcome the back-haul problem may be to generate additional demand in the opposite direction by creative action. For example, a railway line with strongly unbalanced flows may become more balanced when at one end a special tourist attraction point is built. In this example, this is a matter of clever integrated land use and transport infrastructure planning. But note that it may also be the long-run result of relocations induced by differentiated transport pricing strategies.

Several of these policies to cope with the back-haul problem may greatly benefit from information and communication technology (ICT) applications in the transport system. ICT can help carriers to find freight at the right time and for the right market (wait and routing strategies). Also, ICT applications in the field of information provision to travellers may help to overcome information processing problems.

The lower transport fares sometimes found in the low-demand direction of the market may lead to unexpected trade flows. For example, part of the rather unexpected combination of sea–air transport between East Asia and Europe seems to be the result of asymmetric demand in aviation markets.

A final remark on the back-haul problem is that it may also be the result of institutional protection. For example, limitations on cabotage may lead to empty vehicles, even when there is sufficient demand. A well-known example is the limitation on **taxis** to pick up passengers at airports in many countries. Regulatory reform would help to overcome this inefficiency. This particular example of regulation is the cause of back-haul problems, whereas in the price regulation case mentioned above it was a policy response to back-haul problems.

Further reading
Button, K.J. (2001). Economics and transport networks. In K.J. Button and
   D.A. Henscher (eds), *Handbook of Transport Systems and Traffic Control.*
   Amsterdam: Pergamon.
Felton, J.R. (1981). The impact of rate regulation upon ICC-regulated truck back
   hauls. *Journal of Transport Economics and Policy* **15**, 253–67.
Rietveld, P. and R. Roson (2002). Direction dependent prices in public transport:
   the back-haul problem for a monopolistic transport firm. *Transportation* **29**,
   397–417.

Piet Rietveld

basic mobility

Basic mobility (also called basic **accessibility** or essential transportation)
refers to people's ability to access goods, services and activities that society
considers particularly important. Basic mobility typically includes transport for:

- Emergency services (police, fire, ambulances, etc).
- Health care services (medical and dental clinics).
- Basic shopping (food, household goods, clothing, etc).
- Education and employment (schools, training, jobs).
- Mail delivery and goods distribution.
- A certain amount of social and recreational activities.

Basic mobility recognizes that access to some goods, activities and destinations is particularly important to society, and so justifies special policies
and programmes to ensure that such needs are met. This is a particular
problem for people who are mobility constrained (also called transportation disadvantaged), because they have difficulty meeting their basic needs
with the available transportation options. This has several implications:

- Transportation policies and management practices may prioritize
  transportation activities and investments to favour higher-value
  trips over lower-value trips. For example, emergency vehicles may
  have priority over general traffic, and vehicles used by people with
  physical disabilities.
- Transportation **subsidies** may be justified for certain transportation
  activities but not others.
- Transportation systems may be evaluated in terms of their ability to
  provide basic mobility, even under unusual or difficult conditions.

That is, the system is measured based on the quality of transportation services provided to the most disadvantaged people under the worst conditions (for example, the ability of people with disabilities and low incomes to access basic services and activities in an emergency).

Evaluating basic mobility

To evaluate basic mobility for transport planning purposes it is necessary to define and rank the types of activities and services that a community considers essential or 'basic'. These might include:

- Emergency services.
- Public services and utilities.
- Health care.
- Mail and package distribution.
- Freight delivery.
- Basic food and clothing.
- Education and employment (commuting).
- A certain amount of social and recreational activities.

Basic mobility can be evaluated based on transportation adequacy, which refers to whether transportation systems meet minimum standards that society considers necessary, even for people who are economically, physically or socially disadvantaged. Transportation adequacy is affected by:

- Affordability – whether transportation options have financial costs within the targeted users' budget.
- Availability – whether transportation options exist at the location and time users require.
- **Accessibility** – whether transportation options accommodate users' abilities, including people with disabilities and special needs, often called universal design.
- Acceptability – whether transportation options are considered suitable by users.

What is considered adequate reflects geographic and demographic factors, as well as values and perspectives that may vary from one individual or community to another. For example, different people may have different ideas as to how far physically able transit users should be expected walk to access a bus, or how many shopping and recreation trips people need for basic access. For this reason it is usual to involve community members and users when developing basic mobility plans and programmes.

The Table compares the uses of common travel modes. Each is suitable for certain applications. Walking and bicycling are inexpensive, but are slow and limited by physical ability. **Taxis** are relatively expensive. Ride-sharing requires cooperation from drivers. Transit provides mobility for non-drivers who are not very wealthy or fit. This indicates that basic mobility requires providing a variety of modes and services. For example, it requires: adequate and affordable public transit services to accommodate people with low incomes and moderate disabilities; special demand response bus services for people with severe disabilities; and adequate walking and cycling conditions to allow local access by everybody, including users of wheelchairs, walkers and handcarts.

Because non-drivers' mobility is so constrained, increasing their travel provides greater benefit than comparable increases in motorists' travel. For example, a transportation improvement that increases motorized travel by one trip per week represents a 10 per cent increase for a non-driver who otherwise only takes ten trips per week, but only a 5 per cent increase for drivers with comparable travel needs who currently take 20 trips per week.

Although non-drivers on average have relatively low mobility needs because many are retired or unemployed, there are large variations in these needs. A significant portion of non-drivers have education, employment and family care responsibilities that can demand high levels of mobility.

Many communities have special community transportation (also called social transport) services that provide basic mobility to people who are economically, physically or socially disadvantaged. These typically operate demand response (also called **paratransit**) bus services for qualifying clients. Typically, this means that a person who has severe mobility constraints, or a person with minor mobility constraints who lives in a community with poor conventional public transit services, can request a certain number of door-to-door shuttle bus services or subsidized **taxi** rides each month. These services may be operated by religious institutions or other non-profit organizations, by social service agencies or by public transit agencies.

The potential market for community transportation services varies depending on demographic factors (the portion of people who have physical disabilities or financial constraints that limit their ability to drive) and the quality of transportation options (the quality of walking and cycling conditions and public transit services). In a typical community, about 5–10 per cent of the population is severely disabled (for example, being

Mode	Non-drivers	Poor	Handi-capped	Limitations	Most appropriate uses
Walking	Yes	Yes	Varies	Requires physical ability. Limited distance and carrying capacity. Difficult or unsafe in some areas.	Short trips by physically able people.
Wheelchair	Yes	Yes	Yes	Requires pavement (sidewalk) or path. Limited distance and carrying capacity.	Short urban trips by people with physical disabilities.
Bicycle	Yes	Yes	Varies	Requires bicycle and physical ability. Limited distance and carrying capacity.	Short to medium length trips by physically able people on suitable routes.
Taxi	Yes	Limited	Yes	Relatively high cost per mile.	Infrequent trips, short and medium distance trips.
Fixed route transit	Yes	Yes	Yes	Destinations and times limited.	Short to medium distance trips along busy corridors.
Paratransit	Yes	Yes	Yes	High cost and limited service.	Travel for disabled people.
Auto driver	No	Limited	Varies	Requires driving ability and automobile. High fixed costs.	Travel by people who can drive and afford an automobile.
Ride-sharing (auto passenger)	Yes	Yes	Yes	Requires cooperative automobile driver. Consumes driver's time if a special trip (chauffeuring).	Trips that the driver would take anyway (ride-sharing). Occasional special trips (chauffeuring).
Carsharing (vehicle rentals)	No	Limited	Varies	Requires convenient and affordable vehicle rentals services.	Occasional use by drivers who don't own an automobile.
Motorcycle	No	Limited	No	Requires riding ability and motorcycle. High fixed costs.	Travel by people who can ride and afford a motorcycle.
Telecommute	Yes	Varies	Varies	Requires equipment and skill.	Alternative to some types of trips.

Note: Each mode is suitable for certain types of travel. None is a perfect substitute for driving.

legally blind or unable to walk more than 200 metres), and 20–30 per cent of the population has some physical or economic constraint that limits their ability to drive. United States community transportation services appear to generate about 0.24 annual trips per capita.

Further reading

Barnes, G. and H. Dolphin (2006). An exploratory survey of potential community transportation providers and users. University of Minnesota Center for Transportation Studies.

Litman, T. (2001). You can get there from here: evaluating transportation choice. *Transportation Research Record* **1756**, 32–41.

Spielberg, F. and R.H. Pratt (2004). Demand responsive/ADA: Traveler Response to transportation system changes. TCRP Report 95.

Todd Alexander Litman

benefit–cost analysis (cost–benefit analysis)

When Benjamin Franklin was confronted with difficult decisions, he often recorded the pros and cons in two separate columns and attempted to assign weights to them. While not mathematically precise, this moral or prudential algebra allowed for careful consideration of each cost and benefit as well as the determination of a course of action that provided the greatest benefit. While Franklin was a proponent of this technique, he was not the first. Western European governments, in particular, had already been employing similar methods for the construction of waterway and shipyard improvements.

Ekelund and Hebert credit the French as pioneers in the development of benefit–cost analyses for government projects. The first formal benefit–cost analysis in France occurred in 1708. Abbé de Saint-Pierre attempted to measure and compare the incremental benefit of road improvements (utility gained through reduced transport costs and increased trade), with the additional construction and maintenance costs. Over the next century, French economists and engineers applied their analysis efforts to canals. During this time, the Ecole Polytechnique had established itself as France's premier educational institution, and in 1837 sought to create a new course in 'social arithmetic': aimed at the execution of public works that in many cases tended to be handled by a system of concessions and private enterprise. Therefore it was felt engineers should be able to evaluate the local and general utility or inconvenience of each enterprise; and for this they would need a true and precise knowledge of the elements of the investments. The school also wanted to ensure its students were aware of the effects of currencies, loans, insurance and amortization, and how they affected the probable benefits and costs to enterprises.

In the 1840s French engineer and economist Jules Dupuit published *On Measurement of the Utility of Public Works*, where he posited that benefits to society from public projects were not the revenues taken in by the government. Rather the benefits were the difference between the public's willingness to pay and the actual payments the public made (which he theorized would be smaller). This 'relative utility' concept was what Alfred Marshall would later rename with the more familiar term, 'consumer surplus'.

Vilfredo Pareto developed what became known as Pareto improvement and Pareto efficiency (optimal) criteria. Simply put, a policy is a Pareto improvement if it provides a benefit to at least one person without making anyone else worse off. A policy is Pareto efficient if no one else can be made better off without making someone else worse off. Kaldor and Hicks each expanded on this idea, stating that a project should proceed if the losers could be compensated in some way. It is important to note that the Kaldor–Hicks criteria states that it is sufficient if the winners could potentially compensate the project losers. It does not require that they be compensated.

Much of the early development of benefit–cost analysis in the United States is rooted in water-related infrastructure projects. The United States Flood Control Act of 1936 was the first instance of a systematic effort to incorporate benefit–cost analysis to public decision-making. The Act stated that the federal government should engage in flood control activities if 'the benefits to whomsoever they may accrue [be] in excess of the estimated costs', but did not provide guidance on how to define benefits and costs. Early Tennessee Valley Authority projects also employed basic forms of benefit–cost analysis. Due to the lack of clarity in measuring benefits and costs, many of the various public agencies developed a wide variety of criteria. Not long after, attempts were made to set uniform standards.

The United States Army Corp of Engineers *Green Book* was created in 1950 to align practice with theory. Government economists used the Kaldor–Hicks criteria as their theoretical foundation for the restructuring of economic analysis. This report was amended and expanded in 1958. The Bureau of the Budget adopted similar criteria with 1952's Circular A-47: 'Reports and budget estimates relating to federal programs and projects for conservation, development, or use of water and related land resources'.

During the 1960s and 1970s the more modern forms of benefit–cost analysis were developed. Most analyses required evaluation of:

- The present value of the benefits and costs of the proposed project at the time they occurred.
- The present value of the benefits and costs of alternatives occurring at various points in time (opportunity costs).
- Determination of risky outcomes (sensitivity analysis).
- The value of benefits and costs to people with different incomes (distribution effects, equity issues).

The planning programming budgeting system (PPBS) developed in the USA by the Johnson administration in 1965 was created as a means of identifying and sorting priorities. This grew out of a system Robert McNamara created for the Department of Defense a few years earlier. The PPBS featured five main elements:

1. A careful specification of basic program objectives in each major area of governmental activity.
2. An attempt to analyze the outputs of each governmental program.
3. An attempt to measure the costs of the program, not for one year but over the next several years ('several' was not explicitly defined).
4. An attempt to compare alternative activities.
5. An attempt to establish common analytic techniques throughout the government.

Throughout the next few decades, the federal government continued to demand improved benefit–cost analysis with the aim of encouraging transparency and accountability. Approximately 12 years after the adoption of the PPBS system, the Bureau of the Budget was renamed the Office of Management and Budget (OMB). The OMB formally adopted a system that attempts to incorporate benefit–cost logic into budgetary decisions. This came from the zero-based budgeting system set up by Jimmy Carter when he was Governor of Georgia.

Executive Order 12292, issued by President Reagan in 1981, required a regulatory impact analysis (RIA) for every major governmental regulatory initiative over $100 million. The RIA is basically a benefit–cost analysis that identifies how various groups are affected by the policy and attempts to address issues of equity.

It is generally agreed that most modern-day benefit–cost analyses suffer from several deficiencies. The first is their attempt to measure the social value of all the consequences of a governmental policy or undertaking by a sum of dollars and cents, and in particular, the inherent difficulty in assigning monetary values to human life, the worth of endangered species, clean air and noise pollution. The second shortcoming is that many benefit–cost analyses exclude information most useful to decision-makers: the distribution of benefits and costs among various segments of the population. Government officials need this sort of information and are often forced to rely on other sources that provide it, namely, self-seeking interest groups. Finally, benefit–cost reports are often written as though the estimates are precise, and the readers are not informed of the range and/or likelihood of error present.

The Clinton administration in the United States sought proposals to address this problem in revising federal benefit–cost analyses. The proposal required numerical estimates of benefits and costs to be made in the most appropriate unit of measurement, and specify the ranges of predictions and explain the margins of error involved in the quantification methods and in the estimates used. Executive Order 12898 formally established the concept of 'environmental justice' with regards to the development of new laws and policies, stating they must consider the 'fair treatment for people of all races, cultures, and incomes'. The order requires each federal agency to identify and address 'disproportionately high and adverse human health or environmental effects of its programs, policies and activities on minority and low-income populations'.

In recent years there has been a push for the integration of sensitivity analyses of possible outcomes of public investment projects, with open discussions of the merits of assumptions used. This risk analysis process has been suggested by Flyvbjerg in the spirit of encouraging more transparency and public involvement in decision-making.

The Treasury Board of Canada's *Benefit–Cost Analysis Guide* recognizes that implementation of a project has a probable range of benefits and costs. It posits that the effective sensitivity of an outcome to a particular variable is determined by four factors:

- the responsiveness of the net present value (NPV) to changes in the variable;
- the magnitude of the variable's range of plausible values;
- the volatility of the value of the variable (that is, the probability that the value of the variable will move within that range of plausible values); and
- the degree to which the range or volatility of the values of the variable can be controlled.

It is helpful to think of the range of probable outcomes in a graphical sense, as depicted in the first Figure (probability versus NPV).

Once these probability curves are generated, a comparison of different alternatives can be performed by plotting each one on the same set of

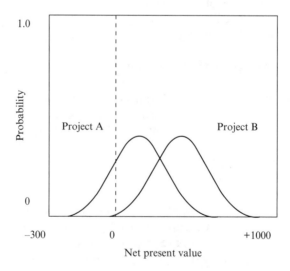

ordinates. Consider for example, a comparison between alternative A and B seen in the second and third Figures. The probability that any specified positive outcome will be exceeded is always higher for project B than it is for project A in the diagrams. The decision-maker should, therefore, always prefer project B over project A. In other cases, an alternative may have a much broader or narrower range of NPVs compared to other alternatives as seen in the second comparison. Some decision-makers might be attracted by the possibility of a higher return, despite the possibility of greater loss, and therefore might choose project B. Risk-averse decision-

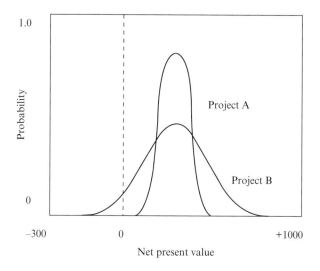

Net present value

makers will be attracted by the possibility of lower loss and will therefore be inclined to choose project A.

Further reading
Dorfman, R. (1978). Forty years of cost–benefit analysis. In R. Stone and W. Peterson (eds), *Econometric Theory Public Decisions*. London: Macmillan.
Ekelund, R.B. and R.F. Hebert (1999). *Secret Origins of Modern Microeconomics*. Chicago, IL: University of Chicago Press.
Flyvbjerg, B., N. Bruzelius and W. Rothengatter (2003). *Megaprojects and Risk: An Anatomy of Ambition*. Cambridge: Cambridge University Press.
Gramlich, E. (1981). *A Guide to Benefit–Cost Analysis*. Upper Saddle River, NJ: Prentice Hall.
Layard, R. and S. Glaister (1994). *Cost–Benefit Analysis* (2nd edn). Cambridge: Cambridge University Press.

David Levinson and *Michael Corbett*

bicycles

Bicycles are two-wheeled vehicles designed to be propelled solely by human power; though three-wheeled forms exist and bicycles can also be power assisted, usually through small electric or, more rarely, combustion engines. The bicycle as a transportation machine was first invented in the early nineteenth century and remained a means of leisure transportation for the reasonably wealthy until the 1880s, when mass production of pneumatic tyred bicycles made them a much more comfortable, safe and affordable option available for the less well-off. Currently, bicycles range from very basic machines used for personal and goods transportation in industrialized and, very prevalently, in many developing countries, to highly advanced racing machines used in competitive cycling events.

In spite of the wide range of personal abilities and cycling purposes catered for by the bicycle industry, there are very great variations in the status that cycling enjoys as a mode of transport in different countries and cities, and consequently also in its modal share. In 2001, the modal share of cycling in Amsterdam over all trips was about 30 per cent, in Copenhagen about 20 per cent and in Munich about 10 per cent; while in London and Paris, it was only between 1 per cent and 2 per cent. In Toronto and New York, less than 1 per cent of trips were made by bicycle in 2001. In Shanghai, bicycles were used for over 60 per cent of all trips in the same year.

The choice of the bicycle as a personal transport mode depends on many factors. Mobility culture plays an important part and this in turn influences factors that act on a more personal level. Among those factors can be included: trip distances; quality and quantity of available infrastructure; the expected quality of the riding experience (affected by type and level of motorized traffic, noise, pollution and spatial qualities); and personal feelings of **safety** and security. The availability of safe bike storage at the trip destination also often plays a very significant role in people's decisions to use a bike.

From the planning point of view, cycling has many characteristics, which make it an important mode, particularly in urban contexts. Cycling is the most efficient form of mechanized travel in terms of **energy** consumption per kilometre and is generally considered suitable for distances of up to 6 km, which the average cyclist can cover in 20 to 25 minutes. Many people's local travel needs can thus theoretically be satisfied by cycling – especially in combination with public transport services.

A further advantage is that infrastructure for both moving and parked bicycles uses considerably less space per traveller than equivalent provisions for the private car. Since space is a valuable commodity especially in city centres, savings in this area can have very real economic implications. Furthermore, cycling creates significantly less external costs – for example in terms of noise, vibration, pollution, accidents or land take – than travelling by motorized modes. Overall, cycling is cheaper to provide and is less expensive for the user than private motorized modes. In some contexts, it can offer the same door-to-door comfort and often be faster than car travel on short-distance trips in congested urban areas.

It has been shown that travelling regularly by bicycle can contribute to reducing the risk of coronary heart disease, obesity, adult diabetes, hypertension, osteoporosis, depression, stress and anxiety – all conditions that are increasingly afflicting people in developed countries due to lifestyle changes, including the way people travel. Though the vulnerability of cyclists as road users is often seen as a barrier to greater use of the mode, the health benefits to be gained are considered to greatly outweigh the risk of injury. Public health costs are rising steeply in most industrialized nations and increasing levels of cycling can thus bring economic benefits for the public sector and health insurance companies.

Lastly, though levels of motorization are rising relatively ubiquitously, even in Western Europe about one-third of the population does not have access to a car. Making cycling a more attractive and feasible transport choice and extending its use by linking it into the public transport **network** – for example through good bike and ride facilities – can thus also have implications for social equity.

Cyclists are in many places represented by active interest groups. Such groups are not always representative of all potential bicycle users, but depending on the local circumstances, their collective expertise and experience can nevertheless be a useful resource for local administrations.

Bicycle use is currently in decline for personal travel but bicycles are gaining popularity for courier and delivery services in urban areas due to their good speed and flexibility over short to medium distances. Public bike hire schemes – often referred to as city bikes – are also increasingly being introduced in cities of various sizes. Prominent examples include Copenhagen, Paris and Barcelona.

Further reading
International Association of Public Transport (2001). *Millennium Cities Database for Sustainable Mobility*. Brussels: UITP and ISTP.
World Health Organization Regional Office for Europe, Copenhagen (2000). *Transport, Environment and Health*. European Series, No. 89. Geneva: WHO Regional Publications.

Philine Gaffron

bus lanes

A bus lane is a roadway right of way restricted to use by buses for certain periods during the day or all hours of the day. The term 'bus lane' is often used interchangeably with other terms including 'transit lane', 'transitway', 'busway', 'dedicated running ways', 'bus-only lanes', and the like.

Bus lanes are used in a variety of forms as part of transit service operations to provide priority treatment to buses in order to improve operational efficiencies for the operating agency, as well as to reduce travel time and improve reliability for the rider. While bus lanes are primarily intended to encourage transit use, other benefits range from reduced **congestion** by reducing car use and environmental consciousness.

Bus lanes can be categorized as the following:

- Designated (or reserved) lanes. The bus lane is designated by traffic control signs, pavement (road) markings, and/or barrier separation to indicate a roadway lane reserved for bus-only use. Examples includes the Minneapolis, Minnesota bus shoulder operations and the Las Vegas MAX route in the United States.
- At-grade transitways. The bus lane is incorporated into a dedicated right of way which is reserved for exclusive use by buses but which does not include grade separation at intersections. Examples include the Los Angeles, California Orange Line and the Eugene, Oregon EMX.
- Fully grade-separated exclusive transitways. The bus lane is incorporated into a dedicated right of way which includes grade-separated facilities for exclusive operation by the buses. Examples include the TransMillenio in Bogota, Columbia and the Brisbane South East Busway in Brisbane, Australia.

These three categories of bus lanes vary greatly in cost between $3 million per mile for designated lanes to upwards of $40 million per mile for fully grade-separated exclusive transitways. These costs exclude right-of-way (ROW) acquisition.

Depending on how the bus lanes are planned and constructed, they can be controversial. For example, opponents of bus **rapid transit** in the United States, which relies on the use of bus lanes, often see the lanes as a poor substitute for light rail transit. Also, many leaders of urban city centres have considered reserving an existing general purpose roadway lane for bus-only use, which may be seen as reducing overall roadway capacity and thereby increasing congestion. However, many successful implementations of bus lanes (notably Minneapolis, Minnesota) have carved out bus lanes from the existing roadway ROW using improved roadway shoulders.

The design and enforcement of bus lanes are important, given that increased bus volumes, especially when buses operate as part of a designated lane on an arterial non-barrier-separated roadway, can have an impact on overall roadway operations including capacity, flow and speed.

Research indicates that the time saved by the installation of bus lanes is a function of how much congestion exists before the lanes were installed. For example, the City of Minneapolis, in the United States, uses shoulders as bus lanes, within an extensive system of around 300 miles, as a way to increase transit speed and, at the same time, reduce traffic congestion.

However, bus lane operations can also be severely hampered by loose enforcement, resulting in violation of the bus lanes by illegal vehicles, stopped vehicles, or illegally parked vehicles. An important component of enforcing bus lanes is to mark the lanes clearly as restricted to bus use only. Cities generally use three different methods for bus lane markings including signage and striping, raised lane delineators, and alternate pavement (road) colour or texture. Currently, there are no consistent methods which localities in the USA use for marking bus lanes, with each developing its own unique method or style. However, there have been attempts to include standardized signs within the *Manual of Uniform Traffic Control Devices* as bus lanes become more prevalent globally.

Bus lanes have been implemented in numerous cities throughout the world, including in London, the United Kingdom and Bogota, Columbia. The London bus lane operation functions alongside a **congestion**-pricing scheme implemented in 2003. The bus lane operations include 24-hour enforcement, with video technology utilizing bus cameras and cameras mounted along bus-only lanes, as well as, more recently, a wireless digital enforcement system. Besides enforcement technologies, London is cited as an example for its investment in engineering and design to improve bus-only lane operations – for example the lanes are clearly marked or paved entirely red. The TransMillenio in Bogota, Columbia consists of 26 miles of fully grade-separated exclusive transitway bus lanes. TransMillenio operates on two-minute headways during the peak period with more than one million daily boardings.

Further reading
Transportation Research Board (1997). *Operational Analysis of Bus Lanes on Arterials*. TCRP Report 26. Washington, DC: TRB.
United States Federal Transit Administration (2004). *Characteristics of Bus Rapid Transit for Decision-Making*. Washington, DC: FTA.

Matthew Hardy

buses

The term 'bus' is used to refer to an increasingly diverse set of public transportation service types and vehicle technologies. All still embody, however, its original meaning of public, collective transportation, short-ened from the French word *omnibus*, meaning 'collective transport'; which was originally derived from the Latin word *omnibus*, meaning 'for all'.

While originally it may have included vehicles on rails or wheels, in the present, 'bus' refers to rubber-tired vehicles of varying sizes operated on a variety of route and service configurations. Typically, riders enter the bus at some point along its route, pay the fare, and ride until they reach their destinations, at which point they depart the bus which continues along the route. Almost always, bus services are available for any member of the public to board at designated bus stops or as 'hail and ride' in certain loca-tions. Sometimes, such as for school or special subscription bus services, only certain persons can use the service. Buses mostly operate on prede-fined, fixed routes, but sometimes deviate from routes in special cases.

Buses are likely the most commonly used passenger transportation mode in the world in terms of passenger trips or passenger mileage. Almost all cities in the world of any significant size have some type of bus system. Even cities with highly developed rail systems typically have extensive bus systems. In the United States, over half of all public transportation trips and passenger-miles are by bus. In many countries, buses are also used extensively for intercity transportation.

Buses are very flexible and can serve a variety of roles within the mixture of transportation services in a region or between regions. Beginning with short-range services, buses, often as smaller 10–20-passenger vehicles, are used to provide access to rail stations, connect locations such as public services with residential areas or shopping nodes, improve circulation within an area such as a university campus or shopping district, or connect a particular destination such as a business park or shopping district to a rail terminal. These services, sometimes called shuttles, circulators, con-nectors, or community service routes, might have designated bus stops or offer 'hail-and-ride' options, where riders can board the bus at any point along the route. Good examples of these kinds of services are the 'Emery-go-round' in Emeryville, California, the 'Deuce' bus route on the Las Vegas Strip, and the Stanford University campus shuttle 'Marguerite'.

Perhaps the most common application for buses is on the medium- to long-distance 'local' routes, typically using 40–60-passenger vehicles (10–15 meters in length) to provide transportation across significant areas of cities or even between bordering or neighboring cities. Here, services operate in mixed traffic, have bus stops every other block or so, and typi-cally run for up to 18 hours per day. All-night service might be provided on a subset of these routes. In **rural areas**, bus routes may deviate from the defined route to bring riders closer to often spread-out destinations, and often these routes only run several times per day.

'Enhanced' and 'bus **rapid transit**' (BRT) routes improve service performance above the 'local' configuration through several modifications, though they typically run on similar routes. Reducing the number of bus stops, reduces the time lost due to stopping and starting. The buses, together with these bus stops, may have special paint schemes to differentiate them from the normal, local service and to add to recognition among the public. Fare payment off-board, typically called proof of payment, reduces boarding times by allowing riders to purchase their tickets before the bus arrives. Sometimes, 'enhanced' routes remove traffic impediments by allowing buses to proceed to the front of the traffic queue or to make turns ahead of traffic, all adding speed to the route's operation. Examples of enhanced bus routes include the Wilshire Rapid Route 720 in Los Angeles and the AC-Transit Line 72-Rapid in Oakland, California.

Moving along the continuum of bus route performance, BRT systems add additional performance to the 'enhanced' configurations by placing buses in traffic lanes segregated from mixed traffic. This allows buses to operate smoothly and quickly without the influence of traffic **congestion**. Additionally, traffic signals at intersections can be modified to prioritize the advancement of the buses to reduce waiting time. Many BRT systems use longer 'articulated' or even 'bi-articulated' vehicles, which expands passenger capacity by adding body sections and axles to the rear of the bus. BRT systems offer similar performance to light rail alternatives at significantly lower costs and construction times.

BRT systems began as simple concepts in Europe and the United States in the 1960s and 1970s and were more fully developed by planners in Brazil. Planners in Curitiba, Brazil applied the BRT concepts to an entire **network**, creating what was called a surface **metro**. The concepts were later applied in Quito, Ecuador and Bogotá, Colombia. The Transmillenio BRT system in Bogotá is the most advanced implementation of the concept. It has two lanes in both directions, segregated from traffic and combines many types of 'express' and 'local' routes while integrating with feeder buses at the system's terminals. This superimposition of services into exclusive lanes provides a carrying capacity greater than most light rail systems. As the cost of rail construction grows and municipal budgets shrink, BRT systems are becoming more popular. Cities in China, Japan, Indonesia, Korea, South Africa, Chile, Mexico and France have all constructed BRT systems since 2000. The more technically advanced BRT systems also incorporate **intelligent transportation** system components such as automated vehicle guidance and collision warning systems, and vehicle location systems for improved vehicle dispatching and traveller information.

Buses are used for commuting using longer-distance, limited-stop, suburb-to-city or suburb-to-suburb routes typically operating during weekday peak hours. These routes, sometimes called express, freeway flyers or commuter, can begin with a short neighborhood tour proceeding directly into the long-distance segment, or begin from a park-and-ride lot affording automobile access. These routes can run in general freeway lanes, separate freeway median busways or high-occupancy vehicle lanes. In many suburban residential areas in the United States, these routes are seen as effective transportation solutions and are expanding as **congestion** and fuel prices rise. Examples of these routes are the Transbay routes offered by AC Transit between Oakland and San Francisco across the San Francisco Bay Bridge, or the West Busway in Pittsburgh, Pennsylvania.

Throughout the world, intercity buses connect most cities of reasonable size. Often, a range of service levels will be available for a range of prices, including 'executive' service with video entertainment and food available on board. In the United States, the Greyhound Bus system is perhaps the most popular, though in vigorous markets several operators may compete for passengers. Brazil and Mexico, being large countries without large rail **networks**, both have well-equipped intercity bus systems.

Bus services, because of their relatively small initial investments, are often provided by the private sector. In the developing world, many cities have bus systems entirely owned and operated by private companies under a variety of public management scenarios. Even in the developed world, private providers may provide services – most likely shuttles, school buses and other specialized services – under the oversight of a public agency.

Buses now include a range of chassis types as well as propulsion technologies. Advanced vehicles offer 'low-floor' configurations which eliminate the need to step-up into the bus by lowering the floor around the wheels, rather than placing it, like a truck, at a level above the wheels. This makes entry easier for all riders, but especially those in wheelchairs, which is important as the United States Americans with Disabilities Act of 1990 requires wheelchair access to all public transit vehicles.

Encouraged by both **energy** use and air pollution concerns, buses employ a surprising diversity of engine types. About one percent of buses in the United States use electric motors connected to overhead wires, called trolleybuses. In 2006, 77 percent of the bus fleet in the United States ran on diesel fuel, 16 percent on natural gas, and the remaining share on a variety of other fuels like methanol and liquefied natural gas. The use of **alternative fuels** for buses has risen sharply since 2000, as only seven percent of buses were run on fuels other than diesel in 1997. Since 2003, **hybrid** diesel-electric buses have grown in popularity, with as many as 1000 hybrids in service in the United States in 2007. In the United States, heavy duty diesel emissions standards got stricter in 2007, encouraging a new set of emission reduction technologies and a cleaner diesel fuel supply.

Further reading
Golub, A. (2004). Brazil's buses: simply successful. *Access* **24**, 2–9.
United States Federal Transit Administration (2006). *National Transit Database: Annual National Transit Summary and Trends*. Washington, DC: FTA.

Aaron Golub

C

climate change and transport

The transport sector is responsible for a large part of global greenhouse gas emissions – 23 per cent of **energy**-related emissions according to the 2007 Intergovernmental Panel on Climate Change (IPCC) report. The breakdown of energy use and emissions among subsectors within transport is as follows: 46 per cent light-duty vehicles and two-wheelers, 25 per cent trucks, 6 per cent buses, 2 per cent rail, 10 per cent ship and 12 per cent air. Reducing emissions from this sector means either reducing the emissions per person-kilometre travelled and tonne-kilometre shipped, or reducing the total demand for person-kilometres and tonne-kilometres or some combination of these alternatives.

The majority of transport greenhouse gas emissions are in the form of carbon dioxide produced from burning petroleum-based liquid fuels. Emissions are chiefly determined, therefore, by the same factors that determine the sector's oil use. These are vehicle **fuel efficiency**, mode of transport chosen, level of transport activity and amount of capacity used. If the sector could be weaned from oil, the greenhouse gas intensity of transport fuels would also play a major role. With alternative materials production and disposal methods, the lifecycle climate impact of transport sector equipment and infrastructure could also be important.

Vehicle air conditioners also leak refrigerant F-gases, contributing between 5 and 10 per cent of transport sector greenhouse gas emissions. These F-gas emissions are projected to decrease over time without further policy intervention.

Emissions reduction options in the transport sector are many. Improving the fuel efficiency of vehicles can be achieved through use of lighter materials, more aerodynamic shapes, better engine designs, drive-train hybridization, or by creating policy incentives for consumers to buy the most efficient vehicles on the market. Passengers will choose more efficient modes if they can be made safe, inexpensive and convenient. It has been argued that policy-makers could encourage these choices by investing in **bicycle** infrastructure, increasing and improving transit service, or increasing **parking** charges and road use fees for single-occupant cars. Shipping companies will generally choose the cheapest and fastest mode for goods transport. They could be encouraged to use more efficient modes with the creation of **intermodal** centres or the use of differentiated shipping taxes by mode. Reduced demand for travel and goods movement can be achieved through more efficient **land use planning** or public education campaigns that promote local products. Vehicle load factors can be increased by optimizing **logistics** for goods delivery and creating incentives for car pooling such as priority use of roadways and/or **parking**. Replacement of petroleum-based fuels with alternatives that have lower lifecycle greenhouse gas emissions is another option, though the large-scale availability and viability of these **alternative fuels** remains uncertain.

Despite this diversity of options to reduce the climate impact of the transport sector, both the level of transport emissions and the sector's share of global emissions are growing. The IPCC report projects an 80 per cent increase in transportation greenhouse gas emissions between 2005 and 2030. The Organisation for Economic Co-operation and Development, that is more developed, countries accounted for approximately two-thirds of transport **energy** use in 2000, but are projected to use only 40 per cent of transport energy by 2050. Leading the growth of this sector are China and India. China's oil demand is projected to increase nearly fourfold between 2005 and 2030. Transport energy demand is the fastest-growing end use sector in India. These projections assume that world oil supplies will not be limited and will meet this growing demand. If this assumption proves to be false, the energy use and emissions in the transport sector will be substantially lower.

It is clear that substantially reducing global greenhouse gas emissions will require a major contribution from the transport sector. In the media as well as in the academic literature, there has been a focus on technological solutions to the problem of climate change. In the absence of an enormous leap forward in either vehicle technologies or alternative fuels, however, substantially reducing greenhouse gas emissions from transport will also require that some behavioural changes will also be needed. One of the main reasons for this is that transport relies so heavily on a single source of fossil fuel – oil. Ninety-five per cent of the fuel used in the transport sector is petroleum-based. This lack of diversity in energy source means that the sector is unable to use fuel switching to reduce its climate impact quickly.

Likely because the options to reduce greenhouse gas emissions from transport are so varied, a comprehensive study does not exist that estimates the global potential for and cost of emissions reduction in the sector as a whole. The 2007 IPCC report summarizes studies that have been done for individual transport technology and policy options. The main finding is that global transport emissions are almost certain to increase in the coming decades, but rigorous policies to curb the rate of growth in the more developed economies could substantially reduce the climate impact of the sector.

Further reading
International Energy Agency (2007). *World Energy Outlook 2007*. Paris: IEA.
Kahn Ribeiro, S., S. Kobayashi, M. Beuthe, J. Gasca, D. Greene, D.S. Lee, Y.
    Muromachi, P.J. Newton, S. Plotkin, D. Sperling, R. Wit and P.J. Zhou (2007).
    Transport and its infrastructure. In B. Metz, O.R. Davidson, P.R. Bosch, R.
    Dave and L.A. Meyer (eds), *Climate Change 2007: Mitigation. Contribution of
    Working Group III to the Fourth Assessment Report of the Intergovernmental
    Panel on Climate Change.* Cambridge: Cambridge University Press.

Deborah Salon

coastal shipping

Coastal, or short sea, shipping is the transportation of waterborne cargo along coasts and within inland waterways, but not in oceans. In Europe, coastal shipping is a viable transportation mode for many shippers – more than 40 per cent of domestic and international cargoes is moved by tonne-kilometres by coastal shipping. The relatively short distances between European countries, coupled with their extensive coastlines, large inland waterway **networks** and numerous ports, provide a favourable environment for a competitive European coastal shipping industry. This industry competes with land modes, particularly in regions where the topography prevents efficient land-based operations, as in the Pyrenees Mountains region bordering France and Spain. Coastal shipping of international shipments between Germany and Denmark utilizes the Baltic Sea.

Europe has been progressive in its use of coastal shipping, integrating it into its multimodal transportation **network**. In 2000 approximately 2 billion tonnes of coastal shipping cargoes were transported throughout Europe, 700 million tonnes of which were transported in the United Kingdom and Italy. Coastal shipping in Europe accounts for 40 per cent of its transportation tonne-kilometres. Further, coastal shipping has contributed to containing the growth in Europe's heavy truck traffic.

Unlike Europe, coastal shipping in the United States is more limited. Only 6 per cent of the domestic and international cargoes in the United States move by coastal shipping. Coastal shipping is being promoted by the Maritime Administration (MARAD) of the United States Department of Transportation via its Short Sea Shipping Initiative. The objective of the initiative is to use the uncongested United States domestic waterway system (coastal and inland) to ease **congestion** on the country's highway and rail systems by transporting cargoes on barges and small coastal vessels.

Coastal shipping in the United States has traditionally consisted of tug and barge operations in the transportation of bulk cargoes (for example agricultural goods and raw materials) throughout its river system, and the use of vessels with deep cargo holds and wide hatches in the transportation of bulk cargoes within its Great Lakes region. However, bulk cargoes are no longer the sole commodities moving via coastal shipping routes; shippers of higher-valued, containerized goods are also utilizing coastal shipping routes. New designs for coastal shipping vessels are being introduced – small-capacity container vessels and roll-on roll-off (ro-ro) vessels that move at faster speeds than tug and barge operations. The former self-propelled vessels do not require a deep draught and thus are capable of accessing inland waterways and smaller port terminals.

United States international cargo trade volumes are expected to double between 2000 and 2020, competing with domestic cargo volumes for transportation capacity. The volume of containerized cargo is expected to reach 30 million **containers** in 2010 and then increase to 40 million containers by 2020. To handle this increase in containers, additional port, truck and rail capacities will be needed. The concern is whether the United States highway and railway infrastructures that are ageing will be able to handle this increase in traffic.

In response to this concern, MARAD has further argued for the promotion of coastal shipping, that is, in addition to its promotion for reducing highway congestion. Specifically, MARAD is promoting the development of the America's Marine Highway, a system of coastal shipping waterways, to expand the United States freight shipping capacity.

United States highway construction has not kept pace with the increases in cargo movements. Coupled with increasing numbers of commuters and strained connections between roads and interstate highways, for example from urban encroachment of ports and marine terminals, the traditional means for transporting cargoes are under pressure. Therefore, the greater time incurred in highway transit, not only for cargoes but also for passengers, has been used as an argument for the redistribution of cargoes from trucks to coastal shipping waterways.

The benefits of expanding coastal shipping in the United States include not only expanding the country's capacity for transporting freight and the reduction in highway **congestion** resulting from the removal of a significant number of trucks from its highways, but also a reduction in transportation pollution. Redistributing truck cargoes to waterborne movements reduces the number of trucks on the highways, thereby reducing truck emissions and total transportation pollution, since coastal shipping is a greener means of transportation per unit of cargo moved than truck transportation. For example, a small container vessel or tug and barge operation transiting along a coast may potentially carry 400

containers, thereby removing 400 trucks from the highways and eliminating the nitrogen oxide (NOx) and sulphur dioxide (SO_2) emissions
that would have occurred from these trucks. Many port authorities are
instituting environmental regulations for trucks that enter their gates;
however, coastal shipping may be a 'greener' alternative. Also, coastal
shipping is a more **energy efficient** means of transportation per unit of
cargo moved than truck transportation.

The expansion of coastal shipping would also benefit United States
shipbuilding-related industries. The United States is a cabotage country,
that is, it has a cabotage law, the Jones Act, which regulates domestic
coastal waterway commerce. Specifically, the Act requires that any vessel
that loads cargo at one United States port and then unloads this cargo
at another United States port must be United States built, flagged and
crewed. Thus, a significant expansion of coastal shipping in the country
will likely result in an increase in the construction of Jones Act vessels, but
also in higher incomes, more shipyards, and merchant marine seafarers,
and growth in various ancillary services albeit at a loss of efficiency compared to using cheaper, foreign sources.

Since coastal shipping vessels are of a shallower draft than deep-water
vessels, they can moor at shallow-water facilities, unlike deep-water
vessels. Thus, shallow-water facilities in communities that were abandoned
because they could not serve deep-water vessels can now be used to serve
coastal shipping vessels. If so, coastal shipping will provide an economic
stimulant to the local economy where these facilities are located.

Along with the perceived benefits of United States coastal shipping,
obstacles exist that can restrict its use. Although the Jones Act would
ensure that many industries would benefit as the demand for domestic
vessels increases, the Jones Act regulations may also result in high costs in
the provision of coastal shipping. If so, high prices will have to be charged
to cover these costs, thereby possibly preventing coastal shipping from
being price competitive with truck and rail modes in the movement of
domestic cargoes. For example, the costs for constructing vessels in the
United States are significantly higher than in many other countries. The
Act by requiring coastal shipping companies to utilize United States-built
vessels, is also requiring that these companies utilize higher-cost constructed vessels.

Union dockworkers, for example the United States International
Longshoremen's Association (ILA) union, may also bargain for the
exclusive right to work – that is, to load and unload – coastal ships while
in port. If so, the port-related costs of providing coastal shipping services
will be higher from the payment of higher union wages. This is likely, since
the ILA has an East Coast contract with a provision that the ILA and only

the ILA is permitted to work container ships while in port from Maine to the Gulf Coast states.

Ports may also have to build separate coastal shipping facilities at their sites. For example, the berths at United States deep-water ports may be restricted for deep-water vessels, given their high rate of utilization by deep-water vessels. Also, coastal shipping vessels may require different pier cargo handling gear than used by deep-water vessels. If so, these ports would incur additional infrastructure and mobile capital costs for the provision of coastal shipping services. Further, coastal shipping vessels may contribute to greater **congestion** at United States ports, for example when deep-water and coastal shipping vessels and their cargoes interfere with one another in the use of port facilities.

Another obstacle to United States coastal shipping is the harbour maintenance tax (HMT). The HMT is a 0.125 per cent tax on the value of cargo, except ongoing exports that are transhipped at a United States port, and is paid by the vessel carrying the cargo. However, if the cargo does not go through a port – that is, it moves from its origin to its destination by truck only – it is not subject to this tax. In addition to the HMT, a vessel carrier that transports domestic cargo will also be subject to the United States inland waterway tax. These taxes add to the cost of coastal shipping and do not always reflect accurately the costs of the water-related infrastructure that is used.

Even if coastal shipping is price competitive with truck and rail, will shippers use United States coastal shipping? That is, will its service be better than that of truck and rail? For high-valued cargoes, the answer is likely no, given the slow speed of coastal shipping versus truck and rail. For **just-in-time** deliveries, the answer is also likely no, especially if a second mode such as truck or rail is needed to deliver the cargo to its final destination – since the services of two modes must be coordinated. Otherwise, coastal shipping is expected to be able to compete in service with truck and rail.

Further reading

Connaughton, S.T. (2007). *Development of Short Sea Shipping.* Statement of the Maritime Administrator before the Subcommittee on Coast Guard and Maritime Transportation of the Committee on Transportation and Infrastructure, House of Representatives. Washington, DC: United States Government Printing Office.

Mulligran, R.F. and Lombardo, G.A. (2006). Short sea shipping: alleviating the environmental impact of economic growth. *World Maritime University Journal of Maritime Affairs* **5**, 181–94.

Sara E. Russell and *Wayne K. Talley*

community severance

Community severance refers to separation or partitions between people, between people and places, or between two places. The purpose of the transportation system is the opposite of severance: its purpose is to join, link or connect one place to another, people to places, and people to each other. But sometimes the transportation system serves to sever rather than connect. Human communities are severed when a new facility, such as a freeway or a rail system, is built through an existing community and local streets are closed to accommodate the new facility. Natural communities may be severed when a new highway is built along a new alignment through an undeveloped area. Such impacts are often referred to as the barrier effect, and may be as much psychological as physical, as much perceived as real. However, the barrier effect and severance are not quite the same thing. In a community that grows up around an existing highway or rail line, the transportation facility may serve as a barrier that impedes the creation of connections between people and places but does not sever connections because none existed at the time it was built. Transportation projects can also contribute to severance by displacing residents and businesses, thus eliminating connections without necessarily creating a barrier.

Severance can also be understood through its converse, at both a physical and a social level. Connectivity is a physical quality of transportation **networks** that takes into account the number and directness of the connections between places served by a network. Good connectivity means that travellers have multiple, relatively direct routes to their destinations. Poor connectivity means few, relatively indirect routes to their destinations. Drivers have some level of connectivity via the road system to practically all destinations, at least within metropolitan areas. Transit riders, on the other hand, might find significant gaps in connectivity to parts of the region that are not served by the transit system. **Pedestrians** and bicyclists may also have connectivity to practically all destinations via the road system, though the poor quality of travel on the road system for these users often creates an effective barrier. As a physical concept, connectivity reflects the potential for movement through the transportation system but does not describe the way that residents actually choose to move through that system.

Community cohesion also represents the converse of severance but takes into account the social implications of physical changes. This concept is often defined as comprising the broader notions of shared values and common goals among members of a community. In a cohesive community, residents have a sense of belonging and feel a strong attachment to the community and their neighbours, and they make use of local facilities and engage in community activities. Although usually defined in social and economic terms, the physical environment plays a role in either fostering or hindering community cohesion in three important ways: by creating borders that help to define the community; by creating barriers that divide a community; and by creating gathering spots that foster community interaction. In these ways, transportation facilities affect the network of social interactions within the community.

Roadways can serve as borders or barriers. Major arterials often help to define the boundaries of a neighbourhood, for example, but projects to widen a road through an existing community or upgrade a surface street to a controlled-access freeway can create a barrier between two halves of a previously cohesive community. Streets within the community are also an important public space and can provide a place for residents to gather and interact. Boulevards and traditional main streets, for example, have long played this role in urban settings. Rail lines also can serve as borders or barriers, and rail stations as well as bus stops may serve to foster interaction in the community. Bicycle and pedestrian facilities also tend to foster interaction, and by doing so are less likely to create a barrier in the community. Whether transportation facilities will serve as borders, barriers or gathering spots depends in part on how residents perceive and react to these facilities.

Further reading
Handy, S. (2003). Amenity and severance. In D.A. Hensher and K.J. Button (eds), *Handbook of Transport and the Environment.* Oxford: Elsevier.

Susan Handy

company cars

Company cars are an important example of fringe benefits provided by employers in many countries. One reason why a firm provides fringe benefits relates to fiscal considerations. When income taxes are high and fringe benefits are not taxed, firms and employees will obviously be interested in the possibility of tax avoidance. Another reason is that fringe benefits may improve loyalty to the firm leading to higher satisfaction of workers, higher **productivity** and lower probability that workers will leave the firm and start working for a competitor. A third reason may be that there are market or regulation failures. For example, fringe benefits may give firms flexibility in situations where salary systems are rigid. A consideration that seems to play a role with company cars is that status effects seem to be involved. Those who are entitled to a company car have a higher status than those who are not. If status is indeed important, putting a company car at an employee's disposal may be a cheaper way to improve his or her satisfaction than the payment of the equivalent amount of additional salary. Based on the idea of a hierarchy of needs it makes sense that once employees have secured a certain salary level they start to pay more attention to the social aspects of life, including their status. The backgrounds to fringe benefits indeed seem to play a role in the case of company cars. For example, the status associated with company cars is underlined by the high economic value, their high visibility and the possibilities to differentiate between different categories of employees.

In Europe, the use of company cars as a fringe benefit is extensive. In countries like the United Kingdom and Sweden the share is above 50 per cent of all new cars that are sold, the average being around 42 per cent. In the United States the share of company cars is considerably lower. The background is probably that the base level of aggregate car ownership in the United States is much higher, and the costs of car use and ownership are considerably lower, making the company car less attractive for employees. After a limited number of years, company cars are sold to other users. Therefore their share in the stock of newly sold cars is considerably higher than in the total stock. On the other hand, their annual kilometrage is higher than that of other cars, so that their contribution to total traffic remains considerable.

Of special importance is the question of what are the consequences of the company car on travel behaviour. A first impact is that it leads to higher car ownership. The effects on kilometres driven depend on the specific arrangement between employer and employee, and on fiscal arrangements. In many cases the employer covers all expenses of the company car irrespective of the actual use made for private purposes. This makes the use of the car rather insensitive to price signals, which is probably part of the background to low elasticity of car use with respect to the cost of its use. Another possible effect is that drivers of company cars have a riskier driving style because their insurance and other costs are often covered by the employer.

Company cars lead to substantial work-related expenditures of employers. The reason that little was done in the past to introduce incentives to stimulate selective use of the company car was that transaction costs related to bookkeeping of kilometres are high.

Information technology may help to overcome the transaction cost problem. For example, if cars were to be equipped with information technology, this would enable the company and the Treasury to get reliable information on distances driven at various parts of the day. The availability of such information may lead to changes in arrangements with smaller adverse effects.

Further reading
Maslow, A.H. (1954). *Motivation and Personality.* New York: Harper & Row, New York.
Rietveld, P. and Ommeren, J.N. van (2002). Company cars and company-provided parking. In W.R. Black and P. Nijkamp (eds), *Social Change and Sustainable Transport.* Bloomington, IN: Indiana University Press.

Piet Rietveld

congestion

In traffic engineering terms, congestion is a condition that affects transportation **networks** when the demand for a facility temporarily exceeds capacity. Congestion is most often observed in large cities, where the demand for travel during morning and afternoon peak periods increases sharply, while capacity remains relatively fixed. Severe traffic congestion is viewed as a problem from the perspective of transportation planners and engineers due to the generation of significant **externalities**, such as degradation of **air quality**, and user costs like time losses and excess fuel consumption.

One useful way to describe congestion is through the use of **queuing diagrams**, which describe the flow of traffic at a specific point, usually some bottleneck where capacity is fixed. On freeways when flow exceeds capacity in these situations there are active bottlenecks. The first figure is called

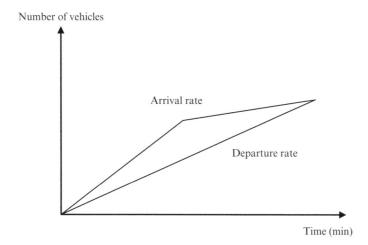

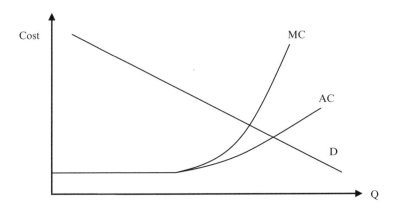

a cumulative input–output diagram and describes the rates of arrival and departure of vehicles at a bottleneck.

The departure rate indicates the rate at which vehicles are able to pass through a section of roadway, while the arrival rate indicates the rate at which new vehicles arrive. When the arrival rate exceeds the departure rate for any length of time, queues begin to form. The length of the queue, in terms of vehicles, can be measured as the vertical distance between the arrival and departure rates. Total delay can also be measured as the area of the triangle formed by the arrival and departure rate curves. Average delay is simply this triangular area divided by the number of vehicles.

While queuing diagrams represent an analytical tool developed by engineers to model congestion, economists have developed their own techniques to model congestion using microeconomic principles. The basic model of congestion on a road (in the short run) is presented in the second figure. Here the flow of vehicles, or volume (Q), is plotted on the x-axis, while the cost of travel, expressed as a generalized cost of time and money, is on the y-axis. The three curves on the graph represent the average cost of travel (AC), the marginal cost of travel (MC), and the demand for travel (D).

In this model that, unlike the **queuing model**, is not dynamic, the user cost of travel is a function of the number of vehicles attempting to use the facility (corresponding to the arrival traffic in the first Figure). Up to a certain point, the marginal cost of accommodating an additional vehicle is zero, or virtually so. However, as volumes rise and approach capacity delays begin to set in and costs begin to increase. The delay that each individual driver faces when entering a congested facility is represented by the average cost curve. Marginal costs, though, increase faster than average costs. When entering a congested facility, a driver also imposes additional costs on other drivers, for example by causing them to slow down slightly in order to maintain a reasonable spacing between vehicles. This dynamic is captured in the marginal cost curve.

This basic model is used to provide insights about optimal pricing and flows on a congested facility. Since tolls are not charged on most urban roads, it is often of interest to find the equilibrium volume of traffic in an untolled case. This equilibrium occurs where the average cost curve intersects the demand curve, which under most circumstances is also the marginal benefit curve. Economists have often advocated tolls set equal to the marginal cost of use as an effective strategy for restraining congestion. In the current example, such a toll or congestion tax would raise the price of use at each level of Q from average cost to marginal cost. Another way of thinking about this is that the external cost of congestion is equal to the area under the marginal cost curve and above the average cost curve at each level of Q. With an optimal congestion toll, the optimal level of traffic would be observed at the intersection of the demand curve and the marginal cost curve.

The analysis refers to a short-term time horizon in which capacity is considered fixed. This analysis can also be extended to the long-term case in which capacity is also variable. In such a case, the objective becomes to optimize the sum of delay costs and capacity costs relative to demand.

A wide variety of policies have been adopted in response to increasing traffic congestion in cities. Supply-side policies that attempt to increase the capacity of the roadway **network** have been among the most common. These include new highways, additional capacity on existing facilities, traffic signal coordination on arterials that are not grade-separated, one-way streets, ramp metering at entry points on limited-access highways, and the use of reversible lanes that provide additional capacity temporarily in the direction of peak traffic flows. A number of demand-side measures have also been adopted, sometimes as complements to the supply enhancement measures, in an attempt to reduce peak-period traffic flows. These include promotion of public transport, carpooling, walking, bicycling, **telecommuting**, **parking** pricing, charging tolls for peak period use of congested facilities or entry into congested areas, and modification of the built environment to reduce travel demand.

The last of these policies, modification of the built environment, is among the most intriguing policies and also among the most uncertain. Such policies are typically adopted with the intention of reducing overall levels of vehicle travel, but are also loosely targeted at reducing peak period trip-making. Policies aimed at altering the built environment have become increasingly common, as many urban planners and environmentalists have contended that traditional, supply-side methods of approaching traffic congestion are ineffective because they simply promote lower-density development and greater vehicle travel.

This latter argument is a variation of the '**induced demand for travel**' hypothesis, that is, that new highway construction will be ineffective at reducing congestion because as supply increases there will be a corresponding increase in the quantity demanded – that is, the demand curve is not vertical. The hypothesis generally assumes that there is some 'latent' demand for the use of a congested facility, and that this demand is usually diverted to alternate routes, modes, departure times or destinations. Hansen and Huang showed a nearly unit elasticity of travel demand with respect to road capacity, and sparked much interest in this phenomenum. The upshot of this line of research has been that road capacity expansion proposals are now often heavily scrutinized, and much more attention has been paid to the implications of new highway projects in terms of their potential effects on urban structure and land use.

The measurement of congestion in terms of aggregate economic costs is an activity that has become well established in recent years in the United States. The Texas Transportation Institute (TTI) at Texas A&M University periodically produces its *Urban Mobility Report*, which estimates the costs of urban congestion in terms of lost time and wasted fuel. The report uses data from the United States Federal Highway Administration's Highway Performance Monitoring System (HPMS) to estimate traffic density and speeds on the arterial highway **networks** for a large sample of cities. The most recent version of the report (2007) collected data on 437 United States cities to provide a very rough estimate of nationwide congestion costs. For 2007, congestion is estimated to have imposed $78 billion in economic losses on cities, based on 4.2 billion hours of additional travel delay and 2.9 billion gallons of excess fuel consumption.

In addition to providing estimates of the cost of congestion, TTI also calculates various other congestion indicators. These include measures of annual hours of delay per peak period traveller, gallons of wasted fuel per peak period traveller, and a 'travel time index', which measures the ratio of peak to off-peak travel times in a given city. In recent years, the set of measures has expanded to include estimates of congestion cost savings due to various construction and operational improvements, as well as demand reduction measures such as public transit improvements. The publishing of these data has gone hand in hand with the advent of sponsorship of the annual study by, among others, the American Road and Transportation Builders Association and the American Public Transportation Association, both of whom are influential lobbying organizations in state and federal transportation policy-making.

Many of the measures that the report produces are based on federal

HPMS data, and thus are available as far back as 1982 for a number of large American cities. This permits the analysis of trends in various measures over time at both the local and national level. Analysis of these trends generally shows congestion worsening in the majority of United States cities.

Further reading

Hansen, M. and Y. Huang (1997). Road supply and traffic in California urban areas. *Transportation Research, A* **31**, 205–18.

Schrank, D. and T. Lomax (2007). *The 2007 Urban Mobility Report.* College Station, TX: Texas A&M University, Texas Transportation Institute.

Zhang, L. and D. Levinson (2004). Some properties of flows at freeway bottlenecks. *Journal of the Transportation Research Board* **1883**, 122–31.

Michael Iacono and *David Levinson*

congestion pricing analysis

Congestion pricing schemes generally rely on the use of monetary disincentives for travelling by a private vehicle during peak traffic periods on congested spatial corridors. The implementation of congestion pricing may lead to complex travel changes: individuals may stop making one or more trips, change the location of their activity participation, change travel modes, change time of day of travel, switch routes, shift responsibilities to other household individuals, chain or decouple activities, or combine these response strategies. Thus, the redistribution of vehicular trips in space and time due to pricing strategies can be examined only through the development of a comprehensive analysis framework to accommodate the many possible responses of road users.

Several different kinds of data sources may be used for congestion pricing analysis and there are several important methodological considerations.

Before–after traffic count data on current facilities with congestion pricing
If the emphasis of the analysis is solely to understand the effects of a potential congestion pricing scheme on particular facilities, then traffic count data from a current facility with pricing may provide useful information. However, a problem with traffic count data is that one cannot identify the reason for the observed changes. Thus, if the intent is to understand the reasons behind the travel changes to predict better the repercussions over the entire traffic system network, before–after traffic count data are inadequate. Besides, transferring aggregate findings from one spatial location to another has its own, rather substantial problems.

Only revealed preference (RP) data

RP data correspond to actual travel behaviour data and represent important information about preferences. Thus, models of activity–travel patterns, including activity and travel generation, activity participation location, travel mode, time of day and route choice, from RP data can be used to estimate the effects of congestion pricing schemes as long as cost is included as a variable in the model. However, there are two limitations of RP data for predicting congestion pricing impacts. First, if the RP data is from an environment with no current congestion pricing policies, use of RP data implies an assumption that the behaviours and responsiveness of individuals will not change due to a changed environment. Second, it is difficult to obtain precise parameters characterizing behaviour due to inadequate observed variation in, and high correlation among, exogenous variables of interest such as times and costs.

Only stated preference (SP) data

SP data refer to self-stated choices in response to controlled exposures to packages of different service levels. The controlled nature of the SP experiments provides the opportunity to collect information on travel responses to congestion pricing along several dimensions and also avoids multicollinearity. However, the limitations of SP data for congestion pricing analysis include 'setting bias' (that is, the choice is made in a hypothetical setting) and 'policy bias' (that is respondents attempt to influence the outcome to favour a certain policy rather than provide objective responses).

Combined RP–SP data

RP and SP data can complement one another. Such data pooling is based on the hypothesis that there is a common preference structure underlying the RP and SP data.

Combined survey and traffic count data

The analyst can also combined survey data (RP only, SP only, or RP–SP) with traffic count data. The traffic count data may be used purely as a validation source for the predictions from the survey data or can also be used to estimate behavioural parameters. Recent methodological advances allow combining disaggregate survey data with aggregate count data for parameter estimation.

The focus here will be on joint RP–SP estimation for congestion pricing analysis, though many of the issues are also relevant for any analysis of pricing strategies. Four important issues need to be recognized in this context.

Firstly, inter-alternative error structure. The literature on joint RP–SP methods has, with few exceptions, assumed a multinomial logit (MNL) structure for the RP and SP choice processes. However, with recent methodological advances, RP–SP methods can be quite easily extended to accommodate flexible competitive patterns through the use of generalized extreme value (GEV) models and/or a mixed MNL approach.

Secondly, scale difference. The second econometric issue in joint RP–SP modelling is that RP and SP choices are made under different circumstances; RP choices are revealed choices in the real world, while SP choices are stated choices made in an experimental and hypothetical setting. Since the RP and SP choice settings are quite different, there is no reason to believe that the variance of the unobserved factors in the RP setting will be identical to that of the variance of unobserved factors in the SP setting.

Thirdly, unobserved heterogeneity (taste variation) effects. The third econometric issue is associated with unobserved heterogeneity effects or unobserved to the analyst taste differences across decision-makers in the intrinsic preference for a choice alternative, preference heterogeneity, and/or in the sensitivity to characteristics of the choice alternatives, response heterogeneity. These unobserved attributes generate a correlation in utility for an alternative across all choice occasions (RP and SP choices) of the individual. The unobserved heterogeneity effects also lead indirectly to non-independent and identically distributed (IID) error structures across alternatives at each choice occasion, so that the independence of irrelevant alternatives (IIA) property does not hold at any choice occasion. Finally, accommodating unobserved heterogeneity allows the identification of a distribution of willingness to pay for travel time savings and travel time reliability.

Fourthly, state dependence effect. The fourth econometric issue in joint RP–SP estimation is the state dependence effect, which refers to the influence of the actual, revealed choice on the stated choices of the individual (the term 'state dependence' is used more broadly here than its typical use in the econometrics field, where the term is reserved specifically for the effect of actual past choices on actual current choices).

The fundamental reason for considering all the four modelling issues simultaneously is that there is likely to be interactions among them. For example, accommodating restrictive inter-alternative error structures rather than flexible error structures can lead to misleading behavioural conclusions about taste variation effects.

Further reading
Lindsey, R. and E. Verhoef (2001). Traffic congestion and congestion pricing. In K.J. Button and D.A. Hensher (eds), *Handbook of Transport Systems and Traffic Control*. Oxford: Pergamon.

Chandra Bhat

congestion pricing practice

Congestion pricing encompasses a wide variety of approaches to bring market-pricing principles to bear on transportation decision-making. Projects that have been implemented or contemplated can be grouped into two broad categories: projects involving tolls, and projects not involving tolls.

Projects involving tolls may include charges for road use that vary by demand although this is often not the case. Charges may vary on a pre-scheduled basis, for example by time of day, or dynamically in response to real-time changes in demand. Whereas toll rates on conventional toll facilities are set primarily to achieve certain revenue targets for financing of the facilities, congestion-priced toll rates are set to achieve specific targets of reductions in demand or to maintain specific levels of performance on the priced facility, for example a target speed range, or a target 'optimum' volume to capacity ratio. Congestion pricing projects involving tolls may be categorized according to their extent of application, as the following.

Priced lanes
HOT lanes involve converting existing high-occupancy vehicle (HOV) lanes into priced lanes called high-occupancy toll (HOT) lanes, or building new HOT lanes. These projects allow vehicles not meeting established occupancy requirements for an HOV lane to 'buy-in' to the lane by paying a toll. Electronic tolling is used to ensure high-speed access to the lane and tolls are set at levels necessary to maintain the lane's speed advantage. HOT lanes provide a high-speed alternative for travelers wanting to bypass congested lanes. They can improve the use of capacity on previously underutilized HOV lanes.

Express toll lanes involve the pricing of new and/or existing highway lanes, generally in conjunction with highway expansion. Users must pay a toll to gain access to the express lanes. Preference (for example reduced-toll access) may be provided for high-occupancy vehicles.

Fast and intertwined regular (FAIR) lanes involve providing toll credits to all highway users based on their monitored usage of free regular lanes adjacent to premium-service HOT or express toll lanes. Accumulated credits would allow periodic free use of the priced lanes by these motorists, so that members of all income groups would obtain the benefits of using the priced lanes in proportion to their travel needs. This approach addresses income-based equity issues. Also, no one is asked to 'pay again' for use of lanes 'already paid for' through taxes – a common objection to pricing of existing free lanes.

If use of priced lanes is restricted to trucks, the lanes are called TOT lanes.

Priced roadways
Priced tollways: this category of pricing introduces variable tolls on all lanes of roadway facilities (for example roads, bridges and tunnels) that already have fixed tolls, or are being constructed as toll facilities. In all cases where variable tolls have been implemented in the United States, variable toll rates have applied only to motorists paying electronically, while cash toll rates have remained fixed all day. The goal is to reduce congestion by encouraging shifts to off-peak periods. Toll authorities have often introduced variable tolls in conjunction with planned increases in the fixed cash toll rate and marketed the variable pricing program as an off-peak discount program for those paying electronically.

High-performance highways: according to the high-performance highway concept, transportation operators charge variable tolls on toll-free highways on all lanes, but only during congested periods on critical congested segments, not on the entire system. The variable toll dissuades some motorists from using limited-access highways at critical bottleneck locations where traffic demand is high and where surges in demand could push the highway over the threshold at which traffic flow collapses.

Zone-based pricing
This project category involves either variable or fixed charges to drive within or into a congested area within a city. With cordon pricing, motorists are charged at a cordon location to enter or leave the zone, but trips made entirely within the zone are not charged. With area pricing, on the other hand, motorists are also charged for trips made entirely within the zone.

Systemwide pricing
This project category encompasses pricing at several locations throughout a metropolitan region, state, or country. Charges may apply only on limited-access facilities, or on both limited-access and lower-class facilities. Systemwide pricing programs are operating on a citywide basis in Singapore and Santiago de Chile. In both cities, charges are adjusted based on speed of traffic. Germany has implemented nationwide tolling for trucks on its limited-access highways, but tolls do not vary based on traffic levels. Revenue-neutral credit-based systems have been conceptualized to address equity and fairness issues that arise with proposals to

impose new systemwide charges, for example a 'FAST miles' approach being studied in Minnesota.

Projects not involving tolls
These include projects that make auto use costs variable. Fixed costs of auto ownership, such as insurance costs, auto lease costs or registration fees generally do not depend directly on the amount the auto is driven. Projects in this category are designed to convert those fixed costs into costs that vary according to the miles the auto is driven, thus giving the driver the incentive to recognize these costs when making the decision to drive. Projects include mileage-based insurance, lease charges, taxes and fees.

The **Parking** pricing project category encompasses parking policies that rely on market forces to influence the decision to drive, including variable pricing of curbside parking, commuter parking taxes, and parking 'cash out' programs that require employers to provide their employees with the option to take the value of free or subsidized employee parking in cash in lieu of using the parking space provided by the employer.

Further reading
DeCorla-Souza, Patrick (2007). *High-Performance Highways*. Available at: http://www.tfhrc.gov/pubrds/07may/01.htm.
Federal Highway Administration (2007). *Congestion Pricing: A Primer.* Available at http://ops.fhwa.dot.gov/publications/congestionpricing/index.htm.

Patrick DeCorla-Souza

congestion pricing theory

Congestion pricing refers to pricing mechanisms designed to induce the economically efficient use of congestible facilities. Examples of congestible facilities include highways, airport runways, shipping terminals and the Internet. They are congestible in the sense that the costs faced by each user tend to increase with the number of users. As such, marginal usage costs can exceed average usage costs, resulting in external costs called congestion **externalities**. If users do not bear the external costs they generate then, in equilibrium, the facility's use will be inefficiently high and a deadweight loss will ensue. Congestion pricing prescribes fees that force users to internalize these externalities to some extent, thereby reducing or eliminating the deadweight loss.

Congestion pricing principles are best illustrated by a common application: the use of tolls to manage highway traffic congestion. For example, consider an urban highway travelled by solo rush-hour commuters – a market for trips, v, both demanded and supplied by travellers. The **generalized price** of each trip is p, which includes travel-time and other non-pecuniary costs, and gives rise to an inverse demand function for trips, (v/k). The cost of each trip is $c = c(v/k)$, where k is the highway's capacity and (v/k) is the volume-to-capacity ratio; $\partial c/\partial v > 0$ indicates that the highway is congestible. The total cost of all trips is then $C = c \cdot v$. Accordingly, c is an average cost function, but it can be interpreted as marginal private cost because it gives the cost faced by each traveller when considering a trip. The **marginal social cost** of an additional trip to road users, however, is:

$$MC = \frac{\partial C}{\partial v} = c + \frac{\partial c}{\partial v} \cdot v \tag{1}$$

comprising the private cost faced by the entering traveller (c), plus the increased cost imposed on all existing travellers ($\frac{\partial c}{\partial v} \cdot v$). This later cost is external to the entry decision and is thus called a congestion externality, measuring a gap between the private and social costs of travel. In equilibrium, entry will occur until:

$$p(v) = c \tag{2}$$

but the efficient level of traffic is the solution to the net-benefit maximization problem:

$$Max \int_{0}^{v} p(v')dv' - c \cdot v \tag{3}$$

yielding the first-order condition:

$$p(v) = c + \frac{\partial c}{\partial v} \cdot v \tag{4}$$

such that the marginal benefit of the last trip taken equals its **marginal social cost** – including the external congestion cost it generates. As such, the equilibrium traffic level indicated by Equation 2 will be inefficiently high. The efficient traffic level can be induced, however, by introducing a congestion toll, τ, levied on each traveller. The new equilibrium condition is:

$$p(v) = c + \tau \tag{5}$$

and it follows from Equations 4 and 5 that the optimal toll is:

$$\tau = \frac{\partial c}{\partial v} \cdot v \tag{6}$$

that equals the congestion externality generated at the efficient traffic level (a Pigouvian tax). This result is generalizable to a **network** of highways and multiple travel periods, and also to a variety of congestible facilities beyond highways. Note, however, that such tolls will not generally eliminate congestion **externalities**; they will instead reduce them to efficient levels.

Congestion-pricing policies often meet public opposition, partially due to the welfare losses they initially impose on travellers, including those priced off of the highway. The tolls levied on each traveller typically exceed the travel cost savings they yield, implying that the bulk of the policy's net welfare gains take the form of toll revenues. As such, congestion pricing is only Pareto optimal if these revenues are somehow returned to those it targets. One way to accomplish this is to invest in additional highway capacity; it can be shown that for travel cost functions like $c = c(v/k)$ that tolls like Equation 6 will generate just enough revenue to cover the cost of optimal capacity expansion. Another way is to use the revenues to reduce distortionary taxes in another market, thereby eliminating two deadweight losses with one toll (a double dividend).

The toll in Equation 6 is a first-best toll because it achieves maximum welfare gains, which is only possible because it is derived without constraints. But such constraints exist in reality, such as an inability to toll some portion of a highway **network**. In such cases the goal is to derive a second-best toll by maximizing objective functions such as Equation 2 subject to these constraints. This second-best approach is particularly useful for analyzing real-world applications of congestion pricing, such as cordon pricing in Singapore and London, and proposed in New York, where tolls are charged only to enter a central business district; and value pricing such as tolled highway lanes in Southern California that run adjacent to non-tolled lanes.

The rush hour example illustrates static congestion pricing, where travellers' departure times are treated as exogenous, implying a fixed-commute-period duration. Endogenizing departure times gives rise to dynamic congestion pricing, which considers how tolls can influence departure times and, thus, the duration of the commute period. In a dynamic pricing framework it has been shown that optimal tolls can eliminate excess congestion (due to departure-time adjustments) if there is optimal road capacity, and that the tolls equal the travel-cost savings they provide – an encouraging result in light of public opposition to congestion pricing.

Further reading
Small, K. and E. Verhoef (2007). *The Economics of Urban Transportation*. London: Routledge.

Verhoef, E., P. Nijkamp and P. Rietveld (1996). Second-best congestion pricing: the case of an untolled alternative. *Journal of Urban Economics* **40**, 279–302.

Seiji S.C. Steimetz

congestion response behaviour

Congestion response behaviour is concerned with a range of reactions of individual travellers and authorities or other public providers to congestion-related changes in travel conditions and their consequent implications. Authorities' behavioural reactions include three basic categories in the following order of usage frequency: reactions related to management of traffic flows (the highest usage); reactions related to activity scheduling; and reactions related to spatial planning. This order can also be considered as an order of perceived difficulty of implementation.

Responses of individual travellers are more complex and can be divided into two general types: preventive and reactive. Each response has a different theoretical implication mainly for modelling choice behaviour. The individual may react in a preventive way when she or he expects, or is informed about congestion prior to departure. Accordingly, a preventive response is adopted in cases of recurrent congestion, as well as in the presence of pre-trip information referring to either recurrent or non-recurrent incidents. A reactive response is adopted in non-recurrent incidents of congestion, or as a response to en route information, usually under time pressure.

Since congestion occurrence, as well as congestion delay, are highly variable from day to day, reactions to congestion are assumed also to be dynamic. Accordingly, decisions are made sequentially whereby the task specification may, either independently or as a result of previous decisions, be contingent on the outcome of earlier decisions, with the implications of any decision having potential future consequences. Dynamic decision-making implies that both choice and knowledge play a major role in explaining the order of response adoption. Choice depends first on the alternatives the traveller subjectively considers to be feasible. These alternatives are constantly changing with the updating of knowledge. Knowledge in this context is a learning from day-to-day, first-hand experience (that is, exposure to congestion), complemented by exogenous information from various media outlets, word of mouth, and others.

Knowledge is directly connected to two types of expectations that may affect the individual's reactions to congestion: expectations about the performance of the feasible alternatives, and expectations about the future solutions to congestion. The first expectation is assumed to affect short-term reactions, mainly those related to daily activity, travel and driving behaviour; whereas the second type of expectation is assumed to affect long-term personal responses such as change in location and / or in lifestyle. It is further assumed that the more frequently practiced reactions are those stimulated more by congestion consequences. The less practiced responses depend on other considerations, mainly personal constraints and the anticipated long-run consequences of the individual's response.

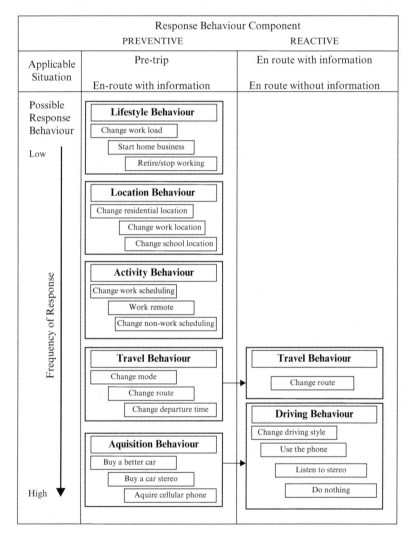

A number of studies of congestion behaviour have mentioned a range of responses for which data on individuals adoption or consideration are available. The Figure classifies these responses into six types of behaviours, ranging from the least to the most frequently practiced, as following:

- Lifestyle behaviour is the least frequently practiced response to a severe and continuous traffic delay caused by recurrent congestion. It involves (in decreasing order) a change in the individual's work load, the start of a home business and, least practiced, retirement. It implies the largest reduction in driving time for the individual.
- Location behaviour is also a response to continuous congestion and it is mainly concerned with changes in the place of residence, work or school. There is empirical evidence of both lifestyle and location behaviours which reflect a spatio-temporal reorganization of space and time.
- Activity behaviour refers to the change of one's daily schedule of either work or non-work activities as a response to non-recurrent travel constraints, either traveller or situational related. It usually changes the frequency and the volume of traffic when forecasting travel demand is concerned.
- Travel behaviour includes the various choices facing the driver as regard to the choice of destination, route, departure time and mode, including substitutes to travel (for example the use of **telecommunication** options). Both activity and travel behaviours constitute the major part of travel demand. They reflect the spatio-temporal patterns and the volumes of the various modes.
- Driving behaviour actually deals with the individual's motoring and overall actions while driving. These are responses to traveller, environmental and situational constraints, both objective and subjectively perceived. They directly affect travel **safety**, but they also affect, in a dynamic way, the momentary situation on the road that may, in turn, affect the individual's decision-making.
- Acquisition behaviour is the most practiced reaction to traffic delays and is highly affected by traveller-related characteristics. It is concerned with the acquisition of a better car (more comfortable and better suited for long trips, safer, and so on), a good stereo system (less boring while queuing), or a phone (better use of time, reduce road **safety**, and so on). It also affects both road safety and the momentary situation on the road.

Efforts to model these responses are based on decision-making mechanisms and have been mainly developed in the field of psychology. One

approach, for example, is the one based on the differentiation and consolidation theory developed by Svenson. Here, the goal of a decision
process is to create an alternative that is sufficiently superior in comparison to its competitors (via restructuring and application of one decision rule only), but making use of a number of rules that are contingent
on the situation and the individual. A more recent approach is the one
based on decision field theory developed by Busemeyer and Townsend,
which aims at understanding the motivational and cognitive mechanisms
that guide a deliberation process involved in making decisions under
uncertainty.

Further reading
Mokhtarian, P.L., E.A. Raney and I. Salomon (1997). Behavioral responses to
    congestion: identifying patterns and socio-economic differences in adoption.
    Transport Policy **4**, 147–60.
Raney, E.A., P.L. Mokhtarian and I. Salomon (2000). Modeling individuals'
    consideration of strategies to cope with congestion. *Transportation Research F*
    3,141–65.
Stern, E. (1998). Travel choices in congestions: modeling and research needs. In
    T. Garling, T. Laitila and K. Westin (eds), *Theoretical Foundations of Travel
    Choice Modeling*. Oxford: Pergamon Press.
Svenson, O. (1992). Differentiation and consolidation theory of human decisions
    making: a frame of reference for the study of pre-and-post-decision processes.
    Acta Psychologica **80**, 143–68.

Eliahu Stern

containers

Containers are metal boxes into which freight of all kinds can be placed to
facilitate shipment. This simple concept has revolutionized transport over
the last 50 years and has made possible the recent explosion of **international trade**. Its success is based in part on the opportunities presented for
reducing handling costs especially in ports, where cargo handling used to
require gangs of workers physically to load and secure individual items in
the holds of ships. By consolidating shipments in boxes of standard shape
and size the handling of freight can be mechanized. The concept is an old
one, however, and there are many examples of freight being placed in
boxes of various dimensions for shipment by train or ship in Europe and
North America that date from the 1920s and 1930s. It is generally accepted
that container revolution was instituted by an American trucker, Malcom
Mclean, who started a shipping service to haul freight from New York to
Houston in 1955, using boxes instead of road trailers, and placing them in

a specially modified ship, the *Ideal X*. It was Mclean who inaugurated the first international fully containerized service across the Atlantic ten years later.

Like many innovations, the initial acceptance of containers as a means of hauling freight was slow. It generated opposition from dockers who saw their jobs threatened. It required significant capital investment in new types of cellular ships and necessitated new types of handling gear in ports. Placing goods of all kinds in a box presented challenges for the regulators and for the pricing of freight rates. In the early years there was a proliferation of box dimensions that made their widespread application difficult. Many shipping services combined containers with break-bulk traffic, thereby negating the efficiencies of containerization.

By the mid-1960s the International Organization for Standardization (ISO) worked to establish common sizes for containers, their fittings and their weight standards. The standards were set at two lengths: 40 foot (12 192 mm) and 20 foot (6096 mm), which in turn has provided the universal measure of container activity, the twenty-foot equivalent unit (TEU). The width of containers is fixed at 8 feet (2483 mm), with their height being originally set at 8 feet. Over time the height has been modified to 8 feet 6 inches for many containers.

An American innovation at the start, international shipping companies began rapidly to adopt the system by the late 1960s. Containers and container ships were deployed increasingly on the transatlantic and later the trans-Pacific trade routes. The shipping lines began to exploit the significant scale economies that the container offered, and from the 1970s up to the present day there has been a rapid progression in vessel capacity, from a few hundred boxes in the earliest ships to over 14 000 TEUs today. This progression of scale in vessel capacity combined with the explosion of container traffic volumes around the world has transformed the industry. Container shipping is dominated by a small number of carriers with the financial capacity to offer global services, and maintaining an extensive fleet of very large ships. For example, the largest container carrier, Maersk, has a fleet of 500 ships and at any one point in time it claims to be carrying cargo worth 3 percent of the world's gross domestic product (GDP). Today, no American carriers remain: they have all been taken over by international shipping lines.

Containers have transformed the port industry. Container terminals are highly mechanized and require extensive storage space so that containers can be assembled to meet the arrival of ever larger ships that are turned around in a matter of hours. They need access to ever deeper navigation channels. These requirements have presented serious challenges to older ports whose sites are ill-suited to container operations. Major ports such as New York and Rotterdam have had to invest heavily to keep up, and others have fallen by the wayside, such as Liverpool and Boston. Today the largest container ports are in Asia, led by Singapore, Hong Kong, Shanghai and Busan.

The container has also facilitated intermodality. The box is easily transferred to trucks, rail and barges. In North America it has revitalized rail freight, with trains providing essential links between the ports and inland destinations, especially since the introduction of double stacking in the late 1980s. Single-stack services on a smaller scale exist from the Dutch and German ports to markets in Central and Eastern Europe. The Rhine river is also an important corridor for containers carried on barges to the gateway ports of Rotterdam and Antwerp.

The container has penetrated all parts of the world and is used to carry all kinds of cargoes. It has transformed the transport industry, especially shipping, and has greatly facilitated world trade. As Levinson said in the subtitle of his book: 'It made the world smaller and the world economy bigger'.

Further reading
Containerisation International (monthly). Informa UK Ltd.
Levinson, M. (2006). *The Box: It Made the World Smaller and the World Economy Bigger.* Princeton, NJ: Princeton University Press.

Brian Slack

contingent valuation

Contingent valuation (CV) is a survey-based or 'stated preference' methodology to place monetary value on non-market goods or services, so that it can be used to evaluate external costs and benefits of projects and policies. In a CV survey, respondents are asked to choose (that is, to state their preferences) among different scenarios of public actions. Their responses provide information that enables analysts to estimate respondents' willingness to pay (WTP).

A number of survey and statistical techniques have been proposed to calculate realistic WTP. In particular, direct elicitation methods (DEM) seek to elicit the WTP amounts for each respondent by simply and directly asking about their WTP.

The most commonly used CV format is the dichotomous-choice model (DCM) where the respondent is asked to choose between two alternatives, one being the status quo policy and the other alternative policy representing a cost higher than maintaining the status quo. In other words, the respondent is asked to state whether they would be willing to pay for the new policy at the offered price. In this case 'yes' means willing to pay, and 'no' means not willing to pay.

Consider a consumer's utility function $u(y, s, j)$, where y is the income, s is a vector of socio-economic characteristics of the respondent and the variable j assumes a value of unity if the respondent is directly affected by the proposed policy and zero if not. It should be noted that the main difference between DEM and the DCM is that the second method relies on the analysis of the characteristics of a large sample to infer respondents' WTP. Thus, the variable j is meant to capture the probability to include in the sample respondents not interested in the output of the policy or of the project. Consequently, the utility function is unknown to the analyst, so that the following expression can be written:

$$u(y, s, j) = v(y, s, j) + e_j \tag{1}$$

where v is the indirect utility function and e_j is an error term.

The respondent will be willing to pay an amount B of money only if:

$$v(y - B, s, 1) + e_1 > v(y, s, 0) + e_0 \tag{2}$$

In this case, the probability distribution of WTP can be expressed as:

$$P_1 = \Pr[v(y - B, s, 1) + e_1 > v(y, s, 0) + e_0] \tag{3}$$

Following Hanneman, assume $\eta = e_1 - e_0$, Equation 3 can be rewritten as:

$$P_1 = F_\eta(\Delta v) \tag{4}$$

where F_η is the probability function for η and for $\Delta v = v(y - B, s, 1) - v(y, s, 0)$.

The previous random utility model can be estimated by considering an econometric specification of Equation 4 where WTP is supposed to be a censored dependent variable in the form:

$$\begin{aligned} WTP_i^* &= 0 & \text{if } WTP_i \leq 0 \\ WTP_i^* &= WTP_i & \text{if } WTP_i > 0 \end{aligned} \tag{5}$$

Thus, the following function can be used to estimate the mean value of WTP:

$$WTP = \mathbf{b}'\mathbf{x} + e \tag{6}$$

where $\mathbf{b}'$ is the vector of parameters to be estimated, $\mathbf{x}$ is the matrix of socio-economic characteristics and income observations and $e \approx N(0, \sigma^2)$ is a random error. In the linear specification Equation 6, the mean of the WTP is:

$$E(WTP) = E(\hat{\beta}'\mathbf{x}) = \hat{\beta}'\overline{\mathbf{x}} \tag{7}$$

where $\overline{\mathbf{x}}$ is the matrix of the mean values for $\mathbf{x}$ and $\hat{\beta}$ is the vector of estimated parameters. In addition, a confidence interval for the WTP can be calculated as:

$$CI_{1-\alpha}[E(WTP)] = \hat{\beta}'\overline{\mathbf{x}} \pm t_{\frac{\alpha}{2}}\sqrt{\overline{\mathbf{x}'\Sigma_\beta\overline{\mathbf{x}}}} \tag{8}$$

where Σ_β is the asymptotic variance–covariance matrix.

It is now widely accepted by analysts that the use of double-dichotomous choice (DDC) questions reduces the need for a large number of respondents. In the DDC model, after the first question, a follow-up offer is made that is doubled if the respondent stated a positive WTP, or halved if it reverses the first offer. By using this method, the mean value of the WTP can be calculated by simply considering a multivariate specification of Equation 4. The main advantage in using this approach is that it provides a larger set of information than in the standard DCM case.

Further reading
Hannemann, W.N. (1984). Welfare evaluations in contingent valuation experiments with discrete responses. *American Journal of Agricultural Economics* **66**, 332–41.

Marco Percoco

cost functions

A cost function is a quantitative measure of costs related to output levels of a firm, and to other variables that influence costs. The costs could be limited to part of a firm – an intermediate activity – but most cost functions focus on aggregate cost relationships, that is, total output and total costs for one firm during one year constitute one data point. There can be multiple output categories.

Economists postulate a production function: a technological relationship between inputs and outputs. Firms combine inputs subject to budget constraints and the prices of inputs. For any given outlay (or specified volume of output), there is some cost-minimizing combination of inputs. A cost function relates levels of costs to different output levels assuming the efficient combination of inputs for any output level.

'Output' in transportation is more complicated than textbook examples of 'widgets'. Transportation deals with a multiplicity of outputs. There are weight and distance dimensions to transportation output and direction, or origin–destination, and multiple markets served. Despite the heterogeneity of tonne-kilometres as an output measure, most cost functions have to work with this aggregated unit of measure. Also, over time it has become important to recognize the influence of **network** characteristics separate from traffic volume.

The simplest cost function would be linear. If there are some costs that do not vary with output ('fixed costs' A), the total cost C of output Y is simply:

$$C = A + b\,Y \qquad (1)$$

where b is the marginal cost per unit of Y. In this example with fixed costs, the average cost of output declines with volume but at a decreasing rate. Because all costs are assumed to be variable in the long run, this is a short-run cost function (but some transport modes, notably railways and pipelines, have investments with very long physical lives, causing the distinction between short and long run to be difficult to establish in practice). Also, costs are influenced by input prices; they can be omitted in Equation 1 if the input prices were fixed across firms and/or over time.

Assuming a linear relationship is convenient, but it is not necessarily accurate. Various other mathematical forms may be used. In discussing cost concepts conceptually, it is customary to use general notation and leave the specific mathematical form to empirical implementation. In general, the costs of a multi-output transportation firm may be written:

$$C = C(y_1, y_2, \ldots y_n;\ w_1, w_2, \ldots w_k, \ldots w_m) \qquad (2)$$

where $y(1 \ldots n)$ are multiple outputs, and $w(1 \ldots m)$ are the prices of m inputs used in the production process. This could be estimated across a number of firms. No fixed inputs are postulated in Equation 2, it is a long-run cost formulation. This assumes that each firm has optimally adjusted all inputs for the level of output each produced. If the latter is not true, the cost function must be reformulated. For example, if firms cannot adjust their capital stocks readily, one can reformulate Equation 2 into a short-run or variable-cost formulation: the price of capital w_k would be eliminated and a measure of the firm's capital stock K would be included.

The cost function represented by Equation 2 estimates the change in costs with respect to output category, reflecting the experience across the firms. One might also make performance comparisons among firms by examining whether a firm's actual costs were above or below what is predicted by the cost function. If there are additional influences on costs not included in the equation, then it is misspecified and additional data and analysis are needed.

It is common to include both a cross-section of firms and also a number of years' data for each firm. This provides a larger data set and enables further analysis to be conducted. Expression 3 rewrites Equation 2 to include illustrative additional influences on costs:

$$C = C(y_1, y_2, \ldots y_i, \ldots y_n; w_1, w_2, \ldots w_j, \ldots w_m; t; N; ALH) \qquad (3)$$

Expression 3 postulates a technological change or **productivity** improvement that is taking place over time, hence time itself t can be used as an index of the technological change (more complex formulations can be developed). The time trend would be the (downward) shift in the cost function over time.

By looking at the relationship between costs and output levels across firms and/or years, how total costs are associated with different output levels can be observed. Firms with higher output will have higher total costs. The interesting question is whether there are differences in the unit costs for different-sized firms. If there are economies of scale, then the total costs of larger firms will increase less than proportionately with the increase in output relative to smaller firms.

Most transport cost functions make a further distinction between firms increasing output over a given **network** N, as opposed to expanding output and expanding the network together. It is common to observe 'economies of density', that total costs increase less than proportionately with volume over a given network. But if both volume and network size increase in the same proportion, would costs rise in the same proportion, or more or less? Scale economies would mean costs increased less than proportionately to the rise in output and points served. Most researchers have found near constant returns to scale, that the recognized tendency for unit costs to decline with volume are explained by economies of density rather than scale. The generic cost function 2 must include terms to indicate the size of the network N (points served or total route miles are common empirical proxies for measuring networks).

In practice there will be idiosyncrasies associated with particular firms' and/or years' data. In order to isolate statistically the precise relationship between costs and outputs corresponding to economists' cost functions, it is necessary to include other exogenous influences on costs such as terrain, weather or other influences that might affect costs of specific firms and/or years. The geographic size of a network will have an influence on costs. It is generally recognized that there are economies of distance in transportation, that is, the average costs per tonne-kilometre will be less for longer-distance trips than for shorter ones, primarily due to spreading the terminal and other overhead costs over the longer journey. Average length of haul (ALH) is another relevant measure to be included in a cost function. Other exogenous variables might be postulated (for example weather, terrain). Some formulations may include 'shift' variables for firms and/or years to isolate the idiosyncratic cost differences of a firm or in a year that would otherwise unduly affect the cost function estimation.

Empirical implementation requires adopting a particular functional form, possibly linear but more likely logarithmic or even more complex forms. Although most transport firms serve a great many markets (outputs), in practice cost functions can only include a few aggregated output categories, for example passengers and freight, and/or a few freight categories thought to have different cost characteristics.

The general formulation of Equations 2 or 3 does not rule out complex cross-relationships among variables influencing total costs. Simple cost functions such as linear (or log-linear) assume that there are separable and unique influences on costs for each variable (output category or input price). But there may be cross-relationships: producing some outputs together might bring some complementarities or diseconomies. These are known are 'economies or diseconomies of scope'. To test for these requires that cost functions allow for such interrelationships. The most common mathematical form used is the translog cost function. The translog for two outputs and two input prices, omitting the technological time trend and **network** characteristics, is written:

$$\ln C = b_0 + b_1 \ln Y_1 + b_2 \ln Y_2 + b_3 \ln W_1 + b_4 \ln W_2$$
$$+ \frac{1}{2}b_5 (\ln Y_1)^2 + \frac{1}{2}b_6 (\ln Y_2)^2 + \frac{1}{2}b_7 (\ln W_1)^2 + \frac{1}{2}b_8 (\ln W_2)^2$$
$$+ b_9 \ln Y_1 \ln Y_2 + b_{10} \ln W_1 \ln W_2 + b_{11} \ln Y_1 \ln W_1$$
$$+ b_{12} \ln Y_1 \ln W_2 + b_{13} \ln Y_2 \ln W_1 + b_{14} \ln Y_2 \ln W_2 \qquad (4)$$

The first line corresponds to a log-linear function with separable influences on costs of outputs and input prices. The second line allows for further non-linearities and the last two lines allow for interaction effects on costs of the variables. For example, if b_9 was negative, it implies economies of scope (costs reduced if Y_1 and Y_2 are produced together). The concepts of returns to density and scale are all more complicated once complex interrelationships in production are recognized. Nonetheless, that may be the reality of multiple output production in spatially diverse transportation markets.

Further reading

Braeutigam, R.R. (1999). Learning about transportation costs. In J.A. Gomez-Ibanez, W.B. Tye and C. Winston (eds), *Essays in Transportation Economics and Policy*. Washington, DC: Brookings.

Oum, T.H. and W.G. Waters II (1996). A survey of recent developments in transportation cost function research. *Logistics and Transportation Review* **32**, 423–60.

William G. Waters II

costing

Costing refers to developing estimates of the costs of supplying transportation services. It might also be labelled 'cost determination', 'cost estimation' or 'cost analysis'.

Cost analysis serves various purposes. One purpose could be measuring economies of scale (will unit costs decline with larger volumes of production?) or for micro decisions including pricing or service decisions, profitability analysis, investment in or abandonment of services, or for regulatory purposes such as setting maximum or minimum price limits. Costing may be carried out for components or activities that are only part of the overall costs of supplying transportation (activity-based costing, see below). Costing usually refers to measuring monetary costs, but it could refer to estimation of environmental or social costs.

Estimating the costs of transportation is difficult because of the heterogeneous nature of output and indivisibilities in production. The act of supplying transportation typically provides a variety of services. A tonne-kilometre of capacity in one direction or on one portion of a route serves different demands. Transporting perishable commodities is a different service than bulk products. There are many indivisibilities, or 'lumpiness' in production: a variety of demands typically are served on a single trip; some input expenditures take place infrequently and are shared among numerous trips (for example periodic maintenance). The consequence is that a variety of outputs are provided and a composite of costs are incurred over some period of time. But it is difficult, and may be impossible to identify a specific level of expenditure with a specific output (the cost-allocation problem).

There are two types of costing studies. The first type focuses on broad cost characteristics, such as the presence or absence of economies of scale. These look for cost characteristics of overall or aggregate operations of a firm (see '**cost functions**'). A second type of study focuses on specific portions of a firm's operation. These are disaggregate studies that focus on the costs of intermediate activities necessary to provide transportation. For example, moving a parcel of goods may require pickup and delivery, loading and unloading operations, shunting operations (if a rail movement), the line-haul, possible switching or transshipment en route, and returning the equipment to the origin upon completion of the journey. Then there would be further activities such as equipment or infrastructure maintenance, marketing and administration. Activity-based costing (ABC) investigates the cost of each activity and how it varies with changes in the quantity and quality provided. Then, the cost of providing a specific transportation service is estimated by summing the costs of required intermediate activities.

Broadly there are three methods for measuring cost–output relationships: use of accounting data, engineering analysis, and statistical analysis of multiple cost–output experience. The methods can overlap.

The accounting approach is easiest, providing data exist. For example, dividing the recorded total costs by the amount of traffic carried provides a measure of average costs. This could be used as a predictor of the costs of increasing or decreasing output levels. However, if some costs were fixed and did not vary with volume, then this approach would overestimate how costs would change with different levels of output. Separating fixed and variable costs would improve this estimate, but it still assumes linearity in cost–output relationships. Also, if the measure of traffic volume included diverse traffic movements, the averaging would overlook differences in the costs of providing different types of service.

The engineering approach focuses on the physical inputs required to produce an output. Multiplying input requirements by the input price provides that portion of the total costs of output. By examining all input–output requirements one can produce a cost function for various output levels. Engineering analysis can make use of physical laws or known engineering relationships (for example horsepower, hence fuel requirements to move specific tonnages) or coefficients can be developed by controlled experiment (for example estimating input wear associated with different output or activity levels).

Statistical or econometric approaches to costing apply statistical techniques such as regression analysis to a data set of multiple cost–output experiences. These might be accounting data for a number of firms and/ or a number of years, possibly adjusted for inflation or other extraneous influences to make a consistent data set. If there are systematic differences among firms or years (for example adverse terrain or weather will make certain firms' or years' cost experience higher than 'normal'), additional variables can be included in the regression to estimate better the coefficient between costs and output. Statistical analysis may be able to separate aggregated costs among multiple outputs.

Further reading
Talley, W.K. (1988). *Transport Carrier Costing*. New York: Gordon & Breach.
Waters, W.G., II (1976). Statistical costing in transportation. *Transportation Journal* **15**, 49–62.

William G. Waters II

courier, express and parcel industry

Over the years, the cargo express service providers have been subsumed under the collective term of CEP (courier, express and parcel) services. The term 'express' is often equated with means of transport of goods or persons with high velocity, whereas the higher celerity arises from the privileged conditioning of goods and persons, and does not refer exclusively to a higher speed of the mode of transport.

The development of CEP services can be ascribed to two constitutive trends. First, since the 1970s the liberalization and **deregulation** of mail services in many countries became predominant, whereby a number of further providers launched the market of fast and reliable forwarding of documents and parcels. Second, the demand for the fulfilment of transport services has changed significantly, particularly in response to new logistic requirements of **just-in-time** and modular manufacturing concepts, and due to increasing spatial division of labour in the course of outsourcing and the **globalization** of procurement and sales markets. The exigencies of transport services, resulting from growing demand for faster, punctual and reliable forwarding of goods, can be outlined as:

- Shortening of the transport cycles by the demand for transport of smallish consignments often with a high frequency.
- Establishment of transnational global **networks** for implementing door-to-door delivery in a globalized economy.
- Organizable runtimes and high standards of services, culminating

in individual services reflecting the rise of the average value of the goods transported.
- Dedication of new information and communication technologies, especially track-and-trace concepts.

The established providers, mostly forwarders, were not able to react adequately to these modified requirements, as their systems were not designed for these kinds of services. In response to changing transport needs, additional providers of transport services launched the market that was hitherto mainly operated by monopolized public mailing companies. The new services defined themselves by the characteristics of short runtimes, reliability and calculability of transports. The industry of CEP services was established with a sophisticated offer that can be delineated in the master segments.

The courier services segment comprises all consignments that are permanently attended on the way from the originator to the addressee by a courier in person. These attended transports can be found on national as well as international routes. A consignment is most often a letter, document or parcel. But to some extent pallets can be under personal attendance too, carrying exhibits, designer chattels or suchlike. 'Courier' includes those providing classic direct courier services, courier **taxis**, and envoys carrying official documents, as well as on-board couriers who carry small, high value packages as part of their baggage on a plane. The city couriers that often deliver consignments by foot or bicycle are a classical courier segment as well. Over the last mile, the deliverer can also be called a courier. More recently the tender of courier services is expanding and contains a multiplicity of added value services, including the forwarding of temperature-controlled goods, medicines, small animals or more intricate logistic services like a regional spare part service. Within this segment, small- and medium-sized businesses that benefit from proximity to the customer often operate.

The segment of express services comprises consignments which are not directly, exclusively or personally attended on delivery, but consolidated by logistic nodes (hubs) and delivered at a definite and guaranteed delivery date. The express transports differ from the forwarders' services by the agreed door-to-door runtimes. The classical offers of this segment can be divided into express services with covenant delivery dates, for example before ten o'clock, and express services without covenant delivery dates but a fixed period of delivery of 24 or 48 hours. These are partly referred to as express freight services and imply further logistic services. Beside this established service range, a multiplicity of customer-oriented and particular offers have been developed, like the same-day, next-day, over-night, in-night, return, proof-of-delivery and special speed services. Such services mostly require flexible and fast means of transport, like road or air transport modes.

Parcel services represent a subsegment of the express services and are distinguished by the consistent rationalization of logistics sequences. These so-called system service providers operate standardized consign-ments (parcels) with delimited measurement and weight (most often up to 20 kg, 31.5 kg, and 70 kg). They are mainly handled by automated or partly automated sorting facilities, using the latest information technolo-gies. The term time for a delivery depends on the transport system chosen. In addition to trucks, seagoing vessels and railways are often used. The creation of parcel services is carried out primarily by medium-sized and big consolidated cargo forwarders.

The distinction between CEP services, consolidated cargo providers and mail service providers is increasingly blurred, noticeably due to further lib-eralization of markets and increasing product diversification. Mail service providers, for example, use similar transport system to parcel service pro-viders. Their **networks** often result in a one- or multilevel **hub-and-spoke system**, as is common for air traffic.

Heike Flämig

D

defence logistics

Defence logistics – or military logistics as it is sometimes called – plays a vital role in a country's national security. One of the earliest writers on the military 'art' following the Napoleonic wars of the early nineteenth century, Baron de Jomini, described military logistics as the 'practical art of moving armies (and sustaining them)'. That definition of nearly 200 years ago applies today with one alteration. Replacing more inclusive 'defence forces' for 'armies' will include maritime, air and special operations forces. In periods of conflict after 11 September 2001, this definition can be expanded further to include also teams from other government agencies, domestic and international, and even non-governmental organizations.

Clearly defence logistics is key to enabling all kinds of operations involving a nation's military forces – from the joint forces conventional war campaign that produced the 'regime change' in Iraq in 2003, to the disaster relief campaign following Hurricane Katrina in Louisiana, United States.

While Baron de Jomini thought of military logistics as an 'art', nations today conceive of defence logistics as a set of processes – not unlike commercial logistics processes. United States forces logistics organizations develop and execute processes to:

- Project land and special operations forces.
- Support the projection of maritime and air forces (some self-deploy).
- Sustain the forces in operations and training.
- Support stabilization and reconstruction operations (as in Iraq and Afghanistan today).
- Redeploy and reconstitute forces following operations.

These are the primary defence logistics tasks that begin with initial campaign planning and operate simultaneously throughout the campaign. The responsibility for both developing and executing force projection processes is shared among several commands, defence agencies and the military services. The regional combatant command which is undertaking the campaign develops the detailed plan for the conduct of the campaign from the reception of deploying units through phases of operations to final accomplishment of the mission. The command prepares a list of units of all the military services necessary to implement the plan in the desired sequence of arrival in the area of operations for employment in the campaign. In the United States, this list is a collaborative effort prepared with the United States Joint Forces Command which oversees all deployable forces of the services, the services that will provide the units, the United States Transportation Command that will provide the air- and sealift to carry the forces' people and equipment and the necessary sustaining supplies, and the regional combatant command which prepares the plan for reception, staging and onward movement of the forces and supplies. The list that results after this collaboration, termed the 'time phased force deployment data' or TPFDD as it is popularly known within the United States military, represents the force projection part of the campaign plan.

The third of the five major defence logistics tasks – sustain the forces in operations and training – sounds simple in concept but requires the establishment and management of multiple **supply-chains** and service provider networks. The supply-chains stretch from sources of supplies domestically and in foreign countries to 'customer' organizations of all services within areas of operations, many of which are continually moving. Sustaining forces in training requires those same supply-chains and service providers to reach organizations around the world where forces are deployed in forward bases.

To understand these sustainment processes, it is useful to categorize them by purpose: sustaining the people engaged in the campaign or training, and sustaining the equipment systems they use. First, the people. Their sustainment includes all the resources needed to preserve the mission readiness of the people, maintaining a healthy, motivated force by providing food, water, clothing, shelter and threat protection, and services to include health care, showers and laundry, morale activities, base lodging, food service, sanitation and other 'municipal' services. In the austere conditions of most campaigns of the present and near future, nearly all the sustainment resources for the people must be brought to the area of operations and distributed.

Sustainment of equipment – weapons as well as support systems – is even more complex and just as essential to the ability of the forces to carry out combat and support tasks. Thus the objective of equipment and system sustainment – as for people – is to maintain mission-ready units, able to accomplish the missions for which they are designed. System sustainment takes place in the units to which the systems are assigned where technicians perform preventive maintenance and repairs requiring component replacement. Component repair is usually accomplished in facilities that are set up in areas relatively free from active combat and accomplished by civil servant or contractor technicians. Key ingredients of effective system sustainment are competent technicians to diagnose failures and make the repairs, and timely access to the necessary replacement components, fuel and lubricants.

The fourth task, also mostly sustainment, is relatively new to military logistics in its potential magnitude – sustaining stabilization and reconstruction operations. While the sustainment tasks for people and systems described above certainly apply to this class of operations, there are unique additions to those supply categories used by other government agencies, the military and possibly non-governmental organizations for stabilization and reconstruction tasks. The range of supplies and services covers humanitarian supplies – food, shelter, medical supplies, construction materials, weapons and equipment for the indigenous armed forces and police, and transportation, protection and training services. The result of the addition of stabilization and reconstruction operations to the sustainment requirement of defence logisticians is the need for them to expand their vision and skills to encompass an ever wider variety of supply-chains and service providers than is required for conventional operations. Distribution of supplies and the very movement of forces and reconstruction teams in austere environments such as Afghanistan or Central Africa are daunting challenges requiring both innovative technology and innovative processes. One such technology with great potential and now under development by the United States Defense Department is a variable buoyancy air vehicle which could traverse hundreds of miles of road-poor countryside with meaningful cargo loads, for example 40–60 tonnes, and land and take off in its own footprint, returning to base without the need to refuel.

The fifth task – redeployment and reconstitution – has become a standard practice among the services' logisticians since 2003. It is deployment in reverse – from the area of operations to a domestic base or an overseas station – followed by the processes of restoring equipment and unit personnel strength to deployable condition.

Finally, the question remains as to how defence logistics organizations can assure the effectiveness of the many processes by which the above tasks are accomplished. Enabling campaign execution and accomplishing its mission and objectives means the timely delivery of forces and sustainment to the combatant commanders (and, of course to the training and support base). That enabling function should ensure freedom of action, extend the operational reach and prolong the endurance of the combatant commander's forces so that the lack of logistics support does not foreclose promising combat or mission options as happened to both Napoleon and Hitler in their Russian campaigns. To assure effective process planning and operation, five principles have been developed to govern defence logistics processes:

- Assign accountability for performance. In large rapidly changing operations where people are constantly moving, it is difficult to fix accountability. When it is done, there is incentive to manage processes much more carefully.
- Develop support processes to produce 'continuously shared knowledge' based on acquisition of accurate and timely data, converted to 'actionable knowledge' through decision tools. Knowledge on the state of readiness of critical equipment and status of people and supplies should feed continuously to process owners and stakeholders from the combat units in the areas of operation to the sources of supply and people.
- Maximize commercial contracting – especially outside active combat zones. Military personnel are a high-cost, critical resource and should only be used for support tasks when the use of civilian employees is impractical; for example, too dangerous.
- Design processes to encourage multinational partners to contribute logistics resources that they can supply in return for other resources such as strategic lift or communications systems.
- Design 'simplicity' into command, financial management and sourcing processes. Too much of the military bureaucracy in those processes is unnecessarily complex, impeding speed of action and obfuscating accountability. The adoption of such commercial techniques as 'lean' has made a great difference in many logistics organizations.

Measuring the performance of defence logistics **supply-chains** can be rather controversial as saving many lives and successfully stabilizing failing states depend on them. Using the most agile commercial firms as benchmarks can be a good start.

Further reading
Tuttle, W.G.T. (2005). *Defense Logistics in the 21st Century*. Annapolis, MD: Naval Institute.

William Tuttle

demand for transport: geographical influences

The demand for transport exits because of the separation of activities, such as living, working, education, shopping and leisure. External issues, as well as personal attributes, influence the demand for transport.

External issues that influence the demand for transport are, for example: gross national product (GNP), infrastructure supply and land-use patterns. Examples of personal attributes that influence the demand for transport are: **gender**, age, education level, personal/household income (see first Figure), lifecycle (that is, care for children), as well as cultural differences. An example of the influence of culture is the fact that, in Africa, certain tribes prohibit married women from cycling. The figure provides an overview of the travel mode choice based on household income levels. The vast differences between income groups clearly illustrate the influence of personal attributes, such as income.

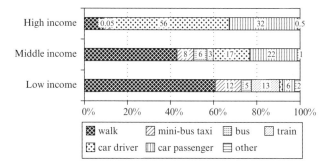

Infrastructure supply and land-use patterns have a severe influence on the demand for transport as well. Planners have investigated several growth patterns for cities over the years. Several theories exist. To illustrate the importance of infrastructure supply and land-use patterns, the city structure growth theory of Newton and Manins is used. They identify six urban growth theories seen in the second Figure of which examples exist around the world.

In the business-as-usual city, new developments occur in any open space. From a transportation point of view, it coincides with the predict-and-provide method. New settlements are added to existing transport models and the travel demand is predicted. Roads or lanes providing for that demand are added to the existing transport **network**. Business-as-usual cities generate long travel distances, mainly with the private car. Therefore, this approach is not considered to be very sustainable.

The main parameter characterizing the form of a city is its density, which has significant effects on travel distances and the **modal split**. The overall characteristics of American and Australian cities are low densities of population and jobs. The city is totally built on a car system. Los Angeles is the most prominent automobile city where business is done as usual. Car ownership is about 700 cars per 1000 inhabitants, the density is as low as about 20 people per hectare, and public transport is virtually unused: 2.2 passenger trips per vehicle km. Los Angeles offers only **buses** as a mode of public transport. The average home–work trip is 15 km.

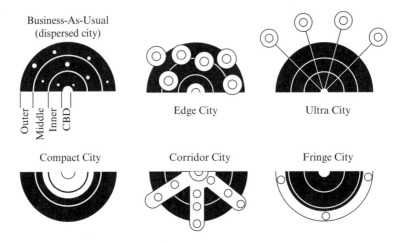

The edge city features growth in population, housing density and employment at selected nodes, and increased investment in freeways linking these nodes. The edge city is considered more sustainable than the business-as-usual city, as the nodes provide level of services closer to home; travel distances decrease. The main negative aspect is the distribution of activity nodes, limiting the possibilities for viable public transport.

Most edge cities can be found in America. Local densities in these cities are higher than in the business-as-usual city. Nevertheless, the overall densities of cities are still low. Denver and Boston are examples of edge cities with an overall density of 20 people per hectare, but a much lower home–work trip distance of around 11 km because of the local concentrations. Moreover, public transport is more important: 1.6 passenger trips per vehicle km for the bus, 4.2 passenger trips per vehicle km for rail and 6.7 passenger trips per vehicle km for the tram.

The ultra city features growth in regional centres within 100 kilometres of the central business district (CBD). **High-speed trains** link the regional centres to the city heart. Although high-speed trains can be an environmentally friendly mode of transport, the ultra city development is not considered sustainable. Valuable open land is used for development, which could have been realized in or closer to urban areas.

Stockholm is the best-known ultra city. The role of public transport is limited: 2.4 passenger trips per vehicle km for the bus and 2.7 passenger trips per vehicle km for the rail system. Stockholm has very high overall density of about 55 people per hectare. Nevertheless, the satellite idea of the suburbs makes travel distances long. Stockholm has an average home–work distance of 11 km. This is the same as the travel distance for Denver and Boston, in spite of much higher density.

Compact cities utilize open spaces within the city. An increase of the population is realized within existing suburbs, therefore the densities increase. In general, compact cities are considered to be a very sustainable way of extending cities and public transport is generally a viable option.

Amsterdam is an example of a compact city. **Accessibility** in Amsterdam is generally not a problem. Public transport is a good option. Using the car and other road-related modes of transport is not always as good because of **congestion** in the region of Amsterdam during peak hours. The municipality increased the accessibility level by improving the main access roads (A10) and introducing a fast train (Thalys) connecting the city centre with Schiphol airport, Paris and Brussels (Vanderschuren et al. 2000). Amsterdam has a density of more than 55 people per hectare and the average home–work trip is 7 km. The passenger trips per vehicle also indicate that Amsterdam is compact and public transport friendly: 3.8 passenger trips per vehicle km for the bus, 2 passenger trips per vehicle km for rail and 11.9 passenger trips per vehicle km for the tram.

The corridor city tries to avoid the negative impacts of the edge city. Growth arises from the central business district. Existing radial public transport links are upgraded. The corridor city is considered to be a sustainable city.

A European example of a corridor city is Vienna. Vienna has a density of more than 75 people per hectare and an average home–work trip distance of 6 km. Public transport is clearly used in the city as well: 2 passenger trips per vehicle km for the bus, 2.1 passenger trips per vehicle km for rail and 3.8 passenger trips per vehicle km for the tram system.

A non-developed world example of a corridor city is Curitiba, Brazil. Since 1965, Curitiba has been working on a transport plan based on the corridor idea. An extensive bus **network** was put into place over the years and settlements were only realized along the bus routes. In 1980, Curitiba had a density of 30 people per hectare and frequent bus use by 79 per cent of the population.

The fringe city has its growth predominantly on the outskirts. Large

Australian cities are known to have distinctive rural–urban fringes and densities are low.

Sydney is one of the most complex and dynamic areas of this kind. Sydney has a density of about 17 people per hectare. Public transport use is limited: 2.2 passenger trips per vehicle km for the bus and 1.5 passenger trips per vehicle km for the rail system. The fringe city is not considered to be a sustainable development policy as travel distances to economic activities are large.

The use of transport is measured in the number of trips or travelled distance per mode of transport. Transport models assist estimate future demand for transport. The effect of the implementation of different demand or supply measures can also be assessed.

Further reading

Newman, P.W.G. and J.R. Kenworthy (1989). *Cities and Automobile Dependence: An International Sourcebook*. Washington, DC: Island Press.

Smith, H. and J. Raemaekers (1998). Land-use pattern and transport in Curitiba. *Land Use Policy* **15**, 233–51.

Vanderschuren, M.J.W.A., L. Langerak, A.M. van den Broeke and G.R.M. Jansen (2000). *Agenda for Research on Tourism by Integration of Statistic/Strategies (ARTIST), the Case Study Amsterdam*. Delft: Inro-TNO.

Marianne Vanderschuren

demand-responsive transport

Demand-responsive transport is undergoing substantial change. Historically, demand-responsive transport referred to **paratransit** or dial-a-ride arrangements that provided customized journeys for passengers within the frame of advanced booking arrangements. Demand-responsive transport was provided for particular categories of transport service clients: the disabled, the **aged** and **rural residents** with no available fixed transport services. In the case of taxis, these have usually been used by the wealthy. The key feature of demand-responsive transport was that its services picked the passenger up and delivered the passenger to the destination outside the framework of a fixed route.

Currently, demand-responsive transport, as a consequence of recent and rapid developments in information communication technology aligned to transport, can offer a range of real-time interactions between clients, dispatchers, drivers and a range of fleets. New information communication technologies open up opportunities for real-time demand-responsive transport systems for wider passenger bases using a wider range of fleets integrated through new software options.

Attention has fallen upon the importance of developing real-time demand-responsive transport systems in relation to two key social transport policy goals. The first of these goals is the reduction of social exclusion: transport has been identified as a primary ground of social exclusion in itself, and inadequate transport coupled with inadequate **accessibility** has been identified as contributing towards other areas and forms of social exclusion. The United Kingdom Department for Transport is now advocating and investigating high technical end demand-responsive transport as a suitable transport policy for reducing social exclusion.

Demand-responsive transport is also seen as important in the reduction of private car-based transport use; it can be used as a part of a demand management package within environmental sustainability goals. It has been argued that new **mobility** effects have generated a new demand for transport: continuous services every hour of the day throughout the year are now required with real-time management and a high degree of comfort, and if the use of the private car is to be curtailed then public transportation must evolve to meet this demand. Demand-responsive transport systems that can aggregate and service these journeys on a real-time basis through flexible routing, and with high levels of personal security clearly have a future.

Further reading
Raje, F., C. Brand, J. Preston and M. Grieco (2003). *Transport and access to health care: the potential of new information technology. Report on literature review.* Transport Studies Unit, University of Oxford.

Margaret Grieco

deregulation

Whilst regulation of transport can be effected through financial, technical, environmental, **safety** or economic instruments, the term 'deregulation' in recent times has been applied more specifically to the processes of reducing or eliminating economic controls such as those restricting entry into the transport industry, and/or setting limits on the prices that could be charged for transport services. Such economic regulation was imposed during the first half of the twentieth century by many national, regional and local authorities for a wide range of reasons, including 'the containment of monopoly power' and 'control of excessive competition'. The long-term effects of such economic regulation were the protection of one mode of transport at the expense of potentially more efficient competitors, benefits accruing to transport owners, management and labour rather than users, and the growth of 'regulatory capture' whereby the regulators developed such close associations with their clients that they were perceived to be protecting the industry rather than its users and shippers or the public interest.

All modes of transport were regulated to varying degrees, with the extent of regulatory control dependent on local conditions, prevailing conventional wisdom and political ideology. The situation was complicated in federal states, with different levels of control exerted over the same mode of transport in different regional or local jurisdictions, overlain by federal regulation of those modes or activities constitutionally in the federal sphere. In Canada, for example, railways were regulated provincially if their operations were within a provincial boundary, but federally if their operations were national in scope or crossed provincial boundaries. Similarly, in the United States, airlines that operated only within a state were not subject to federal aviation economic regulations, a situation which allowed comparisons to be made of airlines' performance under different regulatory regimes.

The move to reduce some of the regulatory constraints over transport operations began in the mid-twentieth century, after road transport had demonstrated in the previous two decades that it could play a much greater role in the movement of passengers and freight, and at the same time as the protection that railways had sought from regulatory authorities was resulting in problems for the railway companies, such as the operation of unremunerative branch lines and passenger services that might be better served by road transport. Regulation of road transport was gradually reduced in many countries and, aided by the construction of new highways and the introduction of improved truck technology, led to new patterns of land transport, with road transport handling local and rural and some long-distance freight more efficiently, leaving the railways to concentrate on bulk traffic. The gradual development of containerized freight was a factor that encouraged intermodal cooperation between road, rail, sea and air transport, emphasizing the need to eliminate any regulatory constraints that might impede the adoption of innovative or cost-saving practices.

Deregulation of road passenger transport was a slower process, as many of the carriers, particularly in urban areas, were public utilities. For the benefits of deregulation to be achieved, a complementary process of corporatization and/or privatization of these entities was desirable, to enable them to compete more effectively for tendered services. **Taxi** services are one of the last bastions of regulated transport businesses in many cities, mainly due to the complication created by 'value' attached to their licences or plates which have been bought and sold.

The most extensively studied example of transport deregulation is that of airlines in the United States, complemented by similar experience in Canada and Australia. The United States Airline Deregulation Act, passed in 1978, initially resulted in a number of new entrant airlines to the national **network**, plus expansion of some that had previously operated only on intrastate routes. The initial benefits of deregulation were lower fares for travellers. Within a few years consolidation began to occur within the aviation industry, offset by the start-up of more new entrants. In Europe, the gradual expansion of the European Union and free movement across national borders has seen a new pattern of low-cost airlines superimposed on the **network** of services provided by national carriers, most of them formerly government-owned enterprises. Deregulation of international aviation is a more gradual process, complicated by the diplomatic machinery and national governments' aspirations involved in international negotiations.

Most railroads in the United States are privately owned and were for many years regulated federally by the Interstate Commerce Commission, but more direct intervention by government was necessary in the 1970s when several north-eastern railroads entered bankruptcy, and Conrail was created. Around the same time the Amtrak corporation was set up by the United States government to relieve the railroads of the loss-making regional and long-distance passenger services. In 1980, the Staggers Rail Act was passed to, *inter alia*, deregulate the railroads, essentially by allowing them to set their own rates and thereby compete more effectively with each other and with other modes of transport. The extent of deregulation of transport in the United States was such that the two major regulatory bodies, for aviation (Civil Aeronautics Board, CAB) and road and rail (Interstate Commerce Commission, ICC) were abolished, with any residual functions transferred to other agencies.

Whether deregulation was necessary, desirable or successful is still debated, despite it having been a significant policy initiative in most modes of transport in many countries. Most commentators agree that deregulation created an environment wherein greater competition resulted in more choices and lower costs. Deregulation has been a prerequisite and/or stimulus for other transport reforms to be implemented, such as corporatization and privatization. One problem in measuring whether deregulation has been successful is the difficulty of separating its impacts from those of other influences such as fuel costs or technological innovation. However there is no doubt that much former economic regulation 'stymied competition by protecting regulated industries' and that deregulation enabled greater competition in transport (and in other sectors of the economy), the benefits of which have exceeded the costs.

Further reading
Button, K.J. (2010). *Transport Economics*. Cheltenham, UK and Northampton, MA, USA: Edward Elgar.
Windle, R.J. (2005). Economic deregulation in the USA. In K.J. Button and D.A. Hensher (eds), *Handbook of Transport Strategy, Policy and Institutions*. Amsterdam: Elsevier.

Derek Scrafton

disaggregate models

A disaggregate model in transport analysis is a mathematical description of travel choices of individual decision-making entities such as a person's and households. For example, a disaggregate model of mode choice could relate via a mathematical equation the decision of a person to drive alone, car-pool or ride the bus to his or her socio-economic characteristics and the travel times and costs by the different modes for the journey under consideration. This is in contrast to an 'aggregate model' which is a description of the collective outcome of the choices of a group of travellers. For example, an aggregate model of mode choice could relate the fraction of all travel between a pair of locations by each of the available modes to the land use and transportation system characteristics. Characteristics of individual travellers are not included in aggregate models.

Aggregate models are generally purely statistical relationships simply replicating observed aggregate patterns. They have limited behavioural underpinnings. A classic example is the **gravity model** for trip distribution. This aggregate model apportions trips among zonal pairs based on measures of zonal attractiveness and the interzonal travel impedances (friction factors) so as to reproduce the observed trip-length distributions. On the other hand, disaggregate models generally represent more fundamental behavioural relationships. A good example is a multinomial-logit model for mode choice which is based on the utility-maximizing behaviour (that is, a decision-maker chooses the mode which provides him or her with the highest utility).

Disaggregate models address the issue of 'aggregation bias'. This issue broadly refers to the difference between the disaggregate- and aggregate-level relationships between the same factors and includes the possibility of a complete reversal in the directionality of impact of an exogenous variable due to aggregation. This bias in the aggregate-level relationship could be because of unobserved characteristic patterns of the aggregate units. For instance, one may find that the average vehicle trip rate of a zone is negatively correlated to the average zonal income even though higher-income households in the same region are generally found to make more vehicle trips. This could happen, for example, if higher-income persons live in zones that are more conducive for non-motorized travel and this factor is not controlled for in the aggregate model.

The development and application of disaggregate models require substantial amounts of data. For the estimation of models, surveys have to be conducted to elicit data on the travel choices of the individuals. Consequently, the survey methodology has a strong bearing on how representative the models are of the relationships that exist in the population. At the same time, tremendous developments in the field of econometrics have enabled us to develop very flexible model specifications from the disaggregate data. The application of disaggregate models for forecasting requires individual-level data on the explanatory factors used in the empirical specification. For example, if age, **gender** and income are used as explanatory variables in a disaggregate model for mode choice, then the application of the model requires the details on these attributes for each person in a future year (an aggregate model may simply require zonal averages of the explanatory factors). Population synthesis methods are increasingly being used for forecasting such detailed demographic characteristics. Nonetheless, the ability to obtain quality forecasts of the explanatory variables should be considered during disaggregate-model development.

The final issue with disaggregate models relates to the aggregation of the model outputs over the population of interest. Disaggregate models represent individual-level relationships and hence the outputs are probabilistic. For example, a mode-choice model would predict the probability that a certain traveller would choose each of the available modes. Analysts, however, are interested in predicting the overall mode shares and this requires aggregation of the individual-level probabilistic predictions. **Micro-simulation** methods are being increasingly used for this purpose. Multiple simulation runs have to be performed to reduce the effect of the random simulation errors leading to higher computational times and costs.

In summary, disaggregate models represent more fundamental, stable and behavioural relationships and hence may be expected to produce accurate travel forecasts. Further, the disaggregate models are also able to capture heterogeneity in responses to policy action as the characteristics of each decision-maker are explicitly incorporated in the models. At the same time, the availability, cost and quality of input data should be critically factored into assessing the overall benefits of disaggregate models developed for any specific purpose. Finally, the econometric structure of the model and the use of **micro-simulation** methods for model application may determine the model run times and hardware and software requirements.

Further reading
Ortuzar, J.D. and L.G. Willumsen (2001). *Modelling Transport*. Chichester: John Wiley & Sons.

Sivaramakrishnan Srinivasan

discrete choice models

Discrete choice analysis is the study of behaviour in situations where individual decision-makers face discrete choice problems. Discrete choice problems involve the selection of alternatives from finite sets of mutually exclusive and exhaustive discrete choice options. In a transport context, examples include the selection of transportation modes for home-to-work trips, the automobile ownership decision and shopping decisions. Over the past decades quite a large body of methodological and empirical research on discrete choice problems has been developed.

The classic discrete choice analysis assumes that a population I of decision-makers is defined and each member $i \in I$ faces a common finite set A of discrete choice options. With each individual $i \in I$, and alternative $a \in A$, is associated a vector z_{ia} of observable continuous or discrete variables that characterize the pair (i, a). Let $z_i = (z_{ia}, a \in A)$ be the matrix of observable attributes describing i's choice problem and let $Z = (z_i, i \in I)$ be the collection of such matrices faced by the various individuals $i \in I$. In applications, the definition of I, A and Z varies considerably. In an analysis of transportation modes for home-to-work trips, for example, I may include all workers travelling on a particular day to their place of employment. The choice set may include modes such as driving alone, public transport and car-pooling. The attributes may include functions of time, cost and so on associated with each mode and functions of individual characteristics such as income and car ownership.

The basic probabilistic assumption of discrete choice analysis is that the frequency distribution of choices $a \in A$ and attribute matrices $z \in Z$ in the population I can be characterized by a generalized probability density:

$$F(a, z) = P(a|z, \theta)\,(z) \tag{1}$$

defined over $A \times Z$, where $p(z)$ is the marginal attribute distribution. $P(a|z, \theta)$ is called the canonical discrete choice model and gives the conditional probability that in the choice context characterized by z alternative a will be chosen. Prior knowledge of causal structure is assumed to allow the analyst to specify the discrete choice model $P(a|z,.)$ up to a parameter vector θ.

The tasks of model specification and parameter estimation may be quite intractable unless the form of the probabilities is very much restricted. Thus, the only probability models used in practice are the well-known logit, probit and nested logit models. These models can be derived from the hypothesis of random utility maximization which postulates that the choice among discrete alternatives is the result of individual preference (utility) maximization, with preferences influenced by unobservable variables.

Random utility models assume that the decision-maker has consistent and transitive preferences over the alternatives that determine a unique preference ranking. Thus, a real-valued utility index U_{ib} associated with every alternative $b \in A = \{1,\ldots, A'\}$ can be defined such that alternative $a \in A$ is chosen if and only if $U_{ia} > U_{ib}$ for all $b \neq a, b \in A$. Using Lancaster's approach, or the concept of an indirect utility, the utility function can be defined in terms of attributes, that is $U_{ia} = U(z_{ia})$ with $z_{ia} = z(x_a, y_i)$, where x_a is a vector attributes of a and y_i a vector of characteristics of i.

The utility function associated with each decision-maker is fixed but the utilities are not known to the analyst with certainty and are thus treated as random variables. Utilities are treated as random variables, not to reflect a lack of rationality of the decision maker, but to reflect a lack of information concerning the choice context. In this setting the analyst can place a probability distribution on the unobserved utility vector $(U_{ia}, a \in A)$, conditional on the known matrix $z_i = (z_{ia}, a \in A)$ and on an unknown parameter vector $\boldsymbol{\theta}$, and derive – from the utility function distribution – choice probabilities:

$$P(a|z_i, \boldsymbol{\theta}) = \text{Prob}[U_{ia} \geq U_{ib}, b \in A|z_i, \boldsymbol{\theta}] \tag{2}$$

for each $a \in A$. In applications the random utility function has generally been assumed to be of linear additive form:

$$U_{ia} = z_{ia}\Phi + \varepsilon_{ia} \tag{3}$$

with the distribution of $\boldsymbol{\varepsilon}_i = (\boldsymbol{\varepsilon}_{ia}, a \in A)$ conditioned on z_i specified to lie within a parametric class $F(\varepsilon_i \mid z_i, \Psi)$. The first term of the right-hand side of Equation 3 is termed the systematic component and the second term the random component of utility. Therefore, $\boldsymbol{\theta} = (\Phi, \Psi)$. Given Equation 3, the functional specification of the choice probabilities (Equation 2) depends on the distributional family F chosen for e.

Different distributions result in different additive random utility choice models. Three important cases may be distinguished: the multinomial logit (MNL) model, the generalized extreme-value (GEV) model and the multinomial probit (MNP) model. The simplest assumption is the hypothesis that F is the independent and identically distributed (IID) type I extreme value, or Weibull, distribution:

$$F(\varepsilon_i|z_i, \Psi) = \prod_{a \in A} \exp(-\exp(-\varepsilon_{ia})) \tag{4}$$

Then the resulting choice probabilities have the form:

$$P(a|z_i, \Phi) = \frac{\exp(z_{ia}\Phi)}{\sum_{b \in A} \exp(z_{ia}\Phi)} \tag{5}$$

for $a \in A$. Model (Equation 5) is called multinomial logit (MNL) and allows easy computation and interpretation, and thus, has been by far the most widely used discrete choice specification in practice. The MNL model is evidently in accordance with Luce's choice axiom of independence of irrelevant alternatives (IIA) stating that the relative probabilities of every two alternatives $a, b \in A$ depend only on their systematic components of utility and are independent in the choice set, thus:

$$\frac{P(a|z_i, \Phi)}{P(b|z_i, \Phi)} = \frac{\exp(z_{ia}, \Phi)}{\exp(z_{ib}, \Phi)} \tag{6}$$

This property is both a strength and a weakness of the MNL model. It is a strength because it permits the introduction and/or elimination of choice alternatives without re-estimating the utility function parameters and thus greatly facilitates estimation and forecasting.

In choice contexts, however, where some of the alternatives are close substitutes for each other the MNL model may lead to counterintuitive behavioural predictions. The classical example refers to a decision-maker who has to choose between two alternatives a and b with $z_{ia}\Phi = z_{ib}\Phi$. In this case the MNL choice probability for a is one half. Now include a third alternative c that is identical to b in all choice relevant respects. One would expect the choice probability for a would remain one half, but the MNL probability is only one-third. These counterintuitive results are not caused by the IIA property as such, but are common to all choice models with IID random terms.

As a consequence many attempts have been made to relax the IIA-assumption and thus to overcome the problem of similarities between alternatives. Such research efforts resulted in generalizations of the MNL model, such as the generalized extreme-value (GEV) model and the multinomial probit (MNP) model. In the GEV model the cumulative distribution function is the multivariate extreme-value distribution:

$$F(\varepsilon_i \mid z_i, \Psi) = \exp\{-G[(\exp(-\varepsilon_{ia}), a \in A), z_i]\} \qquad (7)$$

where G is a non-negative, homogeneous-of-degree-one function that satisfies certain regularity conditions. The GEV choice probabilities consistent with utility maximization under Equation 7 are given by:

$$P(a \mid z_i, \Phi) = \frac{\partial}{\partial z_{ia} \Phi} \ln G(\exp z_{ia} \Phi, \ldots, \exp z_{iA} \Phi) \qquad (8)$$

Different specifications of the function G lead to different GEV choice probabilities. A prominent example is the nested multinomial logit model that takes a recursive sequential choice structure for granted where results of the decisions on lower-choice levels feed into those of higher levels.

The most general random utility model that circumvents the IIA problem can be obtained by assuming the random disturbances to be multivariate normally distributed with zero mean and an arbitrary variance-covariance matrix. This assumption directly leads to the multinomial probit (MNP) model that shows the attractive feature of allowing the random terms of utility to be correlated and – unlike the GEV model – to have unequal variances. Moreover, it permits variation in tastes among decision-makers with identical observed attributes.

But in contrast to the MNL and GEV models the functional relationship between the choice probabilities and the measured attributes cannot be computed in an analytically closed form, except for the binary case. The primary difficulty in applying the MNP form is the lack of practical, accurate procedures for approximating the choice probabilities when the number of alternatives is large, as is usually the case in destination and route choice contexts. Thus, MNP models have been considered as theoretically appealing and flexible, but practically less manageable specifications in discrete choice modelling.

Once a discrete choice model $P(a \mid z, \theta)$ has been specified the parameters θ have to be estimated from the observed choice of sample of individuals. The method of estimation depends on the functional form of $P(a \mid z, \theta)$, the way in which the sample was drawn (random sampling, stratified sampling and choice based sampling), and the extent of prior knowledge of the distribution of the exogenous variables z. Predictions of choice probabilities can then be made for different populations of individuals, or for the same population following changes in the z-variables.

Further reading
Billot, A. and J.-F. Thisse (1999). A discrete choice model when context matters. *Journal of Mathematical Psychology* **43**, 518–38.

Fischer, M.M. and P. Nijkamp (1985). Developments in explanatory discrete spatial data and choice analysis. *Progress in Human Geography* **9**, 515–51.

Manski, C.F. (1981). Structural models for discrete data. In S. Leinhardt (ed.), *Sociological Methodology*. San Francisco, CA: Jossey-Bass.

Manski, C.F. and D. McFadden (1981). Alternative estimators and sample designs for discrete choice analysis. In C.F. Manski and D. McFadden (eds), *Structural Analysis of Discrete Data with Econometric Applications*, Cambridge, MA: MIT Press.

Manfred Fischer

distribution centres / consolidation depots

By definition, a distribution centre (DC) is a physical facility used to complete the process of product line adjustment in the exchange channel. These centres may also be known as consolidation depots (CDs) or transhipment depots. While many distribution centres are serviced purely by road transport, there are also examples where the centre is able to facilitate multimodal transport. A distribution centre at a port may receive goods from the hinterland by a variety of transport modes, before loading products into a container for onwards transport by sea. Equally, a rail-connected facility may receive a train load of products for different customers, with road transport used for the deliveries to specific customers. Primary emphasis is placed upon product flow in contrast to storage. DCs are the modern successors of warehouses. In the traditional world of distribution, warehouses were needed to keep goods in stock, due to the limited capability of vendors to predict supply of and demand for commodities. Storage took place close to one of the two ends of the logistics chain: either at the place of production or at the place of consumption. Due to this, inventory was predominantly held by manufacturers or by retailers. Following the emergence of more complex, often buyer-driven markets, inventory in manufacturing and retail has been reduced almost completely, which was primarily made possible by information and communication technologies.

In using a distribution centre, companies are looking to trade off transport, inventory and customer service costs within their logistics operations. Despite the emergence of the throughput economy, storage remains necessary in many situations, particularly because it is becoming increasingly difficult to predict the demand for certain goods. The more varied and differentiated the markets, the larger the market areas are supposed to be and the more competition there is, the more important is a finely tuned goods flow, and the greater is the need to establish a buffer between the supply and receiving of commodities.

As well as delivering economic benefits, there is also the potential for distribution centres to provide environmental benefits for the logistics **network**. According to Kohn and Brodin, there are three main opportunities from the use of distribution centres. By using a distribution centre, it is possible to reduce the total distance travelled by vehicles within the logistics **network**, through increased efficiency. Second, the use of a consolidation centre may enable the introduction of a multimodal transport solution, so goods can be moved by more environmentally-benign transport modes. Finally, there is a reduction in emergency shipments, which often use faster modes of transport that are not so environmentally friendly. Distribution centres, however, also have a negative impact on the environment, both in terms of emissions and visual pollution.

The core activities in a DC can be distinguished as flow-oriented, stock-related and with regard to added value. A primary function of a DC is the consolidation of incoming freight and its immediate shipping to final destination. Such 'cross-docking' is practised by large trucking and freight forwarding companies, in order to fulfil customers' desires as fast as required. Storage is limited to certain commodity groups that may not be delivered within short term, for example in a DC of a hardware retailer, in a refrigerated warehouse or in the warehouse of a non-food wholesale chain. Added value is increasingly realized in post-production and pre-distribution processes, including assembly and customization (labelling, assembly, assortment), **packaging** and ticketing or product return and repair. Although such activities have been a core manufacturing function, it is increasingly shifted towards the distribution business.

Average DCs consist of a building, featuring high-cube space with clear heights of about 10 metres, an extremely flat warehouse floor and a certain load capacity (often about five metric tonnes). Dock doors and ramps are providing for space for unloading and loading trucks. Many DCs operate a racking system for storage, and also conveyor belts for picking and internal movement of commodities. In-house ground transport is operated with forklifts and pallets. Information and communication technologies are becoming standard; items have to be identified via barcode and radio frequency transmission. To reduce costs and to increase the speed of transaction, warehouse and DC operations are increasingly automated.

Also for cost reasons, the number of facilities being used for consolidation of freight flows is steadily declining, whereas the average size of the facility is becoming much larger than in the past. The size of DCs is variable, certainly dependent on the composition of the **network**, the size of the market area and the volume of transhipments. Because of the tendency towards concentrated **supply-chain** functions, and thus to a decreasing number of DCs, the average size of a facility is increasing. This is simply following the law of economics of scale. Large DCs can achieve a magnitude of 45 000, 70 000 or even more, square metres. Whereas regional DCs can go beyond the threshold of 1 million sq ft, large-scale or nationally oriented facilities are likely to exceed even that. This property of modern DCs raises many conflicts in terms of planning, infrastructure provision or the environment.

The main use for distribution centres has been as part of a wider distribution network, either at a national, regional or global scale. Such networks have tended to evolve over time due to changing pressures in the logistics network. An example of where this has occurred is in the United Kingdom grocery retail sector. Until the 1970s, each supplier would deliver directly to the retail outlet, with weekly delivery frequencies and high inventory levels at stores. During the 1980s, distribution centres were introduced to improve the efficiency of the logistics **network**. As well as offering transport and inventory savings, this change also enabled retailers to increase their selling space. With the introduction of **just-in-time** deliveries from suppliers, problems with delivery bay **congestion** arose at these centres. Consequently, the 1990s saw primary distribution centres developed. These are between suppliers and the main distribution centres and are used by the smaller suppliers nearby.

More recently, there has been the development of urban distribution centres. These centres are used to receive goods from a variety of suppliers before onwards deliveries into the centre of urban areas. These have proved particularly popular in Europe, with schemes implemented in many different countries. While the majority of these have focused upon retail deliveries, there have also been developments in other sectors, such as the London Construction Consolidation Centre that by reducing the number of deliveries to construction sites aims to reduce congestion in the city centre. Geographically, DC development underlies functional concentration and spatial dispersal. Thus DCs represent major nodes in distribution networks that are increasingly designed and operated at a large-scale level. As a consequence, the average distance between the points of transhipment and delivery is increasing. Therefore, DCs are often located outside non-urban areas. Size, traffic requirements and working shifts are driving DCs and modern warehouses out of core cities into sub- and non-urban areas, to locations at highway intersections or **intermodal** facilities. Concomitantly, DCs are mainly being served by trucks and parcel vans. An increasing share of warehouses and DCs is devoted to the consolidation of air freight. Bulk freight carriers such as railroads or inland waterways, at least outside of the United States, are rarely as efficient or as competitive as the customers demand.

Further reading

Bowersox, D., E. Smykay and B. LaLonde (1968). *Physical Distribution Management. Logistics Problems of the Firm*. London: Macmillan.

Hesse, M. (2004). Land for logistics: locational dynamics, real estate markets and political regulation of regional distribution complexes. *Journal of Social and Economic Geography* **95**, 162–73.

Kohn, C. and M.H. Brodin (2008). Centralised distribution systems and the environment: how increased transport work can decrease the environmental impact of logistics. *International Journal of Logistics: Research and Applications* **11**, 229–45.

Andrew Potter and *Markus Hesse*

driving licences

A driving licence is an official document issued by the government to authorize its holder to drive a motor vehicle. In most countries, in order to have a driving licence, individuals are required to take formal or informal training, and to pass mandatory examinations. These examinations usually have both theoretical and practical elements. The driving licence defines the category of motor vehicle that may be operated by the holder (for example car, **motorcycle**, light truck, heavy truck). Bus drivers, **taxicab** drivers, freight transport drivers and others who drive commercially are usually required to have specialized licences.

A well-documented statistic in many countries is that young drivers are more likely to be involved in car accidents than any other age group. Young drivers are most likely to engage in risky behaviours, such as speeding and drink-driving. Due to the high accident risk among young drivers it is not surprising to find age restrictions on car driving, where the minimum driving age in most countries is between 16 (not uncommon in American states) and 18 years (in most European countries). Regardless of a driver's age, studies have found that the amount of experience is related to crash risk. The combined effect of inexperience and lack of skills or knowledge magnifies this risk. Beside a driver's skills and the amount of experience, other factors that influence young drivers' risky behaviour include their level of development and maturity, and their social situation and lifestyle. This provides the main rationale for introducing licensing systems that address behavioural factors related to young and novice drivers.

Licensing systems can be classified into four main categories:

1.   Single-phase systems provide a full licence to a driver who has taken theoretical and practical training ('phase 1') and successfully passed the mandatory examinations.

2. In systems with probationary licences the first phase is followed by a probation period. Drivers who hold a probationary licence may have restrictions such as a night-time curfew. At the end of the probation period the driver becomes fully licensed.
3. Two-phase systems are similar to the above, but to become fully licensed the driver is required to pass mandatory examinations at the end of the probation period.
4. Graduated driving licensing (GDL) was developed to provide young and novice drivers with supervision during their initial months on the road, and to control certain elements of risky behaviour. At the first stage the driver is provided with training and has to pass mandatory exams. This is followed by an 'intermediate' stage, during which unsupervised driving is subject to certain restrictions, different from country to country. Typical restrictions are a night-time curfew, a limitation on the number of passengers in the vehicle, and situations in which the driver is required to be accompanied by a licensed and experienced adult. A full, unrestricted, licensure is provided at the end of this stage.

In most countries, licensing systems fall under one of the first two categories. Different versions of GDL systems have been introduced since 1990 and they are in use in most of the US states and Canadian provinces, as well as in Australia, New Zealand, Sweden and Israel. Evaluation studies of probationary licence systems and GDL systems provide evidence that the number of accidents for young and novice drivers decreased after such licensing systems were introduced.

Due to its effect on **mobility** and lifestyles, social and political dimensions of driver licensing systems have a strong impact on policy-making. In some countries GDL was rejected by the government because of its limited political and public acceptability.

Suspension of a driving licence is one of the measures affected by the government against a driver who has accumulated a certain number of traffic offences, such as drink-driving and speeding. In many countries, penalty points systems are used to monitor the number and the severity of traffic offences made by an individual driver. One objective of licence suspensions is to reduce the number of traffic violations; another objective is to reduce the number of accidents during the period for which the driving licence is withdrawn. It has been found that driving licence suspension has led to a reduction of 17 per cent in the number of accidents. To many people, suspension of a driving licence may have a significant effect on their routine activities and mobility, and might mean the loss of their job. Both **safety** and mobility arguments have effects on the public and political acceptability of measures of licence suspension.

Further reading
Elvik, R. and T. Vaa (2004). *The Handbook of Road Safety Measures*. Oxford: Elsevier.
Gregersen, N.P. and H.Y. Berg (1994). Lifestyle and accidents among young drivers. *Accidents Analysis and Prevention* **26**, 297–303.

Erel Avineri

dynamic traffic assignment

Dynamic traffic assignment (DTA) is the descriptive modelling of time-varying flows of traffic on road **networks** following established traffic flow and travel demand theories. Such flows describe network users entering and exiting both arcs and routes of the network. Time-varying flows allow arc volumes, link traversal times and **congestion** costs to be calculated. Such information is useful in many applications including transportation planning, network design and congestion pricing.

DTA models may seek system optimal solutions or user equilibrium solutions. Dynamic system optimal (DSO) models determine departure times, routes and flows that minimize total congestion in the network. By contrast, dynamic user equilibrium (DUE) models determine departure times, routes and flows that are consistent with a non-cooperative dynamic or moving equilibrium among travellers on the network of interest. The resulting solution assures that departure time–route choice pairs for a given origin–destination pair have the same disutility. In DSO models, it is assumed that there is a central authority that controls the traffic network. DUE models are used to describe networks without centralized control.

The dynamic network user equilibrium problem has become a foundation element in operations research, essential for describing time-varying flows on vehicular networks in applications ranging from real-time traffic control to deliberate transportation planning that recognizes within-day fluctuations in traffic. DUE is recognized as a type of dynamic Nash equilibrium in which each user acts rationally and selfishly in an effort to minimize their own experienced congestion through the departure and route choices at their disposal. Generally speaking, DUE flows are considered more difficult to articulate and solve than DSO flows.

There are many different approaches to constructing computable mathematical DTA models, including, optimal control problems, variational inequalities (VI) formulations, non-linear complementarity problems (NCP) and simulations. A representative and much-cited analytical DUE model (as opposed to a simulation-based DUE model) is that of Friesz which takes the form of a dynamic VI. However, this model is but one of many that have been proposed to date.

While the approaches to representing DTA may differ, all models typically have the same four components: a delay model, flow dynamics, flow propagation constraints, and a route and departure time choice model. The delay model represents the time it takes to traverse an arc of the **network** given the current traffic volume on that arc at the time of entry. Flow dynamics keep track of the arc volumes as functions of the arc entrance and exit flows. The flow propagation constraints ensure first in, first out (FIFO) conditions and relate the flows entering or exiting arcs at different instances of time. Invariably, both analytical and simulation models of DUE encounter computational challenges that are directly proportional to their intrinsic level of modelling realism when they are implemented. Thus, despite much effort to develop so-called real-time DTA models, meaningful dynamic traffic assignment cannot be performed in real or near-real time. This means that, relative to potential applications, the future of DTA lies in deliberate planning and in the derivation of decision rules that can inform tactical and real-time analyses.

Algorithms for solving DSO and DUE models run the gamut from the simplistic to the esoteric. One of the most fundamental decisions to make in solving analytical DTA models is whether to employ a discrete or a continuous time representation. Somewhat surprisingly, there have been recent limited successes with continuous time computation that leave open the ultimate verdict of which representation is computationally preferable. Beyond the choice of discrete or continuous time, one may select among fixed point algorithms, gradient projection algorithms, sequential linearization/Lemke's method, agent-based simulation and discrete event simulation as numerical philosophies for extracting solutions; at this time, there is no general consensus regarding which of these numerical perspectives is best.

Recently, much DTA-related research has focused on dynamic congestion pricing, which is of great interest as a mechanism for controlling congestion. The purpose of dynamic congestion pricing is to determine time-varying tolls for particular arcs, routes or areas encompassing multiple arcs of a **network** that reduce congestion while forcing users to pay the true social costs of the congestion they create. Dynamic congestion pricing models must be constrained by DUE models in order to avoid the Braess paradox of network design. Models of dynamic congestion pricing constrained by DUE generally address passenger vehicles on road networks in urban centres, but other modes and other decision environments may be considered using the same modelling tools.

Further reading

Friesz, T.L., D. Bernstein, T.E. Smith, R.L. Tobin and B.W. Wie (1993). A variational inequality formulation of the dynamic network traffic equilibrium problem. *Operations Research* **41**, 179–91.

Peeta, S. and A. Ziliaskopoulos (2001). Foundations of dynamic traffic assignment: the past, the present and the future. *Networks and Spatial Economics* **1**, 233–66.

Terry L. Friesz, Matthew A. Rigdon and *Changhyun Kwon*

E

e-commerce

Electronic commerce is broadly defined as the buying and selling of goods using electronic transaction processing technologies. More narrowly, electronic commerce uses transaction-processing technologies that rely on the Internet and the World Wide Web (WWW). It includes both business-to-business transactions and business-to-consumer transactions. Mobile commerce (also known as en route commerce) is electronic commerce conducted while travelling from one point to another. Whereas traditional electronic commerce involves two stationary (for example desktop) computers, mobile commerce involves at least one mobile (for example in-vehicle or handheld) computer.

Electronic commerce transactions can be broken into two stages. In the first stage the customer transmits an electronic order and an electronic payment. In the second and final stage, the vendor ships or delivers the product to the customer, or a third party designated by the customer. Critical to this process is the fact that the customer, or third party, can be associated with a delivery address. Mobile commerce transactions are quite different because the customer cannot be associated with a delivery address. Hence, there must be another way to identify the person that will accept delivery, and this leads to two possible three-stage processes.

Prepaid mobile commerce transactions proceed as follows. In the first stage of this process the user transmits an electronic order and an electronic payment to the vendor. Then, in the second stage, the vendor takes the product out of inventory, putting it aside for the customer, and transmits an electronic voucher back to the user, in lieu of being able to ship the actual product. In the final stage of the process, the customer arrives at the vendor, transmits the electronic voucher back to the vendor, and is given the product. Payment-on-delivery mobile commerce transactions are somewhat different. In the first stage of this process the customer transmits an electronic order to the vendor. Then, in the second stage, the vendor transmits an electronic quote, that is, a guaranteed price, back to the customer. In the third stage, the customer arrives at the vendor, transmits the electronic quote and electronic payment, in the amount of the quoted price to the vendor, and is given the product. In this second process payment need not be made electronically. That is, after the customer supplies the vendor with the electronic quote the actual payment can be made in cash.

The primary difference between prepaid and payment-on-delivery transactions relates to the notion of trust as it is commonly used in the information assurance literature. In particular, vendors that do not trust their customers actually to take delivery of the product that they have put aside will insist on prepayment. For example, a restaurant might not want to start preparing a meal that it has not been paid for. On the other hand, customers that do not trust the vendor to provide the product at the quoted price will insist on payment-on-delivery. For example, a driver may not trust a gasoline station to actually provide gasoline at the quoted price.

There are numerous ways in which people can and will use mobile commerce technologies. For example, while driving one might:

- Obtain information about the pricing and availability of nearby hotel rooms, reserve a particular hotel room, prepay for the room, and obtain an electronic key and obviate the need to check in.
- Obtain information about nearby restaurants, obtain menus from each of the restaurants, determine an estimated time of arrival, reserve a table for that time and order food.
- Find nearby gas stations, determine which one has the best prices and/or services and/or location, prepay, and obtain a voucher that could be used to verify payment at the pump.
- Find a suitable **parking** facility, reserve a space and pay the bill (either upon arrival or departure). One can even imagine that some parking lots would auction spots to the highest bidder as is now popular at many electronic commerce sites.
  As another example, while flying one might:
  - Reserve DVD movies or video games for a handheld player at the start of the flight, and arrange for drop-off at the end of the flight. One can even imagine that discounts would be offered to entice people to transport movies from one airport to another.
  - Reserve a **taxi**, contact a 'red cap' (hotel porter), tip the 'red cap', and obtain fare information from a reliable source.

The social and economic impacts of mobile commerce are not well understood. People have hypothesized that it will reduce vehicle-miles and vehicle-hours of travel by eliminating unnecessary search, for example circling around looking for a **parking** space; improve **safety**, especially near interchanges, by eliminating the need to visually search for desired services; increase transit usage by offering more convenient payment options and real-time information; and increase the use of **alternative fuel** vehicles by making it more convenient to locate fuelling stations and purchase fuel.

Further reading
Bernstein, D. and A. Kornhauser (1998). Personal travel assistants and en-route commerce. NJ TIDE Center Technical Report.
Sadeh, N. (2002). *M-Commerce: Technologies, Services, and Business Models.* Hoboken: John Wiley & Sons.

David Bernstein and *Terry L. Friesz*

economic development and transport

Economic development may be defined as a process of improvement in the economic well-being and **productivity** of the population in a region or country. Economic well-being includes not only income but also levels of education, access to health and social services and a healthy environment. Increasingly the definition of development has been expanded to cover measures of equity such as the distribution of income and the level of participation in the political process.

Given the pervasive role of transport in the economy, improvements in the cost and quality of personal and freight transport services naturally play important roles in economic development. The general consensus is that transport activities do not directly cause economic development, but rather play an enabling role in the development process. That is to say, good and cheap transport eliminates impediments to economic processes that drive development.

Accessibility, defined as the ease of reaching desirable destinations from a particular location, embodies the link between transport and development. The greater is the accessibility of a person or firm, the wider is the range of economic opportunities that can be pursued and therefore the higher is the level of productivity that can be achieved. Accessibility is enhanced both through increasing **mobility** of the population and through the rational spatial layout of economic activities. Investments in transport infrastructure can contribute to both.

While the theoretical link between transport investment and productivity is compelling, until recently there has been a dearth of empirical support. Beginning with Aschauer a series of statistical analyses on mostly developed economies has provided evidence of the productivity impact of public expenditures on road and other infrastructure. While results are varied and controversies remain, studies in the United States indicate that the **productivity** benefits are high but declining through time as **networks** become built out. Thus developing countries with relatively sparse networks are likely to reap greater development benefits from infrastructure investments.

A typical historical sequence of economic development in the former colonial countries starts with the export of some resource commodity such as rubber, furs, or spices for which there is a demand in affluent countries. Over time an industrial complex builds up around that commodity, leading eventually to a more diversified and highly integrated economy with its own substantial consumer demand. Taafe et al. proposed a complementary historical sequence of transport network development. At an early stage all road and rail links converge upon one or more port city in the form of a branching network. This is an efficient system for commodity export. Over time service towns develop at the nodes of this network. However, the branching network is only efficient in connecting these towns to the port, not to each other. As the economy becomes more diversified and integrated, links are added to the network allowing efficient interaction among peripheral towns and a more complex pattern of goods and personal movement.

A more highly connected transport network enables a higher level of internal economic integration. This includes a substantial movement of intermediate goods among firms within the country or region and a recirculation of earnings through purchases of domestically produced consumer goods. Increasing integration is an important component of the development process because it leads to greater economic multiplier effects from growth impulses in export industries.

Unfortunately the colonial heritage of many developing countries has left them with transport systems geared exclusively to commodity export, with little provision for domestic connectivity. This is particularly the case in Africa. Furthermore, colonial systems had little need for transport links between neighbouring countries. For this reason opportunities for trade among African countries are still retarded by the lack of international surface transport infrastructure.

In many developing countries, poor reliability of transport services constitutes a major impediment to economic efficiency. Uncertainty about the delivery of goods must be offset by maintaining inefficiently high inventories and thereby incurring carrying costs in the forms of interest, insurance and warehousing costs. Reliability depends not only on the state of transport infrastructure but also on institutional factors such as the existence of transport monopolies and excessively high duties on new transport equipment.

In an era of globalization, economic development is increasing driven by **international trade**. For firms to participate in global logistical chains they need access to very high levels of transport service. Tight production schedules necessary for the coordination of production at a global scale leave little room for unreliability in ports and airports. For example, the highly efficient ports of many Southeast Asian countries give that region a strong advantage in international markets over South Asia and Africa, whose ports generally have long turnaround times and often lack the technology to deal with electronic identification or in some cases even containerization.

The developing world is undergoing a rapid increase in urbanization. In some countries urban growth is concentrated in a mega-city of 10 million people or more. While urbanization is part of the process of economic development, it poses severe challenges for the creation of transport systems. On the one hand, **rural transport** infrastructure is needed to help spread the economic growth that is occurring in the cities to the countryside, where incomes are generally much lower and access to services is poor. On the other hand, improvements in urban transport are needed to prevent the agglomeration benefits of urbanization from being lost to **congestion** and environmental degradation.

The construction of roads through low-income peripheral areas has been a standard instrument of regional policy in both the developed and developing countries. The goal is to improve access to urban markets so that, for example, farmers can receive higher prices for their produce. While these policies generally yield benefits, there is the danger that by making the countryside more accessible to efficient urban producers, rural handicraft industries may be damaged or destroyed. Better access may also accelerate rural outmigration, which may have a positive effect by drawing off excess labour supply or a negative effect by attracting away the young and most productive.

In the largest cities of the developing world, urban transport is in a state of crisis. As incomes increase among the urban middle classes, automobile ownership increases rapidly, leading to massive congestion. As the middle class abandons public transport and the streets become more congested, the quality of transport for the poor deteriorates. In Mexico City, for example, it is not unusual for low-income workers to travel three hours both to and from work. This represents both a waste of human resources and a detriment to the quality of life. At the same time urban traffic contributes to critical **air quality** problems with dire health impacts in cities like Delhi, Cairo and Mexico City. In Latin America, however, cities like Curitiba, Brazil and Bogotá, Columbia are addressing these problems through transit-centred planning programmes.

The role of transport in achieving equity goals in developing countries is problematic. In principle increased **mobility** should improve access to facilities and opportunities for all. In practice, however, transport plans are often geared to the needs of the urban elite and middle class, who are more politically active than the poor. This is especially true of the construction of roads to be used by the minority of the population that own cars. The majority who do not own cars cannot reach economic activities that develop along these roads. Thus, infrastructure investments may serve to widen the gap between the rich and the poor in terms of access to economic opportunities.

Further reading
Aschauer, D.A. (1989). Is public expenditure productive? *Journal of Monetary Economics* **23**, 177–200.
Lakshmanan, T.R., U. Subramanian, W.P. Anderson and F.A. Leautier (2001). *Integration of Transport and Trade Facilitation: Selected Regional Case Studies.* Washington, DC: World Bank
Leinbach, T.R (1995). Transport and Third World development: review, issues and prescription. *Transportation Research A* **29**, 337–44.
Taafe, E.J., R.L. Morrill and P.R. Gould (1963). Transport expansion in underdeveloped countries: a comparative analysis. *Geographical Review* **53**, 503–29.

William P. Anderson

economic regulation

Transport supply has traditionally been very heavily regulated. The regulatory structures are often broken down into economic regulations ('quantity regulations' in Europe) and social regulations ('quality regulations'). The former are used to deal with more conventional market failures such as monopoly power or excessive competition, whereas social regulations focus on such things as environmental protection, **safety** and meeting the larger 'needs' of society. Economic regulation can take many guises.

Economic regulation in its current guises really became important with the advent of rail and canal transportation in the nineteenth century, although there were certainly controls over such things as road provision, tolls, and port charges and investment in many countries going back at least to Roman times. Railways and canals were seen in many cases as natural monopolies and thus having the potential for exploiting users by levying high charges and prices. Later, with the advent of the bus, motorized **taxi** and truck, the focus shifted in the other direction, and there was concern that potential excessive competition between many small suppliers, while keeping the price of transport down, would result in an unstable supply of services.

In the context of monopoly power the most direct form of economic regulation involves state ownership of the transport system ('nationalization'). This was a widespread policy in the former Soviet states and is practised to varying degrees elsewhere. In the United States roads are largely publicly owned (by the federal or state governments), as are sea and **airports** and the **air traffic control** system. In other countries railways are often nationally owned. The aim of this is that the state can directly control the prices customers pay, the level of capacity and the types of service that are offered. In other cases, the scale of investment required may be so large that the private sector does not have the capability to finance it and public ownership becomes a practical necessity. Public ownership may also result from the perception that the transportation market is excessively competitive and that supply needs to be constrained to prevent cycles of over-and undersupply, or to ensure that the quality of service offered customers (for example reliability) is optimal. This argument is often extended to embrace situations where there are problems of coordinating services, and it is felt that some centralized authority needs to be in command.

A weaker form of control is to allow private ownership but to control who supplies the transport services, the form they take and the prices that are charged. Ideally, given the interactions of supply and demand, there is no need to regulate both capacity and price, although this is often done. Licensing has been widely used to control who supplies the market and is often implicitly codetermined with the level of capacity in that new entrants have to show that there is a demand for their services on the particular routes in question. Control over prices traditionally involved some form of 'rate-of-return' regulation whereby suppliers could only charge prices that covered their costs and gave them a reasonable rate of return. The difficulty of this is that it offers little incentive for the supplier to keep costs to a minimum, as they can just be passed on. More recently 'price caps' have been introduced that allow periodic price changes that, averaged across a range of services, produce downward pressures on fares or rates. The idea is that costs fall with time as technical and managerial changes increase efficiency, and that this economic benefit should be passed on to the transport users. The periodic downward adjustment in prices also acts as a stimulus for more innovation. The estimation of the appropriate deflator, however, remains largely an arbitrary exercise.

In recent years there has been a trend to what in the United States is called **deregulation,** but is known as liberalization elsewhere. This has involved a combination of **privatization**, albeit with some other less direct controls often replacing it, and less rigid price, capacity and entry controls. The changes, which began in the late 1970s, are partly a reflection of empirical evidence that many regulations were not achieving their desired objectives, new concerns that the bureaucrats overseeing regulation were motivated by self rather than public interest, and developments in economic thinking indicating that regulation may not be needed in many circumstances. In particular, the ethos was rather more on seeking out workable competition where markets were only to be subjected to economic regulation when it is demonstrably clear that this results in a more efficient outcome than the imperfect market. Even then, regulations were to be targeted.

Further reading
Button, K.J. (2004). *Wings Across Europe: Towards an Efficient European Transport System*. Aldershot: Ashgate.
Winston, C. (1993). Economic deregulation: days of reckoning for microeconomists. *Journal of Economic Literature* **31,** 1263–89.

Kenneth Button

education in transport

Education in the field of transport is generally available in a variety of programs of study. The range of such programs reflects the broad, multidisciplinary nature of the transportation sector. Transportation engineering courses are typically associated with civil engineering programs and emphasize the planning, design and operation of transportation facilities and systems, including highways, airports, ports and public transit systems. Urban planning programs generally focus on urban design, and as such, include the relationship between transportation facilities and services and the development of communities. Business programs sometimes offer studies in freight transportation and increasingly also the broader issue of **supply-chain** management. Business programs may also offer emphases in real estate development, which could include elements of site access and circulation. **Tourism** programs may include a focus on transportation, both for purposes of accessing tourist destinations and travel as a form of tourism, such as hiking, cycling, motoring, boating and taking cruises. Psychology programs may offer studies in human factors and human–machine interfaces. Military or **defense logistics** programs typically include some emphasis on transport as a subdiscipline that supports the fielding, supply, maintenance and staffing of weapons systems. Some programs in public policy and administration offer degrees in transportation policy. Aspects of transportation are also present in a number of other academic disciplines, including scheduling, computer science and information and communication technology (ICT), economics and finance.

Typically, transportation education programs are graduate, or post-baccalaureate, programs, leading to either a master's degree or a doctorate. However, some civil engineering or urban and regional planning programs offer bachelor's degrees with either minors or options in transportation at the undergraduate level. Programs such as the Bachelor of Science in Civil Engineering in the Transportation Engineering Division at Texas A&M University or the Bachelor of Science in Civil Engineering with an emphasis in transportation at UC Berkeley offer engineering students the opportunity to develop a specialization in transportation prior to graduate study. There are also a small number of international programs that offer bachelor's degrees in transportation engineering such as the Technion Faculty of Civil and Environmental Engineering in Israel.

Historically, transport education is strongly linked to civil engineering education. Civil engineering was first developed as an offshoot of military engineering, focusing on the construction of armaments, fortifications and infrastructure. The French founded a National School of Bridges and Roads (Ecole Nationale des Ponts et Chaussées) in 1747, and the Ecole Polytechnique in 1794. The Ecole Polytechnique marked the beginning of a new era of civil engineering education, based on a vision of technical development and the use of systematic, analytical approaches. The Germans followed suit in 1799 by establishing the Bauakademie in Berlin. King's College, London was the first British university to teach civil engineering in 1838, followed by the University of Glasgow in 1840. In the United States, Rensselaer Polytechnic Institute was the first university to offer civil engineering coursework in 1824. Rensselaer exemplified an American approach to engineering education that emphasized practical, industrial and agricultural experiences for students, with comparatively less emphasis on mathematics and science.

Though originally part of civil engineering, advances in technology and changing needs led to the development of the transportation engineering subfield which included not just civil engineering but also traffic engineering. In the United States, the Bureau of Street Traffic Research played an important role in early traffic engineering education. The bureau dates back to the Erskine Bureau of Street Traffic Research at Harvard University in 1925. The mission of the bureau focused on the 'three E's' of traffic control: engineering, education and enforcement. Although the bureau changed its name and location twice, its mission never changed. After becoming the Bureau of Street Traffic Research at Yale, the bureau also took on the task of diffusing American engineering styles to Europe after the Second World War. The program also adjusted its curriculum as the transportation system developed. After a second name and location change, the Bureau of Highway Traffic closed in 1982 due to funding problems and the inability to recruit students for the program. During its 57 years, the bureau turned out 823 students in transportation engineering studies.

Not only is transport education found in a variety of disciplines, but its scope has also been augmented several times over the years. During the 1970s, for example, the expansion of transit systems in the United States and the increased role of the public sector in the development of these systems led to the expansion of the curriculum to include issues surrounding public transit. In addition, advances in new technologies have also led to the broadening of the curriculum in areas such as **intelligent transportation systems** (ITS) and **geographic information systems** (GIS). In the 1990s, the concept of the 'new transportation professional' began to replace the narrower concept of the transportation engineer. This 'new transportation professional' is an individual who will have a broad understanding of technology, systems and institutions in the transportation domain and in-depth knowledge in one of the specialties (such as transport logistics or ITS). Contemporary issues in transport such as greenhouse gases, bicycle and pedestrian transportation, and land use continue to expand the scope of transportation studies.

Further reading

Crawley, E.F., J. Malmqvist, S. Ostlund and D. Brodeur (2007). *Rethinking Engineering Education*. Springer Science+Business Media, LLC.
Kaiser, F. (2005). Early traffic engineering education or 'How did those old guys get so smart?!'. Ohio/WV Section of Institute of Transportation Engineers.
Seely, B. (2004). 'Push' and 'pull' actors in technology transfer – moving American-style highway engineering to Europe, 1945–1965. *Comparative Technology Transfer and Society* **2**, 229–46.
Sussman, J.M. (2000). The new transportation faculty: the evolution of engineering systems. CEE New Millennium Colloquium, Massachusetts Institute of Technology.

Jonathan L. Gifford

elasticities of demand for transport

An elasticity is a measure of responsiveness; specifically the percentage change in one variable in response to a 1 per cent change in another. For **transport demands**, the own-price elasticity of demand is the percentage change in quantity demanded in response to a 1 per cent change in its price. The own-price elasticity of demand is expected to be negative, that is, a price increase decreases the quantity demanded. Demand is 'price-elastic' if the absolute value of the own-price elasticity is greater than unity, that is, a price change elicits a more than proportionate change in the quantity demanded. A 'price-inelastic' demand has a less than proportionate response in the quantity demanded to a price change, that is, an elasticity between 0 and -1.

Economists distinguish between ordinary and compensated demand elasticities. For a consumer demand such as the demand for leisure travel, a change in price has two effects: a substitution effect and an income effect. The substitution effect is the change in consumption in response to the price change, holding utility constant. A change in price of a consumer good or service also has an income effect, that is, a reduction in price means a consumer has more income left than before if the same quantity were consumed. This change in real income due to the price change will change consumption. The compensated elasticity measures only the substitution effect of a price change along a given indifference surface (Hicksian demand), whereas the ordinary demand elasticity measures the combined substitution and income effects of a price change (Marshallian demand).

The concepts are the same for freight transport demands although the terminology differs. A change in the price of an input to a production process, such as freight transport, has a substitution effect as well as a scale or output effect. The substitution effect is the change in input use in response to a price change holding output constant. But a reduced price of an input increases the profit-maximizing scale of output which, in turn, increases demand for all inputs including the one experiencing the price change (freight transport inputs). As with passenger demands, a compensated elasticity measures only the substitution effect of the price change, while an ordinary elasticity measures the combined substitution and scale or output effects of a price change.

The own-price elasticity is distinguished from cross-price elasticities. The latter is the percentage change in quantity demanded for, say, rail traffic in response to a percentage change in the price of another service such as trucking. For substitutable goods and services, the cross-price elasticity is positive. If two products were unrelated to one another in the minds of consumers, the cross-price elasticity demand would be zero, and cross-price elasticities are negative for complementary goods and services.

Another elasticity concept is the income elasticity. This is the percentage change in quantity demanded with respect to a 1 per cent change in income, all other variables including prices held constant. If consumption increases more than proportionately with income (income elasticity greater than 1), it is a 'luxury' or 'superior' good, for example, the demand for luxury cruises. If consumption declines with an increase in income, it is called an 'inferior' good.

It is important to distinguish between the overall market elasticity of demand for transport and the demand facing individual modes of transport. The market demand refers to the demand for transport relative to other non-transport sectors of the economy. The price elasticity of demand for individual modes is generally more elastic (or less inelastic) than the market elasticity of demand. Competition among modes and firms makes the elasticity of demand more sensitive to individual firms than for the market in total.

There is also a distinction between short-run and long-run price elasticities. In the long run consumers or firms are better able to adjust to price signals than in the short run. Hence long-run demand functions tend to be more elastic (less inelastic) than short-run demand.

Finally, one can estimate quality elasticities, that is, the responsiveness of demand to changes in quality. **Travel time** and waiting time are two readily quantifiable quality measures for passenger travel. Quality can take a variety of forms, sometimes difficult to measure. But in many markets, quality variables can be more important than price. The thriving air, motor freight and **container** markets, which generally are more expensive than alternate modes, are testimony to the importance of service quality relative to price in many markets.

Further reading
Oum, T.H., W.G. Waters II and Xiaowen Fu (2007). Transport demand elasticities. In D.A. Hensher and K.J. Button (eds), *Handbook of Transport Modeling*. Oxford: Elsevier.

William G. Waters II

elderly and transport

Modern societies are undergoing a major demographic transition. A larger proportion of the population is reaching old age. For nearly all countries of the Western world, the elderly already make up over 12 per cent of the population, and this percentage is projected to increase substantially by 2010. In the international comparison, Italy is the leader with 18.3 per cent of its population being 65 or older, whereas the United States has a comparatively young population, with only 12.6 per cent of its people being older than 65 years. An increasing number of these individuals are licensed to drive, and they drive more than their age cohorts a decade ago. A reasonable level of **mobility** is viewed by most of the elderly as essential to their quality of life.

The process of ageing is accompanied by waning strength, by the increased risk of declining sensory abilities, and restriction of physical mobility. In view of the constantly increasing number of old and very old people in our societies, it is no surprise that their mobility behaviour has become an issue of public and scientific interest. On the one hand, mobility (the ability to move about) and traffic (the transportation of people, goods and news) have become an even more important precondition of ensuring the ability to lead one's everyday life, keep up social relations, take part in every kind of activity outside one's own four walls, and seek out places subjectively significant or objectively central to provide for daily material needs and health care. On the other hand, mobility is increasingly jeopardized as a person ages.

Different perspectives can be chosen to analyse the relationships between influencing factors and elderly people's outdoor mobility and traffic behaviour in general. One focuses on 'causal factors'. For example, what sociodemographic and psychological characteristics are associated with the driving behaviour of the elderly? This perspective is chosen frequently in traffic research studies. Another perspective might be called a segment-specific approach: can the elderly as a group be subdivided into homogeneous subgroups? For example, are there variables that characterize those elderly people who have a positive attitude toward public transport? It is important to bear this second perspective in mind, since the elderly – and particularly the very old – are a heterogeneous group. This helps us to identify and understand their different mobility needs, their diverse driving behaviour, and the variety of their compensatory strategies. This perspective allows for determining the size of the different homogenous subgroups of the elderly, and identifying the characteristics of these subgroups as a basis for improving traffic **safety** and options for outdoor **mobility**.

Different projects have been able to identify homogenous groups of elderly persons on the basis of lifestyle differences. Based on lifestyle differences – for example stimulation-seeking, intellectually curious, indifferent, passive and negativistic – it is possible to isolate different types of mobility patterns of the elderly.

Beside lifestyle variables like the interaction between each individual and his or her personal competencies, aspects of the physical and social environment have to be taken into account when trying to maintain outdoor mobility for the elderly. Therefore, research projects in this area have to combine different data sources and data collection strategies: standardized questionnaires and mobility diaries can be used to assess various forms of mobility and the essential features of the community. Demographic aspects, social **networks**, personality measures and sensory ability or disability have to be assessed as well.

Typological approaches prove the existence of groups of the elderly deserving special attention with regard to intervention, rehabilitation and prevention. Single-living older persons, women, persons with impaired health and low economic resources, and rural older adults tend to be particularly at risk of losing their ability to move around.

Thus, improvements of the mobility situation of the elderly tend to focus as much on transport policy and socio-political measures as on appropriate urban development planning. It is seen as important to create flexible, user-centred options for mobility that offer a genuine alternative to both the private automobile and traditional local public transport services, and provide for neighbourhoods that also respond to the needs and wishes of an ageing population. For elders, whose life space contracts with advancing age because of their inability to overcome environmental obstacles, it is necessary that the areas near their homes have readily accessible stores, medical and care services, appropriate public transport, and other facilities that will allow them to continue leading independent lives and being full members of society.

Further reading
Rudinger, G. (2002). Mobility behavior of the elderly. In W.R. Black, and P. Nijkamp (eds), *Social Change and Sustainable Transport*. Bloomington, IN: Indiana University Press.
Schaie, K.-W., H.-W. Wahl, H. Mollenkopf and F. Oswald (eds) (2003). *Independent Aging: Living Arrangements and Mobility.* New York: Springer Publishing.

Georg Rudinger and *Stefan Poppelreuter*

elements of movement

The stream of actions which form our day are aggregated both in daily language and in the related scientific analysis into identifiable blocks of time: movement (travel) and, by implication, stationary activity. While time use analysis sees only activities, transport modelling and analysis maintains this division in spite of some difficulties arising from additional activities performed while moving – phoning, talking with fellow travellers, working, relaxing, eating on the train or plane, and so on.

Axhausen suggested the following elements to describe movements consistently:

- A stage, unlinked trip is the movement with one mode or means of transport, including any pure waiting times during or after the stage. Walking is understood as a mode of transport. Means are in particular vehicles.
- A trip is a sequence of stages between two activities. A walk-only trip has one stage, while all trips involving a vehicle have at least three; walking to it, using it, walking to the activity.
- A tour is a sequence of trips from and then back to the same location.

- A journey is a special tour to and then back to the reference location, that is, the home.

This set of definitions needs definitions of activity and reference location:

- An activity is a sequence of purposeful actions within in the same spatial and social context.
- The reference location is the place to which the person returns at the end of the day. This is as a rule the home, but might be the room in the student dorm, the hotel room or some other temporary base for the person involved. In the case of movement to a new reference location, one observes journeys with possibly only one trip.

Daily language identifies activities at a relatively rough level: work, shopping, visiting a friend. **Transport planning** normally tries to match this level with its seven to ten categories for activities, but time user research has been able to use category lists nearly one and a half orders of magnitude larger. This dependence makes **travel survey** results dangerous to compare unless it is clear that the implied levels of activity categorization are similar.

Where movement is the purpose of the activity – for example walking the dog, jogging, **bicycling**, a drive in the car – it should be coded as an activity, unless there is a break dividing the activity. The walk to the vehicle should be coded as a trip. Only in the case of going for a walk and similar activities does one have two activities following each other without a trip separating them. Secondary activities performed during movement are normally ignored in transport analysis, but good practice would note them to enrich the modelling of mode and route choice.

In principle, the definitions provided above can be applied in the case of long-distance travel as well, in particular if the travel involves the use of a new reference location. Still, daily language aggregates the whole into the term 'journey', 'trip' or 'round trip'. Surveys of long-distance travel need to be especially careful in this case to avoid confusing the respondents.

It is recommended to invite the respondents to report in the first instance at the colloquial level of journey, and then ask them to describe the movement to the new reference location in more detail. In general, trips at the destination are rarely the subject of long-distance surveys. In line with this coarser detailing, the detailed activities and activity locations are summarized in locations at the level of villages, cities, and sometimes even regions.

For public transport undertakings it is necessary to subdivide customer trips with respect to those stages for which the customer paid. This is especially necessary when multiple operators provide services to this one customer during one trip, or if the fare depends on this definition. This definition is obviously linked to all financial controlling and benchmarking of such enterprises.

A customer movement is a continuous sequence of stages on vehicles of one undertaking, including the walk stages between the vehicles.

It is also sometimes useful to define customer movements with regards to types of service, or types of vehicle, for example bus or tram, within a larger system.

Further reading
Axhausen, K.W. (2000). Definition of movement and activity for transport modelling. In D.A. Hensher and K.J. Button (eds), *Handbook of Transport Modelling*. Oxford: Elsevier.
Axhausen, K.W. (2003). Definitions and measurement problems. In K.W. Axhausen, J.L. Madre, J.W. Polak and P. Toint (eds), *Capturing Long Distance Travel*. Baldock: Research Science Press.

Kay W. Axhausen

energy efficiency

Over time, humans have become more dependent on a continuous increase in energy consumption, which has run counter to the need for energy efficiency. More recently, energy efficiency has become associated with emissions of CO_2, which is considered by the scientific community as a greenhouse gas contributing to global **climate change**.

Most of our transport modes use liquid hydrocarbon fuel, with a few using gaseous hydrocarbon fuel. In addition, many rail-based systems use electric power which can be generated from a variety of fuels, either hydrocarbon, or not (for example nuclear, hydro, geothermal, wind, solar). Vehicles using liquid fuels need to carry their fuel onboard and this creates a restriction that makes **fuel efficiency** important – the more efficient the vehicle is in using fuel, the further it can travel before the need to stop for refuelling. In most transport businesses, stopping a vehicle constitutes potential lost revenue and is therefore best avoided. For transport modes that enjoy an external power supply, as with electric vehicles powered by overhead cables, this is less of an issue.

Energy efficiency has always played a role in transport operations, as energy use represents a cost. For this reason, it has been of particular concern in areas such as road haulage and air transport. In these activities, fuel costs can represent up to half of the operating cost of a business and therefore, minimizing such costs has been an important objective. In addition to drive-train design, energy efficiency is influenced by two factors: vehicle weight and vehicle resistance. The latter can be broken down into rolling resistance for land-based vehicles, and air or water resistance for land-, air- and water-based vehicles. Weight plays a role in acceleration, while air and water resistance affect speed. The higher the resistance that needs to be overcome, the higher the cost in terms of fuel used. This has always put a pressure on commercial transport operations, although reducing weight and resistance has to be offset against practical business considerations. For example, an aerodynamically optimized truck may be energy efficient, but may have a restricted or impractical carry capability. On the other hand, the lighter the vehicle for a given gross weight, the higher the potential payload, which is an added business benefit.

Motor sport is another area where energy efficiency has long been of interest, as here vehicles do not race when they are being fuelled. The longer they can run without the need for refuelling, the more competitive the vehicle, although this can be offset by the weight of the fuel and a balance, therefore, has to be struck.

Both trucks and aircraft have become significantly more energy efficient since the 1980s as a direct result of pressure from operators on manufacturers of vehicles, aircraft and engines. By comparison, fuel consumption per private vehicle has seen only minimal improvement as here the gains in specific **fuel efficiency** of engines has been offset by increases in vehicle weight and increases in performance in terms of speed and acceleration. In most cases, private individuals do not have the same pressures as businesses to reduce costs. This only becomes an issue at times of rapidly rising fuel costs or shortages.

Energy efficiency for private vehicles became an issue after the Organization of Petroleum Exporting Countries (OPEC) energy crisis of 1973–74 and supply constraints after the Iranian revolution in 1979. At these times, shortages at the pump prompted action on the part of governments. In the United States, for example they led to the Corporate Average Fuel Economy (CAFE) standards whereby manufacturers were made responsible for ensuring the cars they sold in a given year reached a standard of fuel consumption set by federal agencies. Penalties were payable if the standard was not met, although credits were tradable by firms that did better than the set standard. In addition, certain fuel-inefficient cars attracted a 'gas-guzzler tax' to discourage potential buyers. In other parts of the world, such as Europe, high fuel **taxation** has kept fuel prices high, thus inducing fuel users toward more fuel-efficient vehicles.

Thus far, few economies have recognized any natural limits to the growth in energy use. Whilst energy is abundant in some respects – the sun delivers large amount to us on a daily basis – our reliance on fossil sources does mean that there are limits, as these are ultimately finite sources of energy. In recent years these fossil hydrocarbons have also become associated with global **climate change**, which is, at least in part, attributed to the release of CO_2 from fossil sources into the atmosphere. This has prompted regulation to encourage carbon reduction from transport in a number of jurisdictions around the world, including China, Japan, and the European Union. These are effectively fuel efficiency measures and they are likely to spread to other countries, as energy efficiency increasingly is becoming a global concern.

Further reading
Henson, R. (2006). *The Rough Guide to Climate Change; The Symptoms, The Science, The Solutions*. London: Rough Guides.
Roberts, P. (2004). *The End of Oil: The Decline of the Petroleum Economy and the Rise of a New Energy Order*. London: Bloomsbury.

Paul Nieuwenhuis

environmental costs

Environment is now a major concern of our societies, and transport is one of the most important sources of environmental damages. So it is not surprising that environmental costs play a central role in transportation policy, and that considerable resources have been and are devoted to estimating these costs and mitigating their impacts. The list of these costs has increased over the years. A decade or two ago, in the 1990s, the main concern was about local air pollution. Now the list is much longer and includes:

- Aesthetic effects resulting from new infrastructure and vehicle use. These effects are subjective. They are usually viewed as negative intrusions, though in some cases they are positive.
- Habitat and community fragmentation, for animals, plants and humans. Animal and plant migration is inhibited by building of roads and other infrastructures.
- Soil and underground water pollution from construction and use of transportation and fuels infrastructure (leakage from fuel tanks and pipes, water run-off from roads, and so on).
- Water pollution, for example from tanker collisions, spills and discharges, including such dramatic accidents as *Exxon Valdez, Amoco Cadiz* or *Erika*.

- Noise and vibration caused by vehicles of all modes in the water, on land and in the air. Road vehicles are most troublesome in dense urban areas, recreational (off-road) vehicles in pristine areas, and aircraft near airports.
- Air pollution primarily from vehicle exhausts, but also from upstream production of energy and the manufacture of vehicles and facilities. The principal concern is with road traffic, because of the large volume of pollution emitted and because it is in close proximity to people. About half of the air pollutants emitted in urban areas are from vehicles. Air pollution can damage human health, as well as vegetation and buildings.
- Climate change caused by large emission of greenhouse gases, especially CO_2. About 20 to 30 per cent of greenhouse gases in Organisation for Economic Co-operation and Development countries are from transportation, largely from fossil fuel combustion in cars and trucks. Climate change effects have been small so far, but the continuing build-up of these gases is creating a growing threat.

Many of these costs imply non-market goods such as morbidity or value of human life. In this last classical expression, the value of human life is a statistical concept which represents the marginal value of an unidentified life, corresponding to the valuation of a small risk.

If environmental impacts were ruled by competitive market mechanisms with full property right allocation, prices would ensure a correct allocation of resources and would correct the oversupply of these effects. The absence of markets for environmental damages can be a case for public action if public authorities can devise better mechanisms to respond to this absence of a competitive market. In technical terms devise mechanisms able to internalize the environmental effects, and thus induce the agents to behave in a more optimal way. In this purpose, it is necessary first to assess the importance of these costs.

Several levels of assessment can be implemented. The first one is to describe the phenomenon. For certain impacts, for example landscape aesthetic impacts, this may be the extent of a particular analysis. It is possible however to translate impacts such as aesthetic losses into monetary terms, for instance through **contingent valuation.** The next step is to quantify physical impacts, that is, to measure impacts in units such as decibels of noise imposed on residents, tonnes of various pollutants released, or changes in **energy** consumption.

The most complete assessment is to monetize, that is, to measure in money values, such impacts; it allows for more easily incorporating them in economic analysis. Impacts that are not monetized, sometimes called intangibles, tend to be forgotten and underestimated in economic evaluation. Attempts to monetize non-market goods is increasingly common for planning and policy analysis, allowing more consistent and equitable decision-making.

There are several methods to monetize the environmental effects. Their bases are the trade-offs that agents make in some situations between these effects and other market goods. Following Quinet and Vickerman, these methods can be classified into three categories.

Firstly, surrogate markets, which can be dealt with in a number of different ways:

- The cost of trips necessary to benefit from an amenity can be used to value that amenity; this method is traditionally used for the evaluation of leisure parks.
- **Hedonic prices**: the price of some marketed goods depends on their exposure to characteristics such as air pollution or noise. Variations in the price of the marketed good with respect to variations in the environmental factor can thus be used to estimate the implicit value which individuals attach to the environmental quality. This method is especially used for noise, and to a lesser extent for local air pollution.
- Estimates of the cost of environmental protection. Observing the amount which individuals pay to abate negative environmental effects provides an estimate of their implicit valuation.

These methods pose several difficulties. For instance, there is the problem of distinguishing the individual impacts of each of the environmental variables, which are often closely linked to each other. Moreover, assumptions need to be made for accurate hedonic valuations that people are well informed and aware of the damage caused by the nuisance at stake. Last but not least, the results of these methods are very sensitive to the econometric procedures and the underlying hypotheses of behaviour of the agents.

Secondly, **contingent valuations** consist in asking people what they are willing to pay to avoid the nuisance, or what they are willing to receive in order to continue suffering from it. They can be used for a large variety of costs, such as aesthetic consequences, air pollution and valuation of non-market goods such as the statistical value of human life. Difficulties of implementation are, however, numerous:

- To get reliable answers, it is necessary to devote a lot of care to devising the questionnaire, and to administer it through very sophisticated controlled procedures.

- Psychological biases lead to the result that willingness to pay to avoid a nuisance is consistently lower than the willingness to accept compensation to continue to suffer it.
- As is the case for other methods, the results can be biased by insufficient knowledge of the actual damage.

Thirdly, these methods can be combined, for instance for the estimation of local pollution costs. The procedure implies two stages. The first one is technical and aims at estimating the consequences of the nuisance in physical units for instance, in the case of air pollution, the frequency and significance of any impacts on health, or the damage to buildings. The second stage is the monetization of the damage, either through the market prices for the damaged goods, or through the cost of repairing the damage, such as the health care costs of injured or sick people; or through **contingent valuations**, for example the value of human life.

A lot of studies have been achieved to estimate these monetary values. The Figure shows some results from a recent CE Delft study related to the European Union countries. They compare average road and rail external costs, according to several different situations differing by the time or the location.

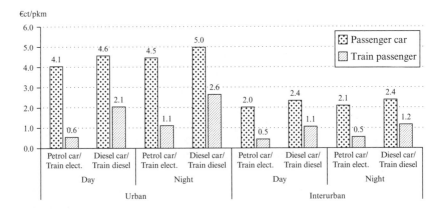

Monetization allows for setting the scope of the public action towards environmental costs. Public action has to answer successively to different questions. First, to what extent should the environmental costs be abated? The answer is that environmental costs should not be cancelled, but reduced to the point where the cost of abatement of the last unit equals the benefit from the reduction of the last unit, namely where:

Marginal cost of abatement = Marginal benefit from the abatement

Public intervention can follow various channels, which, according to a classification close to Button, can be characterized as:

- Direct public management. This approach is widely used for many types of modal and intermodal terminals (road, airports, buses and rail).
- Regulation of actions by individuals and organizations, such as limiting emissions from cars and trucks.
- Economic instruments. These include mechanisms that alter price signals, such as fuel taxes, **congestion** fees, and payments for scrapping old polluting cars; and mechanisms that create property rights and new markets for environment goods, such as marketable credits for emissions, so that the Coase theorem could become operative, and bargaining leads to an efficient result.

Adoption of any particular instrument implies a variety of trade-offs that are difficult to measure and foresee, given that the physical laws to which impacts are subject are in general complex and little known, in particular with regard to their long-term effects, and beset by the kind of unreliability that always surrounds large-scale models with multiple parameters; and also that any measure has equity effects which are not easily balanced with efficiency effects, let alone the magnitude of transaction costs, the side-effects and the equity and distributional issues.

Conventional wisdom in both the political and professional arenas is gradually shifting from command-and-control to greater use of market instruments. Examples include use of tradable credits for vehicle emissions, fuel taxes, modulation of vehicle taxes and tolls, and voluntary agreements with industry to reduce CO_2.

In this respect, it becomes more and more clear that economic instruments, and especially pricing, should be built on very different bases according to the type of effect. For instance, global warming can be quite effectively internalized through a tax on fuel. But a tax on fuel is not appropriate to internalize local air pollution, for which the proper tax should take into consideration both the neighbourhood and the type of vehicle. Unfortunately technology has not for long been able to provide other devices than fuel taxes, vehicle taxes and, for specific infrastructures such as on motorways and other infrastructures such as sea ports and airports. These tools were not at all appropriate to master effects such as air pollution or noise. It is one of the reasons why up to now the mastering of external effects has been built mainly on regulations. Regulation of car emissions, for instance, has been dramatically strengthened over recent decades. In less than 20 years, their incidence has increased by orders of magnitude, although varying according to the type of pollutant involved. But things are rapidly changing in this field. Technological progress allows us now to take into account and price more precisely almost all **externalities** through the new technologies of information and communication (NTIC).

Further reading
Hensher, D.A. and K.J. Button (eds) (2003). *Handbook of Transport and the Environment*. Oxford: Elsevier.
Maibach, M., C. Schreyer, D. Sutter, H.P. van Essen, B.H. Boon, R. Smoker, A. Schroten, C. Doll, B. Pawlowska and M. Bak (2007). *Handbook on Estimation of External Cost in the Transport Sector: Internalisation Measures and Policies for All Axternal Cost of Transport (IMPACT)*. Delft: CE.
Quinet, E. and R. Vickerman (2004). *Principles of Transport Economics*. Cheltenham, UK and Northampton, MA, USA: Edward Elgar.

Emile Quinet

environmental justice and transport

Environmental justice is an element of planning policy that seeks to establish fairness for underrepresented and disadvantaged groups. While the union of environmental justice with transportation is a fairly recent development, transportation has always played a large role in community social and economic outcomes. For example, in *An Overview of Transportation and Environmental Justice*, the United States Department of Transportation (USDOT) identified three fundamental environmental justice principles related to transportation:

- To avoid, minimize or mitigate disproportionately high and adverse human health or environmental effects, including social and economic effects, on minority populations and low-income populations.
- To ensure the full and fair participation by all potentially affected communities in the transportation decision-making process.
- To prevent the denial of, reduction in, or significant delay in the receipt of benefits by minority populations and low-income populations.

Within the United States, transportation inequities can be traced back to segregation of certain minorities on trains and buses. Not only were minorities, primarily African Americans, forced to use separate transportation facilities, but also the quality, **safety** and reliability of such facilities were inferior. These trends have still not been completely resolved. Frequently transportation facilities used predominantly by under-represented groups are of lower quality and minority and low-income groups often shoulder a disproportionately large share of negative transportation effects (for example pollution, decreased pedestrian safety, social disruption and cost burden).

One of the most notable protests during the civil rights struggles of the 1950s was over inequitable public transportation. Rosa Parks's refusal to relinquish her seat to a white passenger in 1955 sparked the Montgomery, Alabama bus boycott. However, Parks's statement went beyond the elimination of segregation on public buses. The demands of civil rights activists in Montgomery also included the need for equal representation in hiring black bus drivers. Crucial service improvements activists campaigned for included better minority neighborhood access to bus routes, increased facility safety and service quality, and greater service frequency. Particularly demeaning to protestors were the payment practices that forced blacks to pay at the front of the bus but to board at the back. The protestors' demands not only addressed the psychological damage due to segregation, but also the economic and social effects of inequitable public transportation.

The economic impacts of inequitable transportation conditions were summarized in the Kerner Report, a federal investigation into the causes of urban race riots that took place in the United States from 1965 to 1968. The report concluded that inadequate public transportation service was partly to blame for high rates of unemployment and poverty among blacks, leading to social discord and high crime rates. Martin Luther King, Jr. noted in 1968: 'Urban transit systems in most American cities have become a genuine civil rights issue. . . If transportation systems in American cities could be laid out so as to provide an opportunity for poor people to get meaningful employment, then they could begin to move into the mainstream of American life.' King's observation was recognition of a racial divide in transportation that existed throughout the country.

Around the same time as the civil rights movement, Congress passed the Interstate Highway Act. This important piece of legislation authorized 40 650 miles of interstate highways and appropriated $24.8 billion for construction. Built in response to urban **congestion**, highways reduced congestion but also accelerated the suburbanization of metropolitan areas. As urban flight and automobile reliance increased, transit services declined. The increased dispersion of origins and destinations within a metropolitan area weakened transit's ability to meet ridership needs. In many metropolitan areas, minority communities were disproportionately impacted or relocated during highway construction. In some instances, this dispro-portionate effect was due to routing through low-cost areas, while other occasions were a result of targeted slum clearing and 'urban renewal'. Displaced residents were sometimes relocated to housing projects.

In response to the civil rights movement, the Civil Rights Act was passed in 1964. Title VI of the Act explicitly prohibited discrimination in any federally funded program or activity on the basis of race, color or national origin. In accordance with Title VI, USDOT passed several regu-lations banning discrimination in transportation, including racial bias in the selection of households displaced by highway construction and their resulting compensation, inequitable highway facility access, and dispari-ties in public transportation service frequency, station quality, and route location.

The passage of the National Environmental Policy Act (NEPA) in 1969 signified a new emphasis on environmental quality and protection within the United States. The Act required that federally funded projects provide environmental impact statements (EIS) during the planning stage for the purpose of taking a 'systematic, interdisciplinary approach' when consider-ing environmental and community factors in project decisions. Furthering the interaction of environmental considerations with transportation plan-ning, the Clean Air Act Amendments of 1970 required that states develop state implementation plans (SIPs) for areas in violation of **air quality** standards. Transportation was recognized as having far-reaching effects not only on congestion relief, but also on environmental quality. This realization among planning officials initiated inclusionary planning proc-esses for transportation projects, drawing in environmental and air quality planners. In 1970, the same year the Clean Air Act Amendments were passed, Congress passed the Federal-Aid Highway Act. This legislation required states to consult with local officials when planning for urban highway projects and to account for adverse environmental, social and environmental effects such that 'decisions on the project are made in the best overall public interest'. Important adverse effects listed by the Act to be avoided or minimized included the destruction of both man-made and natural resources, along with adverse effects on employment, losses in tax and property value, injurious displacement of homes and businesses, and the disruption of desirable community and regional growth.

As these important pieces of legislation were being developed, 'freeway revolts' took place in several metropolitan areas, notably San Francisco, Seattle and Boston. Begun as protests against urban neighborhood disrup-tion during the late 1960s, the battle against interstate highway projects was taken up by activists protesting the disproportionate negative effects on minority communities, increased urban pollution, and disruption of downtown business economies. Freeways were seen as tools of suburban convenience at the cost of urban quality. As a result of these protests, many highway projects were withdrawn. Formal changes in Federal regulations were established in 1973 and 1976 with passage of the Federal-Aid Highway Act, which allowed for federal funding of transit projects in place of highways, and extended the idea of building community-sensitive projects by allowing for the substitution of other highway projects in place of interstate highways.

While NEPA and the Federal-Aid Highway Acts of the 1970s provided the foundation, environmental justice was not formally defined as a federal goal until 1994. Presidential Executive Order 12898 directed that all federal agencies 'develop an agency-wide environmental strategy. . . that identifies and addresses disproportionately high and adverse human health or environmental effects' on minority populations and low-income populations. To provide a context for environmental justice within transportation, USDOT published the *DOT Order to Address Environmental Justice in Minority Populations and Low-Income Populations.* The order mandated that environmental justice be an integral part of all projects undertaken, funded or approved by the Federal Highway Administration (FHWA), the Federal Transit Administration (FTA), or any other USDOT divisions. Environmental justice applies to all project phases including policy, planning, development, design, construction and maintenance for the purpose of creating community sensitive projects. Enforcement is accomplished through 'state action' requirements for states to maintain and staff a civil rights unit and to have administrative procedures to handle civil rights violation complaints.

The movement in environmental justice and transportation in the early twenty-first century is oriented toward building projects that best serve the needs of a community beyond criteria accounted for in cost–benefit analyses. Accounting of impacts is accomplished by using an inclusive planning process: one that involves all aspects of the community, particularly under-represented and minority groups. Because different socio-economic groups have different transportation needs, transportation project impacts must be considered using accurate project assessments in order to prevent inequitable results. For instance, environmental justice for one community may mean extending transit service hours at an employment centre so that workers have a means of transportation after late-night shifts. In another community, environmental justice may mean that a transit authority converts its buses to run on natural gas instead of diesel so that **air quality** is improved for those living in close proximity to the bus depot.

In most examples of environmental justice projects, aggressive public outreach must be employed to establish trust within the community, in order for citizens to feel as if they have a voice that is being heard. Creative approaches in gathering public support must be utilized in order to capture hard-to-reach groups, particularly persons for whom English is not a primary language. Techniques can range from advanced contact through community organizations such as churches and local supermarkets to offering childcare and transportation to the meeting. Methods to receive public input include community meetings, workshops, creating field offices, and hiring community advocates and conflict mediators.

Although there are many definitions of environmental justice, the goal for social, economic and environmental equity remains paramount in the United States. The processes for evaluating transportation plans and relationships between communities and federal, state and local planning authorities continue to be refined. Environmental justice, much like social equality, is an ongoing struggle. Through context-sensitive planning and community participation, the goal of an equitable society is one step closer to realization.

Further reading
Baida, A.H. and J.B. McDaniel (2003). Civil rights in transportation projects. *NCHRP Legal Research Digest*. June.
Davis, J. (1997). Consequences of the development of the interstate highway system for transit. *TCRP Research Results Digest*. Issue 21.
Kelley, R.D.G. (1996). Freedom riders (the sequel). *Nation* **262**, 18–22.
Sánchez, T.W., R. Stolz and J.S. Ma (2003). *Moving to Equity: Addressing Inequitable Effects of Transportation Policies on Minorities*. Cambridge, MA: Harvard University Press.

Andrew Lee and *Debbie A. Niemeier*

environmental standards

Environmental standards – usually established by some public body – aim to control unwanted side-effects of human activities. In principle, any environmental impact caused by transportation could be limited by standards. In practice, it is **air quality** and **traffic noise** that have triggered standards.

Air quality standard is a prescribed level of atmospheric pollution allowed for a certain compound during a specific time in a specific geographical area. The combination of pollutants and exposure can be made in many different ways resulting in divergent standards in different countries (as an example of current environmental standards in the **European Union** see the Table).

Pollutant	Averaging period	Air quality standards
NO$_2$	1 hour	200 µg/m^3 not to be exceeded more than 18 times a calendar year
	calendar year	40 µg/m^3
PM10 [a]	24 hours	50 µg/m^3 not to be exceeded more than 35 times a calendar year
	calendar year	40 µg/m^3
CO	8 hours	10 mg/m^3
Ozone	daily 8 hours max	120 µg/m^3 not to be exceeded more than 20 days per calendar year
Benzene	calendar year	5µg/m^3
Lead	calendar year	0.5 µg/m^3

Note: [a]PM10 is the fraction of suspended particulate matter with a diameter smaller than 10 micrometres.

As examples of probable differences between developed and developing countries, it can be pointed out that in Egypt the allowed concentration of PM10 for 24 hours is 70 µg/m^3, compared to 50 in the European Union. For lead the corresponding figures are 1µg/m^3 annual average in Egypt, against 0.5 in the EU.

Over time air quality standards have tended to have become stricter by including new pollutants and decreasing concentrations and/or exposure. This tendency reflects increasing accumulated knowledge of the health impacts of air pollution, improved administrative capabilities and improvements in **air quality**. As an example, the steps of Clean Air Act in the United States can be described. The Federal law in 1970 authorized the United States Environmental Protection Agency to establish National Ambient Air Quality Standards. The Act was amended in 1975 by prolonging the dates for achieving attainment of the standards. In 1990 the Act was amended to meet problems like acid rain, ground-level ozone, stratospheric ozone depletion, and air toxics. In 1995 the standards for ground-level ozone and particulate matter (PM) were reviewed.

A quite different type of action is related to the Kyoto Protocol of 1997 on climate change. Developed countries then agreed to reduce their greenhouse gas emissions by an overall 5 per cent compared to 1990 levels by 2009–12. The future of this protocol is still open.

In principle, a standard alone will not have much impact without related governmental and industrial activities. The reduction of road transport emissions and the consequent improvement in air quality has mainly been achieved through technological development triggered by environmental standards. Also environmental standards are considered to be the most important factor that might stimulate the market introduction and use of new transport technologies in the future.

The promises of strict standards on exhaust emissions in Europe were quite striking: 90 per cent reductions in new cars' emission rates. In real-world conditions the reductions were more modest – even though quite remarkable – because:

- old cars without catalytic converters are still used in many countries;
- most cars used today no longer meet as stringent emissions standards as when they were new;
- vehicles' emission control systems do not perform as well in real road conditions as they do in laboratory tests.

The use of old cars without catalytic converters is not a problem any more in the United States, where the converters were first made obligatory. It still is a problem in some Southern and many Eastern European countries, as well as in developing countries.

As a car gets older, there are many possible reasons for deterioration in its emission control system. In the worst case the system may be totally out of use or give only partial results depending on the quality of maintenance. To handle these instances there is a need for a governmental control system including regular inspections and/or roadside tests. Otherwise poor maintenance can counteract the positive impacts of technological progress.

It is likely that without some technological innovations, technological development alone will not provide any more big reductions – comparable to the effect of catalytic converters – in the car fleet's exhaust emissions. More improvement can be expected for trucks and other diesel engined vehicles where the current reductions have been relatively modest.

Further reading
Heyma, A. (2000). Barriers and challengers for new urban transport technologies. Seville, IPTS Report 47 European Commission, Joint Research Centre.

Veli Himanen

equity issues in transport policy

Equity plays a role in transport policies in two ways. First, equity problems may be an unintended side-effect of policies to address transport problems such as **congestion** and environmental nuisance. For example, opponents of road pricing may claim that it has adverse equity effects since it will hurt the poor more than the rich. Second, equity may be the explicit aim of certain transport policies such as the construction of infrastructure in lagging regions, **subsidies** to public transport or the provision of special facilities for handicapped persons. In this case equity is more than a side-effect: it is the main motivation for a policy.

In both cases there is a clear need for a proper definition of equity in a broader context where overall efficiency is also considered. However, the meaning of 'equity' is not unambiguous. This is a short inventory:

1. Horizontal equity. Comparable individuals should be treated in a comparable way.
2. Territorial equity. This results from the notion of individual equity when it is projected on relatively homogeneous regions. For example, comparable regions need to get similar funds for public transport.
3. A related fairness concept that is sometimes proposed is that all modes should be treated in the same way. This is often meant to imply that it is unfair when road transport pays high fuel taxes, whereas no fuel tax is imposed on aviation, and rail transport receives subsidies.
4. Longitudinal equity. This concept calls for a long-term view. Lifecycle considerations have to be included, when gains and losses of certain measures vary in the course of time.
5. Vertical equity. This means that disadvantaged individuals deserve protection. People should be burdened according to their ability to contribute, and this may lead to schemes where taxes are more than proportional with income.
6. Transport users should pay their way. As indicated by Gomez Ibañez this concept is usually interpreted in terms of average costs implying that the collective of all transport users pays for the aggregate costs.
7. Individuals that are negatively affected by policies need to be compensated. This principle takes its starting point in the status quo and says that winners have to compensate losers.

Of these equity considerations, the first two are largely unchallenged. The third principle, also known as the level playing field, has intuitive appeal, but it appears not so easy to apply since transport sectors differ in many respects. The fourth concept is convincing, but its application is not easy given the long-term perspective and the uncertainties involved. The fifth one may lead to controversies, in particular because it still leaves open many interpretations on how progressive the tax system should be.

The sixth concept makes perfect sense to most people, but its implications are often not well understood, in particular its departure from marginal cost pricing and economic efficiency. The seventh concept often plays a large role in political debates on transport policies. It is clear that the various equity concepts are not always in harmony. For example, the fifth and the seventh may well be conflicting.

There is a large gap between the efficiency concept as used in **benefit–cost analysis** and the equity concepts mentioned above, in particular numbers 5, 6 and 7. Standard cost–benefit analysis is based on adding the sum of net benefits among all winners and losers. By doing so, equity issues are ignored. A positive net benefit means that in principle the winners can compensate the losers. However, this is a hypothetical compensation, and therefore a policy alternative with a clearly positive aggregate net benefit may have serious equity consequences. In order to improve the systematic search for and development of promising policy alternatives, there is a clear need for a tool where in addition to efficiency concerns as reflected by cost–benefit analysis also equity concerns are operationalized.

Further reading

Gomez Ibañez, J.A. (1997). Estimating whether transport users pay their way: the state of the art. In D.L. Green, D.W. Jones and M.A. Delucchi (eds), *The Full Costs and Benefits of Transportation*. Heidelberg: Springer-Verlag.

Rietveld, P. (2003). Winners and losers in transport policy: on efficiency, equity, and compensation. In D.A. Hensher and K.J. Button (eds), *Handbook of Transport and the Environment*. Oxford: Elsevier.

Viegas, J. (2002). Making urban road pricing acceptable and effective. *Transport Policy* **8**, 289–94.

Piet Rietveld

European Conference of Ministers of Transport

The European Conference of Ministers of Transport (ECMT) was formed under the auspices of the Organisation for Economic Co-operation and Development (OECD) in 1953, with the aim of improving the efficiency of the transport system in Europe, through joint decisions and through cooperation in research. It comprised 44 full member countries from throughout Europe and seven associate members – the non-European countries of the OECD. It comprised a Council of Ministers, a Committee of Deputies and an administration based at the OECD in Paris. Besides formal meetings of ministers, it was well known amongst transport researchers for its published research on specific topics, its occasional conferences, and particularly for its series of Round Tables on specific themes, at which three or four researchers from different countries presented reports on a theme debated amongst a wider international gathering of experts, the results being published.

For many years, ECMT acted as a bridge between the European Union and the wider European community, facilitating policy coordination between them, but as the European Union expanded, this role became less important. In 2004, its research arm was merged with the Road Transport Research programme of the OECD to form the Joint Transport Research Centre. In 2006, ECMT was transformed into the International Transport Forum (ITF) with membership open to all members of the OECD and former members of the ECMT.

Christopher Nash

European Union transport policy

The European Union is a union of 27 member states, which retain autonomy regarding issues that are not deemed to affect the union as a whole (the so-called principle of subsidiarity). Thus in terms of transport policy, laws applying to the union as a whole are only passed relating to decisions which are seen as important in terms of achieving fair competition and economic and social convergence between the member states. These issues include regulation, transport pricing for commercial traffic and investment in key international corridors. However, the Commission does encourage best practice in other areas, including for example urban transport.

The most recent comprehensive statement of transport policy was the White Paper of 2001, which adopted the following objectives:

- Shifting the balance between the different modes of transport;
- Eliminating bottlenecks;
- Placing users at the heart of the transport policy; and
- Managing the **globalization** of transport.

Progress on this was reviewed in 2006, and many saw the review as somewhat watering down the original policies. For instance, the objective on modal shift was replaced by the concept of co-modality, under which each mode should perform the role for which it is most suitable. However, the policy of internalizing **externalities** through pricing was restated in the 2008 greening transport package.

Regarding regulation, the policy has been to deregulate entry into transport markets whilst maintaining and strengthening **safety** and environmental regulation. Free entry has largely been achieved in the airline and road haulage markets, as well as for rail freight. **Deregulation** of rail passenger services will start in 2010 for international services only. For local transport services, competition by means of competitive tendering is generally favoured, but it was not possible to get agreement to make this compulsory; however, transparent contracts must now be awarded for any subsidized services even if the process is one of negotiation rather than tendering.

Since the mid-1990s, EU pricing policy has been to internalize externalities in transport prices. Starting with the Commission's Green Paper *Towards Fair and Efficient Pricing in Transport*, and continuing with the *Common Transport Policy White Paper*, there is a strong emphasis on pricing policy to reflect the full social costs of transport use, but progress has been slow. Within the rail sector, short run **marginal social cost** is taken as the basis for track access charges. Electricity generation is already included in the European emissions trading scheme regarding greenhouse gases; there are proposals to extend this approach to air transport and possibly also to water. Otherwise, there are currently no proposals to internalize the costs of environmental externalities in prices for the air and water modes.

For the road sector, following adoption of a Directive on road charges, the European Union allows the introduction of heavy goods vehicle tolls on all roads. Differentiation is possible according to **congestion** and accident costs and the environmental performance of vehicles, indicated by the EURO category of the lorry. This differentiation has to be designed in a way that the total revenues from tolling do not exceed the total allocated infrastructure costs, except that a surcharge of up to 25 per cent, which can be used to fund alternative modes of transport, is permitted in environmentally sensitive areas such as the Alps. Further proposals on this, to amend the above Directive to allow full charging of external costs of congestion, noise and air pollution, with any additional revenue to be used for improving the environmental performance of the transport system, were brought forward by the European Commission in July 2008. Charging for the private car is regarded as a matter for individual member states.

As regards investment, the development of the Trans-European Networks is the most important issue for the European Commission, as it is the only transport infrastructure for which there is explicit European funding, although there is greater funding of transport from structural and cohesion funds designed to benefit poorer and peripheral countries. A set of priority projects has been defined, which favour rail on account of its superior environmental performance. But EU funding only makes a small contribution to this investment progress, and progress in implementation is again slow.

Further reading
Commission of the European Communities (1995). *Towards Fair and Efficient Pricing in Transport*. Brussels: CEC.
Commission of the European Communities (2001). *White Paper: European Transport Policy for 2010: Time to Decide*. Brussels: CEC.
Commission of the European Communities (2006). *Keep Europe Moving – Sustainable Mobility for our Continent. Mid-term Review of the European Commission's 2001 Transport White Paper*. Brussels: CEC.

Christopher Nash

external costs of transportation

An external cost is a cost not included in the market price of the good or service being produced, that is, a cost not borne by those who create it. As a consequence, third parties that are neither on the demand nor on the supply side of the market transaction have to bear these costs without being compensated. A typical example for a transportation externality is airport noise imposed on those living near major airports and below aircraft flight paths and for which, for those affected, there is no full compensation.

Economists distinguish between private cost and social cost. In our example, while the private cost for air travellers consist only of the air fare, the social cost also comprises the cost imposed on bystanders. The difference between social and private cost is defined as external cost.

The Figure clarifies the distinction between private and social cost and its implication. In a demand and supply market the supply curve is identical with private marginal cost ($MC_{private}$), that is, the cost that is incurred by the producer. Typically, the market reaches an equilibrium at point A, where the demand and supply curves meet.

In contrast, if the social cost is considered, that is, private plus external cost, point B could be reached, the social optimum. Compared to this socially desired outcome, the market outcome does not reflect the true marginal cost and yields quantities that are too high and prices that are too low. Thus, the market is driven by incomplete supply and demand

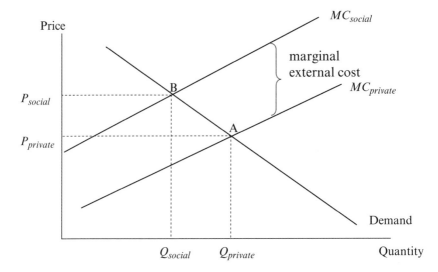

incentives resulting in welfare losses. Economists call this market short-coming a type of 'market failure'.

The transportation sector exhibits a variety of different **externalities** which can be grouped into the broad categories of **congestion** costs, accidents, air pollution, global warming, noise and other external costs. In quantitative terms the majority of these costs are automobile-related; other modes of transportation playing a comparatively minor role.

Externalities can arise from a temporary or permanent over-demand for scarce infrastructure leading to congestion costs. The best-known example is highway traffic congestion. On an underused street motorists neither experience nor cause **congestion costs**. However, when traffic gets denser each additional motorist not only incurs his or her private congestion cost but also imposes additional cost on all other automobile users on the respective highway. Although traffic jams are mostly a temporary event, they impose a major cost on automobile users – they are a 'club bad' in technical terms. In 2005, highway congestion caused urban Americans to travel 4.2 billion hours more and to purchase an extra 2.9 billion gallons of fuel, leading to an overall cost of $78.2 billion. This makes traffic congestion the single most important externality in the transportation sector. Automobile-induced congestion costs have been estimated to amount to $0.05 per vehicle mile travelled (VMT) or $1.05 per gallon of gasoline. However, the congestion problem is not confined to highways. For aviation, airport and airspace congestion has increasingly become a major problem.

Traffic accidents are a predominantly highway-related issue. In 2006, 99.6 percent of all accidents and 99.3 percent of all traffic-related fatalities were linked to highway travel. The annual number of traffic fatalities in the United States has stayed persistently above 40 000 for almost 50 years. For the year 2000, the overall social cost of highway accidents (that is, fatalities, injuries and property damage and travel delays), were estimated at $433 billion, which equals 4.3 percent of the United States gross domestic product (GDP). However, not all of this can be deemed an externality. External accident costs are costs that are not covered by risk-oriented insurance premiums. Therefore, the level of external costs depends not only on the level of accidents but also on the insurance system. Recent studies put the marginal external accident costs in the United States in the range between 13 percent and 44 percent of this amount; an equivalent of $0.02 to $0.07 per VMT or $0.63 per gallon of gasoline.

Air pollution costs are caused by the emission of air pollutants such as particulate matter, NOx SO_2 and volatile organic compounds (VOCs) and consist of health costs, buildings and materials damage, crop losses and costs for further damage to the ecosystem (biosphere, soil, water). Health costs are by far the most important cost category. Due to increasingly stringent US federal emission standards for new vehicles, vehicle emissions of all local pollutants have fallen dramatically. However, air pollution is often regionally concentrated and reaches peak levels at certain times. The United States, especially the Greater Los Angeles area where the air can be in an 'unhealthy range' on more than 200 days a year, faces a substantial pollution problem. Estimations of the overall external pollution cost of automobiles range between $0.01 and $0.08 per VMT or $0.42 per gallon.

Carbon dioxide, which is released by burning fossil fuels such as gasoline or diesel, is the leading greenhouse gas. Globally, the transportation sector contributes to about 20 percent of all global CO_2 emissions; by far the largest part of which is due to automobile travel. The external cost of carbon is estimated in the range of between $20 and more than $300 per ton. The external global warming cost of automobiles in the United States averages at about 0.3 percent VMT or about $0.06 per gallon.

Noise is annoying and imposes a health externality on bystanders. Noise occurs locally and is often confined to certain time periods. It can be caused by all motorized modes of transportation. For automobiles the average external effect is thought to range between zero and $0.004 per VMT or zero to $0.08 per gallon.

Further reading

Parry, I.W.H, M. Walls and W. Harrington (2007). Automobile externalities and policies. *Journal of Economic Literature* **45**, 373–99.

Schrank, D. and T. Lomax (2007). *Urban Mobility Report 2007*. College Station, TX: Texas Transportation Institute, University of Texas.

United States Department of Transportation (2007). *National Transportation Statistics 2007*. Washington DC: Bureau of Transportation Statistics.

Karl Storchmann

externalities

Externalities are effects that economic agents have on each other's activities that are not reflected in the market transactions. Externalities occur when there is a divergence between **marginal social cost** and marginal private cost. In transportation, externalities refer to costs associated with transport that are not fully, directly borne by those generating them, and therefore creating a divergence between social and private marginal cost. Most of the externalities are characterized by a feedback effect: the level of the externality itself affects the behaviour of the economic agent, as in the case of **congestion** where the time cost affects travel behaviour. Button makes the distinction between two types of externalities: pollution and congestion. In pure pollution some users, the drivers, abuse the medium; while others, the public, are relatively passive victims of such abuse. In pure congestion, such as in traffic congestion, all users, the drivers, are using the road, each contributing to increasing the travel time for others as well as for themselves.

Within this range five main categories of transport externalities can be identified: congestion, accidents, environment, land use and road damage. **Traffic congestion** can be regarded as an external effect that travellers impose on each other. A traveller does not take into account the impact they have on the travel times of other travellers. The resulted reduced speed also affects the operating costs and non-transport users through effects on emissions and noise. Congestion cost is evaluated by calculating the travel times lost on the **network** converted to monetary units, using a value of time.

Accidents external costs are categorized into three main types. First, costs to the injured person including costs of treatment and cure. These also include indirect costs such as economic loss to the injured person's place of work, and the value of life in cases of death. Second, accident costs including damage to the car and other property, time loss, congestion cost and environmental damage. Third, other transport users may adapt their behaviour when confronted with a changed traffic situation. How much of these various costs are external depends on the liability, compensation rules and type of insurance adopted.

Environmental costs include the costs imposed by the emission of air pollutants and **traffic noise** on society in general, and on future generations in the case of climate change. The emissions of air pollutants from traffic consist mainly of exhaust emissions, but there are also impacts of fuel that evaporates from the fuel system and emissions that result from the contact between the tyres and the road surface. Some of the emissions have purely local impacts such as particulates and carbon monoxide; others contribute to regional scale effects such as ozones or even the global scale, such as CO_2. The largest effort devoted to the determination of air pollution costs was developed in the European ExternE Transport Study using the 'impact pathway approach' (tracking impacts along the path: emissions, air pollution concentrations, quantitative impact and monetary value), which found the resultant costs to be dominated by damage to human health.

Land use external costs can be categorized into three types. First, effects that are induced partly or wholly through the changes in **accessibility** resulting from transport projects including changes in land use. This is a major benefit of transport projects that contributes to economic growth. Second, land values and property rights. And third, visual impact and other local effects, such as severance. Road damage external costs are only significant in the case of heavy vehicles that cause damage to the road surface.

Externalities can cause market failure because in their presence social marginal cost is greater than private marginal cost. Governments can make use of several instruments to deal with externalities. The three main approaches are pricing, regulation and infrastructure policy. The last category is very broad and includes infrastructure expansion and spatial planning. These various instruments are often complementary.

So far, the main approach to dealing with environmental externalities in the **European Union** and North America has been regulatory, mainly by progressively tightening emissions standards for new vehicles. In regard to greenhouse gases the main policy measure is a voluntary agreement with the car manufacturers to reduce average carbon dioxide emissions. **Congestion** externalities need a real market approach, as it is argued that by failing to take account of external costs, transport prices have led to excessive growth of the use of private cars, and constrained the growth of environmentally friendly modes. Governments must consider all transport external costs to avoid bias towards polluting and congesting modes.

Further reading
Button, K.J. (2010). *Transport Economics* (3rd edn). Cheltenham, UK and Northampton, MA, USA: Edward Elgar.
Shiftan, Y., M. Ben-Akiva, G. De Jong, S. Hakkert and D. Simmonds (2002). Evaluation of externalities in transport projects. *European Journal of Transport and Infrastructure Research* **2**, 285–304.

Yoram Shiftan

F

ferry services

Ferry services are scheduled transport services provided by marine vessels over a fixed water-route between two or more origin–destination points. Ferry services of different forms are found throughout the world. The vessels may be passenger, passenger–auto and cargo ferries – dedicated to transporting passengers, passengers and their autos, and cargo, respectively. By the late 1990s there were 134 million annual ferry passengers in the United States. Washington State Ferries, the largest United States ferry operator, operates 28 ferries with a passenger capacity of 37 500 passengers. Ferry services are provided between points where a bridge does not exist or where the width of the body of water would make a bridge impractical. Ferry services are usually found in coastal urban regions, but also may be found in intercoastal and interisland regions.

Public interest in expanding existing or starting new ferry services in coastal urban regions has grown. This interest reflects the increase in highway **congestion** at bridges and tunnels and the fact that the construction of the latter has become increasingly cost-prohibitive or politically infeasible. Ferry services are less costly alternatives to bridge and tunnel construction for adding urban water-crossing capacity. Also, ferries are more time-responsive than fixed crossings to transport demand, for example, in adding and reducing ferries, and changing routes.

The interest in ferry services has also been spurred in many countries by the deployment of high-speed (exceeding 30 knots) ferries, known technically as high-speed crafts (HSCs). The HSCs come in a variety of shapes and sizes from small hovercrafts to large HSCs that can carry the same number of passengers and vehicles as a conventional ferry. The hovercraft is supported by a cushion of air, having boundaries defined by the rubber skirt in which the craft sits. Lift is provided by a fan system which blows air into the cushion and propulsion is provided by engines. The catamaran is the most commonly used HSC by passenger ferry operators. A catamaran is a twin-hulled vessel with slender hulls or pontoons. Its advantage is its stability – it is not as susceptible to adverse sea conditions as single-hulled HSCs.

Ferry service is not only an alternative to bridge and tunnel water-crossing infrastructures, but also an alternative urban transit service to land transit services such as bus, heavy, subway rail and light, streetcar rail. Urban transit services are urban passenger transport services that are fixed-route, scheduled, shared by passengers and for hire. The urban ferry is the largest urban transit vehicle. Bridges and tunnels are often among the most congested segments of an urban highway system. Thus, the ferry may be a viable alternative to the transit bus and the auto for reducing urban passenger work-trip times where bridges and tunnels exist. Further, since urban transit services are usually subsidized by government, the subsidized lower-fare of the transit ferry makes ferry service more price-competitive with auto travel.

The concern for the **safety** of ferry services has increased with their expansion. The concerns include vessel instability and insufficient fire protection. Roll-on roll-off (for example passenger–auto) ferry vessels have giant doorways that allow for the loading (roll-on) and the unloading (roll-off) of automobiles and other cargoes that preclude vertical water-tight bulkheads that are standard features on most commercial vessels. If water gets in and causes a pronounced list, the vessel will capsize and sink. If their loading doors are breached, they can sink without warning; 60 per cent of roll-on roll-off ferries sink within ten minutes when involved in an accident. Among types of ferry accidents – fire and explosions, collisions, material and equipment failures and groundings – a fire or explosion accident has the highest number of fatal and non-fatal injuries. Every 100 fire or explosion accidents are expected to result in 6.1 fatal injuries, while each fire or explosion accident is expected to result in one non-fatal injury.

In addition to safety concerns, there are also environmental concerns with ferry services, in particular air pollution emissions from marine engines. Diesel-powered ferries without emissions controls are estimated to produce more NOx emissions, but less carbon monoxide (CO) emissions, per passenger trip than a car passenger trip.

Further reading
Corbett, J.J. and A. Farrell (2002). Mitigating air pollution impacts of passenger ferries. *Transportation Research D* **7**, 197–211.
Talley, W.K. (2002). The safety of ferries: an accident injury perspective. *Maritime Policy and Management* **29**, 331–8.

Wayne K. Talley

four-stage traffic modelling

There are a number of reasons why transportation analysts may need to model the flow of traffic or travel demand in a transportation system. They may, for example, need to predict levels of traffic flow or travel demand to anticipate needs for infrastructure and infrastructure maintenance or to determine the appropriate frequency and routing of public transit service. Transportation analysts and planners may also need to understand how travel demand responds to various policy measures – such as **congestion** pricing, tolls, or dedicated traffic lanes – in order to manage congestion effectively. To engage in effective land-use planning and development, they must understand how land use and travel demand are interrelated, a relationship which a properly specified model of traffic or travel demand will capture. Finally, transportation researchers may have need of traffic models to conduct thought experiments to help determine as efficiently as possible what the potential effects of a wide range of changes in a transportation system may be.

The approach to modelling traffic flows most commonly taken is the so-called 'four-stage' one. The four stages are 'trip generation', 'trip distribution', '**modal split**' and 'trip assignment'. These stages represent logically distinct 'moments' of a comprehensive analysis, which may or may not be conducted individually or sequentially. The first stage of the modelling concerns estimating the volume of trips generated in or attracted by areal zones of a transportation system. Trip estimates may be based on characteristics of particular transportation system users and the activities they engage in or on characteristics of entire zones. In computing such estimates in the former, disaggregated case, one may use coefficients of trip generation associated with particular types of households or attributes of households (for example income level or number of vehicles owned) or of business and other travel activity generators. Micro-level measures may also be used to estimate the level of travel attraction to zonal destinations. To estimate trip generation at the aggregate level, multivariate regression techniques are frequently used with aggregate measures to detect and characterize relationships between zonal, usually demographic, characteristics and travel demand. The typical trip generation model at the aggregate level is of the form:

$$O_j = a_{0j} + \sum_{i=1} a_{ij} X_{ij}, \tag{1}$$

in which O_j denotes the number of trips generated in zone j, X_{ij} the ith aggregate characteristic of zone j, and a_{ij} the empirically estimated coefficient giving the number of trips generated from zone j per unit of associated characteristic i. In the absence of data supporting such analyses, coefficients may be taken from the Institute of Transportation Engineers *Trip Generation* manual. In estimating trip generation at the aggregate level, attributes of the transportation system should also be included, because it is likely that the level of service of this system, that is, the spacing of public transportation stops, flow capacity of streets, and so on, will affect travel demand. Trip generation may be usefully disaggregated by trip purpose – for example work-based and non-commuting.

Generally, trip generation models calibrated for one area are not portable to another, and the appropriateness of coefficients' values will depend on how zones are defined. Model specifications should take account of any special travel generators, such as airports, governmental facilities, major shopping centres and industrial plants, when they are present.

Whereas the first stage of the traffic modelling process concerns prediction of travel activity levels on the basis of characteristics of travellers and areas that constitute the origins and destinations of travel, the second stage concerns the distribution of trips, once the levels generated and attracted are given. The organizing question of the second stage is 'How many (or what proportion of) people departing some location *i* arrive at another location *j*?' Typically, what is used to predict trip distribution is a spatial interaction model, the most popular instance of which is the **gravity model**, which is formally akin to Isaac Newton's model of the same name. Following Oppenheim's exposition, the general mathematical form of this model is:

$$I_{ij} = k_i l_j O_j D_i F(d_{ij}). \tag{2}$$

The equation states that the volume of interaction between areas *i* and *j*, I_{ij}, is directly proportional to the capacities of these areas to produce and attract interaction, O_j and D_i, given the degree of difficulty of interaction (or impedance of such) between *i* and *j*, $F(d_{ij})$, which is a function of some measure of the (effective) distance between *i* and *j*, d_{ij}. In Equation 1, k_i and l_j are scaling factors related to areas *i* and *j*, respectively, which reconcile units of measurement. O_j and D_i may not be direct measures of observable quantities but may be indices, which may assume various functional forms. The impedance function, $F(d_{ij})$, also may assume various functional forms. The scaling factors, k_i and l_j, may be eliminated by imposing constraints on O_j and D_i. Coefficients of the various indices involved in Equation 1 are usually estimated from empirical data. But in the absence of data on spatial interaction, gravity models calibrated with parameters taken from the literature may be used to forecast trip distributions.

The third stage of the traffic modelling process involves determining which proportions of trips taken in the transportation system are taken by the different available modes of travel. The two most commonly used models of mode choice are the 'probit' and 'logit' models. In the simplest case of just two travel modes, the probit model equates the probability that a given traveller chooses travel mode 1 instead of mode 2 to the cumulative probability that a standard normal random variable takes on a value less than a given value, called the utility of mode 1. The model can be formally expressed as:

$$P_i = \Phi(G_k), \tag{3}$$

in which Φ (. . .) denotes the value of the cumulative standard normal probability distribution for its argument and the argument G_k denotes the utility derived from the use of mode 1 by travellers in some population group k. G_k is usually specified as a linear function of the relative attributes of the transportation modes, X_s^1 and X_s^2, and personal characteristics of travellers in group k, Y_t^k, such as:

$$G_k = a + \sum_s b_s(X_s^1 - X_s^2) + \sum_t c_t Y_t^k \tag{4}$$

The values of the coefficients of probit models of mode choice are usually estimated from empirical data by maximum-likelihood methods.

The other commonly used model of mode choice, the logit model, expresses the probability that a traveller of type k will choose mode 1 as:

$$P_1^k = \frac{1}{1 = e^{G_2^k - G_1^k}} \tag{5}$$

In Equation 5, G_i^k is a function of mode i's characteristics, as evaluated by a traveller of type k. This function can assume various forms. The parameters of P_i^k, which is formally a logistic function, can also be readily estimated from data by maximum-likelihood methods.

Once trips have been generated, distributed and modal usage has been allocated, the next logical step in traffic modelling is to determine the routes by which travellers will arrive at their destinations; hence, what flows of traffic each link in a transportation **network** will bear. This stage of traffic modelling is termed the trip assignment problem and several approaches to it may be taken. However, each approach embodies the basic principle that traffic should be distributed such that 'travel effort' between zones is minimized, both for individual travellers choosing between routes for their trips and for the entire population of travellers. Thus, the first determination to be made in solving the trip assignment problem is the least-effort route between any two zones, given the efforts associated with each link. This determination can be made by applying the shortest-path method. When traffic is dispersed over a **network**, a route-choice model similar to a modal-choice model may be employed.

The effects of individual travellers' choices on transportation systems need to be systematically accounted for in reliable traffic models. Feedback effects of increased traffic on links can be captured by **congestion** functions of the so-called 'Bureau of Public Roads' form:

$$T^k = T_0\left(1 + 0.15\frac{V_k}{C_k}\right)^4, \tag{6}$$

in which T^k denotes the time it takes to traverse link k, T_0 denotes the free-flow travel time, V_k is the traffic volume on link k, and C_k is the link capacity.

Further reading
Donaghy, K.P. and L.A. Schintler (1997). Managing congestion, pollution, and pavement conditions in a dynamic transportation network model. *Transportation Research D* **3**, 59–80.
Institute of Transportation Engineers (2003). *Trip Generation* (7th edn). Washington, DC: ITE.
Oppenheim, N. (1980). *Applied Models in Urban and Regional Analysis*. Engelwood Cliffs, NJ: Prentice-Hall.

Kieran P. Donaghy

fourth-party logistics

Business process outsourcing (BPO) is commonplace for non-core business functions such as human resources, accounting, payroll and information technology management. Firms with complicated global **supply-chains** frequently outsource traditional logistics operations to third-party logistic providers (3PLs) – to improve customer service, reduce inventory, increase inventory velocity and improve cash flow. Many companies, however, have become increasingly concerned that the service levels and business benefits of logistics outsourcing are not matching expectations and in the mid-1990s, the idea for an additional, higher level of supply-chain management provided by a non-asset-based, and theoretically neutral, service provider emerged.

In 1996, Andersen Consulting, now Accenture, developed and trade-marked the 4PL concept, with the following definition: 'A supply-chain integrator that assembles and manages the resources, capabilities and technology of its own organisation with those of complimentary service providers to develop a comprehensive supply-chain solution'.

In its original concept 4PL was designed to overcome some of the shortcomings associated with earlier 3PL outsourcing models. Namely, to provide a single point of contact across the **supply-chain** rather than multiple and separate functional service contacts, to provide a platform for continuous improvement and renegotiation of service level agreements. The 4PL business model brings together a selected combination of principal parties with a number of minor equity parties with specialist capabilities. As such the 4PL is normally established as a joint venture, owned and operated by the clients and their partners where profit sharing is used to align management goals. The clients submit selected assets, working capital and operational staff while the partners provide logistics strategy, re-engineering, logistics best practice and IT systems development. Supplementary services are purchased by the 4PL from external providers including traditional 3PL service providers.

The business operations of 4PLs differ from those of asset-based 3PLs. 4PLs do not own warehouses or truck fleets, but their expertise resides in managing information and coordinating transactions. 3PLs have traditionally focused on the transportation and distribution of finished products, inbound-cargo operation, procurement and hinterland transportation movements, whereas 4PL operations are involved with the raw materials stage through to the end-product distribution stage of the **supply-chain**. The range of products and services provided by a 4PL is extensive yet specific to client needs. What should be common to all 4PL relationships are knowledge transfer, business development and functional support. The key benefit sought from 4PL is in increasing shareholder value.

By using knowledge-process outsourcing and their supply-chain management expertise and skills, 4PLs are able to manage manufacturers, transportation providers, freight forwarders, customs brokers and even 3PLs on behalf of their customers. By doing so, 4PLs act as the sole contact point for all supply-chain management operations and monitor the efficiency of these operations for their customers. 4PLs are responsible for delivering innovative and company-tailored solutions while at the same time reducing costs for their customers. Key performance indicators are used by 4PL users to aid in the monitoring and benchmarking processes. As a result, the customers of 4PL are able to focus their efforts on core competencies such as product design and/or manufacturing.

In 2000, for example, General Motors (GM) entered into a contract with CNF Inc. to provide 4PL services to reduce GM's $6 billion logistics costs. To do so, CNF Inc. created the 4PL, Vector. With GM's **just-in-time** manufacturing operation, 12 000 suppliers ship 180 million pounds of production material daily to over 70 GM manufacturing sites. The actions of Vector resulted in GM changing production and ordering schedules while at the same time renegotiating their transportation rates with railroads, truck carriers and ocean shipping lines. Of the $1.7 billion in GM logistics expenditures addressed by Vector, $128 million was eliminated by Vector. In 2007 GM purchased CNF's interest in Vector and brought the operations in-house. Much of the synergies between the customer, the 4PL and other parties have largely been made possible by advances taking place in telematics, web-enabled information technology (IT) solutions and the ability to synchronize and integrate with enterprise resource planning systems.

The success of 4PL has been mixed. Many of the current 4PL business models look nothing like the original concept, having been either scaled down or developed sequentially over a long period of negotiation and readjustment, or even taken back in-house. The original **supply-chain** scope was often too broad to manage and many clients became fearful of the loss of control. What has emerged from companies' experiences with 4PL are new business models to supply-chain outsourcing.

Further reading
Armbruster, W. (2002). *4 PL, Journal of Commerce*. June 24–30.
Bauknight, D.N. and J.R. Miller (1999). Fourth party logistics: the evolution of supply-chain outsourcing. *CALM Supply-chain and Logistics Journal* (Summer).
Gattorna, J. (2006). *Living Supply-Chains: How to Mobilize the Enterprise around Delivering what your Customers want*. Upper Saddle River, NJ: Pearsons Education Ltd.

Sara E. Russell, Wayne K. Talley and *Melvyn J. Peters*

fuel efficiency of transport

Energy efficiency refers to the amount of transport that is produced with each energy unit used in the process. In Europe, energy efficiency is usually measured by comparing the number of kilometres each transport mode can move a tonne of freight per litre of fuel. In the United States, the British thermal unit (BTU) is also used. This displays the number of BTUs that each transport mode consumes per ton-mile.

In the Table, a comparison is given between fuel efficiency of barge transport in the United States and Europe. However, the American data date back to 1981 and since then considerable progress has been made. Furthermore, in these numbers, the pre- and end-haulage is not included, while barge transport is almost always dependent on road transport for the first and last part of the trip. Therefore, the actual fuel efficiency of

Fuel efficiency characteristic	Barge United States	Barge European Union
Distance 1 gallon fuel moves 1 ton	514 miles	238 miles
Distance 1 litre fuel moves 1 tonne	216 km	100 km
British thermal units/ton mile	433	n.a.
British thermal units/ton mile	344	n.a.
British thermal units/ton mile	412	n.a.
Energy use (Megajoules) to move 1 tonne/1 km	n.a.	0.3

barge transport, when compared to road transport, will be less favourable. Rail transport efficiency will experience the same problems as barge transport.

During the last decades, the fuel efficiency of all transport modes has showed considerable improvement. It has been shown by Tolliver that the difference between rail and barge fuel efficiency has been decreasing considerably. In another study by Baumel and Gervais it has been shown that barge transport fuel efficiencies had the least technological improvements since 1985. The exact fuel efficiency of barge transport considerably depends on particular circumstances (upstream, downstream, loaded, unloaded, weather, and so on). When transporting raw materials, barge transport is claimed to be the most fuel-efficient method of transport.

Due to increased regulation, especially of road modes, and technical developments, all transport has improved its fuel efficiency. Barge transport has followed this trend with the adoption of more fuel efficient engines and operating practices.

In the future, fuel efficiency of transport modes is likely to increase further. Several alternatives for burning fossil fuels are under investigation. Sun and wind energy, biofuels, electricity and hydrogen may give fuel efficiency a complete different dimension in the long run.

Further reading
Baumel, C.P. and J. Gervais (1999). Estimates of fuel consumption transporting grain from Iowa to major key markets by alternative modes, Iowa State University
Tolliver, D. (2000). Analysis of the energy, emission and safety impacts of alternative improvements to the Upper Mississippi and Illinois waterway system. Report to the Army Corps of Engineers, Washington, DC.

Bart Wiegmans

G

gender issues and transport

Women have traditionally been less mobile than men. This is changing, however, particularly in the industrialized world where in per capita terms the distance travelled by women is becoming more similar to that experienced by men. Moreover, much of the increased travel being done by women is by motorized vehicles, such as cars and vans. In developed nations, the enhanced **mobility** of women can be largely attributed to the feminization of the workplace. While in aggregate terms the travel patterns of men and women look quite similar, at a disaggregated level there are distinct differences in overall mobility levels, trip frequency, mode of transportation used, the complexity of trip making and trip purpose. These distinctions stem from factors such as changing family structures (for example, rise of single-family households), women's concerns for **safety** and security, their continued role as primary caretakers of family and home, and the value they place on community and local environment. In the developing world, in sub-Saharan Africa, Central America and parts of Asia, gender differences are much more distinct than those found in developed nations. This is because there tend to be a more well-defined gendered division of labour, cultural norms and beliefs that limit the travel choices available to women, and impoverished conditions that further constrain women's travel opportunities.

In most nations, women continue to travel generally less distance overall than men. This pattern, though, varies by age group. While the **mobility** levels of men and women look very similar for the younger driving-age population, the levels diverge as women enter into the prime of their domestic and child caretaking years. The responsibilities associated with this part of a woman's stage in life lead to more localized travel, including shorter commutes to be able to conduct multiple activities in a short amount of time. There are also gender differences in terms of the modes of transportation used. Females still travel more than males by less prestigious modes, such as mass transit, and as passengers in cars and vans. At the same time, women are also becoming increasingly motorized and travelling greater distances by car and van.

Women have more complicated patterns of trip making, and more often than men tend to do trip chaining. This is true even for married couples where both spouses are employed in paid work. The types of trips made by females are also often quite different than those of men. Women are more inclined to run errands related to household duties and child care.

This pattern exists regardless of the size of the household or the structure of the family. Trip chaining raises some issues. One is that it can have detrimental implications for the environment due to the amount of cold starts that are generated by the activity. Another is that because trip chaining involves frequent stops, multiple destinations and the need to drop off or pick up items or children, transit, biking and walking are not viable modes of transportation. This is one reason why women are trending towards a greater use of motorized vehicles.

In developing nations, the situation is somewhat different. The role of women in these countries, particularly in **rural areas**, typically centres on laborious activities such as gathering water, firewood and other essential resources. In addition to this, women are also the primary caretakers of children and the household and are more involved in local community activities. Taking care of these responsibilities is typically done using inferior means of transport, such as travelling by foot, bus or non-motorized transportation, for example rickshaw **taxis** or bicycle. While this is similar to what is seen elsewhere in the world, the situation in poorer nations is more often guided less by choice and more by cultural norms and values. Vehicle ownership is generally lower in less wealthy countries and in households that do own an automobile, men have priority over its use. In some nations, local customs preclude women from using **bicycles** and women are required to board **buses** after men. Women are further disadvantaged because their trips tend to be more localized, where the availability and quality of roads and paths are inferior to those that exist at a regional level.

The travel needs and patterns of women could change even further in the future. The population as a whole is ageing and older individuals now make up the fastest-growing age cohort in many nations. Women make up a large share of these baby boomers, and in some countries the female population already exceeds that of men and their life expectancy is higher. As a consequence, the share of older females on the road will continue to rise and they are expected to be more educated, wealthier, healthier and more mobile than their senior counterparts of the past. One implication of this trend is that trip purpose could focus less on domestic duties and caring for children and more on other types of trips, such as those related to leisure or longer-distance travel.

There is some evidence to suggest that men and women differ in terms of certain psychological attributes, and this may help to explain some gender differences in transportation. Psychology affects decision-making and problem-solving. As such, it plays an important role in determining travel behaviour. Women tend to be more risk-averse than men and because of this they are cautious in making choices related to travel. For example, concerns for **safety** and security can limit women's choices regarding mode or route choice. Women are physically smaller than men and they often travel with vulnerable children. Night travel is also a concern for women, particularly for those who are moonlighting. A few studies have also shown that women are more risk-averse in terms of changing their behaviour once en route – for example switching routes due to unexpected **congestion**. Women are also believed to be more ambivalent than men and this in turn leads to more creative problem-solving on the part of females.

One issue that is receiving increasing attention is the incorporation of women's needs, values and travel behaviour into travel **demand models** and evaluation methods. Traditional transport models, like the four-step process, do not adequately capture the demographic, psychological and other factors that distinguish men's patterns from those of women. Also, travel time-valuation used in transport models and to evaluate transportation improvements are focused on commuting and the opportunity costs associated with paid work, that is, wages or salaries. For many women, the valuation of time is quite different, related to non-paid work and non-work-related travel. Another concern is that gender differences in objectives, needs, values and psychology are not considered in conventional models. In route choice modelling, for example, route choice is based on the notion that individuals make decisions on what route to take based on travel time minimization. Because of the role that many women play in domestic and child caretaking, **accessibility** rather than **mobility** could be a more important concern. Lastly, transportation plans are often targeted at addressing peak-hour **congestion** and improving the mobility of commuters, and less on the needs of women.

Further reading
Root, A., L. Schintler and K.J. Button (2000). Women, travel and the idea of 'sustainable transport'. *Transport Reviews* **20**, 369–83.
Turner, J. and P. Fouracre (1995). Women and transport in developing countries. *Transport Reviews* **15**, 77–96.

Laurie Schintler

generalized cost

The concept of generalized cost often has different meanings in the literature according to context. Basically, it is the sum of all the costs involved in an action, buying a good or service, or making an investment. It includes not only all the costs paid to other agents, but also the equivalent monetary values of all effects on the decision-maker's own cost. In transport analysis, the best example of such a factor or attribute is the cost of transport time. In the case of a business trip, its value per hour may be estimated by the labour cost to the firm. The trip generalized cost is then equal to all the expenses paid for travelling (gasoline or rail pass, wear and tear on the car and so on) plus the firm's labour cost during the trip. The 'generalized cost' terminology, however, is customarily associated with an average value. In the simplest case, it is presented as the sum of the unit price paid for a service plus the additional average cost of its use.

For a private journey, the travelling time is also a factor bearing on the decision whether to travel or not, and how to travel, so that the generalized cost of the various alternatives may be helpful to understand and model the choices that are made. In this case the value of time is somewhat more subjective, but it still may be empirically estimated by comparing choices made between alternatives with different money costs and different travelling times. The value of **travel time** differs among people and among firms.

Time is only one of the factors that could be taken into account. In some circumstances, the reliability, the **safety** or the comfort of transport may play an important role. Reliability, frequency of service, safety and time of transport are also factors that play a role in freight transportation. In some studies, (average) transport time may well represent part of these factors, but if sufficient information is available, their specific equivalent monetary values should better be included in the definition of the appropriate generalized cost. In principle, this comprehensive concept of cost should be applied in every choice evaluation made by consumers or service users, or by producers. Likewise, it can be useful for public decision-making.

The concept of generalized cost is distinct from the concept of external costs, which may be simply defined as the costs imposed on other people by an individual transport activity. Obviously, they must be taken into account for assessing the full economic cost of a public service or investment, or of a regulation policy. They are generally not included in the concept of generalized cost since they are not priced like a user's cost in individual decision-making. Examples are the social costs of local and atmospheric pollution, of **noise**, of accidents and **congestion**.

In **cost–benefit analyses** of public investments, the market price or cost of a service is sometimes adjusted to reflect the unit gain in generalized and external costs contributed by a new infrastructure. This adjustment permits easy evaluation of the potential gain in consumer surplus by computing the difference between the initial market price and the adjusted price below the demand function. In such a framework of analysis, this adjusted price is often called 'generalized cost'. Note that this convenient procedure applied on an aggregate demand can only provide an approximation. Its relative quality will depend on the validity of the constant unit gain that is used and assimilated to a given variation of price. Actually, different people and firms may attach different money values to factors of generalized costs as well as to external costs. These differences must be taken into account in computing the change in total surplus. A likely fair approximation can be obtained by using an average value, rather than a marginal value, over the considered population, or by segmenting the demand between homogenous subgroups of agents.

Further reading
Beuthe, M. and Ch. Bouffioux (2008). Analyzing qualitative attributes of freight transport from stated orders of preference experiment. *Journal of Transport Economics and Policy* **42**, 105–28.

Jansson, J.O. (1993). Government and transport infrastructure – pricing. In J. Polak and A Heertje (eds), *European Transport Economics*. Oxford: Blackwell.

Quinet, E. and R. Vickerman (2004). *Principles of Transport Economics*. Cheltenham, UK and Northampton, MA, USA: Edward Elgar.

Michel Beuthe

geographical information systems

Geographical information systems (GIS) are fundamentally an application-led technology for capturing, processing, analysing and communicating information. Geographic information (GI) is defined as information referencing to specific locations on the surface of the Earth. Time is optional, but location is essential and the element that distinguishes GI from all other types of information. Locations are the basis for many of the benefits of GIS: the ability to visualize in form of maps, the ability to link different kinds of information together because they refer to the same location, or the ability to measure distances and areas. Without locations, data have little value within a GIS.

The existence of GIS relies on the widely shared view that GI is unique and requires a specific type of information processing. Two unique properties of GI are worth noting in this respect: spatial dependency and spatial heterogeneity. Spatial dependency is the tendency for things closer in geographic space to be more related, while spatial heterogeneity is the tendency of each location in geographic space to show some degree of uniqueness. These features imply that the systems and tools to support GI processing and decision-making must be tailored to recognize and exploit the unique nature of GI.

The functional complexity of a GIS is what it makes it different from other information systems. Without geo-visualization capability, the system would be merely a database management system (DBMS) endowed with power to extract some meaningful relationships between data entities in geographic space. Without analytical and/or geocomputational capabilities GIS would be reduced to some form of automated mapping. Without DBMS characteristics, GIS would not be able to capture spatial and topological relationships between georeferenced entities if these were not a priori defined.

A GIS is essentially a geographical DBMS. Its heart is the data model. A data model is an information structure that allows the user to store specific phenomena as distinct representations, and enables the user to manipulate the phenomena when held in the system as data. Data modelling involves three different levels of abstraction: conceptual, logical and physical levels.

Conceptual data models describe the organization of data at a high level of abstraction, without taking implementation aspects into account. The conceptual data models supported by GIS are extensive, but more specialized than those in the larger world of database management systems. There are two broad classes of conceptual data models that are widely used: field models that represent continuous variation over the surface, and discrete models according to which discrete entities (points, lines or polygons) populate space. Fields and discrete objects are distinct conceptual views of geographic phenomena. To build a digital representation, it is necessary to make choices about what to represent, at what level of detail, over what time period; but also about how to translate the conceptual data model into a database scheme. The raster and vector spatial representations are common logical data models for handling digital geographic data. These are linked to attribute data often stored in a relational format. The widely used georelational model design separates spatial and attribute data into different data models.

GIS have grown over the decades from their initial commercial beginnings as simple off-the-shelf packages to a system with well-defined components: software, hardware, people, institutions and **networks**. The most fundamental component today is the network without which no rapid communication or sharing of digital GI could occur within institutions and beyond. GIS rely strongly on the Internet and the momentum that the web has generated. The Internet has proven to be a very popular vehicle for delivering GIS applications of various types including a new generation of mobile and handheld applications for personal use, sometimes known as location-based services.

GIS is a generic location-based technology, designed to provide useful functions across a wide range of transport application domains. GIS-T, the application of GIS to research, planning and management in transportation, represents one of the most important and rapidly growing. The vast majority of applications have used GIS as a platform for integrating and displaying data on fixed transportation infrastructure like roads, or on **safety** such as traffic accidents. These applications utilize the traditional strengths of GIS such as graphical display, spatial query and selection, and polygon overlay. But GIS-T, once the sole domain of public sector planning and transportation agencies, is increasingly diffusing into broad commercial and consumer transportation markets including trip planning and travel directions applets, vehicle tracking and routing applications, and often real-time products, services and applications. The synergy between cellular telephones, mobile positioning systems and thin client computing will create entirely new GIS-T markets.

To realize its potential fully, GIS-T faces several challenges. The representations implemented in today's GIS databases are rich, but fall well short of the full range needed to build a comprehensive set of GIS-T applications. The popular node–arc representation of transportation **networks** cannot fully capture the complex road geometry such as ramps or non-planar features like underpasses or overpasses, or positional information resolved to the individual lanes within each segment. Therefore, the first research challenge is to derive representations for the full range of information types needed for a comprehensive approach to GIS-T.

Navigational applications require navigable data models. A second research challenge is, thus, to develop navigable data models for intelligent transportation systems. Navigable data models are digital geographic databases of a transportation system that can support vehicle guidance operations of different kinds. The data model must be able to support best route calculation and this requires a high level of spatial data accuracy including traffic regulations. The data model must also support route guidance and provide other information about the transportation system. This is a challenging task in real time because the system has to process the traveller's current position, perform address and map making and then provide navigational information.

If GIS-T is to succeed as a transportation technology, it has to be able to integrate different levels of **network** representation and data attribution and have the ability to link with other transportation technologies. Transportation systems are essentially linear phenomena. The need to manage, analyse and understand transportation information in a linear context will persist. GIS-T must be able to manage and communicate linear referencing and two- or three-dimensional global positioning system (GPS) coordinate systems. The challenge is to develop improved algorithms for unambiguous and accurate transformation.

Special problems arise when multiple linear referencing systems are used with different network representations at different scales and levels of spatial precision.

Further reading
Fischer, M.M. (2003). GIS and network analysis. In D.A. Hensher, K.J. Button, K. Haynes and P. Stopher (eds), *Transportation Geography and Spatial Systems*. Oxford: Pergamon Press.
Longley, P.A., M.F. Goodchild, D.J. Marguire and D.W. Rhind (1999). *Geographical Information Systems: Principles, Techniques, Management and Applications*. New York: Wiley.
Longley, P.A., M.F. Goodchild, D.J. Marguire and D.W. Rhind (2001). *Geographic Information Systems and Science*. Chichester: John Wiley & Sons.
Miller, H.J. and S.-L. Shaw (2001). *Geographic Information Systems for Transportation. Principles and Applications*. New York: Oxford University Press.

Manfred Fischer

globalization

Globalization refers to the increasing geographical scale and intensification of economic, social and political interactions across the world. It is a process that increasingly has transcended political boundaries, thus diminishing the importance of nationalism. Thomas Friedman identifies globalization as a new international system, replacing the Cold War system that had previously defined international political, economic and social relationships. Globalization has changed the world through the integration of markets, transportation and communication systems that enables corporations, countries and individuals to reach around the world farther, faster, deeper and cheaper than ever before.

There are many dimensions to the globalization process, including the economic, political and cultural, each having both positive and negative ramifications. Most often globalization is thought of in economic terms, particularly the growing acceptance of global capitalism and market economies, accelerating internationalization of trade and capital flows, and the increasing power of large multinational corporations. Politically, globalization has been facilitated by states forming and joining supranational organizations such as the World Trade Organization (WTO) and the International Monetary Fund (IMF) at the global scale, and the **European Union** (EU), the North American Free Trade Area (**NAFTA**) and the Asia Pacific Economic Cooperation (APEC) forum at the mega regional scale. Furthermore, states have enacted governmental policies promoting **deregulation**, liberalization, and **privatization** that have been a *sine qua non* of globalization. Culturally, globalization is having the effect of creating a more homogeneous 'global culture', featuring the dominance of the English language and Western (largely American) norms and values. Globalization has engendered a fair degree of criticism, most visibly in the form of massive, and sometimes violent, protests at international economic forums, such as meetings of the WTO and IMF.

The role of transportation in globalization processes is critical, although it can be difficult to determine the direction of cause–effect relationships. Transportation plays a central role as a space-adjusting technology that acts as a catalyst in enabling the globalization process. While new communication technologies are most often cited, the degree of globalization currently being experienced would simply not be possible without transportation. The increasing efficiency of freight and passenger movements over time has resulted in increased time–space convergence, and thus greater integration over space. Transportation and logistics systems facilitate huge volume flows of goods and people that allow innovative practices, such as **just-in-time** production systems, to be utilized. Improved transportation also allows companies to outsource manufacturing and other operations to lower-cost locations that in turn place a greater reliance on the efficiency of long-distance trade.

Likewise, transportation is subject to general globalization processes that occur for a variety of other technological, economic, political, social and cultural reasons. Transportation companies, particularly in the airline and maritime industries, have created global strategic alliances that result in better **network** system connectivity. The volume of trade flow and freight transport has increased dramatically as a result of global and regional free trade agreements, thus impacting the maritime, railroad, trucking and air cargo industries. Air passenger traffic has increased as a result of more liberalized bilateral and 'open skies' air service agreements.

The combination of strategic alliances and **network** restructuring is probably the most potent manifestation of globalization processes in the transportation industry. Strategic alliances allow transport companies to establish coordinated global operations and integrated networks that they otherwise would not be able to, due to economic and/or regulatory constraints. In the airline industry, for example, the top three global alliances: Star Alliance (including Lufthansa, Singapore Airlines, United Airlines); Oneworld (including American Airlines, British Airlines, Cathay Pacific); and SkyTeam (including Air France, Delta Airlines, Korean Airlines) account for nearly two-thirds of the world's airline traffic. Airlines that are part of a global alliance typically have code-sharing, joint ticketing, marketing and baggage handling agreements amongst themselves that facilitate integrated networks and services. In some instances, equity shares are owned by alliance partners.

Global alliances and multinational mergers also characterize the maritime container shipping industry. British-based P&O merged with the Dutch line Nedloyd, while NOL of Singapore acquired United States-based APL. Today, five global alliances dominate the industry: SeaLand-Maersk, the Grand Alliance (Hapag-Lloyd, P&O-Nedlloyd, MISC, OOCL), the United Alliance (Hanjin, DSR-Senator, ChoYang), the New World Alliance (HMM, APL, MOL) and the grouping of COSCO, Yangming and K-Line. These alliances are both driven by and a reflection of globalization processes.

Further reading
Goetz, A.R. and B. Graham (2004). Air transport globalization, liberalization, and sustainability: post-2001 policy dynamics in the United States and Europe. *Journal of Transport Geography* **12**, 265–76.
Janelle, D.G. and M. Beuthe (2002). Globalization and transportation: contradictions and challenges. In W.R. Black and P. Nijkamp (eds), *Social Change and Sustainable Transport*. Bloomington, IN: Indiana University Press.

Andrew Goetz

governance

While governance is generally not defined in economics dictionaries and texts, free market economists use the term to capture the adoption and enforcement of rules governing conduct and property rights. Governance is often confused with government. It may be imposed by governments or adopted voluntarily by groups or associations. The systems, structures and processes that organize groups of individuals to a common purpose is the governance of the group, society or voluntary organization. At the other end of the continuum, the legislation and regulations imposed on a business or non-for-profit entity by government are also forms of governance. The structures and processes put in place by national laws, such as requirements of open procurement processes, form part of the governance of government. Most frequently, the term 'governance' is used to refer to corporate governance.

The Organisation for Economic Co-operation and Development defines corporate governance as:

> the system by which business corporations are directed and controlled. The corporate governance structure specifies the distribution of rights and

responsibilities among the different participants in the corporation, such as the board, managers, shareholders and stakeholders, and spells out the rules and procedures for making decisions on corporate affairs. By doing this, it also provides the structure through which corporate objectives are set, and the means of obtaining those objectives and monitoring performance.

Therefore, corporations are not expected to deliver the social welfare or public policy objectives of government.

In the private ownership model, corporate governance is the structure, roles and responsibilities that provide the means by which the organization is managed as an economic entity, based on the objectives of the corporation. The corporation is in business to meet the objectives set by the board to the benefit of owners; it is not in business to meet the objectives of government, regulators or other stakeholders. In the not-for-profit model, these objectives are set by the members of the associations or organizations, or the trustees of foundations, to deliver the aims of the organization. The area of corporate governance is widely researched and there exists a wealth of information on how it is implemented in various countries and under various models.

Further reading
Keasey, K., S. Thompson and M. Wright (1999). *Corporate Governance*. Cheltenham, UK and Northampton, MA, USA: Edward Elgar.
Organisation for Economic Co-operation and Development (1999). *OECD Principles of Corporate Governance* (SG/CG(99)5). Paris, Organisation for Economic Co-operation and Development.

Mary R. Brooks

governance and transport

Governance has changed character, as both an academic concept and governmental activity, in recent decades. In its traditional form, the hierarchy of the organizational unit (the state, the corporation, the project) formed the spine of the governance structure. Rules and regulations, procedures and processes reflected that hierarchy. The assumed power distribution allowed strict control from top to bottom. But from the 1970s the flaws and failures of pure hierarchical governance surfaced. It did not reflect the modern democracy, in which voicing and voting made power as much bottom-up as top-down. In most democracies power had become decentralized and the spreading affluence in the late twentieth century further loosened the control potential of government. Governance became a matter of organizing the interplay between the various actors in the **network**. The view on government changed from ruler to coordinator. Hierarchical governance was supplemented with network governance.

At the same time, a second approach to the flaws and failures of pure hierarchical governance was developed: the market. As the bureaucratic machines of hierarchical governance proved to be failing with respect to efficiency and innovation, the flexibility and agility of the private sector became attractive. The approach, under its original moniker of new public management, was not to share the power in the **network**, but rather to reformulate the role of government to goal-setting and rely heavily on the market to execute policy. This asked of government two major things. First, it had to reduce its foothold in various sectors through **deregulation** and **privatization**. Second, goal formulation had to allow for contracting: clear controllable goals for which a contractor could be held accountable.

When looking at transport, two newer forms of governance are observed: network and market. First, government's role in transport is important in the field of infrastructure development. The authorities developing infrastructure that had traditionally only been accountable to the responsible political leadership, had to open up because of the increase in network governance. Most countries now have clear rules on the role of different stakeholders in decision-making on infrastructure projects. The interests of inhabitants of an area, wildlife conservationists, emergency services, taxpayers and also the users of the network, are all secured in intricate systems of permits, procedures and processes. Network governance has become the standard in democracies when it comes to infrastructure development.

In addition, the role of the private sector in infrastructure development and management has become much more diverse as a result of a growing interest in market governance. Traditionally most countries limited the role of the private sector to the construction of infrastructure. Since the 1980s, there have been increasing movements to expand that role, under the widely used term of '**public–private partnerships**'. For road **networks**, many governments seek privately designed, built, financed and maintained roads, tunnels and bridges, possibly paid for by tolling. This form of governance with a strong role of the private sector is widely observed, for example, in Australia, Japan and the Philippines. Countries like Germany, however, traditionally at the other end of the spectrum, have also experimented with this approach. There have also been movements to bring specific tasks to the private sector, like road maintenance in Finland and the United Kingdom.

For development of rail networks, market governance has gained importance, where governments set general goals and routes but private parties again design, build and maintain (DBM) lines and networks, or in addition also operate (DBOM) them. Examples are to be found on **high-speed rail** systems (Netherlands: Thalys route as DBM); however there are many more on **metropolitan rail systems** (Colombia: Bogota; United States: Bergen Count; Portugal: Lisbon and Porto; Denmark: Copenhagen; Greece: Thessaloniki).

Not only has infrastructure development and management of the operations of public transport services gained in strength over the last decades, but so has its governance, especially in Europe. In the twentieth century, operation had developed under a clear hierarchical governance model. Operators, many beginning as private companies, had gradually been absorbed within the public sector. This resulted in a direct line of hierarchy between the responsible political leadership and operations. From the late 1960s, European legislation pushed public service obligation as a governance instrument: a contract that clearly described the obligations and remunerations for the operator. This put the operators more at arm's length from the whims of politics. From the 1990s, legislation was supplemented by a push for competitively awarding contracts, especially in regional public transport. In Europe, tendering of regional rail and bus services has become a widely used governance model.

Numerous changes in the recent history of transport are driven by the recognition that hierarchical governance is vulnerable. The separation of **network** and operation of European rail operators, programmes like the United Kingdom's private finance initiative, the spread of tendering of public transport services, and more open decision-making on infrastructure development, are only a few examples. The move to more network and market governance also provided a drive for different technical solutions. Network governance means that more stakeholders can influence technical developments, with market governance allowing for a wider range of more innovative solutions.

The transport sector when dealing with issues of emissions, **congestion**, casualties and inertia design governance structures considering:

- How to decide on governmental ambitions, goals and policies, including the matter of how various stakeholders are included in that process.
- How to execute the policy; inside the public sector, using semi-autonomous bodies, or the private sector.
- How to incentivize the executor of the policy in a way that their execution is aligned with the original goals and fits the conditions of other stakeholders.
- How to realize governance that can deal with changing priorities and insights.

Further reading

Frederickson, H.G. (2005). Whatever happened to public administration; governance, governance everywhere. In E. Ferlie, L.E. Lynn and C. Pollitt (eds), *The Oxford Handbook of Public Management*. Oxford: Oxford University Press.

Heffen, O. van, W.J.M. Kickert and J.J.A. Thomassen (eds) (2000). *Governance in Modern Society; Effects, Change and Formation of Government Institutions*. Dordrecht: Kluwer Academic Publishers.

Osborne, D. and T. Gaebler (eds) (1992). *Reinventing Government: How Entrepreneurial Spirit is Transforming the Public Sector*. Reading: Addison-Wesley.

Wijnand W. Veeneman

gravity model

The gravity model belongs to the class of empirical models concerned with the determinants of spatial interaction. In its most general formulation, it explains a flow *Fij* (for example migration, commodity flows, passenger movement, telephone traffic, money) from an area *i* to an area *j* as a function of the characteristics of the origin (*Oi*), the characteristics of the destination (*Dj*) and some separation measurement (*Sij*):

$$Fij = f(O_i, D_j, S_{ij}) \text{ with } i = 1,\ldots, \text{I}; j = 1,\ldots, \text{J} \qquad (1)$$

The unit of measurement for *Fij* varies according to the type of flow or interaction that is being analysed (for example number of people, tonnes of freight, number of money transactions). Variables often used to express the characteristics of origin and destination are socio-economic in nature, such as population, number of jobs available, floor area, industrial output or gross domestic product. Variables often used to express the transport friction or decay are distance, transport costs or travel time.

The inspiration for a general formulation of spatial interactions stems from Newtonian physics, more specifically from the law of universal gravity, according to which the attraction between two objects is proportional to their masses and inversely proportional to their respective distance. When applied to, for instance, flows of goods between countries, by analogy, the gravity model stresses that trade increases with size and proximity of the trading partners. The resulting model is given as (Haynes and Fotheringham, 1984):

$$F_{ij} = k \frac{P_i^\lambda P_j^\alpha}{d_{ij}^\beta} \qquad (2)$$

where:

- P_i and P_j are proxy variables or attributes of weight reflecting the importance of the location of origin and the location of destination.
- d_{ij} is the distance between the location of origin and the location of destination.
- k is a proportionality constant which is determined from the data set by simple arithmetic methods.
- β is the transport friction reflecting the degree of attenuation of a process with distance. A beta of 0 means that distance has no effects. A high value implies that friction of distance is very important. In Newton's gravitational equation, beta equalled 2. This implies that, if for instance transport costs on a certain relationship are cut by half, traffic on that relationship will quadruple.
- λ and α reflect, respectively, the potential of the origin to generate movements and the potential of the destination to attract movements. A value of 1 implies a linear relationship. Any value higher than 1 implies an exponential growth of the interaction level as P increases.

A gravity model measures interactions between all the possible location pairs. In this respect, gravity models differ from potential models that measure interactions between one location and every other location, and retail models – for example William J. Reilly's law of retail gravitation – that calculate the breaking point between two locations (so-called market boundary) where customers will be drawn to one or another of two competing commercial centres.

Customarily the gravity model is estimated in log-linear form, but other approaches do exist. Calibration consists in finding the value of the parameters (constant k and exponents α, β and λ) that insure that the estimated results are similar to the observed flows. However, planning applications have revealed that often poor fits with the real data sets could be observed, resulting in a series of ad hoc adjustments to the original form of the model. These adjustments relate to the relationship with distance (using an exponential function for distance decay) and a change to the P terms to ensure that the flows predicted by the model either from destinations, or to origins (the destination or origin constrained model), or both (the double constrained model), equal the actual flow. The adjusted model usually takes on the following form:

$$F_{ij} = A_i\, P_i\, B_j\, P_j \qquad\qquad (3)$$

where A_i and B_j are calibrating constants which have to be empirically determined by an iterative procedure. Clearly, the resulting adjusted model has but few links with the original model from physics, hence requiring a stronger rationale for its particular form.

Besides allowing for different model specification adjustments, another 'family' of gravity model focuses on a randomization of the Fij-relationship through the inclusion of an error theory. Sen and Smith, for instance introduce the Poisson gravity model that is estimated by maximum likelihood methods.

Although a gravity model cannot be confirmed scientifically, cannot be applied to hypothetical, new situations and is not a method for predicting movement because it is biased toward historic ties (perpetuation or intensification of existing patterns) and toward the largest population centres, it is widely used in transport planning. This is partly a result of the availability of a large variety of possible mathematical formulations offering fairly accurate fits to empirical data.

Further reading
Haynes, K.E. and A.S. Fotheringham (1984). *Gravity and Spatial Interaction Models*. London: Sage Publications.
Sen, A.K. and T.E. Smith (1995). *Gravity Models of Spatial Interaction Behavior*. Heidelberg: Springer-Verlag.

Frank Witlox

greenhouse gas emissions from transportation

The greenhouse effect is a phenomenon whereby certain gases are thought to trap excess heat from the Sun within the Earth's atmosphere. This leads to **climate change** phenomena of various types. The concept was first mooted in the 1890s, but did not come into the public and political consciousness until the 1980s. It was considered at the Rio Earth Summit in 1992 and subsequently led to the Kyoto Protocol, an attempt to reduce human emissions of greenhouse gases under a binding international agreement.

Transportation contributes to greenhouse gas emissions principally through its emissions of carbon dioxide, nitrogen oxides and methane. Although methane is primarily an issue of natural gas vehicles, and on a well-to-wheel basis of electric vehicles using **energy** generated by natural gas, it is considered to be 20–25 times more powerful as a greenhouse gas than carbon dioxide. According to the United Nations Intergovernmental Panel on Climate Change, the transportation sector generates a third of all CO_2 emissions globally and these are growing at around 2 per cent a year. Road vehicles are the fastest-growing element within this, although air transport is also increasingly causing concern. By 2005, carbon emissions from flights leaving the United Kingdom equalled about half of the emissions of all United Kingdom housing. In addition, it is believed that emissions at high altitude have a greater impact.

There are a number of ways to reduce CO_2 emissions from transportation. One option is to reduce the total kilometres driven by restricting car use in some way. Other than this, when using conventional fossil carbon-based fuels, improved fuel consumption is the only option. This can be achieved in a number of ways, notably weight reduction, reduced air and rolling resistance, and/or improved efficiency of engine and transmission (including tyres). Another option is to use **alternative fuels**, which are either lower in carbon content, and hence in carbon emissions, or which can be considered 'carbon-neutral'. Among the latter are the renewable fuels, such as biofuels, provided that they are produced with a minimum of fossil fuel input in their production, such as for transport, processing and fertilizer.

Considerable resources are now being dedicated to the search for and implementation of various **energy efficiency** technologies and alternative transportation energy sources. Gaseous transportation fuels such as LPG or propane, compressed natural gas (CNG) or liquefied natural gas (LNG), though still fossil fuels, already offer a reduction in carbon emissions compared to conventional gasoline or diesel and they are therefore used as a partial solution in several countries. Biofuels offer another viable carbon reduction option. Research suggests that on a well-to-wheel basis, Brazilian bioethanol from sugar cane has one of the best greenhouse gas saving potentials of any biofuel, which has been put at up to 90 per cent. This compares with a more modest 50 per cent for biodiesel from palm oil and 30 per cent for biodiesel from soy. The latter two feedstocks have been associated with rainforest destruction and rising food prices, however.

Another alternative under consideration is hydrogen, which is a non-carbon fuel. It can be used in an internal combustion engine, or to power a fuel cell, which then produces electricity to drive the vehicle. Hydrogen fuel cells are regarded by many inside and outside the automotive industry as the best future powertrain solution. Hydrogen does not occur naturally on Earth and has to be extracted from hydrocarbon fuels or water, both of which are energy-intensive processes, and when using a hydrocarbon feedstock, carbon is released. Therefore much of the hydrogen for these fuel cells would be derived from conventional fossil fuels, potentially involving higher carbon emissions than conventional fuels. Alternatively, the car industry may decide – in a bid to preserve the tried and trusted internal combustion engine – to go for **hybrids** instead. In these an internal combustion engine is used to generate electricity, which in turn powers the vehicle through electric motors. In this context the plug-in hybrid which can in addition be recharged from the mains, is particularly promising.

Battery electric vehicles are another option. Electric powertrains have a number of inherent environmental advantages over any of the proposed alternatives, as converting primary energy into motion via an electric powertrain can be more efficient than using an internal combustion engine. The precise gains depend on how the electricity is generated; coal gives higher well-to-wheel carbon emissions than hydro or wind, for example. The fact is that electricity can be generated from non-fossil feedstocks, while traditional automobile fuels only have the option of the less efficient hydrogen route. These simple facts may serve to support the electric vehicle option in favour of internal combustion, as the need to reduce carbon becomes a more pressing policy priority in global efforts to reduce greenhouse gas emissions from transportation.

Further reading

Commission of the European Communities (2007). *Biofuels Progress Report; Report on the Progress made in the Use of Biofuels and other Renewable Fuels in the Member States of the European Union – Communication from the Commission to the Council and the European Parliament, COM (2006) 845 final.* 10.1.2007. Brussels: Commission of the European Communities.

Henson, R. (2006). *The Rough Guide to Climate Change; The Symptoms, The Science, The Solutions.* London: Rough Guides.

Intergovernmental Panel on Climate Change (2007). *Climate Change 2007: The Physical Science Basis.* Cambridge: Cambridge University Press.

Paul Nieuwenhuis

H

hazardous materials transportation

Some materials or products have risks associated with their transport; classic examples would be explosives, gasoline, toxic materials and radioactive wastes, among many others. These hazardous materials or 'hazmats' need to be transported, but doing so imposes risks on drivers, handlers or to the public at large. Harm can arise through incidental leaks or spillage through routine handling and transport, or through more severe spillages in crashes. In some cases, the consequences can be catastrophic.

There are many materials or substances that could be labelled 'hazardous', for different reasons. The United Nations places hazmats in nine categories (with some subcategories, and some with packaging performance requirements):

- Class 1 – explosives and pyrotechnics;
- Class 2 – compressed and liquefied gases;
- Class 3 – flammable liquids;
- Class 4 – flammable solids;
- Class 5 – oxidizers and peroxides;
- Class 6 – toxic and infectious materials;
- Class 7 – radioactive materials;
- Class 8 – corrosive materials;
- Class 9 – miscellaneous dangerous substances and articles.

There can be a variety of hazmats with differences in characteristics within these categories. Regulations and related issues are available from government departments.

The dangers associated with hazmats differ significantly. A major complication is that the degree of harm is a function not solely of the physical properties of the hazmat, but also of the amount that is released and, especially, the circumstances associated with a spill.

Virtually all countries have hazmat regulations, but details differ. Generally shippers are required to inform carriers and any other relevant agencies of the hazmat and why it is labelled as such. Vehicles may be required to have an external label or placard to identify the hazmat. Shippers may have to supply a 24-hour phone number so that they may be contacted in an emergency to provide details about the hazards associated with the particular shipment, along with instructions on how to deal with spills or other emergencies. In some cases, large shippers may have emergency response teams available. In most cases, hazmat emergencies must be dealt with by local community resources such as by fire departments.

Generally companies are required to report the volumes of hazmat movements and any spills or incidents. Although statistics have been compiled for many years, there are often gaps or weaknesses in the data. Must all spills be reported, or only those above some threshold amount? Because most spills are small, the number of recorded incidents can differ considerably depending on the criteria. Even if statistics are accurately compiled, note that there are unavoidable challenges in developing predictions about low-probability, high-consequence events.

Quantitative risk assessment (QRA) is employed to evaluate the risks and associated costs of hazmat movements. QRA refers to the framework employed to evaluate the risks. It is a process of analysis rather than a specific analytical technique.

Analysts begin by trying to identify and portray all possible causes of spills and outcomes. The next and crucial step is establishing the probabilities of various events taking place. Providing data exist, historical records can be used to develop probability estimates. Alternatively, engineering analysis, simulation models or simply judgement may be necessary to develop these estimates. Obviously the reliability of the estimates can differ, and hence so can confidence in the final result. Next, there are various environmental factors that affect the outcome. It is necessary to identify these environmental factors and probabilities of different combinations being present.

Finally, there are issues in the valuation or measurement of the costs associated with the outcomes. In some cases, this is relatively straightforward such as clean-up costs, damage to equipment and adjacent property. In other cases, even if the consequences might be predicted with confidence, for example the number of fatalities, there are still issues of valuation in monetary terms.

Once estimates of risk exposure probabilities are established, combining these with measures of harm provides a measure of the risk exposure to society. Then one can explore different actions that can be taken to reduce the risks or mitigate the consequences of any spill. Spills and tragedies will occur. But they are rare enough that they are newsworthy events rather than commonplace. Diligence by shippers and transport operators, government oversight, and refinement of data and analysis, can make hazmat emergencies even more rare than they already are.

Further reading
Waters, W.G. II (2002). Transportation of hazardous goods and materials. In D.A. Hensher and K.J. Button (eds), *Handbook of Transport and the Environment*. Oxford: Elsevier.

William G. Waters II

hedonic prices

The hedonic price method is used to provide a monetary estimate of a particular good or bad under conditions of absence or failure of markets, that is, in the presence of a divergence between market price and social cost. Thus, price hedonics is a useful tool in economy–environmental analysis of project and policy design in estimating the monetary value of external costs and benefits.

In particular, the hedonic price method assumes that goods are valued according to a given set of attributes or characteristics. Hedonic prices are then defined as the implicit prices of attributes and are revealed to economic agents from observed prices of differentiated products and the specific amounts of characteristics associated with them.

The basic idea of the price hedonics approach is that one can use data from existing markets as proxies for the relevant values. The main assumption, for both theoretical and statistical reasons, is that the considered surrogate or implicit market must be sensitive to external effects that one is trying to monetarize and that the variations induced by a given project or policy should be observable and quantifiable.

Assuming a class of goods and an associated set of n observable and objectively quantifiable characteristics, that is, for each good a vector of coordinates $\mathbf{z} = (z_1, z_2 \ldots z_n)$ with z_i measuring the amount of the i-th attribute for the considered good. A model of characteristics affecting the price of the good can be expressed by the hedonic price function:

$$p(z) = f(z_1, z_2, \ldots, z_n) \tag{1}$$

The change in the price of the good that results from a change in a particular attribute is called the hedonic price of the attribute. In a perfect market, the hedonic price can be interpreted as the additional cost of purchasing a good that is marginally better in terms of a particular attribute. It should be noted that, in the case of transport infrastructure appraisal, housing is often the good whose price behaviour is analysed through the hedonic price method to provide a monetary estimate of external effects.

This choice is supported by the evidence that the value of a transportation facility, especially in an urban context, can be measured by observing the reaction of housing prices (that is, the variation in the willingness-to-pay of consumers) to a change in the level of a given attribute, for example environmental quality.

The hedonic pricing model in Equation 1 can be represented in a multiplicative functional form:

$$p(z) = \beta_0 \prod_{i=1}^{n} z_i^{\beta_i} e^{\varepsilon} \tag{2}$$

The vector of parameters b is a vector of **elasticities** measuring the change in the price of the good resulting from a change in the amount of any given characteristic. The hedonic price of a particular attribute is the slope of Equation 1 with respect to that attribute. For the multiplicative model in Equation 2, the hedonic price of i-th attribute is:

$$r_{z_i} = \beta_i \frac{p(z)}{z_i} \tag{3}$$

Under the assumption of perfect and complete markets, consumers with utility-maximizing behaviour are supposed to purchase the good so that the hedonic price of a particular attribute, the marginal cost, equals the willingness to pay for a marginal increase, the marginal benefit. Thus, the hedonic price of a particular characteristic is the willingness-to-pay for a marginal variation in that attribute.

In perfect market, utility-maximizing consumer will purchase the good so that their willingness-to-pay for a marginal increase in a particular attribute equals its hedonic price. Consequently, in equilibrium, the hedonic price of an attribute can be interpreted as the willingness of the households to pay for a marginal increase in that attribute.

The hedonic price model can be operationalized by log-linearizing the multiplicative model in Equation 2. In this case the following hedonic model is estimated:

$$\ln(p) = \sum_{i=1}^{n} \beta_i \ln(z_i) + \varepsilon \tag{4}$$

where p is the housing price. The parameters in Equation 4 can be estimated by simple ordinary least squares. Once the hedonic regression parameters are estimated, the hedonic price of the i-th attribute can be computed by substituting the housing price p, the amount of z_i and the estimate of i.

The main problem with Equation 4 is that often vector **z** presents some zero values in some attributes for some observations. In this case, the estimation procedure cannot be operated because of the non-existence of some values. To overwhelm this problem, a semi-log model can be adopted:

$$\ln(p) = \beta_0 + \sum_{i=1}^{n} \beta_i z_i + \varepsilon \tag{5}$$

This can easily deal with situations where some attributes have zero values. A disadvantage is that the semi-log model does not derive from a manipulation of a multiplicative hedonic function $f(\mathbf{z})$. Thus, it is not possible to impose constant returns to scale.

Further reading
Rosen, S. (1974). Hedonic prices and implicit markets: product differentiation in pure competition. *Journal of Political Economy* **82**, 34–55.

Marco Percoco

high-speed trains/railways

An often stated principle of the high speed trains (HST) is often defined as providing transport services to passengers at a speed twice that of the car and half that of the plane. Often high speed is considered to be over 200 kph, although this does not correspond to all definitions. Some of the HSTs in operation, like the French TGV, can achieve a maximum operating speed of above 350 kph. HSTs in service are a development of the common train using the same but more advanced technology; it is an incremental improvement to the basic steel wheel on steel rail technology used in Victorian times. To allow trains to travel at high speed the tracks, as well as the trains, are upgraded, and in this respect the term 'high-speed rail' (HSR) might be more appropriate. Although not yet in commercial service on long-distance routes, a new technology to propel trains exists that can allow operating speeds of over 500 kph, these Maglev use magnetic levitation for propulsion.

The HST originated in Japan in 1964 with the introduction of the Shinkansen 'New trunk line' system, also known as the Bullet Train, on the 560 km Tokaido route between Tokyo and Osaka that runs at speeds of 210 kph. In Europe, it was the French in 1981 that first operated HSTs as currently understood when the Train a Grande Vitesse (TGV) was inaugurated on the route between Paris and Lyon. The introduction of

HST services usually leads to around 50 per cent reduction in travel time by rail.

The main features of a HST route usually include a dedicated railway for a train running at high speed between two densely populated metropolitan areas a few hundred kilometres apart, where there is substantial demand for travel between them. The Japanese Shinkansen usually follows these features. The French TGV deviates from this by sharing the tracks with conventional trains as it enters and leaves cities. The Swedish X-2000 tilting train uses conventional rail lines throughout the route but the train is specially designed to tilt as it goes through tight curves – hence the term 'tilting trains' – allowing it to achieve relative high speed compared to other trains, but slower than the Shinkansen or the TGV without the requirement of new dedicated track.

In Europe, the emerging HST **network** is seen by the European Commission as one of the main tool to 'bring Europe together', and accordingly the development of a European HST network is an important element in **European Union transport policy**. In China, development of the HST network started relatively late compared to Europe and Japan but the scale of development will make its network the largest in the world in the near future. HST is also now being considered for several corridors in the United States.

The introduction of HST services usually leads to passengers shifting to it from the road (car and bus) and the air. It usually also results in generation of new traffic. Three years after the introduction of the Paris–Lyon HST service, rail share on the route increased from 40 percent to 72 per cent; car and bus share decreased from 29 per cent to 21 per cent; and air share decreased from 31 per cent to 7 per cent although this also coincided with a move of Lyon Airport further from the city. The same pattern in modal shift occurred on the Madrid–Seville route three years after the introduction of HST services in 1992. The HST is also envisaged, by the European Union, as a way to relieve **congestion** at major airports and to reduce the negative environmental impact of aircraft operation through substitution of short-haul aircraft services with HST services.

The HST is considered a cleaner mode of transport compared to the car and the aircraft, because it has a lower impact in terms of **climate change** and local air pollution. Since almost all HSTs use electricity as the source of energy they do not contribute to air pollution along the route, but only at the location of **energy** production, often away from populated areas. HSTs' impact on air pollution and on **climate change depends** on the sources of energy used to generate the electricity to power the HST.

There is no agreement, and the evidence is mixed, on the extent to which the HST can generate wider socio-economic impacts in addition to its direct impact as a mode of transport and through changes in **accessibility**. It appears that under certain conditions HST development can result in positive economic impacts at the terminal cities, and this is an important factor in planning and designing HST lines, and especially in deciding on the station location.

Further reading
COST 318 (1998). Interaction between high-speed rail and air passenger transport. Brussels: European Commission Directorate General of Transport.
Givoni, M. (2006). The development and impact of the modern High Speed Train. *Transport Reviews* **26**, 593–612.
Spiekermann, K. and M. Wegener (1994). The shrinking continent: new time–space maps of Europe. *Environment and Planning B* **21**, 653–73.

Moshe Givoni

HOV and HOT lanes

Growing urban congestion has created the demand for innovative and beneficial capacity expansion to improve traffic flow. Because the addition of new general-purpose lanes is very costly and problematic due to environmental impacts and social concerns, new management and operational strategies based on existing freeway facilities, such as managed lanes, have been gaining increasing interest among public agencies.

The concept behind 'managed lanes' is to employ various management tools and operational strategies on a limited number of freeway lanes to improve traffic efficiency on those lanes. General forms of managed lanes include high-occupancy vehicle (HOV) lanes, value priced lanes such as high-occupancy toll (HOT) lanes, and exclusive lanes. The operational strategy of exclusive lanes is to provide special lanes for certain vehicle types, normally **buses** and large trucks.

HOV lanes are separate lanes designed for the vehicles with a specified minimum occupancy, which is normally posted on a traffic control sign. These lanes help move more people in fewer vehicles based on the existing highway facilities. Usually, HOV lanes require at least two occupants in vehicles to use the facility legally, though during peak travel times some facilities require three or more occupants. Generally, **motorcycles** are allowed to use HOV lanes even when carrying just one person. HOV facilities are usually designated for service during peak traffic periods, and at other times non-HOV vehicles are allowed to use such a facility. HOV lanes can be in many forms when implemented on freeways, such as separated roadways, concurrent-flow lanes and contraflow lanes. Contraflow HOV lanes have been used worldwide, such as the contraflow HOV lanes on the Katy Freeway in Houston, Texas. In this system, a 13 mile one-lane reversible facility separated from the main lanes and provides access between downtown Houston and the Galleria area. Two or more occupant restriction is effective during 6–11 a.m., Monday through Friday in the inbound direction, and 2–8 p.m. in the outbound direction. The three or more occupant restriction is effective during the peak periods, which are from 6.45–8 a.m. and 5–6 p.m.

HOV lanes have been implemented in many areas of the world to improve freeway efficiency by encouraging ride-sharing. They offer choices that provide travel time savings and trip reliability, and improve **safety** by reducing levels of congestion. Moreover, they protect the environment by reducing fuel consumptions and emissions, which is contributed by the reduction of delay. However, poorly utilized HOV lanes degrade the performance of both HOV and general-purpose lanes. In this case, HOV lanes do not satisfy the objectives of reducing **congestion**, especially during peak hours. Another form of HOV operation, known as HOT lanes, has been utilized to reduce traffic congestion and delay.

HOT lanes are parts of a highway system that can be used by motorists who are willing to pay a toll to gain access to these lanes, which are separated from the mainstream traffic and likely to provide faster travel. Incorporated with the operational concept of existing HOV facilities, HOT lanes utilize both the number of occupancy eligibility and congestion pricing to regulate traffic demand. Congestion pricing is a concept of charging drivers a fee for the use of the highway facility. HOT lanes encourage the vehicles which do not satisfy minimum occupancy requirements to use the available underused capacity by paying a fee, which could be dynamically changed according to traffic conditions in those lanes. One example of HOT is the 8-mile facility on the I-15 in San Diego, California, which stretches between State Route 52 and State Route 56, originally operated as HOV lanes but converted to HOT lanes in 1996. In restricted hours, usually during the peak periods, the solo-occupancy vehicles (SOVs) must pay an access fee, and HOV travel is free of charge. The toll rate is adjusted in response to the current flow status in the lane, to ensure smooth traffic flow. All users must register first to use the system.

Besides the benefits of the traditional HOV lanes, HOT lanes are designed to manage the demand dynamically and to better utilize the capacity of the managed lanes. It may divert some single-occupancy vehicles from the general-purpose lanes if those drivers choose to pay. The revenue generated from HOT lanes can be used for other transportation facilities improvements. Furthermore, they provide a superior level of service and save travel time compared to general-purpose free lanes.

HOV and HOT lanes hold great promise as effective tools for traffic demand management, and many applications have been implemented successfully in many countries. However, some public opinion leaders argue that HOT lanes benefit the wealthy, and some motorists have questioned the need for this tool, wondering instead if it is indeed merely another tax. Privacy is also a concern for motorists, because of the registration requirement needed for some HOT systems.

Further reading

Collier, T. and G. Goodin (2004). *Managed Lanes: A Cross-Cutting Study.* FHWA-HOP-05-037, Washington, DC: Federal Highway Administration.
Kuhn, B., G. Goodin and A. Ballard (2005). *Managed Lanes Handbook*. FHWA/ TX-06/0-4160-24. Austin, TX: Texas Department of Transportation.

Yan Zhou

hub-and-spoke networks

Hub-and-spoke networks are networks that involve serving a range of geographically dispersed locations through a central hub. Rather than operate direct services between locations, carriers often find that it is feasible to serve markets more cheaply, and with greater frequency, if they connect locations indirectly through a central hub. Thus the hub-and-spoke networks of airlines are well known, and cities such as Atlanta, Amsterdam and Singapore are noted for being airline hubs. Ports such as Hong Kong and Hamburg function as hubs for container shipping traffic. Most urban passenger rail networks are set out as hub-and-spoke networks. Some, though not all, road freight and urban bus networks work on a hub-and-spoke basis and postal services have deployed them from their beginning.

Hubs come about as a result of the cost conditions underlying transport operation. Very often, the unit costs of operation of larger aircraft, vessels or vehicles are lower than those of smaller ones. Thus it can be cost-effective to concentrate traffic, especially on long-haul routes. In addition, frequency of service is valued by users, and hub-and-spoke networks can offer high frequency between centres which do not generate much traffic between them. As against this, hub-and-spoke networks involve costs of connections between services for passengers, or **transhipment** costs for freight. In addition, they involve longer overall trip lengths than direct services. For many transport tasks, hub-and-spoke networks dominate, though not always. The move to hub-and-spoke networks after United States airline **deregulation** was estimated to be a substantial source of increased efficiency.

Regulatory factors influence whether hub-and-spoke networks come about. International aviation has long been operated as a pattern of hub-and-spoke networks; this has come about partly because, due to regulatory restrictions, airlines were not permitted to serve routes directly. Thus, a German airline could fly passengers from Copenhagen to Nice via Frankfurt, but not directly. Some regulatory arrangements have prevented the formation of hubs and spokes; the most significant example of this was with the United States airline industry. Before deregulation in the late 1970s, airlines were restricted in the routes they served, and it was only after deregulation that they had freedom to choose their networks – and most settled on hub-and-spoke networks.

The emphasis on hubbing varies over time, reflecting the relative advantages of large and small equipment. After the introduction of the Boeing 747, airlines emphasized hubs, but when smaller long-distance aircraft, such as the Boeing 767, Boeing 777 and Airbus A330 became available, many airlines reduced their relative reliance on hubs and introduced more direct services. If the unit cost savings of the very large container vessels now being introduced to service are significant, this could lead to a greater emphasis on high-density routes with smaller ports being served by feeder vessels transhipping at large hubs.

The hub-and-spoke approach does not suit all operators. In the airline industry, the **low-cost airlines** have been steering away from this network, preferring direct services between cities. The low-cost carriers (LCCs) see connection costs at airports as being high, since they like to have quick turnarounds, and they gain little from concentrating traffic on the major routes, since they tend to operate the same size of aircraft on all routes. Thus for them, hub-and-spoke operations do not deliver economies. This has led some of the legacy carriers to reconsider their reliance on hubs, especially since they can be highly reliant on busy and congested airports.

The preference for hub-and-spoke networks has implications for the performance of transport infrastructure, especially that of the hubs. This type of network concentrates traffic through a hub, which works well if capacity is adequate. When it is not, there is a demand management problem. Sometimes this is handled through slot allocation mechanisms at airports and ports. Alternatively, pressure of demand can lead to extensive delays, especially if a first come, first served system of allocation of capacity is used.

The reliance on hubs can lead to hub dominance by one or a small number of carriers. This can have both undesirable and desirable consequences.

Hub dominance gives carriers market power in routes from the hub city, and they use this to raise prices – often it is cheaper to travel or send goods from one city to another via a hub than it is to travel or send goods to the hub. On the other hand, if one operator is very strong at a hub, it has a clear incentive to coordinate its services so that they do not create costly delays that it mainly bears.

Further reading
Tretheway, M. and T. Oum (1992). *Airline Economics: Foundations for Strategy and Policy*. Vancouver: Centre for Transportation Studies, University of British Columbia.

Peter Forsyth

hybrid engines

A hybrid propulsion system combines an internal combustion engine with an electric motor and battery. It normally uses the following technologies:

- The electric motor in a hybrid may either provide additional power to assist the engine or simply drive the wheels alone in low-speed driving conditions when the internal combustion engine is inefficient. Current that the electric motor uses to drive the wheels comes from the battery, which is charged when the engine drives the generator. The electric motor can be smaller than that for an all-electric vehicle as the hybrid motor only provides current for short periods. It enables the use of a smaller and more efficient internal combustion engine.
- The hybrid engine can be turned on and off as needed. For example, the engine could be turned off when the vehicle comes to a stop and turned back on when the accelerator is pressed. This saves **energy** from idling.
- The hybrid allows regenerative braking. The electric motor in a hybrid engine functions as a generator in this case. It first applies resistance to the drivetrain slowing down the wheels. The motor then converts the energy into electricity and thus recharges the battery. This prevents energy loss caused when coasting and braking, and thus reduces wear on the brakes.

Hybrid engines would seem to enjoy a promising market future. First, they are already placed in an advantageous position for market entry as they modify existing technologies with gradual changes. Second, vehicles with hybrid engines could be competitively priced if all the costs during the life of a hybrid are taken into account. The fuel-saving technology in a hybrid electric vehicle (HEV) is likely to eventually help offset the initial higher cost. Tax deductions or credits offered by governments to encourage potential hybrid consumers also lower the cost of purchasing a hybrid vehicle. Third, hybrid engines can save energy and have significant environmental advantages. Major current barriers to market development include higher maintenance cost and lower engine performance. Power level is a major concern about the market acceptance of the hybrid engines in the United States. American customers accustomed to 'muscle cars' may not be satisfied with the cars with hybrid engines such as the hybrid Toyota Prius and Honda Civic that are rated at about 85 horsepower.

Hybrid engines can play a significant role in environmental protection and improvement because they consume considerably less fuel than many gasoline ones and thus increase fuel economy. Although they are not true zero-emission engines because of the existence of the conventional internal-combustion ones, hybrid engines will significantly lower CO_2 emissions and other global-warming pollutants. The hybrid electric technologies in current models will become more advanced and further reduce emissions.

Automobiles with hybrid engines are already on the market. Toyota Prius, a five-passenger vehicle, was the first hybrid engineered vehicle (HEV) available to the public. It was first introduced in Japan in 1997 and has been well received there and later in the United States since 1999. The Honda Insight, introduced in late 1999, was the first HEV in the United States automobile market. Honda introduced its second HEV, Civic Hybrid in 2002. All these HEVs meet the standard of the second strictest regulations called ultra-low-emission vehicles (ULEV) compared to the strictest standard called zero-emission vehicles (ZEL). Both Toyota and Honda produce a limited volume of their HEVs. Most of the HEVs are sold in Japan and the United States so far. All major automakers are now working on hybrid vehicles (both light-duty and heavy-duty). Sport utility vehicles (SUVs) and light trucks with more horsepower are the newest hybrid vehicles to enter the market. The automobile industry is now faced with pressures from both environmental protection groups and individual consumers who favour automotive use. Some environmental protection groups pursue air pollution reduction and increased fuel economy through regulation whereas some individual consumers oppose measures that lessen automobile use such as fuel taxes. The advantages of hybrid vehicles such as **energy** saving and emissions reduction enable the automobile industry to address the concerns from both sides and ensure the continued growth of the industry.

The development of the hybrid engines are expected to help address major policy issues faced by governments around the world, including air pollution, **climate change** and increased dependence on imported oil. Hybrid engines are probably the best green or clean alternative to replace conventional gasoline engines at this time. The HEVs therefore probably provide the best near-term path for **sustainable transport**. Governments at different levels can facilitate the development of hybrid electric technologies and the adoption of these technologies in the automobile industry through various policy tools such as tax incentives in the purchase of HEVs, fuel tax and emission regulations.

Further reading

Burke, A. (2004). Present status and marketing prospects of the emerging hybrid-electric and diesel technologies to reduce CO_2 emissions of new light-duty vehicles, California. Institute of Transportation Studies, University of California-Davis.

United States Department of Energy (2004). How do hybrid electric vehicles work? Washington, DC: USDOE.

Roger R. Stough and *Guang Yang*

I

induced travel

Roadway construction is a controversial measure for reducing traffic **congestion** in cities. On the one hand, proponents argue that construction is necessary to keep pace with the travel demands of a growing population. On the other hand, critics charge that capacity expansion provides only short-term relief. That is, within a few years, roads are just as congested as they were before the investment. The reason for this is that new capacity generates new automobile traffic, and attracts traffic from other routes, times and modes. The former is known as induced travel, and the latter, diverted travel. Collectively, they are referred to as generated traffic for the given route.

Downs formulated the theory of triple convergence to explain why new capacity fails to alleviate congestion during peak periods. Assuming that people minimize their travel time, three behavioral responses occur immediately following a road improvement (see Table). First, drivers who were using other routes switch to those incorporating the newly improved road (that is, spatial convergence). Second, drivers who were traveling at off-peak periods switch to the peak (that is, temporal convergence). Finally, public transport users switch to driving their automobiles (that is, modal convergence).

At the facility level, over the short run, most generated traffic consists of diverted trips, whereas over the long run, induced trips comprise an increasing proportion of such traffic. At the same time, diverted trips can increase, decrease or have no effect on vehicle kilometers of travel (VKT). Conversely, induced trips always increase VKT.

Economists have long recognized the potential contribution of induced travel to traffic congestion. The reason for this is that induced travel is based on the concepts of supply and demand. New **network** capacity, that is, an increase in supply reduces the **generalized costs** of travel by reducing travel times. As the cost of travel declines, the quantity demanded increases. In other words, when confronted with additional capacity, drivers undertake both new and longer trips.

Although economic theory posits its existence, induced travel remains a center of debate between proponents and critics of roadway construction. Initially, the debate focused on the fundamental existence of induced travel as verified by empirical evidence. This debate was complicated by two factors. First, there was some disagreement concerning the definition of induced travel. That is, should induced travel include only new trips or

Response	Type of automobile trip	Change in VKT
Short run		
Route switching: new route is shorter than previous one	Diverted	Decrease
Route switching: new route is longer than previous one	Diverted	Increase
Rescheduling of trips from non-peak to peak periods	Diverted	No change
Public transport users switch to their automobiles	Induced	Increase
Drivers choose to travel to farther, existing destinations	Diverted	Increase
New trips by automobile to existing destinations	Induced	Increase
Long run		
Drivers choose to travel to farther, new destinations	Diverted	Increase
New trips by automobile to new destinations	Induced	Increase
New trips by automobile due to reduced public transport service	Induced	Increase
New trips by automobile due to rising ownership levels	Induced	Increase

should it also include diverted trips? Second, induced travel effects must be disentangled from other factors that drive travel demand growth. Such factors include population and employment growth, increases in income and increasing numbers of women in the workforce.

Beginning in the late 1990s, several studies were undertaken to verify empirically the existence of induced travel. Although they varied methodologically, the majority of such studies measured induced travel as the elasticity of VKT with respect to lane kilometers. For example, an elasticity of 0.5 would suggest that for every 10 percent increase in lane kilometers, VKT increases by 5 percent. The **elasticities** documented in these studies found that there is a significant relationship between new road capacity and VKT growth after controlling for other factors driving VKT growth. In other words, these studies verified the existence of induced travel.

Given the overwhelming evidence supporting the existence of induced travel, concern has now shifted to policy – specifically, the extent to which current travel demand forecasting models are able to account for induced travel. Many cities forecast travel demand using some variant of the urban transportation modeling system (UTMS), which represents the state-of-the-practice in such modeling. In the vast majority of cases, the modeling system is calibrated for the morning peak period only, which implies that it is unable to forecast travel at other times of the day. Given its rigidity, UTMS is unable to encapsulate all of the behavioral responses to new capacity, which give rise to induced travel. This implies that current travel demand forecasting models will overstate the purported benefits of new capacity in terms of travel time savings, reduced **congestion**, and reduced emissions of harmful air pollutants. In turn, if induced travel is to be encapsulated in its entirety in travel demand forecasting models, thereby increasing the reliability of forecasts, new approaches to such modeling are needed. Two promising approaches are integrated transportation and land-use models and activity-based travel **demand models**.

Further reading
Downs, A. (1992). *Stuck in Traffic: Coping with Peak-Hour Traffic Congestion.* Washington, DC: Brookings Institute.
Scott, D.M. (2002). Overcoming traffic congestion: a discussion of reduction strategies and behavioral responses from a North American perspective. *European Journal of Transport and Infrastructure Research* **2**, 317–38.

Darren M. Scott

information systems in the United States

Information technology as applied to surface transportation systems is known as **intelligent transportation systems** (ITS). The promotion of ITS was established as a United States federal government policy objective in the 1991 Intermodal Surface Transportation Efficiency Act (ISTEA) and the follow-on 1997 Transportation Equity Act for the 21st Century (TEA 21), under each of which the federal government has spent about $200 million annually on ITS for research, testing, national planning, establishment of national technical standards and deployment of systems throughout the nation.

ITS technologies generally fall into one of four categories: advanced traveller information systems, advanced traffic management systems, commercial vehicle operations and advanced public transportation systems.

Advanced traveller information systems (ATIS)
These are techniques for electronically collecting and communicating traffic information. Traffic information has traditionally been collected through magnetic resonance loop detectors embedded in roadways, but

new technologies include roadside radar units and video cameras, and the tracking of cellphone traffic emanating from travelling vehicles, thereby permitting a measurement of speed. These newer techniques promise cheaper installation, less maintenance, and potentially greater accuracy.

Traditional methods of communicating traffic information are traffic broadcasts by commercial radio stations, electronic variable message signs positioned above or alongside roadways, and highway advisory radio, which are low-powered transmitters with a range of only a few miles broadcasting information about traffic conditions in the immediate areas. Newer methods include cable television displaying current traffic conditions, provision of route-specific current traffic information to cellphones and pagers in en route vehicles, and in the United States the nationwide '511' number (akin to the 411 information and 911 emergency numbers), which travellers can call to receive current traffic information.

ATIS also includes the provision of traveller information via electronic databases about hotels, restaurants, tourist attractions, hospitals and gasoline stations. The database can be search according to specific characteristics, such as proximity to the driver, prices and product offerings, for example, type of food. This service is sometimes called 'electronic yellow pages'.

Advanced traffic management systems (ATMS)
The most traditional function of ATMS is traffic signalization. Newer signal technologies include systems in which a control centre can adapt signal timing instantaneously throughout a whole region to accommodate changing traffic patterns. Another innovation is 'adaptive' traffic signals, which include sensors around an intersection permitting the signal to adapt automatically, without human intervention, to changing traffic patterns.

An important new ATMS tool is electronic toll collection, which permits traffic to pass through toll booths without stopping. Electronic toll collection technology also permits so-called 'variable', or '**congestion**', pricing, whereby tolls are continually adjusted to ensure that traffic does not become congested on the tollroad. Thus, as traffic volume builds, tolls are raised, thereby discouraging additional traffic.

Commercial vehicle operations (CVO)
The most economically important CVO technology is fleet management, whereby a control centre keeps track of the location of en route trucks throughout a region, or even throughout the nation. This method typically relies on a satellite-based global positioning system on each truck, and is called automated vehicle location, or AVL. This location information has several uses. The centre can dispatch en route trucks to new pickup or delivery destinations to satisfy newly received orders. Alternatively,

customers can be kept informed of the exact location of their shipments. And management can maintain tighter control over driver efficiency.

Another important CVO technology is the electronic review at US state border crossings of a truck's licence and **safety** credentials, permitting the truck to maintain its speed rather than stopping for a manual inspection. Similarly, electronic 'weigh-in-motion' technologies eliminate the need for trucks to stop at state police weigh stations.

Advanced public transportation systems (APTS)
Automated vehicle location systems (AVL) have several important applications in transit. First, AVL permits much-improved control of en route transit vehicles, permitting, for example, a control centre to mitigate bunching of buses, a frequent problem in heavy traffic.

Second, AVL can help protect the security of drivers and passengers. For example, in case of a robbery or assault on a bus, the driver can send an immediate distress signal to a control centre which, knowing the exact location of the vehicle, can then direct police, fire, ambulance or other needed emergency support to the vehicle.

Finally, AVL systems are used to provide expected time of arrival information to travellers waiting for a bus or train, a service which can mitigate impatience and anxiety among waiting passengers.

This survey of ITS is not exhaustive. Other technologies include radar-controlled braking and steering that is activated when a vehicle faces an imminent crash from a nearby vehicle; mayday systems whereby an AVL-equipped vehicle automatically sends a distress signal to a control centre in case of an accident; and use of fleet control technologies to dispatch snow removal vehicles in the case of severe storms.

Further reading
Benson, B.G. (2001). Transportation information systems. In K.J. Button and
    D.A. Hensher (eds), *Handbook of Transport Systems and Traffic Control.*
    Oxford: Pergamon.

Brien Benson

infrastructure

Infrastructure usually identifies civil and social structures such as schools, university, hospitals, but also energy **networks** and sewerage systems, as well as transport and **telecommunications** networks and services. In economic theory, infrastructure has always been interpreted as an important element for economic growth, in terms of income, **productivity** and employment growth. The most common way of conceptualizing the role of infrastructure in **economic development** is to include infrastructure in a traditional production function, and to treat it as an input factor:

$$Y = f(K, L, I)$$

where Y is the level of production, K and L represent the traditional neo-classical production factors, respectively capital and labour, and I represents the infrastructure endowment in an economic system – a nation or a region.

In regional economic theory, the role of infrastructure on regional development has been emphasized by different economic approaches; in all of them infrastructure is excepted to play a strategic role on regional competitiveness, by enhancing local attractiveness and therefore new investments and new business activities in an area. Moreover, for what concerns only transport and **telecommunications networks**, they are generally interpreted as strategic instruments for peripheral area to increase **accessibility** to core market area, and therefore to enhance local competitiveness.

The supply of infrastructure is usually characterized by large indivisibility (it cannot be offered on a small scale), non-substitutability (it cannot be replaced at low cost), immobility (it cannot be removed) and polyvalence (it can be an input for a large number of production processes). On the basis of these characteristics, in economic theory infrastructure is generally defined as that part of the overall capital stock of national and regional economies that, because of its 'publicness', is normally not provided by free markets at all or only inefficiently. Thus, its provision, or the control of its provision, is left to the public sector, and infrastructure is also defined as 'social overhead capital'.

Many empirical studies are devoted to the measurement of the impact of social overhead capital on economic growth. Starting from the pioneering contribution of Aschauer, many attempts have been made in different countries to measure the impact of infrastructure on economic growth, applying different methodologies to different databases. Simple correlation analyses developed in different Organisation of Economic Co-operation and development countries witness a positive relationship between infrastructure endowment and economic growth. The intensity of the correlation very much depends on the type of infrastructure analysed: influencing more directly the efficiency of private investments, economic infrastructure (transport, energy, telecommunications infrastructure) has a higher correlation with economic growth than civil and social infrastructure. The latter have a direct impact on quality of life and quality of human capital, but have a less immediate influence on the efficiency of private investment, and therefore on production. Moreover, empirical analyses measure the impact of infrastructure on factor productivity, by estimating through econometric models the increase of gross domestic product (GDP) due to one unit of increase in infrastructure (the elasticity of GDP to infrastructure). Applied to Italy, the elasticity of GDP to infrastructure is measured at around 0.20.

The role of infrastructure in the regional development process has, for a long time, been rather uncertain. Long periods of regional development policies based on the creation of infrastructure in lagging regions have failed to make much impression on regional divergence. These failures have led to the identification of some conditions in order to achieve regional development through infrastructure creation, namely: the need to plan new infrastructure endowment on the real productive vocation of the area; the need to have favourable existing preconditions for new development in the area where infrastructure is created; the need to take into consideration that new infrastructure in an economically weak region may now run the risk that the region will suffer from strong competition from enterprises in more distant regions; and the need to take into consideration that infrastructure investments only have a discriminating effect on regional development if the competitive position of a region is enhanced. A simultaneous improvement of infrastructure in both central and peripheral areas is not necessarily beneficial – in a relative sense – for peripheral regions.

Infrastructure is therefore a necessary condition for economic growth. However, the idea that infrastructure creation is also a sufficient condition for **economic development** is usually wrong and even dangerous: wrong, since a series of other important factors have to be present (among which are entrepreneurship, specialization and innovative capacity) to guarantee efficiency and effectiveness to infrastructure policies; dangerous, since it risks influencing regional development policies towards the creation of 'white elephants' in lagging regions, with no real impact on local growth.

Further reading
Aschauer, D. (1989). Is public expenditure productive? *Journal of Monetary Economics* **23**, 177–200.
Biehl, D. (1986). *The Contribution of Infrastructure to Regional Development*. Brussels Regional Policy Division. Brussels: European Community.
Vickerman, R. (ed.) (1991). *Infrastructure and Regional Development*. London: Pion.

Roberta Capello

inland water transport

Inland waterways **networks** are made of rivers and canals. In Western Europe, there are about 29 000 km of waterways that are regularly used. In the United States, about 40 000 km are usable for commercial navigation; this number includes the intracoastal waterways but excludes the rivers of Alaska. Nowadays, waterways are only used for transporting goods, with the few exceptions of some river commuter services, such as in Paris, and tourist boat operations in some cities or on some panoramic rivers.

The capacity of waterways varies alot. About 50 per cent of the waterway network of Belgium and the Netherlands allows the use of boats of more than 1000 tonnes of deadweight; in France, this percentage falls to 25 per cent. The typical self-propelled boats on the main European waterways, like the Schelde, the Maas or the Rhine, are rated at 1350 tonnes, but there are many bigger boats that may exceed 3000 tonnes. Barges of all sizes also are pushed or towed on these waterways; on the largest rivers, up to six barges of 2000 tonnes linked together can form a convoy. Convoys of many more barges, 20 and more, can be operated on a river like the Mississippi. On large rivers or canals close to seaports, small-sized sea vessels can navigate inland to some distance. Through the St Lawrence seaway in Canada, some sea vessels can even reach the American Middle West. Specially adapted short sea shipping and **coastal vessels**, with a collapsible wheelhouse, can reach far inland on the main rivers and canals of Europe.

In the European Union (EU-15), the inland water transport share of the freight transport market was only 6.7 per cent in 2001 (in tonne-km), compared to 75.5 per cent for road, 13.1 per cent for rail and 4.7 per cent for pipelines. The share of intra-Europe sea transport amounts to 40.4 per cent of the total European transport market. However, the relative importance of water transport varies greatly from one country to another, according to their **networks** of rivers and canals, and how these networks extend into other countries. Within the **European Union**, its importance in terms of tonnes-kilometres varies from 0 per cent in Denmark and 0.1 per cent in United Kingdom to 43.4 per cent in the Netherlands. This very large share is the exception, since the next-largest shares are 13.5 per cent in Belgium and 12.8 per cent in Germany.

In United States, road transport has a smaller share (32.2 per cent), which leaves a larger market to other modes: 41.3 per cent for rail, 16.3 per cent for pipelines and 10.2 per cent for water transport. This can be partly explained by the geography of the region, and differences with Europe in terms of population density and spatial distribution. Water transport in United States benefits from the extensive networks of the

Missouri–Mississippi–Ohio–Tennessee rivers systems as well as extensive intracoastal systems that allow the use of larger barges than are possible in most of Europe. These factors impact on the average length of haul of water transport, which is estimated at about 300 km in Europe versus 780 km in United States (including very long hauls over intracoastal waterways).

In the early twenty-first century, global freight transport volumes have increased at an annual rate of about 3 per cent in both regions. However, water transport growth was slower than that average, which was dominated by a rapid growth of road transport. It was only 0.3 per cent in United States and somewhat better at 1.9 per cent in Europe, where water transport is used more for traffic related to the major harbours, and where it is progressively seen as an alternative to road transport that is increasingly affected by **congestion**.

At the same time that the volume transported over inland waterways in Europe increased, there were important reductions in the fleet, at least in the number of the boats. Between 1970 and 2000 the number of self-propelled boats, tugs and pushers, as well as of barges was halved although the size of the boats increased with the progressive elimination of smaller and older units. This was a policy supported by a European programme of fleet modernization. This evolution led to an increase in **productivity**, which was necessary to sustain the competition of water transport relative to other modes, and the progressive **deregulation** of transport markets.

The choice of a mode depends on the type of goods to be moved, the network's **accessibility** and the destination sought. Given the large capacity of boats, their relatively low speed, but low cost per tonne, inland water transport is well adapted for transporting bulk goods of low value, including minerals, building materials, petroleum products, and iron and steel products. Also, it is increasingly used for transporting **containers**, from and to harbours; this is particularly the case of empty containers that are repositioned in terminals. When an origin and/or destination is not on the waterway, this type of transport is handicapped by the additional cost and time of carrying the goods to and from the terminal on the river. For that reason, it is less competitive for transporting goods over short distances.

Further reading
European Commission (2003). *EU Energy and Transport in Figures* 2003. Brussels: European Commission.

Michel Beuthe

integrated ticketing

Integrated ticketing permits passengers to make journeys that involve transfers within or between different transport modes or transport operators with a single ticket that is valid for the complete journey. By simplifying the public transport journey in this way, the public transport journey can be made more attractive *vis-à-vis* the private car. Integrated ticketing can perform an important function in a demand management package designed to reduce the use of the private car or at least limit the growth in its use.

The better integration of ticketing is possible as a consequence of the rapid and recent developments in information communication technologies aligned to transport; however, institutional difficulties such as legislation designed to preserve competition amongst transport operators can work against the introduction of integrated ticketing systems. In the United Kingdom, with the exception of London, the fracturing of the national transport system into a system of competing commercial transport operators has worked against the introduction of integrated ticketing systems even within the **network** structure of transport and at a point of time in which technical developments made such integration a much simpler affair. In contrast, in Europe integrated ticketing has fared much better: not only do many cities have integrated ticketing arrangements for public transport but a number are also moving towards the 'smart card' option.

Both efficiency and equity arguments can be made for integrated ticketing: simplifying the ticketing system will remove barriers which discourage travellers from making the journey by public transport and will increase patronage of public transport services – integrated ticketing reduces the costs of travel to the socially excluded by enabling the purchase of a lower cost through ticket rather than the purchase of full fare ticket for the separate legs of a journey. Integrated ticketing has emerged in policy discussion as an important instrument in addressing transport and social exclusion concerns.

Further reading
Smogbusters, A. (2001). A ticket to ride: Getting passengers on-side and on-board with Integrated Public Transport Tickets. Brisbane: Queensland Vision Statement.

Margaret Grieco

integrated transport planning

Until the 1970s, planners treated transport as an independent phenomenon, unrelated to its spatial and social conditions. Transport modes were also generally regarded independently of each other. The expansion of traffic networks planned using this sector-based transport approach tended to be automobile dominated. Other transport modes were hardly noticed.

The first step towards 'integrated transport planning' included all means of transport in the analyses, and subsequently in plans and concepts as well. Transport was increasingly regarded as a means to an end, namely the realization of activities. Consequently, the spatial distribution of opportunities became a subject of transport analyses.

Integrated transport planning is now seen as an intercoordinated planning of settlement structures and transport systems. Settlement structures and transport are regarded as an intertwined system that can be affected by bundles of measures and holistic actions rather than just by single, isolated projects.

With the emergence of integrated planning, the aims of transport planning changed. Besides the primary goal of sectoral planning – the fast and frictionless flow of traffic – ecological and social protection requirements became important including such things as **safety**, conversation on the street, undisturbed sleep, healthy forests and climate protection. One narrow concept of sustainability requires decoupling economic growth and transport demand. It needs the reduction of the transport intensity of economic activities. Three strategies shall contribute to this:

1. reduced traffic – by reducing travelled distances (this does not mean avoiding activities);
2. modal shifts to more environmentally friendly modes;
3. making motorized traffic city-compatible.

Concepts include a large variety of construction and infrastructure, organizational, financial, legal, regulatory and informational approaches. They may be centred directly towards travel demand, or they may affect travel demand indirectly, that is, by the spatial distribution of functions. Bundles of measures are aimed at encouraging action patterns resulting in short distances and environmentally friendly transport modes, and they discourage long-distance and car-oriented action patterns (push and pull).

While investment may be financially costly, non-construction approaches are particularly important because of their low costs. For instance, housing and working might be assigned in a coordinated manner not only on the structural level of land use, but also on the individual level, for example by housing location management or workplace exchange.

Transport planning as a cross-sectional task is complex. It needs interdisciplinary work and the integration of a multitude of actors. The participation of affected citizens and enterprises at an early stage of the planning process is important. Some preliminary achievements as perceived in some European exercises include:

- traffic calming in urban residential areas;
- the allocation of costs to transport means;
- efforts to improve public transport;
- temporal and spatial restrictions for cars in cities;
- improvements in vehicle use and technology, particularly with respect to **safety** and emissions.

Traffic growth, however, seems unlikely to be stopped. This is partly a result of ambivalent policy and planning strategies. In particular, measures that reduce the attractiveness of the car are frequently planned but not realized, in many cases they are simply wrong sighted. So far, the parallel promotion of public transport and individual motorized transport has to be advocated, for example the expansion of light rail and road **networks** at the same time but has singularly failed to stop the growth in car use.

In the future, four key aspects may be crucial for an improved balance and greater efficiency in applying policies:

- Moving away from fixed positions in the political arena.
- Strengthening intercommunal cooperation at the regional level instead of 'parish-pump' politics.
- Supporting the political insight that the constant shortage of public means requires small, decentralized concepts instead of prestigious albeit ineffectual large-scale projects.
- Acknowledging that the key to **sustainable transport** development does not primarily lie within the transport system, but at a number of different levels that require cooperation between various actors; for example housing developers and employers.

Three guiding principles for an integrated transport planning for **ageing** and shrinking societies are often stressed:

- **Accessibility** and **safety** are more important than speed.
- The maintenance of the existing infrastructure is more important than new infrastructure.
- Sustainability requires consistent actions.

Further reading
Greiving, S. and R. Kemper (1999). *Integration of Transport and Land Use Policies: State of the Art.* Dortmund: IRPUD.
Holz-Rau, C. (1996). Integrierte Verkehrsplanung – die herausgeforderte Fachplanung. *Informationen zur Raumentwicklung* 7: 391–415.

Christian Holz-Rau and *Joachim Scheiner*

intelligent transport systems

The term 'intelligent transport systems' (ITS) refers to a wide range of detection, identification, location, charging, enforcement, communication and control technologies applied to travel and transport. The general aim of ITS is to increase the efficiency, reliability and **safety** of transport operations and to provide users with appropriate knowledge before, during and after travel. Increasingly, ITS systems and services are being used to address **climate change** issues.

Many people make trips based on limited knowledge of the alternatives available, and these trips are often by car. ITS systems and services can give comprehensive information before and during travel and this can lead to more sustainable travel choices provided effective public transport services are available.

The Internet is the main source of pre-trip information, and public and private services may both be accessed by static or portable devices. The information may be general, such as timetables, or bespoke by providing solutions to specific requirements. The services may also involve booking and payment. Once a journey is started, the traveller may access information to confirm journey details such as at interchange points or to recover a journey if there is unexpected delay or cancellation. The first of these is relatively straightforward and many public transport services have information screens at key points and on vehicles. The second is much more difficult to deal with as the service providers themselves are often unaware of how a problem will develop and, whilst general information on the problem may be available, the best response actions for a specific traveller may not be clear. Both these issues are the subject of substantial research and it is likely in the foreseeable future that improved operational models, combined with hand-held mobile devices will enable such services to be introduced. However, the many problems which need to be overcome include better **network** state estimation and forecasting, improved procedures to respond to incidents, improved power availability and more, effective human machine interaction (HMI) with hand-held devices and improved technology to locate and communicate with individuals. The use of global positioning systems (GPS) base stations to locate individuals better, and ubiquitous Wi-Fi and WiMAX systems will enable more non-transport-related calls for such things as emergency services to be integrated with transport calls and this provide a better business case for their provision.

A key area of ITS is road traffic management. Traditionally, vehicles have been detected at specific locations on the network for immediate local control decisions such as at traffic signals, and/or longer-term monitoring for policy and planning purposes. Detectors on the approaches to traffic signals are used to create online profiles of demand which are communicated to a roadside signal control unit, which triggers changes to signals aspects according to a performance function which usually incorporates the minimization of delay.

Older, isolated intersection systems are relatively simple and rapidly reach fixed-time operation as traffic demand increases. Some systems are more sophisticated and online modelling with more comprehensive detection. An example of this is the MOVA system in the United Kingdom where vehicle positions on the approach arms are monitored at 100 m and 40 m from the stop lines, and signal timings are altered to minimize delay using a simulation model in the local controller. However, more sophisticated systems are more normal in urban areas, in which adjacent signals are linked. In these systems, the three factors of cycle times, green times and the offsets are varied to achieve a more global optimization. (Offsets are the time delays to the start of a cycle for the next downstream signals.) These values may be determined offline using a computer model such as TRANSYT from which a series of fixed-time programmes can be determined for the different demand conditions that may be encountered. The most appropriate programmes may be determined by time of day or be triggered by flow or queue measurements at key points in the **network**. Whilst TRANSYT, which is used throughout the world, has been found to reduce network delays by some 20 per cent, the step changes in network conditions when moving between plans causes discontinuities between the arrival of platoons of vehicles at a stop line and the start of green time. Also, plans age because traffic demand changes. TRANSYT-type programmes are still used in many areas and have particular value in the control of large interchanges.

Most modern urban signal networks are now controlled by demand-responsive online systems. Typical examples are SCOOT that has central control, and UTOPIA which has more distributed control. Both systems use detectors on the approaches to estimate arrival patterns and hence delays in an online model. As with TRANSYT, optimization is achieved by changing green times, cycle times and offsets. This is done in SCOOT in an incremental way to avoid discontinuities in arriving platoons of vehicles. The SCOOT model can deal best with network conditions which are not oversaturated, whereas UTOPIA addresses oversaturation at a junction level; although both work well over the whole range of demand and many other network control models are available. Typically, the SCOOT and UTOPIA systems can save an additional 20 per cent of delay over TRANSYT. However, a traffic signal control model is only part of an urban traffic management system which can have additional functionalities to address incident detection and management, **parking** management, traveller information, **network** monitoring, environmental management, interurban traffic manage- ment, public transport priority and demand management. Together these ITS systems enable the control of urban traffic to be effective at meeting the increasingly sophisticated transport policies and objectives that are being applied. Key to all these systems is the need to know what is happening in a network, and detection for network state estimation is an essential ITS function.

A wide range of detectors are available, but the most common are wire loops buried in the road which are triggered when a vehicle crosses the field created. They can vary in size to cover one or more lanes, and can be configured and timed to measure speed and vehicle type. Microwave detec- tors are often used in conditions where the presence of steel in the road as reinforcement or decking precludes the use of loops. Also, microwave detectors are less vulnerable to damage during roadworks. Infrared and microwave detectors are particularly important for monitoring pedestrian movements. Video-based systems have never been particularly successful, other than in providing control centre operators with additional informa- tion on selected areas of the **network**. They are also used to read number plates for identification and enforcement of **speed limits**, red light running, access control and charging.

Within urban traffic management the location and identification of indi- vidual vehicles is becoming increasingly important. For priority, many bus fleets are fitted with either global positioning system (GPS)-based auto- matic vehicle location (AVL) or beacon- or transponder-based units that can identify and locate individual vehicles. This enables online priority at signals to be allocated when necessary; either for 'gating' that is, priority access to roads, or for cycle times to be changed to reduce bus delay and increase journey time reliability. Such priority schemes often have a 100 per cent first-year rate of return. Similar systems can be used with other vehicle types to control access and/or to charge.

On motorways, ITS systems are commonly used to identify incidents and warn approaching drivers by using variable message signs or in-vehicle systems, to change and enforce speed limits, and to control lane use and access using slip-road ramp metering. Ramp metering systems measure main carriageway traffic and control the ramp access flow using traffic signals so that the flow downstream does not exceed capacity and lead to flow breakdown with associated delays and enhanced accident risks. Speed cameras that read number plates at two or more points can be used to estimate average journey time and are very effective at calming traffic at roadwork sites (50 per cent reduction in accidents).

Since the 1970s, there have been extensive programmes by the vehicle manufacturers to develop new systems that provide information to the driver, support driving functions and control the vehicle. These range from climate control and sophisticated audio systems to systems that initiate braking. Systems may be fitted when the vehicle is new or as after-market products, although technologies such as brake assist or stability control, which automatically initiate braking, and other related **safety** functions are only available as first fit to new vehicles. Systems, such as driver monitoring or navigation, may be fitted after-market.

Technology-based safety features that are now commonly available include the anti-lock braking system (ABS) in which the vehicle takes over control of braking in an emergency, and a variety of stability control systems. There are benefits from many of these systems, but some concerns remain which relate largely to the ability of the driver to cope with the workload generated by the extra systems, and long-term behavioural changes in which drivers begin to display an over-reliance on the technology. Other concerns include cost, long-term reliability and the ability of drivers to cope with the use of similar functions which have different performance characteristics depending on the vehicle or manufacturer. In the foreseeable future, vehicle-based systems will only ever have limited awareness of the surroundings because of software and hardware constraints. For example, technologies cannot determine the 'intent' of a pedestrian with the same degree of subtlety as a driver.

For the future, ITS systems are being developed that are enhanced by vehicle–vehicle and vehicle–infrastructure communications that will inform drivers of route conditions ahead and of more immediate traffic problems. This will enable information from one vehicle to be used to warn another driver. For example, the operation of a windscreen wiper or the anti-lock braking system on one vehicle may be used to inform other approaching drivers of the onset of rain, or of an icy road surface.

Vehicle–infrastructure systems are already used, commercially, to charge for road use and pay-as-you-go insurance. Such systems fall into two broad categories: beacon-based, which use microwave communications and have generally local but secure communications; and global positioning system (GPS) or global system for mobile communications (GSM)-based systems. Both types are currently used for tolling. Stumbling blocks for major deployment exist in developing a business case and funding timeline that meets the need of both owners and operators of infrastructure, service providers and manufacturers.

Further reading
Hounsell, N. and M. McDonald (2001). Urban network traffic control. *Proceeding of the Institution of Mechanical Engineers, Part 1, Journal of Systems and Control Engineering* **215**, 325–34.
McDonald, M., H. Keller, J. Klijnhout, V. Mauro, R. Hall, A. Spence, C. Hecht and O. Fakler (2006). *Intelligent Transport Systems in Europe: Opportunities for Future Research.* Hackensack: World Scientific Publishing.
Miles, J. and K. Chen (eds) (2004). *The Intelligent Transport Systems Handbook* (2nd edn). Swanley: Route 2 Market.

Mike McDonald

intelligent transport systems evaluation

An estimated $2 billion per year is spent by government and industry on **intelligent transport systems** (ITS) in the United States, and perhaps $5 billion worldwide. Therefore, some impressive efforts at evaluating ITS have been made, but none highlight the fact that ITS can be evaluated from two very different perspectives: ITS as a collection of individual technologies, and ITS as an integrated national system. There have been some striking successes of individual ITS technologies, but efforts to achieve national standards and national integration have thus far not been overly successful.

Among the most successful individual applications of ITS are in-vehicle navigation devices using a global positioning system; electronic toll collection; fleet control systems, whereby a control centre keeps continual track of the location of all vehicles in a fleet, typically using satellite-based global positioning systems; and electronic certification at state border crossings of commercial vehicles, obviating the need for the vehicle to stop at an inspection station.

Other emerging ITS technologies show promise, including traffic sensors relying on radar, sonar, video cameras and tracking of transponders on individual vehicles; electronic weighing of trucks, permitting them to pass a weigh station without stopping; and electronic posting of time-of-arrival information at transit train and bus stations.

In contrast to the numerous successes of individual ITS technologies, the effort to establish a nationwide system and national standards has been struggling. Many early US champions of ITS envisioned a national system that would combine the integrated road **network** of the interstate highway system with the systems engineering developed during the Apollo moon shot programme. Reflecting this thinking, the 1991 United States Intelligent Vehicle and Highways Systems Act called for a national ITS plan and national standards, and the 1998 ITS Act followed up with implementing requirements.

An elaborate national systems architecture has been prepared for the United States, but actual interoperability of equipment among competing firms is very limited. A major barrier to deployment of a national system is lack of national technical standards that are accepted in the marketplace. On paper, many technical standards have been agreed to – 82 as of June 2004 – but these standards are the product of standards development organizations, and few have been fully accepted in the marketplace.

One important reason for this failure of adoption is inadequate testing of standards before they were promulgated. As a key study by the **Transportation Research Board** (TRB) notes: 'formal testing, observation of in-service applications, or other verification of functioning may or may not be considered a routine part of a particular standard's development process'.

A second problem is lack of sufficient detail in the standards. For example, a general purpose device may conform to the National Transportation Communications for ITS Protocol (NTCIP), but to gain competitive advantage the manufacturer adds on a new feature which may not adhere to the ITS Protocol.

A third problem is that, as explained in the aforementioned TRB study:

> many ITS functions do not require interactions among system components above a local or regional level. There is no compelling reason, the committee observed, why a traffic information and management centre in Boston, for example, should be able to communicate directly with its counterpart in Phoenix. Why, then, should agencies in either region be expected to compromise on the functional requirements they seek to purchase or the cost they must pay for their systems so that their hardware and software will meet national standards?

Finally, many ITS technologies are evolving so rapidly that they are not yet ripe for standardization. As argued by Carl Cargill:

In a market that is growing explosively and is dynamic to the point of instability, internal relationships are unclear, and there are no guarantees that tomorrow's market will be based on today's activities. In this atmosphere, planning is impossible; it is a speculator's market. No standards can be written for this type of environment: standards are postulated on a recognized growth path and certain continuity of progress; in a high-growth, highly dynamic market, there is nothing but discontinuity. If standards, voluntary or otherwise, are introduced into this environment, they will fail, since standards act to stabilize a market.

Of course, there have been some successes in standards setting. An excellent example is protocols for vehicle-to-roadside communications, which promote standardized electronic toll collection systems. Nonetheless, at present the successes of individual ITS technologies far surpass those in the construction of a nationally integrated intelligent transport system.

Further reading
Cargill, C. (1989). *Information Technology Standardization*. Newton, MA: Digital Press.
Transportation Research Board of the National Academies (2004). *Development and Deployment of Standards for Intelligent Transportation Systems: Review of the Federal Program*. Washington, DC: Transportation Research Board.
United States Federal Highway Administration (2000). *What Have We Learned about Intelligent Transportation Systems?* Washington, DC: USFHWA.

Brien Benson

intermodal freight transport

Intermodal transport is generally defined as the movement of goods in one and the same loading unit, which uses successively two or more modes of transport, without handling the goods themselves in changing modes.

By association, the term intermodality widely used in European Union documents describes a transport system, whereby two or more transport modes are used to transport the same loading unit or truck in an integrated manner, without loading or unloading, in a (door-to-door) transport **supply-chain.** Thus, the definition of 'intermodal transport' is based on loading units, instead of individual items, moving between different transport modes. This distinguishes the term 'intermodal transport' with other terms that signify either combined transport, which is a restricted type of intermodal transport, focused on the use of rail or maritime and inland waterways transport for the greater part of the journey and limiting the road leg to the initial pickup and final delivery of the loading unit with journeys as short as possible; or 'multi modal' transport, which is mainly related to the transport of goods that are not containerized by different modes. The key issues defining intermodal transport are the types of loading unit, and the forms of loading and unloading processes.

Loading unit
There is a great variety of types of loading units available, and their use depends on the transport mode and the type of cargo. The most commonly used are:

- Container: a standardized box that carries freight, strengthened and stackable and allowing horizontal or vertical transfer. **Containers** are widely used for rail and maritime intermodal transport. Containers are carried on flat wagons, International Organization for Standardization (ISO) deep sea containers, and tractors with articulated chassis for the road part of journey.
- Swap-body: a freight-carrying unit, not strong enough to be stackable, which travels on truck–trailer combinations and is carried on railways, usually on flat wagons.
- Semi-trailer: a trailer without a front axle, connected to an articulated vehicle, used for freight that is transported primarily by road and rail; these raise **safety** concerns for damage and theft.

Forms of loading and unloading process

- Roll-on roll-off (ro-ro): the process of a vehicle or train transfer to the inside or outside of a ship. Also, this applies to train services, when the truck or trailer is boarded on a train platform.
- Lift-on lift-off (lo-lo): the process of loading and unloading an intermodal transport unit with the use of lifting equipment.

Integration of different transport modes at different levels
Intermodal transport presents an ideal combination of advantages, which relate to the nature and characteristics of each different transport mode; for example road, rail, inland waterways, open seas, air. The objective is to develop a framework for the optimal integration of different transport modes, whilst favouring competition between transport operators.

More specifically, rail, maritime and inland waterways transport offer constant average speeds unaffected by road traffic, time savings in most cases, significant capacity, and are economically efficient, safe and environmentally friendly. On the other hand, road transport is the most flexible type of freight transport, offering a door-to-door service, without having a fixed pattern of operation. The aim is, therefore, to integrate intermodal transport patterns, often supporting alternatives to road transport, particularly for the longest section of the journey, thus moving goods in a more efficient way.

Bespoke intermodal transport
Until recently, generic policies for improving the competitive position of intermodal transport have not always been successful. The focus on the **supply-chain** and an individual, tailor-made approach is likely to be more effective in attracting traffic from road to intermodal transport. The critical challenges for intermodal transport are the following.

Congestion on the road **network** and access to intermodal terminals and ports is a major challenge. Many motorways experience long delays, especially within and near urban centres. The objective is to reduce road congestion through modal shift and the promotion of interoperable transport services. Ports, airports and rail terminals are particularly prone to peak congestion periods. Therefore, optimization of their capacity and efficiency of infrastructure, interoperability and access will improve terminals and establish the reliability of the **network**.

The increasing transport demand in recent years, the unequal growth in the use of different modes of transport and congestion have caused harmful effects on the environment. An optimally functioning intermodal transportation system can contribute to the reduction of vehicle emissions and noise pollution.

Road transport generally has higher accident rates than those sustained by other modes. By developing intermodal systems, a significant reduction in accidents may be accomplished.

Success in the highly competitive market predicates low transport costs and reliability for delivery times. Intermodal transport can be a tool for satisfying the new logistics requirements of final customers, which are **just-in-time** delivery, customized production, and concentration of supply and distribution centres. Based on the transport of unitized cargo, intermodal transport seeks to supply efficient uninterrupted functioning of door-to-door transport supply-chains, using various alternative modes. Moreover, intermodal transport can enhance the economic performance of a transport chain by using modes in the most productive and **energy efficient** manner.

Intermodal transport enhances the links and the efficiency of **supply-chains**. Remote regions can face severe isolation and there may be political need to improve links with central markets. The development of intermodal transport contributes to the distribution of economic activity and social cohesion.

The **globalization** of production and economic growth are creating demand for transport services on a global level. Therefore, governments and public authorities, as well as private companies, are often pressurised to invest in transport. More efficient infrastructure, services and transport operations offer the potential for significant savings in public expenditure. An intermodal transport supply-chain consists of the following steps:

- *Composition.* Initially, different local suppliers use flexible modes, such as road trucks, to transfer loads to distribution centres, in order to be forwarded to higher capacity modes such as rail, airplanes and maritime or inland waterways shipping. Activities such as **packaging** and warehousing are also included in the composition process.
- *Connection.* This involves a consolidated modal flow, such as on a freight train or a containership, between at least two terminals. It may be part of either a purely domestic freight distribution system or an international system.
- *Interchange.* The terminal is the point where interchange facilities are provided for transfer of freight from one mode to another. The function of the terminal is to provide an efficient continuity within a transport **supply-chain**, as well as the necessary equipment and infrastructure for the transfer of goods to take place as economically, quickly and safely as possible.
- *Decomposition.* Once a load of freight has reached a terminal close to its destination, it has to be fragmented and transferred to the local or regional freight distribution system. This function, which is linked to the function of consumption, occurs mostly within metropolitan areas and involves unique distribution problems also known as **urban logistics**.

Intermodal transport is often used as a broader term in providing 'door-to-door' transport services for both goods and passengers. The intermodal transport chain for the passenger flow follows the same pattern as that for the freight flow. Intermodal passenger transport should focus on the quality and cost of the facilities and services it provides, in order for it to be viable: it should be convenient, cost- and time-effective. The main objective of intermodal passenger transport is to encourage passengers to use public transport instead of private car for all or part of their journeys, by transferring from one transit mode or line to another as smoothly as possible.

Historically, national transport systems were designed in part for national **defence** purposes; thus technical designs (for example rail track gauge) and operations strategies (for example ability to use locomotives across national boundaries) have often been incompatible.

For the development of an intermodal transport system the focus is now more on reducing barriers to the flow of freight and people, whilst improving **safety** and efficiency. Transport policy is increasingly adopting a 'bottom-up' approach in transport planning, considering it in terms of the greater whole. The transport system concept now more often focuses on the coordination of transport modes and the interoperability of the transfer facilities and transport **networks** in terms of infrastructure, operations and administrative procedures and legislation.

Well established intermodal transport is a systems approach stemming back to use of sacks for mail and the use of foot, horse and water transport by the postal services applied to the modally oriented transport system, where any change of mode within a journey involves a change of transport system, rather than just a technical transhipment. In this context, intermodal transport creates 'friction costs', which often makes intermodal transport uncompetitive in comparison to unimodal haulage.

The weakest links in the intermodal transport chain are the terminals where the transfer between modes takes place. Many problems are also related to the access to these terminals. The current system is largely funded and managed separately by each mode; therefore strengthening those links is challenging.

Successful integration of the operators in complex intermodal transport chains is generally supported by adequate and harmonized regulations but a harmonized legal and technical framework for international intermodal transport has yet to be implemented.

Governments and public bodies could expand financing methods for intermodal transport projects. The planning process is also increasingly embodying market research and technology development. The necessary infrastructure would seem to be in need of upgrading and expansion. Moreover, opportunities to use information systems for capacity management and **telecommunication** and information exchange would seem to be continually growing.

Further reading

European Commission (2006). *Communication on Freight Transport Logistics in Europe – The Key to Sustainable Mobility*, COM(2006) 336 final (2006). Brussels: European Commission.

Tsamboulas, D. (2004). Intermodal transport markets and sustainability in Europe. In P. Rietveld and P. Stough (eds), *Barriers to Sustainable Transport*. New York: Spon Press.

United Nations (2001). *Terminology on Combined Transport*. New York: UN.

Dimitrios A. Tsamboulas

international trade and transport

Some economists have suggested a causal connection exists between transport and trade. Such causality, it is argued, arises from the effects that the costs of moving goods have on the observed amounts of volume and value of international trade. Transport costs are composed of direct elements – freight charges and insurance; and indirect elements – such as the financial cost of the time goods are in transit, and their inventory cost. Other trade costs include transaction costs such as search costs, legal fees and currency exchanges, among others.

Research to verify the existence of causality has been limited. Academic interest was revived during the 1990s as a complement to other work by international economists to measure the effect of lower tariffs on trade following the end of the Second World War and the end of the Uruguay Round of Multilateral Trade Negotiations in 1994. These works encompassed the development of trade theories and the empirical assessment of international trade models based, predominantly, on David Ricardo's theory of comparative advantage and the Heckscher–Ohlin general equilibrium mathematical model of international trade. The results of such works have provided some evidence that currently observed trade levels are lower than those predicted by the models. Some economists refer to this as the mystery of 'missing trade' and have attempted to quantify the effects of changes in trade costs, including those of transport costs, when analysing international trade flows.

On a very simplified level, econometric models of international trade and transport can be grouped in two broad types of analysis, adapting David Ricardo's theory of comparative advantage to two countries, A and B: country A has limited endowments of natural resources and specializes in the production of manufactured goods while B has abundant natural resources specializing in producing agriculture goods. The first type of analysis includes classical economic trade models with zero trade costs and uniform tastes in both countries. In this scenario, agricultural goods will move from B to A whereas manufactured goods will move from A to B when countries move from autarchy to trade. These models typically do not control for geography and assume that firms charge the same free-on-board prices to all markets and apply a common trade factor cost across goods. In essence, transport and other trade costs do not change relative prices. In equilibrium, agricultural prices will fall in country A as imports from country B expand supply. Moreover, employment and output in A's manufacturing sector will increase as labour moves from agriculture to manufacturing. Country B is the mirror image of A and will benefit from lower prices for manufactured goods. As the result of trade both countries will be better off.

The second approach is essentially Keynesian in its orientation and its modern application is linked to the New Growth Theory. Taking the initial conditions of countries A and B, this approach argues that not only will higher trade levels not be attained (missing trade) but that there may be cases where trade flows diverge further (only North–North trade increases while North–South trade remains unchanged or even declines).

Under this framework of analysis, trade flows are usually impeded not only by geography and high transaction costs but also by differences in consumers' tastes. The role of transport in these two scenarios is different. In the classical trade theory framework it is considered to be ubiquitous and free. In the Keynesian-style scenario it is seen as a major cost that will usually encourage unidirectional trade flows only from developed-country A's products to developing-country B. This occurs as shippers in country A will likely face lower transport costs than their counterparts in country B due to differences in infrastructure levels. Bidirectional trade flows will increase only between countries with overall low transactions costs; that is, North–North trade.

A major limitation in exploring the ties between transport and trade has been the complexity in estimating the **generalized costs** of freight transport, largely due to the lack of publicly available disaggregated data by type of good and mode; for example air, ground, sea or multimodal. Furthermore, freight charges can vary depending on the weight–value ratio of the goods, fuel prices, time of the year and trip direction. Attempts to estimate freight charges include calculations based on trade statistics of: transport costs per unit of weight or value of the shipped good; transport costs in *ad valorem* terms (percentage of the good's retail price); and estimations of **elasticities** of relative prices with respect to transport costs. Such attempts have provided some empirical evidence that historically transport costs tend to decline over time, especially those of air freight. Hummels, for instance, has reported that the average revenue per tonne-kilometre airshipped dropped by 92 per cent between 1955 and 2004. In the case of ocean shipping, freight charges changed only slightly from 1952 to 1970, increased substantially from 1970 through the mid-1980s, and declined steadily thereafter.

Further reading

Anderson, J.E. and E. van Wincoop (2004). Trade costs. *Journal of Economic Literature* **42**, 691–751.
Hummels, D. (2007). Transport costs and international trade in the second era of globalization. *Journal of Economic Perspectives* **21**, 131–54.

Henry Vega

International Transport Forum

The International Transport Forum (ITF) was established by transport ministers at the 2006 ministerial meeting of the **European Conference of Ministers of Transport** (ECMT) with membership open to all member countries of the Organisation for Economic Co-operation and Development (OECD) and the former members of the ECMT. In 2008 it had 51 member countries with discussions under way for membership of India, China and Brazil. The ITF has a mandate to work on transport economics and global policy issues across all modes of transport. It holds an annual ministerial forum in Leipzig at which researchers, stakeholders and policy-makers consider a specific important transport issue. The first of these was on the subject of transport, energy and **climate change** and was held in May 2008.

The ITF and the OECD continue to operate the Joint Transport Research Centre, organizing a range of research activities that include: joint working groups of transport ministry and transport research agency experts to review critical transport policy issues; round table meetings where researchers debate specific topics at the interface of economics and policy; a triennial transport research symposium; and databases on road **safety** and transport statistics. The research undertaken by the centre is published in a series of reports and discussion papers available on the web.

Further reading
www.internationaltransportforum.org

Christopher Nash

investment criteria

Since transport is a capital-intensive sector, decisions on investment are critical to its efficient operation. Investment in transport is distinguishable from investment in most other sectors because of the wider impacts, positive and negative, on those outside the sector which are not fully captured by a normal financial appraisal. This has led to the use of techniques such as **cost–benefit analysis** (CBA) (or **benefit–cost analysis**) and **multicriteria analysis** (MCA).

The basic analysis of investment, whether a financial appraisal or a CBA, requires the comparison of a stream of future revenues or benefits with the capital expenditure which might take place in a single outlay or itself be spread over a number of years. Expenditure incurred or revenues received in a future period do not have the same value as those of the present period. The comparison of costs and benefits that occur over time requires discounting to produce present values that can be compared. Hence for a given discount rate, r, the present value, PV_0, in year 0 of $\$X_1$ received in year one is given by:

$$PV_0 = X_1 / (1 + r)^1 \tag{1}$$

where X_i is the difference between the revenues R_i and costs C_i in year i. For a stream of net receipts over the lifetime of a project to year n, given an initial outlay of C_0, and a residual value RV_n in year n, the net present value can be written:

$$NPV_0 = \sum_{i=1}^{n} \left(\frac{X_n}{(1 + r)^i} \right) - C_0 + \frac{RV_n}{(1 + r)^n}. \tag{2}$$

For a financial appraisal the R_i will be the revenue received in year i and the C_i will be the direct costs to the operator. For a CBA the definition of both the revenues and the costs has to be widened to take into account the wider impacts on the economy. In CBA these wider effects need to be monetized so as to treat them consistently with the direct money costs and revenues. For transport projects the most important benefits will be the time savings to users over and above any which can be charged for directly as part of an enhanced quality of service, and the reduction in accident costs. The most important costs will be the negative impacts on the environment through impacts on greenhouse gas emissions, local air pollution, noise, vibration and landscape impacts. Some of these are simpler to monetize than others.

A critical decision is that of the most appropriate discount rate. The discount rate should be one that reflects the time preference of the community making the investment, since any long-term capital investment requires the deferment of current consumption in the interest of a higher future level of income. However, it is also important to recognize that the commitment of funds to investment in transport capital cannot easily be changed if circumstances change – such capital has a low, often zero, opportunity cost, meaning that it cannot easily, if at all, be changed in use. The commitment of funds, particularly public funds, to such an investment has to take account of other possible uses of that capital; for example, commitment of funds to the building of a new road needs to be compared not just with a new railway or airport, but also with public expenditure on schools, hospitals and so on. Often this is allowed for explicitly by introducing a term representing the marginal cost of public funds, reflecting the alternative uses to which the funds could have been put. This is equivalent to any external constraint on the cost of credit. Similarly, it may be necessary to allow for the distributional effects of an investment by weighting the benefits and costs to different groups.

The *NPV* criterion used above assumes that the future stream of revenues and costs are known with certainty and correctly valued by the market. Where there are imperfections in the market, such that price is not equal to marginal cost, the expected return may over- or underestimate the true return.

Because of these potential problems with the *NPV* criterion, two possible alternatives can be put forward, based on the same underlying principles. Instead of using a predetermined discount rate to estimate *NPV*, Equation 2 can be rewritten as:

$$0 = \sum_{i=1}^{n} \left(\frac{X_n}{(1 + r)^i} \right) - C_0 + \frac{RV_n}{(1 + r)^n} \tag{3}$$

where *r* is the unknown. Solving Equation 3 for *r* generates the internal rate of return which can be compared with the ruling interest rate *r** to determine whether or not to accept the investment according to $r > r^*$ or $r < r^*$. This can produce different rankings of projects from the *NPV* method according to the profile of net returns through time.

A variation on this method is the payback period. Given the length of life of most transport investments, and the uncertainty surrounding future revenue and cost streams, Equation 3 can be solved for *n* for a given *r*, in order to determine how long it takes to pay off the initial investment. An extreme version of this, usually used for comparing alternatives for the same project, is the first-year rate of return where *r* is solved by setting *n* = 1 in Equation 3.

Where all the elements cannot be monetized, or where the values associated with some of the wider effects are subject to uncertainty or debate, **multicriteria analysis** can be used. MCA involves taking all the characteristics of a project and, on the basis of the stated preferences of decision-makers, estimating the implicit trade-off between these characteristics by placing weights on each one. MCA is usually used as an adjunct to a more formal investment appraisal technique, but helps to counter the criticism often made of CBA approaches that they depend on arbitrary monetary values of intrinsically non-traded outcomes.

Further reading

Keeney, R.L. and H. Raiffa (1976). *Decisions with Multiple Objectives: Preferences and Value Trade-offs.* New York: Wiley.

Varian, H.R. (1992). *Microeconomic Analysis* (3rd edn). New York: Norton.

Roger Vickerman

J

just-in-time distribution

Initially, just-in-time distribution was a term used to describe the outcome of a reliable process of production or distribution that completed its task just at the programmed time. A typical and very old example is the production process of a daily newspaper which must be provided to carriers and postal operators at a deadline time for distribution early in the morning. The carriers and distributors must also organize themselves to deliver the newspapers speedily to shops and postal boxes. Speed and good timing are essential in such a process.

More generally, 'just-in-time' is used nowadays to designate in brief an efficient organization of production and/or distribution in a chain of coordinated operations, which reduces the need and cost of intermediate and final inventories. In logistics analyses, several types of inventories are distinguished: cycle stocks of inputs to feed production between deliveries, in-transit stocks during transport, and safety stocks to meet delays and incidents. In business-to-business transactions, or even within large integrated corporations, 'just-in-time' organization aims at providing the necessary inputs just in time for their use in the next step of the production process, so that no intermediate stocks of inputs, or only small ones, are needed to insure the continuity of the process. It also allows the reduction of lead-time for ordering goods ahead of production or consumption.

Just-in-time coordination is an important element of so-called 'lean logistic processes' that strive to minimize the cost of production and distribution of goods by all means available: rational organization of the successive production processes; electronic communication between plants; reduction of inventories by fluid deliveries of materials, parts and final goods; electronic identification and spatial localization of shipments; standardization of loading units and equipments, and so on. Lean logistics is made of strenuous cost minimization of all elements affecting the **supply-chain**, with continuous communication between involved agents, good timing and speed.

Speed in transportation is an important factor in just-in-time logistics, but it is not the only element to be considered. The choice between transport modes or means is conditioned by their relative costs and qualitative characteristics in relation to the goods' own characteristics such as weight, value, fragility, bulk or finished product, dry or fresh food, dangerous or not, and so on. Transport **safety** is important for more fragile goods, reliability of delivery is essential for just-in-time logistics, flexibility of service allows for meeting unexpected needs, and frequency of services is needed for handling a continuous flow of small shipments as in cases of commerce through the web. These qualitative factors and speed affect the level of the safety stocks. On the other hand, transport time and frequency of service bear upon the size and cost of cycle and in-transit stocks. Naturally, all stocks are particularly costly when comprised of valuable goods.

Demand characteristics also matter, and supply logistics may be different whether the demand is regular or not, whether it is an industrial demand of an input or individual consumers' demand, and whether it is a seasonal or temporary demand. In summary, the choice of a transport means is conditioned by its appropriate insertion and cost-saving contribution in a specific logistic chain between producer and users. Hence, the value to the shippers or users of a transport qualitative attribute, like transport time, depends on the goods transported, and may also differ substantially according to whether it is evaluated from the point of view of a carrier or from the point of view of a shipper or consignee.

Most of these qualitative requirements are better met by road transport, which is particularly cost-competitive for shipments over short distances. However, just-in-time logistics may be compatible with other modes particularly for bulk and heavy commodities of lower value per weight. An interesting example is given by a steel-making firm that, in a just-in-time delivery contract, ships heavy sheet coils by inland navigation to feed an automotive assembly line on a continuous work schedule. In that case, the low transport cost of inland navigation over the distance is the main factor of choice, besides its good reliability and **safety**. But this set-up is supplemented by occasional expensive road transports when, for some reasons, the coils production itself is affected by delays.

Further reading
Ballou, R.H. (1999). *Business Logistics Management: Planning, Organizing and Controlling the Supply-chain*. Upper Saddle River, NJ: Prentice-Hall.

Beuthe, M. and Ch. Bouffioux (2008). Analyzing qualitative attributes of freight transport from stated orders of preference experiment. *Journal of Transport Economics and Policy* **42**, 105–28.

Michel Beuthe

L

labour unions and transport

Labour unions are organizations of workers whose primary objectives are to improve the wages and working conditions of their members. A labour union bargains with an employer on behalf of its members over the terms and conditions of employment – for example wages, benefits and policies regarding overtime, promotion and job assignment – and will call a strike to achieve its objectives. A union gives workers: greater bargaining power versus the employer than a non-union system of individual bargaining; greater job and income security; a more equitable pay structure by reducing arbitrary wage determinations by management; and protection from the unilateral authority of management. Unions can be classified into industrial and craft unions. The industrial union represents the majority of workers in an industry or firm regardless of their occupations, and a craft union only represents workers in a single occupational group.

Transport labour unions are unions whose members work for transport carriers (for example airlines, railroads and truck carriers), ports and terminals (sea and air), government and other employers in the provision of passenger and freight transportation services. Transport labour unions tend to be organized as craft unions. In the United States airline pilots are represented by the Air Line Pilots Association (ALPA), flight attendants by the Association of Flight Attendants (AFA) and mechanics by the International Association of Machinists (IAM). Union railroad workers belong to the craft unions: the Brotherhood of Maintenance of Way Employees (BMWE), the Transportation Communications Union (TCU), the Brotherhood of Locomotive Engineers (BLE) and the United Transportation Union (UTU) that represents conductors. By contrast, truck carriers bargain almost entirely with the craft union, the International Brotherhood of Teamsters, which represents truck drivers. At United States East Coast **seaports**, union dockworkers belong to the International Longshoremen's Association (ILA) and at West Coast seaports they belong to the International Longshore and Warehouse Union (ILWU).

The bargaining power of a transport labour union relative to that of its employer is partly affected by the extent and the role of government intervention in the provision of transportation service. The economic regulation of transport carriers, for example, provides the opportunity for carrier unions to bargain for higher wages than in a deregulated environment. By government regulators allowing regulated transport carriers to maintain a stated return on investment, higher wage costs may be passed forward to transport users in the form of higher passenger fares and freight rates. Further, entry restrictions may provide regulated carriers with above-normal profits that may be used to finance higher wage costs. In the United States, the real hourly wages of union truck drivers were 15.8 per cent less and the real weekly wages of union railroad engineers were 11.6 per cent less in the post-**deregulation** period.

An exception to the argument that the real wages of transport labour unions are lower in a deregulated than in a regulated environment is the case of United States dockworkers. The United States Shipping Act of 1984 deregulated ocean transportation service by shipping lines in United States waters. Following passage of the Act, competition among container shipping lines intensified and container rates soon declined. A by-product of shipping **deregulation** has been its effect on seaport dockworkers. The significant growth in containerized cargo from lower container rates and major seaport capital improvements and expansions lead to an increase in demand for dockworkers, which was followed by an increase in the real hourly wages of union dockworkers in the post-deregulation period.

In addition to economic regulation, government ownership and subsidization of transport carriers are also forces that potentially enhance the bargaining power of transport labour unions. Unions in the public sector may inherently have more power than in the private sector, since wages are determined within an environment in which public officials respond to public workers as an organized lobbying and voting bloc with specific interests. In the United States urban transit firms are generally owned by local governments and **subsidized** by local, state and federal governments. These firms are highly unionized, with the majority of vehicle drivers belonging to the Amalgamated Transit Union (ATU). Not only does public ownership of the transit industry lower resistance to high wage demands, but also subsidization of the industry helps to finance these demands.

Further reading
Kaufman, B.E. and J.L. Hotchkiss (2003). *The Economics of Labor Markets* (6th edn). Madison, WI: Thomson/South-Western.
Talley, W.K. (2001). Wage differentials of transportation industries: deregulation versus regulation. *Economic Inquiry* **39**, 406–29.

Wayne K. Talley

land use and transportation modelling

Land use and transportation modelling is the process by which spatial and mathematical representations of past, present and future land use and transportation phenomena are developed. These models contain key variables and relationships rather than replicating the entire structure. Land use and transportation models are used by scholars and practitioners to predict and manage future land use and transportation. Land use and transportation modelling is distinguished from land use and transportation planning.

Land use modelling, at the most fundamental level, is used to predict where people will live and work in the future. Land use modelling requires data on existing land use, planned land use, and special land use requirements or restrictions. Advances in **geographic information systems** (GIS) have made more sophisticated land use modelling possible. The land use modelling process requires the disaggregation of the planning area, the prediction of population and employment growth, the allocation of population and employment growth, and the aggregation of the planning area.

A land use modelling area usually needs to be disaggregated into smaller areas so that a more precise land use model can be constructed. These smaller areas can be identified by political boundaries, administrative processes or GIS tools. An urban land use model may represent a region with several adjacent incorporated cities or towns. Administrative processes such as those of the United States Census divide populated areas into successively smaller areas of tracts, block groups and blocks. And using GIS tools, a **land use planning** area can be divided into a grid with constant cell sizes of an acre or less.

Population growth is usually represented by households, and employment may be linked to different land uses (for example industrial, office, retail). Growth of population and employment can be endogenous or exogenous to a land use model. In endogenous growth models, growth of population and employment is predicted by the model itself, based on analyses of previous land use models, Census data, and other historical trends. In exogenous growth models, growth of population and employment are specified a priori for the entire land use modelling area and then allocated to smaller areas.

After growth has been predicted, it must be allocated to land units based on their ability to absorb that growth. A common technique for estimating the parameters allocating growth in population and employment is the use of logistic regression. The underlying log-linear model is calibrated by computing coefficients for predictors of previous population and employment growth (for example access, visibility, infill pressure, proximity to infrastructure, and public policy) and applying those coefficients to predict future growth. The resulting probabilities suggest whether a given land unit will be developed for residential or employment purposes.

Land use models based on relatively small spatial units such as grid cells or Census blocks, block groups or tracts will probably need to be aggregated up to a higher level before they will be useful for land use planning or transportation modelling. Land use planners may need to compare multiple models that have been aggregated to regional analysis zones (RAZs) to visualize the effect of different land use policies on predicted growth. Transportation modellers will need aggregated land use as well as socio-economic data (for example households and employment) as the basis for any transportation model.

Understanding differential land use necessitates effective transportation models to link people and resources. The geographic area of a transportation model consists of transportation analysis zones (TAZs) and each TAZ is characterized by socio-economic and land use variables. Although a transportation model is comprised of TAZs, the unit of analysis may be much smaller (for example individual or household). Transportation models subject land use models and transportation **networks** to the following series of trip-generating, trip-distributing, mode-splitting and network loading activities in the **four-stage traffic** framework.

The first step in this approach to transportation modelling is determining how many trips are made in the transportation planning area. A trip is made between a TAZ that produces the trip and a TAZ that attracts the trip. The context of household trip production is typically reduced to from-home-to-work, from-home-to-non-work, and all other trips. The two most common techniques for determining trip generation, regression and category analyses use similar data elements (for example households, vehicles and workers in a TAZ). Trip attraction is often estimated at the TAZ level based on the factor analytic results of travel surveys.

The distribution of trips between each zone is typically accomplished through application of one or more of three models. Growth factor models simply adjust the number of trips to and from a zone based on predicted changes in traffic volume. **Gravity models** are an adaptation of Newton's Law and base trip distribution proportionally on the population of each zone and inversely proportionally to the separation between each of the zones. The intervening opportunity model derives probabilities that an individual will stop at any of the available and comparable destinations rather than just the closest one.

Having predicted the number of trips that will be taken and their origins and destinations, the mode of travel (for example private car, public transit and common carrier) must be established. The two general types of mode split models are trip-end and trip-interchange. Trip-end models precede trip distribution and determine the percentage of trips by each mode that will begin in each TAZ. Trip-interchange models estimate the mode split for individual origin and destination TAZ pairs based on variables such as the time and cost of travel via transit versus automobile, income of traveller and purpose of trip.

The final step is assigning the trips to the transportation **network**. Because the origin and destination of many trips are not in adjacent TAZs, a route for each trip that minimizes travel time through intermediate TAZs must be identified. The basis for highway and transit trip assignment is the minimum path algorithm. The minimum path algorithm computes all possible routes for each trip and assigns the trip to the path with the shortest travel time. Transit trips are similarly assigned, but also included in the minimum path algorithm is the time it takes to walk to or between bus stops in a transit trip.

Land use and transportation modelling are iterative and recursive processes. The predicted growth in a 20-year land use model may be modelled in four increments of five years, with each successive increment building upon the previous model of population and employment. Similarly, the predicted growth in a 30-year transportation model may be modelled on the anticipated budget identified in five-year regional transportation improvement programmes. And symbiotically, transportation infrastructure depends on land use while land use depends on the **accessibility** provided by transportation infrastructure.

Ultimately, land use and transportation models suggest what is possible rather that what is preferable, and various evaluation perspectives can be used to assess model preference. A common evaluation perspective involves benefit–cost analysis. Both land use models and transportation models reflect costs (for example public services and roadway construction) and benefits (for example open space and **safety**). Other criteria, such as doing the least harm, may be applied to the environment (for example **air quality**), community facilities (for example sewer systems), society (for example neighbourhood dislocation), and hazards (for example flood control).

Further reading

Hensher, D.A. and K.J. Button (2007). Introduction. In D.A. Hensher and K.J. Button (eds), *Handbook of Transport Modelling* (2nd edn). Oxford: Elsevier.

Kaiser, E.J., D.R. Godschalk and F.S. Chapin (1995). *Urban Land Use Planning*. Chicago, IL: University of Illinois Press.

Werner, C. (1985). *Spatial Transportation Modeling*. Beverly Hills, CA: Sage.

Robert S. Done

land use planning and transport

Almost all travel stems from a derived demand, in that individuals are mostly travelling to do their activity engagements. The way individuals compose their travel is strongly influenced by the individual's daily commitments, levels of **accessibility**, and the resources they have, and the location of the activities. Adjusting activity locations will influence the origin–destination of the travel and also the individual's potential mode choice. Therefore land use and transport are interlinked.

To have an efficient and effective transport system implies getting the land use planning right; similarly planning urban development implies getting the transport access right. Superb spatial development without support of good transport planning would cause various transport, social and economic problems. For example, an excellent eco-town development that is located far away from the work and other main activity locations will increase travel distance, road **congestion** and devalue the overall eco-town benefits. On the other hand, superb transport infrastructure that is not well integrated with wider spatial development will reduce the efficiency of the whole system and create excessive and unnecessary trips. The different policy spheres and disciplines have to work together to deliver the best results for the functioning of a town or city.

There is a variety of land use planning measures available for influencing **mobility**. These range from the large-scale planning of whole settlements down to the detailed design of urban design features such as buildings and 'streetscape' features. Those measures can be considered under the following themes.

Firstly, changing the urban concentration or densification, by increasing the number of people and/or jobs per unit of land area. This affects travel behaviour by increasing the number of potential destinations are located within a geographic area, increasing the number of travel options feasible and available in the area and reducing the automobile **accessibility** to move within the area.

Secondly, initiating diversification and settlement containment, such as mix development policy. The diversification of the land uses can result in reallocations of housing, commercial and other activities together, allowing individual to carry out their activities locally.

Thirdly, improving regional accessibility. This refers to an individual site's location relative to the regional urban centre (either a central city or central business district), and the number of jobs and public services available within a given travel time in and around this area. Although regional accessibility tends to have little effect on total trip generation (the number of trips people make), it tends to have a major effect on trip length and therefore per capita vehicle travel. Polycentric development and job–housing balance policies are examples of various policies that people use in improving regional accessibility.

Fourthly, improving the overall urban structure, such as increasing the degree of centeredness and connectivity. 'Centredness' refers to the portion of employment, commercial, entertainment, and other major activities concentrated in multimodal centres, such as central business districts (CBDs), downtowns and large industrial parks. Such centres reduce the amount of travel required between destinations and are more amenable to alternative transport modes, particularly public transport. People who work in major multimodal activity centres tend to commute by **public transport** modes significantly more than those who work in more dispersed locations, and they tend to drive less for errands. Connectivity refers to the degree to which a road or path system is connected, and therefore the directness of travel between destinations. This would reduce private vehicle travel by reducing travel distances between destinations, and by improving walking and cycling access, particularly where paths provide shortcuts so that walking and cycling are more direct than driving.

Fifthly, transit-oriented development (TOD), a mixed-use residential or commercial area designed to maximize access to public transport and non-motorized transport. A typical TOD has a rail or bus station at its centre, surrounded by relatively high-density development, with progressively lower-density development spreading outwards by a quarter to half a mile, which represents pedestrian scale distances.

Sixthly, urban design features and development controls which support car-free-travel, such as **parking** supply and management, roadway design, better walking and cycling infrastructure, promoting shared space and home zones, and so on.

Interestingly, whilst the effects of the above themes on travel are generally acknowledged, the robustness of each measurement is not necessarily consistent between case studies and the exact extent of cause and effect is not conclusive. Even where results appear to show clear correspondence between indicators, this clarity does not necessarily prove a straight-forward underlying relationship. Often there is a complexity of factors involved, such as self-selectivity, culture and need issues, relating to particular people and localities involved. Nevertheless, there is a general view that the denser the urban structure, particularly when locating a mix of uses in close proximity to each other, the less the dependence on the car. Such urban forms result in densities that are high enough to support public transport services, and can encourage greater levels of walking and cycling. Neighbourhood design features that also claim to enable residents to make fewer and shorter car trips vary in scale and type. At the master planning scale, it is argued that high-density developments within existing built-up areas can enable most people to live near amenities, facilities and employment, therefore reducing the need to travel. Mixed-use developments are advocated for similar reasons. In addition, the appropriate design of the movement framework is seen as the best way to ensure that car use is limited. This means transport **networks** that are well integrated with the surrounding area, have dedicated, convenient and direct routes for **pedestrians** and cyclists, and are linked in a grid or deformed grid pattern rather than cul-de-sac configurations. They also need to be able to accommodate public transport and offer direct routes to interchanges.

Considering its effects, land use planning has been promoted as one of the main solutions in managing travel demand. However, these may take a long time to take effect. The conversion of existing building stock and neighbourhoods takes place at a slow rate of change – a typical figure for the rate of turnover of the urban fabric is 1 per cent per year. Therefore the switch from, say, a policy of minimum housing density and maximum **parking** standards, to a policy of maximum housing density and minimum parking standards, will take some years to have an effect, since a large proportion of the existing urban development will already be laid out to previous standards. On the other hand, this long-term nature implies that land use planning measures can set the physical pattern upon which **mobility** patterns are based for generations. Put another way, once good practice has been invested in, it is harder to undo. The suburbs of the early twentieth century – built to low density but before mass car ownership – have meant that car-orientation has been 'built in' to those localities for decades. This also implies that if sustainability-oriented (for example travel-minimizing) features can be 'built in' to new developments, these could be a worthwhile investment prevailing over decades to come. Moreover, while land use distribution along with the design of development may not necessarily itself cause shifts towards more sustainable travel behaviour, it can provide choice and support more sustainable behaviour.

Further reading

Litman, T. (2008). *Land Use Impacts on Transport, How Land Use Factors Affect Travel Behavior*. Victoria: Victoria Transport Policy Institute.
Marshall, S. and Y. Lamrani (2003). *Planning and Urban Mobility in Europe: Land Use Planning Measures. EU Project Report City of Tomorrow*. Brussels: European Union, PLUME Consortium.

Yusak O. Susilo

last-mile problem

The terminology 'last-mile problem' was coined in the context of liberalization of **telecommunications** markets, but it refers to a general issue, regarding all **network** industries, including more traditional transportation situations. In the logistics case, for example, it is often linked to the problem of delivery within cities after an extended trunk haul. It can also refer to multimodal transport movements, for example the difficulties of getting to a final destination by road or transit after a long flight.

The telecommunications market has long been considered a natural monopoly, because of the existence of large fixed infrastructure costs. Accordingly, telecommunication services were provided, in most countries, by public or private regulated monopolies. Historically, market entry first took place in the long-distance communications segment, in the United States. Entry was made possible by the introduction of low-cost technologies, as well as by the price-discrimination policy of the incumbent, keeping high the price of long-distance calls.

To make a long-distance service available, however, entrants need access to the infrastructure connecting the local switches to the customers' premises. The alternative of building a parallel, costly link in the 'last mile' of the network is – in general – neither privately nor socially desirable. However, the ownership of this critical link by an incumbent could allow them to prevent entry in the market, simply by refusing to interconnect.

This case is an example of what can happen when a firm owns an essential facility in a vertical industrial relationship; that is, when services or goods are produced through a series of stages: market power in a single segment of the production process may allow the acquisition of market power in some other, related segments.

To avoid this effect, access regulation is often necessary. An access is regulated when the incumbent is obliged to provide access at some specified conditions. Normally, the incumbent cannot discriminate between applicants, and receives compensation for the infrastructure usage through the payment of an access fee, the level of which is set by a public market authority.

Determining the socially optimal access fee is not easy, because of the conflicting policy goals that may drive the choice. Major objectives are:

- entry efficiency;
- allocation efficiency;
- dynamic efficiency.

An entry is efficient when the entrant firm is at least as efficient as the firms already in the market. An access fee that achieves this objective is the one determined by the efficient component pricing rule (ECPR). Under this scheme, the incumbent is compensated by the opportunity cost of providing access to a competitor. A discussion of the implications of the ECPR is not offered, but it should be noticed that, in this case, the incumbent is just indifferent between providing the service directly and allowing entry. As a consequence, entry under the ECPR does not reduce market power.

An allocation is efficient when the marginal consumer faces the marginal cost of resources usage. This would call for a marginal cost pricing rule, which is problematic because of the existence of large fixed sunk infrastructure building costs. Many regulatory norms in the United States and **European Union** state that the access fee must be cost-oriented. In practice, this entails setting the access fee on the basis of a rule like the total element long-run incremental cost (TELRIC) one, where marginal costs are estimated by an engineering model, considering the best available technology at the present time and some forecast of future demand growth.

Since these cost estimates, however, may be well below the actual historical cost borne by the incumbent, a too-low access fee would have effects similar to a partial expropriation, hampering the incumbent's incentives for building new infrastructure, or for appropriately maintaining the existing one.

Another danger, more likely to occur when the access fee is lower than the incumbent opportunity cost, final consumer services are sufficiently close substitutes, and there is asymmetric information between the incumbent and the regulator, is the emergence of sabotage behaviour. This refers to a wide class of actions that the incumbent may undertake, lowering the competitors' profit without directly affecting their own: interconnection delays, quality deterioration, imposition of inferior technical standards, and so on. Sabotage behaviour may be difficult to detect and anti-sabotage norms may be difficult to enforce.

Further reading
Laffont, J.J. and J. Tirole (2000). *Competition in Telecommunications*. Cambridge, MA: MIT Press.

Roberto Roson

leisure time mobility

Leisure time is one important factor of human contentment and well-being, together with family, friends and work. Leisure time balances work life and offers social relationships. Long-term trends in developed countries have been rising income, rising consumption per capita, a major expansion in free time and ageing populations with decent incomes, abundant leisure times and increasing confidence to travel. Leisure time activities, travelling and all leisure-related services and goods production have an important and increasing economic role. The share of consumption directed to leisure time activities, recreation, traffic, and travelling has grown throughout the last centuries.

Leisure time mobility is responsible for a significant share of trips made in passenger traffic. In many countries work trips are no longer the largest trip group, nor are they as fixed by the time of day or week as they used to be. Leisure time travelling is to a high degree car-bound, and responsible for between 40 and 50 per cent of all mileage travelled in most Western economies. Leisure time travelling is naturally also responsible for a significant share of the **environmental costs** of passenger traffic. Also, some share of environmental impacts of industrial and service production and goods transportation can be regarded to be caused by leisure time activities, services and consumption of commodities.

Both a contributing factor to and an implication of the neglect of leisure travel issues in transport policy-making and research is that any attempt to focus on leisure travel is beset at the outset with the vast problem of identifying what is meant by leisure. The term appears to encompass a variety of recreational pursuits, from going out for a walk, evening entertainment, visiting friends and relatives, day trips, and short- and long-stay breaks. Even shopping can be regarded as a leisure time activity. At the very least, a definition that clarifies the boundaries and a better documentation of the trends are necessary if policies are to be designed and targeted effectively. While the older, pedagogical discussion of free time (whereby free time is connected with leisure time) is full of normative implications, a system-theoretical view is instructive because it undertakes a revealing change in perspective. According to this perspective, actions are observed not from the viewpoints of the protagonists, but from the functional perspective of the systems. In this meaning leisure becomes a necessary 'time out' provided by social subsystems in order to save the individual from being constantly busy. Seen from this perspective, it becomes evident that it is not the content of the activity that determines what is leisure. It is far more the case that the same activity can possess different qualities for people with different role responsibilities.

No debate of any significance has taken place with respect to the development of a meaningful definition of leisure in terms of travel purpose, consequential journey characteristics, and policy approaches. The leisure journey appears to comprise all journeys that do not fall clearly into other well-established categories of commuting, business, education, escort, and sometimes other personal business and shopping. Leisure travel embraces all 'discretionary' forms of travel, regardless of the fact that not everyone regards such activities as pleasurable. Sustainable **rural transport** and **tourism** is now beginning to ascend the policy agenda; without, however, much clarification of what is meant by leisure or any understanding of the particular car-dependent attitudes associated with it. Contradictory and ambivalent attitudes and cultural issues remain inadequately acknowledged in attempts to find solutions to the special conflicts generated by leisure travel demand.

To understand leisure time travel demand in depth it is necessary to synthesize quantitative data (statistics of measurement) with behavioural indices (statistics of understanding), which means that a shift from hard scientific approaches toward softer and more socially based methods is indicated. Since leisure travel may be less influenced by such factors as **accessibility** and price elasticity as is assumed or proven to be the case with other journey purposes, psychological issues linked with the expression of identity and practical issues concerned with the timing of decison-making and journeys should take precedence. Identity, personal values, decision-making strategies and attitudes are basic influence factors of how people spend their leisure time. Leisure time mobility is deeply affected by these variables. It is only likely to be understood, and managed, if these variables are taken into account.

Further reading
Anable, J. (2002). Picnics, pets, and pleasant places: the distinguishing characteristics of leisure travel demand. In W.R. Black and P. Nijkamp (eds), *Social Change and Sustainable Transport*. Bloomington, IN: Indiana University Press.

Stefan Poppelreuter and *Georg Rudinger*

licensing

A licence gives authority to undertake certain activities. In the field of transport, licensing is commonly a way of imposing **safety** or other quality controls. Thus it is necessary to hold a driving licence to be permitted to drive a vehicle, and individual vehicles must be licensed to be allowed to be driven on the roads. Within the **European Union**, road transport operators are required to hold an operator's licence, and with the liberalization of the rail industry has come a Directive requiring all train operating companies to be licensed.

However, licensing may be used as a way of controlling access to the market for reasons other than safety. During the 1930s, it became widely accepted that in the transport field free access in the market led to wasteful or destructive competition; wasteful because it created excessive capacity with resultant low load factors, and destructive because charges were driven down to short-run variable costs, leading to losses and bankruptcies. At the same time the rapid growth of road transport was causing major financial problems for the rail mode, and many commentators believe that this was the real reason for the spread of controls on road transport. For whatever reason, in many countries around the world, licensing systems were introduced whereby it was necessary to have a licence to operate transport services. For instance, in Britain, under the 1930 Road Traffic Act it became necessary to have a route licence to operate a bus service. The licence specified the route, the timetable and the fares, and to change any of these required application to the public authority responsible for administering the system, the Traffic Commissioners. To obtain a licence it was necessary to satisfy the Traffic Commissioners that it was in the public interest; generally if there was an adequate existing service they would conclude that this was not the case. For road haulage, it was necessary to have an A or B licence to carry goods for third parties; C licences that permitted carriage of goods on own account were freely available. Most European countries had similar systems, and to operate international road haulage or bus services required acquisition of a permit for each country visited en route.

Britain became one of the first countries to remove the use of licensing as a way of controlling the quantity of transport supplied to the market as opposed to the quality of the operators; restrictive licensing of road goods vehicles was removed under the 1968 Transport Act, and of long-distance and local bus services under the Transport Acts of 1980 and 1985 respectively. Liberalization of international road haulage became a priority of the European Commission as an important ingredient of the integration of European markets, and is now virtually complete. However, most countries still have licensing systems designed to restrict entry to the local bus sector.

Licensing systems may also be used as a way of restricting the number of private cars entering a particular area in order to reduce **congestion**. Such a scheme is referred to as a supplementary licensing system, whereby in addition to the regular licence a supplementary licence must be purchased and displayed on the vehicle to be entitled to drive in a particular area and at a particular time of day. This approach to congestion charging was used in Singapore for many years, but has since been superseded there by electronic road pricing, and the latter approach, or approaches based on automated number plate recognition as in London, are now the norm for congestion charging.

Further reading
Button, K.J. (1984). *Road Haulage Licensing and EC Transport Policy*. Aldershot: Gower.
Dodgson, J.S. and N. Topham (eds) (1988). *Bus Deregulation and Privatisation: An International Perspective*. Aldershot: Avebury.
Glaister, S. and C. Mulley (1983). *The Public Control of the British Bus Industry*. Aldershot: Gower.

Christopher Nash

Lill's law of travel

Eduard Lill was an Austrian military and civilian Austrian mathematician and engineer during the middle of the nineteenth century. At the Paris World Exhibition of 1867 he presented an auxiliary apparatus for the solving of non-linear equations and a pantograph, and in the same year published articles in which he presented a graphical technique for the determination of the roots of algebraic equations. In 1889 *The Basic Laws of Passenger Transportation* appeared, in which he formulated his 'law of travel', which was refined and extended in subsequent publications. Lill's law of travel provides a **gravity model** including intervening opportunities. It says that trips $T(i)$ from a city (i) decrease with distances x to other stations according to a hyperbolic curve, 1, x, $T(i) = M(i) / x$ where $M(i)$ is the trip value, based on the size and other qualities of the city. The trips from an originating city and to a specific city and its station (j) at the distance $x(j)$ are calculated as the difference between the probability $P(j - 1)$ of stopping at the station (j) and to the probability $P(j + 1)$ of passing the station, $P(j) = P(j - 1) - P(j + 1)$ Trips $t(i, j)$ between (i) and (j) are derived as $t(i, j) = M(i) s(j) / x(j) 2$ where $s(j)$ is the station distance for the city (j) in relation to surrounding stations.

Lill's graphical solutions for equations have been applied by the Italian mathematician Margherita Piazzolla Beloch in the context of the solution of cubic and quartic equations by paper-folding. Lill's law of travel did not play an important role in the study of transportation up until the 1950s, when models for calculating trip distribution based on it were developed, known later as the intervening opportunity model and the competing opportunity model. In 1969 an English translation of *The Law of Travel and its Application to Rail Traffic* was published and then Lill's work became increasingly significant to the development of geographic models of spatial interaction. Gunnarsson calls Lill one of the 'pioneers in travel modelling', and his work 'fundamental'. Besides that, Lill's graphical works of railway statistics are true masterpieces of painting.

Further reading
Gunnarsson, O. (2000). Studies in travel behaviour and mobility management need a special scientific discipline: 'Mobilistics'. *IATSS Research* **24**, 69–75.
Lill, E. (1891). *The Law of Travel and its Application to Rail Traffic* (translated by L. Hoppner in 1969), Harvard Papers in Theoretical Geography: Geography and the Properties of Surfaces. Number 25. Cambridge, MA: Harvard Graduate School of Design,

Bernhard Hachleitner

location and transport

From the earliest writings on industrial location by Alfred Weber, transportation costs have been listed as one of the prime factors in determining optimal facility location; the others include labour costs, and savings due to agglomeration economies. In the case of industrial location, the desire to avoid costly transportation pushes the factory towards the site of the raw material source, the market location, or in some cases to intermediate transhipment positions. The following, in brief, are the conditions leading to these various outcomes: if a raw material loses weight during processing, it makes sense to process the material close to the source, for example smelting near a mine; to the extent that a finished product requires special handling or gains weight or bulk from the addition of ubiquitous inputs (for example water) during manufacture, it makes sense to locate near a market (for example cement plants, or bottling facilities where syrup is added to water). If a shipment has to be interrupted as a result of physical mode change, there may be advantages to making some processing steps at the same time as the transhipment. Optimal intermediate locations occur at break-of-bulk terminals, for example milling at a lake shore transfer point when transhipment or **intermodal** handling gives an advantage to these places.

The interaction of facility location and transportation also arises in the derivation of optimal locations for warehouses, distribution centres, and freight terminals and hubs. In the United States, several regional gateways have developed by exploiting their position as preferred points of access to road, rail or water transportation. Atlanta, Georgia, comes to mind as the quintessential crossroads in many modes of land transportation. This region's advantage for truck transport also makes it ideal for positioning distribution centres, logistical supply points and service centres for trucking equipment. Another area, the Ohio River Valley (between say Louisville and Pittsburgh) is centrally located in the United States, providing excellent **accessibility** to the nation, and is the site of many air express hubs (UPS in Louisville, DHL in Cincinnati, and Emery Air Freight in Dayton). Globally, other examples of **hubs** include Subic Bay (Philippines), Frankfort (Germany) and Anchorage (Alaska).

In viewing facility location as an optimization problem, one naturally focuses on areas where the overall lowest costs are found. If the objective function of such a problem can be expressed in terms of continuous convex functions, classical optimization techniques can be used to devise the conditions to be satisfied by the location at optimality; an iterative process called the Weiszfeld procedure is used to solve simple cases. The so-called centre of gravity of the points has mistakenly been thought to solve the Weber problem; it does not. It is known that for problems such as the Weber problem, the objective increases fairly slowly as one moves away from the minimum cost area. The contours or so-called 'isodapanes' describing lines of equal transport costs could be used to zero in on the low-cost regions; this is known as a 'site generation' problem.

Alternatively, and more likely in practical application, the list of potential commercial feasible sites or regions is preset, and the analyst performs a comparison of the costs for various solutions; this is known as a 'site selection' problem. The field of locational analysis has a long history, and the methods used today, while more computerized and analytical, survive from foundations well known from the earliest years of the twentieth century. If the problem is set up with a linear objective function, and inequality constraints, powerful integer programming techniques can be put to use to devise simultaneous facility location, routing and supply region planning for complex multifacility problems.

Intermodal facilities are a modern phenomenon, at a scale unimaginable in previous centuries. The major **intermodal** facility in Brampton, Ontario, for example, combines transfer from rail to truck, and very extensive warehouse and distribution capabilities. The location of facilities near such points of extraordinary transport access has also been observed as an emerging trend: it makes sense to stockpile specialized parts, pharmaceuticals and emergency supplies at points of high connectivity such as air express hubs.

It is perhaps easiest to appreciate the role of transport in location whenever new linkages are opened or new modes connect markets. Thus, new roads and interchanges confer added **accessibility** to places that in turn become preferred locations for retail as well as industrial activities needing highway access. Conversely, the critical importance of transportation flow to the effective operation of industrial and distribution **supply-chains** emerges at those times when conventional systems break under extreme stress. It is apparent that ports are the throughput locations for extraordinary quantities of material moved from source to sink (for example production in the Pacific Rim moves into the United States through Los Angeles). Thus, cargo handling and **intermodal** facilities are the basing point for immense flows of materials to industrial centres. These systems periodically grind to a halt, stranding tons of produce and seasonal commodities when a strike causes a backlog at these ports.

Transport and location can be priced in analytical terms by devising a 'cost per unit of flow' coefficient C_{ij} that links source i to sink j. That cost coefficient can be a constant, or can exhibit various rate-breaks for longer hauls while preserving an analytically convenient linear model. Once the rates begin to exhibit flow-based economies of scale, however, more complex objective functions and model formulations could be anticipated. In fact the optimal location literature has become quite sophisticated and can handle all manner of cost functions, including fixed charges, multilevel distribution systems and logical constraints such as those required by capacity or infrastructure limitations. In any event, tapering freight rates with respect to distance or to bulk discounts, as always in the fundamental logic of cost minimization, encourage the user to make extensive use of the cheap input (bulk, long-distance freight) while economizing on the expensive input.

Transportation, so far, has been primarily viewed as moving products to, from and between factories, with a view to providing connections between sources and sinks; but transport and location are intermeshed in other ways. The collection of grain from spatially distributed growing regions into grain elevators (silos), and ultimately for transhipment to bulk freight, opens yet another spatial analytical question: what facilities are chosen to serve which parts of the growing region? Originally these areal allocations could be constructed as hinterland or supply regions using Thiessen polygons or Voronoi diagrams, but increasingly one has to consider the equilibration of delivered price and the spatial variations in rates and costs. Furthermore, as in the case of industrial location, there are issues of simultaneity that can make this problem quite challenging. As one opens transport corridors, the ability to grow or harvest material for supply to certain locations becomes more apparent. Thus, a new linkage can make some areas, once thought to be unsuited to supply urban markets, profitable places from which to procure supplies. In the case of perishable commodities such as fruits and dairy products, and extensive literature on the optimal location of processing plants arose in the mid-twentieth century. These methods are now entrenched in the basic analysis of the preferred location and source and sizing of multi-plant firms.

No review of transport and location would be complete without mention of the importance of the perspective from which the questions concerning efficiency are asked. For a consumer, one looks to the source or factory from which the material can be procured at least cost, including freight charges. For the agents arranging or providing the transportation services, the question becomes one of finding the best mode to achieve the desired movement of commodities within the requisite time and service standard. Clearly the price set for such a service must be determined in the context of competition, regulation and the intrinsic amount of effort needed to overcome the spatial separation. Such markets will only emerge when the value of the goods shipped warrants the transaction costs. For the firm considering the logistical implementation of its locational layout, it has to be said that it is interested both in the current ability to reach markets from fixed distribution centres, or sources, and in analysing the potential savings from rearrangements of these systems. If the plants in a multiplant firm are to be examined from the point of view of their transportation efficiency, then one gets into the trade-off between the fixed costs of the facility and the obvious lowering of the size of catchment areas as the number of such facilities increase. At some stage the optimal mix of number, size and location of plants to optimize facility costs can be achieved, and there exist powerful analytical modelling tools for making such optimizations.

Further reading
Drezner, Z. and H.W. Hamcher (eds) (2002). *Facility Location: Applications and Theory*. Berlin: Springer.
Love, R.F., J.G. Morris and G.O. Wesolowsky (1988). *Facilities Location: Models and Methods*. New York: North-Holland.
Weber, A. (1929). *Theory of the Location of Industries*. Translated with an introduction and notes by Carl J. Friedrich. Chicago, IL: University of Chicago Press.

Morton E. O'Kelly

location-based services

Location-based services (LBS) are the new face of the wireless Internet. LBS – sometimes called location-based mobile services (LBMS) – are an emerging technology combining information technology, **geographical information systems** (GIS), positioning technology, **intelligent transportation systems** (ITS) technology and the Internet. LBS combine hardware devices, wireless communication **networks**, geographic information and software applications that provide location-related guidance for customers. They differ from mobile position determination systems, such as global positioning systems (GPS) in that LBS provide much broader, application-oriented location services, such as:

'You are about to join a ten-kilometre traffic queue, turn right on Washington Street, one kilometer ahead.'
'Help, I'm having a heart attack!' or 'Help, my car has broken down!'
'I need to buy a dozen roses and a birthday cake. Where can I buy the least expensive ones while spending the minimum amount of time on my way home from the office?'

One consulting firm predicted that by 2005, the LBS market would reach $11–$15 billion in revenue and as many as 1 billion Internet-enabled handsets would be in use. While the market for LBS seems to be rapidly emerging and many services have been introduced to the market, there remain issues that have yet to be researched and developed to provide efficient services for users and providers. To appreciate the diversity and common framework elements of location-based services, a sample set of scenarios has been compiled below.

Disasters are unforeseeable events that can happen in many different ways and take many different forms including incidents such as earthquake, flood, terrorist attack, tornado, cyclone, nuclear explosion, forest fire, toxic contamination of the environment such as a nuclear plant leak or a train derailment involving toxic product containers. When faced with a disaster situation, quick and efficient reaction times are essential to save lives and minimize propagation of the disaster.

LBS can enable the people working around a problem to communicate with each other critical information such as: what are the regions affected, what are the restricted areas, what facilities are still useful, to what extent they are being used, how many injured people there are in a specific area, what kind of emergency workers are needed, and a priority order for target areas. In short, a large quantity of diverse information could be shared. The information can be available in real time to the emergency workers, the rescue teams and the control centre, thus eliminating the delays that would otherwise occur.

LBS can provide a means for locating and rescuing people hiking or travelling in mountainous regions who may have lost their way, been injured or be suffering from sudden health problems. In a wider sense, LBS as a navigation tool and geographic information broker can also prevent such situations. This includes people being guided along safe hiking paths, being guided to mountain hotels and to other important points of interest, and being warned about dangerous precipices and so on.

A traveller would like to go from some origin, not necessarily where they currently are, to some destination, given certain constraints and/or requirements, which could be fuzzily or well defined, static or dynamic. The traveller could be a person, with or without transport, with the ability to make decisions; or an object being sent through a system, such as a parcel or freight, without any intelligence, but which either people monitor or this is done automatically.

A specific scenario for an application of location-based services that expands upon the intelligent routing scenario is the case of a visually impaired or **elderly** traveller using individual and/or **public transport**. Such applications typically propose to increase efficiently the **mobility** of visually impaired **pedestrians**, particularly in an unknown urban environment. To achieve this aim a combination of pre-journey planning and journey positioning and routing is required. Travel planning as well as navigation has to meet the special needs of visually impaired people in choosing an optimal route, being guided along the route and being informed about objects in the vicinity whilst en route. As an essential component of the system, visual sensors and the use of a digital three-dimensional (3D) city model can fill the gap in the disabled persons' perceptual capabilities by supporting conventional satellite-based and terrestrial positioning sensors, by identifying large obstacles on the pavement (sidewalk), and by recognizing important warning and information signs.

Location-based services can assist travellers to solve their routing problems by providing them with real-time traffic conditions, real-time public transport vehicle locations, and pedestrian navigation instructions. Considering the case of a traveller who would like to use public transport for their journey, the traveller may require a LBS to:

- determine an appropriate mode and/or route for their journey;
- restrict their journey to include or exclude a particular mode and/or route of transport that they wish to use or not to use;

- assist them to plan a trip, or investigate trip alternatives prior to travelling; or
- provide timetable look-up information for a nearby stop or station.

Tracking can be triggered by some event or by the passage of time, depending on the scenario. For example, a natural disaster event could trigger tracking of the disaster and its modelling so that people in areas likely to be affected could be warned. On a less dramatic scale, the tracking of public transport vehicles and passengers could be used to help passengers choose alternative routes if vehicles are delayed. The form of tracking position would vary depending on the object or person being tracked, and could be a position or coordinate in a particular reference system, address or affected area or polygon extents.

Further reading
Kim, T.J. (2004). Multi-modal routing and navigation cost functions for location-based services (LBS). In L. Der-Horng (ed.), *Urban and Regional Transportation Modeling: Essays in Honor of David Boyce*. Cheltenham, UK and Northampton, MA, USA: Edward Elgar.

Ostensen, O. (2001). The expanding agenda of geographic information standards. Geneva, *ISO Bulletin*, July.

VanderMeer, J. (2001). Location content drives wireless telecommunications. http://www.geoplace.com/bg/2001/0201/0201pay.asp.

Tschangho John Kim

logistics

The term 'logistics' originates from the French term *logis*, meaning the quarters of the forces, and covers all operations which are necessary for the movement and maintenance of the military. Against this background logistics has a long history. Its significance has particularly increased since the early 1990s, as in the first Gulf War a huge amount of material and troops had to be moved in short time-frames. Now, in all areas of life logistics plays an important role.

In general logistics describes a system of transformation of objects in space and time. Logistics can involve the movement of people as well as the shipping of goods, and information as well as materials. Logistic processes are associated with organizing resource flows (material, goods, persons and so on), information flows (information about the resources in real time) and transaction flows (for example money transfer). Following a functional point of view, logistics include three main functions: transport, handling and storage. The main characteristics of logistic systems are the conjunction of movement and storage, which originates **networks** between nodes and edges according to three main structures. In a single-level logistic system the goods flow is directed between the shipper and the recipient. In a multilevel logistic system the flow is organized in an indirect way, going through a consolidation or a break bulk point. Combined systems are also possible.

At the macro level logistics covers all logistic systems of a national economy, also referred to as macroeconomics. One example is the freight traffic system within a national economy. It consists of nodes (ports, airports, freight yards and villages, and so on) and edges (transport infrastructure). The material and goods flows take place on the edges, connecting the nodes. Thus one of the main drivers of a freight traffic system is the spatial division of labour. The main actors are the freight forwarders and logistics providers who offer the logistics and transportation services, also public authorities, particularly state and municipalities that provide the transport infrastructure.

On the micro level logistics covers all logistic systems of individual economic units, mostly in terms of microeconomics. Examples are military logistics, business logistics or logistics of other institutions (aid organizations, public authorities like hospitals, administrations and so on) or households. The main actors are the sender and the recipient of a shipment. In this context, three main definitions of logistics exist: a flow-oriented, a service-oriented and a life-cycle-oriented definition.

The flow-oriented definition is adapted from the system-based philosophy of logistics. Logistic systems consist of elements and flows between these elements and describe systems where processes of transformation in time and/or space take place. In this sense logistics not only means the change between at least two addresses (transport), or the change in time (storage) but also includes the processes once changing the quantity or the composition of an object (handling). According to a very broad definition logistics includes the changing of form of materials or goods (production) also.

Initially, business logistics functions that emerged in the 1960s included warehousing, materials handling and industrial handling activities within a company. The main cost drivers were transport and inventory costs. The flow-based perspective concentrated on the physical distribution system of outbound logistics, because normally the value of a finished good is higher, analysed from a cost perspective.

At that time logistics consisted of the functions of purchasing (demand forecasting, purchasing, requirements and production planning, manufacturing inventory) as well as of the functions of distribution (finished goods inventory, distribution planning, order processing, transportation, customer service), these being highly fragmented from each other.

In the course of **deregulation** and liberalization of trade and transport, inbound logistics gained in importance and added the inbound logistics to the outbound logistics. The combination of inbound and outbound transportation means that the sourcing of material and supplies all over the world is cheaper and easier than before.

Between the 1980s and 1990s the service-oriented understanding of logistics was gaining even more importance. Inbound and outbound logistics actually became merged, due to the rise of the value concept. Its main idea is that the inbound and outbound logistics provide a value for the firm's customers. Logistics thus became enlarged by the so-called value-added-services (labelling, finishing and so on). Because of its cross-sectional orientation and process view, the extended range of tasks as well as the growing understanding of logistics, the term '**supply-chain** management' was established.

The American logistics society (Council of Supply-Chain Management Professionals, CSCMP) defines logistics management as a part of supply-chain management: 'Logistics management is that part of supply-chain management that plans, implements, and controls the efficient, effective forward and reverse flow and storage of goods, services and related information between the point of origin and the point of consumption in order to meet customers' requirements.'

Not least through the 'carbon footprint' concept, the life-cycle-oriented definition has received increasing attention. This product-based view considers the life cycle of a product from the cradle to the grave. In the past this mostly concentrated on resources and the impact on the environment of the product and the production process. Since the awareness of **climate change** and resource constraints has increased considerably, logistics processes aim at paying attention to the full life cycle of a product.

These three definitions reveal that there is no 'one and only' definition of logistics. Mostly, the definitions describe different concepts of how to manage the flow of materials and information between logistic nodes, actors or stages from the cradle to the grave of a product. The objectives of the different management tasks and strategies vary between cost, quality of service and environmental performance.

Logistics ensures that required resources are positioned in the right quantity and right quality at the right time, the right place – and to the right price. Logistics has to provide a service function within the context of time and space, or, in other words, regarding both economy and ecology. Over recent years the targets of logistics management may have shifted from economic scores to more comprehensive success factors, particularly sustainability. That means that the efficient use of resources and the environment as well as the conditions of labour and the society are being considered, besides profit maximization and the long-term well-being of the company.

Business logistics in trade or production implies the designing, planning, implementing, controlling and verifying functions of all processes related to the movement of goods and the associated flow of transactions and information, including the producer (importer and so on), the distributor (wholesaler, retailer, and so on) and the customer, and also the backward functions. As a consequence of technological advancements, the information flow determines the actual flow of goods. This can be a pre-information flow, for example the order placed by a customer, an accompanied information flow, for example a delivery note, or a post-information flows, for example customer invoice.

Following a more traditional functional perspective, business logistics provides a service function for the procurement, production, distribution and disposal of commodities. Recently the logistics of spare parts, redistribution, or reverse logistics, and recycling have moved into focus. The phase-specific, functional subsystems of physical logistic systems follow the different sequences of the goods flow from the sourcing market and the production processes towards the sales market, and vice versa.

The first phase is the procurement logistics, which is directly connected with the distribution logistics of the supplier. Procurement logistics has a supply function for the whole company, so the sourcing strategy is its main object. Procurement logistics covers the goods flow of raw, auxiliary and operating materials as well as the flow of all kinds of commodities and spare parts directed towards the receiving store. Due to new utilization concepts, for example life extension of products by maintenance or repair, intensified utilization of goods by rent, lease or share, the spare part supply is becoming increasingly important.

The second phase consists of the production or manufacturing logistics. It organizes the internal material flow between the receiving store and the production unit to the finished product storage of the considered company. The production logistics depends on the organizational structure of the production process itself. The main objectives are to fulfil the order in the least lead-time, at a minimum of total costs and at the highest possible quality.

The third phase includes the distribution logistics and is directly connected with the procurement logistics of the customer or with the end-customer itself. Central to distribution logistics is the supply of an external customer (often) with the finished goods. The main subject of distribution logistics is the transportation and **network** design.

The redistribution logistics covers all return flows and the disposal as well as the reverse logistics. Disposal logistics includes the disposal and recycling of containers, valuable materials, finished products and waste. The reverse logistics covers all flows of used or unsold products. Circulation economy and new utilization concepts make additional demands on logistics, such as concerning the treatment of defective electronic modules. In the context of spare parts and repair, redistribution or reverse logistics are continually gaining importance – that is, if this is to be seen as a category distinct from procurement logistics.

These fields of action reveal that the application of logistics is closely intertwined with other fields of management. Thus logistics ought to be understood as a cross-sectional function within company management. However, in recent years the focus has shifted from an end-customer view of consumption to utilization, and to the treatment of goods and information after utilization. In doing so, logistics is situated in between goods preparation through the production processes – extraction, manufacturing and processing processes – and the goods utilization – in companies, institutions and households. It covers the supply and the transfer processes as well as the return processes. In the framework of this comprehensive definition, the logistics system plays an exceptionally important role in service provision, for related costs and regarding the impact of production concepts and trade strategies on the environment.

Further reading
Coyle, J.J., E.J. Bardi and C.J. Langley (2003). *The Management of Business Logistics. A Supply-chain Perspective* (7th edn). Madison, WI: South-Western Thomason Learning.
Pfohl, H.-C. (2004). *Logistiksysteme. Betriebswirtschaftliche Grundlagen* (7th edn). Berlin: Springer.

Heike Flämig

low-cost airlines

There is no single definition of low-cost airlines, although this generally refers to a situation where an airline operator has lower costs compared to traditional scheduled, full-service airline operators. Low-cost carriers (LCCs) are sometimes referred to as 'no-frills' operators. Airline operators may offer tickets at a reduced rate on particular routes from time to time, but this does not necessarily mean that they are low-cost airlines. Low-cost carriers emerged in the United States in the 1970s with the specific aim of operating with a lower cost structure than traditional operators, as a means of offering lower fares. The concept was initiated by PSA in California although now Southwest Airlines, established in Texas in 1971, the market leader in the United States, operates 500 aircraft, carrying close to 100 million passengers a year.

The concept proved to be viable both financially and operationally for short-haul operations, and as such Europe experienced a growth in LCCs from the mid-1990s onwards. This phenomenon originated in the United Kingdom and Ireland with the establishment of easyJet and Ryanair. A sympathetic economic regulatory framework was conducive to the development of these low-cost airlines, as was consumer demand. In addition, entrepreneurs namely Stelios Haji-Ioannou (easyJet) and the Ryan family and Michael O'Leary (Ryanair) were instrumental, as was underutilized airport capacity, and the privatized, commercialized United Kingdom airports' keenness to attract low-cost airlines by offering attractive airport charges, so as to benefit from increased passenger spend at the airports' retail outlets.

According to the European agency responsible for air navigation (EUROCONTROL) the market share of LCCs in Europe was 19.5 per cent of air passenger kilometres in May 2007, with a two-percentage-point increase per year being the average. Low-cost airlines have lower costs than traditional operators by undertaking a number of strategies, most notably:

- The operation of one type of aircraft. This affords economies in aircraft maintenance, training and flexibility in terms of crew utilization.
- The efficient utilization of their aircraft, for example by faster turnaround times. This is achieved by using uncongested secondary airports, by not carrying cargo which is time-consuming with respect to loading and unloading, no on-board catering facilities (or passengers having to pay for food and drink), and, in the case of a number of operators, by not having seating allocations, resulting in a speedier check-in process.
- The use of alternative airports rather than the hub airports. As well as the uncongested nature of these airports, they invariably charge operators less for landing their aircraft.
- Operating a single class with no business class seats. This means that more passengers can be carried, with fewer cabin crew required in attendance.
- Lower rates of employee unionization, which impacts on the airlines' pay structure.
- Offering a point-to-point service with no connections.
- Cost savings by selling tickets directly to their customers, rather than through travel agents, thus avoiding the payment of commission. The use of Internet booking and e-ticketing is a strategy which has been adopted throughout the sector in recent years.

Individual LCCs differ in terms of these features. For example, some low-cost airlines will allocate seats or operate more than one type of aircraft. Increasingly many aspects of low-cost operators are being adopted by the traditional carriers: aspects such as the use of e-ticketing and no meal service.

While the target for low-cost airlines has been the price-elastic leisure market, they have also attracted business users. This has placed pressure on the scheduled airlines to lower their fares. Some of the low-cost operators have been established 'from scratch' such as Ryanair and easyJet, while others have been set up as subsidiaries of existing companies, keen on obtaining a share of the low-cost market. These have included companies such as Ted which is part of United Airlines (United States) and bmibaby part of bmi (United Kingdom). In this situation the degree of cost minimization is dependent on the cost structure inherited from the parent airline, not least in terms of fleet make-up and employee union agreements. In terms of the future, this is likely to be one of consolidation, with traditional airline operators responding to the LCCs by cutting their costs or setting up their own low-cost subsidiaries.

Further reading

EUROCONTROL (2008). Low cost carrier market update, June 2007. Accessed at: www.eurocontrol.int/statfor/gallery/content/public/analysis/LowCostMark etUpdateJun07_V01.pdf.

Francis, G., I. Humphreys, S. Ison and M. Aicken (2006). Where next for low cost airlines? A spatial and temporal comparative study. *Journal of Transport Geography* **14**, 83–94.

Stephen Ison

M

marginal social cost pricing practice

Existing pricing practice in the transport sector rarely starts with a calculation of marginal social cost. In the roads sector, charges are usually
levied through a combination of annual vehicle licensing charges, fuel tax
and tolls on selected roads. Tolls are most frequently based on the need
to finance the road in question. Where public transport is provided on a
purely commercial basis, charges are obviously designed to cover costs,
although where **yield management** methods are used to price according to
the strength of demand for particular services this may achieve an outcome
not too far from that of marginal cost pricing by ensuring that empty
seats are filled wherever someone is willing to pay even a small amount
to travel. Regulated public transport fares are set according to a variety
of criteria: social, political and public acceptability as well as economic
efficiency.

It is in the roads sector that proposals for the implementation of marginal social cost pricing have been most common as a way of coping with
the problem of **congestion**, and something approaching the principle has
been adopted in a small number of cities (it should be noted that where
prices are set on the basis of a social **benefit–cost analysis**, then the optimal
will be marginal social cost-based pricing even if this is not explicitly given
as the objective of the pricing policy). Since the marginal social cost of congestion varies substantially in time and place, nationally set tax rates are
not capable of reflecting it in charges. The first city to move in the direction
of congestion charging was Singapore, which initially adopted a simple
paper-based supplementary charge for driving into the city, but later went
for an electronic version able to cope with more sophisticated variation of
charges in time and space. Within Europe a number of Norwegian cities
implemented tolls for entering the city centre, but these were calculated to
raise funds for investment. It was London in 2003 and Stockholm a few
years later which were the first European cities to implement road pricing
in the form of a charge to enter the city centre with the explicit aim of
reducing congestion; the general perception is that these measures have
been broadly successful, with a 20 per cent reduction in traffic and a larger
reduction of congestion in both instances.

Marginal social cost pricing has also been influential in transport pricing
policy at the European level, since 1998, when the European Commission
published a White Paper proposing its phased introduction on all modes
of transport infrastructure. A Directive in 2001 stated that charges for the

use of rail infrastructure by operators should be based on the direct cost of operating the train in question (which is widely interpreted as marginal cost), and could include explicit charges for **environmental** costs and for the use of scarce capacity. Since then, a number of countries (including Britain, Sweden, Finland, Austria and Switzerland) have undertaken research on the measurement of marginal social cost in order to implement this Directive. By contrast, the Directive on charges for heavy goods vehicles agreed in 2006 still ties average charges to average infrastructure cost excluding **externalities**, although it does allow charges to be varied with vehicle type according to the environment, **congestion** and accident costs. There is a particular issue in heavy goods vehicle charging in that wear and tear costs are an important component of marginal social cost and they vary with vehicle characteristics in a way not well reflected in relative fuel consumption. Switzerland, Germany and Austria have already implemented systems of charging heavy goods vehicles for the distance they travel, using a variety of technologies; and a number of countries, including Britain, Sweden and the Netherlands, are looking at nationwide road pricing systems either just for heavy goods vehicles or for all vehicles.

Further reading

Niskanen, E. and C. Nash (2008). Road pricing in Europe: a review of research and practice. In C. Jensen-Butler, B. Sloth, M.M. Larsen, B. Madsen and O.A. Nielsen (eds), *Road Pricing, the Economy and the Environment.* Berlin: Springer.

Verhoef, E. (2008). Road transport pricing: motivation, objectives and design from an economic perspective. In E. Verhoef, M. Bliemer, L. Steg and B. van Weeds (eds), *Pricing in Road Transport: A Multi-disciplinary Perspective.* Cheltenham, UK and Northampton, MA, USA: Edward Elgar.

Christopher Nash

marginal social cost pricing theory

Economic theory shows that in a first-best world in which all the conditions for Pareto optimality are met, price should be equal to marginal social cost for all commodities. In this case, since costs represent the compensation needed for those incurring them to do so willingly, with marginal social cost pricing those users who value their use above the costs they impose by adding to traffic flows will travel. Those who value their use below that cost will not travel or will use some alternative means. Consequently, when expanding traffic to the level implied by marginal social cost pricing, users could fully compensate all those bearing costs by the move and still be better off. Similarly if traffic were currently at a higher level than that implied by this principle, those suffering the costs of the higher level of traffic would be able to compensate marginal users fully for giving up their journeys and still be better off. Key applications of this principle in the transport literature are Hotelling on rail and Walters on roads.

To ensure optimal use of existing infrastructure, prices should be based on those costs that will be incurred by adding additional traffic to a constant infrastructure – in other words, short-run marginal cost pricing. Thus, three components of cost for the addition of extra traffic to the existing infrastructure need to be measured: firstly, the extra maintenance, renewals and operating cost imposed by additional use on the infrastructure provider; secondly, the marginal cost imposed on other infrastructure users, in terms of delays, and opportunity costs of slots on those modes where there is a physical limit to the number of slots available; and thirdly, the cost imposed outside the transport system; that is, mainly **environmental** cost, but also any other costs such as accidents, where these are borne in part by the police or health service and not recovered from users.

The same sort of approach may be taken to scheduled transport services. When traffic is added to these, there are three possible results: load factors rise, or larger vehicles or longer trains are operated, or services are increased. In the first two cases marginal costs to the operator are far below average costs; in the third, there is a benefit to existing users from a better service as traffic rises. In each case, marginal social cost is likely to be below average cost, except where capacity constraints (for example track capacity) bind, and an unsubsidized competitive outcome will not be optimal.

One factor that many people find unacceptable about short-run marginal cost pricing is that it totally ignores the capital costs of expanding the system. There is an alternative, long-run marginal cost pricing, which charges the costs imposed by the extra traffic when the infrastructure is optimally adjusted to the new traffic level. This will therefore include marginal capital costs, but compared with short-run marginal cost the **congestion** cost, and possibly some of the other external costs, will be reduced. It is easy to show that if capacity is optimally adjusted, then short-run marginal cost and long-run marginal cost are equal. There is therefore only an issue between the two as a basis for charging when capacity is not always optimally adjusted to demand.

There are many reasons why pure marginal social cost pricing may not be a sensible policy in practice. These include the fact that it may lead to deficits if marginal cost is less than average cost, and these deficits have to be funded by distorting taxes; the presence of distortions in the price of related goods which cannot be removed; and the complexity of the resulting price structure which may be administratively expensive and difficult to understand. These lead to the need to adopt second-best pricing principles.

Further reading
Baumol, W.J. and D.F. Bradford (1970). Optimal departures from marginal cost pricing. *American Economic Review* **60**, 265–83.
Hotelling, H. (1938). The general welfare in relation to problems of taxation and of railway and utility rates. *Econometrica* **6**, 242–69.
Walters, A.A. (1961). The theory and measurement of private and social cost of highway congestion. *Econometrica* **29**, 676–99.

Christopher Nash

metro systems

Metro systems refer to heavy railway systems serving the urban areas of cities. The term 'metro' originated from the first of these systems built in London – the Metropolitan Railway (now part of London Underground). When compared to the automobiles and other means of public transport, metro systems are distinguished by their exclusive rights of way, high-capacity, high-speed and environmentally friendly characteristics. As most metro systems are built underground, they are also commonly known as undergrounds and subways. Due to their off-road nature, metro systems can play a significant role in relieving downtown traffic **congestion**. Furthermore, metro systems can release valuable road space for other uses. When used at capacity, metro systems are highly efficient. They offer frequent and high-speed services to many passengers in a short period of time. Last but not least, most metro systems are powered by electricity and, hence, neither directly consume petroleum (a non-renewable **energy** source) nor contribute to global warming and **climate change** (with carbon emissions), as most internal combustion vehicles do.

Metro development projects, however, are highly technology- and capital-intensive. The hardware and software associated with the development of a metro system are multifarious. Typically, the hardware includes the civil engineering, electrical and mechanical engineering, and electronics engineering. These technological inputs are crucial, from the early geotechnical engineering to the actual construction work and the installation of power and signalling systems. Depending on the local geology, economic situation and the complexity of the system, the reference figures for constructing a metro system ranged from $60 million to $180 million per kilometre of track in the late 1990s. These reference figures were readily exceeded by the mid-2000s. In general, the railway infrastructure alone accounted for 30 per cent to 70 per cent of the overall costs of metro systems. Apart from the hardware, the software consists of project management, contract management, quality management, environmental management and customer services. Metro systems are mega infrastructural projects that require multidisciplinary inputs and a highly organized management. Nonetheless, these software skills are lacking in many developing economies, where metro systems can have a high potential in face of the rapid urbanization and income growth.

Apart from the huge initial capital cost, the cost of operation and maintenance can also be substantial. For a metro system to be financially sustainable, it should be able to generate enough revenue to recover the capital investment in the medium run and to pay for the cost of asset improvement and assent replacement in the long run. Nonetheless, the fare of a metro system has to be competitive to ensure that it can have sufficient patronage and does not lead to social inequality. Hence, the fare of a metro system has to be set in relation to the other public modes, particularly buses. Under such financial circumstances, most metro systems are operating at a loss and are supported by government **subsidies**. Notable exceptions include Hong Kong and Tokyo.

In view of the technological, financial and affordability issues, metro systems need long-term planning and prudent management. In general, metro systems should only be considered for large cities (more than 5 million population), where the income per capita has reached a threshold (over $1800 per capita at 1990 prices). Moreover, due consideration should be paid to the urban form of the cities and the **network** alignment. Compact urban form with walkable communities and/or linear urban form with high-density development are favourable to railway patronage. A railway network with high connectivity and a well-integrated intermodal transport system are important characteristics of rail-based transit-oriented societies. Where automobiles represent the dominant mode of urban transport, the building of a metro system alone is unlikely to change people's travel behaviour dramatically. Hence, metro systems should be completed and in operation before automobiles become the major mode of urban transport. In particular, metro systems typically have a long lead-time, at least seven years, from initial planning to revenue generation. It is notable that the huge upfront capital cost would mainly be offset by the economic benefits in the form of time savings, which continue to rise as the value of time increases in the society.

Further reading
Allport, R.J. (1990). The metro: determining its viability. In J.H. Margaret (ed.), *Developing World Transport*. London: Grosvenor Press International.
Loo, B.P.Y. and D.Y.N. Li (2006). Developing metro systems in the People's Republic of China: policy and gaps. *Transportation* **33**, 115–32.

Becky P. Y. Loo

metropolitan transport planning institutions

Metropolitan transport planning institutions are those public organizations set up to plan and develop infrastructure and services for **mobility** or **accessibility** in a given urban or metropolitan area. They analyse future mobility demand, existing infrastructure facilities and transport services, and plan infrastructure and service changes based on that analysis and policy goals in the region.

These organizations found their basis in the planning, developing and managing of, mainly, road infrastructure, with the aim of facilitating mobility. However, from the late 1960s three major developments in most Western countries changed the role of these organizations. Firstly, **automobile** ownership and use rose dramatically and it became apparent that keeping up with this growth by building road infrastructure would be costly and have all kind of negative side-effects, including danger, **traffic noise**, smog, acid rain and **climate change**. Secondly, public transport, which in many cities started off as a private initiative, had become more and more under the influence of the public sector. It had become a policy instrument. Thirdly, the role of urban planning developed strongly. As a result, metropolitan transport planning institutions became less facilitators of mobility and more policy-driven: transport policy would become the key driver of the choices made by these institutions. This broadened their role, from infrastructure planners to planning and regulating **mobility** more in general.

Metropolitan transport planning institutions show a great deal of variety in their form. Firstly, especially larger urban regions are characterized by multilevel planning. In one metropolitan area, municipal, regional and even state or national governments all have their own transport agendas and subsequent transport policies. As the policies all relate to the metropolitan transport system, many interdependencies exist and effectiveness depends on good coordination between these levels. This is strengthened because transport systems are governed by different layers of government, with local roads in the hands of the municipalities and highways in the hands of state or national governments. As a result, metropolitan transport planning institutions at various levels have to cooperate closely, often resulting in a metropolitan transport planning approach or even a metropolitan transport planning entity.

Secondly, transport is a multimodal system and transport planning is needed for the various modes. As the car proved problematic, for example in many urban areas public transport was again positioned as an alternative. Generally, planning **public transport** is carried out as a separate task, by a separate planning entity. This can be carried out by public transport authorities and operators with different division of roles in various metropolitan areas around the world.

Thirdly, transport and **land use planning** are closely related and coordination is needed, connecting the different policy fields. As a result, metropolitan transport planning institutions are often closely linked or even a part of spatial planning departments. In the case of a larger new urban development project, organizations are often set up to realize an integrated approach for the new development, with transport planners becoming part of the project team, securing coordination on a project level.

Finally, metropolitan transport planning institutions provide the link between the political choices made about transport policy and the execution of the plans in projects and operation. Because of the above characteristics, governance of metropolitan transport planning is often an issue. How should the planning best reflect the policy choices made by various governments with responsibility in the region? The link with the political demands of various governments in the region is often secured through a board of elected officials from the various local governments.

There are several ways in which metropolitan transport planning institutions organize funding for realization of their plans. Some regions have earmarked regional taxes, from which transport projects and public transport operation are funded. But often a regional tax base is not available. Some regions build up funds from municipal contributions, and larger projects are often funded by national or federal authorities, with the metropolitan transport planning institution playing a key role in securing those funds.

For the urban regions of many developing countries the challenge is not to find the right coordination between urban and transport planning over different levels of government. Rather, for them the challenge is the initial building of viable, workable institutions *per se*.

Further reading
Banister, D. (2002). *Transport Planning*. London: SPON Press.
Weiner, E. (2008). *Urban Transportation Planning in the United States: History, Planning and Practice*. New York: Springer.

Wijnand W. Veeneman

metropolitan transport planning organizations in the United States

One of the major institutional changes in the United States brought about by the Intermodal Surface Transportation Efficiency Act (ISTEA) of 1991 was the empowerment of **metropolitan planning organizations** (MPOs) to conduct and coordinate transportation planning in their metropolitan areas. According to federal law, each urbanized area (contiguously built-up areas with a central city greater than 50000 population) must have an MPO for transportation planning purposes. MPOs are typically housed by regional councils of local governments, individual city or county planning organizations, or independent single-function transportation planning organizations. Prior to 1991, MPOs had served a mostly advisory role in transportation planning. ISTEA elevated that role by providing larger MPOs with more than 200000 inhabitants increased funding and project selection authority, while all MPOs were given primary responsibility for developing the long-range regional transportation plan and the short-range regional Transportation Improvement Program (TIP) in cooperation with state Departments of Transportation (DOTs), regional transit agencies and local governments. Through ISTEA, Congress intimated that metropolitan transportation problems were best handled at the regional scale, with direct participation from local and state agencies.

The importance of a regional approach to metropolitan transportation planning has been recognized since the early twentieth century, though formal recognition took much longer. Section 701 of the Housing Act of 1954 was the first time when federal funds were made available to regional planning agencies to begin collecting region-wide data for planning activities in housing, urban renewal, transportation and other issues of regional concern. The Federal Aid Highway Act of 1962 stipulated that federal highway funds for urbanized areas were contingent on the 'establishment of a continuing and comprehensive transportation planning process carried out cooperatively by state and local communities' (the '3-C' planning process). This process also identified the entire metropolitan region as the appropriate scale for urban transportation planning. The Housing and Urban Development Act of 1965 extended and expanded Section 701 grants to regional planning agencies for purposes including mass transit planning and coordination between highway and transit system planning.

Formal designation of MPOs occurred in the 1970s. The Federal Highway Act of 1973 dedicated a small portion of each state's funding (one half of one percent) from the Highway Trust Fund for the creation of MPOs in metropolitan areas with populations greater than 50000. In 1975, the Urban Mass Transportation Administration (UMTA) and

Federal Highway Administration (FHWA) issued joint regulations concerning annual certification of MPOs, the development of a long-range plan, a short-range TIP, and a Unified Planning Work Program (UPWP) (for metropolitan areas with populations greater than 200 000). The TIP regulations designated MPOs as the focus of the 3-C planning process for each urbanized area, to develop the multiyear TIP as well as annual transportation projects for each year. The TIP would then need to be approved by the state and United States Department of Transportation. The Clean Air Act Amendments of 1977 got MPOs more involved in **air quality** planning by prohibiting them from approving any transportation project not in conformity with a state's implementation plan for achieving or maintaining federal air quality standards in that region.

As a result of funding cutbacks and other changes in the 1980s, the role of MPOs in regional planning was reduced significantly. New regulations allowed the federal government to withdraw from specifying how the transportation planning process should be performed, thus permitting states and MPOs to self-certify their processes. These and other changes had the effect of de-emphasizing the role of MPOs, as states became more proactive in raising transportation funds and deciding which projects would be built.

The promulgation of ISTEA in 1991 brought MPOs back into the mainstream of metropolitan transportation planning. ISTEA gave MPOs expanded funding for planning purposes and more authority to select projects eligible to receive federal highway funds. MPOs representing metropolitan areas of greater than 200 000 population were designated as Transportation Management Areas (TMAs) and were given authority, in consultation with the state DOT, to allocate some of the several new categories of funds that ISTEA created. TMAs were authorized to allocate Surface Transportation Program-Metro funds for highway, transit, or other transportation projects to be built within the metropolitan area. Some states permitted TMAs to take the lead in allocating funds in the Congestion Mitigation and Air Quality (CMAQ) program, intended for projects and transportation control measures in **air quality** non-attainment areas that would enable compliance with the State Implementation Plan and conformity to national air quality standards, as well as for Transportation Enhancements. ISTEA also required MPOs to 'begin serious, formal transportation planning', and to constrain fiscally their long-range plans and short-term TIPs.

Since ISTEA's promulgation, MPOs have been adjusting to the new reality of increased responsibilities regarding **intermodalism** and regional transportation planning. Regulations enacted shortly after ISTEA identified 15 planning factors, later reduced to seven as part of the Transportation

Equity Act for the 21st Century [TEA-21] of 1998, that MPOs were required to consider as part of their long-range planning process. These factors required MPOs to pay more attention to intermodal concerns, such as improved connectivity within and between modes and explicit consideration of access to ports, airports and intermodal transportation facilities, as well as methods to expand and enhance transit services and to increase the use of such services. MPOs thus find themselves in a position of collaborative leadership among other transportation agencies and providers, identifying plans and projects to address the expanding transportation needs of metropolitan populations.

Further reading
Dempsey, P.S., A.R. Goetz and C. Larson (2000). Metropolitan planning organizations: an assessment of the transportation planning process, a report to Congress, Volumes 1, 2, and 3. University of Denver Intermodal Transportation Institute and National Center for Intermodal Transportation.
Solof, M. (1998). *History of Metropolitan Planning Organizations.* Washington, DC: Association of Metropolitan Planning Organizations.

Andrew Goetz

microsimulation models

Road users make different types of choices – strategic, tactical and operational – at various moments in times. Strategic choices, such as purchasing a vehicle or making a trip, are made long before the road user enters the public space. Tactical decisions, such as the departure time or route choice, are generally made as the trip starts. Some tactical decisions, such as the route choice, may be changed during the trip due to information that becomes available (for example **congestion**). Operational choices, such as accelerating, decelerating, lane changes and so on, are constantly made during the trip.

Over the years, five types of models, applying to different decision-making levels and driver decision-making levels, have been developed (see Figure):

- Sketch planning models are tailor-made decision support tools exploring questions such as the effect on **mobility** of changed fuel levies. These models are applied on a large scale (country or province).
- Macroscopic models (the traditional four-step model) explore the effects of measures, such as **network** changes. The application level

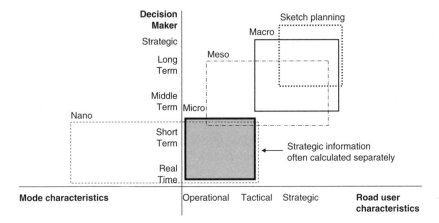

is metropolitan areas. Results are mostly aggregated, calculating (peak) hour volumes on links and overall delays.

- Mesoscopic models include more detail, regarding specific issues such as intersections. Results are often available for smaller time periods (for example five minutes). Typical outputs are volumes and (stop line) delays. Typical application areas are corridors (part of the metropolitan area).
- Microscopic models include individual vehicles. Outputs can be provided for a vehicle, per lane or at a specific point in the **network**. Information such as the distance between leading and following vehicles can be established. The effects of measures such as **intelligent transport systems** can be explored with microscopic simulation models. Typical application areas are small areas with a limited number of intersections or highway junctions.
- Nanoscopic models add vehicle characteristics to the application area of microscopic models. Information such as acceleration and deceleration details, or the behaviour of a vehicle through a curve, is added. Nanoscopic models are developed by vehicle manufacturers and are generally not commercially available.

Microscopic simulation models include a representation of individual vehicles and traffic dynamics through vehicle interaction and movement. Driver behaviour is included in a more detailed way, often via driver classes. Departure times of vehicles are available for every one to five minutes. Information from macroscopic simulation models, such as an origin–destination matrix, is used as a starting point and split in time. During every calculation time step (for example 0.1 seconds), the position of all vehicles in the network is calculated. The outputs provide possibilities to follow vehicles and get link, lane and point information. Moreover, information such as shockwaves, headways and time-to-collision is calculated. Strategic driver information is often not included in microscopic simulation models. Microscopic models are dynamic.

Most of the listed parameters in microscopic simulation models appear in submodels representing car-following, gap-acceptance and lane-changing behaviour. The parameters include desired speed, desired headway (distance between two vehicles), reaction times, rate of acceleration and deceleration, different types of gaps (minimum, critical, willingness to create), lane changing, level of compliance, aggression and awareness.

Further reading
Bonsall, P., R. Lui and W. Young (2005). Modelling safety-related driving behaviour – impact of parameter values. *Transportation Research A* **39**, 425–44.
Vanderschuren, M.J.W.A. (2006). Intelligent transport systems in South Africa: impact assessment through microscopic simulation in the South African Context. Delft TRAIL Research School.

Marianne Vanderschuren

mobile emissions

Air pollution arises from engines, industries, and commercial and residential operations that emit harmful gases and particles (pollutants) into the air. Pollution sources that move, or can be moved from place to place, are referred to as mobile sources, which in turn produce mobile emissions. Examples of mobile sources include vehicles that operate on roads (that is, 'on-road' light-duty automobiles and trucks, large heavy-duty trucks, buses and **motorcycles**) and non-road vehicles, engines and equipment (that is, recreational, construction, logging, agricultural and recreational marine equipment, as well as aircraft and locomotives). Other non-mobile sources of air pollution, for example power plants, factories, manufacturing and residential processes, are usually known as point and/or stationary sources. Mobile emissions are released from sources through combustion exhaust emissions and fuel evaporation. Motor vehicles and non-road equipment typically burn gasoline or diesel fuels, mixtures of hydrocarbons, in an engine to generate power. Ideally in 'perfect' combustion all the hydrogen and carbon in the fuel would react with oxygen in the air to form water and carbon dioxide. In reality, the combustion process is incomplete and engines emit several types of pollutants as combustion by-products. In addition, fuel readily evaporates and fuel molecules escape into the atmosphere from the fuel storage and delivery system. This results in evaporative emissions especially when fuels leak or spill, or when fuels get hot and evaporate from the fuel tank or engine.

Criteria pollutants are those atmospheric pollutants regulated by the United States Environmental Protection Agency (USEPA) through national ambient **air quality** standards. Of the criteria pollutants, mobile emissions include carbon monoxide (CO), lead (Pb), particulate matter (PM), and sulphur dioxide (SO_2). Mobile sources also emit total or reactive organic gasses, and nitrogen oxides (NOx), which react in the presence of sunlight to produce another criteria pollutant, ozone (O_3). These criteria pollutants have been shown to harm human health, damage the environment, and impair property. For example, CO reduces oxygen delivery to the body's organs and causes visual impairment, headaches and reduced work capacity. Fine particulate matter, also known as PM2.5 (less than 2.5 microns in aerodynamic diameter), can reach the deepest regions of lungs and cause adverse health effects including asthma, difficult or painful breathing, and chronic bronchitis, especially in children and the **elderly**. Exposure to ambient ozone contributes to a wide range of adverse health effects such as lung function decrements and respiratory symptoms, as well as aggravation of asthma.

In addition to contributing to criteria pollutants, mobile sources produce several other important air pollutants such as air toxins and greenhouse gases. Air toxins, like benzene found in gasoline, are known or suspected to cause cancer or other serious health effects, such as reproductive problems or birth defects. Greenhouse gases, including carbon dioxide (CO_2), trap heat in the Earth's atmosphere, contributing to global **climate change**.

Mobile emissions contribute significantly to air pollution and are in fact the primary cause of air pollution in many urban areas. According to USEPA, at present in the United States, mobile emissions are responsible for up to half of the smog-forming volatile organic compounds and NOx, more than 50 per cent of the hazardous air pollutants, and up to 90 per cent of the CO found in urban air. The European Environmental Agency reported that in 1996 mobile emissions accounted for 74.6 per cent of NOx and 60 per cent of CO emissions in France, and 59 per cent of NOx and 88 per cent of CO emissions in the United Kingdom. In Canada in 1995, transportation sources emitted 40 per cent and 52 per cent of national CO and NOx emissions, respectively.

Various regulatory efforts have been under way to bring ambient pollutant concentrations within acceptable limits. In the United States, for example, the Clean Air Act, first enacted in 1970, requires states to prepare State Implementation Plans (SIP) to set forth their strategies for attaining and maintaining NAAQS. As the primary sources of air pollution, mobile emissions have long been targeted for control. The regulations governing implementation requirements pertaining to mobile emissions are included in the US Environmental Protection Agency's transportation conformity rule, the Intermodal Surface Transportation Efficiency Acts and more recently the Transportation Efficiency Act for the 21st Century metropolitan planning regulations. The transportation conformity rule establishes detailed requirements which apply to numerous metropolitan areas to ensure that transportation plans, problems and projects do not worsen **air quality** or interfere with attainment of air quality standards.

Establishing the degree and type of mobile emissions controls requires estimating mobile emissions inventories. Emissions inventories are used to establish the relative contributions, current and projected, of mobile sources and stationary sources, as well as to help identify and evaluate potential control measures. Ozone, for example, is photochemically produced in the atmosphere from precursor VOCs and NOx emissions. To develop an effective ozone control strategy, air pollution control agencies require information on the main mobile sources that emit these precursor pollutants.

Simplistically, mobile emissions inventories are calculated by multiplying emission activities by their associated emission factors. An emission factor represents the amount of emissions that are released per unit of emission activity, that is, emission rate. For example, grams of CO emitted from a given vehicle or fleet of vehicles operating on-road in a given period of time (for example, day, year) are estimated by multiplying the number of vehicle miles travelled, emission activity, with CO emissions factors. Due to the wide variety of mobile emission sources and their complex emission characteristics, however, the methodologies for estimating an inventory of emissions from different mobile sources will vary depending on whether they are on-road or non-road sources.

On-road mobile sources are distinguished by vehicle size, weight and use, as light-duty vehicles, light-duty trucks, heavy-duty trucks, motorcycles, and so forth. In most urban areas, highway vehicles represent the largest single source of CO emissions and contribute significantly to VOCs, SOx and NOx. Emission estimates for on-road vehicles are usually based on the combination of two fundamental measurements: travel activities and their emission factors. Both measures reflect complex patterns of behaviour. The three main types of travel activity are: the pollution of vehicles, the number of vehicle miles travelled (VMT), and the number of vehicle starts. The corresponding emission factors are grams per vehicle, grams per mile, and grams per start.

The USEPA and the United States Department of Transportation Federal Highway Administration have developed a series of tools and models to estimate emission factors and the amount of travel activities. The USEPA and the California Air Resources Board maintain large data collection programmes for emission factors. Both organizations have used this information to develop emission factor models which provide emission factors for different pollutants from assorted vehicle types under various conditions. Traffic monitoring sources and travel **demand models** are used to generate the necessary travel activity data. The accuracy of the emissions inventory will be no better than that of the estimates of either the emission factors or vehicle travel activities. None of the factors is static: technology is continually evolving, leading to changing in-use emission performance. Changes in fuel prices and economic conditions lead to changes in vehicle sales and travel patterns.

Non-road mobile emissions are emitted from engines, motorized vehicles and equipment that are normally not operated on public roadways for construction, agriculture, recreation and many other purposes. The emission activities for developing non-road emission inventories include: equipment populations, annual hours of use, load factors, horsepower, and so forth. Equipment populations can be derived from relationships between economic activity indicators and equipment category populations. The emission factor is defined as the average emissions of each pollutant per unit of use (gram/horsepower-hour) for each category of equipment. The United States has a model that provides emission factors for tailpipe exhaust, refuelling, evaporative and crankcase emissions with adjustments to account for in-use non-road emissions. Estimating emissions from aircrafts and locomotives requires consideration of specific emission characteristics.

Technological advances in vehicle and engine design, together with higher-quality fuels, have achieved dramatic success in reducing mobile source pollutants – compared to an uncontrolled passenger car of 1970, an average car on the road today emits 60 to 90 per cent less pollution over its lifetime. However, the amount of driving in the United States has more than doubled since that time.

Further reading

United States Environmental Protection Agency (1992). *Procedures for Emission Inventory Preparation Volume IV: Mobile Sources.* EPA420-R-92-009. Washington, DC: USEDP.
United States Environmental Protection Agency (2000). *National Air Pollutant Emission Trends, 1900–1998.* EPA-454/R-00-002. Washington, DC: USEPA.
United States Federal Highway Administration (2000). *Transportation Conformity Reference Guide.* Washington, DC: USFHWA.

Oliver H. Gao and *Debbie A. Niemeier*

mobility

Mobility refers to the movement of people or goods. Mobility is measured in person-kilometres, tonne-kilometres, and in travel speeds (kilometres per hour). It generally assumes that more and faster physical travel is desirable. It can apply to any travel mode, including walking, cycling, ride-sharing, public transit and air travel for passenger travel, and truck, rail, ship and air for freight travel. Mobility is sometimes measured door-to-door, taking into account each link of a trip, including walking to a **parking** lot or transit stop.

Mobility represents a broader perspective of transportation than just considering vehicle traffic, but not as broad as **accessibility**, which reflects the overall ability to reach desired goods, services and activities. Mobility recognizes the potential transport system benefits of shifts from low- to higher-occupancy travel modes. For example, mobility-based transport planning allows a transit investment that can potentially attract 2000 **peak period** passengers out of single-occupant automobile travel into a transit vehicle to be considered of equal value to a new highway lane that accommodates 2000 additional peak-period vehicles.

The concept of mobility, however, assumes that travel is an end in itself, rather than a means of achieving access, and so does not recognize the potential transport system benefits of mobility substitutes such as **telecommuting**, or of land use management strategies that reduce the amount of travel required to reach common destinations. Using mobility to evaluate transportation system quality tends to favour longer-distance travel over local travel, and motorized modes over non-motorized modes (walking and cycling), since they serve short trips and are slower than motorized modes.

Further reading
Litman, T. (2003). Measuring transportation: traffic, mobility and accessibility. *ITE Journal* **73**, 28–32.
United States Federal Highway Administration. Performance Measures Website, www.ops.fhwa.dot.gov/Travel/Deployment_Task_Force/perf_measures.htm.

Todd Alexander Litman

mobility and ageing

Some would argue that one of the principal requirements for a high quality of independent living in old age is the ability to achieve full access to services, resources and cultural opportunities. Others would suggest that technological advances now make it possible to obtain information, participate in passive entertainment activities, engage in communication and initiate the provision of many services without ever leaving the confines of one's home. To address the latter argument one has to examine the extent to which home-based interactions are of a virtual kind and are a good substitute for actual interaction.

The mobility needed to maintain connectedness with one's community and culture requires that older individuals retain a physical and psychological personal infrastructure that remains at least minimally effective. These characteristics also require that the environment be organized in such a way that the reduced capability of older people can be compensated for in terms of providing suitable personal and mass transportation options that support personal mobility. Six major goals of maintaining mobility have been identified to be important for many older persons.

Reduction of personal isolation
A major psychological issue for older people is their perceived and actual isolation. Next to physical dependency, loneliness is one of the greatest fears that people associate with old age, and social isolation is a major cause in the deterioration in the health of the **elderly**.

Increased isolation coincides with increasing longevity, and sociocultural changes that have occurred over the past century that has led to the demise of the extended families. Older adults are also more likely to remain in rural environments when their adult children move to the cities. There has also been growing resistance to parental co-residence on the part of both generations.

Some older people seek reduced social isolation by joining retirement communities. But such communities are relatively expensive. For most individuals maintenance of mobility depends on the availability of convenient forms of mass transportation or continued use of personal transportation.

Participation in cultural and recreational activities
Although the mental stimulation for most elderly people comes from the passive experience in front of their television sets, there is evidence that the maintenance of cognitive function in old age requires more active forms of intellectual stimulation. More often this involves attending live performances, individual or group travel to sites of cultural and touristic importance, participating in senior colleges, or being active in social and political organizations and volunteer community activities. All such activities require retention and/or enhancement of personal mobility. There is also evidence that physical activities and exercise programs involving group participation are important in maintaining health.

Access to full choices of goods and services
Older people living in non-urban areas are particularly dependent on their personal automobiles. Hence, maintenance of driving abilities is a requirement for quality living. Because of declines in sensory processes and response speed, many people in their late seventies or eighties either give up driving voluntarily or lose their driving licenses. The resulting reduction in mobility leads to increased dependence on others and reduces access to a wide array of goods and services.

Choice of health services and personal care facilities
Exercising a choice of health care specialists or care facilities requires transportation, for normal health care as well as emergency situations. Some older people's preference is for non-traditional health care resources, whether naturopaths, acupuncturists or faith healers. These resources are not necessarily available in close proximity and lack of mobility can preclude their use. Mobility restrictions similarly impair access to other personal care specialists such as beauticians, cosmeticians, physical therapists or health spas.

Access to financial and other personal consultants
It is possible to pay bills and conduct other financial transactions over the Internet but many elders are reluctant to manage their life's savings via the impersonal algorithms of web banking. They, throughout their lives, have based financial decisions on face-to-face interactions with professionals whom they trusted because of such personal relationships. Given the need for elders to adjust financial planning to the demands of a prolonged life, direct consultation with financial and legal advisers becomes even more pressing. Few of these professionals are likely to make house calls. Most older people also need to interact with various government agencies regarding their pensions, retirement benefits and insurance problems.

Direct participation in religious worship and spiritual experiences
For many older people religious beliefs and activities can be central to their lives. The elderly may attend church less frequently due to health problems, but they remain active in other dimensions of their devotions. Solitary spiritual activities increase in frequency but do not always satisfy the important role of religious communities as a resource for reducing isolation. Because of the ritual nature of most religious worship, many people find it essential to their spiritual welfare to participate in organized religious activities. This may be one of the principal avenues for many single old people to retain their feelings of connectedness.

Further reading

Fozard, J.L. and S. Gordon-Salant (2001). Sensory and perceptual changes with aging. In J.E. Birren and K.W. Schaie (eds), *Handbook of the Psychology of Aging* (5th edn). San Diego, CA: Academic Press.

Schaie, K.W. and M. Pietrucha (eds) (2000). *Mobility and Transportation in the Elderly*. New York: Springer.

K. Warner Schaie

modal split models

Modal split models estimate the probability $p^i(m/c)$ that a traveller making a trip i will choose a specific mode m of travel from a given set of modes c. Most modal split models are **disaggregate, discrete choice models**. Given an individual making a trip of category i from zone o to zone d in time period t, these models will determine the probabilities of each mode being chosen out of a finite set of modes. In many practical applications the model is estimated based on disaggregate data and then applied in a semi-aggregate approach. In this approach, given a trip table of a specific purpose and time of day, for each origin–destination the model will predict the shares of each mode for each socio-economic group. Advance travel **demand models** moves more and more toward agent-based approaches with a full **disaggregate** application.

Modal split models provide the tools to evaluate a priori the effectiveness of various transport policies by estimating mode shares shifts in response to such policies. Analysing modal split models can help policy-makers identify the variables that will encourage a shift to **sustainable** modes including public transportation, **bicycling** and walking.

In the traditional **four-step travel demand** modelling, mode choice modelling is the third step following trip **generation** and trip distribution, and preceding trip assignment. When time-of-day modelling precedes mode choice modelling, the latter can account for the level of service for the actual time of day. In more advanced travel demand model systems known as **activity-based models**, travel decisions become part of a broader activity scheduling process based on modelling the demand for activities rather than merely trips. These models estimate the travel choices of each trip segment within the context of all trips taken during a day, or at least within a tour, usually defined as a set of subsequent trips starting at home and ending at home. While this complicates the task of mode choice modelling it also provides more realistic results, as the mode of each trip segment is highly dependent on the modes of the other segments of the tour and other attributes of the tour.

Most choice sets include at a minimum public transport and auto. More advanced models include various submodes of the public transport system including distinctions between local bus, express bus, light rail and heavy rail. Choice sets can also be defined by access and/or egress modes. These usually include **park-and-ride**, drop-off points, bus and walking. The analysis of transit auto access is very important in the context of analysing modal shift to public transportation of people with auto availability. With increasing interest in **sustainable transport** many models also include non-motorized modes, mostly walking and bicycling. The inclusion of all these modes means that the model can easily have a large number of alternatives. Identification of the relevant alternatives, the choice set, depends on the transport system under study, the policy at question and data availability. For example, intracity models will include modes that would not be included in intercity models such as walk and bicycling, while the latter will include modes such as **high-speed rail**. In mode choice models the choice set has to be identified for each decision-maker, as not all modes are available for all trips.

Modes can always be available; for example, driving is not a possibility for a person without a driver's licence. They can also be unavailable because they are not perceived as an alternative for a specific trip; for example, heavy rail will not be considered for a few blocks' trip. When there are a large number of alternatives where some of them share common attributes, it is common to define nested model structures. At the highest level the person chooses between private auto and public transportation. At the next level they may choose between drive alone and car pool if they choose private auto, or between bus and rail if they choose **public transportation**. At the last level they may choose between various access modes.

Mode choice models have two main types of explanatory, independent variables: attributes of the individual and of the alternative travel modes that may also be considered as policy variables. These two types of variables can also appear interactively; for example it is common to include a variable of modal cost divided by income representing the travel cost relative to one's income.

Attributes of the travel decision-maker are mostly socio-economic attributes such as **gender**, age, income, car availability and life cycle variables where the latter represent the family stage in life, such as presence and age of children and working status of the household members. It is common to segment the population to various markets and estimate a model for each market (market segmentation) to account for the different values that various groupings in the population give to different attributes. Common examples for market segmentation are by **auto ownership** and income. Another dimension of segmentation is by trip purpose, to represent the different behaviour in mode choice decision-making for different trip purposes.

Most attributes of the alternatives are level-of-service measures describing the level of service they provide to the traveller. These include travel time, travel cost, number of transfers, service reliability and others. **Travel time** is usually decomposed into various components such as in-vehicle time, waiting time, transfer time and walking time, as they have different weight on persons' utility. These attributes have negative coefficients since they usually represent disutility for the traveller. Level-of-service variables depend on the specific route the traveller will choose to take under each choice of mode. This is done by using the expected utility of the route choice, which, in logit or nested logit models, is the log-sum variable.

Another type of attributes of the alternative modes is alternative specific constants, known as modal preferences variables. They account for qualitative characteristics of each mode or for perception differences among modes. For example a **metro** may have a higher perceived non-measured quality, such as comfort, than a bus.

Value of travel time is derived from mode choice models by calculating the ratio of the marginal utility of time (dU/dt) – the time coefficient in a linear utility model; and marginal utility of cost (dU/dC) – the cost coefficient; giving:

$$\text{VOT} = (dU/dC) \, / \, (dU/dC) \tag{1}$$

This shows the marginal trade-off people are willing to pay in order to save time while keeping their utility at the same level. This value is an important input for appraisal purposes, as the monetary value that people put on their time. Ratios between other coefficients of level of service are also interesting, showing the relative importance of each attribute. For example the coefficient of out-of-vehicle time is usually two to three times larger than the coefficient of in-vehicle time, showing that people are willing to pay more to shorten their wait or walk time than their in-vehicle time.

Finally, land use and urban form variables of the origin and destination of the trip can be proxies for both service-level variables, representing for example friendliness of walking; and for the individual, representing for example the type of neighbourhood they are residing in.

The process of building a mode choice model involves a number of steps. The first is model design, in which the alternatives, model structures, independent variables and the data to be used are defined. Mode choice models are usually based on the random utility theory. They assume that individuals make decisions that maximize their utility. The utility of an alternative mode is expressed as a function of the various explanatory variables. The most common model structures within this framework are the logit and the nested logit models, but advances in computing have allowed more flexible model structures to be used, including probit and mixed logit. The next step is model estimation, where the parameters of the model are determined to fit the data best. This is usually done by the maximum likelihood method. The last step is validation, where the model is validated against an independent data set and compared to available aggregate traffic data.

Mode choice models are best estimated by using revealed preference data where the actual mode choices people made are observed. However, many mode choice models are designed to evaluate new modes and policies that do not currently exist in a specific area. In such cases it is common to use stated preference data, where people are faced with hypothetical alternatives and are asked to state what would be their choice under various level of service attributes of these new modes. To minimize potential bias with stated preference data it is recommended to use a combination of revealed and stated preference data.

Further reading

Ben-Akiva, M. and R.L. Lerman (1985). *Discrete Choice Analysis*. Cambridge, MA: MIT Press.

Hensher, D.A. and W.H. Greene (2003). The mixed logit model: the state of practice. *Transportation* **30**, 133–76.

Yoram Shiftan

motorcycles

A motorcycle is a two-wheeled, single-tracked vehicle powered by an internal combustion engine. First attempts to power **bicycles** with steam engines are recorded from the mid-nineteenth century. In 1885 Gottlieb Daimler took out a patent for the first motorcycle with an internal combustion engine, which at 264 cubic centimetres produced about 0.4 kW. This was sufficient for about 20 km/h maximum speed. The first motorcycles produced in serial form came on the market at the end of the nineteenth century. In the twentieth century motorcycles became a means of transport accessible to all social classes. In Europe and North America the importance of motorcycling as a means of transport declined from the 1950s on, when affordable cars came on the market. The role of motorcycling was reduced to a leisure activity for a small group. During the 1990s motorcycling started a comeback and sales numbers boomed, for example the number of licensed motorcycles in Germany grew at a rate of about 6 per cent per year.

Motorcycles comprise a wide range of different types: from mopeds powered by engines of 50 cubic centimetres, scooters with engines of 50 to 250 cubic centimetres and motorcycles with cubic capacity up to 1000 cubic centimetres and even more. They can also be subdivided into several types: choppers, touring bikes, cross-country bikes, naked bikes, racers, and so on. Most motorcycles are powered by four-stroke engines. Two-stroke engines are only common in smaller motorcycles up to about 250 cubic centimetres. Motorcycling as a sport comprises cross-country competitions (moto-cross, trial, enduro, rally, hill climbing); speedway on ash, sand or grass tracks, road races in different formulas and with different cubic capacities; and acceleration competitions. Since 2000 or so, the specific power increased from 1.5 kW per litre for Gottlieb Daimlers patent to about 50 kW per litre for middle-class motorcycles and to about 100 kW per litre for the most powerful motorcycles available for use on public roads. Fuel consumption ranges from about 1–2 litres per 100 kilometres for mopeds, to about 3–5 litres per 100 kilometres for middle-class motorcycles.

The role of motorcycling in third world countries is quite different from Europe and North America. Especially in Asian cities, motor two-wheelers are the dominant mode of transport. In India the number of registered motor two-wheelers was growing at a rate of 15 to 20 per cent per year from the 1950s on. This growth rate was much higher than that of other motor vehicles. During the 1990s, 60 to 70 per cent of all registered motor vehicles were two-wheelers.

In Europe motorcycles are not only used as leisure or sports vehicles. Especially in the urban agglomerations of Southern Europe, motorcycles play a substantial role in transport. For example, in Athens about 7 per cent of all trips are made by motorcycle. But also, in agglomerations with a high level of **congestion** like Paris the relevance of motorcycling is increasing. Motor scooters are especially popular in Paris.

The power to weight ratio of today's motorcycles is much higher than that of today's cars. This leads to high speeds. Motorcyclists are not protected by a car body only by a leather or carbon suit and a helmet, and in several countries not even that. **Safety** is thus an issue. The chance of getting killed when involved in an accident is about four times higher on a motorcycle than in a car (see Figure). In Austria the use of helmets became obligatory for motorcycles in the early 1980s. This measure reduced the number of motorcycling fatalities by about 30 per cent. In Greece and Portugal, where motorcycles are used as daily means of transport and where people rarely wear helmets, the share of motorcycling fatalities is the highest.

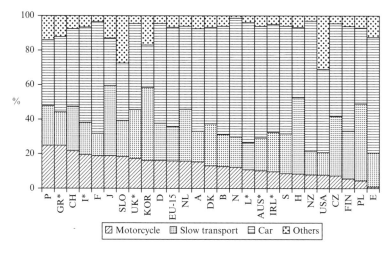

Note: *2000, **1999.

Motorcycling is very popular as a sport and a leisure activity for wealthy people in all parts of the world. Motorcycles have the potential to relieve some of the problems of densely populated urban regions, mainly the space consumption of **parking** and flowing traffic. At the current low car occupancy rate in Western countries, the use of small- to middle-class motorcycles also has the potential to reduce fuel consumption.

Further reading
Kuratorium für Verkehrssicherheit (2003). *Unfallstatistik 2003.* Kuratorium für Verkehrssicherheit (KfV) Institut für Unfallstatistik, Reihe Verkehr in Österreich, Heft 34 Vienna.

Paul C. Pfaffenbichler

motorway and freeway history

A motorway or freeway (sometimes called an expressway or throughway) is a multilane divided road that is designed to be high speed, free flowing, access-controlled, built to high standards, with no traffic lights on the main carriageway. Some motorways or freeways are financed with tolls, and so may have tollbooths, either across the entrance ramp (slip-road) or the main carriageway. However in the United States and Great Britain, most are financed with gas or general tax revenue.

Though there were major road **networks** during the Roman Empire and before, the history of motorways and freeways dates from at least as early as 1907, when the first limited-access automobile highway, the Bronx River Parkway, began construction in Westchester County, New York (opening in 1908). In this same period, William Vanderbilt constructed the Long Island Parkway as a toll road in Queens County, New York. The Long Island Parkway was built for racing, and speeds of 60 miles per hour were accommodated. Users however had to pay a then expensive $2 toll (later reduced) to recover the construction costs of $2 million. These parkways were paved when most roads were not.

In 1919 General John Pershing assigned Dwight Eisenhower to discover how quickly troops could be moved from Fort Meade between Baltimore and Washington to the Presidio in San Francisco by road. The answer was 62 days, for an average speed of 3.5 miles per hour. While using segments of the Lincoln Highway, most of that road was still unpaved. In response, in 1922 Pershing drafted a plan for an 8000-mile interstate system which was ignored at the time.

The United States highway system was a set of paved and consistently numbered highways sponsored by the states, with limited federal support. First built in 1924, they succeeded some previous major highways such as the Dixie Highway, Lincoln Highway and Jefferson Highway that were multistate and were constructed with the aid of private support. These roads however were not, in general, access-controlled, and soon became **congested** as development along the side of the road degraded highway speeds.

In parallel with the United States highway system, limited access parkways were developed in the 1920s and 1930s in several United States cities. Robert Moses built a number of these parkways in and around New York City. A number of these parkways were grade separated, though they were intentionally designed with low bridges to discourage trucks and buses from using them.

German Chancellor Adolf Hitler appointed a German engineer Fritz Todt Inspector General for German Roads. He managed the construction of the German Autobahns, the first limited-access high-speed road **network** in the world. In 1935, the first section from Frankfurt am Main to Darmstadt opened; the system today has a length of 7125 miles.

The Federal-Aid Highway Act of 1938 called on the Bureau of Public Roads to study the feasibility of a toll-financed superhighway system (three east–west and three north–south routes). Their report *Toll Roads and Free Roads* declared that such a system would not be self-supporting, advocating instead a 27 190-mile free system of interregional highways; the effect of this report was to set back the interstate program nearly 20 years in the United States.

The German autobahn system proved its utility during the Second World War, as the German army could shift relatively quickly back and forth between two fronts. Its value in military operations was not lost on the American generals, including Dwight Eisenhower.

On 1 October 1940, a new toll highway using the old, unutilized South Pennsylvania Railroad right-of-way and tunnels opened. It was the first of a new generation of limited-access highways, generally called super-highways or freeways that transformed the American landscape. This was considered the first freeway in the United States, as unlike the earlier park-ways it was a multilane route as well as being limited access. The Arroyo Seco Parkway, now the Pasadena Freeway, opened 30 December 1940. Unlike the Pennsylvania Turnpike, the Arroyo Seco parkway had no toll barriers.

A new National Interregional Highway Committee was appointed in 1941, and reported in 1944 in favor of a 33900-mile system. The system was designated in the Federal Aid Highway Act of 1933, and the routes began to be selected by 1947, yet no funding was provided at the time. The 1952 Highway Act only authorized a token amount for construction, increased to $175 million annually in 1956 and 1957.

The United States Interstate Highway System was established in 1956 following a decade and half of discussion. Much of the network had been proposed in the 1940s, but it took time to authorize funding. In the end, a system supported by gas taxes (rather than tolls), paid for 90 percent by the federal government with a 10 percent local contribution, on a 'pay-as-you-go' system, was established. The Federal Aid Highway Act of 1956 had authorized the expenditure of $27.5 billion over 13 years for the construction of a 41000-mile interstate highway system. As early as 1958 the cost estimate for completing the system came in at $39.9 billion and the end date slipped into the 1980s. By 1991, the final cost estimate was $128.9 billion.

While the freeways were seen as positives in most parts of the United States, in urban areas opposition grew quickly into a series of freeway revolts. As soon as 1959 (three years after the Interstate Act), the San Francisco Board of Supervisors removed seven of ten freeways from the city's master plan, leaving the Golden Gate bridge unconnected to the freeway system. In New York, Jane Jacobs led a successful freeway revolt against the Lower Manhattan Expressway, sponsored by business interests and master builders such as Robert Moses among others. In Baltimore, I-70, I-83 and I-95 all remain unconnected, thanks to highway revolts led by now Senator Barbara Mikulski. In Washington, I-95 was rerouted onto the Capital Beltway. The pattern repeated itself elsewhere, and many urban freeways were removed from master plans.

In 1936, the Trunk Roads Act ensured that Great Britain's Minister of Transport controlled about 30 major roads, 4500 miles in length. The first motorway in Britain, the Preston by-pass, now part of the M6, opened in 1958. In 1959, the first stretch of the M1 opened. Today there are about 6300 miles of trunk roads and motorways in England.

Australia has 490 miles of motorways, though a much larger **network** of roads. However the motorway network is not truly national in scope (in contrast with Germany, the United States, Britain and France); rather it is a series of local networks in and around metropolitan areas, with many intercity connections being on undivided and non-grade-separated highways.

Outside the Anglo-Saxon world, tolls were more widely used. In Japan, when the Meishin Expressway opened in 1963, the roads in Japan were in far worse shape than in Europe or North America. Today there are over 3800 miles of expressways, many of which are private toll roads. France has about 6200 miles of motorways, many of which are toll roads. The French motorway system developed through a series of franchise agreements with private operators, many of which were later nationalized.

Beginning in the late 1980s with the wind-down of the United States interstate system (regarded as complete in 1990), as well as intercity motorway programs in other countries, new sources of financing needed to be developed. New (generally suburban) toll roads were developed in several metropolitan areas.

An exception to the dearth of urban freeways is the case of the Big Dig in Boston, which relocates the Central Artery from an elevated highway to a subterranean one, largely on the same right of way, while keeping the elevated highway operating. This project is estimated to be completed for some $14 billion, which is half the estimate of the original complete United States Interstate Highway System.

As mature systems in the developed countries, improvements in today's freeways are not so much a matter of widening segments or constructing new facilities, but of better managing the road space that exists. That improved management takes a variety of forms. For instance, Japan has advanced its highways with application of intelligent transportation systems, in particular traveller information systems, both in and out of vehicles, as well as traffic control systems. The United States and Great Britain also have traffic management centers in most major cities that assess traffic conditions on motorways, deploy emergency vehicles, and control systems like ramp meters and variable message signs. These systems are beneficial, but cannot be seen as revolutionizing freeway travel. Speculation about future automated highway systems has taken place almost as long as highways have been around. The Futurama exhibit at the New York 1939 World's

Fair posited a system for 1960. Yet this technology has been 20 years away for over 60 years, and difficulties remain.

David Levinson

multicriteria analysis

Multicriteria analysis (MCA) is an established support tool in decision and choice problems that are characterized by: a set of distinct choice alternatives; a set of mutually incompatible, conflicting, decision criteria; the presence of different priorities, weights, attached to the various decision criteria; and the need to identify the 'best possible' choice alternative. The information necessary to perform a multicriteria analysis is normally included in an effect or impact matrix that contains the expected outcomes of each alternative to be considered for all relevant choice criteria. In addition, it is necessary to have insight into the decision-makers' preferences for each of the decisions criteria.

Multicriteria analysis implies a systematic assessment of the impacts of various policy alternatives. This impact assessment may include direct and indirect, and short-term and long-term impacts, as well as their social or geographical distribution.

In addition, knowledge of the decision-maker's preference structure (weights set) is a central element in multicriteria analysis. This can be based on stated preference techniques, posteriority analysis, simulation analysis and so on. In a multi-decision-maker context, the assessment of weights is not easy, and is the reason why in practice 'fictitious' weights are often deployed to analyse 'what-if' conditions.

Another critical element in multicriteria analysis is the accuracy of measurement of both the impact or effect table and the weights set. The precision of measurement may range from cardinal to ordinal, from crisp to fuzzy, and may also contain alpha-numerical information. The appropriate level of measurement is essential for the type of methodology to be used in a multicriteria analysis. Dozens of multicriteria decision support tools have been developed, showing some commonalities but also differences regarding the treatment of information. A wide variety of software packages has also been developed offering an operational decision support system to planners and decision-makers.

Multicriteria analysis has been applied to a wide array of evaluation problems, for example in the fields of environmental management, energy policy, industrial planning, **land use planning**, and public facilities management. It has also found a wide application in the field of **transportation planning**.

Transportation provides many illustrations of the applicability of MCA in complex decision-making. Transportation projects are usually discrete-choice projects, which have a variety of relevant dimensions for balanced and multifaceted decision-making, such as cost items, security and **safety** aspects, land use dimensions, environmental factors, and social, distributive elements.

During the 1980s transportation **network** analysis was mainly conducted using single-objective approaches, such as the minimization of transport cost. In some cases, the conclusion was that such an approach is not satisfactory, and multi-objective programming methods were used to find solutions for a transportation network problem, for example finding the optimal pattern of home-to-work trips in a certain region.

The introduction of the notion of sustainability resulted in the operationalization of this concept in MCA focusing on transportation-related decision problems. In these cases not only were environmental consequences included, but also the impacts on, for example, social structures or cultural heritage were taken into consideration.

More recently, the integration of multicriteria analysis in participatory decision-making procedures has been observed – for example participatory multicriteria evaluation (PMCE) and social multicriteria evaluation (SMCE). In traditional multicriteria analysis approaches, a relationship is assumed between the analysis and one decision-maker. The PMCE and SMCE approaches aim at establishing relationships and interactions with the social environment in which the decision is taken. An important goal of SMCE is to establish a multicriteria decision-making procedure that is as participative and transparent as possible.

To conclude, multicriteria analysis gradually evolved from a decision support tool used for assisting one decision-maker, into a participative decision-making procedure for the integrated evaluation of policies or alternatives.

Further reading
Munda, G. (2008). *Social Multi-Criteria Evaluation for a Sustainable Economy*. Berlin: Springer-Verlag.
Nijkamp, P., P. Rietveld and H. Voogd (1990). *Multicriteria Evaluation in Physical Planning*. Amsterdam: Elsevier.

Peter Nijkamp

N

NAFTA transport policy

When the North American Free Trade Agreement (NAFTA) came into effect in 1994, it promised new trade opportunities, significantly improved access to the Mexican market for Canadian and United States exports, and increased total trade through the phased elimination of tariffs over ten years. In addition to the promise of more goods to carry by virtue of freer trade in goods, NAFTA provided a timetable for the removal of standards-related barriers, in particular with respect to the provision of land transport services between NAFTA countries. The three countries agreed to encourage cooperation between private standards organizations for mutual acceptance of test results and certification procedures, and to establish a trilateral committee, the Land Transport Standards Subcommittee, to achieve these goals and act as a forum for consultation and cooperation.

What was important about the agreement was the milestones that were negotiated, the conditions and standards that were agreed for each milestone, and whether they were fully implemented over the phase-in period. For international cargo, NAFTA proposed to phase out rules against moving international cargo from Canada through the United States into Mexico, and vice versa. The timetable was to be phased in, with three years before Mexico would allow United States and Canadian operators to make cross-border deliveries to, and pick up cargo in, Mexican border states. The United States would allow Mexican truck operators to perform the same services in its border states by the end of that period. This timetable was not met, and President Bush ran for office in 2000 promising to meet the much-delayed access obligation.

NAFTA never intended that domestic traffic would be made available to foreign carriers. Under NAFTA, the United States maintained its moratorium on operating authorities for truck carriage of domestic cargo and for passenger service. The maintenance of cabotage was clear, and for more than just the trucking industry: under the United States Merchant Marine Act 1920, also known as the Jones Act, domestic marine services are also reserved for American owned, flagged, crewed and built ships. Air services and, therefore, air cargo activities were also excluded from NAFTA's liberalizing agenda.

Other exclusions from NAFTA prevent greater liberalization of transport services. These include, for example, immigration restrictions (each country's immigration requirements for crews to change at or near their borders); harmonization of vehicle weights and dimensions and other such standards; and cabotage provisions (preventing the free movement of transport entities carrying domestic cargo).

Prior to NAFTA implementation, ownership restrictions in the United States were more liberal than in either Canada or Mexico. Phased changes would partially level the field. While each country would accord NAFTA investors and their investments national treatment, exceptions were granted to Canada and Mexico in the areas of investment screening. It was the area of ownership restrictions that became a major disappointment in the road to liberalization. The Mexicans made a significant promise to liberalize the ownership of surface transport companies and develop a phased timetable for liberalization, with 49 per cent foreign ownership allowed by 18 December 1995, and two further improvements in 2001 and 2004. However, the implementation of investment legislation was derailed by the 1995 trucking dispute and the United States failure to live up to its obligations on Mexican truck access. Further improvement in the currently limited investment provisions is dependent on widening United States access to Mexican trucks, a trade irritant that continues to deter full implementation of NAFTA today.

As road is the primary mode for trade within NAFTA, the most important factor of NAFTA became its promise of resolving non-tariff barriers and cargo access problems in the trucking industry. Since signing, the Land Transportation Standards Subcommittee agreed on a number of items including a common legal age for a vehicle operator in international commerce (21 years); common format and contents for driver logbooks; reciprocity of medical standards; drivers to have the language of jurisdiction; and substantial harmonization of regulations governing the transportation of **hazardous materials**. It formed several working groups to address vehicle and driver standards, weights and dimensions, **hazardous goods transport** and traffic control systems, for example. Advances in cross-border facilitation, data exchange (including driver **safety** data and port state control data), and the development of transportation technology, however, have been made, and these were not part of the original mandate of the subcommittee. Unfortunately, progress since about 2002 has been limited and the subcommittee's demise became inevitable.

While the transportation provisions of NAFTA were not fully implemented when its final milestone of 1 January 2004 arrived, and there remained much to do to liberalize trade in transport services in the region, a new vision of security and prosperity, including some measures of transportation regulation, developed in 2005. Progress here has also been limited and the vision of a liberalized transport region, as seen in Europe, remains unlikely in North America.

Further reading
Brooks, M.R. (2008). *North American Freight Transportation: The Road to Security and Prosperity*. Cheltenham, UK and Northampton, MA, USA: Edward Elgar.
Brooks, Mary R. and S. Kymlicka (2007). *Unfinished Business: A NAFTA Status Report*. Halifax, Canada: Atlantic Institute for Market Studies.

Mary R. Brooks

networks

Networks provide the infrastructure for the movement of people, goods and services. They come in many forms from transportation networks (road, rail, waterway, air) to **telecommunication** networks, including the Internet, as well as a variety of energy networks (electric power, gas, oil, and so on) and logistical networks, including **supply-chains**. Networks have evolved throughout history and form the conduits by which people interact and conduct their economic and social activities.

The emergence and the evolution of physical networks over space and time have given rise to elegant theories and scientific methodologies for the modelling, analysis and solution of such problems. Mathematically, network problems are modelled and studied by making use of graphs, which abstract reality, and consist of nodes and links that connect the nodes. In a transportation context, nodes correspond to points of origin or destination, as well as intersections or transhipment points. Links correspond, depending on the type of transportation network, to roads, railways, shipping routes, and so on. Networks also consist of flows, which can take the form in transportation of vehicular traffic, freight, airplanes, and so on. Transportation networks may be multimodal in nature, as in the case of urban transportation networks with private and public modes of transportation. Associated with the links are, typically, costs, which may reflect **congestion**.

Networks may be utilized and managed in a centralized or decentralized manner, depending upon the application with the former leading, if optimization is the desired goal, to a system-optimized (S-O) solution and the latter to a user-optimized (U-O) solution. In the U-O problem, in a (congested) transportation context, one seeks to determine the path flows and link flows such that the demand is satisfied for each origin–destination (O/D) pair of nodes and all used paths, sequences of links, connecting each

O/D pair have equal and minimal travel costs (or travel times). Hence, no user would have any incentive to alter their travel path. This condition is commonly referred to as traffic or transportation network equilibrium. In an S-O network problem one also must satisfy the demands, but it is the total cost in the network system that is minimized.

An excellent example of the difference between U-O behaviour and S-O behaviour is captured in the well-known Braess paradox in which the addition of a new road or link (assuming U-O behaviour) results in the travel cost increasing for all the users in the network, despite the fact that now the travellers have a new path from their origin to their destination. Such a paradox has also garnered the interest of computer scientists in the context of the Internet, a large-scale decentralized network.

Policies, such as tolls, may be imposed on transportation and other networks in order to alter users' behaviour so that the U-O solution (after the imposition of tolls) coincides with the S-O solution. Clearly, any improvements or enhancements that are made to a network must take into consideration the behaviour of the users of that network.

Networks may be interrelated as in the Internet being interwoven with transportation networks; as in electronic commerce; or with financial systems, as in electronic finance. Networks may have flows that consist of multiple modes of transportation (private, public, and so on). Demands may be fixed or elastic where the attractiveness associated with travelling between an O/D pair may depend on the volume of the associated demands.

The network equilibrium concept, originating in transportation, is also applicable in different contexts, including spatial or interregional commodity trade, **supply-chain** networks and electric power generation and distribution, as well as in the flow of financial funds. Recently, it has been shown that financial network problems with intermediation as well as electric power **supply-chains** can be reformulated and solved as transportation network equilibrium problems.

The first mathematical models that focused on transportation networks typically assumed that the costs associated with shipping a unit of the commodity on a link were fixed and independent of the volume of flow on the link. Such classical transportation network problems were linear programming problems and spearheaded special-purposes algorithms for their solution, which exploited the network structure. Generalizations of such network models included quadratic and non-linear programming formulations.

Equilibrium problems on networks, with a transportation focus, were originally formulated as non-linear optimization problems. More general transportation network equilibrium problems in which the cost on a link could depend on the flow on that link, but also on the flows on other links in an asymmetric fashion, were subsequently formulated and solved as variational inequality problems. Variational inequality formulations have also been obtained for multimodal traffic network equilibrium problems, with either fixed or elastic demands, and a plethora of other network equilibrium problems.

Since networks provide the foundation for the functioning of our societies and economies it is essential to be able to determine their vulnerability due to, for example, natural disasters, deteriorations due to ageing or poor maintenance, attacks, and so on. Indeed, the identification of the most important nodes and links can assist decision-makers in terms of which network components should be better secured and maintained since disruptions to these components may have the greatest impact.

Finally, it is important to emphasize that network concepts and models may also be utilized to abstract decision-making on networks, and to capture similarities and differences of systems through their network representation.

Further reading
Boyce, D.E., H.S. Mahmassani and A. Nagurney (2005). A retrospective on Beckmann, McGuire and Winsten's *Studies in the Economics of Transportation. Papers in Regional Science* **84**, 85–103.
Nagurney, A. (1999). *Network Economics: A Variational Inequality Approach* (2nd revised edn). Boston, MA: Kluwer Academic Publishers.
Nagurney, A. (2006). *Supply-chain Network Economics: Dynamics of Prices, Flows, and Profits.* Cheltenham, UK and Northampton, MA, USA: Edward Elgar.

Anna Nagurney

non-motorized travel demand modelling

Pedestrian and **bicycle** travel planning has been receiving increasing attention in the past decade at the local, regional and national levels because of the potential **environmental**, social and health benefits of non-motorized travel. Specifically, pedestrian and bicycle travel can provide a safe and convenient alternative to automobile travel, thus reducing traffic **congestion** problems and mobile source emissions. Similarly, non-motorized travel can contribute to the improved health of society, serve as a recreational outlet, and foster a socially vibrant community through increased opportunities for interaction among individuals. At the same time, however, the limited resources for funding transportation improvements require that planners and policy-makers estimate the usage and benefits of improvements in non-motorized transportation options against other alternative transportation projects. Such estimations require a good understanding of non-motorized travel behaviour, and the development of non-motorized travel demand models to predict future travel needs as well as to assess the impact on travel mode of policy actions aimed at encouraging bicycle and pedestrian travel.

Non-motorized travel behaviour analysis and demand forecasting is in its infancy relative to motorized travel, as pointed out by several recent reviews of non-motorized travel methods. These studies highlight the importance of collecting accurate data on non-motorized travel, understanding the behavioural elements of non-motorized travel, and developing quantitative models of non-motorized travel for both planning purposes (prioritizing projects, estimating reduction in automobile emissions, time and cost savings to travellers, and so on) as well as for **safety** analysis, for example, developing exposure rates from which measures of accident risk can be developed.

Many different sources of data may be used for non-motorized travel analysis. Among these, metropolitan household surveys provide detailed individual and household-level information about non-motorized travel usage for both work and non-work purposes. However, some practical limitations of typical metropolitan household surveys for non-motorized travel analysis are: no recording of purely recreational trips, such as walking or bicycling for exercise; under-reporting of short work trips; limited or no information on non-motorized travel patterns of young children; and inability to assess the impact of weather conditions on non-motorized travel because of the narrow time period of survey data collection. In addition, metropolitan household surveys typically collect information from about 1000–2000 households, and such a small sample size does not provide adequate data for non-motorized travel analysis. Thus, an important consideration in non-motorized demand estimation is to identify a data source that includes purely recreational trips, children's travel patterns, an extended period of survey collection to encompass different kinds of weather conditions, and an adequate sample size of non-motorized trips.

The importance of predicting and influencing non-motorized travel suggests the need for a detailed and comprehensive modelling of non-motorized travel demand. A three-step procedure may be used. The first step is to bring all the non-motorized trips from the survey into a geographic information system (GIS)-based platform. In addition, this step should include overlaying the land use, urban form, traffic analysis zone configuration, and the auto or transit **network** over the spatial layer representing non-motorized trips within the GIS platform.

The second step is to use the GIS platform to analyse non-motorized travel behaviour, which should include aggregate characterizations of non-motorized travel (such as number and percentage of non-motorized trips by activity purpose; number and percentage of individuals who bike or walk by activity purpose; trip length and time-of-day distributions of non-motorized trips; and location characteristics of the origin and destination of non-motorized trips) and cross-classifications of non-motorized travel indicators with land use, urban form, facility attributes and the demographic characteristics of individuals.

As part of this second step, the analyst should specifically differentiate between non-motorized travel for utilitarian activity purposes (such as walking or biking to the transit station and/or to work) and recreational activity purposes (such as walking or **bicycling** for exercise or to enjoy the outdoors). The third step is to develop and estimate a demand modelling framework for non-motorized travel. The framework should consider the joint effects of: household or individual demographics; employment characteristics; weather; and season of year. It should also consider community or neighbourhood characteristics such as: size and density; land use mix and **accessibility** to activity opportunities using non-motorized modes of travel; **safety** from crime; school quality and accessibility measures; street network measures; and street scale and aesthetic attributes. In addition, the modelling framework should accommodate the self-selection of individuals and households into neighbourhoods based on inclinations toward non-motorized travel. That is, individuals who are highly inclined toward walking and bicycling may search for communities and neighbourhoods with non-motorized-friendly facilities. If this were true, but not accommodated in the analysis, it could lead to a spurious causal effect of community or neighbourhood effects on non-motorized travel.

Further reading
Cervero, R. and C. Radish (1996). Travel choices in pedestrian versus automobile oriented neighbourhoods. *Transport Policy* **3**, 127–41.
Zahran, S., S. Brody, P. Maghelal, A. Prelog and M. Lacy (2008). Cycling and walking: explaining the spatial distribution of healthy modes of transportation in the United States. *Transportation Research D* **13**, 462–70.

Chandra Bhat

P

packaging

A strategic component of freight transportation is cargo packaging, which attempts to ensure that products arrive at their destinations without damage and ready for store shelves. In the United States, packaging is a $5.8 billion business with an annual growth rate of 2 per cent. Consequences of improper packaging may include higher costs in the form of damaged shipments, lost shipments and higher insurance premiums. It is imperative that all parties within a **supply-chain**, from product design to the transportation of products, are familiar with the transportation modes that transport products and with storage facilities from which and to which products are transported. This knowledge will likely ensure that products are properly packaged to avoid damage when transported. The packaging industry in recent years has emphasized sustainable business practices, cargo security and consumer product **safety**.

Three levels of packaging exist – tertiary, secondary and primary. These forms of packaging are used at different points within the supply-chain. Tertiary packaging or transport packaging serves to protect cargoes throughout their transportation movements. **Containers**, steel drums and fibrous bags are examples of tertiary packaging. Secondary packaging is the next level that includes, for example, palletizing cargo and using boxes that hold multiple primary packaged units. Primary packaging is the packaging of individual products by means of boxes, bags and seals. Primary packaged products are displayed on store shelves.

Packaging serves three main purposes: to protect goods during their transit, facilitate careful handling operations and provide customer service. For international shipments, all Incoterms, that is, terms of trade identifying risk and responsibility in an international transaction, state that packaging is the responsibility of the exporter. Transported products must be able to withstand: the rigours of transit, for example water infiltration during ocean voyages; changing temperatures and altitudes, for example as in the case of air cargo; and possible tampering, theft and pilferage.

For containerized cargo, various mechanisms in addition to the steel container box can be employed to prevent pilferage, for example electronic cargo seals (e-seals), bolts and radio frequency identification (RFID) tags. E-seals and RFID tags may be read at **transhipment** points, along rail lines and roadways, allowing shippers to monitor for possible route deviations and sabotage. In the case of unauthorized seal removal or tampering, alerts are sent to shippers notifying them of such activities and providing them with the time, date and location of the event.

The second purpose of packaging is to allow for proper handling of the cargo. Markings displayed on products to be transported are attempts to ensure that the products are not misdirected or mishandled at any point in their movements. Such markings may include the weight and dimensions of the product and important handling descriptions such as the International Organization for Standardization (ISO) handling pictorials. Detailed product information that might invite higher levels of theft should be avoided.

Packaging also provides a level of customer service. From a marketing perspective, packaging captures the attention of consumers, peaks their interest, communicates various product attributes and leads to sales. Packaging can leverage the brand. For example, innovative designs, colour schemes and pertinent information on the packaging materials of products may draw consumers, thereby enhancing the likelihood that they will be purchased when displayed on store shelves.

In 2006 more than 251 million tons of waste were produced in the United States, equivalent to over 4.6 pounds per person per day. Packaging represents about 65 per cent of United States waste. Firms, including Wal-Mart, the world's largest retailer, have called on their suppliers to reduce packaging as well as to utilize green packaging, that is, packaging materials that are recyclable or compostable. Wal-Mart has mandated that suppliers cut packaging by 5 per cent by 2013. If so, this would translate into a significant operational cost savings for Wal-Mart – for example fewer **containers** being used in the shipping process, fewer truckload deliveries to stores, a reduction in fuel costs and improved spacing on retail outlet store shelves. Re-engineered packaging designs can save 12 per cent in carton space, reduce packaging materials by 10 per cent and save 20 per cent in transportation costs.

Overcoming the prevalent challenge of using too few versus too many packaging materials is the conundrum for firms focused on sustainable packaging. Using too few packaging materials may result in damage and the theft of products. Using too many packaging materials will result in the greater use of packaging materials than is necessary, thereby resulting in higher packaging costs and greater amounts of waste.

As a result of the cost savings associated with reduced packaging and an emphasis on cargo and consumer **safety**, re-engineered packaging mechanisms will remain industry trends. Moreover, as eco-friendly business practices become traditional business activities, it is conceivable that the polluter-pay principle will be emphasized in global packaging policies, therefore encouraging the use of less packaging and renewable resources.

Further reading

Mongelluzzo, B. (2009). New dimensions in savings. *Journal of Commerce* **10**, 54–7.

United States Environmental Protection Agency (2007). *Municipal Solid Waste Generation, Recycling, and Disposal in the United States: Facts and Figures for 2006*. Washington, DC: United States Government Printing Office.

Sara E. Russell and *Wayne K. Talley*

paratransit

Paratransit is an alternative mode of public transportation that is provided by private or public operators for a certain group of users or to the general public. This mode of public transport is adaptable in its routing and scheduling to individual users' and/or operators' desires in varying degrees. Whilst the implementation and the use of this mode differs in developed and developing countries, ultimately this mode aims to fill the gaps left among private cars, **buses** and other fixed-track systems. Typically vans or minibuses are used to provide paratransit service, but also shared **taxis** and jitneys are important providers.

In developed countries, paratransit is often used for **demand-responsive** systems such as shared-ride **taxis**, dial-a-ride and subscription or community buses. When it was introduced in the 1970s, it was thought to be an ideal public transport service provision for all users in areas of low-density land use and low-density demand (areas not served cost-effectively by conventional transit systems). Recently it has been used as a public transport system for users or commuters with special needs, such as disabled travellers and the **elderly**.

In developing countries, the lower standard of living, higher population density, and availability of a cheap labour force have together provided a bewildering array of transport modes bridging the gap between undeveloped 'fixed' **public transport** system and private automobiles. More than half of the public transport demand in many cities in developing countries is carried by paratransit. Rapid increases in urban population, low per capita income, along with inadequate existing transport infrastructures have stimulated their usage as inexpensive and convenient public transport modes.

The delivery of paratransit services may vary considerably on the degree of flexibility they provide their customers. Basic paratransit offers a service from a user-specified origin to a user-specified destination at a user-specified time. The basic service is modified to offer service only to provider-specified destinations, or in some cases one destination, such as a site for social or medical service provision. In practice, the simplest service may consist of a **taxi** or small bus that runs along a more or less defined route and stops to pick up or allow passengers to alight on request. At the other end of the spectrum – fully demand-responsive transport – the most flexible paratransit systems offer an on-demand call-up door-to-door service from any origin to any destination in a service area. In developing countries the form of paratransit modes range from simple non-motorized human, mainly hand-drawn or pedal-driven, or animal-powered vehicles to motorized minibuses. These paratransit modes are designed to provide flexible and frequent services to small communities and through narrow streets where no other services operate at a relatively low fare.

In terms of functional characteristics and service patterns, the paratransit modes can be classified into three separate groups. The first is the 'individual' type of paratransits which provide a door-to-door service. In the second and third groups, the 'shared' and 'collective' types, the routes are generally fixed but vehicles often deviate from the route on passenger demand. The collective type of paratransit services sometimes cut routes to pick up opposite-direction passengers.

Paratransit services can be operated by public transit agencies, community groups or not-for-profit corporations, and for-profit private companies or operators. Private individuals and cooperatives own the vehicles used for paratransit. Survey results in developing countries indicate that most drivers rent the vehicles from small-scale enterprises, with very few drivers owning their vehicles. For example, only 9 per cent of the jeepney drivers in Manila, 18 per cent and 13 per cent of *becak* drivers in Bandung and Jakarta, and 1 per cent of *samlor* drivers in Bangkok, are estimated to own their vehicles. Mostly, the fares of 'individual' types of paratransit modes are decided through negotiation between passengers and drivers. Some countries, such as India and Nepal, have metered autorickshaws. But in the case of 'shared' or 'collective' types of paratransit, fixed fares are received from passengers although in some countries the system can be more flexible, depending on the operator or driver.

Each transport mode has its positive and negative consequences. Although the characteristics of paratransit modes are different based on their functions in different cities, commonalities include that these modes are the usual means of movement among low-income individuals, with cheap fares, low **energy** requirements and higher labour intensity. Moreover, in some cities in developing countries, the paratransit sector also generates a considerable number of employment opportunities. For example, in India and Bangladesh the share of employment generated by cycle rickshaw services is 12 and 12.9 per cent respectively. This percentage was more in case of Chiang Mai (Bangkok), about 13–20 per cent, in the minibus and *samlor* services. Unlike a conventional bus service, the parat-ransit modes have no obligation to provide a service on those routes where demands are low. The operator provides services only where and when it is profitable for them. Often, to achieve more profitability, the 'shared' and 'collective' types paratransit modes do not leave the terminal until the vehicles are full; though the operator profitability and environmen-tal effects are good, this approach does lead to longer passenger waiting time.

At the same time, however, the paratransit system has negative impacts to the overall transport systems. Because the system is mostly developed by the community or market initiative, it is also harder for it to be regulated by the government, leading to difficulties not only in standardizing the level of service but also in other practical aspects, such as fares and the size and vehicle type of fleets. Other negative effects are the overall reduction of the traffic speed and decrease of road capacity which can cause appreci- able **congestion**. In many developing countries, paratransit indiscriminate stopping and starting may hamper the normal flow of traffic. For example in Jakarta, in terms of road space utilization per passenger, it is estimated that *bajaj* or *bemo* is 10 to 13 times more inefficient than a conventional bus. There is also some indication that the use of paratransit significantly contributes to the road traffic accident rate.

Whilst modern rapid mass transport systems such as tram and modern urban rail may relieve transport and traffic **congestion** problems, these systems need a huge amount of capital investment; something which is almost impossible for most developing countries and low-density areas in developed countries. In such circumstances, paratransit modes will still be able to serve the community in a much better way than the fixed public transport system.

Further reading
Shimazaki, T. and M. Rahman (1995). Operational characteristics of paratransit in developing countries of Asia. *Transportation Research Record* **1503**, 49–56.

Yusak O. Susilo

park-and-ride facilities

The park-and-ride concept, developed in the 1970s, involves driving a private vehicle to a suburban public transport station, **parking**, and then boarding a bus, train, light rail or **ferry** to complete the journey. Park-and-ride facilities serve as the collection point for individuals transferring to means of public transport or another vehicle containing at least one person. These facilities are designed to accommodate public transport, rail, car-pooling, van-pooling and shuttle services. Infrastructure facilitating this concept may consist of bus stops, transit stations, but also travel information signs, security and lightning to address security concerns that users may have about leaving their vehicles. Key public transport and railway stations at the urban fringe seem to be most ideal sites for park-and-ride facilities. **Parking** is generally free or significantly less expensive than in urban centres.

Governmental involvement in organization and financing of park-and-ride programmes is generally high. Local or regional governments together with regional or local transportation agencies are usually involved in implementation and organization. However, there are successful examples of **public–private partnerships** and even full private provision – park-and-ride facilities are profitable in Bath (United Kingdom) and Philadelphia (United States). A range of policy aims has been identified for the provision of park-and-ride facilities, including **economic development**, providing additional or replacement parking facilities, **traffic management** (that is, measures to mitigate the effects of vehicle use which do not necessarily seek to result in less traffic) and car traffic reduction. A major drawback of these schemes refers to the environmental impact of constructing large car parks in sensitive land on the urban fringe.

There has been considerable debate about the necessity and effective-ness of park-and-ride facilities. Park-and-ride may increase the passenger occupancy of vehicles driven to an urban centre, and reduce the pressure of traffic growth on the road **network**. On the other hand, most people would perceive that the fringes of urban areas are more pleasant without the presence of large surface car parks than they are with them. Evidence from the United Kingdom (park-and-ride schemes in York and Oxford) shows that unintended effects may occur. There was lack of evidence for traffic reduction, and the abstraction from modes other than the car (car use to reach the facility) increased. **Congestion** has remained persistent in the cities and there is concern that total travel may have been increased rather than reduced.

More recently, research finds that park-and-ride can have traffic-reduction benefits in the urban area. This effect is dampened by an increase in urban fringe vehicle traffic as motorists detour to reach facilities or make additional trips. It is concluded that the main effect of the schemes is traffic redistribution, and that their role within traffic restraint policies is unlikely to be directly one of traffic reduction. Park-and-ride seems to be an appropriate way to encourage public transport and decrease urban traffic problems, but policy-makers should be aware of serious redistribu-tion effects that may even lead to a negative overall effect.

The park-and-ride concept may seem attractive at first glance, but needs careful consideration because of the opposing effects. It tends to be most effective as part of a comprehensive effort to encourage ride-share commuting and use of public transport. An important guideline for a more successful implementation of park-and-ride programmes seems therefore to be the development of an overall **public transport** and ride-share improvement strategy. Security needs to be part of this package and may, for instance, be improved when locating facilities within view of businesses or homes.

Further reading

Parkhurst, G.P. (1995). Park and ride: could it lead to an increase in car traffic? *Transport Policy* **2**, 15–23.

Parkhurst, G.P. (2000). Influence of bus-based park and ride facilities on users' car traffic. *Transport Policy* **7**, 159–72.

Parkhurst, G.P. and G. Stokes (1994). Park and ride in Oxford and York: report of surveys. Transport Studies Unit, Working Paper 797, University of Oxford.

Barry Ubbels

parking

Parking is the storage of a vehicle at the end of a leg of a trip allowing its user to undertake an activity outside the vehicle. The vehicle can be an automobile, truck, bicycle, **motorcycle, bus**, tram or train. All vehicles must park at some point in time, and it is this fact that makes parking such an important consideration for all transport users.

Parking requires space to store the vehicle. The size of the parking space is directly related to the size of a standard vehicle, with additional space at the sides and back to allow entry and exit of people or goods into the vehicle. The space at the side and back of the vehicle may be influenced by the activity that the occupants are undertaking. For instance, an automobile parking space at a shopping centre where goods have to be loaded and unloaded frequently, may be wider (for example 2.6 m x 5.4 m) than that for a parking space at a business (for example 2.4 m x 5.4 m) where people may only enter and leave the vehicle once or twice a day.

Entry and exit of the vehicle into or out of a parking space requires an area to manoeuvre the vehicle. This consists of a manoeuvring area in the proximity of the parking space, and roads providing access to the manoeuvring area. In an automobile parking lot the roads in the vicinity of the parking space are termed 'aisles' and those providing general movement in the lot are termed 'circulator aisles'. The design of aisles and circulator aisles is related to their prime purpose. Circulator aisles are designed for movement while the aisles are designed for manoeuvring into and out of the parking space.

The land use where the vehicle occupant wishes to undertake their activity is often used to guide the amount of parking required for the land use. The desired number of parking spaces per unit of activity in the land use is termed the parking rate. This rate is determined by measuring the parking usage associated with a land use and dividing it by a measure of the level of activity, for example, parking spaces per gross floor area. To determine parking usage at a land use the parking rate is multiplied by the total measure of activity in the land use. Although this approach has considerable theoretical limitations, it is a practical, easy-to-measure approach and is generally supported by the parking industry.

The decision of the location, amount, type, duration and cost of parking provided in an area can be used to manage the demand for a land use and, indirectly, the method of travel to that land use. This decision comes under the heading of parking policy. Parking policy can influence the economic climate; the efficient use of transport, land and public resources; **mobility** and access; equity; environmental goals; and amenity in an area. For this reason, parking policy should be integrated with **land use and transport** policy, and aimed at obtaining a sustainable urban structure. Parking policy is usually implemented at the local level of government. The coordination of parking policies between local governments in conjunction with higher levels of government is essential to ensure a sustainable urban structure.

Parking provision is often seen as a blight on the urban landscape. Large areas of black bitumen can be viewed as ugly, they are an area where pollutants from vehicles tend to accumulate, and people may use them as sites for undesirable activities when the parking area is not in common use. The appropriate design of parking facilities may overcome these concerns by designing them to be integrated into the urban landscape and to allow the pollutants to be collected and disposed of; while access control of entrances and exits and video surveillance may reduce undesirable activities.

The behaviour of vehicle drivers in a parking facility is influenced by the design of the parking facility, regulations describing appropriate behaviour and the enforcement of these regulations. Enforcement of the regulations is an important aspect of the monitoring of behaviour in a parking facility and has a considerable impact on the performance of the transport, parking and land use systems.

The use of information technology, improved mechanical devices and data collection technology have improved the performance of parking facilities. The automation of parking payment has reduced inconvenience to drivers, and reduced fraud in the parking industry and **congestion** at parking entrances and exits. Driver behaviour can also be assisted through the provision of information on the type, location and availability of parking spaces. Parking guidance systems using automatic vehicle detection contribute considerably to the efficient use of parking facilities.

Data describing parking demand and supply can be obtained by many methods. Origin destination, patrol and usage surveys using human observers are common approaches. Automation of the collection of parking charges and measuring vehicle flow at entrances and exits are allowing data to be collected more efficiently in order to increase the efficient performance of parking facilities.

Further reading
McCluskey, J. (1987). *Parking: A Handbook of Environmental Design*. London: E. and F. Spoon.
Wendt, R.A. and H.S. Levinson (1990). *Parking*. Washington, DC: ENO Foundation.
Young, W. (1991). Parking policy, design and data. Department of Civil Engineering, Monash University.

William Young

peak loads

Peak loads of traffic can be defined as higher demands for travel imposed on any given system. This is valid for any **network** and mode of transport, be it urban and interurban bus and rail services, airport and airlines services, road traffic and urban and interurban roads, and so on.

Since the **demand for transport** is predominantly a derived demand, and the activities with which transport is associated vary over time, the demand for transport services is not constant over time, resulting in peaks and troughs. The demand for travel varies by time of the day, day of the week and by season (see Figure for the typical pattern). The daily peak period, for example, is caused by people going to and coming from work. Commuters travel in the morning peak not because they choose to do so, but because they need to get to work by a certain time, and there is usually a penalty for arriving late. In the short run, increasing the price of trips, for example by imposing a **congestion** charge, would not alter these trips to work. Some people might change the mode they use, for example from car to bus, but they would still travel to work during the morning rush hour. Employers are also unlikely to change working hours as there

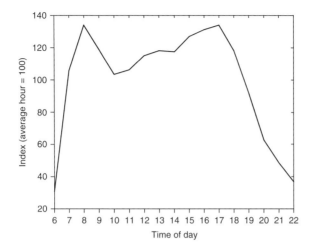

are significant advantages to working at approximately the same time as everyone else. However, they are typically not forced to take into account the effects of this on **congestion**. Light and heavy goods vehicles are similarly constrained by the normal hours of work of commercial and industrial establishments. The peaks for commercial vehicles do not coincide exactly with commuting trips although there might be some overlap. The Figure shows a typical town road traffic profile for a weekday.

It can be seen on the Figure that peak loads occur during the morning and evening rush hour, when demand is highest. There is also usually an inter-peak, when demand is still high but lower than the maximum values it reaches during the morning and evening commuting times.

The weekly and seasonal peak loads occur because demands for trips during weekdays are usually work-related, whereas those during weekends tend to have shopping or recreational purposes. In the same way, long-distance trips, for example to summer or winter resorts, are usually linked to summer or winter holidays.

The fact that demand for travel is a derived demand also implies that the distribution of trips in space depends on the location of residences, businesses, recreational activities, and so on. In this sense, the same route may have a peak load in one direction only during the morning rush hour, and in the opposite direction during the evening rush hour.

During times where there are peak loads on the system, marginal costs tend to be higher. Efficient pricing requires that prices equal **marginal cost**. Even when fares are not set equal to marginal costs, operators will try to maximize their profits during peak times and to increase demand during off-peak times. Airline operators charge higher fares during peak periods, and make special offers during off-peak periods. Travellers arriving in London before 10 a.m. pay higher train fares, and the same policy applies to most cities throughout the United Kingdom.

Peak loads become a problem when demand exceeds the capacity of the system. When this happens, queues build up, resulting in further delays and higher costs. Although this **queuing system** could be seen as an allocation method, it does not guarantee that the most valuable trips are the ones that will be completed. Adding capacity in an attempt to satisfy demand during peak times will result in excess supply during off-peak times. Ensuring marginal costs are covered will reduce demand and guarantee that only the most valuable trips, that is, those for which marginal cost equals marginal benefit, will be made; whilst others will change time or mode of travel, or be cancelled altogether. In the case of roads, for example, car users could pay a **congestion** charge to reflect the true social cost of their trips at peak times, which impose delays on other road users.

Further reading
Button, K.J. (2010). *Transport Economics* (3rd edn). Cheltenham, UK and Northampton, MA, USA: Edward Elgar.
Glaister, S. (1981). *Fundamentals of Transport Economics*. Oxford: Basil Blackwell.
Small, K. and E. Verhoef (2007). *The Economics of Urban Transportation*. London: Taylor & Francis.

Georgina Santos

pedestrian zones

Pedestrian zones or precincts are squares, plazas, streets or street **networks** reserved solely for pedestrian use. They are predominantly found in urban centres, and the associated traffic regulations generally allow access for delivery and service vehicles. This is normally restricted in time to avoid vehicular traffic during the busiest hours. Examples of pedestrian zones also exist in which the pedestrian traffic is mixed with **buses**, **trams** and/or **bicycles**, but where **pedestrians** still have legal priority over other modes. Access restrictions may be enforced through the use of moveable physical barriers, which allow vehicular entry via key card or remote control systems.

In principle, pedestrian zones are a reiteration of the original form of urban settlements in which movement on foot was the predominant form of locomotion. During the nineteenth century, street layouts in urban centres were progressively adapted to accommodate horse-drawn carriages and, later, the **automobile**. The idea of separating pedestrian spaces from motorized traffic – and the associated drawbacks of danger, noise and exhaust emissions – was first popularized by the Garden City Movement of the late nineteenth and early twentieth century. Here, the concept related mostly to small- to medium-scale residential or mixed-use settlements, though.

The idea of separating through traffic from local traffic found further favour in post-war planning during the middle of the twentieth century, and several concepts were devised which employed the idea of neighbourhoods, areas or precincts designed for certain functions and accessible only for local circulation. The so-called Radburn layout (after the United States American garden town of the same name), which envisaged completely separate circulation systems for pedestrians and **bicyclists** on the one hand and motor vehicles on the other, was hardly ever repeated on a large scale. Exceptions are found, for example, in British new towns such as Cumbernauld, Scotland.

A few exceptions apart, the construction of pedestrian precincts in Europe only became prevalent in the late 1960s, often in conjunction with the reconstruction of urban centres damaged or destroyed during the Second World War. The implementation generally started by closing the main shopping street to car traffic and progressively extending the restrictions to surrounding streets and areas over the following years and decades. Apart from providing greater comfort for pedestrians, the impetus for pedestrianization often also derived from the simple fact that pedestrian volumes in these streets became too great for the pavement (sidewalk) space available.

Over time, the perceived function of pedestrian zones grew beyond the idea of areas with largely commercial functions, as urban spaces were rediscovered as outdoor living areas, as places with social functions. Not only did shopping become a leisure activity in itself, but pedestrian zones also became enhanced through actively designed public spaces with opportunities for meeting, resting and 'watching the world go by'. This function was enhanced by the increasing presence of cafes, restaurants, bars and bistros, which offered outdoor seating or at least a view on the world outside.

Commercially speaking, pedestrian zones are virtually always associated with increased turnover for local restaurateurs and retailers – although creating such zones from scratch still often meets with opposition from exactly these groups, who see themselves in competition with out-of-town shopping facilities that offer unrestricted access to the car. Conversely, where pedestrian zones already exist, traders in adjoining areas are often keen to be included in the scheme as they see a competitive disadvantage in not being situated within the zone itself.

In addition to local users, tourists are a very important group frequenting pedestrian zones. Many towns and tourist boards use the existence of such areas – especially but not exclusively those in historic town centres – as an important attractor in their marketing strategies. They also increasingly become arenas for special events such as seasonal markets or street-based festivals. In some cities, the pedestrian zone has become inextricably linked with the experience of the city that is expected by and sold to visitors. Brussels, Copenhagen, Venice, Vienna and York are all prominent examples.

The downside of this high commercial viability can be that rents increase, and retail space is taken over by shops, cafes and restaurants belonging to big chains that can afford to pay higher rates. The effect can be a loss of the local identity provided by independent traders. Furthermore, it is not enough simply to ban car traffic from central shopping streets in order to save an ailing urban centre. Such strategies must go hand in hand with transport and land use planning elsewhere in the municipality.

The advantages of the social as well as commercial opportunities afforded by well-designed pedestrian zones are mostly greater than the potential problems, and pedestrian zones have in some places contributed to reviving town centres which were suffering from losing their human scale in favour of car-oriented spaces.

Further reading

Gaffron, P. (1998). The transport crisis in Britain: pedestrian solutions or solutions for pedestrians? In B. Turton (ed.), *Transport Geography Research Group Papers Presented at the Third Postgraduate Seminar*. London: Royal Geographical Society.

Monheim, R. (2003). The role of pedestrian precincts in adapting city centres to new lifestyles. In R. Tolley (ed.), *Sustainable Transport: Planning for Walking and Cycling in Urban Environments*. Cambridge: Woodhead Publishing.

Philine Gaffron

pedestrians

Walking is the most basic form of human locomotion, and in terms of numbers, pedestrians form the largest transport 'user group' anywhere on earth. Even in industrialized countries, where motorized modes have the highest modal share in terms of distance travelled, virtually every trip begins and ends on foot. In developing or threshold countries, walking generally plays a much greater role than in industrialized nations due to lower levels of motorization and less-developed **public transport** systems, but is also less well studied in these contexts. Differences in culture and tradition apart, the basic needs of pedestrians everywhere can be summarized as comfort and **safety**.

In urban contexts, pedestrians are generally exposed to emissions from motorized transport such as noise, particles, nitrous oxides, ozone and carbon monoxide, all of which are detrimental to human health and are associated with sustainability concerns on a wider scale. Encouraging more people to walk for short- to medium-distance trips will help to reduce these emissions, which in turn will enhance the quality of the urban experience and make walking more attractive. Since 2005, **European Union** citizens also have a legally enforceable right to certain **air quality** standards.

While pedestrians are physically exposed and potentially vulnerable road users, walking does provide a form of exercise which is available to all. In fact, the health benefits of walking regularly for half an hour per day are generally considered to outweigh the risks of physical injury in accidents, through contributing to a reduction of cardiovascular diseases, obesity, diabetes, stress-related syndromes and depression. Making walking for utility purposes as attractive as possible to as many people as possible is the most likely way of encouraging this type of exercise on a regular basis.

Depending on the context, pedestrian comfort and **safety** will demand varying solutions, while the factors to be considered are constant. Comfort is affected by topography, weather, distance from origin to destination and the quality of the (urban) environment. This includes factors such as noise and pollution, which in urban contexts are very directly related to motorized traffic. On the more detailed level, directness and signposting of routes, frequency and quality of road crossings, as well as quantity and quality of walking surfaces and types and distribution of street furniture all influence pedestrian comfort. Pedestrian safety is mostly affected at points of contact with motorized traffic (though the quality and maintenance of walking surfaces are also important, particularly for people with limited **mobility** and the **elderly**). Consideration must therefore be given to the layout of junctions and crossings, the levels and speed of motorized traffic, the allocation of road space to different user groups and the prioritization of modes, for example in the context of traffic calming or pedestrian zones. Feelings of personal security also play an important role. These, too, are affected by spatial qualities but also, for example, by lighting and the possibility of social supervision.

Pedestrians travel at an average speed of 8 km/h, though this figure will vary according to health, age, fitness and loads carried. For planning purposes, a trip length of about 20 minutes (an average of about 2.6 km) is generally considered to be the distance most people are prepared to consider for a walking trip. Thus planning for pedestrians is closely linked with spatial planning and particularly the concept of the 'city of short distances', with its emphasis on maximizing **accessibility** of destinations (education, jobs, shops, and so on) rather than the **mobility** of the citizens. Since existing spatial patterns oriented towards motorized travel will persist for some time, though, while the practical activity radius of pedestrians will not grow significantly, pedestrian travel should also be considered in conjunction with other modes, particularly public transport.

Pedestrians as customers play an important economic role in urban centres and central business districts, particularly in connection with traffic calming measures and **pedestrian zones**. Pedestrian travel is also comparatively cheap to provide for, and free to the 'user'.

Pedestrian travel is furthermore linked to social equity. Pedestrians are generally not a homogenous group, with some relying more on walking than others and thus also suffering disproportionately from inadequate provisions for pedestrian travel. Connections exist between the reliance on walking and age (that is, the young and the old), **gender** and socio-economic factors.

Due to low levels of personal identification with walking, pedestrians generally do not have strong lobby groups, which means that their concerns are often less well represented compared to other road users. This problem is often exacerbated by a bias against walking implicit in many survey methodologies that only measure trips over certain distances, or concentrate on modes used for the main component of a trip chain. **Pedestrian travel demand** is furthermore difficult to consider in most current transport models.

Further reading
Tolley, R. (ed.) (2003). *Sustainable Transport: Planning for Walking and Cycling in Urban Environments*. Cambridge: Woodhead Publishing.

Philine Gaffron

privatization

Public ownership (nationalization) of transportation infrastructure has been common in many countries; public ownership of operating modes less so. In the former Soviet Union state ownership was ubiquitous, and it is still widespread even in what are largely considered 'market economies'. In the past, national ownership of roads and ports was seen as important for military logistics and political control. In their heyday, for example, the Roman Empire, for example, had 37000 miles of state-owned paved roads to move troops and carry communications throughout the Empire. More recently, and particularly since the Industrial Revolution, economic considerations have played a bigger role. To muster the necessary assets to construct transport infrastructure, public monies were often needed and this generally also involved public ownership. In the twentieth century the concern to coordinate transport facilities, embracing implicit ideas of **intermodality**, interoperability, and interconnectivity, has been used to justify state provision. In some cases state ownership transport was used as part of larger land use and economic planning strategies, with transport being supplied to give access to places where it was clear that the market would not invest.

The long-held view was that provided those managing publicly held assets were given the right incentives, this would ensure that the public interest would be served and that social, economic and political goals would be achieved. What became apparent, however, was that it is very difficult to define clear goals for management; there was no single objective of profit maximization as found in the private sector. Attaining multiple objectives generally involves making numerous trade-offs. This is not always conducive to maximum efficiency. The problem can be compounded when the set of objectives are frequently poorly defined or the subject of unpredictable change, as is often the case when politics become involved. In addition, there was increased academic interest in the 1960s in the motivations of those who managed publicly owned transport undertakings, with the traditional idea that they were solely concerned with meeting the public interest being questioned. Given the lack of dividend and other income, the motivations, it was argued, could well shift to seeking larger bureaucracies.

Privatization of transport assets began on a large scale in the 1970s in places such as the United Kingdom and New Zealand in efforts, depending on the transport involved, to inject private finance into investments, enhance efficiency, to reduce **subsidies** and to raise cash from asset sales. Subsequently, there has been mass privatization on an altogether different scale in the former communist countries.

Privatization can take a variety of forms largely depending on whether there are scale economies of retaining large-scale enterprise, and the future demand prospects for the mode. There are also differences in accompanying institutional changes with price or capacity regulations being introduced if the privatized undertaking has the potential to exercise monopoly power. Large **airlines**, for example, have usually been privatized through a stock issue and without any attempt to break them up; they may benefit from **network** economies but most now operate in competitive markets and thus cannot exercise any monopoly power. In other cases, as with the United Kingdom bus industry and rail operations, privatization was through sales of assets, often in the form of management buyouts because there appeared to be few scale economies.

Privatization has not always involved the sale of assets, it can also entail allowing private companies to supply transport services in markets formerly the single domain of a state-owned supplier. Legislative changes in many countries have, for example, allowed companies such as UPS and FedEx to transport letters and packages in competition with former post office monopolies. In other cases, there has been outsourcing as state-owned transport undertakings have unbundled services and brought in private sector contractors to undertake activities formerly done in-house – road maintenance is often an example of this. Joint **public–private** ventures represent a form of privatization if the investment would have been made by the public sector anyway. To date, public–private initiatives have been mainly limited to the private sector building and operating infrastructure that ultimately reverts to the state, and technically it is difficult to define a firm counterfactual reflecting what would have happened if a cooperative arrangement had not emerged.

The results of privatization have been mixed. Some shifts in ownership, such as the privatization of container transport in the United Kingdom, have been clear successes with cheaper, more efficient services emerging. Opening the transportation of letters beyond post office monopolies has introduced widely used premium services, and outsourcing **road maintenance** has generally resulted in low costs and more rapid repair work. In contrast, efforts to privatize rail track in the United Kingdom proved to be costly. In many cases the outcomes have been mixed. From the transport industry's perspective, many privatized airlines have gone bankrupt or have encountered severe financial difficulties, but customers have gained significant benefits as fares have fallen and the range of services has increased.

Further reading
Gómez-Ibáñez, J.A. and J.R. Meyer (1993). *Going Private: The International Experience with Transport Privatization*. Washington, DC: Brookings Institution Press.
Winston, C. (2010). *Last Exit: Privatization and Deregulation of the U.S. Transportation System*, Washington, DC: Brookings Institution Press.

Kenneth Button

productivity measurement of transport

Productivity is a measure of performance, usually expressed as a ratio of outputs compared to inputs, for example tonne-kilometres transported per employee. There are several purposes of productivity measurement and various methods of measurement. The purposes are various types of performance assessment, for example comparing performance among individuals or teams (activities performed per hour), performance improvement of a company over time, or performance comparisons across plants or companies (and even across countries).

Firms may employ a myriad of performance ratios as partial measures of performance: cargo handled per unit of time might be a measure of dock or loading or unloading performance; cars switched per switch engine hour might be used for rail yard operations; average repair time and/or downtime of equipment might be used as an indicator of maintenance performance. The possibilities are immense. Note that high performance in one dimension could reflect weaker performance in some other dimension, for example high labour productivity typically reflects higher capital inputs. To assess performance more accurately requires tracking both labour and capital productivity.

For this reason, economists have looked for comprehensive measures of productivity. Broadly, there are two approaches: comparisons of total outputs with total inputs via index numbers, or estimating shifts in production or cost functions. These two approaches are related but not identical in concept. Total factor productivity (TFP) is measured by the growth of a revenue-weighted index of all outputs compared to the growth of a cost-share weighted index of inputs. There are many computational issues in index numbers as well as challenges in ensuring data consistency over time and/or among companies being compared. TFP measures the overall productivity change whatever its cause, whether productivity results from eliminating inefficiencies with existing technology, shifting outputs to those requiring fewer inputs, or by real advances in technical knowledge.

The alternate approach to productivity measurement confines the measure to actual shifts in productive abilities, as opposed to efficiency improvements using existing knowledge. This is illustrated in the Figure, a hypothetical production function showing the maximum output y that can be produced with any amount of input x, denoted $F(x)$. The Figure postulates increasing returns, that is, the ratio of y/x increases with the scale of output. Productivity can be measured as the ratio of output to input, indicated by a ray from the origin to various points in the Figure. The upward rotation of the ray from the origin to point A and then B, C

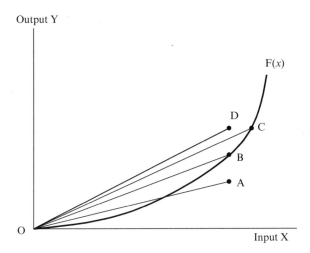

and D shows increasing productivity. The move from A to B eliminates inefficient input use with existing technology. The rise in productivity from B to C reflects economies of scale inherent in the current technology. Point D is attainable only if there is a shift in production technology that enables higher output per input indicated by OD compared to OB, a 'technological change'.

In comparing OA to OD (on an undrawn new production frontier), the index number approach would measure this as a productivity gain, whereas the production shift approach would only measure OD/OB. By identifying sources of productivity measured by the index, the two approaches can be reconciled.

There are two caveats. The first is that productivity performance and financial performance can differ. Productivity compares quantities of output to quantities of inputs. Financial measures compare revenues of output with expenditures on inputs. Changes in prices of outputs and inputs can result in financial results differing from productivity performance.

The second caveat is that productivity abstracts from quality changes. Quality improvements may require increased inputs, so apparent deteriorating productivity could reflect increased quality of what is being produced. A quality adjustment can be incorporated into productivity measures, but quality is much more difficult to measure than quantities of outputs or inputs. It is important to be aware of possible changes in quality in assessing how meaningful a productivity measure is.

Further reading
Coelli T., D.S.P. Rao and G.E. Battese (1998). *An Introduction to Efficiency and Productivity Analysis*. Boston, MA: Kluwer.
Oum, T.H., M.W. Tretheway, and W.G. Waters II (1992). Concepts, methods and purposes of productivity measurement in transportation. *Transportation Research A* **26**, 493–505.

William G. Waters II

public participation

Public participation is the process in which individual members of the general public become involved in the decision-making process for government plans, programmes and projects that may affect them. The mechanisms and importance of public participation differ considerably between countries. Here we focus on America. The United States Department of Transportation provides guidance on a variety of public participation techniques in transportation decision-making. A common technique is to establish a core group of participants through community-based organizations, citizen advisory committees, citizen representatives on committees and collaborative task forces. Members of the core group should reflect affected interests and provide linkage to the represented community. Meetings, whether with a core group or members of the general public, are the foundation of public participation. Hearings, open houses, conferences, workshops and retreats provide alternative formats to involve the public. Techniques for communicating more directly with the public include open houses, mailing lists, key person interviews, newsletters and speakers' bureaus. The choice of which techniques are the most effective can depend on the nature of the information and the need for feedback.

Special public participation efforts may be indicated by Title VI and environmental justice considerations. Transportation plans, programmes and projects funded at least in part with federal funds must comply with Title VI, environmental justice, and other legal requirements. Title VI refers to protection provided by federal law against discrimination in federal programmes and activities based on race, colour or national origin. Additional protection is provided by executive and administrative orders for low-income and minority populations, as well as those with limited English proficiency. Other federal laws protect against discrimination based on **gender**, age, religion and disability. There are a variety of ways to involve these members of the public, perhaps most importantly techniques that recognize the significance of culture. This can be achieved by tailoring typical public participation techniques to reflect local customs and language. In addition, community and religious organizations can serve as gateways and forums for public participation activities.

More than just providing information to the public, public participation requires feedback from the public. Feedback can suggest how well the initial message was communicated and whether additional information or clarification is needed. Feedback can be obtained from the public through the Internet, hotlines and drop-in centres. The convenience of Internet technology allows the public to provide feedback via e-mail or online comment forms. Telephone hotlines that are staffed and provide toll-free access allow the public to provide feedback on an individual basis without cost. Local drop-in centres provide for even more individualized feedback in locations that are convenient to the public. Feedback can be structured with scripted tools such as public opinion surveys, or more flexible tools such as focus groups, facilitation, negotiation and mediation. Focus groups allow the public to provide feedback in an informal setting, while facilitation, negotiation and mediation are structured forums for the public to participate in dispute resolution.

Public participation efforts can be enhanced with special techniques such as holding events, changing meeting approaches and finding new ways to communicate. Transportation fairs engage the public with dynamic displays, videos and models of projects, as well as providing opportunities for the public to give feedback. Other special events such as games and contests can be held at transportation fairs or as independent events to stimulate public involvement. Although meetings are critical to public involvement, alternative meeting agendas that include role-playing, site visits and non-traditional activities can improve attendance and participation. Role-playing requires the active participation of the public in the dramatization of hypothetical situations. Site visits and other non-traditional activities allow the public to participate in field trips and other interesting events. Finally, advances in technology create new opportunities to communicate. Geographic information systems, simulations and visualizations allow the public to compare alternative transportation scenarios and make more informed decisions.

Public participation is required by federal transportation law and policy. The Safe, Accountable, Flexible, Efficient Transportation Equity Act: A Legacy for Users provides specific guidance for public involvement. Public participation efforts must include organizations that represent transportation employees and commercial users; representatives of **pedestrians**, bicyclists and the disabled; and affected public agencies. Transportation agencies must solicit input on public involvement plans, hold public meetings at reasonable times and locations, use visualization techniques to communicate transportation plans and provide public information in electronic formats. Similarly, the United States Department of Transportation's Federal Highway Administration and Federal Transit Administration have jointly committed to a policy of continuous public participation. This policy promotes active roles and mutual obligations for the public and transportation agencies, ensures that state and metropolitan programmes provide for public participation that goes beyond commenting on draft documents, encourages transportation agencies actively to engage the public with innovative techniques, provides assistance and evaluates public participation processes.

Further reading
United States Department of Transportation (2002). *Public Involvement Techniques for Transportation Decision-Making.* Washington, DC: USDOT.

Robert S. Done

public–private partnership

Public–private partnership (PPP) is a contractual agreement between a public agency and a private sector entity to deliver a service or facility for the use of the general public, according to which all or part of the investment is contributed by the private sector and each party shares risks, responsibilities and rewards. The relationship between the two parties (the public and the private sector) in PPPs is made up on the basis of a long-term collaboration for a project with large financing requirements.

In traditional infrastructure development cases (design–bid–build), design and construction responsibilities are awarded to independent contractors following a tender procedure. In these cases the public sector retains responsibility for financing, operating and maintaining infrastructure.

The innovation of the PPP delivery approach is the financial involvement and the greater responsibility and risk taken by the private sector. Expanding the private sector role implies that the assets of the public and private sectors are shared for developing, financing, operating and preserving the facility or service.

The financial and technical resources and management skills of the private sector are applied to serve the objectives of the public party, such as financial viability of the project, greater certainty for success and on-time implementation, specialized expertise, more effective methodological approach, innovative technology application, and so on. At the same time, part of the risk is transferred to the private developer.

The extent of private sector involvement varies and PPP, and it can take many forms from simple commercialization to full **privatization**. Two main archetypes of PPPs can be distinguished.

Firstly, joint venture type PPP. This is a joint commitment of the public and private sector throughout the project's life-cycle. The investment participation by the private sector is thus less than 100 per cent. Both parties share responsibility, risk and financing as shareholders in a public enterprise, which is usually called a special-purpose company (SPC) or vehicle (SPV). In most cases, the risks and profits are allocated according to the share of each party in the project. Both parties are equally concerned for the objectives of the project and share the same risks; therefore, the management of responsibilities and risks becomes a critical issue.

Secondly, pure concession type PPP. This is a form of partnership where the private sector takes on all the investment, and public and private parties divide the identified responsibilities and risks. The private developer usually bears the construction and commercial risks, such as delivery delays and construction cost overruns. The main actions of the public sector involve regulatory configuration and protection of the public interest. The public sector is able to provide public assets and other provisions for a specific period in the agreement, to assist the private sector in the process of accomplishing a particular service. The public sector is also able to absorb large amounts of risk and to compensate retrospectively for major uneven income distribution that may occur, through **taxation** or other policies. Nevertheless, the allocation of project risks between the parties involved is a critical issue that requires careful consideration and should be explicitly defined in the contract.

A more restrictive type of PPPs is typified by the United Kingdom's private finance initiative (PFI), whereby the government becomes a purchaser of services instead of physical assets. The terms PFI and PPP are commonly used interchangeably to refer to any aspect of private involvement in provision of public sector infrastructure or services. However, PPPs are any projects where the public and private sectors are working together in a partnership, and where the private sector undertakes at least part of the costs and expenses. On the other hand, a PFI project is one for which the private sector, being a contractor mainly, undertakes the design, build, finance and operation (DBFO) of a new infrastructure or provision of services, in most cases through the installation or provision and operation of equipment, and it is paid by the public sector within a pre-agreed time period for the full cost of services rendered or infrastructure construction and operation.

The development of a PPP project normally involves a number of phases:

1. Project preparation includes the decision to start the project, scope of the project, market consultation, public enquiries, first formulation and preliminary designs.
2. Tendering and negotiation involves tender preparation, selection of a preferred tender, negotiations with the preferred tender and signing of a contract. In a joint venture type PPP, tendering takes place at a relatively early stage of the project since the project is further developed and defined in a joint effort by private and public sector.
3. Design and construction includes final design activities, if needed, and all construction activities.
4. Operation involves activities related to the exploitation and maintenance of the infrastructure.

The private sector is involved in at least the construction and the exploitation phase, for both joint venture and concession type PPPs.

The most commonly used PPP type of agreement is the build–operate–transfer (BOT), where the private sector is responsible for the financing, design, construction, operation and maintenance of the facility for a specified period of time. Many variants can also be found in current practice such as:

- Build–own–operate–transfer (BOOT). The private sector finances, builds, owns and operates a facility or service for a specified period of time, after which ownership is transferred back to the public sector.
- Build–own–operate (BOO). The private sector finances, builds, owns and operates a facility or service for the facility's entire lifetime.
- Build–own–operate–sell (BOOS). The private sector is responsible for the financing, design, construction, operation and selling of the facility.

A number of incentives may exist for the public sector to form public–private partnerships for transport projects:

- Transport projects encounter obstacles with regards to financing that can lead to serious delays or even cancellation of the project's implementation. Public administrations have been encouraged to collaborate with the public sector in order to increase the budget of transport projects.

- PPPs increase certainty of outcomes by the reduction of project duration and 'on time' project delivery. Moreover, reduced life-cycle costs and protection from the exposure to cost overruns contribute to a successful outcome.
- Benefits on service efficiency and project quality. The operating efficiency can be improved by the best possible combination of the expertise and skills of each sector, and the introduction of competition to the provision of transportation facilities and services, which leads to quality improvement.
- Transfer of risk to the private sector is one of the main incentives for the public sector to form PPPs. These risks involve the final design, construction, financing, operation and maintenance.
- Flexibility to meet changes in the future and to conform to the current and anticipated future market structure.
- The major social benefit of PPPs is their potential to expedite the delivery of transport facilities and services and to reduce capital and operating costs. Therefore, **mobility** can be improved and the environmental impacts can be minimized (reduction of **energy** consumption, **congestion**, air pollution).

Equally, there are a range of possible incentives for the private sector to participate in public–private partnerships. The intention of the private sector to participate in a PPP depends on how attractive and appealing the investment might be. The main objective of the private sector is to achieve the maximum investment return with the minimum risk and cost. Private parties will provide the financial investment, as long as the interplay of risk taken and financial reward matches with its investment strategies and interests. In order to motivate the participation of the private sector, some actions should be taken to increase the revenues of the project and the confidence of the private sector, without harming the public benefit.

A fundamental prerequisite is the public awareness that the PPP approach is necessary, environmentally sound, and the only feasible means of immediate-term implementation. Mutual trust and collaboration between the public and the private sector is vital for the project's success. Coordination between the private and public partners should be achieved from the very early stages. Rational allocation of risk is one of the most critical elements for PPPs' success. Risk should be allocated according to the skills and risk control abilities of each sector. Project evaluation is necessary, in order to prove that the different objectives of the two parties are met, and to estimate the investment return to the private sector. A key issue is to find a balance between the public interest (socio-economic benefits) and the financial rewards. **Environmental** impact constraints should be defined in the design and planning stage, and impact costs should be estimated. Firm political support and commitment for the implementation of the project will ensure project viability. Government support has many elements, for example setting up the appropriate legislative structure, and the provision of some protection and indirect benefits to private partners. Regulatory and legal stability are necessary conditions for success. Market-based financial instruments for project funding are often important to enhance the confidence of the private partner and to lead to successful project implementation.

Further reading

Tsamboulas, D. and S. Kapros (2003). Freight village evaluation under uncertainty with public and private financing. *Transport Policy* **10**, 141–56.
United Nations (2007). *Guidebook on Promoting Good Governance in Public–Private Partnerships*. New York: UN Publications.
United States Federal Transit Administration (2007). Report to Congress on the costs, benefits, and efficiencies of public–private partnerships for fixed guideway capital projects. Washington, DC: USFTA.

Dimitrios A. Tsamboulas

public transport

Broadly speaking, a public transport service can be viewed as a system set up to convey people by using dedicated resources (infrastructures and/or vehicles). The most important distinguishing feature of public transport is that it is **accessibile** to everyone, thus it excludes systems targeted to specific groups such as school transport or services for company employees. In many countries public transport systems and infrastructures have traditionally been owned and operated by public bodies, but there is a general trend to involve the private sector more.

Several kinds of public transport have been used at different times. Stagecoaches were replaced in the nineteenth century by trains for intercity travel, marking a golden age of public transport concerning both its market share and its technological superiority over other forms of transport. Industrialization and urbanization processes caused the expansion of historical cities well beyond traditional town walls, inducing the need to provide public transport services for urban as well as intercity trips, generally through horse-powered and then electric tramways.

The coming of the automobile age in the twentieth century radically changed the situation, leading to the end of the dominance of public transport in almost all market segments. Rail systems have been particularly hit in urban areas, and most tramways were dismantled and substituted with **buses**. Decreasing patronage and increasing costs led to public **subsidies**. The progressive erosion in the share of trips served by public transport accelerated in Europe from the 1960s. Concerns about the environment, **congestion** and social access in the 1970s, however, led to improved services.

The capability of the public transport to alter modal splits substantially seems to be limited; particularly in those countries or cities where past policies have supported private transport and has led to travel patterns that are difficult to serve with public transport. This integrated approach has led to more stress and to more focus on transport demand management techniques.

Traditionally public transport systems are characterized as surface, air and waterborne public transport. Within surface public transport, several modes can be distinguished: road transport, including **buses** and vans; **railways**, including **tramways**, subways and suburban and intercity lines, and funiculars. Another important distinction is based on the scale of the territory covered: urban, suburban, regional, intercity or long-distance systems. New organizational forms of public transport have been made possible by developments of information and communication technologies, and in particular of **intelligent transport systems** that have made them more responsive and efficient.

These new forms, often called **paratransit**, were originally introduced to overcome the limitations of traditional services as effective alternatives to private modes, through improved flexibility. Initial enthusiasm has been tempered by serious financial problems, and they are now mainly used to serve specialized groups such as the disadvantaged and elderly.

Further reading
Pucher, J. (2004). Public transportation. In S. Hanson and G. Giulian (eds), *The Geography of Urban Transportation* (3rd edn). New York: Guilford Press.
Stern, E. and T. Tretvik (1993). Public transport in Europe: requiem or revival? In I. Salomon, P. Bovy and J.-P. Orfeuil (eds), *A Billion Trips a Day: Tradition and Transition in European Travel Patterns*. Dordrecht: Kluwer.

Marco Diana

public transport demand

Increasing environmental concerns, particularly with regard to **climate change**, are stimulating the desire to promote public transport in many countries. However, public transport use varies considerably from one country to another. **Car ownership** is frequently cited as an explanatory factor for public transport use (see the Figure), but the variance around the curve is very high as many other factors also explain public transport demand. These factors can be organized with reference to three dimensions.

The characteristics of transport supply influence the transport mode that is chosen. Usually, in modelling, transport supply is defined in terms of the journey time and the cost of travel. In order to add these two dimensions, the concept of **generalized cost** (C_g) is introduced:

$$C_g = P + T*V \tag{1}$$

where: P is price of trip, T is the journey time and V is value of time.

The price of the trip considered in the **generalized cost** is a price perceived by the individual. This is generally different from the real cost. The journey time is also a perceived time (deduced from the behaviours of individuals) to take account of the fact that different parts of a journey are perceived more negatively than others. For example, in the case of public transport, time spent walking or waiting appears to be at least twice as stressful as time spent in the vehicle.

It is this time which is used to estimate the generalized cost. It is then

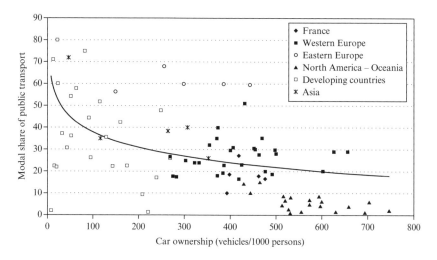

multiplied by the value the individual ascribes to their time. This value obviously varies from one individual to another, but also varies for different trips or, more accurately, different activities at the destination. Depending on the aim of the study and the available data, either a single value of time (for each class of individual or each class of trip), or a distribution of values of time within the population of individuals or trips is used.

It has been assumed that all individuals actually have a choice between different transport modes. This is not the case in reality. Thus, **modal choice models** usually take car ownership into account. This can be done either by applying an average level or by segmenting the population on the basis of the number of cars owned by the household or an estimate of the real availability of a car for a given trip.

The models estimate the available public transport for a given trip using a description of the network based on a zoning of the urban area. Consequently, it is necessary to calculate an average public transport access time for individuals in the zone both at the origin and the destination, a waiting time and a time spent in the vehicle. A weighting is then applied to each of these to indicate how they are perceived by users of public transport.

Parking supply is also an important determinant for modal choice. It has been shown in France that individuals with a parking space at their place of work use public transport to travel to work half as much as individuals who do not. The difference is even greater when the individuals in question live in the centre of a major city with high-quality public transport. This partly explains the success of Bern and Zurich where public transport use is considerably higher than in many European cities. In spite of its importance, models do not always consider **parking** supply as it is frequently unknown, particularly when private.

Other, more qualitative factors are also influential. Examples are comfort, **safety** and reliability, which are often difficult to measure. Usually they are taken into account implicitly in the generalized cost formula. It is, nevertheless, possible to estimate these factors using the type of surveys that have been developed for marketing or **stated preference methods** that allow their utility to be estimated.

Trip origin and destination are important factors in modal choice, as the level of supply of motorized modes varies considerably from one place to another. Public transport's share of the travel market therefore decreases as one of the trip ends becomes more peripheral. If both trip ends are considered, public transport has the highest market share for trips that take place within the centre. This share is still reasonably high for radial trips. However, it becomes very low for trips with both ends in peripheral areas.

Thus, urban sprawl tends to reduce public transport's market share. The location of activities and households' residents therefore has a considerable effect on transport mode use.

The use of modes is also differentiated according to trip purpose. Traditionally, public transport use has been higher for school- and work-related trips. However, these trips account for a smaller proportion of all the trips that are made, due to an increase in the number of leisure trips, with a consequent drop in public transport's market share.

The time of day and the day the trip is made also affect modal choice insofar as the relative performance of the two principal motorized modes varies in the opposite direction. Public transport performs best during weekday peak hours because of higher frequency, while the car is adversely affected by **congestion**. On the other hand, public transport supply is reduced as traffic levels fall, but traffic flow improves.

Lastly, although analyses of **modal split** are usually concerned with trips, more and more research approaches modal choice on the basis of tours (all the trips and activities performed between leaving and returning home), or the individual's sequence of activities during the day (activity-based analysis). There are many of these. The most important involve car ownership and the socio-economic characteristics of the individual and their household.

Car ownership is an important factor in modal choice. There is general agreement that there is a very strong link between car ownership and modal choice, even though there is still debate about causality – do people buy a car in order to use it or use their car because they have one? Most predictions are that car ownership will rise throughout the world, without any clear perception of approaching saturation. In the United States there are now more cars than driving licence holders. Growth in gross domestic product (GDP) is obviously the dominant explanatory factor, but others also play a role: for example the increase in the number of women going out to work which is often accompanied by car purchase, generational renewal leading to the prevalence of groups for whom the car has been dominant throughout their lives, urban sprawl, and so on.

The status of the individual is a variable that has emerged from travel analysis research. It combines a number of socio-economic factors that influence travel practices: sex, age, occupation, position in household, the presence of children and so on. This variable is of interest because it is closely linked to the individual's role in the household, in particular as regards the division of tasks within the household, and the nature of the constrained activities performed by each class. Modal use is extremely contrasted according to status.

Habit is not generally regarded as a socio-economic determinant for individuals. It is, however, a characteristic of individuals that is closely linked to their position in the life cycle. Even if the economic theory which provides the basis of most forecasting models stipulates that individuals are rational, and therefore permanently question their choices as the performance of transport modes changes, it has to be admitted that moments of choice are rare, or more precisely that individuals rarely question their choices.

International comparisons also reveal the importance of density and the organization of space in terms of the location of jobs and residential areas. The urban sprawl which can be witnessed in most cities thus explains a considerable increase in car ownership. A study conducted in Lyon, with some 1.2 million inhabitants, showed that the market share of public transport remained stable between 1975 and 1995 despite investment totalling over €2 million. By analysing the explanatory factors it has been possible to quantify the effect of urban sprawl (-9 per cent), car ownership (-8 to -14 per cent) while the improvement in supply has led to an increase of between 10 per cent and 15 per cent. This analysis has shown that almost all the trends that affect the explanatory factors for public transport use are unfavourable to this use. Thus, while increased supply is a necessary condition for an increase in public transport use it is by no means a sufficient one. Only limiting the role of the car (for example reducing supply or speed, or by pricing measures) has been shown to have a beneficial long term impact on public transport use.

Further reading

Bonnel, P. (1995). Urban car policy in Europe. *Transport Policy* **2**, 83–95.

Goodwin, P.B. (1984). *Changes in Transport User's Motivations for Modal Choice*. ECMT Round Table 68, Paris: European Conference of Ministers of Transport.

International Association of Public Transport (2001). *Recommendations and Analysis of the Millennium Cities Database for Sustainable Transport*. Brussels: UITP.

Joly, I., S. Masson and R. Petiot (2003). La part modale des transports en commun dans les villes du monde, Une analyse de la base UITP sur les systèmes de transports urbains de 100 villes du monde. Lyon, Laboratoire d'Economie des Transports.

Patrick Bonnel

Q

queuing theory

A queue can be formed whenever the demand exceeds the capacity, such as cars waiting for car wash service, planes waiting for take-off or landing, calls waiting for answering at call centres, people waiting for security checks, and vehicles queuing up at the traffic lights. In other words, **congestion** occurs when the service rate is less than the arrival rate for a period of time. On the other hand, a queue will not dissipate until the service rate is larger than the arrival rate for a period of time. Here, arrival represents input or demand for a queue, whereas service can be substituted by output, supply, release, discharge or capacity. Rooted in operation analysis, queuing theory studies the formation, behaviour and consequence of queues in a wide variety of disciplines, including in the operations of various transportation modes.

Introduced by Kendall, the notation of $A/S/n$ becomes standard for queuing classification and analysis. As the inputs, A and S represent arrival and service process or time distribution, respectively, and n represents number of servers (for example number of counters for check-in or check-out, number of tollbooths for toll collection). Typical distributions for arrival and service rate include Markov (notated as M), Erlang (notated as E), and Deterministic (notated as D). For example, the simplest stochastic queuing system $M/M/1$ indicates that one server serves the arrival and service events that both follow the Markov prossess, also known as the Poisson process (that is, the arrival and service time intervals and number of arrival and service events in a fixed time interval are negative exponentially distributed).

Though most real-world queuing systems are stochastic and should be analysed using probabilistic analysis technique, a few transportation queuing problems can be simplified by assuming that both arrival and service distribution are deterministic, that is, $D/D/n$ queuing system. In those cases, the analyst assumes the exact time distributions of arrival and service events are known. For example, constant arrival and service rates for intersections, and linearly increasing and decreasing arrival rates for peak and non-peak period traffic changes on the highway, are assumed for simplified analysis.

Deterministic queuing analysis embraces two approaches: macroscopic and microscopic. The macroscopic approach assumes that the arrival and service flows are continuous, and analyses a collective of vehicles, which usually compose a high rate flow. On the other hand, a microscopic approach analyses discrete arrival and service events of individual vehicles when the flow rate is low. The microscopic analysis usually requires the trajectories of discrete arrival and service events of individual vehicles. Flow diagrams can visually aid the understanding and analysis and the deterministic queuing system. The inputs of arrival and service rate distribution are depicted in a flow rate versus time diagram. Then cumulative vehicle versus time curves for arrival and service events can be developed by computing the integral of the arrival and service flow rates. In other words, the slopes (first-order derivative) of the arrival and service cumulative vehicle curves are the arrival and service flow rate curves. The area enclosed by the service and arrival curves in a cumulative vehicle diagram represents the total delay of the queue. The typical performance measures for queuing analysis include average individual delays in seconds or minutes, and total delay in vehicle-seconds or vehicle-hours. Additional information such as service policy, also known as queue discipline, and queue capacity is also critical for queuing analysis. Examples of service policy include first in, first out (FIFO), first in, last out (FILO), service-in-random-order (SIRO) and priority first (server-defined priority such as shortest distance and most urgent).

Although it has been applied in the transportation field for almost half a century, queuing theory is still a valuable tool to help transportation professionals to accommodate the ever-increasing traffic demands. Transportation operations often deal with many queuing situations, such as at intersections, toll plazas **parking** facilities, freeway bottlenecks, traffic incident sites, and merging and weaving areas. These situations may greatly impact upon **mobility** and **safety**. Adequate queuing analysis can facilitate the effective planning, design and operation of the transportation system. For instance, the performance of various **intelligent transportation system** (ITS) technologies, including intelligent signal controls, electrical toll collection, advanced commercial vehicle operations, incident management and **congestion** alleviation, can be analytically studied using queuing theory and then could help the management and control of flow of vehicles and people in an effective and efficient fashion.

Further reading
May, A.D. (1990). *Traffic Flow Fundamentals*. New York: Prentice Hall.
Medhi, J. (2002). *Stochastic Models in Queuing Theory* (2nd edn). Amsterdam: Academic Press.

Yongchang (Max) Ma

R

railways

The term 'railways' is synonymous with 'railroads', the latter is the American terminology but both terms are used throughout the world. Rail technology refers to a pair of parallel steel rails held in position on 'ties' or sleepers, that is, wooden or concrete or steel supports nestled in a bed of crushed rock or, rarely, concrete slabs. The train is guided by the rails, so operation of the train is limited to propulsion and stopping. Traffic control is necessary so that only one train occupies a section of track. There are some variations in technology such as cog railways for steep inclines, or magnetic levitation which eliminates direct contact between the train and the roadbed, but the traditional fixed-rail guideway remains dominant the world over.

Rail transport offers inherent high efficiencies in transport because of the low rolling resistance of steel wheels on steel rails. Relatively modest power is required to move large loads, providing that the gradient is very low. Grades of 3 to 4 per cent are the maximum desirable and less gradient is preferable, also modest turning radii. Therefore terrain can be very important in the feasibility and cost of railways, for example large bodies of water usually cannot be crossed, and mountain ranges require circuitous routing and/or costly tunnels. Locomotives are additive so train size is very flexible, from a few rail cars to trains with over 200 cars or waggons. Their long length and heavy loads mean that rail cars tend to be strong and heavy, causing trains to be slow in acceleration or deceleration, and necessitating the low gradients. Expansive rail yards are required to store cars and assemble them into specific trains. Especially for mixed freight operations, considerable time and expense are incurred in assembling or 'breaking' trains. Hence, except for unit-train operations, most rail equipment is sitting rather than moving for much of its life.

Railways were the defining technology of the nineteenth century and remained the dominant mode of transport until about the mid-twentieth century. Railways were an intimate part of the Industrial Revolution in England and Europe and its export to the rest of the world, especially North America. The railway conquered distance with speeds that enabled economic and political linkages among distant points. Railway construction is credited with providing a significant stimulus to nascent iron and steel production, as well as many other industries. Railways brought development to the vast hinterlands of North and South America, Eurasia and Australia. Railways brought us standard time zones. Arguably, they were our first experience with real time management of large-scale, far-flung enterprises. Finally, the evolution of public sector participation and/ or regulation of railways formed a model for transport policy that persists to this day and for other modes.

Railways continue to play a significant role in modern economies. Although motor and air transport have come to dominate most transportation markets, rail is still important in a few markets.

The basic distinction is between freight and passenger operations. They are usually specialized trains, rather than sharing passengers and freight on the same train. There are significant differences among countries in organization, size of trains, what is carried, and so on, particularly between North America where rail freight is the dominant traffic and Europe where passenger services are predominant. Most countries have some of both types of services.

For passenger transport, a further basic distinction separates urban operations from intercity service. Urban rail transport is very capital-intensive and only suitable for very large-volume movements. Because of the high-volume movements, traffic control is the biggest technical challenge in urban rail operations. Trains of different priority with more or fewer stops must share track space. Passenger systems are scheduled systems, so it is possible to plan and allocate 'train paths' in advance. Nonetheless, there are inevitable delays or breakdowns that require adjustment to handle the multiplicity of passenger train movements. Parallel three- or four-track systems are common in urban rail passenger markets. Note that trains may not be confined to one direction only on a specific track. It is more efficient to have crossovers and allow trains to operate in either direction over any section of track, but strict traffic control is required (if capacity is available, **safety** concerns may confine passenger service to single-directional track).

For intercity passenger travel, in most markets traffic volumes are much smaller than in urban areas, hence train service is less frequent than in urban operations. High **subsidy** levels are common in rail passenger services, especially for suburban services, where fares are usually kept very low, and for **rural** or other low-density services.

Freight or goods movement is a totally different market from passengers. Cost and reliability rather than time convenience is the priority of most rail freight movements, although there are distinctions between large-volume low-valued bulk shipments compared to high-priority express trains moving high-valued goods such as ship **containers**. Trains may be dispatched on a random or scheduled basis. The most efficient are the bulk trainloads of a single commodity in round-trip unit trains, such as coal trains. Coal is the largest single commodity transported in the North American rail system. For countries that have substantial rail passenger service, typically passenger service gets track priority, thus hampering the level of service that can be provided to freight customers.

Most railways are vertically integrated: the same company owns and maintains road and track, and operates trains over it. Because of the very large investment before any traffic can move, there is tendency toward monopoly or at least a limited number of firms serving a market. Most railways in the world were owned and operated by governments; North America was the major exception. Historically, railways were a technology to open up new lands and transport agricultural or resource products over long distances. Profitability was doubtful, hence public sector involvement was often needed, sometimes indirectly such as land grants to foster North American rail development in the nineteenth century. For many railways, some traffic, especially passenger services, was never profitable and public subsidy was required, hence rail ownership was retained in the public sector.

In North America, private railways became subject to extensive regulation for much of the twentieth century. But the growth of the economy and the rise of alternate transport modes eventually led to substantial **deregulation** of railways. Residual regulation is limited primarily to situations of market dominance, but the majority of traffic moves under unregulated commercial contracts. There has been substantial consolidation in the long-distance freight rail industry in North America, so there is some debate about possible regulatory reform.

The long-standing concern for monopoly power in vertically integrated rail companies has generated interest in rethinking the industrial organization of rail transportation. Some countries, notably Britain, Sweden and Australia, are separating ownership of the track from operations over that track. The analogy is like privately owned trucks using publicly provided highways. The trucking industry is highly competitive because firms do not need to finance the investment in roads before they operate. The government levies user charges (usually licence fees and fuel tax), but this converts what would be a high fixed cost of road infrastructure into a variable charge paid by **trucking** companies. If they do not operate, they do not pay. There are still the risks and fixed costs to bear, but these are assumed by government, which has given rise to long-standing debates over the efficiency and equity of truck–rail competition because the latter provides its own infrastructure whereas truckers do not bear this risk. Several countries have acknowledged the natural monopoly element is the track infrastructure. Therefore it can be placed under a separate company, either a regulated private monopoly or a public enterprise, and then various private companies are free to pay a fee for access to the track and provide services.

The analogy with truck operations and competition is obvious, but there are some dissimilarities. Individual truck movements are very small relative to road capacity, so traffic management of assigning trucks to specific operating times does not arise. In contrast, rail operations are larger units of supply relative to track capacity, and access times and traffic control are significant concerns. Thus a high degree of regulation and coordination is necessary to accommodate multiple ownership and operation of vehicles. There is also wide belief that there are cost interdependencies between track investments and train operations, which may be lost if these are not under joint management. A variation on the principle is the concept of regulated access to existing rail lines by other operators. The challenge here is how to promote efficient competition that is not simply confiscation of the investors' property.

Further reading
Nash, C.A., M.R. Wardman, K. Button and P. Nijkamp (eds) (2002). *Railways.* Cheltenham, UK and Northampton, MA, USA: Edward Elgar.

William G. Waters II

rapid transit

Rapid transit is a generic term used to describe a group of public transport modes which operate over a fully exclusive right of way and hence have superior reliability, speed, capacity and **safety** performance. Superior performance is relative to public transport modes that are partly or wholly operating over a shared right of way. Here other modes including auto traffic, **pedestrians** and other public transport modes compete for space and interact with each other. An exclusive or private right of way is one in which the vehicles do not share the right of way with other vehicles. This includes exclusivity in crossing points across the right of way. No roads or footpaths impede the path of a rapid transit vehicle at all. Common exclusive rights of way are tunnels and elevated roads, guideways or railways; however they can also include an 'at grade' or surface right of way as long as they are completely separated from access by other modes.

The term 'rapid transit' is sourced from the post-Civil War United States where the substantial growth in cities such as New York made travel in streets very ineffective for buses and trams (streetcars). As central business districts (CBDs) grew upwards with skyscraper developments, demand for travel increased in volume and density until on-street shared movement became slower and less reliable. The answer was rapid transit, which in this case referred to trains or **trams** using elevated rights of way or subway trains using tunnels, grade-separated from street-level **congestion**.

Traditionally rapid transit has referred to railway technologies such as subways and elevated heavy or light rail. In general it has also been related to urban passenger transport. Some reference to rapid transit in relation to regional or intercity rail has been made although this is rare.

Major urban rapid transit systems have included the subways, metros and underground railway systems of some of the world's largest and oldest cities, such as London, Paris, Moscow and New York. Today there are over 160 systems using rail of this type. The London underground system, commencing in 1863, was the first. However the term 'rapid transit' is rarely used in English to refer to this system. The terms 'underground' or 'Tube' are more common. In Germany 'underground' is abbreviated to U-Bahn or Untergrundbahn. 'Subway' is a common North American means of referring to underground railways as is 'rapid transit'; however 'subway' has also been used in Asian contexts such as Japan and South Korea. Several Asian cities also refer to 'mass rapid transit' or MRT, for example the Singapore MRT. In these contexts the term 'mass' is emphasizing the capacity of the system to carry substantial passenger volumes.

The term 'rapid' has generated a positive association with quality. Hence the term has been adopted by new technology systems aspiring to play a greater role in mainstream urban transport. Examples include bus rapid transit (BRT) and personal rapid transit (PRT).

Some people have taken the view that 'rapid transit' refers only to rail-based technologies and that BRT technically does not exist in pure terms. While many BRT systems have exclusive rights of way (or busways), it is common for some sections of the right of way to include on-street operations, for example within central business districts (CBDs). Hence they are not 'fully exclusive' as is required by the definition. The term 'bus semi-rapid transit' has therefore been suggested. This technicality may require review over time, with an increasing number of BRT systems being developed and expanded with exclusive rights of way. For example the Brisbane busway **network**, one of the world's largest BRTs, now includes a fully grade-separated set of CBD tunnels which provide fully exclusive rights of way from suburban catchments for many of its bus routes.

Trends in technology have tended to blur traditional definitions of transit modes and services. This has occurred as urban planning authorities innovatively seek quality solutions to complex urban **accessibility** problems within limited budgets. In these cases the technology has been adapted to address the problems identified, rather than generating solutions which fit traditional and historical paradigms.

The superior quality features of rapid transit have made them popular additions to increasingly congested urban areas. Indeed of the 160-plus subway or **metro rail rapid transit systems** built since 1863, over half have been built since the late 1960s. Recent growth has been at the rate of over 20 new systems every decade.

The major constraint in urban rapid transit system development has been establishing an exclusive right of way within a context of existing high-density city development. Planners generally want to avoid the dislocation associated with removing existing buildings to create new exclusive rights of way for transit. Construction has occurred where an alignment is available, for example adjacent to freeway reserves or as part of a freight rail corridor. Even river valleys and canals have been adopted as a path for an exclusive right of way in some cases. Generally these options lack a direct path between major trip generators. In addition they can have negative environmental impacts.

Elevated structures are expensive to construct and can also act to blight streetscape views. They also require passenger access from street level, generating access barriers (stairs, elevators and escalators). Subways have the same access problems but are not obstructive to surface views. However they are generally more expensive to construct compared to elevated structures.

Cost has also been a major constraint on rapid transit system development. Construction costs make only the rarest of rapid transit projects financially viable from a fare box revenue perspective. Government **subsidies** and funding from **taxation** have thus been the primary source of rapid transit investment. Hence this is constrained by political concerns and the competing demands on government investment from all other aspects of government service. As a result many rapid transit investments have been the focus of national or federal investment, rather than state- or city-focused.

While most rapid transit systems are operated by government agencies there have been a number of efforts to introduce private sector commercial participation in operations and management. A number of systems have been corporatized (Hong Kong, Seoul, Vancouver, Beijing). Here governments transfer authority to corporations who adopt commercial principles at arm's length from direct political influence. Some have privatized, where control is more decentralized to a commercial organization. This has included a vertical separation model where operations are separated from track infrastructure and either or both are franchised to private concerns. Another model is the BOT or build–operate–transfer model whereby a concessionaire wins a tender to build and operate a new rapid transit system that includes the right to generate revenue from the operation for a period of time. Bangkok Metro was developed using this model.

A number of major concerns have been the focus of management and operations of rapid transit systems. Older systems have faced considerable challenges in updating century-old infrastructure with modern technologies and practices. Even the largest systems have sought to expand their footprint as urban development spreads beyond the catchment of rapid transit system passengers. Many systems have faced critical challenges as demand has outgrown the capacity of the system to carry more passengers. Overcrowding is now common in London and in Japanese systems. **Safety** is a concern when passenger volumes accumulate on platforms or access passageways at a rate that exceeds the volume of departing services.

Since the international security concerns of the 11 September 2001 terrorist attacks in New York City, security concerns have been a major focus for the management of many rapid transit systems. Terrorist bombings on rail services in Madrid in 2004 and London in 2005 have resulted in the adoption of measures to monitor and respond better to attacks in most rapid transit systems.

It is likely that rapid transit systems will play an increasingly more important role in urban travel as world urbanization continues. The capacity advantages of rapid transit make them an essential part of the economic future of all the world's larger and increasingly more congested cities. The majority of rapid transit systems use electric traction and can therefore be efficient from an air pollution and carbon monoxide (CO) or equivalent greenhouse gas emission viewpoint, depending on the nature of the electrical power source.

Further reading
Currie, G. (2006). Bus rapid transit in Australasia: performance, lessons learned and futures. *Journal of Public Transportation* **9**, 1–22.
Vuchic, V.R. (2007). *Urban Transit Systems and Technology*. Hoboken, NJ: John Wiley & Sons.
Walker, J.B. (1918). *Fifty Years of Rapid Transit* (reprinted in 1970). Manchester: Ayer Publishing.

Graham Currie

road accident locations

Accidents are one of the negative **externalities** of road transport; they generate important economic and social as well as environmental costs, but are unfortunately too often neglected in transportation management. Traffic collisions are one of the leading causes of premature death in most developed countries. Identifying dangerous accident locations and profiling them in terms of accident-related data and location and environmental characteristics is one way of providing insights into the complexity and causes of road accidents.

It is well known that the occurrence of an accident is a complex function of the road users (age, health, behaviour, vulnerability), the vehicles (type, crash-worthiness, on-board distractions) and the road infrastructure, as well as the environment of the place of accident (including traffic flow, weather and speed conditions, and level of urbanization). Most countries only record road accidents involving deaths or injuries, the definition of the casualty varying from one country to another. Transport and mobility practises as well as the quality and the location of the emergency services (medical, police) influence the level and type of casualty as well as the quality of the data; for example **bicyclists** falling alone are seldom reported in the censuses.

The location of a road accident is nowadays accurately known by global positioning system (GPS) technology or, more traditionally, by milestones on numbered roads and by postal addresses on other roads, leading to a quite interesting field of research for spatial analysts due to the development of **geographical information systems**. It is indeed important to describe and to explain spatial concentrations of road accidents in order to orient prevention.

Accident hotspots can be defined at three levels of spatial data aggregation, each leading to different methodologies as well as practical use:

- 'Black surfaces' (2D) correspond to states, countries, regions or communes, that is to say, data aggregated by surfaces. At this level, epidemiological analyses can be performed, countries and regions compared, and prevention campaigns gauged. However, international comparisons are difficult due to the heterogeneity of the data.
- 'Black zones' (1D) correspond to road segments characterized by an 'abnormal' concentration of road accidents. These segments vary in length and dangerousness or risk indices. Geostatistical indices enable better definition of locations, lengths and intensities (for example kernel methods, local autocorrelation indices). On average, black zones concentrate 30 per cent of all accidents. Their location enables suggestions for road enhancements, or a better fit of the road to its physical and human environment.
- 'Black spots' (0D) correspond to point locations characterized by a 'high' number of accidents. A black spot is often – but not always – defined as a 100-metres segment of road characterized by three accidents within a year. This enables accurate location of dangerous spots and hence suggests local planning and management. It is

well known that, due to their definition, black spots are very mobile in space and time, and represent less than 10 per cent of the total number of accidents.

Each level of spatial aggregation has its advantages and drawbacks, and its specific uses. When aggregating, however, the shape and size of the spatial units influence the statistical results ('modifiable areal unit problem') and there is no way to predict what they are at a higher level given the values at a lower level. This affects statistical descriptors as well as maps and statistical explanation. Although the problems of representing and integrating data at different scales are well known, the continuing emphasis placed on scale-related issues in human and physical geography suggests that problems remain. This is especially true for accidents.

Explaining the observed concentrations necessitates not only good databases but also adequate statistical techniques in order to take into account the Poisson nature of the distribution of road accidents as well as the spatial autocorrelation and the multivariate nature of the explanation. Multilevel analysis, logistic autoregressive techniques and weighted regressions are some of the many techniques explaining the observed differences in road accident concentrations. Compared with traditional, frequentist methods, the Bayesian approach is more flexible in structuring complicated models and provides a better estimation when simple aggregation techniques are performed on rare events, such as road accidents (that is, when large variability is observed from one unit to another).

In conclusion, a road accident is the result of a complex process involving many actors and factors, and hence is difficult to model. Reducing the number of accidents is nowadays a governmental objective, but there is no unique way of achieving it. Education, enforcement and engineering are the most classical ways of acting, at the global or local level. Hence, space is one element for the **safety** jigsaw, keeping in mind that 'vision zero' (no accidents) can only be achieved when no one moves (staying home, or stuck in traffic jams).

Most studies show that about 30 per cent of the accident concentrations are to be explained by transportation infrastructure and spatial environment. Each spatial scale of analysis brings its explanatory elements in terms of risk and **mobility**. Increasing mobility means increasing speed, and hence reducing time of transportation, but also increasing operational costs, pollution (noise and air) as well as road accidents; all have a spatial component. The spatial variation of the transportation and environmental components is one of the key elements in transport and mobility planning and decision-making.

Further reading

Flahaut, B., M. Mouchart, E. San Martino and I. Thomas (2003). Identifying black zones with a local spatial autocorrelation index and a kernel method. *Accident Analysis and Prevention* **35**, 991–1004.

Lassarre, S. and I. Thomas (2005). Exploring road mortality ratios in Europe: national versus regional realities. *Journal of the Royal Statistical Society A* **168**, 127–44.

Miaou, S.-P., J.J. Song and B.K. Mallick (2003). Roadway traffic crash mapping: a space–time modeling approach. *Journal of Transportation Statistics* **6**, 33–57.

Okabe, A., T. Satoh and K. Sugihara (2009). A kernel density estimation method for networks, its computational method and a GIS-based tool. *International Journal of Geographical Information Science* **23**, 7–32.

Isabelle Thomas

road finance

Road finance has taken various forms in the course of time. In Roman times, road construction and maintenance was paid through what was called *corvée*: the duty for road users to build and maintain roads. From the twelfth to the seventeenth century, roads were to be constructed and maintained by the owners of the land over which roads passed. Over time, various direct road tolls have been levied, but the measure was in most cases unpopular and abandoned and collection caused bottlenecks in the road network. Moreover, strong control was needed to avoid evasion and vandalism (for example breaking down turnpikes). In a large number of cases, roads have been sponsored by wealthy and/or religious people as a gift. Sometimes, funds raised from specific activities, for example lotteries, or taxes, for example a tax on wool, were used to build roads.

In more recent times, in Europe, there was a tendency to use general government revenues for road construction and maintenance. Only in a few cases has tolling (for example France) or flat-rate vignettes (for example Switzerland) been introduced. The general tendency in the United States has been to allocate specific taxes to road purposes (local property taxes for local roads and fuel taxes for inter-urban roads), although a trend towards more general budget funding has been observed. In Asia, funding is in most cases provided from general government budgets, although much more from local sources than in Europe and the United States.

Tolling however is an option which is regaining ground, in many cases driven by technological developments. Four major motivations back this upsurge of interest in tolls: shrinking public budgets, more accurate estimation of charges, modernization of toll collection systems, and the economic feasibility of tolling through more efficient systems. Criteria used to achieve toll variability include spatial, vehicle and trip characteristics.

Tolls, depending on the criteria used to calculate them, may serve more purposes than just providing funding for construction and maintenance. This also reflects in the names given to the concepts most often used nowadays: **congestion charges** on individual facilities, congestion charges on cordon areas, electronically calculated weight–distance charges and general purpose distance-based user fees. The advantage is that a well-elaborated toll system allows for achieving various goals at once, although the lack of a direct link between payer and user of funds tends to be inefficient.

The political interest seen in the early part of the twenty-first century in road pricing systems largely eminates from local, state or national authorities, whereas an efficient road pricing system would cross borders if one wants to avoid unintended negative effects like traffic diversion. In Europe, the European Commission is trying to establish common principles on road tolling, but in the meantime national or local initiatives are taken, that make it harder to develop a common platform.

Two more points need to be addressed in creating effective road pricing systems. Initially, a first-best solution putting a levy on all users causing some kind of external cost, based on that cost, is socially the most desirable, but hardly feasible in practice; not least because there is often disagreement on the basis for pricing and because of the costs of implementation. In most cases, marginal costs are suggested. However, even the content of this concept is subject to debate. Therefore, one often has to recur to second-best solutions where external costs are approximated and levies are refined as better, scientifically founded estimates become available. Secondly, a social optimum is reached when all persons bearing external costs get refunded according to the burden that they experience; essentially a Coasian trading outcome. This too is practically unworkable.

An alternative method of finance, especially in view of the large capital costs involved in building roads, is the issuing of bonds. Two options are possible: bonds issued directly by governments for roads they manage, or bonds issued to prefinance private operators who need to pay back the capital upon receipt of toll income. Instruments such as temporary or permanent tax rebates are available for making this kind of financing more attractive to the wider public.

Further reading
Sörenson, P. and B. Taylor (2006). Innovations in road finance: examining the growth in electronic tolling. *Public Works Management and Policy* **11**, 110–25.

Thierry Vanelslander

road maintenance

The major recent trends in road maintenance have revolved around decreasing public maintenance budgets and the growing influence of the private sector in maintenance work. A consequence has been the need for management systems to more explicitly take into consideration the economic and financial analyses of maintenance works. Appropriate models are required to calculate and predict economic costs throughout the life cycle of road structures. To this end a number of models have been developed.

Budget constraints have imposed short-term constraints in road maintenance, which have affected road users through higher user costs immediately, and road management through higher road maintenance costs in the future.

Cost streams are composed of:

- Periodic maintenance costs, which are the costs of planned measures including reconstruction.
- Routine maintenance costs, which can be calculated as a function of the condition and traffic.
- Road traffic costs, which can be calculated as a function of the condition and traffic.

An effective road maintenance management system aims to achieve the following under budget constraints:

- high levels of road condition;
- reduced user costs;
- reduced accident levels and consequent costs;
- protection of the environment in terms of reduced noise and emissions;
- reduced administration costs.

Road maintenance measures are used to prevent, stop or repair condition deterioration. In the beginning, mostly simple and cheap routine maintenance measures with relatively low frequency are used, preferably with a preventive purpose. Later on, bigger or more frequent measures are needed, and their purpose is restoration of a deteriorated condition. The measures are still directed to the surface – either to the roadway (pavement) top layers or to the road drainage.

When the strength of the road construction or its drainage system are collapsing, an extreme maintenance measure is needed – reconstruction. The road is rebuilt, and its condition is usually restored to the original level. The reconstruction marks the end of one life cycle and the beginning of a new one, but it is still a maintenance measure. No permanently improved functionality is achieved, only the original functionality is restored. If the functionality of the road is permanently improved at the same occasion, for example through widening or better alignment, the measure is called improvement instead of maintenance.

A maintenance strategy is defined by a single maintenance action, or multiple series of maintenance actions, with the application of the action or actions specified by time or condition level (trigger level). The action or combination of actions specified should be chosen to address the deficiencies in the segment or element over the lifespan of the road (pavement) section, and should constitute appropriate maintenance actions in the context of the deficiencies present. For a given section, with its current condition parameters, the optimum maintenance strategy is the best treatment, or combination of treatments, over a defined lifespan to minimize the net present value (NPV) of combined agency costs and user costs while addressing the deficiencies of the section.

The lifespan of the road is an important factor in this definition. Roads are usually designed for a lifetime of 25 to 40 years. In effect, after that period the structural strength has expired, the lifetime is achieved and a reconstruction is needed. In reality, the lifetime can vary from less than two years for catastrophic failures to hundreds of years for good-quality construction in extremely favourable circumstances. Forty years can be seen as a median value. It is quite common that the lifespan is shortened because the volume of heavy traffic, axle loadings and tyre pressures have increased much more than the road design had allowed for. Roads that are anticipated to have several years of remaining life are suddenly candidates for reconstruction.

The lifespan may be specified as an actual duration (for example 25 years) or qualitatively (for example time to next reconstruction). Effectively, a maintenance strategy is akin to a series of maintenance projects over a specified lifespan for a particular pavement section. Condition trigger levels tell how poor the condition should be before maintenance is needed. Trigger levels are defined for each condition indicator, and they may be different for each road class. Setting up of the trigger levels will probably be performed on a country-specific basis, using local engineering expertise and knowledge. A recent review of European road administrations showed that the most popular collected road condition data were rutting, roughness, skid resistance, deflection and cracking.

A typical range of road maintenance activities includes:

- surface dressing (seal coat, single surface dressing, double surface dressing, and so on);
- pothole patching;
- restoration of road widths;
- reprofiling;
- overlay (several thicknesses have to be defined);
- milling and replacing;
- reconstruction;
- improvement of the road transverse and/or longitudinal profile;
- improvement of skid resistance;
- restoration of hard shoulders;
- restoration or installation of drainage.

A newly constructed road has good condition in all characteristics. Afterwards, the road deterioration starts. Different condition characteristics are deteriorating at different rates. The rates depend on many factors. Typically, the most important are traffic, temperature changes, water influence (drainage) and ageing effects. The deterioration in condition must be modelled mathematically if a life-cycle economic analysis of the maintenance strategies is to be carried out.

Maintenance effects models are also required for the economic analysis. The derivation of these relationships mirrors the development of the deterioration curves. Essentially, the maintenance effects illustrate the effect on the immediate condition, and on the subsequent behaviour of the road (pavement) in terms of condition deterioration. These maintenance effects are crucial in the determination of optimum maintenance standards, as they directly affect the calculation of road user costs, particularly those costs (for example vehicle operating costs) that are directly related to condition.

Further reading
American Society of State Highway and Transportation Officials (2008). *AASHTO Maintenance Manual for Roadways and Bridges* (4th edn). Washington, DC: AASHTO.
World Bank (1987). *The Highway Design and Maintenance Standards Series*. Baltimore, MD: Johns Hopkins University Press.

Kieran Feighan and *Aisling Reynolds-Feighan*

roads

A road is a path connecting two points. The English word 'road' comes from the same root as the word 'ride' – the Middle English *rood* and Old English *rad* – meaning the act of riding. Thus a road refers foremost to the right of way between an origin and destination. In an urban context, the word 'street' is often used rather than road, which dates to the Latin word *strata*, meaning pavement (the additional layer or stratum that might be on top of a path).

Modern roads are generally paved, and unpaved routes are considered trails. The pavement of roads began early in history. Approximately 2600 BC, the Egyptians constructed a paved road out of sandstone and limestone slabs to assist with the movement of stones on rollers between the quarry and the site of construction of the pyramids. The Romans and others used brick or stone pavers to provide a more level and smoother surface, especially in urban areas, which allows faster travel, especially of wheeled vehicles. The innovations of Thomas Telford and John McAdam reinvented roads in the early nineteenth century, by using less expensive smaller and broken stones, or aggregate, to maintain a smooth ride and allow for drainage. Later in the nineteenth century, application of tar (asphalt) further smoothed the ride. In 1824, asphalt blocks were used on the Champs-Elysees in Paris. In 1872, the first asphalt street (Fifth Avenue) was paved in New York due to Edward de Smedt, but it was not until bicycles became popular in the late nineteenth century that the 'Good Roads Movement' took off. **Bicycle** travel, more so than travel by other vehicles at the time, was sensitive to rough roads. Demand for higher-quality roads really took off with the widespread adoption of the automobile in the United States in the early twentieth century.

The first good roads in the twentieth century were constructed of Portland cement concrete (PCC). The material is stiffer than asphalt (or asphalt concrete) and provides a smoother ride. Concrete lasts slightly longer than asphalt between major repairs, and can carry a heavier load, but is more expensive to build and repair. While urban streets had been paved with concrete in the United States as early as 1889, the first **rural** concrete road was in Wayne County, Michigan, near to Detroit in 1909, and the first concrete highway in 1913 in Pine Bluff, Arkansas. By the next year over 2300 miles of concrete pavement had been laid nationally. However over the remainder of the twentieth century, the vast majority of roadways were paved with asphalt. In general only the most important roads, carrying the heaviest loads, would be built with concrete.

Roads are generally classified into a hierarchy. At the top of the hierarchy are freeways, which serve entirely a function of moving vehicles between other roads. Freeways are grade-separated and limited access, have high speeds and carry heavy flows. Below freeways are arterials. These may not be grade-separated, and while access is still generally limited, it is not limited to the same extent as freeways, particularly on older roads. These serve both a movement and an access function. Next are collector and distributor roads. These serve more of an access function, allowing vehicles to access the **network** from origins and destinations, as well as connecting with smaller, local roads that have only an access function, and are not intended for the movement of vehicles with neither a local origin nor a local destination. Local roads are designed to be low speed and carry relatively little traffic.

The class of the road determines which level of government administers it. The highest roads will generally be owned, operated or at least regulated (if privately owned) by the higher level of government involved in road operations; in the United States, these roads are operated by the individual states. As one moves down the hierarchy of roads, the level of government is generally more and more local (counties may control collector and distributor roads, towns may control local streets). In some countries freeways and other roads near the top of the hierarchy are privately owned and regulated as utilities; these are generally operated as toll roads. Even publicly owned freeways are operated as toll roads under a toll authority in other countries, and some United States states. Adjoining property owners and neighborhood associations often own local roads.

The design of roads is specified in a number of design manuals, including the American Association of State Highway and Transportation Officials (AASHTO) *A Policy on Geometric Design of Streets and Highways* (or Green Book). Design standards vary by country. Relevant concerns include the alignment of the road, its horizontal and vertical curvature, its super-elevation or banking around curves, its thickness and pavement (road) material, its cross-slope and its width.

Further reading
American Association of State Highway and Transportation Officials (2004). *A Policy on Geometric Design of Streets and Highways* (5th edn). Washington, DC: AASHTO.

David Levinson

route guidance systems

Route guidance systems provide information to drivers regarding the routes they should take to reach their destinations more efficiently. The information required will be different depending on the nature and character of the journey and levels of familiarity with the routes available. Information may be provided before the journey starts and/or during travel, and systems may describe aspects of the road **network** conditions and provide journey time estimates and route alternatives.

Before setting out on an unfamiliar journey a driver may use a conventional road atlas or seek a route itinerary from a motoring organization. They may also seek information from sources including the Internet, friends and colleagues, and radio and television travel broadcasts. This latter type of information generally relates to incident situations such as accidents and roadworks, which affect the usual **road** conditions and are particularly relevant to journeys made regularly. During a journey, drivers may receive information from within the vehicle by radio or dedicated route guidance systems or outside the vehicle via variable message signs (VMS).

Dedicated in-vehicle route guidance systems require vehicle location that is generally satellite based, making use of geographical positioning technology, with map-matching technologies. Essential elements are a sound digital map base of the road **network** including one-way roads and banned movements, knowledge of the location of the vehicle relative to the network, and a human machine interface (HMI) to interact **safely** and effectively with the driver. Systems have different styles of presentation, with audio as well as visual feedback to drivers and voice control to minimize workload and distraction. Menus allow bespoke settings for both HMI and route choice conditions. Increasingly, route guidance systems are being factory fitted to new vehicles with a display common to other vehicle functions such as the radio. This enables a more coherent approach to HMI and the management of driver workload, than with after-market systems.

Two-way communication enables routes to be changed in response to evolving traffic conditions, and this type of service is growing. For these services to be credible and effective, the service provider must have a sound knowledge of network conditions and how they are likely to change in the short term. Some such services are provided by government agencies (also responsible for VMS), with information usually collected using traditional roadside detectors. Others are provided by the private sector, where additional sources of information are utilized such as number plate recognition for section journey times and/or probe vehicle data taken from the users. Usually, a wide range of data sources are fused and may include information provided by the police, planned roadworks and, more recently, estimates based on mobile telephone usage.

VMS continue to play an important role in route guidance and they are used to impart information to drivers at specific locations. The signs may be used to inform, advise or control, and may contain text, be diagrammatic or a mixture of both. VMS may be controlled at some central location or locally, by human intervention or triggered automatically by some local detector identified event. They are usually located at the roadside or on overhead gantries and are sited so that drivers can prepare to react or divert to another route if necessary. Incident information usually contains three elements: the nature of the incident, its location and it potential impact – for example 'Expect Long Delays'.

VMS can be used to give advice on conditions ahead or simply to advise drivers of changes from the norm. A typical example of the latter is the ROMANSE system in Southampton, United Kingdom where the base message is 'No Reported Incidents'. Thus, when travelling in a peak period, drivers will expect their usual journey times even though these may include substantial delays from recurring **congestion**. Messages of this nature are valuable for regular users who have some significant knowledge of **network** conditions. In other applications, VMS may display journey times to the next junction or destination.

The main benefit of VMS and route guidance more generally is to enable drivers to make alternative decisions to avoid problems on the route ahead. Such decisions may be related to time change, mode change or route change. Time change may occur by a driver choosing to stop for a rest break until a problem has cleared. **Mode choice** may occur by a driver choosing to divert to a **park-and-ride** site. Route choice changes have been studied extensively. Diversion rates vary considerably because of the network alternatives available, the incident location relative to the individual's destination, and overall levels of network congestion. Simulation shows that optimal benefits are typically produced when the diversion rate reaches about 30 per cent, although this is scenario-specific. Most VMS systems have a very short payback period and first-year rates of return may be 100 per cent. However, some studies have shown that drivers are often sceptical about the validity of real-time information and only prepare to divert when they see the effects of the problem themselves.

Further reading

Richards, A and M. McDonald (2007). Investigating limits of benefits provided by variable message signs in urban network. *Transportation Research Record* **2000**, 25–34.

Wren, A.C. and K.G. Laughlin (1998). ROMANSE – Monitoring and evaluating ITS. Proceedings of the 4th World Congress on Intelligent Transport Systems, Berlin.

Mike McDonald and *Andy Richards*

routing problems

The operation of almost any kind of transport implies defining the path that the vehicles will have to follow through a given **network** to reach their chosen destination, and this generally requires the solution of a routing problem. In most cases, a routing problem is not solved from scratch. For example, public transport service routes are partly the result of historical evolution, in which single lines have been gradually extended or added to accommodate urban sprawl and changes in travel patterns. It is likely that the resulting configuration of the services offered is not the best possible, given prevailing demand on the road network, but a complete redesign would be problematic or even impossible in the case of rail systems. On the other hand, there are examples where there are fewer constraints, such as parcel deliveries or paratransport services. In those cases, the best vehicle routes are sought that minimize a given objective function, such as the number of vehicles needed or the length of travel.

The solution of a routing problem usually uses mathematical programming techniques. The objective function, generally related to service cost minimization, and service constraints, are expressed as a combinatorial optimization model. The basic idea at the core of a routing problem is the choice of the 'best' path to go from an origin to a destination through a given network. The best path is intended to be the 'shortest' (as defined by the objective function) succession of arcs and nodes in the **network**. It is often of interest to find the shortest path between a node in the network and all the others, or between all pairs of nodes, leading to the solution to the shortest-path problem (SPP). The SPP is the core of all routing problems, and also of other important transport-related concerns such as traffic assignment or location of facilities.

The simplest routing problem is the travelling salesman problem (TSP), which consists of finding the shortest tour that starts and ends at a given node and visits a defined subset of nodes in the network. Using such a basic problem it is possible to model a number of transport services, such as postal deliveries. The classic TSP formulation has been extended in several different ways, to take into account a variety of real-life services. This in practice means adding sets of constraints to the model, which in turn increases its computational complexity; there is thus a trade-off between the degree of realism of the modelling exercise and the ease of the optimization problem.

One extension of the TSP is to limit the length of the tour, which means postulating the existence of more than one salesman, leading to a multi-TSP in which the sum of all the path lengths are minimized. Another common generalization is to introduce a capacity constraint for vehicles and a load function to nodes being visited, obtaining a vehicle routing problem (VRP). The latter is of particular practical importance in studying backhaul services or passenger transport systems such as school buses. Many possible variations are possible for both the TSP and the VRP, such as imposing different starting and ending points to the routes (multi-depot problems), defining a non-homogeneous fleet of vehicles or jointly considering related issues such as crew rosters. A more challenging problem is when precedence constraints are introduced among pairs of nodes, so that the visiting sequence is no longer arbitrary: the corresponding pickup and delivery problem (PDP) and dial-a-ride problem (DARP) are, for example, used to model **paratransit** services.

Two further practically relevant variants are: problems in which nodes must be visited within a specified time interval, a time window, so that the routing and scheduling aspects of the service are treated together; and stochastic and/or dynamic problems, when for example the travel times of arcs or load functions at nodes are not deterministically known, or change during the service deployment. These extensions allow analysts to model almost any kind of transport service, although the corresponding solution techniques often pose severe limits to the maximum dimension of the problem that can be solved, at least to an acceptable approximation.

Further reading
Ball, M.O., T.L. Magnanti, C.L. Monma and G.L. Nemhause (1995). *Handbooks in Operations Research and Management Science, Volume 8: Network Routing*. Amsterdam: North-Holland.
Larson, R.C. and A.R. Odoni (1981). *Urban Operations Research*. Englewood Cliffs, NJ: Prentice-Hall.

Marco Diana

rural transport

Transport in rural areas is generally characterized by: low levels and densities of population, economic activity and traffic; long distances between nodal points, such as service centres; high unit costs for service delivery, operations and maintenance; sometimes difficult physical terrain; and greater adverse weather conditions.

Accessibility, in addition to **mobility**, is particularly important in rural areas relative to urban ones. People in general, but especially the less mobile such as non-car owners or the mobility-impaired, suffer relatively low accessibility to essential services, employment opportunities and other desired activities or destinations. This is due to high **generalized**

transport costs needed to reach the activities. These include financial costs (for example input costs such as fuel prices), time, discomfort, reliability and other risks, and are often linked to limited economies of scale, fewer alternatives and longer distances travelled. These high costs may be only partly compensated for by low levels of **congestion** or environmental costs, although in some cases these can potentially lead to relatively low marginal social and private costs of travel per distance travelled.

Improvements in transportation infrastructure in, or leading to, a rural area may increase market and supplier access, including **accessibility** for **tourism**. However, there may be negative economic and population effects ('Appalachian Highway' or two-way effects) as improved access leads to firms from other areas capturing some of the local market, services being centralized into urban areas and/or local people commuting to cities, or even moving there as they can now more easily return at weekends. The effects will depend on specific local and national circumstances.

The balance between economies of scale and economies of scope is important for the delivery of rural transport services. A lack of economies of scale results in relatively low levels of service and high unit costs. In low-density rural areas fixed-route and fixed-schedule **public transport** normally cannot meet transport demand. However, economies of scope may be achieved through public transport operators joining together to provide combined public, school, health and social (for example for **elderly** or disabled people) transport services for a combination of clients or markets rather than having a series of separate services. In some developing countries informal transport, and waiting for vehicles to be full before travelling rather than following a schedule, are common. Similarly goods transport services may capture scope economies by combining together services to different customers, or goods with passenger transport, so as to improve efficiency. A system-wide, coordinated approach, using appropriate geographic boundaries, should improve the achievement of both economies of scope and scale in rural areas.

Other significant forms of public transport aimed at dealing with low passenger numbers in rural areas include community-operated transport schemes and demand-responsive transport (for example where journeys are booked in advance by telephone or through the Internet). Where the origins and destinations of travellers are close, ride-sharing or car pools (with drivers not being compensated, but costs being shared) may provide similar travel times to individual car trips. Technology changes such as mobile communication, **geographical information systems** (GIS), automated booking systems and so on are likely to increase the viability of more flexible transport systems. Further rural transport policies seek to reduce the need to travel, for example through the use of information and communication technologies to provide medical diagnoses, information and services; changing school opening times to improve school transport efficiency; and improved **land use planning**.

Car ownership and usage is generally higher in rural areas in developed countries, although road **safety** is worse. The fatality rate for United States rural areas is over twice that of urban areas (per 100 million vehicle km of travel), due to factors including speed, road conditions, alcohol use and accident response time and/or time to receive medical treatment.

There are many different types of rural areas, each with different implications for transport analysis and policy. A simple three-way division is, first, remote rural areas that have few or no major population centres and virtually no commuting to major employment and population centres, often characterized by poor **accessibility** and limited public transport. Second, developed rural areas that tend to have some small towns or cities with a mixed industrial and service local economy and a surrounding agricultural and natural resource base, and a more diverse transportation infrastructure (including goods and passenger links to some urban centres). Third, peri-urban, or urban boundary, rural areas that border metropolitan areas and are highly developed in economic and transport terms with strong commuting, **logistics** and economic links to the metropolitan core or suburbs and sometimes highly developed public transport. Some sparsely populated remote areas exist along interregional transport corridors and have relatively good links to other areas, while others may be in 'cul-de-sac' areas where there are no through transportation links and subsequently poor external connections.

Ronald W. McQuaid

S

safety in transport

Even though the safety risks have fallen by at least half in all modes of transport since the 1960s, the absolute level of harm is still very high. In the United States, one in 6000 of the population dies each year in a transport crash (note that safety professionals prefer the word 'crash' to 'accident' because the latter suggests that occurrence is due to pure fate and cannot be influenced by human decisions). The annual death toll represents half of all accidental fatal injuries when one includes workplace injuries, but excludes homicides and suicides. Studies have found that just the direct costs of highway crashes are equivalent to 2.6 per cent of gross national product.

The vast majority of the fatalities, 85 per cent, occur when private highway users, pilots and mariners are involved in single vehicle/aircraft/ vessel crashes or collide with other private users. A further 13 per cent of fatalities occur in situations where these private users are in collision with commercial operators, such as when trucks collide with cars, or trains collide with cars at grade crossings. Only about 2 per cent of fatalities exclusively involve commercial transport, and nearly all of the casualties are employees. Therefore, despite receiving a considerable amount of press attention, the number of aviation, **bus** and train passenger fatalities is, in the global scheme of things, quite small.

When fatality counts are expressed relative to passenger miles, bus and commercial aviation have the best passenger safety records. In the United States the risk is about one fatality for every 5 billion passenger-miles. Riding the train is four times more risky, and driving is 12 times more risky, than taking the train. Employment in transport is also relatively risky. Employees in the maritime and **trucking** industries face twice as much risk than they would if they were working in construction. In contrast, **railroad** and aviation employees face much less risk, but these risks are still higher than in manufacturing industries. It is not surprising that much of the public concern for safety has originated from organized labour.

While the level of harm is substantial, one cannot tell from risk data whether transport safety is 'a problem'. To the economist, if a person knows of, and can evaluate, both the benefits and the risks and still decides to travel, then there is no inherent problem. Consequently society only minimally intervenes in the decisions made by private aviators and recreational boaters. The case for intervention is much stronger when one or more of the following six market failures are present.

The first failure occurs when people are not knowledgeable about the risks. This is more likely in commercial passenger transport where crashes are rare, and passengers do not have the knowledge and access to understand crash data. In contrast, freight shippers are repeat purchasers who deal with carriers on a daily basis to settle claims for minor loss and damage to their products.

The second possible failure is that even fully informed people may make poor choices due to cognitive processes. People have a tendency to overestimate the possibility of low-probability events and events that kill multiple people at any one time. Working in the opposite direction is the possibility that some people underestimate risk because the consequences are too horrendous to contemplate, and have a feeling of invincibility that bad outcomes 'will not happen to me'. It is not an understatement to suggest that much of society's intervention is to protect people from themselves rather than from avaricious carriers and third parties.

The third failure is myopic behaviour by some carriers. Avaricious carriers can take advantage of imperfectly informed consumers by reducing expenditure on safety but masquerading as offering high safety and charging a premium price. As crashes occur rarely, even for careless carriers, it may take some time before consumers become aware and either shun the carrier or demand a lower price. In the meantime a myopic carrier can earn short-term profits.

The fourth possible failure occurs when crashes cause oil spills or result in the release of explosive or toxic materials that impose **external costs** on bystanders. Work by psychologists suggests that bystanders are much more intolerant of the risks that they face than are people who derive some benefit from the risky activity, either as users or as employees.

The fifth possible failure is associated with collisions between private users, and when private users have crashes with commercial carriers. These collisions are called bilateral crashes because the actions of both parties influence the probability of occurrence. There is a complicated literature in law and economics that discusses the socially optimal actions of both parties, and the role of legal mechanisms to compensate victims, penalize perpetrators and generally give both parties the correct incentives to take appropriate care.

The sixth and final possible failure is concerned with the amount of competition. Individual drivers, passengers and shippers may have varying tastes for the amount of safety that they desire. In some markets, such as **trucking**, there are thousands of carriers of every ilk, and shippers can find a service that matches their taste. However, in other markets there is less competition and such a matching of tastes is unlikely.

The applicability and magnitude of the six market failures vary significantly by mode. Consequently, public policy prescription in each mode needs to be tailored to the market failures that are present.

Public policy on private automobile travel is often characterized using a 3-by-3 matrix. The categories on one axis are the driver, the vehicle and the highway. The other axis is composed of actions before a crash (crash avoidance), the crash phase and the post-crash phase. Traditionally, policy has been directed to the top left-hand cell of this matrix, and the minority of drivers who do not appreciate the risks and do not conduct themselves in a prudent manner. These problem drivers can be divided into four categories. The first are young drivers, especially males, who are both inexperienced and prone to risky behaviours. The second group is the growing ranks of older motorists, whose driving performance deteriorates markedly after the age of 65. The third group comprises people who drive while under the influence of alcohol. The final group consists of drivers who fit into none of the above categories yet seem to be more risk-loving and/or accident prone than other drivers.

Starting in the 1960s there was a conscious move to attack traffic safety via other cells in the matrix. For example, a significant reduction in fatality risk has come from improved medical response in the post-crash phase. Highway design is clearly important in both promoting crash avoidance and mitigating the harm when a crash occurs. Regulations were promulgated that imposed automotive solutions that promote crash avoidance and increased survivability in the event of a crash.

In analysing commercial transport safety, one needs to consider the economic incentives for carriers. Safety is just one attribute of the transport product, and one that is valued by consumers but costly to provide. A monopolist, such as an infrastructure provider, would decide on the optimal safety to provide by equating the marginal revenue from providing a higher-quality service with the marginal cost of doing so. In a competitive market it is possible that vertical differentiation may emerge whereby some carriers offer high quality at a premium price, and others offer lesser quality at lower prices. There is a growing literature on how safety is produced. In particular, there is a concept of 'organizational accidents', whereby firms make conscious choices on the inherent safety of their production processes and the layers of 'defences' that they build into their systems to protect against naturally occurring human and environmental errors.

As described earlier, imperfect consumer information allows the opportunity for some carriers to act in a myopic fashion. Not all carriers will act in this way, as they would not wish to lose future custom if their reputation is sullied, and they fear legal suits and increased insurance premiums in the event of a crash. However, in most modes there is a need for governmental intervention to supplement market discipline. One, traditionally underutilized, option is to attack the root cause of the problem by providing safety ratings and crash information directly to consumers. More common is direct regulation. There is a plethora of regulations in every mode that define acceptable safety standards, and provide for inspections to certify compliance. Traditionally, the designated standards have been expressed in terms of the quality and quantity of staff and equipment. There is a discussion as to whether switching to 'performance standards', which designates minimum acceptable crash rates, would lead to a more efficient delivery of safety without sacrificing effective enforcement.

Further reading
Evans, L. (1991). *Traffic Safety and the Driver*. New York: Von Nostrand Reinhold.
Lamm, R., B. Psarianos and T. Mailaender (1999). *Highway Design and Traffic Safety Handbook*. New York: McGraw-Hill.
Maurino, D.E., J. Reason, N. Johnson and R.B. Lee (1995). *Beyond Aviation Human Factors: Safety in High Technology Systems*. Aldershot: Ashgate.

Ian Savage

school transport

Transport to school can consist of journeys by foot, cycle, car, bus, **taxicab** or other modes such as rickshaw or boat, but the vast majority of the world's children walk to school. Walking, often for several miles each way, is the normal form of transport for most children in Asia, Africa, South America and many other parts of the developing world. In the developed nations, walking was normal until the arrival of mass car ownership in the 1960s. According to one survey published in the United Kingdom, 54 per cent of girls aged up to 11 travelled to school on foot, compared to 49 per cent of boys, and 41 per cent of school trips were made by car (National Travel Survey, 2006). United Kingdom estimates are that school transport increases traffic by about 20 per cent at peak hours, four times as high a proportion as 20 years before. Hillman when looking at travel to school, found that there was an 80 per cent fall in the number of ten-year olds allowed to go to school unaccompanied between 1971 and 1990.

The impacts of such changes are varied – there is the use of non-renewable fossil fuel in the vehicles, contributing to **climate change** emissions and air pollution, and also more crashes. Given that car engines emit more when cold, school journeys are responsible for a disproportionate amount of **climate change** gases. Climate change has altered the climate in many parts of the world (for instance, in south-east England snow that lies on the ground is now a rarity, up to the 1980s it was a regular winter occurrence. Similarly, **climate change** is associated with more severe and unpredictable weather events, for instance in the early part of the twenty-first century there have been increases in hurricanes and cyclones (for example Hurricane Katrina), droughts (for example in Australia) and flooding (in parts of Asia, Central America and several European countries). Vehicular air pollution also aggravates some respiratory diseases and contributes to early death.

The switch to motorized school transport diminishes the amount of physical exercise children take, contributing to obesity, diabetes and various serious health outcomes such as greater incidence of heart disease and stroke. The greater number of vehicles on the roads contributes to more deaths and injuries due to crashes, and also adds to fear of travelling except by vehicle, thus deterring **bicycling** and walking, so forming a 'vicious spiral' in which death and injury and the fear of such so-called 'accidents' contributes to greater use of cars for **safety**, so escalating the likelihood of fear of danger from traffic. Finally, the use of cars for school travel also reduces the amount of time that children are likely to spend away from adults who are directly responsible for them. This, in turn, is associated with the reduction of children's social skills and independence as their interactions with each other and non-related adults becomes more heavily mediated by adults, so reducing children's opportunities to develop their own social skills independently.

There is debate about the reasons for this increase in the use of cars as school transport. Undoubtedly the increase in car ownership and, indeed, young people getting their own cars as soon as regulations allow a provisional licence, which can be as young as 14 in some American states or 17 in the United Kingdom, plays a part. Cars have glamour, and usually higher status than alternatives such as buses or bicycles. Similarly women's higher employment levels, combined with their greater levels of caring and domestic responsibilities, can lead to greater numbers of multimodal trips. These in turn mean that taking and collecting children from school by car might seemingly saving time in a busy day. There is also the issue of fear of attack or sexual molestation, so-called 'stranger danger', for unaccompanied children. However, research indicates that children are no more likely to be attacked by predators now than they were in the 1980s. There have also been policies that have encouraged the motorization of transport: perhaps most famously, these involved the busing of black children into predominantly white urban areas in the United States between the 1950s and 1980s in the largely vain hope such mixing would encourage greater racial integration. More recently policies supposed to encourage 'parental choice' of schools have also increased the distances travelled to school for many students, as parents can opt for schools outside traditional catchment areas.

All these policies are controversial: as it is predominately women who drive children to school trips then some contemporary concerns may be motivated more by misogyny than traffic reduction. Other controversial policies have included lowering the costs of children using **buses** or other forms of **public transport**, or encouraging younger children to form 'walking buses'; there are also plans to charge more for **parking** outside schools to drivers who take their children to school in 'gas-guzzler' 4x4 vehicles. There are also successful campaigns run by local authorities and non-governmental organizations like SUSTRANS to identify safe routes to school and publicize them, and to encourage students to walk or cycle to school at least once a week, even if they travel in a car on other days.

Further reading
Hillman, M., J. Adams and J. Whitelegg (1990). *One False Move*. London: Policy Studies Institute.

Amanda Root

seaports

A seaport may generally be regarded as a gateway through which goods and passengers are transferred between ships and the shore. The economic function of a seaport is essentially to benefit those whose trade passes through them; that is, by providing increments to consumers' and producers' surpluses. The throughput of a port is usually defined in terms of number of passengers or freight tonnage handled per time unit (year, month, day).

Jansson and Shneerson divide the process of cargo throughput in a port into seven important subprocesses: approach of the vessel along a river or canal and subsequent mooring along the quay; unloading of the cargo from the ship's hold onto the quay; transportation of cargo from the quay to transit storage; transit storage; transportation of cargo from transit storage to loading platforms; loading of cargo onto the inland transportation mode; departure of the inland transportation vehicle from the port. Furthermore, seaports provide a number of supplementary, non-water-bound services, including customs clearance, storage in the port area and cargo preparation (pre-slinging, stripping and stuffing of **containers**).

The port product, then, may be regarded as a chain of interlinking functions, while the port as a whole is in turn a link in the overall logistics chain. Within the port itself, the relative significance of the constituting links has clearly changed in the course of time. This is due to, among other things, important technological developments (for example the increasing degree of containerization, the growing dimensions of ships, more speedy handling) that have improved efficiency.

A chain is as strong as its weakest link – a truism that also holds for the production of port services. What this means in practice is that the capacity of the various links should be optimally balanced. If the relative capacity of a particular link increases through an innovation (for example the deployment of a new generation of gantry cranes), the other links in the chain must follow suit. Only then can the original innovation achieve its full potential.

Hence, capacity is a crucial concept within the logistics chain approach to seaport activity. A distinction is to be made here between the general port capacity and the capacity of the port's constituting parts. Often, one distinguishes further between physical capacity, effective capacity and economic capacity. The physical capacity is the maximum capacity at which a structure can operate on a permanent basis in the absence of external restrictions. It is, in other words, an intrinsic capacity, determined only by the size and other physical properties of that structure. Effective capacity is the maximum capacity at which a structure can operate given a number of external restrictions on its physical capacity (working hours, maintenance, repairs, legal requirement and so on). Economic capacity, finally, refers to that part of effective capacity that is utilized in an economically and commercially viable way.

Within a **logistics** chain, the port cost usually constitutes only a fraction of the total cost. Overall demand for port services in a particular range will therefore be inelastic, especially in the absence of alternatives. On the other hand, competition between goods handlers, ports and countries within the same range is often fierce. The possibilities for substituting one port for another are often so great that the price-elasticity for a specific port may be quite substantial after all.

In view of the considerable number of players within any given port (port authorities, management, consignors, shipping lines, trade unions), each of whom pursues different objectives, the nature of port activities is inevitably heterogeneous. Consequently, the goals of a port authority are determined in part by the degree to which it is, directly or indirectly, exposed to foreign influences, external control or competition from other ports. Not surprisingly, then, these goals may differ quite considerably and indeed may change profoundly in the course of time.

Port management used to be almost exclusively in the hands of the port authorities. However, over the years, and especially since about 2000, an important evolution has unfolded in this respect. In general, the position of port authorities has weakened. They are now controlled more by the stronger players, notably shipping companies and terminal operators. In this context, it is interesting to consider how port management has changed, especially in terms of the objectives pursued and the tools applied.

The objectives of a port authority are closely connected with what is considered to be the economic purpose of a seaport. In the past, these goals were restricted mainly to increasing throughput, generating value-added, creating local employment and maximizing operating profits. However, today's reality is more complex and more dynamic than that, particularly as a port authority often needs to compromise between the priorities of the various market players. As the relative strength of those market players may change over time, so too might the objectives of the port authority.

At the same time, evolutions in port managerial structures are also a direct consequence of technological developments and changes in the socio-economic environment. The British port sector is a case in point: it was nationalized after the Second World War and grouped together into the British Transport Docks Board, then privatized as Associated British Ports in 1981, before a government decision in 1991 sanctioning the privatization of the most important ports. While matters did not evolve quite as dramatically in continental Europe, there was clearly a trend towards more autonomy for port authorities and a greater private stake in goods handling.

Far-reaching mechanization and sweeping technological change have also resulted in a sharp decline in the employment of dock workers, and indeed in a thorough reorganization of the work itself. A typical example of this trend is found in container throughput. After all, the capital-intensive nature of liner shipping demands that capacity utilization be maximized with a view to achieving a satisfactory return on investment. Ports and terminal operators are thus forced to strive constantly for a further improvement of efficiency and **productivity** of labour. Under this considerable pressure, an important part of port activity has become capital-intensive, requiring a very substantial level of investment in infrastructure and cargo-handling equipment.

It follows from this evolution that the role of government has changed. Much attention has been paid in this respect to possible financial or other support from government for port authorities and the consequences this may have on the competitive balance between companies and ports.

It is very hard, however, to make sensible comparisons between ports, as they usually operate in different economic, legal, social and fiscal environments. Consequently, there is today a considerable degree of variation in the management of European ports: the Anglo-Saxon tradition of independent port authorities; the Latin tradition of centralization in France, Spain and Italy; and the municipal Hanseatic tradition in Germany, the Netherlands and Belgium.

These different traditions have resulted in two important, but diametrically opposed, philosophies. First, there is the Continental approach whereby the port in the strict sense of the word is managed and operated by the port authority, while the maritime access routes and inland connections are more the responsibility of the central authorities, and cargo-handling and various other port-related services are in private hands. Diametrically opposed to this continental tradition stand the ports that are run as 'total organizations' (for example such British ports as Felixstowe), whereby the maritime access, the port itself and cargo-handling services are the responsibility of a single organization that supervises all port operations.

Thus, seaports possess characteristics of public utilities on the one hand, and of private enterprises on the other. Cargo-handling and related activities are commercial operations that, under normal circumstances, need no subsidizing. By contrast, port infrastructure has many public good characteristics and is thus approached from a socio-economic rather than a purely business perspective (that is, the application of socio-economic **benefit–cost analyses** to determine whether or not an investment is justified).

Further reading

Goss, R. (1990). Economic policies and seaports: 1. The economic functions of seaports. *Maritime Policy and Management* **17**, 207–19.

Jansson, J.O. and D. Shneerson (1982). *Port Economics*. Cambridge, MA: MIT Press.

Meersman, H. and E. Van de Voorde (2002). Port management, operation and competition: a focus on the North European continent. In C.T. Grammenos (ed.), *The Handbook of Maritime Economics and Business*. London: Lloyd's of London Press.

Suykens, F. and E. Van de Voorde (1998). A quarter of a century of port management in Europe: objectives and tools. *Maritime Policy and Management*, **25**, 251–61.

Eddy Van de Voorde

settlement structures and transport

The historical development of transport systems, settlement structures and travel demand is characterized by close interrelations. From the horse-drawn bus to the **railway** and later on to the car, economic and social interconnections expanded in space, and cities spread out and constituted intertwined regions. Initially, this development took place along the main axes of public transport. Then, more dispersed settlement patterns emerged with mass motorization. Hence, transport might be understood as part of a spiral of location choice, traffic infrastructure and travel demand.

This system is characterized by manifold interdependencies, which have been studied intensely since the 1980s. The focus of the research lies on the dependence of travel behaviour on spatial structures (aspects like density, city size, location, land use) at an individual's place of residence, and on the impact of traffic on spatial development (for example suburbanization because of noise emission and pollution in inner-city areas).

Most of the studies rely on cross-sectional comparisons between speci-fied areas. Longitudinal analyses are rare. They may be classified by at least three attributes:

- Scale: comparisons range from the international level to internal structures of cities.
- Level of generalization: case studies with idiographic character versus studies based on settlement types (for example region types, city size categories).
- Attributes of travel demand: mostly, the focus lies on covered dis-tances and **mode choice** for job, shopping, leisure and/or educational trips. Less intensely studied are business trips and freight transport. Neither are primarily caused by settlement structures.

The findings can be summarized into two key conclusions:

- The essential spatial factors for short distance behaviour are density, compactness and mixed land use. As far as centre-oriented activities (working, and to some extent shopping and education) are concerned, the covered distances increase with the distance from the next centre.
- Density, compactness and mixed use are also essential factors for a high proportion of environment-friendly transport modes (by foot, **bicycle**, **public transport**).

The reason for these findings is that the high potential of activity oppor-tunities (workplaces, retail, leisure facilities) in dense and mixed structures is a precondition for a traffic-saving lifestyle. At the same time, dense and compact settlement structures are necessary for an efficient high-quality **public transport** supply that facilitates a car-free life. Both of the key conclusions, though, have to be differentiated, and they imply problems concerning interpretation and consequences for planning.

Firstly, there is a lack of knowledge on the relevance and the inter-relation of various factors. The close correlation between settlement density and fuel consumption might likewise be interpreted as a correlation between fuel price and fuel consumption – the really decisive factor remains unknown. It is fairly well established that density without mixed use does not facilitate a reduction of travel demand: the inhabitants of high-density large-scale housing developments of the 1960s and 1970s mostly cover long and short distances – the monofunctionality of these quarters does not allow short distances, especially regarding job trips.

Secondly, there might be substitutive relations between travelled distances for different trip purposes. Some researchers consider high density and lack of free space as the reason for 'escape **mobility**' in leisure time: short job trips on weekdays, but escape to remote green areas on weekends. Besides that, residential location decisions are partly based on the desire for green and quiet neighbourhoods. Thus, excessive density might contribute to suburbanization and therefore to increasing travel volume.

Thirdly, traffic-saving behaviour of the residents of certain area types (for example the centres) does not imply that these area types save traffic. The residents of these centres might cause little traffic, but the surplus of centrality attracts considerable incoming traffic. Therefore, low transport volume (outgoing and incoming traffic) essentially depends on a well-balanced mixed use in the region as a whole.

A reasonable scale of mixed use varies by the degree of specialization of activities and supply facilities. A small-scale mix of housing, retail and other facilities is particularly important to secure the mobility of non-motorized or low-motorized population groups (children, adolescents, **elderly**). With demographic **ageing**, small-scale **accessibility** will gain importance compared to large-scale high-speed connections.

The impact of settlement structures on transport has tended to decrease since the late 1950s due to the revolutions of accessibility (cars, traffic infrastructure, **telecommunication** systems). As a consequence, the relevance of settlement structures for the explanation and manipulation of transport demand is discussed intensely. There is a tendency towards some doubt after a couple of years of settlement structure euphoria. The causality of an impact can hardly be proven, because settlement structures are not invariant frame conditions for an individual: they can be changed by relocation.

For the future evolution of the settlement structure and transport system, the further decoupling of suburbs from the core cities by the sub-urbanization of trade and services is often seen as of primary importance with tangential traffic flows and outcommuting from centres to suburbs further increasing.

Further reading

Holz-Rau, C., P. Rau, J. Scheiner, K. Trubbach, C. Dörkes, A. Fromberg, P. Gwiasda and S.S. Krüger (1999). Nutzungsmischung und Stadt der kurzen Wege: Werden die Vorzüge einer baulichen Mischung im Alltag genutzt? Bonn: Werkstatt Praxis No. 7.

Stead, D. and S. Marshall (2001). The relationships between urban form and travel patterns: an international review and evaluation. *European Journal of Transport and Infrastructure Research* **1**, 113–41.

Christian Holz-Rau and *Joachim Scheiner*

shipping conferences

Shipping conferences are defined by the United Nations Conference on Trade and Development (UNCTAD) Code of Conduct for Liner Conferences as:

> a group of two or more vessel-operating carriers which provides international liner services for the carriage of cargo on a particular route or routes within specified geographical limits and which has an agreement or arrangement, whatever its nature, within the framework of which they operate under uniform or common freight rates and any other agreed conditions with respect to the provision of liner services.

While countries may have alternate definitions in national legislation, this one serves the purpose of laying out the key features of conferences.

First and foremost, those who offer liner shipping are providing a scheduled service. The business model assumes that if vessel owners offer cargo owners reliable sailing schedules, business can be grown that will be mutually beneficial. In the mid 1800s, the development of the steam engine removed the unreliability of wind propulsion from trip planning and enabled ship owners to offer reliable transport services. Early liner opera-tors plied the trade routes from the United Kingdom to Asia and back, but the rapid expansion of the business led many shipowners to chase too little cargo and, finding that fixed costs were high, they tried cut-throat marginal pricing to secure business. Instability grew, and in 1875, in an effort to rein in the volatility of the business, the conference system was born with the formation of the UK–Calcutta Conference.

Early conferences employed a common tariff and attempted to control capacity and pool revenue. Because of this, they came under the scrutiny of both British and American regulatory authorities. In the United Kingdom, the 1909 *Report of the Royal Commission on Shipping Rings* concluded that the conference system should be supported, but urged that shippers' bargaining powers be strengthened. In the United States, the Shipping Act of 1916 established a regulatory regime for conferences that meant they were exempt from antitrust; oversight of the new regime was by a body separate from the Department of Justice. Both investigations determined that liner conferences possess such uncommon features that they should be exempt from competition legislation.

Over the course of the twentieth century, governments and multilateral organizations have sought to counter what is perceived to be anti-competitive activities by conference operators. The United States Shipping Act of 1984 introduced the concepts of independent action and service contracts as the means to limit the market power of the conferences and the Ocean Shipping Reform Act of 1998 (OSRA) made substantial changes to the United States regulatory approach to conferences, by allowing confidential contracting and electronic tariff publication. The intention was to create a more market-driven, efficient liner industry.

On the European side, conference regulation followed quite a different path, driven in part by Europe's efforts to cooperate more deeply and broadly within its own community. Here the activities of liner operators fall under the Competition Directorate of the Commission rather than the Transport Directorate. Council Regulation 4056/86, however, provided block exemptions to the full force of the competition rules for liner conferences, and safeguards were put in place to ensure that this privilege was not abused. The Commission went further than United States regulators in that it recognized that alliances between liner companies were becoming the dominant form of cooperative activity in the industry; it concluded that these too should be regulated. Commission Regulation 870/95 on 20 April 1995 granted immunity from antitrust regulation to a long list of activities, typical of joint ventures; price-fixing was not on the list. In sum, by 2000, conferences enjoyed a block exemption from antitrust scrutiny for certain activities including price-fixing, and consortia (alliances) had a block exemption for another list of operational activities like slot-sharing under successor rules.

Since 2000, the power of shipping conferences has eroded and conference usage has decreased as regulatory changes have been introduced and large, global shippers have used their power to negotiate volume contracts. Key shipper groups, believing that liner shipping is not sufficiently unique to be treated separately from a regulatory point of view, convinced the

European Commission to remove antitrust immunity for conferences, effective from 18 October 2008. Liner conferences calling into Europe are now subject to the competition rules embodied in Articles 81 and 82 of the EC Treaty. The United States Antitrust Modernization Commission has also called for the end to antitrust immunity for conferences. Given the capital-intensive, high-fixed-cost nature of the shipping business, and the problems operators have adjusting to short-term changes in demand, particularly because the market demands regular, fixed-day sailing schedules, it is unclear in the economic downturn whether the appetite exists for further changes to the rules governing consortia and alliances; the European review is under way in advance of the 2010 expiry of Regulation 823/2000 affecting consortia.

Further references
Brooks, M.R. (2000). *Sea Change in Liner Shipping: Regulation and Managerial Decision-Making in a Global Industry*. Oxford: Pergamon Press.
Brooks, Mary R. (2009). Liberalization in maritime transport. Paper to the International Transport Forum 2009 on Transport for a Global Economy: Challenges and Opportunities in a Downturn. Leipzig: Joint Transport Research Centre of the Organisation for Economic Co-operation and Development.
United Nations Antitrust Modernization Commission (2007). *Report and Recommendations*. Washington, DC: Antitrust Modernization Commission.

Mary R. Brooks

short sea shipping

There is no consensus on the definition of short sea shipping (SSS). Some definitions focus mainly on the operational maritime aspects of SSS, and examine specific characteristics of this maritime operation. For the most part, they consider a classification based on length of route, type and size of **containers**, nature of load, membership of ports of the same state, and type of demand distinguishing between 'feeder traffic' and intraregional movements. Within these classifications, short sea shipping is viewed as the shipping of cargo or goods for relatively 'short' distances or to nearby coastal ports.

Recent trends in production, however, such as global sourcing, **just-in-time** deliveries and fragmented production chains, have produced clear patterns in relation to the negative environmental impacts of freight transport. A general increase in tonnes-kilometres of goods shipped via, road transport, has been observed, even though this is among the most expensive and environmentally polluting, resource-consuming transport modes. **Congestion** is a growing problem in overland carriage and can limit economic growth. One alternative strategy is to revitalize short sea shipping to alleviate traffic congestion and enhance **economic development** by maintaining freight flow efficiency. Because ship transport offers fuel economies and lower emissions of harmful pollutants, SSS is considered to be one of the most environmentally benign and economically competitive modes of transport. However, only with the inclusion of private and external costs in transport costs can short sea shipping have an effective economic advantage in relation to road transport system.

From this perspective, short sea shipping, either as unimodal alternative or as part of an **intermodal** freight transport **network**, is often regarded as a component in the reduction of the external costs associated with freight transport. Sobremisana has given a broader definition, which includes the advantages of SSS:

> a commercial waterborne transportation that does not transit an ocean. It is an alternative form of commercial transportation that utilizes inland and coastal waterways to move commercial freight off already congested highways, thereby providing more efficient and safer roadways for car passengers while alleviating congestion at critical choke points. A secondary effect of SSS would be reduction of air pollution and overall fuel consumption through economies of scale.

A primary characteristic of short sea shipping therefore as a link with road and/or rail within the context of national and international transport systems. By considering the transport system as a whole, SSS acts as a non-deep sea segment substitute and/or as a complement of other transport modes. It is a complement of other modes such as **truck** and **rail** services, but conversely, SSS is a competitor when providing alternative transport services in the same point-to-point market also served by road, conventional rail services or even air transport. **Intermodalism** therefore assumes a relevant role in the identification of the use and capability of SSS as a freight movement alternative and complement.

Despite numerous advantages, SSS is not regarded as especially attractive by some freight handlers although it does carry 40 per cent of European Union tonnage; the industry therefore faces various challenges. First, many shippers still view it as an old-fashioned mode of transport. Second, full integration of short sea shipping into door-to-door multimodal systems remains to be accomplished. Third, the complexity of documentary and administrative procedures in short sea shipping that can pose problems. Fourth, the efficiency of ports, port services and port–hinterland connections are often suboptimal.

To take full advantage of SSS requires overcoming these disadvantages. A number of factors are often seen as necessary to fully exploit SSS. SSS is particularly competitive over certain type of distances and in relation to the time taken for the door to door movement. Moreover, the ships have to meet certain conditions. Not every kind of product is likely to be transported via SSS and to obtain a seamless intermodal transport service, it is necessary to overcome administrative obstacles. Finally, port infrastructure is the central link between modes in the development of an efficient chain. To the extent that ports can fulfill this role they must be able to accomdate coastal ships and carry out efficient handling.

Further reading

Henesey, L. and M. Yonge (2006). Short sea shipping in the United States: identifying the prospects and opportunities. Paper to the 85th Transportation Research Board Annual Meeting, Washington, DC.

Sobremisana, C.J. (2003). Short sea shipping initiative. To the United States Federal Highways Administration, Talking Freight Seminar, Washington, DC.

Francesca Medda and *Lourdes Trujillo*

simulation

Webster's Revised Unabridged Dictionary in 1913 defined simulation as 'the act of assuming an appearance which is feigned, or not true'. In the area of computing, simulation means the attempt to analyse, understand and/or predict aspects of some system by running an approximate computational model of it (computer simulation).

Computer simulation is preceded by modelling, which means the construction of a usually abstract representation of the system. Most systems of interest are too complex to be fully described; then, the process of modelling includes the selection of the presumably most important entities, interactions and parameters of the system.

At the core, computers only understand algorithms, that is, sequences of computational actions. The corresponding computer languages, called procedural, or imperative, are the most prominent and efficient ones. Software layers can remove the computer user from that technical core, usually at the cost of degrading performance.

Many computer simulation models are not developed as algorithms. In such situations, there needs to be a translation into algorithmic form. For example, discretisation translates differential equation models into algorithms. Often, computer simulation refers to running the model forward in time (dynamical system). There are also simulations of static systems; for example, a virtual environment can be a simulation of a real environment.

Important simulation techniques include differential equations, **queuing systems**, cellular automata or multi-agent systems. Prominent uses of simulation in transport are for physical systems (car traffic, rail traffic, air traffic, freight movement, engine design, and so on), but also where human behaviour is concerned (for example activity-based demand generation). The use of simulation is increasing because of enhanced computational capabilities, but also because of the increasing availability of digital data, for example from **intelligent transportation systems** (ITS) or from digital maps.

There are several types of possible errors in the area of simulation. Modelling errors occur when the model is too simple, or concentrates on the wrong aspects of the system. Algorithmization errors occur when the original model is not given in algorithmic form, as explained above. Implementation errors occur when the implemented version of the model does not correspond to its specification. Rounding errors occur because floating decimal point numbers have finite precision in a computer. Interpretation errors occur when predicting real-world aspects from computer simulations.

To reduce errors in a simulation, the following steps can be taken. Verification tests how far the implementation corresponds to the model. If the model is too complex to do formal verification, then at least limiting cases need to be tested. During calibration, parameters of the simulation are adjusted so that they match some actual data as well as possible. Validation means that the simulation is used to predict some real-world data. In principle, these data should be different from the data used for calibration. Sensitivity testing refers to running the simulation with different initial conditions, different parameters or even with different models. The goal is to find out how stable and thus reliable the results are under those changes.

There is discussion in the community which of these steps should be taken under which conditions, and how. In a data-poor situation, withholding data from calibration in order to do validation may be problematic; and calibration may be done by reducing the distance to some real-world numbers in the least-square sense, but also by visual comparison with real-world images.

This discussion is particularly critical in the context of emergent phenomena. There is no accepted exact definition of emergence, but intuitively it refers to system behaviour that is difficult to describe at the level of the microscopic entities. Examples of emergent phenomena in the area of transport and planning are traffic jams, road capacity or fractal dimensions. Emergent phenomena are difficult to calibrate – for example, fractal dimensions are often not easy to change at all once the model is given.

Other important topics in the area of simulation include stochastic (Monte Carlo) simulations which generate distributions of results rather than a single result. Often, there are not enough computational resources to obtain a good estimate of the complete distribution. Simulation models, even when deterministic, can display completely different behaviour after small changes (chaos). Such behaviour limits the predictive capability of simulation models and therefore needs to be well understood.

Further reading
Gilbert, N. and K.G. Troitzsch (1999). *Simulation for the Social Scientist.* Buckingham: Open University Press.

Kai Nagel

slow transport

Slow transport includes the non-motorized modes of walking and bicycling. The term 'slow transport' for walking and cycling is a bit misleading. Surveys from Middle European cities show that in urban areas the average speed of cars (29 km/h) and public transport (16 km/h) is not that much higher than that of walking (4 km/h) and **bicycling** (10 km/h).

Walking is the oldest form of human transport. For millions of years the only possibility to overcome distances was to walk. Walking consumes only physiological energy. The average total energy consumption varies depending on the walking speed from about 900 to 1300 kJ per hour. This energy is supplied by ingestion. Walking does not require any exogenous energy, and has several advantages. The flexibility of **pedestrians** is high. Walking requires little space. **Pedestrians** have a higher hill-climbing ability than other modes. Walking is safe. Walking does not produce emissions or noise. The weakness of the walking mode is its sensitiveness to detours, gradients and weather.

In 1817 the predecessor of the bicycle was invented by Freiherr von Drais. First **bicycles** with pedals were developed around the year 1860. The pedals of the first generation of bicycles were directly connected to the front wheel. To reach higher speeds the front wheels had to be huge. This design made cycling difficult and dangerous. In the late nineteenth century the bicycle already had its current design. The main features are chain drive, a diamond frame and pneumatic tyres. Cycling became easier and attracted a broader segment of the population. Experiments with two-geared transmissions in the pedal bearing started around 1870. The breakthrough came with the use of sun-and-planet gear units in the hub of the rear wheel. In parallel, the first systems using derailleurs and cog sets were developed. Both systems have survived in reworked versions. Being able to change the gear ratio while driving made hill climbing much easier. The technical improvements were responsible for the cycling boom around the turn of the nineteenth century. The popularity of the mode declined with the coming of **motorcycles** and cars in the early twentieth century.

The comeback of the bicycle as a serious means of transport began after the oil crisis in the 1970s. The operation of a bicycle requires only physiological energy. The **energy** consumption on a flat surface varies from about 800 kJ/h (10 km/h) to about 8000 kJ/h (50 km/h). The operation of the cycling mode neither produces **climate change** gas emissions nor consumes non-renewable resources. Compared with other modes only a small amount of external energy is required to produce a bicycle (see Figure). The primary energy consumption and emissions per lifespan person-kilometre for the production of a car are more than five times that for producing a bicycle. The operation of the car mode requires about eight times the space of the bicycle mode. One of the weak points is that cyclists are very sensitive to detours, wind and hill climbing.

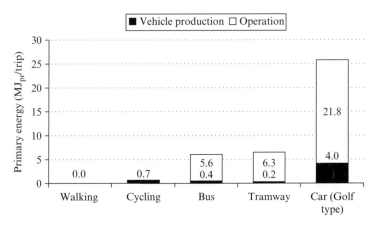

During the period following the Second World War, planners tended to forget about slow transport. Instead they focused exclusively on motorized modes and in particular on the car. Politicians and the public followed this view. But in contrary to this thinking, the contribution of non-motorized transport to daily transport is still significant. In Western European cities such as Vienna about a third of daily trips are by walking or cycling. The share of slow transport in North American cities is less, but generally is higher in cities in the Southern Hemisphere; for example in Indian metropolitan areas up to 60 per cent of the daily trips are slow transport. During the 1990s the notion of sustainability gained popularity amongst planners and politicians. The promotion of slow transport is often seen as necessary to achieve the objective of sustainability in the urban transport system. Walking and cycling can contribute substantially to the protection of the environment, liveable streets and neighbourhoods, **safety**, equity and social inclusion.

Further reading
Knoflacher, H. (1995). *Fußgeher- und Fahrradverkehr – Planungsprinzipien.* Wien: Böhlauverlag.
Pfaffenbichler, P.C. (2001). Verkehrsmittel und Strukturen. *Wissenschaft and Umwelt Interdisziplinär* **3**, 35–42.

Paul C. Pfaffenbichler

social costs of transportation

The concept of social cost of transportation (often called the full cost of transportation) aims at encompassing all costs of transportation on the society. It is akin to the economic concept of resource cost, as opposed to the narrow private cost of transportation, which is the cost borne by the users. It is relevant when public policy issues are at stake, while private costs are relevant when users' behaviour or welfare is relevant.

The private costs largely comprise time costs (travel time, cost of late or early arrival), which use the value of time. In the case of private transport, they also include operating costs of vehicles (capital costs, running costs). In the case of **public transportation**, they include the monetary costs paid by the users, that is, the fare or the ticket price. It has been acknowledged that private costs do not cover the full costs for the society, and that several items should be added to the private costs to cover the social costs.

First, they must be corrected by indirect **taxes**, charges and **subsidies**; these are common and large in the transportation sector. Especially in the case of public transportation, the fares often differ from the suppliers' costs due to operation subsidies.

Second, the social costs should include the infrastructure costs. They usually are not directly paid, or at least only partially paid, by the users. The typical example is the case of roads, the use of which is free, except for toll motorways, bridges and tunnels; though not, or not entirely, paid by the users, the infrastructure costs of roads are borne by the society, through the taxpayers. However, this is not always the case: United States' freight railroads, for example, provide their own track.

Accidents are another important part of the social costs of transportation, both through their uninsured monetary consequences (material damage, administrative costs, medical care, production loss) and through non-monetary costs (pain and suffering, risk value); the main parameter is the statistical value of human life, estimated either through **contingent valuation** methods or through human capital methods.

Environmental costs are a recent concern, with current interest dating back to the 1970s. They include an increasing number of items: aesthetic impacts of infrastructures; habitat and community fragmentation for animals, plants and humans; soil and underground water pollution; **noise nuisance** and vibration caused by vehicles; air pollution both from vehicle exhausts and from upstream production of energy and manufacture of vehicles and facilities; and **climate change** caused by emissions of greenhouse gases, especially CO_2. Recently, the **European Union** has sought to bring these items together within a single framework – the Unification of Accounts and Marginal Costs for Transport Efficiency (UNITE) project.

The work to date show that estimates of social costs are uncertain. Calculations of non-market goods such as the value of time, value of life and environmental effects entail a lot of uncertainty. Social costs also vary widely according to the specific situations: differences in the neighbourhood (for instance urban versus **rural**), the time (peak and non-peak hours), the type of vehicle (new or old cars) are dramatic.

Despite the uncertainty and the variations of the estimates it appears clearly that social costs largely differ from private costs, by ratios varying according to the situations but on average of two or three to one. This is the reason why social costs of transportation play an important role in public transport policy issues, in which social costs are more pertinent than private costs. They are now widely used by public authorities in their decision-making process, both for strategic orientations (the modal split, the public funds to be devoted to each mode or zone) and for specific decisions such as project appraisal or infrastructure charges.

Further reading
Greene, D.L., D.W. Jones and M. Delucchi (eds) (1997). *The Full Costs and Benefits of Transportation*. New York: Springer.

Emile Quinet

space–time prism

The space–time prism (STP) is the set of all locations that are reachable by an individual in space and time given known starting and ending points in space–time and a maximum travel speed. For example, if an individual decides to walk to a restaurant for lunch at noon, but must return to work one hour later, all restaurants within a 2.5 km radius of work are reachable if the individual is able to maintain a maximum walking speed of 5 km/hr. Restaurants beyond 2.5 km lie outside the individual's STP unless they are able to walk faster or use another mode of transport. Restaurant arrival time increases with distance from work, which means that the time available for eating lunch decreases with distance, becoming zero at 2.5 km from work. As this example illustrates (see the first Figure), the STP determines where, when and for how long an individual can conduct an activity given their constraints and resources for travel.

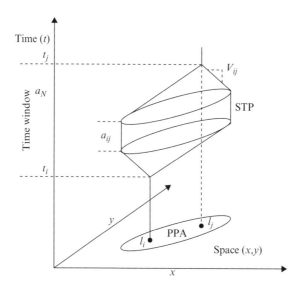

The STP concept was developed by Torsten Hägerstrand and his colleagues at the University of Lund in the mid-twentieth century as part of time geography, which focuses on the constraints on human spatial behaviour in space and time as a means for understanding that behaviour. Time geography distinguishes between fixed and flexible activities based on their degree of flexibility in space and time over the short run – for example, a day. A fixed activity is one that cannot easily be rescheduled or relocated, whereas a flexible activity is amenable to changes in its timing and/

or location. Work is an example of the former, and shopping the latter. Spatio-temporal coordinates (that is, *x-y-t* coordinates) derived from two consecutive fixed activities are the anchors for an STP (that is, the starting and ending points noted above). By definition, the prism formed by these anchors delimits possibilities for participating in flexible activities.

A general STP with notation is shown in the Figure. Graphically, the STP is a volume with crisp boundaries. In the Figure, the first and second anchors are defined for two different locations, l_i and l_j. However, they can also be defined for the same location – that is, $l_i = l_j$. The temporal coordinate for the bottom of the prism is given by the end of the first fixed activity, which is time t_i. Likewise, time t_j, that is, the start of the next fixed activity, helps define the apex of the STP. Since time is linear, the interval (t_i, t_j) defines a time window, which corresponds to a specific period of time, typically some part of a day. Returning to the above example, a person who leaves work at noon for lunch and must return to work no later than 1 p.m. has a one-hour time window corresponding to the period 12 p.m. to 1 p.m. The time window defines the time budget, which is the amount of time available for travel and activity participation (that is, $t_j - t_i$). The trade-off between space and time, and thus the spatial extent of the STP, is governed by the maximum travel speed that an individual can achieve during the time window (that is, v_{ij}). In reality, this implies that spatial extent is a function of travel conditions (for example, free-flow versus congested traffic, weather) and travel mode (for example, car, **public transit**, **bicycling** and walking).

Prism boundaries determine the earliest time of arrival, the latest time of departure, and thus, the maximum time available to participate in a flexible activity at a specific location. As shown in the first Figure, the minimum time required to complete an activity, a_{ij}, can be considered in the derivation of a STP. This time reduces the time budget and thus the prism's spatial extent. Projecting the STP onto the two-dimensional (2D) geographic plane delimits the potential path area (PPA), which is the spatial manifestation of the prism.

Many attempts have been made since the 1970s to operationalize the STP. While early efforts relied on mathematical and geometrical methods, **geographic information systems** (GIS) have been used since Miller published his pioneering work on the subject. The strength of a GIS in this regard lies in its ability to replicate a realistic spatial environment that includes both travel conditions over a road **network** and the locations of opportunities for engaging in flexible activities. Most of the effort to date has focused on implementing 2D PPAs rather than 3D STPs, presumably due to their direct application in studies concerning individual measures of space–time **accessibility**. Two types of methods exist for deriving PPAs in a GIS: those based on overlay analysis and those based on shortest paths.

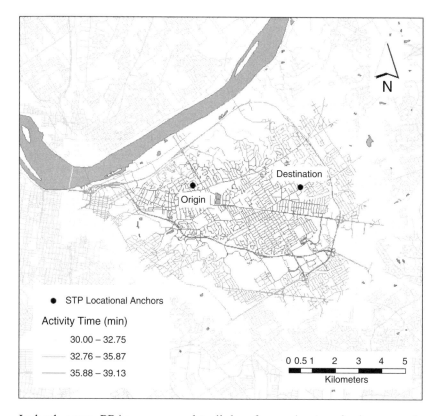

In both cases, PPAs correspond to links of a road network. An example of such a network-based PPA is shown in the second Figure. In this case, the spatial extent corresponds to a reduced time budget of 15 minutes after considering a minimum activity time of 30 minutes (that is, the original time budget is 45 minutes). Links are shaded according to the amount of time available for participating in a flexible activity somewhere between the locations of the first and second fixed activities, which are labelled respectively as origin and destination.

Further reading
Miller, H.J. (1991). Modelling accessibility using space–time prism concepts within geographical information systems. *International Journal of Geographical Information Systems*, **5**, 287–301.
Scott, D.M. (2006). Constrained destination choice set generation: a comparison of GIS-based approaches. Paper to the 85th Annual Meeting of the Transportation Research Board, Washington, DC.

Darren M. Scott

speed limits

Many argue that speed limits have a significant influence on highway **safety** and operational efficiency. However, setting speed limits has been a controversial issue because the different stakeholders, including traffic engineers, public safety officials, enforcement personnel and the motoring public, do not always agree on the appropriate balance between travel efficiency, convenience and safety. The optimal balance depends on the type of **road**. For example, roads in residential subdivisions provide access, while collector roads distribute local traffic between neighbourhoods and arterial street systems. On these roads, low operating speeds are necessary to accommodate **pedestrians** and bicyclists and provide local access. On the other hand, on limited-access roads built to the highest standards, there may be greater emphasis on reducing travel times without compromising **safety**.

Speed limits can be set system-wide or for a particular roadway section. System-wide speed limits are set for the general highway system and are established by legislation at the national level, state level and municipal level. Setting speed limits for a particular roadway section has been traditionally accomplished through engineering studies.

Most studies that looked at the effect of system-wide changes in speed limits in the United States concluded that the decrease in interstate speed limits in 1974 was associated with a significant reduction in fatal crashes, while the increases in speed limits in 1987 and 1995 were associated with an increase in fatal crashes. On the other hand, the few studies conducted in the United States to study the effect of changes in speed limit on non-limited-access roads seem to conclude that changes in speed limit have very little effect on the frequency and severity of crashes.

Instead of fixed speed limits that apply all the time, some countries in Europe have been experimenting with variable speed limits that depend on traffic conditions, time of day, weather, construction activities and other factors. Variable speed limits have had very limited application in the United States.

Some have argued that as a general proposition, speed limits should be set at levels that are self-enforcing so that law enforcement officials can concentrate their efforts on the worst offenders. The *Manual on Uniform Traffic Control Devices* (MUTCD) argues that: 'when a speed limit is to be posted, it should be within 10 km/h or 5 mph of the 85th percentile speed of free-flowing traffic'. However, the MUTCD also indicates that other factors including road geometry, the pace speed, roadside development, **parking** practices and crash experience may be considered in addition to the 85th percentile speed when establishing speed limits, but does not provide specifics on how to account for these variables. Due to lack of specific guidance and procedures from the MUTCD and other documents, engineers often rely on their experience and judgement in considering many factors when deciding on an appropriate speed limit. The use of subjective procedures by decision-makers with various levels of experience sometimes leads to inconsistencies in how speed limits are set in different jurisdictions. In order to reduce these inconsistencies, some have proposed the use of expert systems as an aid to the decision-maker.

Expert systems for speed limits were first introduced in Victoria, Australia, in late 1980s. Since then, similar programmes have been developed for other provinces in Australia. Recently, an expert system was developed in the United States by making use of the knowledge, experience and expertise of several individuals with backgrounds in engineering, enforcement, research and public policy. This system takes into account the site characteristics including operating speed and crash statistics in recommending the appropriate speed limit for a roadway section. This expert system is web-based and can be accessed by anyone with access to the Internet and web-browsing software.

Automated enforcement, as a complement to traditional law enforcement, has been proposed as one way to reduce speeding. Automated enforcement typically involves cameras at fixed locations or mobile systems. The system can be covert or overt. Very few jurisdictions in the United States have implemented automated enforcement due to several concerns, including whether the system provides a **safety** benefit or is mainly a revenue-producing tool. Most of the studies that have tried to evaluate the impact of automated enforcement have concluded that automated enforcement is effective in reducing speeds and injury due to crashes.

Further reading

Parham, A.H. and K. Fitzpatrick (1998). Handbook of speed management techniques. Research Report 1770–2, Report FHWA/TX-99/1770-2, College Station, Texas Transportation Institute.

Srinivasan, R., M. Parker, D.L. Harkey, D. Tharpe and R. Sumner (2008). Development of a web-based expert system for setting speed limits in speed zones. Paper to the 87th Annual Meeting of the Transportation Research Board, Washington, DC.

Raghavan Srinivasan

Speed–flow functions

Traffic tends to slow down as its volume increases. Speed–flow functions ('correspondences' would be a more correct term) aim to capture this regularity by establishing the relation between traffic flow and the speed at which traffic moves. Although attempts have been made to determine 'area-wide' speed–flow relations for full **networks**, most efforts have considered single road segments, a focus also chosen here.

Imagine a single homogeneous **road** with identical users, on which stationary traffic conditions apply. Three important characteristics of these conditions are traffic flow (*F*, measured in vehicles per hour), traffic density (*D*, in vehicles per kilometre) and speed (*S*, in kilometres per hour). For stationary traffic conditions, these three characteristics are identically related through:

$$F = S \cdot D \qquad (1)$$

that can be verified by checking units.

The so-called fundamental law of traffic **congestion** states that speed declines as density increases. The behavioural motivation is provided by **safety** considerations. Because of Equation 1, a parametric plot of speed and flow, both as a function of density, will then have the general shape shown in the Figure.

The backward-bending shape arises because at relatively low densities, an increase in density causes a relatively small decrease in speed, so that their product, flow, increases. The opposite occurs at relatively high densities. Note that a zero flow is possible both because there are no vehicles, or because there are so many that speed has fallen to zero. Engineers often refer to the lower segment of the speed–flow function as 'uncongested' and to the upper segment as 'congested', whereas economists often speak of the 'normally congested' and 'hypercongested' segments, respectively. The particular combination of speed and density that maximizes their product defines the road's capacity, as well as the critical speed that separates the normally and hypercongested segments.

Empirical observations of speed and flow combinations reproduce the general pattern seen in the Figure, although factors such as weather conditions and driver heterogeneity often cause substantial scatter. Various functional forms have been proposed to characterize speed–flow relations. Of historical interest is the Greenshields formulation, which assumes a linear speed–density relation resulting in the following parabolic speed–flow relation:

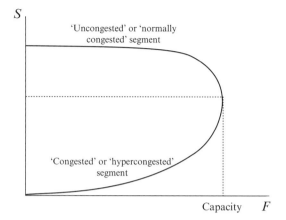

$$F = D_j \cdot \left(S - \frac{S^2}{S_f} \right) \tag{2}$$

where D_j gives the 'jam density' for which speed falls to zero, and S_f the 'free-flow speed'. This functional form is however unable to reproduce the empirical regularity that speeds tend to remain constant or nearly constant up to a considerable flow level (the so-called breakpoint) of around 50 per cent to 75 per cent of capacity. Two widely used, more recent speed–flow relations that do account for this phenomenon are the British COBA9 and the *United States Highway Capacity Manual* (HCM) formulations. Both have piecewise normally congested segments. Up to the breakpoint, the left-most segment is linear for COBA9 and flat for HCM, while between the breakpoint and the capacity another linear segment is assumed for COBA9 and a quadratic one for HCM. Capacities have been estimated at 2000 vehicles per hour per lane for COBA9 and 2200 for HCM.

Speed–flow functions are at the basis of what has become the conventional static economic model of traffic **congestion** and road pricing. Specifically, the speed–flow function of the figure can be translated into a **generalized cost** function, depicting average per user travel cost as a function of traffic flow. An important component of this generalized cost is the value of travel time. Ignoring, without loss of generality, other variable cost components like fuel costs, one can transform the speed–flow function into a generalized cost function by multiplying the inverse of speed by the length of the road and the value of time. Like the speed–flow function, the resulting average cost function (again a correspondence) is backward-bending, but now the upper segment corresponds with hypercongestion and the lower segment with normal congestion. When confronted with a standard downward-sloping inverse demand function, this backward-bending average cost function yields puzzling results, which have given rise to fierce debates. The emergent view is that hypercongestion cannot emerge as a stable equilibrium outcome in the strict single-road setting, and occurs in reality only when a downstream bottleneck is active. From the upward-sloping part of the average cost function, a marginal cost function can be derived that enables identification of the optimum traffic flow and the supporting optimal congestion toll for stationary state traffic.

Further reading
Smith, W.S., F.L. Hall and F.O. Montgomery (1996). Comparing speed–flow relationships for motorways with new data from the M6. *Transportation Research A* **30**, 89–101.
Verhoef, E.T. (1999). Time, speeds, flows and densities in static models of road traffic congestion and congestion pricing. *Regional Science and Urban Economics* **29**, 341–69.

Erik Verhoef

state departments of transportation in the United States

In the United States each of the 50 states has an agency that is charged with providing a statewide multimodal transportation system, including highways, roads, **public transit**, **rail**, maritime and aviation. Typically, these agencies are the state departments of transportation (state DOTs), and together with the federal United States Department of Transportation (USDOT) they are the most powerful and influential government agencies that shape transportation planning and policy, as well as the design, construction, maintenance and operations of transportation systems.

Every state DOT originally started as a Department of Highways, typically in the late 1800s and early 1900s. Prior to that time and throughout much of United States history, the private sector was largely responsible for transportation provision, but eventually federal and state government involvement in transportation was instigated by the need for more and better roads. The 'good roads movement' began in the late 1800s, initially spurred by three major constituencies: bicyclists, who started the movement; railroads; and farmers. Because of this early support, states began to develop road **networks** in the 1890s, including the establishment of state aid systems and state Highway Departments. New Jersey was the first state to establish a Highway Department in 1892.

The newly emerging automobile and truck industry began to provide an increasing impetus for the 'good roads movement' by the early 1900s, and the states and federal government responded to the growing need to develop better roads. In fact, by 1915, 45 states had established state aid systems for highway development and 40 states had created state highway departments. State highway departments expanded road-building throughout the 1920s, spurred by several federal highway Acts that established the first federal aid highway system and by the adoption of state gasoline taxes to help fund state highway expansion programs. Extensive road-building continued in the 1930s due largely to federal New Deal funding that targeted road construction as one of numerous public works projects to provide employment for workers during the Great Depression. Attention to highway building had to be postponed for several years due to the onset of the Second World War, with its attendant gas rationing and travel restrictions.

After the war, as business demand increased and automobile use skyrocketed, there was widespread public support to upgrade the nation's highway system. Existing roads and highways were inadequate to meet the demands of an expanding and suburbanizing population that was becoming increasingly reliant on automobiles and trucks. The Federal-Aid Highway Act of 1956 authorized $25 billion over 12 years to begin building a 41 000-mile National System of Interstate and Defense Highways in accord with high design standards – all roads had to be multilane, limited-access highways for high-speed travel. It also reasserted the federal–state highway partnership, thus providing state highway departments with a new *raison d'être*: building the Interstate Highway System.

The enthusiasm for highways began to wane during the 1960s, as a trickle of public opposition to highway building due mainly to negative environmental and social impacts began to grow into a flood of outrage, triggering the 'freeway revolt' era. The 1962 Highway Act was the first to acknowledge that changes in standard highway operating procedures were necessary, and that state highway departments needed to involve local officials in a broader-based planning process that should be 'continuing, cooperative, and comprehensive' (the 3-C process). There was growing recognition that state highway departments might need to expand beyond highways to embrace other modes of transportation.

After the federal government created the USDOT in 1966, several states changed the names of their highway departments to transportation departments. New Jersey, the first state to create a highway department, also became the first state to change to a department of transportation, in 1967. New York followed shortly thereafter, and by 1973, 20 states had made the change. By 2010 only Nebraska retained such a term in its official name.

By 1990, state DOTs were becoming more involved in aviation, **public**

transportation, rail, water and **intermodal** transportation. The key event that signalled the beginning of the new era in transportation was the promulgation of the landmark Intermodal Surface Transportation Efficiency Act (ISTEA) of 1991. It was the first major piece of federal transportation legislation that used the term 'intermodal' instead of 'highway'. For state DOTs, ISTEA required the planning process to focus on the development and implementation of the intermodal transportation system of the state, and attempted to mandate much greater cooperation with metropolitan planning organization (MPOs) and other local planning organizations in the process of transportation planning. States were required to have a statewide transportation plan that was coordinated with the transportation plans of their metropolitan areas.

Today, state DOTs remain concerned principally with maintenance, construction and **safety** on interstate, federal and state highways as part of the National Highway System. But their focus has broadened considerably to include other modes of transportation, as well as more explicit consideration of environmental and social impacts. Despite the increased roles for MPOs and local transit agencies during the **intermodal** era, state DOTs remain the most important transportation agencies in terms of funding, constructing and operating transportation systems.

Further reading
American Association of State Highway and Transportation Officials (1990). *Moving America Into the Future: AASHTO 1914–1989*. Washington, DC: AASHTO.
Sampson, R.J., M.T. Farris and D.L. Shrock (1990). *Domestic Transportation: Practice, Theory, and Policy* (6th edn). Boston, MA: Houghton Mifflin.

Andrew Goetz

stated preference methods

Stated preference (SP) is a methodological approach to studying choice behaviour. SP recognizes that the revelation of preferences of agents (be they individuals, households, firms, and so on) should not be limited to choices made in real markets (referred to as revealed preference, RP data). Rather, through the design of a preference experiment the agent's preferences can be assessed for combinations of levels of attributes associated with specific goods and services (for example various modes of transport) that may include new (currently not available in real markets) goods and services (for example electric vehicles). Importantly, SP models offer an enrichment strategy to study the preferences and choices of agents that are inadequately represented by RP data settings alone. The RP attribute levels can be 'stretched' to create greater variability in information than is typically observed in real market data, and consequently add knowledge to our understanding of preference revelation and the role of such preferences in determining choices. This gives the analyst greater capability in applying a travel choice model outside of the limits imposed by the market data. Examples of the use of SP methods include determining the demand for high-speed rail where it currently does not exist, valuation of **travel time** savings where RP data lacks the variability in attribute levels for times and costs, and design of new classes of automobiles and fuel types.

There are two broad categories of SP methods: an agent is asked to indicate his preferences among a set of combinations of attributes which define services or products. This judgmental task usually seeks a response on one of two metric scales – a rank ordering or a rating scale; or an agent is asked to choose one of the combinations of attributes. Information is not sought on the ordering or rating of each of the non-chosen combinations. This is often called a first-preference choice task.

In SP experiments, each combination of attributes can be defined as an alternative in the sense of representing a product or service specification that may or may not be observed in the market. It is feasible to vary both the combinations of attributes and levels as well as the subsets of mixes to be evaluated. This can be achieved either by designing varying numbers of combinations or by asking the respondent to eliminate a priori any combinations which are not applicable before responding (soliciting criteria for non-applicability).

In practice, it is common in preference experiments to hold the number of alternative attribute mixes constant and only vary the attribute levels. However, in choice experiments, it is common to vary the number of alternatives, while either holding the attribute levels associated with each alternative constant, or varying them, producing varying choice sets. Fixed choice set designs are also widely used. Central to an SP study are the following elements.

Firstly, the identification of the set of attributes which need to be considered as sources of influence on travel choice.

Secondly, selecting the measurement unit for each attribute. In most cases the metric for an attribute is unambiguous; however there are situations where this requires consideration of alternative metrics.

Thirdly, the specification of the number and magnitudes of attribute levels. As a rule of thumb, one should be extremely cautious about choosing attribute levels which are well outside the range of both current experience and believability. Pivoting levels around known experience gives greater confidence to the outputs.

Fourthly, statistical design is where the attribute levels are combined into an experiment. A combination of attribute levels describes an alternative, referred to in the literature as a profile or treatment. The alternative can be abstract in the sense of being an attribute mix which is not defined for a particular mode (for example a travel time and cost); or it can be mode-specific (for example travel time and cost by car). The former is often referred to as an unranked or unlabelled alternative, and the latter as a ranked or labelled alternative. Alternatives are generated with the aid of statistical design theory. In a statistical experiment each attribute has levels, and it is these levels that are the input data required to construct a factorial design (that is, combinations of attribute levels for all attributes in the design). In practice the full number of combinations is impracticable to evaluate and so a fractional factorial design (FFD) is constructed.

The price one pays for making the experiment manageable is that some statistical efficiency is lost. In designing a fractional factorial experiment, the analyst has to assume that certain interaction effects among the attributes are not statistically significant. This is a very reasonable non-testable assumption for a large number of possible interactions, especially interactions of more than two attributes (for example three-way interactions), and indeed for many two-way interactions. If interactions are statistically significant, their effects in an FFD will be loaded onto the individual main effects, giving erroneous results. This is referred to as confounding main effects with interaction effects. The analyst has to be creative in selecting a limited number of two-way interactions which enable one to include up to that number of interactions to test for statistical significance.

Fifthly, the experiment has to be translated into a set of questions and showcards for execution in the data collection phase. The **survey** instrument can be administered in many ways, such as a computer-aided personal interview (CAPI) or a paper and pencil exercise. Whatever the preferred collection strategy, the design must be translated from a set of orthogonal or near-orthogonal design attribute levels into real information for respondents to comprehend and respond. Where feasible, it is suggested that a respondent be asked both to choose an alternative, and either rank or rate the full set of alternatives (or a subset derived from a prior question on applicability or non-applicability of particular alternatives). The subset issue is particularly important where there are too many alternatives to rank or rate, although it may be of interest in a choice response context to ascertain some additional information on relevant sets. If the request for ranking or rating responses may jeopardize the cooperation across the replications of the experiment, it is more important to limit the task to the first preference choice.

Sixthly, the selection of an appropriate estimation procedure will be dependent on the metric of the response variable and the level of aggregation of the data for modelling.

Further reading
Louviere, J.J., D.A. Hensher and J.F. Swait (2000). *Stated Choice Methods.* Cambridge: Cambridge University Press.

David A. Hensher

strategic seaport planning

Strategic seaport planning (SSP) refers to the long-term planning of seaport development, characterized by substantial uncertainty about the future. Such uncertainty can have a variety of causes, including changes in the port's technological, economic, social and political environments. SSP typically involves multiple stakeholders, because port activities have four components. First, a maritime component, related to the port's maritime **accessibility**. Second, a land component; cargo must be stored on land and, in some cases, is processed further in the port, thus requiring substantial storage facilities and sometimes manufacturing and distribution facilities. Third, a hinterland component; maritime cargo comes from, or has to be transported to, a point of origin or destination in the port's hinterland. Fourth, a **network** component; the port is only one link in a set of broader **supply-chains**, and its development cannot be divorced from the evolution of these supply-chains. SSP generally aims to optimize the port's long-term development, taking into account the above four components simultaneously.

SSP is undertaken to improve the port's long term efficiency as compared to the situation whereby no such planning would take place. It is typically undertaken either by a port authority, a government agency or a set of port operators. SSP involves setting long-term goals for the port's development, and designing actionable plans to reach these goals. Many analytical tools from the strategic management field can be used as aids in SSP, including the analysis of the port's core competences (port-specific advantages or PSAs); value chain analysis; competitive strategy analysis; portfolio analysis; and analysis of strengths, weaknesses, opportunities and threats (SWOT analysis).

It is useful to distinguish between narrow goals, related to the port activities themselves, and broader societal goals. Narrow goals, which dominate SSP in countries such as the United Kingdom, include *inter alia* increasing income for the port authority, improving port **productivity** levels and increasing the port's market share. Broader societal goals are pursued in many European countries, such as Italy, France, Germany and Belgium. Such goals, which may include regional development, trade balance effects and increased adoption of environment-friendly transport modes, are then often used as a rationale for government support to port expansion.

SSP goals can be either demand-driven or supply-driven, or both. Demand-driven SSP implies that the port aims to provide a sufficient and appropriate supply of infrastructure and port services to users as a response to exogenously determined changes in demand (for example growth in industrial production, changes in trade patterns, changes in the composition of the world's maritime fleet, and so on). In contrast, supply-driven SSP aims to alter demand, for example when attempting to increase the port's market share in a seaport range through state-of-the-art infrastructure or superior services. In practice, both supply and demand elements are critical in SSP. On the one hand, successful SSP requires insight into both the size and nature of demand in order to avoid inadequate supply of infrastructure and services. Conversely, the supply side can also be used to improve the port's position vis-à-vis alternative nodal points. More specifically, particular infrastructure and services may provide a PSA to a port vis-à-vis its rivals in a seaport range. A seaport range includes all the ports competing with each other for specific cargo categories. Supply elements available to a port constitute a PSA to the extent that they are valuable, rare, difficult to imitate and difficult to substitute. Such PSAs should be reflected in the port's favourable market share and growth rate.

When comparing a port's present market share and growth rate vis-à-vis rivals in the relevant seaport range, three elements should be taken into account. First, most ports try to develop niches in specific cargo categories (strategic traffic units), so that any market share and growth rate analysis should be performed for each strategic traffic unit separately. Second, all tonnes are not equal. The value-added and other contributions to specific port goals may be different for each strategic traffic unit. For example, identical volumes of general cargo, dry bulk and liquid bulk may have a very different economic significance. Third, as a result of **containerization**, port traffic is becoming increasingly footloose, meaning that it can easily shift from one port to the next. As a result, strategic seaport planning is becoming more important in order to augment the port's attractiveness to port users. SSP is the basis for subsequent investment and pricing decisions, and is therefore the key to seaport competitiveness.

Further reading
Haezendonck, E. (2001). *Essays on Strategy Analysis for Seaports.* Leuven: Garant.
Haezendonck, E., C. Coeck and A. Verbeke (2000). The competitive position of seaports: introduction of the value added concept. *International Journal of Maritime Economics* **2**, 107–18.

Alain Verbeke

subsidies in transport

A subsidy occurs when an individual or a group receives a product or service and pays less than the cost of production. If there is a subsidy then there will be a departure from the free market or competitive outcome. Such departures from economic efficiency can result in a misallocation of resources and may encourage growth of inefficient transportation modes.

Direct subsidies involve payment of cash or other financial assistance from the government to a group of transportation users or carriers. These resources are usually derived from a funding source other than user fees, so costs are borne by taxpayers in general. Accordingly, subsidies are usually justified on political or social grounds rather than for economic reasons.

Public transit receives large direct subsidies for both operating expenses and for purchase of capital. This is usually justified on grounds of social equity – people in low-income groups need public transit for **mobility** and they cannot afford to pay the full cost of the service. Other arguments for transit subsidies are that public transit takes drivers off the road and thus can reduce vehicular emissions and **congestion externalities** that are not fully paid for in the current system of highway user fees. In the United States the federal government 'matches' local funding sources for transit capital by paying up to 80 per cent of the capital cost, creating an incentive for overcapitalization of the transit system. Indeed, it has been argued that the operating and capital subsidies of transit in the United States have inflated the costs of transit service.

The United States maritime industry has received both operating and capital differential subsidies because the cost of United States shipbuilding and maritime labour is higher than that in other countries. Such subsidization of an essentially inefficient industry is considered necessary for reasons of national security. In particular, the United States maritime industry is considered a potential auxiliary to the navy in times of war.

Service to small or remote communities that cannot afford to pay the full cost of transportation service is another argument invoked to justify direct subsidies. In the United States there is an Essential Air Service

(EAS) subsidy provided to carriers that serve small communities. Most of the EAS communities are in very remote areas – some in Alaska are only accessible by air.

Continued large operating and capital subsidies continue to be paid to the United States passenger system, AMTRAK, the intercity passenger rail carrier. Once again, outside of any political consideration the rationale appears to be a combination of the need to provide service to small communities as well as the fact that rail service is a more environmentally friendly form of long-distance transportation than automobiles.

While direct subsidies involve cash outlays to pay for either operating or capital expenses, indirect subsidies may result from a variety of other governmental actions. For instance, United States government policy that has kept gasoline and diesel prices artificially low has resulted in greater use of highway modes relative to rail. Thus, United States energy policy has indirectly subsidized highway transportation.

Cross-subsidization occurs when one group of users pays more than the cost of the service and this overpayment is used to cover costs for other users who pay less than the cost of their service. Cross-subsidization involves a transfer of resources between different groups of users of a transportation service or infrastructure. There are many examples of cross-subsidization in transportation. For instance, passengers flying on the same aircraft may pay a variety of air fares that results in some passengers cross-subsidizing others. Heavy trucks often pay user fees that are considerably less than their contribution to road damage, and light vehicles as a group (passenger cars) often pay more. In **public transit** systems that charge a fixed fee regardless of trip length, short-haul riders are cross-subsidizing long-haul riders.

Although cross-subsidization does not involve a direct payment from the government, it still may cause an inefficient allocation of societal resources. For example, if heavy trucks pay less than their full share of highway costs and are thus able to charge lower prices to shippers, they will gain market share relative to other transport modes such as rail. Further, such inefficient road pricing will lead to trucks overusing the roads and the roads deteriorating faster than they would if pricing were economically efficient and no cross-subsidization took place.

Further reading

Pucher, J., M. Stedt and I. Hirshman (1983). The impact of subsidies on the cost of urban transport. *Journal of Transport Economics and Policy* **27**, 155–76.
Small, K.A., C. Winston and C.A. Evans (1989). *Road Work: A New Highway Pricing and Investment Policy*. Washington, DC: Brookings Institution.

B. Starr McMullen

supply-chain management

The term 'supply-chain management' (SCM) is related to the oversight of all procurement, production and distribution activities, which span from the provision of raw materials, to their transformation into possibly intermediate and finished goods, and to their distribution to wholesalers, retailers and, eventually, customers. The traditional approach to the management of a supply-chain (SC) was based on a series of processes exploited on a sequential basis. Each process was conceived with the aim to increase the added value of the product as it moved along the SC. The firms taking part in a SC normally acted autonomously and were mainly locally and internally focused. Such strategies were perpetuated along with a situation characterized by excess demand and low international competition.

From the 1970s, firms began to face increased competition stemming from globalized markets, excess supply situations, seasonality in demand and shorter life cycles of goods and services. Firms were consequently required to react appropriately and in a timely manner to the changes that characterized markets. It became clear that traditional supply-chain strategies were often leading to excessive inventories; uncompetitive market offers; inefficient utilization of plants, warehouses and transport activities; and dissatisfied customers. The relationships among producers, transport firms, wholesalers and retailers consequently experienced deep changes resulting in new strategies aimed at more efficient planning of activities and to a rationalization of supply-chains.

Nowadays, efficient SCM practices are characterized by an ever-increasing integration and coordination stemming from a continuous process of learning and interacting among firms belonging to an SC, so as to manage the material, informational and financial flows from the acquisition of raw materials to the production and distribution of finished goods. SCM also aims to improve customer service by making informed decisions along the entire SC to provide products in a timely way, to reduce costs and thus to increase the level of profits. For an SCM to be efficient, it is important that all firms belonging to an SC be efficient with respect to cost, quality, delivery speed and reliability and flexibility.

The perspective of procurement, production and distribution are not related in an efficient system to single firm but to the entire SC. To reach this goal, the relevant degree of management integration is needed both within single firms' activities and among firms. In this respect, information and communication technology (ICT) tools acquire an ever-increasing importance to make the networking in the SC effective and to enable firms to share information in a fast and efficient way. Relevant information might be related, for example, to inventory levels; to tracking and tracing of goods; to financing and payments. In this respect, firms are moving towards web-based applications. Examples are represented by e-procurement market places, real-time dedicated discussion forums and advanced intelligent messaging techniques.

Moreover, in the context of SCM, the necessary logistical and transportation sevices to move goods along all the nodes composing a SC play a key role in the fulfilment of the goals in terms of efficiency and timeliness. It is then necessary to think about transportation not in isolation but taking into account the entire SC and, consequently, the entire set of activities coordinated, efficient and feasible and this requires planning. Accordingly, modern SCM does not consider transportation as a residual function. The importance of efficient logistics and transportation activities also emerges in the cases in which one of the other activities composing an SC cannot be delivered as planned. In this case, advanced ICT tools and a sufficiently flexible logistics and transportation structure are required.

Further reading
Brewer, A.M., K.J. Button and D.A. Hensher (eds) (2001). *Handbook of Logistics and Supply-chain Management*. Amsterdam: Pergamon.
Handfield, R.B. and E.L. Nichols Jr. (1999). *Introduction to Supply-chain Management*. Upper Saddle River, NJ: Prentice Hall.

Luca Zamparini

supply-chains – dynamic

Simply put, a dynamic supply-chain is a supply-chain that is not in a steady state; rather, it is either in disequilibrium and moving toward an equilibrium, or it has attained a moving equilibrium. A moving equilibrium is a sequence of equilibrium states visited in succession without transit through any disequilibria.

Dynamic supply-chains may be viewed as dynamic games whose agents are the multiple players involved in supply of inputs to manufacturing and service provision. In dynamic supply-chains, inventories of essential inputs as well as inventories of products made from those inputs are fundamental and critical state variables that devolve from the construction of competitive business strategies. As such the technical literature on production planning and multi-echelon inventory problems is directly relevant to the modelling, planning and operation of dynamic supply-chains.

The most common quantitative tools for studying dynamic supply-chains and crafting dynamic supply-chain decision support systems are discrete-event simulation and agent-based simulation. Dynamic game theory has been employed to model dynamic supply-chains for the purpose of extracting decision rules. However, new developments in computational methods for differential games have awakened interest in the direct use of dynamic game theory to support operation and exploitation of dynamic supply-chains.

Further reading

Swaminathan, J.M., S.F. Smith and N.M. Sadeh (1998). Understanding modeling supply-chain dynamics: a multiagent approach. *Decision Sciences* **29**, 607–32.
Towill, D.R. (1991). Supply-chain dynamics. *International Journal of Computer Integrated Manufacturing* **4**, 197–208.

Terry L. Friesz, Tae Il Kim and *Il Soo Lee*

supply-chains – static

Due to rapid changes in business environments and increasingly complex relationships among diverse business partners and competitors, the supply-chain has become an essential factor in the quest for profits and efficiency. A supply-chain can be defined as a **network** of autonomous or semi-autonomous agents collectively responsible for procurement, manufacturing and distribution activities associated with one or more sets of related outputs. In other words, a supply-chain network is the actual system charged with moving a product or service from supplier to customer. That system will, typically, rely on interdependent organizations, people, technology, activities, information and resources. Supply-chain activities are integral to the transformation of natural resources, raw materials and components into finished products ready for delivery to end users. The various entities comprising a supply-chain operate according to different sets of constraints and objectives, although there may also be constraints and objectives that link and coordinate them. As such, these entities are generally interdependent from the point of view of improving on-time delivery, assuring quality assurance and controlling cost. As a consequence, performance of any aspect of a supply-chain depends on the performance of the rest of the supply-chain.

To say a given supply-chain is static is an abbreviated (and potentially misleading) way of saying that it is in some sort of equilibrium, generally arrived at as the result of a dynamic process that has passed to a steady state. Thus, in a static analysis of supply-chains the emphasis is on a period of time during which no change in supply-chain system parameters is observed. As a consequence, static supply-chain models are able to ignore the problem of characterizing intermediate inventories (and associated costs) before and during a selling season. In addition, it is assumed that the information needed for decision-making is available and transparent to the supply-chain participants and that the overall order lead-time is smaller than the length of the period considered; consequently, all deliveries are de facto provided on time in a static supply-chain. Thus, static supply-chain models are relatively simple and treat all supply-chain agents as well-established fixtures of a given market. In addition, static supply-chains can be relatively well described by the notion of Nash equilibrium. When these assumptions and characteristics are not palatable or mask questions for which an answer is needed, a static supply-chain model should not be employed.

In a static supply-chain, the manufacturer, retailer and customer can be thought of as playing a static mathematical game involving some degree of competition between two or more entities. In fact, a fully general static supply-chain can be **modelled** as a static game with interdependent performance or pay-off functions and coupling constraints, making it a so-called generalized Nash game. However, most theoretical and applied literature on static supply-chain games employs mathematical formulations that are much more conducive to numerical computation than are generalized Nash games. In particular, most static supply-chain games avoid the use of coupling constraints among decision agents, allowing the games to be reduced to complementarity problems and variational inequalities that enjoy excellent numerical solution algorithms. Furthermore, the typical static supply-chain game is not only deterministic but it also employs the notion of simultaneous action by agents or players; this simultaneity arises because each player is assumed to have identical information about the decisions of other players.

On the whole supply-chain games reported in the technical literature tend to be deterministic in nature, although stochastic supply-chain games treating information imperfection and information incompleteness have been examined to a limited degree. Moreover, the applied literature on solving stochastic static supply-chain games has not made use of the notion of subgame perfection to decompose the general supply-chain problem into sequential games dealing with pricing, production and stocking.

In modelling static supply-chains, two schools of thought have emerged. The first of these is concerned only with obtaining rules of thumb useful to supply-chain managers and stakeholders. The second school of thought believes that models of the supply-chain should be solved using actual data, and the numerical results employed for direct decision support of supply-chain managers and stakeholders. In a sense this is nothing more than the eternal debate between practitioners and modellers, but in another sense it speaks directly to the state of art in the modelling of large-scale supply-chain systems. In particular, when one moves from the static to the dynamic world, much greater ambiguity arises with regard to how to model a supply-chain system; supporting data become harder to obtain, uncertainty plays a role that becomes difficult to overlook, and numerical solution of dynamic supply-chain games becomes daunting. Because of the numerical challenges posed by dynamic supply-chain games, many supply-chain simulation models, which capture the dynamic aspects of supply-chains to varying degrees, have been proposed and some have been implemented.

Further reading
Kogan, K. and C.S. Tapiero (2007). *Supply-chain Games: Operations Management and Risk Valuation.* New York: Springer.
Swaminathan, J.M., S.F. Smith and N.M. Sadeh (1998). Understanding modeling supply-chain dynamics: a multiagent approach. *Decision Sciences* **29**, 607–32.

Terry L. Friesz, Il Soo Lee and *Tae Il Kim*

sustainable transport

Sustainable transport most broadly refers to a combination of paradigm shifts and new planning approaches and technologies which result in the consumption of natural resources at or below their natural rate of generation or technical substitution, a production of pollution or wastes at a rate which does not threaten human or environmental health, a more equitable distribution of benefits and costs, and a more accessible and transparent transport planning process, all while supporting economic growth and regional development. This definition results from an appreciation of factors commonly cited as those which make the current transport unsustainable: contributions to global greenhouse gas accumulation and concomitant **climate change**; excessive use of non-renewable resources as fuels and materials; excessive fatalities and injuries; local environmental and social problems; and system **congestion**.

Sustainable transport systems address these impacts by acting along several overlapping policy dimensions. 'Sustainability' is seen as a shift in public and private policy concerns from strictly economic or strictly environmental to a combination of these, while also adding social or distributional issues – together forming the economy–environment–society triad. Some researchers add governance to these three areas to reflect the importance of planning processes in defining and implementing sustainable transport policies. The following paragraphs explore each of these four areas in more detail.

The performance of the transport system, both passenger and freight, is integral to the operation of the economy across all scales. Sustainable transport systems support the economy by improving regional efficiency and competitiveness and by employing efficient and effective management programs and financing mechanisms. Sustainable transport systems try to reduce the large external costs endemic to transport such as regional air quality impacts, congestion delays and traffic crashes and fatalities. An example of such policies is toll lanes that can reduce freight costs by allowing trucks to pay a fee to bypass congestion.

Transport systems have obvious environmental impacts including: facilitating urban sprawl, leading to farmland and natural habitat loss; barrier effects limiting wildlife movements; local air pollution emissions; **climate change** gas emissions; **noise** and vibration; aesthetic impacts of transport infrastructure; pollution from maritime vehicles and polluted surface water run-off, among many others. Sustainable transport systems limit these impacts by employing new technologies, directly mitigating effects, shifting travel to 'greener' modes with few effects, or reinforcing urban development patterns, which in turn shifts travel to greener modes. Examples of these policies include **hybrid-engined** vehicles that are typically 20 to 30 percent more fuel-efficient than similar vehicles, **HOV** (car-pool) lanes which reduce congestion on key roadway bottlenecks, or land-use zoning which allows for higher density near mass transit stations.

The social impacts of transport systems include: inequities among income groups, races or **genders**; the various **accessibility** issues due to disability or age (old and young); social exclusion and the psychological impacts of isolation; and significant **safety** impacts. Also, past failures in including broader sections of the population in planning have significant social impacts. Sustainable transport systems try to address these issues by broadening input to the transport planning processes and providing transport options which meet the needs of a more diverse cross-section of the population. Example policies include: convening a meeting of minority citizens for a regional transport plan; creating a special transit pass for low-income households; and creating a shuttle connecting housing for older populations with shopping and public services.

Governance highlights how the transport planning process works and how infrastructure is managed. The efficient and equitable financing of infrastructure is important for its long-term financial sustainability. For example, agencies may employ a certain pricing regime to affect a more efficient use of some piece of congested infrastructure. A clear and inclusive planning process built on robust modeling, broad public input, honest alternatives analysis, and current data and forecasting tools is another component of governance that adds to sustainability.

While sustainable transport has become a commonly used term, there is still wide debate about how to measure it. Since resource stocks regeneration rates, **climate change** dynamics, future populations' needs and costs, among other factors, are poorly understood, it will be difficult to know what precise effect current policies will have on long-term sustainability. For many, sustainable transport is better thought of as more sustainable rather than absolutely sustainable. Sustainability indicators are being developed and employed by both public and private actors in order to understand current baselines, gauge progress and understand policy trade-offs.

Further reading

Black, W.R. (2005). Sustainable transport: definitions and responses. In Transportation Research Board, *Integrating Sustainability into the Transport Planning Process*. To the Conference on Introducing Sustainability into Surface Transportation Efficiency. Washington, DC: TRB.

Transport Canada (2005). *Defining Sustainable Transport*. Ottawa: Transport Canada.

Aaron Golub

T

taxation

A tax is a compulsory payment imposed by a public authority. Transportation markets are affected by a variety of taxes, especially indirect taxes (related to the physical or monetary volume of a transaction) on the purchase of factor inputs, and on the selling of services.

To help understand the role of taxation in the transportation industry, it is worth remembering the two broad classes of reasons explaining the existence of taxes. Generally speaking, taxes are levied to finance the activity of the public sector (income redistribution, production of public goods and of publicly provided private goods), and to alter the distribution of resources (because of distributive goals, or to correct for the existence of market **externalities**).

When choosing where and how much to tax, the distortionary impact of taxation should be considered. Taxation systems generally cause distortions because in practice they inevitably alter relative prices. Tax pressure is, therefore, not uniform among the various economic sectors; also because some activities are 'informal', they do not give rise to explicit market transactions, and because taxes can be evaded, more or less easily, depending on the circumstances. Both of these issues have interesting implications for the transportation sector.

It may be quite difficult to evade taxes in the transportation sector (for example, fuel taxes or vehicle ownership taxes). Tax rates can also often be adjusted rapidly and at little cost, meaning that taxes in this sector may not always be a consequence of a specific industry policy.

Furthermore, transportation involves a variety of formal and informal activities. Private transportation, for example, typically involves a good amount of self-production, which cannot be directly taxed. As a general rule, the higher the global fiscal pressure, the higher the incentive to shift away from the market, for example replace buying with do-it-yourself.

Distributive goals, often associated with efficiency considerations, have contributed to create a very fragmented picture of taxation in the transportation industry. For example, in most countries, **public transportation** is **subsidized**, whereas private transportation is taxed. Traditionally, arguments in support of this asymmetric policy have been put forward:

- Low prices of public transport allow the achievement of a universal 'right to **mobility**'. However, the actual distributive impact of such a policy depends on the differences in the consumption patterns, among the various transport modes, and of the population groups. If these differences are not very significant, as the evidence seems to suggest, the distributive effect is rather limited and other 'direct' policies (for example vouchers) turn out to be more efficient.

- **Subsidies** are the consequence of economies of scale, the existence of natural monopolies or given for purely political reasons. Even this argument could be questioned: first, economies of scale, if they exist, vary quite significantly among the transport modes, and the amount of subsidization should be related to some measurement of these economies; second, increasing returns to scale often involves some very specific stages of the production process, so that the public intervention should be limited and focused.

From another point of view, subsidization can be interpreted as another way to finance transportation services. In general, the production cost of any good or service can be covered by the owners or users (private production = users pay), or by a broader group of individuals (public production = taxpayers pay). Many transport modes involve a combination of private and public production. The splitting between these two regimes varies between countries, modes, and so on, and it is essentially a political choice linked to the question of why a non-user of transport services should be required to pay a cost share of these services.

Recently, concerns about the environmental impact of transportation activities have stressed the role of taxes as environmental policy instruments. Pollution, as well as **congestion**, in paid for infrastructure wear and tear, and so on, are all negative **externalities**, that is, costs imposed on outside agents. Externalities (both positive and negative) are symptoms of market failures due, for example, to lacking property rights. When externalities are present, market prices are 'too low' or too high, bringing about underconsumption or overconsumption and production.

In the Pigou approach, taxes can be used to bring prices in line with the social marginal cost of resources. For negative **externalities**, this would call for the introduction of indirect taxes, whose level should be set to the social value of external effects.

This value may be very difficult to estimate, and in any case it would vary in time and space. Furthermore, this policy – ideally – would ensure the efficiency of the market equilibrium, not its equity. For example, the tax revenue obtained through the introduction of environmental taxes may not be used to compensate the individuals negatively affected by **noise** and pollution.

Roberto Roson

taxicabs

Taxis are a ubiquitous and important part of modern city life around the world. The circumstances and quality of a taxi ride for visitors in a new city or country often strongly influence their first impression about the place. A taxicab is in general a passenger car for hire with a driver for transporting people between locations of their choice. Taxicabs are an important part of the **public transport** system in a city.

In many countries the taxi industry is organized as a private market sector without the help of public **subsidies**. Nevertheless it is often an extremely regulated sector. In particular, entrance into the market and the determination of tariffs are not free, but strictly bound by rules. The general question for economists is whether those kinds of rules are necessary and whether the market could not itself better organize supply and demand.

The first modern taxi business company was founded in 1897 by Friedrich Greiner in Stuttgart, Germany. He replaced horse-drawn cabs by motorized carriages equipped with taxi meters and built by Gottlieb Daimler. The passengers' demand for motorized taxis encouraged Greiner to invest further. Two years later the company already had a total of seven Daimler taxis. Petrol-powered taxicab companies were founded in Paris (1899), London (1903), New York (1907) and other metropolises. During the first years of the twentieth century, the number of motorized taxies in the large cities increased rapidly. In 1911 7000 cabs already existed in London, in Paris 5000 and in Berlin 2000. It is estimated that there are more than 12000 Yellow Cabs in New York City and more than 50000 taxicabs registered in Germany.

There is a long history of the limitation of entry into the taxi market around the world, sometimes by auction, of licences or medallions to operate. The main arguments for limitation are the potential for overcapacity and the securing of quality standards. There are different experiences around the world with **deregulation** and sometimes re-regulation of the number of taxis in a city.

From a theoretical point of view there are only weak arguments in favour of regulation entry into the market. Comparatively low fixed costs in the taxi industry suggest that the risk of excessive entry is minimal because inefficient taxicabs are able to leave the market quickly.

In general, the real or perceived problem of inadequate pricing is solved with price regulation by metering. The regulated price of the meter is based on some formula relating to distance and time of journey. The taxi meter allows the customer to verify the distance travelled, which is usually the largest component of the fare. A minimum fare or a basic charge for entering the taxi is in general used to reduce the number of refusals on short journeys. There may also be different prices during special times of the day, and premium charges for longer journeys leaving the city limits or for additional passengers. In many countries the rates have to be displayed somewhere visible inside the taxi and can be viewed before the journey is taken.

Often the fares are regulated by a public authority that considers local market conditions, an acceptable rate of return on the time and capital invested by the driver, and the expected number of trips in a typical day's work. Sometimes the fares will also reflect wider social aims, such as **tourism** needs or **congestion** targets. In cases where the meter rates are set by a private fleet organization, the fares will presumably reflect profit-maximizing necessities under consideration of price sensitivities of customers and other rival fleets. Also, the special local situation of competing modes of transport will influence the price.

In the taxicab market there are several aspects of quality. This includes firstly the requirements of the taxi itself, especially **safety**, proper maintenance, cleanness and comfort. Secondly, the requirements of the driver with regard to trustworthiness, road competence and the geographical knowledge to find the shortest way. Under consideration of these, there are clear asymmetries of information between the driver and the passenger. The potential passenger is unable to observe or verify in a straightforward way the quality level of service they are buying. This problem of asymmetric information is even stronger if you are in a different city or foreign country. Therefore, the taxicab service has some characteristics of a credence good and could be subject to direct quality regulation. Medallions and licences can potentially be used as a bonding mechanism to enforce quality standards. In order that this system works, the authorities must be willing to monitor the quality and to suspend drivers or taxi companies which breach the quality standards. Special segments of the taxicab market with distinctive characteristics like access to airports or stations are likely to require separate regulatory approaches. Furthermore many countries grant special tax allowance to the taxicab companies, for example a reduced value-added tax rate for taxi journeys.

Finally, despite or because of the comprehensive regulations in many regions a booming black market in taxi services exists, for example in London with thousands of 'part-time' taxi drivers.

Further reading
Cairns, R. and C. Liston-Heyes (1996). Competition and regulation in the taxi industry. *Journal of Public Economics* **59**, 1–15.

Dempsey, P.S. (1996). Taxi industry regulation, deregulation and reregulation: the paradox of market failure. *Transportation Law Journal* **24**, 73–120.

Häckner, J. and S. Nyberg (1995). Deregulating taxi services, a word of caution. *Journal of Transport Economics and Policy* **29**, 195–205.

Organisation for Economic Co-operation and Development (2007). *(De) Regulation of the Taxi Industry*. Round Table 133, ECMT European Conference of Ministers of Transport, Paris.

Andreas Matthes

telecommunications and transport

New information communication technologies can have a profound impact on travel and transport. New telecommunication technologies have had their impact on the management of the transport system and transport environment, for example in a very short space of time, automatic vehicle identification – the basis of the EZPass system – altered the toll plaza experience of the United States commuter. Original concerns about Big Brother environments were eroded by the experience of the convenience of the system. In terms of freight, clumsy commercial electronic data interchange systems gave way to the client's ability to track goods globally; global positioning system (GPS) and **geographical information system** (GIS) combined with the Internet now provides a routine customer surveillance over the shipping and transport environment.

In terms of travel behaviour, the new telecommunications environment has some important features. Mobile telephones that connect with the Internet enable travellers to be in continuous contact with their social **network** whilst on a journey and to reorganize commitments when there are delays and journey hold-ups. Rescheduling whilst on a journey becomes a very different prospect as a consequence of the advent of the new technology.

The academic work on the exact relationship between travel behaviour and information communications technology is not yet sufficiently mature for a determination to be made as to whether **telecommuting** and other teletransport options increase or decrease or leave unchanged household levels of travel. Whether telecommunications will stimulate new levels of travel or operate as a substitute for travel is an important question for policy making in a situation where there are major concerns about congestion and environmental costs.

Further reading
Grieco, M. (2003). Replacing travel: technology led futures. In J. Hine and J. Preston (eds), *Integrated Futures and Transport Choices*. Aldershot: Ashgate.

Margaret Grieco

telecommuting

Telecommuting has been defined as a salaried employee working at home, or at a location closer to home than the regular workplace, in lieu of commuting to the regular workplace at the regular time. Some researchers use the term more or less synonymously with 'teleworking', while for others telecommuting is a subset of teleworking, with the latter term more broadly construed to include all kinds of work that is distant from the supervisor or client. With respect to transportation impacts, the definition matters a great deal, since some forms of telework (for example after-hours work at home) may have no impact on travel, others (for example working while travelling) may actually be synergistic with travel, and for others (for example home-based self-employment) the impact may be ambiguous (reducing travel if the alternative were a job with a conventional commute; increasing it if the alternative were not to work at all, or if self-employment generated more travel than the conventional job alternative would have). The estimated number of people who.telecommute, and forecasts of future levels of telecommuting, can vary dramatically, depending on the definition. The focus here is on the first, more narrow definition.

A number of possible transportation impacts of telecommuting can be identified. Direct effects can include eliminating the commute entirely (working at home), shortening it considerably (working at a centre or 'third place' close to home), or moving one or both legs out of the congested peak (partial-day telecommuting) – representing effects on trip generation, destination and time of day, respectively. The prospect of obtaining these beneficial effects is the basis for many public sector agencies promoting telecommuting as a transportation demand management (TDM) measure. On the other hand, to the extent that the telecommuter would normally be using transit or non-motorized modes to commute, the removal or shortening of such a trip will have virtually no marginal impact on **congestion**. Further, several types of rebound effects are plausible as well. The time saved by telecommuting may partly be spent on making other trips. At the margin, some car pools may break up and be replaced by multiple single-occupant vehicle trips, if one or more of the car pool members begins to telecommute multiple days a week. In the long term, the ability to telecommute may motivate people to move farther enough away from work so that total commute travel could increase, even while the frequency of commuting decreases.

So far, studies of salaried telecommuters suggest that those rebound effects do not entirely negate the transportation benefits – one aggregate United States study estimated a reduction of vehicle-miles travelled of about 0.8 percent that could be attributed to telecommuting in 1998. One **disaggregate** empirical study of residential location found that telecommuting is more often an effect than a cause of relocating farther from work, and that in any case telecommuters save enough travel to counteract their longer one-way commutes. Thus, on net, telecommuting appears to have a small but genuine transportation benefit, and there are also a number of other public-interest reasons to promote it (for example increasing employment opportunities for **mobility**-limited individuals, and providing contingencies for dealing with extreme events affecting workplaces or the transportation system).

Two caveats are in order, however. First, telecommuting is not simply a technology, but a complex social solution, with ramifications for employers and household members as well as telecommuters. This helps explain why the adoption of telecommuting has not lived up to its earliest enthusiasts' forecasts. In some cases, job type or management resistance has impeded adoption; in other cases the environment at home may be more distracting and/or unpleasant than that of the regular workplace; and in still others the worker themself might not find it appealing, despite a suitable job and willing manager. Some people value the social and professional interaction of the regular workplace; some find it too much trouble to bring needed items back and forth; some find the collateral activities available at the workplace to be desirable (for example shopping or eating out on one's lunch break); and some actually enjoy the benefits that commuting can provide. For these and other reasons, the adoption of telecommuting has been relatively slow compared to its feasibility. On the other hand, one factor that could change that historical trend is rising transportation costs. It is likely that dramatically higher gasoline prices, or the implementation of congestion pricing, will increase the appeal of telecommuting.

The second caveat is that while telecommuting per se seems to reduce vehicle travel modestly, the picture changes considerably when information and communications technology (ICT) more broadly is analyzed. For a variety of reasons (such as the use of travel time savings to make more trips; the increased ease of learning about activities, places and people of interest via the Internet; the increased availability of travel bargains through the Internet; and the use of ICT on the supply side to increase the efficiency of the transportation system), the net impact of ICT on travel appears to be the stimulation of greater travel. Thus, the policy challenge is how to promote the trip-reducing applications of ICT, without simultaneously supporting the trip-generating ones. Pricing travel appropriately is one important element of the solution.

Further reading
Choo, S., P.L. Mokhtarian and I. Salomon (2005). Does telecommuting reduce vehicle-miles traveled? An aggregate time series analysis for the US. *Transportation* **32**, 37–64.
Mokhtarian, P.L. (2003). Telecommunications and travel: the case for complementarity. *Journal of Industrial Ecology* **6**, 43–57.

Patricia L. Mokhtarian and *Ilan Salomon*

telephone surveys

Telephone surveys are one of the four travel survey methods that are normally considered when implementing a travel survey, the other three being face-to-face, postal and web-based. It is usually considered that face-to-face interviews provide the best transport data quality, in particular a higher response rate and better response quality, but they are also the most expensive as the interviewers need to travel. For this reason, but also because telephones are now commonplace in the West, telephone surveys have become widespread there.

Although there is still intense debate between the advocates of the different survey modes, the principal advantages and disadvantages of the telephone survey mode for household travel surveys are listed next.

The principal advantages are seen to be:

- Lower survey costs because, unlike face-to-face interviews, conducting surveys involves no travelling. This increases the productivity of interviewers, so a smaller team of interviewers can be used.
- Better monitoring and checking of interviewers because their work can be monitored in real time.
- A computer-assisted telephone interview (CATI) system provides easier use of online coding aid and real-time validation of survey coherence than in the case of a face-to-face survey or a web-based survey (even if computer-assisted personal interview (CAPI) or computer-assisted web interview (CAWI) systems can provide reasonably similar services.

- It is less intrusive as regards subjects' homes and time than the face-to-face interview (but more so than the postal interview).
- It provides greater flexibility for survey management, allowing interviews to be conducted later during the evening and more easily during the day.
- Data are available more rapidly due to direct input systems.

The main disadvantages are considered to be:

- Coverage of the population is incomplete because of a certain number of non-subscribers, an increase in the number of unlisted numbers and, more recently, the development of the mobile phone. However, the proportion of households without the telephone is very low nowadays (between 2 and 5 per cent in most developed countries). The problem of unlisted numbers can be solved by automatic number generation techniques. Lastly, methods are being developed to cope with the mobile telephone.
- A greater distance separates the interviewer and the respondent, which may reduce the quality of the responses, particularly when collecting data about trips, especially the shortest ones. At the international level large differences are apparent between different countries as regards the number of daily trips (between 2 and 5 trips per day) which cannot be explained just by contextual differences. However, if surveys performed with identical methodologies, except survey mode, are compared the differences are frequently slight and not statistically significant.
- Telephone interviews must be short. A telephone survey must, like a postal or a web survey, generally take less time than a face-to-face survey to avoid refusal to take part in the survey or abandonment in the course of the interview. However, many successful surveys have involved interviews of longer than half an hour.
- Refusal rates are tending to increase, in particular because of the development of telemarketing. Unfortunately the effects of this change are not confined to telephone surveys. The situation nevertheless varies considerably from one country to another, meaning that the local context must determine the methodology.

This account should not be taken as a plea for telephone surveys, rather as a demonstration of their potential value for travel surveys. The choice, however, of a survey mode and, more generally, a methodology, must be the outcome of an in-depth appraisal of the survey's objectives and the constraints in the field to ensure that the methodology with the best cost–quality ratio is chosen. Lastly, it is increasingly common for a single survey to combine different survey modes in order to target the different segments of the survey population. This raises enormous data comparability problems later, but also enriches the range of tools available.

Further reading

Bonnel, P. and M. Le Nir (1998). The quality of survey data: telephone versus face-to-face interviews. *Transportation* **25**, 147–67.

Bonnel, P. M. Lee-Gosselin, J. Zmud and J.-L. Madre (eds) (2009). *Transport Survey Methods: Keeping up with a Changing World.* Bingley: Emerald.

Groves, R.M., P.P. Biemer, L.E. Lyberg, J.T. Massey, W.L. Nichols II and J. Waksberg (1988). *Telephone Survey Methodology.* New York: John Wiley & Sons.

Patrick Bonnel

third-party logistics

As manufacturers continue to source raw materials and establish manufacturing operations farther from their points of sale, **supply-chains** are growing longer and becoming increasingly complex. Furthermore, new international markets for goods and services have followed the elimination of trade barriers and the creation of free trade agreements. Hence, the question arises: how should firms deliver their goods in this environment and manoeuvre through the intricate operations of importing and exporting? One solution is to employ the services of third-party logistics providers (3PLs), businesses specializing in providing such value-added logistical services as transportation, warehousing, distribution, quality control, labelling, **packaging** and international forwarding. By outsourcing logistical services, manufacturers have the opportunity to focus on their core businesses, compete in existing markets and enter into new markets to grow revenues and market share. Third-party logistics providers compete through pricing and the variety and quality of services offered.

Third party logistics providers are categorized as either asset-based or non-asset-based, referring to the manner in which they function. Asset-based 3PLs own the assets, for example warehouses, trucks, trailers and flatbeds, which are used in the provision of their services. Also, the asset-based 3PL may utilize its own personnel to provide customs and forwarding services and handle documentation procedures required for importing and exporting of products by its customers.

Non-asset-based 3PLs do not own the assets that are used in the provision of their services, but rather arrange for outside vendors to provide logistics services for their customers. For example, these 3PLs do not own transportation equipment, but rather contract with local or regional trucking firms or railroads to provide transportation services for their customers. Non-asset-based 3PLs provide information and coordinate the requested logistics services for their customers. These 3PLs have the advantage of being able to customize their logistics services in many locations; that is, they are not constrained as for asset-based 3PLs in having owned assets in many locations where they provide logistics services.

Third-party logistics providers can customize their services to fit the needs of their customers. From an internal assessment of customer logistics needs, a 3PL can provide logistics assistance, resulting in a competitive advantage for the customer. For example, one shipper may need assistance with transportation services while another shipper may need warehousing assistance, another customs brokerage and documentation procedures assistance and another assistance with free trade agreements. Third-party logistics providers enable importers and exporters to reduce their levels of damaged products, missed deadlines and misdirected shipments that could subsequently result in lost sales.

Large retail companies often require that their suppliers provide advanced technological tracking services, for example radio frequency identification (RFID), electronic data interchange (EDI) and advanced shipping notifications. Manufacturers may hire large 3PLs that have invested in these technologies to offer these services to their customers. Small 3PLs are at a disadvantage in being hired by large manufacturers if they do not have the capital to invest in and manage such services. Alternatively, small 3PLs may be able to compete for the business of small manufacturers by providing customized services for niche markets.

Third-party logistics providers may also provide reverse logistics services for their customers. Reverse logistics (characterized as such by the retail industry) is the retrieval of unsold products – for example damaged, recalled or overstocked products – from retail outlets. In the provision of reverse logistics services, 3PLs may reclaim and store or rework goods for either resale, refurbishment, recycling or destruction.

To remain competitive, 3PLs must offer operations visibility to their customers. Specifically, a challenge to 3PLs is to address the customer's need for **supply-chain** visibility. Supply-chain visibility refers to real-time and related information regarding the location of shipments along a supply-chain **network**, for example the current location of shipments and related information such as bills of lading, container numbers, estimated arrival times and inspection details. Interactive web-based computer programs allow 3PLs to update continually the locations and delivery statuses of shipments.

United States-based 3PLs earned $120 billion in revenues in 2007. Globally, 3PL revenues are estimated at $390 billion. Global 3PLs remain focused on Chinese markets. The five largest global logistics providers in 2007 were DHL Logistics (Germany), Kuehne & Nagel (Switzerland), Schenker/BAX Global (Germany), CEVA Logistics (the Netherlands) and Panalpina (Switzerland) with gross annual revenues of $33.4, $17.5, $12.1, $7.8 and $7.2 billion, respectively.

Further reading
Armstrong & Associates (2007). *US and Global 3PL Financial and Acquisition Results and Projections to 2010.* Stoughton, WI: Armstrong and Associates.
Traffic World (2008). Global top 50 logistics providers. 10 March, 24–6.

Sara E. Russell and *Wayne K. Talley*

total logistics costs

A key element in the integrated logistical approach is the concept of total logistics costs. It refers to the idea that all logistical decisions that provide equal service levels should favour the option that minimizes the total of all logistical costs, instead of an option that results in cost reductions in one particular area alone, such as lower transportation costs. To illustrate, when comparing different freight transport modes, a shipper or receiver should not only consider the cost of transportation, but also take into account all other costs in the **supply-chain** that are affected by the choice of transport mode. Examples of these so-called non-transportation logistics costs are the costs of goods handling and **packaging**, the inventory costs, the costs of facility location, the order processing costs, the administration costs, the customer service costs, and so on.

While it is generally seen as the aim of logistical management to consider costs as a whole (that is, transport and non-transport-related costs), simplifications are often used. In the inventory-theoretic approach the trade-offs between transportation costs and inventory costs are being made explicit. The total logistics costs (TLC) of a transport mode are formulated as follows:

$$\text{TLC} = r.T + \frac{a}{s} + u.t.T + \frac{w.s.T}{2} + w.K\sqrt{(s + t).T} \qquad (1)$$

where TLC is the annual logistics costs of a transport mode; r is transport cost per unit (including freight rate, loading and unloading, and insurance); T is the total physical amount transported per year; a is cost of ordering and processing per shipment; s is average annual time between shipments; u is in-transit carrying cost per unit per year; t is the lead time or the average annual time needed to complete a shipment; w is the warehouse carrying cost per unit per year (may differ from u); and K is a constant, depending on the specified probability of no stock-outs during lead time.

The first term in the equation refers to the annual transportation costs. It is found by multiplying the transport cost per unit by the overall order quantity or shipment size. Due to the existence of economies of scale, transportation costs per unit decrease with increasing shipment size and distance.

The second term adds the annual ordering costs. The calculation of the annual order costs is rather straightforward: since s is the average time between shipments in years, $1/s$ orders are placed every year, with an associated order and processing cost of a per order. Clearly, one can reduce the annual order costs by keeping the annual number of orders low, that is, shipping goods in large quantities or grouping orders for different parts into one large shipment; consolidation. The impact of these costs, however, should not be overestimated. In most cases nowadays, the order and processing costs only play a minor role in the total logistics costs. With the introduction of large-scale automation and computerization in logistics, ordering and processing have indeed become much less labour-intensive.

The third term gives the annual in-transit carrying costs. The calculation of these costs is also straightforward. Multiplying the in-transit inventory cost per unit per year u by the average time t in years to complete a shipment yields the in-transit inventory costs per shipment. Multiplying this figure by the number of shipments per year yields the annual in-transit inventory costs. It is obvious that the in-transit inventory costs encourage the use of fast transport modes, such as road haulage or air transport.

The fourth term refers to the annual costs of cycle stock. Average cycle stock is equal to half the shipment size: that is, $s.T$ units are delivered each time and are gradually being used until the next shipment arrives. Multiplying the average inventory $(s.T)/2$ by the annual warehouse carrying cost w gives us the annual cycle stock costs at the destination. While the in-transit inventory carrying costs encourage the use of fast transport modes, the cycle stock costs encourage the use of transport modes with a small capacity. After all, the use of such modes decreases the average time between shipments s, which in turn decreases the cycle stock costs. Given that fast transport modes normally move small quantities (air transport), the distinction between these two logistics costs is not always clear.

A final element of inventory costs are the costs incurred by holding safety stock. The safety stock is the inventory a company holds in addition to cycle stock as a buffer against delays in receipt of orders or changes in customer buying patterns. Two important parameters determined the safety stock: average lead time t and average time between shipments s. The larger these two variables, *ceteris paribus*, the larger the safety stock. The parameter K is a so-called Poisson multiplier.

Some have argued that the Poisson-assumption may be inaccurate and, if not satisfied, results in an overestimation of the required level of safety stock. Therefore, an alternative way to compute the safety stock is often used. A useful approach is to assume that the safety stock depends on the distribution of demand during lead time, which in turn depends on the distribution of lead time and the distribution of demand during a fixed interval, assuming that all distributions are stationary and independent. Under the assumptions that demand during lead time is normally distributed and that the shortage criterion is to keep the probability of a stock-out during any lead time period below a specified value p, the level of safety stock (SS) can be calculated as:

$$SS = K \times \sigma \tag{2}$$

where K is the safety factor, a constant dependent on the stock-out risk one is prepared to tolerate; and σ is the standard deviation of demand during lead time.

Further reading

Ballou, R.H. (1999). *Business Logistics Management: Planning, Organizing and Controlling the Supply-chain.* Upper Saddle River, NJ: Prentice-Hall.

Baumol, W.J. and H.D. Vinod (1970). An inventory theoretic model of freight transport demand. *Management Science* **16**, 413–21.

Fetter, R.B. and W.C. Dalleck (1961). *Decision Models for Inventory Management.* Homewood, IL: Irwin.

Tyworth, J.E. (1991). The inventory theoretic approach in transportation selection models: a critical review. *Logistics and Transportation Review* **27**, 299–318.

Vernimmen, B., W. Dullaert, P. Willemé and F. Witlox (2008). Using the inventory-theoretic framework to determine cost-minimizing supply strategies in a stochastic setting. *International Journal of Production Economics* **115**, 248–59.

Frank Witlox

tourism and transport

Tourism is a difficult phenomenon to describe and there is no universally accepted definition. Tourism can best be described in two general, but inseparable, ways: as an activity and as an industry.

As an activity, tourism reflects the temporary movement of people to destinations outside the places where they normally live and work. It encompasses all travel, with the exception of commuting, including any activity for leisure, business or other purposes such as health, religion or the attendance of events. For the activity to be regarded as tourism, the United Nations World Tourism Organization (UNWTO) puts a time period on this temporary movement of people to stays of between one night and one consecutive year. The activity itself encompasses everything from the planning of a trip, the travel to the destination, the stay itself, purchases made, interactions between host and guest in the destination, the return and even the reminiscences about the trip afterward. People undertaking tourism activities are referred to as tourists, people undertaking day visits to tourist attractions where no overnight stay is involved are called excursionists. The flow of tourists to various destinations shows the attractiveness of those destinations for tourism purposes. Tourist flows can be domestic or international.

Domestic tourism refers to a country's residents undertaking tourism activities within their own borders. International tourism is divided into inbound and outbound tourism. Inbound tourism refers to non-residents arriving in a country for tourism purposes, and outbound tourism refers to residents of a country visiting another country. Since the 1950s international tourism activity has grown by an average of 6.5 per cent per annum, with international tourism arrivals expected to reach the 1 billion mark in 2010. Historically Europe and the Americas have been the most visited regions, but more recently tourist arrivals into Asia-Pacific have grown above the world average and this is forecast to overtake the Americas by 2020 as the second-most visited region. Many factors such as political instability, crime, health concerns and economic fluctuations negatively affect tourist flows to destinations, while popular events and effective marketing can heighten the demand. Tourism demand is met by tourism supply.

Tourism supply is made up of what the destination offers through its unique natural and cultural resources, and what the tourism industry brings to the tourist. The World Travel and Tourism Council (WTTC), whose primary purpose is to document the size and economic impact of travel and tourism globally and which describes tourism as one of the world's largest industries, defines the tourism industry as the **network** of businesses that are engaged in the transport, accommodation, feeding, entertainment and care of the tourist. Together these businesses produce what is often referred to as the tourism product, although this reference is a misnomer in two ways: first, the tourism product is not a single entity but a bundle of products and services; second, the tourism product is a range of intangible services experienced by the tourist, rather than a tangible consumable product. The two main sectors in the tourism industry are transport and accommodation, without which no tourism could take place. The growth of tourism has been directly linked to the technological advancement, increasing capacity and greater speeds achieved in the various modes of transport, particularly air transport. The increased **accessibility** created by road, seaport and airport infrastructure has stimulated tourism growth, including more recently in emerging destinations. The term 'accommodation' does not capture the true nature of its role in tourism and thus the preferred term is 'hospitality'. The hospitality sector includes accommodation such as bed and breakfasts, guesthouses, graded hotels, resorts, casinos and also food services.

A destination is made accessible through its marketing and those that 'package' it such as travel agents and tour operators who supply the information on, and facilitate the arrangements to, the destination. Through their physical locations and electronic channels (websites) they form an important link between the supply and demand sides of tourism. With the advent of the Internet there has also been a shift towards more direct links between destinations, regions and tourist organizations such as airlines and hotels, and their customers and potential tourists.

The economic size of the tourism industry is measured by the use of the Tourism Satellite Account (TSA), the standard used to measure the tourism industry's impact on global and national economies.

Tourism is not strictly separated into demand (activity) and supply (industry) but viewed rather as a system with all its parts being affected by changes, particularly those resulting from its growth. This growth has brought a number of concerns, such as how tourism benefits all people, its impact on the natural environment and its role in the preservation of social and cultural heritage. Sustainable tourism development has become the underlying value and vision for many public and private sector tourism organizations because it is not only concerned with natural and physical environments, but also recognizes the need to maintain the cultures and lifestyles of local people.

Further reading

Mill, R.C. and A.M. Morrison (2006). *The Tourism System*. Dubuque, IA: Kendall/Hunt Publishing Company.
United Nations World Tourism Organization (2008). Facts and figures. At http://www.unwto.org/facts/menu.html.

Berendien Lubbe

track costs

From an economic perspective track costs comprise the capital and variable costs associated with operating existing track (**road** or **rail**) infrastructure to an acceptable level of service. Capital costs comprise depreciation and interest costs derived from the initial costs of construction of the infrastructure. Variable costs comprise the infrastructure maintenance and rehabilitation expenditures associated with keeping the infrastructure operational to a defined level of service. Variable costs associated with traffic operations are excluded. Track cost information is typically used for road and rail cost recovery studies, interproject comparisons, and studies of resources associated with the provision and maintenance of infrastructure.

While sharing a common variable cost component, track costs differ from the related measure of track expenditure because of the treatment of capital items. For the latter, capital items comprise raw expenditures on new construction and reconstruction as these occur. These are not converted, or amortized into an annual cost. The difference between the two measures is that track costs seek to cost the delivery of infrastructure services as they occur, and model the progressive consumption of the infrastructure, while track expenditures measure budgetary outlays associated with infrastructure provision.

The track expenditure definition assumes that inefficiencies that can either overstate or understate required outlays do not occur, this being a practical assumption used to quantify track outlays. Outlay categories are usually relatively well defined and can be quantified with a reasonable degree of certainty, although there is often some concern about being able to discriminate between maintenance and capital costs, which is discussed below. Track costs can also be estimated on a whole-of-life costing basis that uses a life-cycle costing analysis of the track infrastructure requiring the use of life-cycle prediction and cost models for the infrastructure.

Rehabilitation or restoration expenditures are considered to be maintenance costs if they are not a complete replacement of the infrastructure, as full replacement constitutes capital expenditure or a reinvestment in the infrastructure. Capital construction costs usually include earthworks, formation, drainage and bridge costs, signals and any other expenditure necessary to establish and satisfactorily commence operation of the final wearing surface, or track, that carries the users.

Track costs form the basis of costs to be recovered from the users on an annual basis in some form of user charge. Usually the track costs are recovered on a 'cost occasioned' basis; that is, the users, or group of users that cause the costs are responsible for paying for them on either an individual or a group basis. Under a cost recovery system, the track costs are allocated to users, or groups of users, by some form of cost allocation process that aims to allocate the various costs caused by the users. The track costs that are allocated to specific users are termed attributable, or separable, track costs; and these costs vary with the amount of use of the infrastructure. The remaining costs that are not attributable to users are termed non-attributable, or non-separable, track costs, that are generally fixed costs and are allocated to users on a arbitrary basis. Where track costs have not been available, track expenditures have been used in their place for cost recovery, as is the case of pay-as-you-go (PAYGO) road infrastructure approaches.

Track costs may also form part of the basis for developing a pricing system associated with the use of the infrastructure, either as short-run marginal costs (SRMC) or as long-run marginal costs (LRMC) that make up the marginal cost of use. SRMC are based on the incremental cost of maintenance under current traffic capacity, while LRMC include the incremental cost of maintenance and capital required to increase traffic capacity. Costs, other than track costs, such as **externality costs** are included in these marginal cost approaches and can constitute the majority of the costs, although unlike track costs, these costs can be more uncertain to quantify.

Further reading
Small, K.A., C. Winston and C.A. Evans (1989). *Road Work: A New Highway Pricing and Investment Policy*. Washington, DC: Brookings Institution.
Wong, T.K.F. and M.J. Markow (1983). Allocation of life-cycle highway pavement costs. Report FHWA/RD-83/080, United States Federal Highway Administration, Washington, DC.

Tim Martin and *Thorolf Thoresen*

traffic analysis zone

For urban transportation planning purposes, cities are routinely partitioned into spatial units called traffic analysis zones (TAZs). This is accomplished by aggregating smaller spatial units to form a TAZ. More often than not, these smaller spatial units conform to some type of census geography such as census blocks, block groups or even census tracts. The aggregation process is guided by various criteria, the most important of which are:

- Spatial contiguity: smaller spatial units comprising a TAZ should be adjacent to one another.

- Homogeneity: each TAZ should be characterized by a predominant land use (for example residential, retail, commercial or industrial) and homogeneous socio-economic characteristics.
- Compactness: the shape of a zone should be spatially compact.
- Exclusiveness: no zone can be located within another zone.
- Boundaries should conform wherever possible to census boundaries, major roads, railways, canals and other physical barriers.
- Equitable trip production that, typically, implies that TAZs will increase in size away from the city centre and/or other densely populated areas (see Figure showing the Hamilton Census Metropolitan Area in Canada).

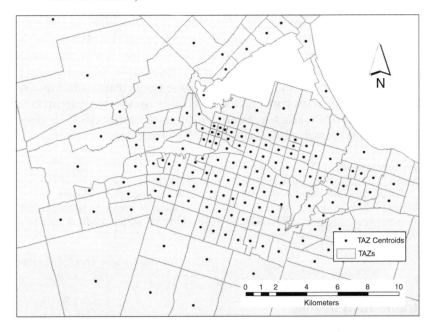

Traffic analysis zones are the foundation upon which **four-stage urban travel demand models** are constructed and used for transportation planning. At the outset of this process, data from various sources (for example a household trip diary survey, a national census) are assembled for each TAZ, which is assigned a unique identifier. These data are then used to calibrate trip generation models, which predict the number of trips originating from and terminating in each zone. These trips are then distributed across zones by mode. Finally, a traffic assignment model is used to assign the automobile trips to links comprising the urban road **network** (that is, traffic assignment). Throughout this process, the relationship between TAZs and the road network is maintained via zonal centroids which are, more often than not, located at the geometric centre of each zone. In turn, this implies that all trips start and end via one point per zone rather than their actual starting and ending locations. Consequently, intrazonal automobile trips are not assigned to the road network, which means that traffic flows on links may be lower than those observed in reality. This is the primary reason why homogeneity above must be considered in TAZ design. Quite simply, homogeneous land use tends to minimize intrazonal trips and maximize interzonal trips.

In most jurisdictions, TAZs are delineated by local transportation officials who have an in-depth knowledge of their city. However, over the past decade or so, an increasing number of researchers have sought to develop methods for deriving 'optimal' traffic analysis zones using the geoprocessing capabilities of **geographic information systems** (GIS) and the criteria noted above. In large part, this work has been stimulated by the recognition that TAZs, like many other zoning systems such as census tracts, suffer from the modifiable areal unit problem (MAUP). This issue arises in transportation analysis because an infinite number of zoning systems can be constructed to subdivide a city into smaller spatial units. In turn, this implies that the data tabulated for TAZs will vary from one zoning system to another, thus affecting the results obtained from urban travel **demand models**. In other words, the outcome from any particular model is merely one manifestation from a range of possible outcomes. MAUP effects can be divided into two components: scale effects and zoning effects. The former relate to spatial aggregation, whereas the latter relate to the configuration of the zoning system given a fixed level of aggregation.

Besides optimal zoning systems, two additional methods have been suggested for handling the MAUP in urban travel demand modelling. The first, assessing zoning system effects, requires data that have been collected for very small spatial units so that the consequences of TAZ aggregation can be measured. The second method is to derive better zonal distance measures. The reason for this is that zonal centroids are unlikely to represent accurately underlying spatial distributions of people and potential destinations for trips. Consequently, MAUP effects are partly due to poor distance measures between TAZs.

Further reading
Ding, C. (1998). A GIS-based human-interactive TAZ design algorithm: examining the impacts of data aggregation on transportation-planning analysis. *Environment and Planning B* **25**, 601–16.

Páez, A. and D.M. Scott (2004). Spatial statistics for urban analysis: a review of techniques with examples. *GeoJournal* **61**, 53–67.

Darren M. Scott

traffic and health

Transportation can affect the health of individuals in two broad ways; through accidents and through the pollution that it causes. The main health effects associated with pollution and environmental impacts of transportation are diverse.

It is estimated that in European cities around 80 000 adult deaths a year are related to long-term exposure to traffic-related air pollution, using the proportion of ambient PM10 concentration due to traffic as an indicator. Both short- and long-term The United Nations World Health Organization **air quality** guideline values are frequently and considerably exceeded in the European Region, in particular for ozone, NO_2 and particulate matter. There is evidence that children living near roads with heavy vehicle traffic have about a 50 per cent higher risk of suffering from respiratory symptoms than those living in areas with low traffic. In 1998, the California Air Resources Board identified diesel exhaust as a toxic air contaminant and in 1989, the International Agency for Research on Cancer concluded that diesel engine exhaust fumes are probably, and gasoline engine exhaust fumes possibly, carcinogenic to humans.

Road traffic is the main cause of human exposure to ambient noise. The proportion of the population in Europe exposed to noise levels of 65 dBLAeq over 24 hours increased from 15 to 26 per cent between 1980 and 1990. About 65 per cent of the European population is estimated to be exposed to noise levels leading to serious annoyance, speech interference and sleep disturbance. Children chronically exposed to loud noise (for example in the proximity of **airports**) show impaired acquisition of reading skills, attention and problem-solving ability. **Noise** can interfere with mental activities requiring attention, memory and the ability to deal with complex analytical problems. Adaptation strategies (tune-out or ignore noise) and the efforts needed to maintain performance have been associated with high levels of stress hormones and blood pressure.

Lack of physical activity is one of the major risk factors for coronary heart disease, which is the leading cause of mortality in Europe. On the other hand, walking and cycling as daily activities can promote health by providing physical activity, decreasing noise and air pollution. The increased use of the private motorcar has reduced physical activities of this kind.

Certain patterns of transportation have a broad range of effects on mental health, including risk-taking and aggressive behaviours, depression and post-traumatic psychological effects of accidents. High levels of traffic can cause social isolation and limit interpersonal networks of support, factors that have been found to be associated with higher mortality and morbidity in the **elderly**. Children who have the opportunity of playing unhindered by street traffic and without the presence of adults have been found to have twice as many social contacts with playmates in the immediate neighbourhood as those who could not leave their residence unaccompanied by adults due to heavy traffic. Lack of this opportunity can hinder the development of children's independence, and reduce their opportunities for social contact and cycling.

Accidents with dangerous goods movements can lead to localized environment and health risks from contamination of air, water and soil. Transportation infrastructures, heavy metals from vehicle exhaust and de-icing substances, vehicle waste (for example old cars, tyres, batteries), fuel spillages, **hazardous material** incidents, as well as tyre and road abrasion, can cause contamination of soil and groundwater, which may affect the quality of drinking water and of agricultural products. Sewage released from ships can cause microbiological contamination of water and shellfish.

The impacts of transportation on health fall disproportionately on certain groups of the population and raise issues of environmental justice. Some are more vulnerable to traffic risks, due to old or young age, to illness or disability. Others use modes of transport associated with greater risks (for example **motorcycles**). Some are more exposed because the areas they live, work or move in have higher levels of pollutants and noise (for example due to the intensifying effect of specific geographical and topographical conditions and settlement characteristics) or other risks, or restrict cycling and walking. Many disbenefits of transportation can accumulate in the same communities, often those that already have the poorest socio-economic and health status.

Further reading
British Medical Association (1997). *Road Transport and Health*. London: BMA.
Kunzli, N., R. Kaiser, S.M. Studnicka, O. Chanel, P. Filliger, M. Herry, F. Horak, P. Quénel, J. Schneider, R. Seethaler, J-C. Vergnaud and H. Sommer (2000). Public health impact of outdoor and traffic-related air pollution: a European assessment. *Lancet* **356**, 795–801.

Kenneth Button

traffic and transportation psychology

Traffic and transportation psychology (TTP) is a young but expanding field in psychology. Whereas traffic psychology is primarily related to the study of the behaviour of road users and the psychological processes underlying that behaviour, as well as to the relation between behaviour and **safety**, transportation (or **mobility**) psychology has as its focus mobility, individual and social factors affecting the movement of people and goods, and travel demand management.

There is no single theoretical framework in TTP, but rather numerous specific models explaining, for example, perceptual, attentional, cognitive, social, motivational and emotional determinants of mobility and traffic behaviour. One of the most prominent behavioural models divides the various tasks involved in traffic participation into three hierarchical levels: the strategic, the tactical and the operational level. The model demonstrates the diversity of decision and control tasks that have to be accomplished when driving a vehicle. In the past most psychological models had a rather heuristic nature, for example risk theories like Wilde's risk-homeostasis and Fuller's task capability model, and were thus not sufficiently precise to allow for concrete behavioural prediction and control. This was partly due to the importance of individual differences, a major topic of psychology that in traffic and transportation has not yet been sufficiently accounted for. On the other hand, social-psychological attitude–behaviour models, such as Ajzen's theory of planned behaviour, have been helpful in identifying determinants of **mobility** decisions. Bringing together the scientific and practical lines of TTP, six areas of traffic and transportation psychology can be distinguished.

First, behaviour and accident research, particularly in relation to different groups of road users (age groups, modes of transport), but also in relation to road design and motor vehicles. Explaining and predicting road user behaviour depends on the development of valid and reliable models about the role of human factors in mobility behaviour and especially driver performance. Psychological traffic accident and behaviour research deals with, for example:

- analysis of the driving task, changing conceptually from a traditionally rather sensomotoric task to a task with high monitoring impact;
- perception, cognition and attentiveness when driving, driver information processing and expectations;
- driver state, workload, alertness and fatigue;
- driver personality, risk-taking, attitudes, motives for driving, arousal and emotion;
- interactions and the social psychology of driving;
- the relation between the personal and environmental background of behaviour, overt behaviour, emerging conflicts and accidents.

Second, accident prevention and improvement of traffic safety, especially education and information, but overall following the '4 E's':

enforcement, education, engineering, encouragement/economy. The main goal here is the promotion of **safety** by influencing and modifying behaviour with legal, educational, vehicle- and road-specific measures: driver training, driving-instructor education, information on traffic issues, campaign design and marketing, and effective enforcement.

Thirdly, research and counselling regarding questions of mobility, transport economy and engineering, the main objectives of which are on user orientation and usable products and design. This includes differentiation between transportation needs of special groups such as the **elderly**, handicapped and young people. The main topics considered include:

- **mobility** needs and travel demand, choice of means of transport;
- travel behaviour research, above all activity-based approaches;
- altering mobility behaviour and **modal split**, problems of habituation and resistance to change, car dependence;
- design and acceptance of travel demand management, above all of pricing measures;
- psychological aspects in **road** design and traffic environment;
- quality management, especially quality of service, usability and well-being.

Fourthly, psychology in car manufacturing traditionally deals with questions of ergonomics, but since the 1980s the effects of new in-car devices, as well as related innovative infrastructure, has emerged as a growing field of interest. Advanced driver assistance systems (ADAS) and new information systems are designed to support the driver in a suitable and user-oriented way. Based on analyses of driving tasks which drivers have to cope with, for example, multiple tasks requiring divided attention, psychologists' primary orientation in the design process is towards human needs defining the technical requirements, human-centred development, usability of ADAS, operability of human–machine interfaces, behavioural adaptation and risk compensation, acceptance of innovations, and social impacts.

Fifthly, psychological assessment, and counselling and rehabilitation, for drivers who have behaved or may in some way behave abnormally. This embraces such things as rehabilitation for drivers who have committed offences such as driving while intoxicated; severe violations of traffic laws; and aptitude assessment for driving, selection and training for professional drivers.

Sixthly, while much of the analysis applies to road traffic there is also to rail and air transport. **Rail** and flight psychology has historically developed in part separately from road-related TTP. One major new direction in rail as well as in flight psychology is the focus shift from the professional operator (selection and training) to the customer perspective (quality of service and usability).

From its very beginning, TTP has followed an interdisciplinary approach and has shared common topics especially with medicine (for example related to driving aptitude), engineering (ergonomics of cars as well as human factors in traffic planning), and economics (for example travel demand management). People as traffic participants are seen as the core of an interactive traffic system also comprising transportation means, routes, traffic environment and regulation. Thus **mobility**, including its positive as well as detrimental impacts, has its origin in people's desires, decisions and behaviour – and these might be influenced. The main accident causes are human error and maladaptive behaviour, accounting alone or in interaction with roadway or vehicle-related causes for more than 90 per cent of all traffic accidents. Recognizing the possible impact of psychology in studying and solving transport problems, traffic and transportation psychology has emerged rapidly since the 1980s.

Further reading
Rothengatter, T. (1997). Psychological aspects of road user behaviour. *Applied Psychology: An International Review* **46**, 223–34.
Schade, J. and B. Schlag (eds) (2003). *Acceptability of Transport Pricing Strategies.* Oxford: Elsevier.
Schlag, B. (ed.) (1999). *Empirische Verkehrspsychologie* (Empirical Traffic Psychology). Lengerich Berlin: Pabst Science Publishers.

Bernhard Schlag and *Jens Schade*

traffic and weather

All transportation systems are designed with some consideration of weather and climate. At the same time, all modes of transportation experience weather-related service disruptions and other incidents. For example, up to one-quarter of all **roadway** delays and an even higher proportion of air delays are weather-related. In addition, the frequency of collisions and other unsafe events tends to increase during inclement weather – sometimes by more than an order of magnitude. A way of thinking about weather and traffic is to consider, first, how weather can destroy, damage or compromise the usability of transportation infrastructure; and second, how weather affects the decisions made by operators of the various systems.

Recent catastrophic examples of weather-related damage include the world's worst train disaster in Sri Lanka following the 2004 tsunami, and numerous aviation crashes linked to wind shear. More regular occurrences include road damage due to heat-related rutting, flash floods or freeze–thaw cycles; cancelled services or closed routes due to storms of various kinds; and conditions that damage vehicles (for example hail or tornadoes) or routes (for example broken **railway** lines due to extreme cold). There is also growing concern over the probable effects of **climate change** on transportation systems, especially in coastal areas that may be susceptible to storm surges; in northern areas that rely on permafrost or ice roads for overland movements; and for inland water navigation that may experience lower water levels.

Operator decisions are also important because these affect both traffic flow (and thus highway capacity and **congestion**) and **safety**. To begin, those responsible for transportation systems do follow a number of weather-related regulations or protocols that address some of the added risk associated with weather, for example: requiring wind shear detectors for commercial aircraft; giving 'slow orders' during extreme cold for rail operators; providing marine forecasts and gale warnings for shipping; and specifying winter maintenance standards for roads. However, the individual operator's interpretations and responses to weather are still important; this is particularly true for roads, because the driving public often has limited training for operating vehicles during inclement weather.

From a road transport perspective, inclement weather refers to conditions that reduce road friction (wet or icy roads), impair visibility (sunlight glare, fog, blowing snow), and/or make vehicle handling more difficult (wind). However, most attention has been given to precipitation because of its frequent occurrence and its extended influence on road conditions.

Various driver adjustments might be taken to reduce risk during inclement weather. One potential response is to cancel or defer a trip, which reduces exposure to risk and affects traffic density with indirect effects on safety. Traffic-count data show that traffic levels are indeed reduced during inclement conditions, with only minor changes during light rain and light snow, but with reductions of 20 per cent or more during heavy snowfall. However, it seems that much of the observed change in volume is due to lower travel speeds rather than trip rescheduling; indeed driver surveys confirm that trip cancellation is rare except in extreme weather or freezing rain. While trip cancellation may be rare, empirical studies indicate that travel speed adjustments during rain and snow are commonplace, albeit relatively modest – typically 5 to 10 per cent, but sometimes higher. There is also evidence of other risk-reducing strategies, including less variation in travel speed, increased headway between vehicles, increased caution and a higher level of driver attention. In summary, research suggests that drivers do compensate for weather.

Numerous studies, however, also demonstrate that inclement weather increases collision risk on both highways and city streets, suggesting that drivers' adjustments to weather are insufficient to offset weather hazards completely. The magnitude of the collision risk increase varies by precipitation type and intensity, but is typically between 50 and 100 per cent. Snowfall has a greater effect than rainfall on collision occurrence, although snowfall-related collisions tend to be less severe because of speed adjustments. Collision risk tends to be highest for freezing rain and sleet (low friction), on the first snowfalls of the season (lack of driver adjustment), and during rain events following extended dry periods (oil accumulation on roads).

Further reading
Andrey, J., B. Mills, M. Leahy and J. Suggett (2003). Weather as a chronic hazard for road transportation in Canadian cities. *Natural Hazards* **28**, 319–43.
Maze, T.H., M. Agarwai and G. Burchett (2006). Whether weather matters to traffic demand, traffic safety, and traffic operations and flow. *Transportation Research Record* **1948**, 170–76.

Jean Andrey

traffic assignment modelling

Traffic assignment modelling aims to determine the number of vehicles and the travel time on different road sections of a traffic **network**, given the travel demand between different pairs of origins and destinations. An application of static traffic assignment modelling is to allow planners to forecast the impact of changes in traffic flows as a result of planned changes. For example, the benefits and impacts of a new road, pedestrianization scheme, **bus lane** or priority measure, or other change to the physical infrastructure may be assessed by such a method, and fed into an economic **benefit–cost analysis**. Another common application is to predict the impacts of a new development, either housing or retail, which will affect the origin–destination trip matrix. A common recent application is in the area of road pricing, where alternative designs may be tested.

To enable such a model to be developed, it is necessary to provide a theoretical abstraction of how drivers choose routes to travel between origins and destinations. The first of two principles articulated by **Wardrop** forms the backbone of all traffic assignment modelling used in practice: 'the journey times on all the routes actually used are equal, and less than those which would be experienced by a single vehicle on any unused route'. This first principle is also often referred to as the 'user optimum principle', following the work of several well-known scholars in the field such as Dafermos, Nagurney and others (though strictly speaking the mathematical definition of this is slightly stronger than Wardrop's).

In the context of the first principle, this is an example of what in game theory is referred to as a Nash equilibrium, in which individual drivers do their best to minimize their journey times. Wardrop alluded to this in his original paper and specifically mentions that: 'no driver can reduce his journey time by choosing a new route'. The resulting equilibrium journey times (more precisely **generalized travel costs**) give a manifestation of a Nash game between users of the **network**.

Therefore, this model represents the viewpoint of the traveller in making route choice decisions. The view of the planner, on the other hand, may be said to be reflected in the second principle articulated by Wardrop. This stated that: 'the average journey time is a minimum', and has become a benchmark for transport planners endeavouring to ensure that the travel time of users on the road network is minimized as they design their policies and transportation strategies to accomplish this goal.

It was the publication of the book by Beckmann, McGuire and Winsten in 1956 that made it possible to put Wardrop's ideas into practice. Among many topics, they gave an equivalent mathematical formulation – in terms of a convex, constrained optimization problem – of a **network** flow model satisfying Wardrop's first principle. This work gave a bridge to the field of optimization, whereby algorithms could be developed for solving realistic scale networks.

At the time the mathematical model was developed, it was carried out with the link cost functions that were separable (that is, the travel time on that link depended on the flow on that link only) and for homogenous traffic. Extensions were later made to allow for link cost functions that were non-separable, as well as to allow for multiple user classes where different drivers perceived the trade-offs between time and distance in route choices differently, or where different vehicle types shared the same road (for example cars and trucks). A major research focus of the last 20 years has been the extension of this model to represent 'dynamic traffic assignment'. This model seeks to determine route choices of drivers so as to satisfy Wardrop's first principle at each departure interval, while at the same time ensuring temporal and spatial consistency of the link flow and travel time profiles that arise, and remains a major challenge.

Further reading
Beckmann, M., C.B. McGuire and C.B. Winsten (1956). *Studies in the Economics of Transportation*. New Haven, CT: Yale University Press.
Boyce, D.E., H.S. Mahmassani and A. Nagurney (2005). A retrospective on Beckmann, McGuire and Winsten's *Studies in the Economics of Transportation*. *Papers in Regional Science* **84**, 85–103.
Wardrop, J.G. (1952). Some theoretical aspects of road traffic research. *Proceedings of the Institution of Civil Engineers Part 2* **1**, 325–78.

Andrew Koh and *David Watling*

traffic engineering

The traffic system involves three elements:

- The person (road user, **pedestrian**, driver, passenger).
- The vehicle (automobiles, buses, **trams**, **motorcycles**, **bicycles**).
- Infrastructure (roads, bicycle paths, footpaths, plazas, railway tracks, bridges, traffic signs and traffic lights).

Traffic is represented by the person and vehicle elements. Traffic engineering focuses on infrastructure and its interaction with the vehicles and people using it. Traffic engineering encompasses the design of traffic infrastructure along with the planning, management, operations and control of the infrastructure **network** to achieve the safe and efficient movement of people and goods. Traffic engineering uses information on the person and vehicle elements in the planning, management, operation and design of the traffic system.

The traffic system must operate under different physical, traffic and social environments, and its performance is defined in terms of **safety**, sustainability and efficiency. These elements of performance can be measured by volume, speed, **congestion**, delay, traffic composition, vehicle occupancy, conflicts, crashes, emissions and/or **energy** use. Generally it is not possible to design for all performance elements, and trade-offs must be made. The priority given to each of these performance elements by the traffic engineer is influenced by the physical, traffic and social environments, and results in the quality of the traffic system provided.

Traditionally traffic infrastructure was provided and designed to meet the demands for motor vehicle traffic for efficient traffic flow but in recent years more emphasis has been given to using traffic engineering to provide a safe environment, particularly for vulnerable road users. **Sustainability** is also becoming more important with traffic engineering being used to provide priority for public transport and to encourage walking and cycling. The fundamental roles of traffic engineering are to:

- manage traffic flow;
- maximize the use of infrastructure;
- provide access and mobility;
- provide a safe traffic system;
- contribute to transport sustainability;
- measure the performance of the traffic system.

Manage traffic flow

To assist in managing traffic flow, procedures have been developed to analyse the capacity and level of service of roads and intersections (Roess et al., 2004). The fundamental relationship between lane flow (Q) (veh/hr) maximum speed (V) (km/hr) and density (K) (veh/km) is $Q = KV$. Intersections interrupt this steady flow situation and use spatial and temporal separation to maximize the movement and **safety** of intersecting traffic. The introduction of intersections complicates the steady flow relationship and moves analysis to include vehicle delay and travel time. More recently, the design of the traffic system to emphasize safety and environmental impacts has resulted in the control of traffic flows in terms of speed, access and movement.

Maximize the use of infrastructure

To maximize the use of infrastructure there have been advances in communication and control procedures through development of **intelligent transport systems** (ITS). These systems monitor the movement of traffic, analyse its performance, determine optimal situations and then inform or guide drivers towards appropriate actions. This information can be provided through traffic signals, roadside variable message signs and in-vehicle **route guidance systems**.

*Provide access and **mobility***

The traffic system provides access (the ability to gain entry) and mobility (the ability to move). Traffic engineering is involved in the planning, design and operation of the traffic system to ensure that appropriate levels of **accessibility** and mobility are provided. This is facilitated through the development of a hierarchy of roads that meets the various needs of traffic. This hierarchy includes motorways, arterial, distributor, collector and local roads. The upper end of the hierarchy has primarily a mobility function and the lower end an access function. The access ends of a trip may provide access to residential, retail and office land uses. The design of a safe, low-speed environment to facilitate multiuse and vulnerable users is paramount here. This can involve management through the design of slow points, roundabouts and rumble strips, as well as direct control of speeds through signage of traffic regulations. The philosophies of traffic calming and local area traffic management found their initial applications at this level of the hierarchy.

The mobility component of the trip focuses on moving the vehicles from their origin to their destination as safely and quickly as possible. The capacity and use of the traffic system can be influenced by its design. Pedestrians, bicycles, public transport and freight movement must all be facilitated in the traffic **network**. Separate priority lanes, priority at intersections, design of entry and exit points and provision for **parking** must all be matched to the needs of the users. This may require limiting use of the traffic system to some users to maximize systems performance. For instance, ramp meters may be used to delay entry onto a motorway to maximize the flow, occupancy and travel time of vehicles on the motorway.

Many trips made by individuals involve the storage or **parking** of a vehicle. The design of parking systems requires traffic engineers to consider the demand, **safety**, circulation and storage of vehicles. The correct provision and design of parking systems can facilitate appropriate use of traffic infrastructure.

Control of movement and parking on the traffic network is facilitated through regulations. Drivers should abide by these regulations and regulatory systems are set up to encourage this adherence. Traffic engineering is involved in the development of these regulations, to ensure that they fit the needs of the user and the requirements of traffic infrastructure.

Provide a safe traffic system

Aligned with movement of traffic is the potential for crashes, and consequently injury and possible death to road users. Traffic safety involves traffic engineering in the design of infrastructure to reduce the number, severity and frequency of crashes. Traffic engineering uses physics and vehicle dynamics to analyse the impact of crashes, and consequently the infrastructure required to reduce trauma. Traffic engineering is often combined with vehicle engineering and human factors to reduce the incidence and severity of crashes.

Contribute to transport sustainability

Traffic movement is a major contributor to emissions and **energy** consumption. Traffic engineering develops infrastructure to guide and control traffic movement to reduce emissions and energy consumption. The linking of traffic signals so that traffic can move steadily along a road can reduce the numbers of stops and create a traffic speed that minimizes emissions and energy consumption. Traffic engineering is also involved in the development of infrastructure to facilitate the use of environmentally efficient modes of transport like public transport, bicyclists and walking. This could include separate right-of-way and prioritizing movement through intersections.

Measure the performance of the traffic system
Measuring the performance of the traffic system is an important dimension of traffic engineering. The measurement of its performance measures can be carried out by human observers using questionnaires and traffic **surveys**. The introduction of **intelligent transport systems** has resulted in the automation of a considerable amount of data collection.

   Traffic engineering is closely associated with urban planning, transport planning, transport engineering, highway engineering and human factors engineering.

Further reading
Roess, R.P., E.S. Prasas and W.R. McShane (2004). *Traffic Engineering*. Upper Saddle River, NJ: Prentice Hall.
Taylor, M.A.P., P. Bonsall and W. Young (2000). *Understanding Traffic Systems*. Aldershot: Gower Publishing.

William Young

traffic management

Traffic includes different forms of transportation such as **bicycles**, walking, **motorcycles**, passenger cars, buses, **trucks** and recreational vehicles. This multiuse requirement of roadways poses a challenge to accommodate these different modes of transportation with different operating characteristics and physical traits. Managing these diverse types of modes and their operators creates the need to manage these elements in an organized fashion through guidance and control, which is accomplished through a concept or programme called 'traffic management'.

   Understanding traffic characteristics is important for implementing effective traffic management measures, which require understanding both the traffic flow elements and the interactions between these elements. These elements are flow, density, speed and headway. Flow represents the number of vehicles passing a specific point in the unit of time, whereas density represents the number of vehicles on a section of highway at a specific time. Speed is defined as the distance travelled by a vehicle in a unit of time. Headway may be defined in two ways: time headway, which represents the time difference in the arrival of two successive vehicles at the same point; and distance headway, which is the distance between two successive vehicles from the same reference points in each of these vehicles. Several traffic flow models have been developed to describe the interactions between these elements in different traffic conditions. Understanding the interactions between traffic flow elements helps to determine different important parameters, such as capacity, that is, the maximum hourly flow rate under roadway, traffic and control conditions, which is important for traffic management.

Traffic moves in highway systems or **networks** to travel from one location to another. Highway systems can be organized by different operational and geometric standards, such as freeways, major highways, street and local roads. Traffic management, which implies improving and sustaining **safety** and **mobility** of the traffic, includes different objectives, such as providing guidance and information and enacting control for achieving safety and mobility. Once a highway or street is constructed and populated by motorized and non-motorized traffic, the task then becomes one of traffic management, involving sustained flow of traffic, support for and recovery from breakdowns, maintenance and safety improvements. As the vehicular and **pedestrian** traffic in the network increases, the risks of breakdowns and accidents also increase, resulting in more demands placed on traffic management.

Different tasks are utilized in traffic management. Various traffic studies, including data collection on the origin and destination of traffic, accidents and their causal factors, traffic flow elements and delay, are conducted to identify traffic management problems and solutions. For example, gridlock at certain locations at certain times can be resolved through different traffic management options. These options include the use of contraflow lanes and shoulders to be used as extra travel lanes during peak **congestion** periods, and metering ramps to control the access of traffic onto the freeway. Additional data can be gathered to determine the causes of crashes at a signalized intersection, such as the absence of a protected left turn in countries that drive on the right.

Federal agencies publish standards and guidance related to devices used for informing and controlling traffic, such as the *Manual on Uniform Traffic Control Devices* (MUTCD) published by the United States Department of Transportation. The MUTCD provides standards, guidance, support and information to ensure uniformity in traffic management in different geographical locations. The MUTCD also includes traffic management tools (for example signs, marking and traffic signals). Different types of signs are utilized to communicate operational and control features and guidance to drivers. For example, regulatory speed limit and stop signs convey the maximum legally allowable speed, and the requirement to come to a complete stop before proceeding on a road, respectively. Warning signs are designed to alert drivers of unexpected conditions on the roadways, such as a sign indicating a narrow bridge ahead. Guide signs are used to direct motorists along their route to reach a destination. Markings on highways and streets provide important traffic management functions in terms of providing guidance, information and supplements to other traffic control devices, such as signs, signals and other marking. Primary categories of marking on highways and streets include road (pavement) and curb markings, object markers, delineators, collared pavements, barricades, channelizing devices and islands. Traffic signals, usually placed at intersections where conflicts are prevalent, are an important traffic management tool. They reduce the conflicts between different traffic streams, which include vehicular and pedestrian traffic, by separating their right of way in time.

Traffic management is applied during periods of recurrent and non-recurrent **congestion**. The former includes congestion that occurs regularly within a certain time range, such as during peak rush hour periods. Non-recurrent congestion may occur at any time due to either a crash or an established work zone, which interrupts the normal flow of traffic. Managing non-recurrent congestion requires prompt identification of the problem or prior knowledge of planned events that can interrupt the flow of traffic.

Many technologies now exist for more effective and efficient traffic management. These management systems include roadside and roadway detection devices that identify traffic abnormalities indicating impending or existing congestion. Modern traffic management technologies include online or real-time traffic management strategies that can be implemented based on prevailing and/or predicted traffic conditions, to minimize the risks of any traffic flow disruptions and **safety** problems. Online traffic management strategies are a part of the **intelligent transportation systems** (ITS) concept that uses technology to support innovative traffic management and safety improvement goals. An example of online traffic management involves a scenario in which real-time traffic data (such as vehicle speed and density) are collected through traffic detection devices and then, through an overarching computer **network**, distributed to traffic management centres. Traffic management centres usually coordinate the procedures for the identification of and response to a traffic operational problem on highways. Traffic management centres receive data promptly from the field sensors and initiate actions to manage traffic in and around the affected areas. For example, once an incident results in congestion on a particular section of highway, traffic is diverted to alternate routes to reduce subsequent congestion from the event. Traffic management centres also support evacuation during emergencies and serve as an important coordinator with emergency management and other stakeholder agencies during both natural (hurricanes) and man-made (terrorism) crises.

With the advent of online traffic management concepts, in which sensors control both vehicle and pedestrian thoroughfares, traffic signals have become more demand-responsive. These signals, primarily computing devices with possible interfaces to field devices and traffic management centres, can support high-intensity response operations. Different types of signal concepts are in use, from signals that change timing using either an existing library of plans, or from feedback used to develop an online signal plan immediately. For large areas, coordinated signals along a corridor, or a hierarchical system in a large network encompassing different highways and streets to improve operations, are in use. Key features of these signal control systems include online optimization of selected operational parameters, and capabilities to predict traffic conditions. In terms of reduction of delay, these systems are changing the face of traffic management in urban areas.

Field operational tests in United States and Europe have shown positive results due to online traffic management using the concepts developed with ITS. These impacts include reductions in delays, the frequency of crashes, air pollution and energy consumption; and increased motorist satisfaction. Because of its promising field results and future potential, ITS is becoming a mainstream tool for traffic management systems. In addition to traffic sensors and cameras as a means for traffic assessment, new technologies have already been considered and some have already surfaced. For example, tracking cellphones or global positioning systems (GPS)-equipped vehicles can now be utilized as mobile traffic sensors, providing an opportunity for gathering more detailed and continuous traffic flow data than before. In addition, the concepts of vehicle and infrastructure integration, in which vehicles and roadside agents communicate through wireless communications, can now provide further improvements in detail and continuous data related to traffic conditions to assess and predict traffic conditions more accurately. This system is also likely to provide an effective traffic management tool in which travellers are kept constantly informed as to current and future traffic problems, and provided with a best course of action to avoid those problems during their trip. Increasing traffic demand and changing distributions of traffic and drivers in massive traffic streams is only expected to make traffic management that much more complex.

Further reading
Chowdhury, M. and A. Sadek (2003). *Fundamentals of Intelligent Transportation Systems Planning*. Norwood, MA: Artech House.
United States Department of Transportation, Federal Highway Administration (2003). *Manual on Uniform Traffic Control Devices*. Washington, DC: USDOT.

Mashrur (Ronnie) Chowdhury

traffic noise policy

Traffic noise abatement policy dates back to the days of the Roman Empire, but here we focus on the recent experiences in America. The requirement to consider traffic noise impacts from highways traces back to the 1970 United States Federal Aid Highway Act, Public Law 91–605. That law modified Title 23, Section 109 of the United States Code to include the following mandate given to the United States Department of Transportation:

> not later than July 1, 1972, the Secretary . . . shall promulgate guidelines designed to assure possible adverse economic, social and environmental effects related to any proposed project . . . have been fully considered . . . taking into consideration the need for fast, safe, and efficient transportation . . . and the costs of eliminating or minimizing such adverse effects as the following: 1. Air, noise, and water pollution . . .

The United States Federal Highway Administration (FHWA) response to this mandate has come in the form of a regulation, which today is found in the Code of Federal Regulations (CFR), entitled Procedures for Abatement of Highway Traffic Noise and Construction Noise (23CFR772). The regulation, commonly referred to by its citing, 23CFR772, includes a five-step process to consider traffic noise impacts on sensitive receptors: identification of existing activities, developed lands, and undeveloped lands for which development is planned, designed and programmed, which may be affected by noise from the highway; prediction of traffic noise levels; determination of existing noise levels; determination of traffic noise impacts; and examination and evaluation of alternative noise abatement measures for reducing or eliminating the noise impacts.

The regulation also includes a table showing noise abatement criteria for a wide variety of sensitive land uses. The most common sensitive land use is Category B, which includes picnic areas, recreation areas, playgrounds, active sports areas, parks, residences, motels, hotels, schools, churches, libraries and hospitals. The Noise Abatement Criteria for this category is 67 A-weighted decibels (dBA) for Leq (the energy equivalent sound level for the noisiest hour), exterior. If a future noise level approaches this value (that is, Leq of 66 dBA), then an impact occurs and possible abatement measures must be evaluated. Also, if the difference in Leq values will significantly increase from before to after the project is constructed, impacts are deemed to have occurred, and abatement must be evaluated. This difference is usually considered to be at least 10 dBA.

The passage of PL-605 was 'technology forcing' in that there were procedures in place to implement its mandates. As a result, there have been millions of dollars invested to quantify future noise levels accurately. The current model used in the United States is TNM 2.5, the FHWA Traffic Noise Model, Version 2.5 (TNM 2.5). TNM 2.5 contains the following elements:

- modeling of standard vehicle types (automobiles, medium trucks, heavy trucks, buses and **motorcycles**) plus user-defined vehicles;
- modeling of constant-flow and interrupted-flow traffic using a field-measured data base;
- modeling of the effects of different pavement (road) types and the effects of graded roadways;
- sound level computations based on a one-third octave-band database and algorithms;
- graphically interactive noise barrier design and optimization;
- attenuation over and through rows of buildings and dense vegetation; and
- multiple diffraction, parallel barrier and contour analyses.

These elements are supported by a scientifically founded and experimentally calibrated acoustic computation methodology, as well as a new and flexible database, compared with that of its predecessor, Stamina 2.0/Optima. The database is made up of over 6000 individual pass-by events measured at 40 sites across the country. It is the primary building block around which the acoustic algorithms are structured. The most visible difference between the TNM 2.5 and Stamina 2.0/Optima, is TNM 2.5's Microsoft Windows interface. Data input is menu-driven using a digitizer, mouse and/or keyboard. Users also have the ability to import Stamina 2.0/Optima files, as well as roadway design files saved in CAD DXF format. Colour graphics play a major role in both case construction and visual analysis of results (TNM 2.5).

Louis F. Cohn

trams

Trams are vehicles running on embedded tracks on the streets in urban areas and powered by electricity. Trams are intended for the transport of passengers but have also been used for cargo. Trams were first powered by horses, then mechanically and now electrically.

The horse tram was the second most widely used mode of public transport, after the horse omnibus, in urban areas in the latter nineteenth century. The horse tram became viable with the solution of the problem of the height of the rail, achieved in 1852 as part of an experiment carried out in New York under the supervision of the French engineer Alfhonse Loubat. This was a significant innovation because the first trams had used rails placed above street level and such rails interfered with other traffic which created public hostility. The horse tram used horse power, the operators' main expense, much more efficiently than the omnibus and it was safer, more comfortable, faster, smoother and less noisy. The **productivity** of the service increased and lower fares were possible but the costs of operation remained high. Fares were above what low-income workers could afford and several attempts to mechanize the tram took place.

Steam power was introduced in some cities, but generally over short periods of time, and had little significance (for example a steam tram in Antwerp between 1888 and 1891, Copenhagen 1884 and 1892, Munich 1883 and 1900). The same happened with the cable tram, with a few exceptions in cities like Chicago, Edinburgh and Melbourne – the largest cable tram systems in United States, Europe and in the world, respectively. The first cable car line in the United States was tested in San Francisco in 1873 and it is still in operation.

The electric tram was the technological innovation that provided a cheap form of transportation and a swift increase in **public transport** utilization. Siemens experimented with the first overhead conductors with copper wire in 1881. At the beginning of the 1880s, in spite of some technical difficulties, some electric tramway systems with underground supply were built in holiday resorts but had operational costs similar to those of the horse tram. In 1888 in the United States, in Richmond, Virginia, the American Julian Sprague built the first **network** capable of providing regular service, without major disruptions, using electric supply from overhead wires. Sprague's system enabled a reduction in working expenses of about 45 per cent. This information spread quickly and Richmond became the mecca of railway operators and investors. Other cities had similar systems built in a few years. Incremental technology and the gains in the phase of learning-by-doing were also important. Fares went down, public transport then became affordable for those on a low income, and utilization increased sharply. The electric tram was a perfect substitute for the horse tram, which entered a period of rapid decline.

A deep consolidation of markets was attained at the time of electrification because, with the exception of larger cities, it was not feasible to have several operators electrifying the streets. The industrial organization of the market became monopolistic or, at least, there was a greater degree of concentration. Consolidation was achieved in one of three ways: monopolies or oligopolies created by private organizations, mergers or acquisitions (for example Porto in 1893, Lisbon between 1892 and 1896, Copenhagen in 1897); granting of monopoly licences to a private operator (for example Milan in 1897, Antwerp in 1902); or municipalization (for example Amsterdam in 1900, Frankfurt in 1898).

The development of the trolleybus and the motor bus resulted in the abandonment of many electric tramway lines, with the exception of some Western European cities. The abandonment of the tramway was mostly related to the huge investments needed for track replacement; but the moment when specific services were abandoned was influenced by several different local factors, internal and external to the industry.

With increasing concern on environmental issues, excessive oil dependence, large **congestion** levels in urban centres, trams have been 'reinvented' since the 1980s, and are referred to as 'light rail systems' or 'light rail transit'. In 2007, Europe had more than 8000 km of **network** in operation, and more than 2000 km in construction or planned.

Strasbourg is commonly referred to as the case study which inspired several cities to develop light rail systems. These systems' success is verifiable not only in growing patronage, but also in the large urban transformation process developed by the local authorities. Technological development, undertaken by rolling stock suppliers, led to an 'upgrading' in the concept of light rail systems, allowing them to operate simultaneously in urban environment at low speeds and in suburban heavy rail infrastructure at higher speeds. These new trams are called 'tram-train' since they combine features of both trams and trains, even though they look like common trains. The city of Karlsruhe was the first to develop this system.

Further reading
McKay, J. (1976). *Tramways and Trolleys*. Princeton, NJ: Princeton University Press.

Álvaro Costa

transborder transport

The term 'transborder' transport is used in reference to transport infra-structure crossing political boundaries and in the description of cross-border passenger and goods traffic. It is regarded from three viewpoints, the primary study objects being: transport, boundaries and international interactions, as reflected in the movement of persons and goods. In the case of transport, the focus is on the functioning of transborder transport infrastructure, with boundaries the centre of political focus, while international transactions touch upon broader problems of the existence of boundaries on the intensity of economic and social links, and on innovation diffusion.

The specificity of transborder traffic is associated not so much with the existence of boundaries per se as with their functions. In 1930s Harsthorne proposed classifying boundaries into antecedent (primary with respect to forms of spatial organization) and subsequent (secondary with respect to these forms). In the former case, transborder transport infrastructure developed slower than the internal infrastructure of the neighbouring countries or regions (in autarchic economies, a gravitation towards a country's own core areas dominated). In the latter case, the cutting of developed transport **networks** took place as for example in post-war Germany. While transborder sea and air transport are becoming global phenomena, overland cross-border traffic has particular significance in many regions including Europe which has a large number of countries included in a network of continental significance. In the nineteenth century and in the first half of the twentieth, the tendency towards formalization of boundaries dominated in Europe. Many countries introduced their own transport standards concerning such things as railway gauge and electric power supply as well as national regulations. This trend was reversed with the initiation of integration processes. Starting in the 1950s, more permeable boundaries emerged stemming from the Benelux initiative that spread with the creation of European Coal and Steel Community and then the European Union.

Transborder transport infrastructure often, and particularly for smaller countries can constitute a large fragment of the domestic transport **network**, or may have specific characteristics. The former often includes roads, **railways**, pipelines and waterways that cross borders, as well as **airports** and **seaports**, while specific infrastructure encompasses objects or network elements, the existence of which is due specifically to a border crossing. These include passenger and cargo border crossing points, customs terminals, reloading stations, and such facilities as fee collection points and truck weight bridges.

The degree to which borders can impact as barriers to transport depends upon their formalization, and degree of permeability. Less permeable borders limit not only cross-border traffic of persons and goods, but also network extensions, and in extreme cases result in a degradation of local infrastructure. Many international transport routes with the former Soviet Union were, for example, left unused over decades and underwent deliberate or natural devastation.

The impacts of boundaries as spatial barriers are often expressed in institutional reactions. These are not only the direct border regime institutions (immigration and customs services), but also bodies responsible for tax policy, spatial planning and the regulation of transport markets, as well as insurance companies and transport operators. Transport is limited by the existence of borders in terms of prolonged transit times at crossing points, higher operating costs, special fees and formalities including the restrictions on cross-movements of import or export of specified goods, and limitations on personal movements. Additionally, numerous political boundaries follow the natural environment, rivers and mountains. Consequently, political barriers frequently overlap with the natural ones, which can increase the costs of infrastructure construction and maintenance.

The impact of formalized and poorly permeable borders is firstly expressed through low levels of cross-border interactions and demand for international transport. If transborder infrastructure is insufficient then bottlenecks develop in the supranational transport system. This, for example, happened with some borders between the **European Union** and Central European countries after 1990. Border **congestion** can, especially when it involves commodity transport, have adverse effects on international trade. Solutions may involve further liberalization, as with the creation of the single European market or the Schengen area within the European Union, or the provision of more infrastructure capacity.

Further reading
Corvers, F. and M. Giaoutzi (1998). Borders and barriers and changing opportunities for border regional development. In K. Button, P. Nijkamp and H. Priemus (eds), *Transport Networks in Europe: Concepts, Analysis and Policies*. Cheltenham, UK and Northampton, MA, USA: Edward Elgar.
Komornicki, T. (2001). Changes in the role and permeability of Polish borders. *Geographia Polonica* **74**, 77–100.

Tomasz Komornicki

transhipment

In its narrow sense, transhipment is the act of shipping goods to an inter-mediate destination prior to reaching their ultimate end use. The term is often used for the ship-to-ship transhipment (unloading of cargo from one merchant ship and its loading into another to complete a journey, even where the cargo may have dwell-time ashore before its onward journey). Such a transportation practice is an essential operation of the **hub-and-spoke system** applied to oceanic shipping: large container ships (mother-ships) call at a few big, hub ports that offer the required depth, berths and equipment for fast unloading and loading operations. Then the **containers** that are not originated from or destined to the port's hinterland are transported to their final destination by smaller, feeder, container ships. Transhipment traffic is welcomed for a port as it is over and above its local traffic, and two quay crane operations for each container transhipped (one for the mother-ship and one for the feeder-ship) are required and charged for. In recent decades, the proportion of transhipment as a percentage of container handling increased due to the growing importance of larger container ships and associated economies of scale, as well as the increasing degree of containerization, even at smaller ports.

Similarly, the term 'transhipment' is used for cargo shifts between other modes (trains, trucks, barges, air freighters) functioning in a hub-and-spoke system (for example trains departing from various Northern European terminals are bound in a Hungarian terminal to form block trains towards Greece or Turkey) or in other operating forms.

In addition, the term 'transhipment' is used to describe cargo transfers between different transport modes, for example rail–road transhipments in a combined transport terminal, or cargo transfers between different modes, served in different terminal types, as in the case of sea-to-air tran-shipments (for example between Malta Freeport and Malta International Airport). Transhipment can also be used to describe operations and areas denoted for cargo handling and transport in a freight village.

Transhipment is normally seen as a fully legitimate transportation practice offering logistic benefits, but can be used illegitimately to disguise country of origin or intent of the goods.

In its wider sense, the term 'transhipment' is used to describe handling systems or elements of these systems that allow for the transfer of cargoes between two transport modes, usually by unloading of one mode with simultaneous loading of the other mode. This operation mainly concerns unitized cargo types like pallets, **containers** (for example the International Organization for Standardization standardized 20 ft and 40 ft units of the maritime sector), swap-bodies (loading unit types used mainly in the internal Europe trade), cranable semi-trailers (that can be handled by grapple-arm spreaders and transported by special wagon types), and air unit load devices (ULDs); platforms, igloos and light containers tailored to be stowage in the belly or the deck of an aircraft.

The term 'transhipment equipment' is used for a wide family of equipment that includes quay cranes, transtainers (rubber-tyred or rail-mounted cranes that can span many container rows), straddle carriers (mobile equipments that can span one row of containers and provide both vertical stacking and horizontal transport of the containers), and reach stackers (mobile equipments with suitable spreaders for the handling of containers, swap-bodies and cranable semi-trailers). Transhipment may also have very specific connotations within the logistics supply chain, including:

- 'Transhipment terminal' (for example cargo transhipment terminal or container transhipment terminal) is sometimes used synonymously with **intermodal** and combined transport terminal. These terminals (for example maritime–barge–road–rail and rail–road) provide the space, the equipment and the operating environment required for the transhipment of loading units between the transport modes served.
- 'Transhipment area' is used (mainly for rail terminals and **seaports**) to define a terminal area dedicated to loading and unloading of transport modes and/or handling and storage of the loading units.
- 'Transhipment system' or 'technique' is used to describe efficient combinations of conventional and innovative handling equipment and transport modes that facilitate the transhipment of loading units either directly or through an intermediate buffer area. Two main clusters exist: the vertical transhipment system or technique (where the loading units are lifted to be transhipped) and the horizontal transhipment system or technique (where the loading units are swift horizontally between the modes).

Further reading

Tsamboulas, D. and S. Kapros (2003). Freight village evaluation under uncertainty with public and private financing. *Transport Policy* **10**, 141–56.
United Nations Economic Commission for Europe (2009). *Glossary for Transport Statistics* (4th edn). Geneva: UNECE.

Dimitrios A. Tsamboulas and *Athanasios Ballis*

transponders / automatic equipment identification

A transponder, short for transmitter-responder, is a communication device capable of electronically responding to predetermined messages and is used as part of **intelligent transportation systems**. These devices can be either passive or active, with passive transponders using magnets to encode identification or other messages, and active transponders transmitting data when prompted. Passive transponders must be used with active sensors; for example, passive transit cards must be used with active card readers. Active transponders are commonly used in location systems for aircraft, trucks, ships, transit vehicles, personal vehicles and emergency response vehicles.

Automatic equipment identification refers to the tagging and locating of transport elements using transponders. Much attention has been given to the automatic identification of en route **rail** cars. Desire for an automatic equipment identification system was demonstrated in the 1970s when the American Association of Railroads introduced Automatic Car Identification. This identification system used an optical sensor to read colour-coded labels on the side of rail cars. Unfortunately, dirt accumulation and wear reduced the accuracy of the system so significantly that efforts towards automatic identification were almost completely abandoned until the mid-1980s. The use of the transponder solved this problem because identification was not constrained by sensor appearance.

Aviation transponders arose during the Second World War to identify aircraft as friend or foe. Further developments brought transponders into civil aviation and with continued technological improvement, transponders now commonly report the altitude, location and direction of aircraft to air traffic controllers.

Transponders used in the trucking industry aid with tolling and are a key component to weigh-in-motion. For example, transponders provide tolling agencies with identification information as the vehicle passes over scales, then receive information either verifying the anticipated vehicle weight or requesting the truck exit to be reweighed. **Trucking** transponders can also transmit information about electronic seals on cargo and truck location, aiding in security.

Maritime transponders help manage ship traffic and provide **safety** benefits. In and around ports, transponders can transmit the location and identity of each ship, at a minimum. These tools can also transmit the ship's next port of call, the vessel length, speed and course, and final destination. Similar transponder uses are being explored for use on vessels travelling inland waterways. While management is commonly the focus of transponder use in ports and **inland waterways**, safety is the focus on the open seas. Search-and-rescue transponders are now commonplace among commercial vessels and follow internationally accepted standards.

Public transportation agencies can use transponders in transit payment cards and road access. Transit payment cards can be active or passive, personal or anonymous. In-vehicle transponders can provide transit vehicles with access to bus-only lanes, **high-occupancy vehicle** lanes and dedicated entrances to **parking** lots such as those at airports.

Personal vehicles can utilize transponders for security, toll payments or parking access. If stolen, equipped vehicles can transmit location data from a hidden transponder to alert police and aircraft of its location. Payment of road and parking tolls are commonly accomplished using transponders. While mainly operated by private companies, this use can greatly improve the efficiency of tolling stations on public or private roads. **Parking** access can also be granted by receiving information from transponders.

Data from transponders can be used to monitor the flow of traffic along roadways, and the information-providing vehicles are termed probe vehicles. For example, data from toll collection transponders are often used to determine the travel times between consecutive toll centres. Because privacy is frequently an issue with sharing this information, removing driver identifications from the data is common.

Finally, transponders can aid in emergency response through access and priority. Hospitals located adjacent to freeways can have transponder-activated entrances for fast access for emergency vehicles to and from the freeway. Signal pre-emption using transponders can provide rights of way to approaching emergency vehicles at a signalized intersection, thus improving their response time and **safety** during response.

Further reading
Fries, R., M. Chowdhury and J. Brummond (2008). *Transportation Infrastructure Security Utilizing Intelligent Transportation Systems*. Hoboken, NJ: John Wiley & Sons.
Pfliegl, R. and A. Back (2006). Increasing the attractiveness of inland waterway transport with E-transport river information services. *Transportation Research Record* **1963**, 15–22.

Ryan N. Fries

transport demand forecasting

Transport demand is the sum of movements of persons or goods within a defined area and within a specified time period, measured generally in terms of transport volume (persons or tonnes) or transport performance (person-kilometres or tonne-kilometres). The transport volume may be measured at one or several points of a transport **network** (for example border crossings) or between two points or zones. Transport performance measures the distance over which persons or goods are moved within a defined area (territorial approach), or by one or several individuals or commercial transport undertakings, for example the residents of country X (national approach). For both measures, a time frame must be given, whether it relates to a year, day or hour, with further qualifications, for example per peak hours or during daylight. Different modes and submodes of transport are available for a journey; it therefore makes a difference whether one is looking at movements independent of the transport mode and vehicle type or at specific modal movements, for example rail trips. Only when the segment of transport demand has been clearly defined can one think about forecasting on these very specific segments.

To consider the future, one has first to observe and analyse the past. How has the segment developed over time? As a general rule, the previous period observed should be as long as the forecast period although if there have been recent sea changes a much shorter horizon is appropriate. If the evolution was steady, approximately 2 per cent growth every year, and no saturation or drastic changes are expected, one can fairly safely extrapolate the trend of the past into the future without worrying about what causes and drives the demand. But transport markets are volatile and not independent from business cycles of the economy. Therefore, things are more complex.

In general, transport demand within an individual country is driven by:

- population and its structure (age, employment, and so on);
- economy (gross domestic product or other suitable macroeconomic parameters, export, import, car ownership);
- **energy**: fuel consumption and prices;
- transport offer and supply (infrastructure, services, prices, quality of service);
- travel behaviour (for passenger transport); **logistics** characteristics (for goods transport);
- transport policies (regulations, **taxation**, infrastructure development).

Passenger transport demand and goods transport demand generally need to be handled separately. Each market is segmented further by transport purpose (for example by trip purpose, passengers and type of goods for freight), transport mode and/or transport type; domestic, international, outgoing and incoming, transit.

Transport demand forecasting initially involves modelling demand parameters as variables that depend on the choice parameters of travellers or shippers of goods, on changes in demographic and economic parameters, and on transport supply characteristics. Such models can be purely statistical, based on time series of empirical data. The **elasticity** concept is often used in this context: the elasticity indicating the proportional responsiveness of the amount of transport demanded to changes in factors influencing demand. Factors influencing the transport demanded may be disposable income, fuel price, motorization or car ownership, or speed. If the number of car trips increases by 5 per cent as a result of an increase of disposable income by 10 per cent, it can be said that the elasticity of trip generation with respect to income is 0.5. Or the elasticity of car usage in terms of annual vehicle mileage with respect to fuel price increases is -0.15 meaning that a fuel price increase of 10 per cent would reduce car mileage driven by 1.5 per cent. **Elasticities** are useful for short-term and medium-term forecasts, but they are not always constant over time and hence not suitable for long-term forecasts.

Changes in transport demand are generally not homogeneous across a transport **network**. A 10 per cent increase in transport performance may be reflected by increases above this in certain parts of the network, and by smaller increases or even drops in other parts. Transport demand in a given base year is computed as origin–destination transport flows between zones; transport flow matrix. Using a modelling procedure reflecting transport levels in terms of infrastructure networks and **generalized cost** functions, these transport flows are assigned to the different transport modes and routes.

The needs for transport demand forecasts are multiple:

- Very long-term forecasts of more than 30 years are used for strategic policy purposes and decisions of long-lasting transport infrastructure investments, for example road tunnels and bridges, railways, inland waterways and ports.
- Long-term forecasts of 10–30 years are used in infrastructure investment planning and for ex-ante evaluation of policy measures.
- Medium-term forecasts of more or less five years are used for corporate decision making and business planning by transport operators.
- Short-term forecasts: for the next two years correspond to business cycle forecasts.
- 'Now casts' are used for the current and previous years to produce

provisional outcomes pending the availability of complete statistical information.

There is no generally accepted method for forecasting transport demand. There are all sorts of procedures, from intuitive informed statements about the future to trend extrapolation to modelling of various levels of sophistication, for example space–time multinomial probit modelling combined with Monte Carlo simulation techniques to evaluate probabilities of occurrence. All forecast procedures have weaknesses and advantages. Here the focus is on long-term trend forecasts at national level to demonstrate the interdependency of variables in passenger and goods transport models.

The objective of urban passenger demand forecasting (see the first Figure) is usually to predict person-kilometres for cars, buses, taxis, urban rail and interurban rail. For the road transport modes, the vehicle stocks and vehicle-kilometres done are forecast. Segmentation by trip purpose is not normally covered in this concept but can be integrated if necessary.

The forecasts are based on past population and **economic development** data, and on past transport performance of each mode, as well as on expected future national socio-economic development prospects. In the process, transport performance indicators related to population, gross domestic product (GDP) and private consumption are predicted as the functional linkages between transport performance and the socio-economic framework. The functional relationships are determined through statistical modelling, often deploying regression analysis of absolute and logarithmic values and growth rates. Anticipated transport policy measures can be integrated into the process. The resulting transport performance is split according to the modal shares of car and public transport with the latter being further split into three submodes. In this procedure, demand is forecast independently of changes in the supply of infrastructure and transport services, other than trends in supply that are already implicitly reflected in previous performance data.

Car ownership per 1000 inhabitants is used in conjunction with the socio-economic variables, but also as a parameter to validate car stock and car mileage forecasts. Additional intermediate variables are average annual mileage per car and an average distance-weighted car occupancy ratio. Autonomous bottom-up forecasts are thus harmonized with the top-down **modal split** forecasts in an iterative process. If transport or traffic performance by nationally registered cars driving abroad and foreign-registered vehicles driving on the national territory is unbalanced, this has to be taken into account.

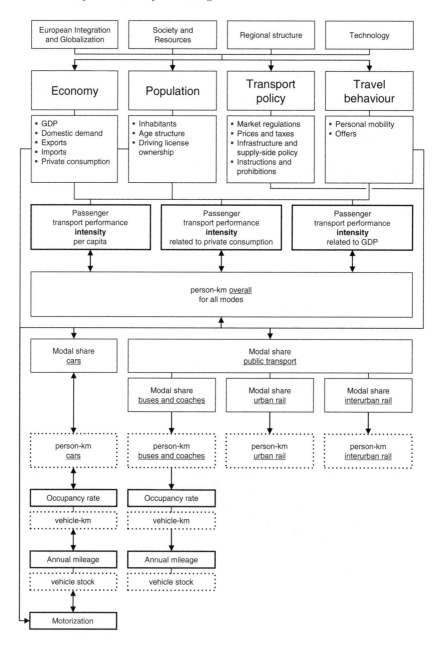

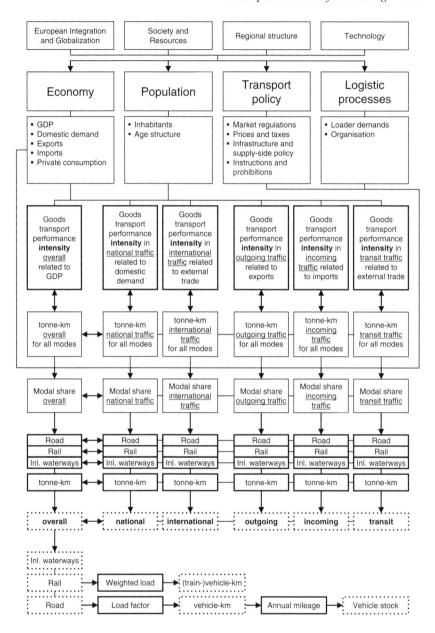

The procedure for long-term goods transport forecasts (second Figure) resembles that for passenger transport. However, modern goods transport is a highly internationalized business and this needs to be reflected in the forecasting procedure. Segmentation by commodity type is not covered in this concept but can be integrated if useful.

The initial step towards forecasting goods transport performance is to establish the overall (all modes and all types of transport) transport link with GDP as the reference parameter. Subsequently, individual transport intensities for all types of transport (all transport modes combined) are forecast, using:

- domestic transport performance per value unit of domestic demand (GDP minus exports plus imports);
- transport performance of international outgoing freight traffic per value unit of exports;
- transport performance of international incoming freight traffic per value unit of imports; and
- transit transport performance per value unit of trade (export plus import).

The overall intensity is initiallly estimated independently. Then the same procedure is performed for each individual type of transport, and the four results are combined. Two transport performance measures are thus obtained for each forecast year. The results are unlikely to be identical, and thus some reconciliation is usually needed.

After completing the **modal split** forecasts for each type of transport, using similar procedures and approaches as in passenger transport, the forecasts of goods vehicle-km and vehicle fleets, and of train-km using estimates of distance weighted average load, are made.

In addition to trend forecasts, so-called scenario analyses are frequently conducted to test for sensitivity. A scenario is a picture of a distant future, defined hypothetically around realistic assumptions about the development of the factors driving transport demand. From these assumptions, transport demand is derived in quantitative terms. Scenario forecasts are used to answer questions like 'What happens if . . .?', but they are sometimes at the limits of what can be imagined, with no way of indicating the probability of their occurrence.

Further reading
Garrido, R.A. and H.S. Mahmassani (2000). Forecasting freight transportation demand with the space–time multinomial probit model. *Transportation Research B* **34**, 403–18.

Ickert, L., T. Erhart, A. Greinus and S. Rommerskirchen (2007). ProgTrans European Transport Report 2007/2008 – Analyses and Forecasts, 37 European and Overseas Countries. Progtrans, Basel.

Quinet, E. and R.W. Vickerman (2004). *Principles of Transport Economics.* Cheltenham, UK and Northampton, MA, USA: Edward Elgar.

Olaf Meyer-Rühle and *Lutz Ickert*

transport demand models

Models are simplified representations of complex phenomena. A model attempts to identify key influences on the subject of interest. For transport demands, one wants to know the most important variables affecting the level of demand, or in some instances, one focuses on the importance of a particular variable separate from other influences.

The demand for transport refers to the quantity of people and/or freight moving between two locations during a time interval. Demand could refer to very specific movements on a route, or an aggregation of amounts of traffic on that and possibly other routes. Expressed in general notation:

$$Q_{itod} = f(P_{itod}, y_{itod}, x1_{itod} \ldots xn_{itod}) \tag{1}$$

where Q is the quantity (volume) of travel type i (say, passengers) during time interval t between origin o and destination d. P refers to the price charged, y represents income level of passengers, and $x1 \ldots xn$ refer to other variables such as speed, reliability, comfort or other influences on the demand for travel. This is demand at a micro level. More typically, some aggregation of that traffic is examined, for example total airline traffic along a route for a period of time.

Various ambiguities arise as individual demands are aggregated. 'Quantity' could be measured in different ways depending on characteristics; people as opposed to freight is an obvious distinction. Freight might be measured either by weight or volume (space required), or in some other standardized quantitative unit (bushels, pallets, 20-foot **containers**, and so on) depending on the specifics of the market. In doing this, there is the ambiguity of aggregating diverse movements into a total, especially if different routes of different distances are aggregated. It is common to use a weight–distance measure (for example tonne-kilometres or passenger-kilometres).

The usual purpose of demand models is to forecast future volumes and patterns of travel based on our understanding and modelling of current and past transport demands in terms of variables and characteristics to explain the historical record. The purpose can be to predict total travel demands, or possibly simply to investigate particular influences on transport demand such as the sensitivity of demand to the prices charged, or the responsiveness of demand to quality variables such as the duration of trip time. Most transport demand studies are of aggregate movements, for example the total demand for transport along some route or even for an entire mode and market.

Forecasting the total volumes and patterns of travel in an urban area is a major example of transport demand models. The problem is so complex that it is customary to break the task into four recursive stages:

Generation –> Distribution –> Mode Split –> Route Assignment

It is somewhat artificial to model these as separate stages but it facilitates analysis and feedback can be incorporated among the stages.

Data on total daily travel by all modes and routes in a region is collected. The urban region is divided into zones and step one analyses total trips originating from (or arriving at) various zones. Total trips originating will likely be linked to the population of a zone, but other variables may influence demand, such as income levels. Similarly, the trips arriving at a zone will depend on a measure of 'attractiveness' of the zone, such as total work trips arriving will reflect the number of employment opportunities in the zone. Stage 2, **traffic distribution**, examines the patterns of travel among zones. Trips between two specific zones are more likely if the zones involve large instead of smaller populations, and less likely if the zones are farther apart.

Stages one and two produce forecasts of traffic volumes to and from all zones as well as how they are divided among the various origins and destinations. Stage 3 models the allocation of traffic between modes: primarily car and **public transport** but it may have further categories such as car passengers, bicycle and walking. The 'mode split' will depend on the relative attractiveness and cost of using various modes. These models can be based on aggregate data comparisons, but often they make use of a different demand estimation approach. An individual choosing a mode is making a discrete choice, one or the other, as opposed to demanding a quantity of something; a continuous variable. These **disaggregate models** focus on a sample of individuals making mode choices and attempt to model the probability of choosing one mode or another in response to the relative prices, travel times, comfort, and so on of the various modes. The modelling of individual choice can be very intricate although **discrete choice modelling** has much wider relevance than just urban mode choice estimation.

The final stage, route assignment, is not really demand per se but part of urban modelling of assigning traffic volumes by mode to specific routes. Various operations research models are employed. Minimizing trip time is an obvious routing characteristic, but feedback is required as **congestion** levels affect trip times.

In summary, there are a variety of transport demand models, from simplistic correlations of total transportation volumes with population levels, to highly complex **network** demand models and models of individual behaviour. Demand models may be simplistic and based on little more than judgements about how consumers will react to a change in price or to changes in underlying circumstances. Alternatively, transport demand models can be constructed on massive databases such as those used in airline seat management. In all cases, demand models are analytical representations of our understanding of various influences on transport demands, both exogenous influences and variables that can be modified to influence demand.

Further reading
de Dios Ortúzar, J. and L.G. Willumsen (2001). *Modelling Transport* (3rd edn). London: Wiley-Blackwell.

William G. Waters II

transport economics

Transport economics has been a recognized subfield of economics for many decades, undergoing shifts of emphasis over time. It is the adaptation and application of economic principles and methods of analysis to the transportation sector broadly interpreted. The focus of transport economics is on microeconomics. Microeconomics is the study of decisions by firms and households regarding resource allocation through pricing and the working of market forces. This includes supply and demand characteristics and their determinants; competition, or its lack, and implications for efficient resource allocation; and the roles of government in monitoring and modifying, and sometimes replacing, market outcomes.

There are a few fundamental characteristics of transport operations and markets that distinguish them from standard economics texts. Transport necessarily involves spatial dimensions of an economy. Origins and destinations are fundamental dimensions of transport measurement, in contrast to the spaceless concept of widgets. Transport is service provided between two or more points in space per interval of time. Measurement is further confounded by indivisibilities in the outputs of demand and supply. The units of supply typically are much larger than the appropriate units for demand. Truckloads or trainloads or shiploads are supplied in transport whereas the sales or demand unit in the marketplace may be only a fraction of the relevant measure for the supply side. A further example, except for pipelines, is that supply nearly always necessarily involves round trips, whereas demand for any movement will be unidirectional. Supply commits to a round trip whatever the demand for the return journey, although triangular routing or serving different markets can reduce this problem. Further, in nearly all cases, transportation involves multiple production; that is, serving a multiplicity of markets with single acts of production. This is in contrast with the single-product focus of basic economics.

The implication of indivisibilities in outputs and multiproduct production is a difficulty or even impossibility of identifying the marginal costs associated with specific services. But comparing prices with costs is a fundamental in microeconomics. **Costing** methods became more sophisticated but it is still common for some costs to be shared by a number of outputs and any allocation is arbitrary. In these circumstances there can be differential markups above what costs can be assigned to specific outputs in order to generate revenue sufficient to cover total costs. These markups will vary with the demand or ability to pay by the respective markets. Optimal prices are a function of costs and demand conditions in multiple markets and cannot be determined by cost considerations alone.

Rail industry issues dominated transportation and transport economics until well into the twentieth century. It was widely accepted that there were substantial economies of scale in the industry, and/or persistent fixed or unallocable costs. The economic efficiency dictum of pricing equal to marginal costs could not sustain the enterprise. **Railways** (and public utilities) were 'affected with the public interest', and government intervention became accepted well before it would arise in other industries. Public intervention took two forms. In the United States and in many other countries this led to extensive regulation of prices and entry controls, and decades of debate over appropriate pricing principles. These were dominant themes in transport economics. In several other countries the solution was public ownership of railways. Debates over pricing principles were a major focus there too, along with issues in determining optimal subsidy levels. But by the mid-twentieth century other transport technologies had evolved and thrived. Competition emerged in many markets. The general growth of population and income levels meant a larger economy with more opportunities for market expansion and diversification.

Also important by mid-century were improved statistical techniques and availability of data. Cost and output data from regulated firms enabled empirical analysis of costs and production. Over the 1960s and 1970s empirical studies showed scale economies to be less important than had been believed, and **productivity** performance was better where competition was present. This led to fundamental changes in transport economics, from an emphasis on regulatory issues to analysis of supply and its cost and demand conditions and the feasibility of reliance on market forces rather than government controls. A **deregulation** movement started primarily in the United States but spread to other countries over the 1980s and 1990s. Where government ownership prevailed, there was **privatization** in some cases, or at least increased commercialization and autonomy in transport management.

Parallel to the developments in cost and efficiency estimation, empirical analysis of transport demands increased significantly after about 1960. This reflected improved econometric techniques. Data availability was a challenge at first and led to greater emphasis on generating data. This was especially so for urban transportation, where large infrastructure decisions warranted extensive analysis of demand. Other advances came in markets involving major expenditures such as air passenger demand. Especially important were the developments in **discrete choice analysis**. Traditional concepts of demand refer to continuous variables (quantities of transport service demanded), whereas many transport decisions involved discrete choices such as choice of mode of travel or choice of residential location. **Discrete choice** requires different methods of analysis; for example data based on individual decision units and estimates of probabilities of choice rather than quantities of travel. Empirical analysis of transport demand has continued to be a major focus of transport economic research.

Modern transport markets have diverse market structures, and both data availability and tools of analysis support more intricate analysis of market equilibria and efficiency than were possible in the past. Early writing tended to emphasize only monopoly or 'destructive' competition outcomes. Oligopoly models and industrial organization analysis are now much more prominent in transport economics.

The emphasis on analysis of the workings of markets and firm behaviour also extends to the roles and performance of government institutions. The emphasis on regulatory failings that characterized research during the 1970s and 1980s was also stimulated by work on and models of regulatory behaviour and the implications for efficiency. In the 1990s and 2000s there has been research on the behaviour and performance of infrastructure suppliers such as ports, airports, roads and rail infrastructure, how ownership and organization can affect performance and how it might be changed.

Public provision of transport infrastructure was analysed extensively from about 1960 onward. Social **benefit–cost analysis** identified and quantified non-market benefits and costs so that they could be combined with market-determined ones. Although measurement controversies could arise, this technique gave a framework for more accurate economic evaluation of infrastructure.

By about the 1980s there arose a number of new emphases on the role of the public sector in transport and related activities, which continue to this day. The continued growth of population and income levels, especially in urban areas, resulted in greater importance of transport **externalities**. Traditional negative externalities were local, for example local air and noise pollution, but by the 1990s and into the twenty-first century there was growing interest in possible macro and even global consequences of emissions leading to **climate change**. Issues of sustainable industrial structures and economies go beyond transport, but analysis of **energy** use and emissions are now important themes in transport economics research. This is accompanied by industrial organization analysis of incentive systems, design of markets and institutions to deal with these problems.

A long-standing externality topic in transport economics is **congestion**, which is especially visible in urban transportation. This reflects another intrinsic characteristic of many transportation markets: the importance of user-borne costs. In many transport markets, a significant portion of the total costs of transport is borne directly by users rather than by supplying firms, such as the time and effort expended by users. These user-borne costs can have different cost characteristics than those borne directly by firms. Congestion externalities are an example. Users of congested facilities perceive their own increased time costs during congestion, but not the similar costs imposed on others. The full marginal costs of using congested facilities are larger than what individuals perceive. The result is inefficient excessive use of a facility. For decades transport economists have advocated congestion taxes to correct this market distortion as well as to link it with the optimal provision of congested facilities. **Congestion pricing** has met strong public resistance. Nonetheless, modern congestion problems are so severe that research on this topic continues.

Once dominated by issues of costs and prices in government-controlled monopoly sectors, transport economics evolved with the transformation of the transportation sector into multiple modes with diverse and often highly competitive market structures, along with diverse government controls and/or direct government involvement such as infrastructure provision. Modern transport economics retains an emphasis on the empirical estimation of costs and demand, and analysis of the economic efficiency of prices and the performance of transport enterprises and public agencies. The increasing importance of **externalities** gives still greater importance to transport economics research.

The increased interest in the study of transport economics has brought with it a number of academic journals. Most notable of the specialized publications are the *Journal of Transport Economics and Policy*, which first appeared in 1967, and the *International Journal of Transport Economics*, but there are also journals such as the *Journal of Urban Economics* and *Regional Science and Urban Economics* that also often carry transport material relating to urban and regional transport issues, *Environment and Planning* and *Transportation Research* that, in their various series, frequently contain material on transport economics. In addition, mode-specific journals have emerged, such as *Maritime Economics and Logistics* and the *Journal of Air Transport Management*, that focus on particular transport industries, or those like the *Journal of Transportation Security*, *Transportation Research D, Transport and Environment* and *Transportation E, Transportation and Logistics Review*, that cover particular transport issues with a strong economic input. Nevertheless, compared to many areas of economic study, transport still remains remarkably neglected.

Further reading
Button, K.J. (2010). *Transport Economics* (3rd edn). Cheltenham, UK and Northampton, MA, USA: Edward Elgar.
Due, J.F. (1982). Major recent contributions to the literature of transport economics: a review article. *Quarterly Review of Economics and Business* **22**, 6–28.
Gomez-Ibanez, J.G., W.G. Tye and C. Winston (eds) (1999). *Essays in Transportation Economics and Policy*. Washington, DC: Brookings Institution.
Oum, T.H., J.S. Dodgson, D.A. Hensher, S.A. Morrison, C.A. Nash, K.A. Small and W.G. Waters (1997). *Transport Economics: Selected Readings*. Amsterdam: Harwood Academic Publishers.

William G. Waters II

transport evaluation

There are four major characteristics of transport that distinguish it from most other economic sectors and that bear special attention in the evaluation of a transport project or programme. First, the basic metric of transport is time. Second, **safety** is a pervasive concern in transport. Third, transport often has major externalities, both positive and negative. And fourth, major transport projects often have very long time frames, therefore perhaps meriting the use of a 'social' rather than a market discount rate.

Time is a critical factor in almost any economic enterprise, but in transport time is the critical factor. The essence of most transport service is to minimize **travel time** within certain cost constraints. When transport operates within a market system – as does most freight transport and some passenger transport – transport time can be evaluated by the marketplace. But most passenger transport occurs on public roads lacking a pricing mechanism. If such roads are to be built, operated and maintained so as to optimize user satisfaction, a dollar value must be placed on the time that people spend travelling.

The most widely used such measure is a function of the income of the traveller, typically about one-third to one-half of a traveller's hourly earnings. For simplicity's sake, an average figure for a region, or even a whole country, may be used.

Alternatively, travel time may be evaluated according to the purpose of the trip, such as work, shopping, vacation or social visits. Various studies have found leisure travel time valued more highly than commuting, and commuting valued more highly when the job has variable hours than fixed hours. Travel time value may also vary with the length of the trip. One study found that travel time is valued more highly on long trips than on short trips.

Finally, demographic factors may affect travel time valuation. One study found that retired people place below-average value on travel time, that adults with children have higher travel time values, and that travel time savings when travelling alone are valued more highly than travel time savings when travelling with a companion. Thus, uncertainty abounds in travel time valuation.

Huge numbers of highway accident deaths and injuries every year throughout the industrialized world, combined with widely publicized airline and railway accidents, have focused public attention on transport **safety**. Transport project evaluation, therefore, almost invariably involves some calculation of safety benefits or hazards.

There are two dimensions to such evaluations. First are technical measures. For example, in road construction these include geometry design, intersection design and traffic control design. In vehicle production, technical criteria typically include crashworthiness standards and other elements of vehicle design, such as placement of fuel tanks.

The second dimension of safety evaluation is placing a dollar value on deaths and injuries. Discounted future earnings have been used to evaluate the cost of death (or the value of life), but a newer evaluation method relies on what people pay for life insurance and the premium workers charge for accepting high-risk trades. The cost of serious injury is typically placed at about one-tenth the cost of death.

Placing a dollar value on the loss of life or limb is not universally accepted as a legitimate tool of evaluation. As Kornai puts it: 'A physician would never think of expressing the general state of health of a patient by one single scalar indicator. He knows that good lungs are not a substitute for bad kidneys . . . Why cannot the economist also shift . . . to that way of thinking?'

Sometimes referred to as the 'circulatory systems' of economies, transport systems may create substantial positive **externalities**. The creation of benefits, however, must not be confused with the transfer of benefits. For example, if a new road opens up opportunities for one business, it may simply be transferring wealth away from another business. Examples of true external benefits include the opening up of huge new markets in the nineteenth-century United States by the transcontinental **railroads**, and the creation of 'economies of agglomeration' by roads, such as the Route 28 corridor around Boston.

Negative externalities most typically involve air, water or noise pollution, or disruption of the human or natural environment. While such costs clearly exist, trying to identify their extent has led to a flood of sometimes conflicting studies. On the subject of air pollution, Small tries to make sense of available work with the conclusion:

> several estimates imply that the air pollution costs of motor vehicles are significant compared with the costs of potential emission-control options, but rather small in relation to the implied value that people place on auto travel. If these results hold up to further refinement, they suggest both a direction and a limitation on policy toward air pollution: namely, that further emission control policies are probably warranted, but that air pollution alone cannot justify sweeping measures to reduce motor vehicle traffic.

Major transport projects may have huge benefits or costs reaching far into the future. For example, metropolitan **airports** and **transit** systems may fundamentally improve a region's economic productivity for generations to come. On the negative side, global warming or loss of biodiversity may lead to massive losses for future generations. In assessing such benefits and costs, the market cost of capital may not be an appropriate discount rate, since it is typically keyed to 30-year bonds and would render insignificant any benefits or costs in the distant future. A lower 'social' discount rate may be more appropriate. But the determination of a social discount rate is essentially a political, not an economic, calculation. This presents an evaluator with a difficult dilemma to which there is no obvious solution.

Further reading

Kornai, J. (1979). Appraisal of project appraisal. In M.J. Boskin (eds), *Economics and Human Welfare: Essays in Honor of Tibor Scitovsky*. New York: Academic Press.

Small, K.A. (1999). Project evaluation. In J. Gomez-Ibanez, W.B. Tye and C. Winston (eds), *Essays in Transport Economics and Policy*. Washington, DC: Brookings Institution.

Brien Benson

transport geography

The geography of transportation may be approached from a number of perspectives. First, overcoming natural barriers in the physical environment, for example by tunnels, canals and bridges, may be emphasized in the construction and arrangement of **networks**. Second, the geographer may choose to develop extensive expertise on a region and all its interconnected transportation aspects, including the role of transportation investment in economic growth and development. Gateways, such as **seaports**, and other transportation infrastructure are always seen as a critical element of a region's ability to compete for trade and commerce. Finally, the geographer may take an analytical, map-based view, extracting the nodes, linkages, hinterlands and hierarchies that shape a generic description of many evolving networks. In keeping with this later view, the geographer would attempt to integrate many features of the spatial organization of a system, to describe, explain and ultimately prescribe preferred transportation solutions. In all of these endeavours, one should pay attention to the analysis of economic underpinnings, as well as be cognizant of the institutional and historical context in which the transportation puzzle is being tackled.

Transport geography pays special attention to the stages of development associated with emerging interconnections in a growing economy. Thus, geographers pay special attention to the critical date of 1825 when the Erie Canal provided a route connecting the agricultural bounty of the Midwest to the vast markets on the East Coast through a combination of a canal route and the fortunate alignment of the Hudson River Valley (connecting New York to the interior at Albany, south of the otherwise impassable Adirondacks). Significant events such as the perfection of a steam-powered boat (Fulton in 1808) followed much later by the completion of the subway system in New York, are examples of the kinds of studies that a transport geographer would integrate within the particular place-specific details in getting to know a region's transport. It is fair to say that the steamboat opened the scene for the Industrial Revolution in the nineteenth century, and the subway and mass transit opened the way for the massive urban residential growth in the twentieth century. Transportation geography examines the integration of various social, economic, political and physical engineering processes.

Cronon provides an account of the integration of such processes and the emergence of a place-specific geography, influenced by transport. He weaves the many natural resource endowments, accidents of fate, the entrepreneurial spirit, and the alignment of transhipment routes that came together to make Chicago one of the most remarkable success stories in transport geography.

One exceptionally clear way that geographers and economists interested in **network** theory have aided understanding is through recognition of the fundamental equation governing feasible arbitrage for the movement of goods. Assuming, for simplicity, regional production functions and a set of regional prices, the linkage of a potential supplier (source) to a demand location (sink) cannot work out unless the transport costs required to overcome the spatial separation are smaller than the spread in prices. In various guises, this rule explains many aspects of **international trade**, the regional specialization of production, and the absolute interdependence between economies, and the ability to provide suitable shipment arrangements. Price spread and transport costs provide the preconditions for trade; of course trade and flow cannot as easily take place in the presence of tariffs or other institutional barriers. Versions of the same rule appear in the complementary slackness conditions, dual feasibility and variational inequalities that are at the bedrock of network equilibrium models.

It is in the later area that the transportation geographer moves beyond the basic description of network flows, to the optimization of the least-cost solution for commodity shipment and allocation. The transportation problem of linear programming is exactly designed to make a match between a set of spatially distributed sources (supply locations – factories or warehouses) to deliver desired quantities of goods to sinks (demand locations – cities or destinations) at lowest overall cost. This is typical of the basic calculation that underlies multiplant multimarket distribution systems and can be expanded to cover quite realistic models for multiple commodities, economies of scale and 'less than truck load' movements. In all cases the necessity to overcome the geographical or spatial separation between areas rich in resources endowments (mines, forests, agricultural regions and so on) to the places where these commodities need to be provisioned is the fundamental problem in spatial economics and optimization. Many extensions, such as allowing for endogenous determination of regional prices, stem from the base case.

Geographers have traditionally dealt with the regional trade and interaction patterns that give rise to, and provide the preconditions for, interregional flow. Thus, hubs in **networks**, ports, canals and **intermodal** transhipment faculties are set up to facilitate the movement of goods or people and, increasingly, information.

Air passenger movements hold special interest for geographers. The levels of spatial interaction between places in a system of urban nodes are modelled as systematically related to the spatial separation (distance or cost), the level of common interest between the two places (perhaps using population or business size as surrogates) and the ever-important role of various forms of spatial competition including intervening opportunity, traffic shadow and competing destinations effects. (All of these are explained in the current literature on spatial interactions.)

Geographers have directed large amounts of research to the network planning and interaction that accompanies continental-scale networks. The range of such endeavours is truly panoramic, from early studies in the design for the United States Interstates, to analysis of the European TGV and the provision of oil and gas pipeline networks in difficult geopolitical circumstances.

For trade to be considered, the price spread $V_j - U_i$ must cover the transport cost, or in a sense the transport costs have to be low enough to make it worthwhile to ship the goods. Eventually, however, a situation known as space price equilibrium will drive the price spread down to the level of the intervening transport costs (that leaves enough money for the transport agent to make a living because the return to the initiative taken by the transportation agent is built into the normal rate of profit in C_{ij}). Transportation geographers are fascinated by this basic core inequality which arises in many ways – as the dual feasibility condition in the linear program (LP) ($V_j - U_i$ compared to C_{ij}). In fact there are numerous examples of transportation services being called forth in response to the perceived opportunity to link spatially spread-out sources and sinks (oil tankers, container ports). Opportunities for arbitrage occur when transportation services exist and the entrepreneur links a cheap source to a ready market.

Increasingly, transportation geographers have turned to the study of urban transportation **networks** as a topical arena for their studies. Thus, one expects transportation geography to describe and explain, and ultimately attempt to optimize, urban **accessibility** in transit and auto networks. Geographers have been at the forefront of the linkage of behaviour and psychological choice theory in the analysis of trip **distribution, modal choice** and route choice for the urban networks that are so critical; and often the most congested and contested transport networks are a natural place to explore issues of efficiency and equity.

A recent revival in the area of economic geography has linked economic theory and the spatial processes that are the basis for so much work by geographers. Such research sometimes treats the transport sector as a necessary evil that does no productive work. The economist Von Thunen, who noted that a wagon team would need to consume some of the transported hay as the journey progressed, proposed such an idea long ago. Suffice it to say that this device (and its modern incarnation in Krugman's iceberg model of transport) is simply a way to avoid the separate analysis of a transportation production sector. That view perhaps distracts attention from an important insight, as one can readily see that the **economic**

development impacts of new roads are in their labour-intensive construction, and in the emergence of a new transport freight and service sector. Entrepreneurs, potentially, could begin with a beaten-up old truck, and become behemoths of the trucking industry. Hoteliers at convenient junction points can see the through-flow of passengers expand.

Transport geography studies the development and organization of linkages, nodes and **networks**, and does so either from a place-based specialization or more commonly through intensive analysis of thematic aspects of the movement of goods and people. Thus, it is common to find geographical studies of particular modes and types of commodity shipment.

Further reading
Cronon, W. (1999). *Nature's Metropolis: Chicago and the Great West*. New York: Norton.
Hood, C. (1993). *722 Miles: The Building of the Subways and How They Transformed New York*. New York: Simon & Schuster.
Taaffe, E.J., H. Gauthier and M.E. O'Kelly (1996). *Geography of Transportation* (2nd edn). Upper Saddle River, NJ: Prentice Hall.

Morton E. O'Kelly

transport law

Transport law is concerned primarily with legal requirements placed upon transport by governmental organizations at all levels. Here we focus on the transport laws of the United States by way of illustration. Perhaps the oldest of these laws were the laws governing the manner in which land could be used for moving transport vehicles. The earliest of these date from the 1600s and pertained to roads. The land so used was referred to as a right of way, and such a right was generally granted by a government unit to several individuals to construct a road, which usually meant at the time to cut down trees on the right of way. These laws usually placed a requirement on landowners or parishes located along the road to maintain it. The power of government to 'take' an individual's land for a public use is often referred to as the power of eminent domain.

Railroads of the early 1800s were often granted such eminent domain powers by governmental units so that they could locate a route for their track. There is some ambiguity as to whether the railroad continued to own the land after abandonment, and this depends on the precise wording of the charter under which the railroad was organized.

Roads, canals and railroads were initially built for profit and each of these required its own special Act of the appropriate state legislature in the

United States. By the middle 1800s general laws governing the creation of such transport operations had been enacted by most states. In general the most critical factor in creating a transport operation was a demonstration of financial responsibility.

States passed numerous laws that affected the operation of railroads. There was a tendency for locomotives accidentally to kill livestock and most states enacted fencing laws that required fencing along the right of way. Some states enacted laws that required a set number of individuals to operate the trains. These full-crew or 'featherbedding' laws were usually enacted by labour-friendly state legislatures if the railroads refused to agree to such concessions during labour negotiations (Ely, 2001). Such laws often required a fireman to fuel the locomotive furnace; this requirement continued in many cases even after the locomotives no longer used wood or coal as fuel.

Although roads became public in most cases (some toll roads continued) and canals began to fail due to a loss of traffic, railroads were to remain private operations in the United States. In most cases communities had only one railroad serving them, and this led to certain monopolistic practices with regard to providing service and the prices charged. This led to the federal enactment of the Interstate Commerce Act in 1887, the first piece of economic regulatory law enacted in the United States. In general this law governed entry, exit (abandonment) and pricing in the railroad industry for nearly a century. The title 'interstate commerce' is more meaningful than the names given to many other pieces of legislation in that it recognizes the power of the federal government to oversee interstate commerce. This meant that local commerce, commerce within a state, could be governed by state law, and as a result short-line railroads operating within a single state answer to that state and not to the federal government.

Economic regulatory laws were passed during the twentieth century governing all modes of transport involved in interstate commerce. In an attempt to allow the transport modes to be more competitive, these laws were also repealed during the last quarter of that century: the Airline Deregulation Act of 1978, the Staggers Act of 1980 which deregulated the railroads, and the Motor Carrier Deregulation Act of 1982 were among the most significant of these.

Another major area of transport law governs the **safety** of vehicles and their operation. This area includes operations at grade-crossings, operator testing, hours of service provisions and the like. This body of law has not been tampered with except to make it more inclusive to keep up with technological change in the transport industries.

There are several other areas of the law that are not explicitly transport-based, but they do have significant impacts on the sector. First, there are a series of antitrust laws. These basically prevent transport carriers from getting together to set rates on traffic. These laws also come into play when two railroads, airlines or motor carrier companies decide to merge into a single operation. This may lead to regional monopolies, and as a result these proposals are reviewed for their antitrust implications. Second, there are numerous administrative laws. These have to do with employee health and safety, environmental protection, transporting of **hazardous materials** and similar statutes. Third, there are insolvency and bankruptcy laws, which often are handled quite differently in the transport case. For example, railroads are often of such major importance that they are required to continue operating even after they have gone into bankruptcy. This was the case with the Penn Central Railroad and seven other railroads in the Midwest and Northeast that were reorganized into the Consolidated Rail Corporation (Conrail) under provisions of the Regional Rail Reorganization Act of 1973 and the Rail Revitalization and Regulatory Reform Act of 1976.

Another body of state and federal law that has fluctuated over the years is that concerned with financial aid to the railroads. Major land grant laws at the federal level in the United States of the 1860s were intended to provide a revenue source for the construction of western railroads. Decades earlier many states passed internal improvement acts to provide state funds for the construction of canals, roads and railroads. More recently, rail freight lines that were found to be economically unviable were offered operating **subsidies** with federal and state programmes. Several states have low-interest loan programmes for railroads, and most states that have Amtrak rail passenger service do so under subsidy.

Another body of law that has not seen as much use in the United States as it has elsewhere is **privatization** laws. Throughout the world, national governments have found that they are not well equipped to operate transport modes. In many cases these operations have excess employees and they are a drain on the national funds. Each situation is rather unique, but the national government usually allows firms to bid on providing the service once offered by the government. In some cases the nation may retain control of some aspect of this operation. In the case of British Rail, there are now more than 25 operators providing service over the former **network**; the government retains ownership of the physical plant (that is, the tracks, trestles and the like).

There are suggestions that a new body of law concerned with re-regulation may appear in the future. This is due in part to the excessive consolidations that occurred after **deregulation** in the United States. Airline competition in particular may require the creation of partial regional monopolies if airlines are to be sustainable. There is also some belief that the privatized rail system in the United Kingdom is costing more than the previous government-operated system, and this may lead to some re-regulation in that part of the world.

Further reading

Black, W.R. (1986). *Railroads for Rent: The Local Rail Service Assistance Act.* Bloomington, IN: Indiana University Press.

Ely, Jr., J.W. (2001). *Railroads and American Law.* Lawrence, KS: University of Kansas Press.

Gunadolo, J. (1983). *Transportation Law* (4th edn). Dubuque, IA: William. C. Brown Company Publishers.

William Black

transport network design

Transport network design (TND) is a form of normative analysis that identifies an optimal, or at least an improved network configuration; that is, in network design one determines the arcs, nodes and/or the characteristics of arcs and nodes that make a network optimal or at least improved. Optimality or improvement is determined relative to a chosen performance criterion, such as **congestion** costs or environmental and sustainability objectives, and also requires any imposed constraints to be satisfied. TND plays an important role in transport since it allows for reorganizing current supply configuration to utilize existing resources efficiently. Transport network design problems can occur at strategic, tactical and operational levels. At the strategic, long-term level the problems involve the design of the underlying physical network. Typical questions of interest include:

- Where should facilities be located?
- What resources should be acquired?
- What type of services should be offered?

At the tactical, medium-term level one does not consider day-to-day operations, but aggregate information over time. From this data one tries to find an efficient and rational allocation of existing resources. Network design problems at this level ask questions like:

- Which lanes to close or open during evacuations?
- Where should empty vehicles be positioned in transit systems?

Network design problems are also present at the operational level (short term). A typical example is the operation of series of signalized intersections in a downtown area. The signal timings should be set so that the total travel time of all vehicles in the system should be minimized. The traffic between any two points should also be routed as cost-efficiently as possible, at the same time ensuring that the heterogeneity of drivers is considered. Additional objectives such as minimizing the maximum number of stops can also be considered. In short, the network design problem is a core problem that allows us to solve planning, design and operational transport problems such as lane widening and addition, signal settings, **congestion** pricing and lane reversal in evacuation problems. Solving these problems requires solving some variation of the TND problem.

The TND problem is especially relevant when travellers are autonomous agents that compete non-cooperatively on transport networks in the presence of congestion (**queuing**). It is necessary to distinguish clearly between descriptive modelling of that competition and normative modelling to determine optimal network design. The Braess Paradox clearly demonstrates that, if this distinction is ignored, actions that decrease congestion locally may actually result in a global congestion increase. Avoiding the Braess Paradox requires that an appropriate network design model be employed that includes constraints describing the behaviour of autonomous agents, because such constraints typically describe a Nash equilibrium of a non-cooperative game. The resulting model is bi-level in nature and takes the form of a Stackelberg leader–follower game or a so-called mathematical program with equilibrium constraints (MPEC). While the Braess Paradox might be a mathematical artefact, it was indeed observed in Stuttgart, Germany after investments into the road network in 1969: the traffic situation did not improve until a section of newly built road was closed for traffic again.

Typically, the TND problem is posed in three forms: (1) a discrete form dealing with the addition of new roadway segments, a road closure scheme, the provision of a new public transport service such as a new set of links, and the construction of a new road and rail links; (2) a continuous form dealing with the optimal capacity increases of existing roadway segments; and finally (3) a discrete or continuous form involving both addition of new roadways and widening existing roadways. These are typically non-linear mathematical programs with resource, flow conservation and non-negativity constraints. The models may or may not employ integer variables, depending on whether it is a discrete version of the problem or a continuous TND. The structure of these problems is typically represented as an MPEC. Solving the TND problem is complex since it involves solving the bi-level problem that is shown to be a linear program hard problem. However, with the research since the late 1970s, there are now excellent static network design models available for transport network design. Early attempts to solve the TND problem involved developing linear approximations to the travel time and construction cost functions of the upper-level problem and solving using a bi-level linear programming heuristic. Others have developed a heuristic method, called equilibrium decomposed optimization, which finds locally optimal solutions with less computational effort.

Other approaches to solve this complex problem are the use of traditional local search methods, such as branch-and-bound. Unfortunately sequential branch-and-bound procedures cannot solve larger-dimension problems. These local search methods were applied to particular problem classes, and did not give results beyond the first local optimum. Moreover, these generally require significant computational times. Due to these difficulties many have applied meta-heuristic and other approximation techniques, such as tabu search, genetic algorithms, and simulated annealing, to solve the static TND problems. Using meta-heuristic approaches, one can solve multi-objective TND problems that are formulated and solved to include other **externalities** in addition to **congestion** costs.

Recently, the research in TND is burgeoning in multidisciplinary avenues. There are versions of dynamic network design models which account for the temporal variation of traffic flow – for instance the dynamic disequilibrium network design problem was used in a variety of applications, and the dynamic transport network design based on a linear programming approach with an embedded traffic cell transmission model are perceived to advance the notion of dynamic traffic flows. In addition to single-level network design models, there are a handful of multilayer, coupled infrastructure models that deal with design to varying degrees.

Further reading
Ben-Ayed, O., D.E. Boyce and C.E. Blair (1988). A general bilevel programming formulation of the network design problem. *Transportation Research B* **22**, 311–18.
Braess, D. (1968). Über ein Paradoxon aus der Verkehrsplanung. *Unternehmensforschung* **12**, 258–68.

Satish Ukkusuri and *Terry L. Friesz*

transport planning history

Transport planning is closely tied to **economic development**, and the environmental and social aspirations of a society. Thus, the history of transport planning has been one of reflecting on the relative importance of these concerns in transport investment decision-making.

Many examples in history illustrate the thought that has been given to the role of transport infrastructure in meeting some need; for example, the ancient Roman road **network**, the canals of the Middle Ages, and the street grids of many eighteenth-century North American colonial cities. However, transport planning as part of professional practice first started in the early 1900s with the comprehensive urban planning movement in both Europe and North America. Largely in response to the urban health and socio-economic consequences of the Industrial Revolution, many city officials and planners developed new concepts of urban development that often separated land uses and in some cases created satellite cities. Both road and **transit** facilities and services were instrumental in connecting these new urban sites to the central city, and became part of the formal comprehensive urban planning process.

Transport planning became a major field of the transport engineering and planning professions after the Second World War. With significant growth in population in the 1950s and 1960s, and with much of this growth resulting in even more significant increases in automobile use, many metropolitan areas began developing regional transport plans that detailed the transport system investments that would be necessary over a 25–30-year time horizon to handle expected growth in travel demand. This formative era of formal transport planning had several defining character-istics that are still found today in many transport planning efforts.

Regional transport studies required the collection of large amounts of data on travellers and on system performance. This early era of transport planning developed the survey methods and traffic counting techniques that provided input to the analysis process. Because of the nature of the technical capabilities at this time – computers were primitive – much of the data analysis was aggregated into travel flows rather than predicting what individual travellers would likely do when facing different travel options.

A formal modelling procedure was developed to predict future travel flows. Although often defined in slightly different ways, this modelling procedure generally consisted of four major steps, predicting: how many trips would be produced; where these trips would go; what mode of travel would be used; and what path through the transport **network** would be taken.

The primary focus of the planning process was on developing trans-port strategies for improving the performance of the transport system. Even though it was recognized that land use and urban design charac-teristics influenced when and where people travelled, land use strategies themselves as a means of influencing transport demand were generally not considered.

The planning time horizon for transport plans was usually 20–25 years. Very little attention was paid to shorter-term issues or how to manage better the operations of the existing transport system.

In many cases, the models used to prepare transport plans were based on data and evidence relating to travel behaviour from the previous decades, that in the 1950s and 1960s indicated significant automobile use and thus the need for more highways. This led to transport plans, especially in the United States, that were heavily focused on highway construction.

The early transport planning process was dominated by technical experts, individuals who understood the modelling applications and presumably the 'best' solutions to the transport problems facing a community. However, as some of these solutions ran into community opposition in the late 1960s, laws and regulations were passed that provided opportunities for more citizen input into the transport planning process.

Beginning in the 1960s, doubts were being raised in some metropolitan areas and countries about the effectiveness of a transport investment strategy heavily reliant on providing more highway capacity. A 1963 report prepared for the United Kingdom Department of Transport, *Traffic in Towns*, was a highly influential critique of this continued focus on highway expansion. It was one of the first reports to suggest that increasing highway capacity actually made **congestion** worse by attracting additional trips, and that there were environmental impacts associated with increasing traffic volumes. By the late 1960s, several cities in the United States were facing highway revolts in which the traditional transport planning process was being questioned as to highway bias and the lack of transparency in the process itself. Laws were passed that required the transport planning process to be multimodal considering more than just one mode of travel and for there to be ample opportunities for the public to participate in the process.

Increasing environmental concerns in the 1960s and 1970s also resulted in laws and regulations aimed at avoiding or reducing the impact of the built environment on the natural environment. The disruptive effects of building transport facilities and the negative impacts of their use such as motor vehicle pollutant emissions led to requirements on the transport planning process to consider strategies and actions that would alleviate such negative impacts. Thus, in the 1970s and beyond, the transport planning process began to consider a range of actions that could result in reduced **environmental** impacts. Beginning in the 1990s, and especially in Europe, the concern for the environment as well as for community and social development resulted in many planning efforts placing transport planning within a broader context of **sustainable** development. Strategies considered as part of the transport planning process included encouraging the use of modes of travel other than the automobile; promoting travel demand management strategies that would influence the timing and travel paths of trips; considering the use of road pricing as a means of changing travel behaviour; and more closely examining the impact of land use and urban design decisions on travel patterns.

One of the most important influences on transport planning since the 1990s has occurred in the technical capability provided through the use of ever more powerful and higher-speed computers. The microcomputer provided transport planners and engineers with an ability to analyse more complex transport system phenomena and travel behaviour. New travel **demand models** were developed based on individual trip-making behaviour; simulation models examined complicated travel flows on transport **networks**; and more advanced models were applied to assess the environmental consequences of different transport investment strategies. The analysis capability available in most of the current transport planning efforts allows transport planners, and indeed anyone familiar with the analysis software, to evaluate a range of alternatives for a particular transport problem.

Another trend that has characterized transport planning since the late 1990s has been an increasing concern for improved transport system management. With limited financial resources, and in many cases physical constraints in adding new transport facilities, transport planning has begun to look seriously at how the existing transport system can be managed more effectively. This has included the consideration of strategies to reduce or manage travel demand, for example pricing; applications of advanced technologies that provide better information to system users on the best path through a network; and the use of incident response strategies to remove disabled vehicles and thus reduce the amount of disruption to the rest of the network.

Transport planning today continues the trend of examining transport's role in the context of much broader socio-economic issues. For example, although many contemporary transport plans focus on strategies and projects aimed at improving transport system performance, some also give considerable attention to transport's role in achieving sustainable development goals, reducing the environmental footprint of the transport sector, and enhancing **economic development** opportunities in a community. It seems likely that the transport planning process of the next few decades will be dealing with a large number of similar issues, including:

- Targeting transport investment in a way that promotes a comprehensive urban strategy for providing **mobility** and **accessibility**, including actions that can be undertaken in land use and urban design to enhance transport system performance.

- Linking transport investment to broader sustainable development goals.
- Applying new technologies to the transport infrastructure and the use of in-vehicle navigational and communications technologies for better managing system operations.
- Examining the role of the transport sector's contribution to greenhouse gas emissions and the types of strategies that should be considered in reducing this impact.
- Providing a more comprehensive consideration of goods and freight movement in the context of transport system performance (especially for metropolitan areas serving as gateways for global trade flows).
- Considering different types of funding strategies for providing transport infrastructure, including innovative combinations of both public and private investment funds.

Further reading
Banister, D. (1994). *Transport Planning in the UK, USA and Europe*. London: E&FH Spon.
Hall, P. (1998). *Cities in Civilization*. New York: Pantheon.
United Kingdom Ministry of Transport (1963). *Traffic in Towns*. London: HMSO.

Michael D. Meyer

transport security

One of the main threats to transport, especially in recent years, is terrorist attacks. The threat extends to all modes of transport, here we focus on the American aviation sector, systems vary elsewhere. Security policy has a fairly long history. In 1976, the International Civil Aviation Organization (ICAO), for Safeguarding Civil Aviation against Acts of Unlawful Interference, adopted its Annex 17 requirements on aviation security. Aviation security will include an observative and executive measurement to prevent criminal activity onboard aircrafts. Criminal activity includes acts such as hijacking, damaging or destroying aircraft, airports and properties, and assault on passengers and aviation employees.

From 2001, a series of major global and economic events have affected the air transportation industry. During this period, the industry has endured a recession as a direct result of the 11 September terror attacks. The events of 11 September curtailed airline travel in various ways. First, they reduced the demand for air travel as a result of the increased concerns about security. Second, they reduced air travel by exacerbating the mild recession that began in March 2001. Third, the cost of travel was increased because of the necessity of arriving earlier for departures, the increased frequency of delays resulting from security breaches, new security surcharges and the cost of making aircraft and aviation infrastructure more secure. The result was substantially less air travel for both work and leisure purposes.

Historically, aviation security prior to 11 September had been provided by three main partners: airlines, airports and the United States Federal Aviation Administration (FAA) in the United States. Generally, providing security has been the responsibility of air carriers and airports. Government, via the FAA, performed primarily a regulatory role and a background role in terms of national security. The airlines were responsible for passenger and baggage screening, both carry-on and checked. The usual practice was for airlines to contract with private companies which provided trained screeners at security checkpoints. The airlines were also responsible for security from the screening checkpoints to the aircraft. Airports were responsible for law enforcement and general security in the airport vicinity, including exterior areas, **parking** areas, the airport perimeter and interior areas up to the security checkpoints. Airports also hired law enforcement officers for the security checkpoints. The FAA was responsible for providing threat information; establishing security policies, regulations, and protocols; conducting security audits of airlines and airports; supporting research and development of security technology; and overseeing the installation of security equipment and devices in airports.

Since the 11 September attacks, new regulations involving airlines, airports and air traffic control have escalated to reduce the probability of similar events occurring again, and changes in airline and airport security were immediately applied. Overreaction and misunderstanding inevitably led to wasted efforts initially, and were sometimes counterproductive for the aviation sector. As a result, large amounts of money were used in a suboptimal way on misguided programmes, for example, to distinguish regular travellers from suspected terrorists.

Further reading
Gorman, S.P. (2005). *Networks, Security, and Complexity: The Role of Public Policy in Critical Infrastructure Protection*. Cheltenham, UK and Northampton, MA, USA: Edward Elgar.

Thierry Vanelslander

transport statistics

In its broadest sense, the discipline of stochastic analysis lies at the intersection of transport and statistics. As such, anything to do with transport as well as data or probability is part of transport statistics. According to this definition, much of the study of transport falls under the purview of transport statistics. Particular attention is given to the collection and dissemination of transport data and the use of data to inform policy in the United States. Other countries use similar general procedures but they do differ in detail.

Transport data can be collected via **surveys**, whether responses are voluntary, as in the case of household travel surveys, or mandatory, as in the case of data on aviation and **trucking** collected by the United States Bureau of Transport Statistics (BTS) of the United States Department of Transport (USDOT).

Data can also be administrative data, which are based on information collected for other purposes, like those on vehicle registration or those on traffic fatalities which are based on police reports. Sometimes additional items, mainly of statistical value, are inserted into administrative data-gathering instruments.

Data can be part survey and part administrative. For example companies, states or other entities could be surveyed to obtain their administrative data.

Automated – mainly electronic – methods also exist for transport data collection. Older examples include turnstile and fare data for transit and under-pavement loop detector data to measure highway **congestion**. In recent years, data from automated toll collection have become available. Probes, or devices that measure location via **geographical information systems** (GIS), can be used to collect a wide variety of information, including origin–destination, route choice and travel or transit times for both passenger travel and freight. Such devices are in use for equipment location and to measure real-time congestion, but have somewhat unexplored potential in a wide variety of other data-gathering contexts.

Transport data collection faces the usual challenges of all data collection efforts. However, it also has some unique challenges. Transport is spatial and, complicating matters further, it involves several points in space for the same unit of information – origin, destination, route, transfer points. Depiction of this is difficult even using GIS tools.

Another consequence of the spatial nature of transport data has to do with confidentiality or disclosure. Disclosing information in which an individual's or business's information can be identified is often prohibited by law and, at any rate, is bad practice since it makes respondent cooperation more difficult. Consider the collection of origin–destination data for a metropolitan area. Typically the vast majority of origin–destination pairs have no observations and several have just one or two. If somehow one were able to find out who was in the sample, in many cases one would find out where the respondent went, by what mode, and so on. This problem can be alleviated by making origin and destination zones bigger. But then the value of the data declines, since transport solutions are typically location-specific. No completely satisfactory solution to this problem has yet been found.

The BTS – sometimes jointly with United States Census Bureau – collects data on travel and freight movements, as well as detailed data on the aviation and trucking industries, including the particularly well-known data on airline delay and its causes. The Census Bureau collects commuting data through its household survey (The American Community Survey). It also obtains origins and destinations of workers from employment data. The United States National Highway Traffic Safety Administration and other administrations within the USDOT collect a wide range of data including those on accidents and fatalities for each mode, detailed data on transit agencies, and on the condition and use of highways. Individual states and metropolitan areas also collect a variety of data including detailed origin–destination data. Private companies also collect a vast amount of data but most are not made public. However, many trade associations, like the Association of American Railroads, disseminate transport data.

Agencies collecting transport data, which are not principally data-collecting entities, often do so for their own purposes and frequently do not have the budget for widespread dissemination. Since data do not get disseminated, the quality, although often adequate for the specific needs of the agency, is often not high for other applications.

One of the mandates of the BTS is to disseminate data and it set up a data delivery system, TranStats, explicitly for the purpose. International data on transport are available from the International Road Federation and other mode-specific organizations; private sources, such as the *Journal of Commerce*; the United Nations and the World Bank; Eurostat; national statistical agencies and other sources.

Transport data has a role to play in determining if things are going as expected, identifying unexpected occurrences and helping formulate policies that address problems. Much of the support for policy formulation is done through one-time analyses, while determining how things are going is typically done through statistics that are issued repetitively. How things are going might also be assessed by comparing performances of different entities (for example transit agencies or regions) through benchmarking. An example would be to compare like transit agencies using data in the National Transit Database maintained by the United States Federal Transit Administration (USFTA).

An example of a one-time analysis is analysis conducted to determine what the United States federal government needed to compensate the airline industry for losses involved with the grounding of airplanes following the terrorist attacks on the World Trade Center in New York. Analysis had to be produced quickly with no prior warning that such analysis would be needed. This required the right data to be available, and a good understanding of the industry on the part of those involved.

The example illustrates some of the issues involved in the one-time use of transport statistics in informing policy. Data needs appear suddenly, but data collection efforts can take a long time. Thus, data collection agencies need to be aware of potential needs while improving the speed of data collection. Statistics that are issued repetitively might be broadly classified into three classes. One class consists of descriptive statistics – often displayed as tables that are based on a recently collected data set and issued shortly after the data are gathered and processed.

Another class of repetitively issued statistics consists of compilations of tables and state of transport reports issued at regular intervals but not linked specifically to a data collection effort. Often the tables or other statistics are based on several data sets. Examples include the *Transport Statistics Annual Report* and *National Transport Statistics*.

A third class consists of time series data. Such data are those that are presented explicitly to illustrate changes over time. The classes of statistics mentioned above, because they too are available over time, also constitute time series but are not always displayed or treated as time series.

Several time series are associated with the Government Performance Results Act. Under this Act, a number of performance measures were created. Statistics on these measures presented as a time series enables one to see if things are getting better or worse and if an intervention is needed. These statistics are presented to the United States Congress along with annual budget requests.

The BTS also publishes a number of other transport indicators such as the Transport Services Index (TSI) and the Air Travel Price Index (ATPI). Other government agencies, industry associations and universities also disseminate transport indicators. An indicator on cost of traffic **congestion** is put out by the Texas Transport Institute.

Since transport is an economic activity, useful transport-related indicators are provided by several economic and other data agencies within the United States government, including the Bureau of Labor Statistics, Bureau of Economic Analysis, Bureau of the Census and the Energy Information Administration.

Further reading
United States Department of Transport, Research and Innovative Technology
    Administration, Bureau of Transport Statistics (annual). *Transport Statistics
    Annual Report*. Washington, DC: BTS.
United States Department of Transport, Research and Innovative Technology
    Administration, Bureau of Transport Statistics (annual). *National Transport
    Statistics*. Washington, DC: BTS.

Ashish Sen

Transportation Research Board

The Transportation Research Board (TRB) is a private organization
dedicated to promoting innovation and progress in transportation through
research. Its formal mission is: 'to provide leadership in transportation
innovation and progress through research and information exchange, conducted within a setting that is objective, interdisciplinary, and multimodal'. It is one of six major program units of the National Research Council,
which is the administrative body of the United States National Academy
of Sciences (NAS), National Academy of Engineering (NAE) and Institute
of Medicine (IOM), which are together called the National Academies.

The TRB is respected for the independence of its policy analysis and
advice, for the extent and quality of its research and exchange activities, as
a publisher and as a research manager. One key role has been to identify
critical issues facing the industry, to provide focus for the TRB's activities
and the broader transportation industry. Its most recent list includes: **congestion**, emergencies, **energy** and environment, equity, finance, human and
intellectual capital, infrastructure, institutions and **safety**. This list of issues
reflects the broad range of activities that fall within the TRB's scope.

In addition to these critical issues for the transportation sector, the TRB
as an organization also faces both threats and opportunities. Maintaining
funding in an environment of increasingly scarce resources from its traditional government sponsors is a key challenge. So, too, is maintaining its
relevance as an organization in an environment of proliferating special-
purpose organizations and advocacy groups that are more focused on
single issues. The TRB also has the opportunity to add value in a 'complex,
transitional era in transportation', taking advantage of new information
technologies to support its mission.

As an organization, TRB activities fall into four major areas. In the area
of fostering information exchange, the TRB supports more than 200 stand-
ing committees and task forces that focus on specific aspects of the transportation sector. It also organizes an annual meeting in Washington, DC,

in January with approximately 10000 participants from around the world. The TRB also sponsors other conferences and workshops, electronic **networks**, and a program of field visits to state departments of transportation, academic and research institutions, and other transportation-related agencies and organizations.

The TRB also manages a program of research sponsored by government and private agencies. The oldest of these programs is the National Cooperative Highway Research Program (NCHRP), established in 1962 to manage research related to the planning, design, construction and maintenance of highways. The NCHRP is sponsored by the state highway and transportation departments, and conducts in excess of $30 million in research per year. The Transit Cooperative Research Program (TCRP), established in 1992, manages approximately $8 million per year in research sponsored by the United States Federal Transit Administration. Additional cooperative research programs focus on airports, freight, **hazardous materials**, and commercial truck and bus safety.

In addition to these ongoing cooperative research programs, the TRB also manages the Strategic Highway Research Program 2 (SHRP 2), a seven-year program (2006–13) of approximately $150 million focused specifically on highway safety, renewal, reliability and capacity. SHRP 2 is a follow-on program to an earlier Strategic Highway Research Program in the 1990s, which the TRB also managed.

The TRB's third major activity is providing policy analysis and advice to the United States government, states and other organizations. Since 1982, the TRB has conducted more than 100 studies on topics requiring expert analysis and advice, such as counterterrorism, **truck** size and weight regulation, airport capacity, transit use, **high-speed rail**, airline **deregulation**, dredging, environmental policy, school transportation safety and automotive **safety**. An independent committee of experts conducts each study, with staff support provided by the TRB. A key feature of these committees is their independence. The TRB selects the committees to include an appropriate balance of expertise and perspective. Preservation of the independence of these committees, and their ability to meet in closed session to develop findings and recommendations, has at times excited considerable controversy as advocates for particular perspectives or interests have sought to influence committee membership and deliberations.

TRB's fourth major area of activity is as a publisher of reports and periodicals. TRB publishes approximately 200 items per year, including the *Transportation Research Record*, conference proceedings, reports from the cooperative research programs and circulars. These publications are increasingly available electronically.

The TRB was founded in the 1920s as the National Advisory Board on Highway Research, renamed as the Highway Research Board in 1925. In 1974, it became the Transportation Research Board, reflecting its expanding scope to transit and other modes.

The TRB is governed by an Executive Committee appointed by the Director of the National Research Council. Its full-time staff of approximately 140 is led by an Executive Director. Its annual budget in 2007 was approximately $75 million.

Further reading
www.trb.org.

Jonathan L. Gifford

travel behaviour modelling

Travel behaviour modelling involves understanding how and why people make choices regarding their travel plans. This includes how much they travel, for what purposes, where to, at what times and by which mode. Another aspect asks how people make such decisions for the transport of commodities. As a field, travel behaviour deals with theoretical constructs, behavioural assumptions and methodologies for the analysis, representation and inference of the way travellers behave and the interrelationships of this behaviour with their activities, land use and the transportation system. The understanding of these various aspects requires an interdisciplinary inquiry, engaging geography, engineering, statistics, urban and regional studies, economics, psychology and sociology. The analysis of travel behaviour is important for estimating various aspects of travel demand.

While the basic travel technology, the car, has changed relatively slowly, many other factors have induced significant changes in travel behaviour. In modern life there is more leisure time, and more engagement in non-work out-of-home activities. Work hours have become more flexible and more women are in the labour market. Information and communication technologies provide travellers with better information and enable them to substitute travel for all purposes. Work trips are no longer dominant, as there are more trips for shopping, social and leisure purposes. Residential, commercial and workplaces are being decentralized. The world's population is growing and people are travelling more, use faster modes and travel longer distances compared to a few decades ago. The number of trips has increased, trip chaining is more frequent, and traffic peaks are often smoother.

These changes have made household travel patterns more complicated by significantly increasing the number of alternative activity and travel patterns households can choose from. The relaxation of some constraints, such as the need to commute at fixed hours, provides more degrees of freedom and more alternatives, thus making the analysis of travel behaviour more complicated. At the same time, these changes significantly increase **congestion** and air pollution from motor vehicles, raising as a result the need to develop new objectives of policy and planning toward **sustainable transport**.

The growing complexity in travel patterns and the need to estimate changes in travel behaviour in response to new policies, in addition to new infrastructure and services, calls for a better understanding of travel behaviour. This includes issues such as: How is travel behaviour affected by new information and communication technologies? How does land use and growth management affect travel behaviour, and how do travellers respond to auto restraint policies such as congestion pricing and **parking** regulations? Understanding such effects is essential for a better design of new policies. In this regard travel behaviour analysis lies at the core of procedures for the analysis and evaluation of transportation-related measures aimed at improving urban **mobility**, environmental quality and a wide variety of social objectives.

Historically, the field has changed over time, parallel to changes in transportation systems, planning goals and travel behaviour. In the 1960s the development of the American interstate highway system has led to the development of an operational macro-level system of models providing planners and engineers with travel demand forecasting tools. This system, also known as the four-step process, relies on statistical tools and enables the forecast of various travel behaviour elements in an aggregate manner, given a land use structure and socio-economic characteristics of the population. In the late 1960s additional emphasis was given to economic approaches motivated by the need to understand travel behaviour better and to derive a value of behavioural travel time saving for **benefit–cost analysis**.

In the 1970s the economic theory of the allocation and valuation of time developed toward an econometric approach providing a framework for modelling travel behaviour. This approach was based on random utility modelling (RUM). Thereafter a growing interest and the need to understand better the motives for travel behaviour prompted the involvement of psychology among other social sciences. These studies question whether the RUM paradigm can accurately represent the set of decisions travellers use. They develop the rules-based paradigm as an alternative method. In both approaches there is a move towards an activity-based framework where there is an effort to understand travel behaviour as derived from activity participation and time use behaviour. Quality data on travel behaviour, collected by various types of travel **surveys**, is an essential element to all these efforts. Recently there are attempts to use panel data to understand better the change in travel behaviour over time.

Further reading
Garling, T., L. Thomas and W. Kerstin (1998). Theoretical foundation of travel choice modelling. In T. Garling, L. Thomas and W. Kerstin (eds), *Theoretical Foundation of Travel Choice Modeling*. Oxford: Elsevier.

Yoram Shiftan

travel surveys

Surveys are one of the principal sources of transport data. As such, they often constitute the critical starting point of any transport planning process, since the availability of data sets of good quality and which correspond to the objective is a prerequisite to carry out any analysis successfully. Unlike most subsequent activities, shortcomings and errors in this initial phase of a transport study can seldom be corrected at a later stage. Beyond this, travel surveys are frequently costly and methodologically problematical. These two elements can be explained by the considerable effort going into improving the cost–quality ratio of data production. Travel surveys therefore represent a well-established research field, with a series of scholarly conferences being organized roughly every three years by the International Steering Committee for Travel Survey Conferences (ISCTSC), a very active **Transportation Research Board** Committee in the United States, and several ongoing international and national research projects carried out by different research teams.

There are a variety of data collection procedures in the transport sector, that vary according to the kind of **mobility** that is targeted (persons versus goods; urban versus long distance), the study object and therefore the kind of data that the researcher wants to collect (actual mobility behaviour versus preferences or attitudes; trips versus traffic flows). Methods used to implement surveys also vary. The focus is mainly on personal surveys and exclusively on surveys targeting mobility behaviour. Preferences and attitudes are usually investigated through different instruments, often derived from the marketing approaches; for example **stated preference** methods or focus groups and other qualitative data collection techniques. On the other hand, traffic flows do not generally require a travel survey but are monitored through specific devices such as magnetic loops or traffic counters.

Personal trip analysis and forecasting represent a very significant effort both in time and in monetary terms in many transport studies. It is anticipated, however, that contemporary analytical techniques often imply working on mixed data sets, so that hybrid surveys are more and more commonplace, investigating for example both revealed and stated preferences.

Travel surveys can be implemented through a variety of methods. Concerning the sampling strategy, the use of census surveys, in which all the persons are interviewed, is confined to particular cases where this is feasible and necessary: for example, when designing mobility management services inside a firm, where the analyst needs to know the actual travel patterns of all the workers. However in transport planning the universe is normally the population of a city, region or even nation. To increase the precision of data, the sample is generally stratified on household location and, when available, on socio-economic characteristics like car ownership or household size. Strict respect for the sampling method is a condition for applying inference methods in order to expand the collected data to the whole population. The possible sizes of the study area implies potentially wide variations in the scale of the survey, typically ranging from urban to national.

Concerning the statistical unit to consider, observations can be referred to households, persons or private motorized vehicles, usually cars. Household surveys are preferred for more general surveys, since they can control for interactions among household members and their influence on **mobility** behaviours, essentially due to the fact of sharing the use of cars. Either all or a part of the members of the sampled households can be actually interviewed. Car ownership and car use surveys provide complementary information useful in understanding the patterns of consumption of such goods and their impact on the economy or the environment. They are sometimes coupled with household surveys.

Traditionally, transport surveys are cross-sectional, that is, implemented at a given time point. Researchers have lately debated on the benefits of continuous surveys, where the same surveying activity is regularly implemented, typically on a yearly basis, each time drawing a new sample. If the same sample is kept across different survey waves or if it is only partially renewed, then a panel is obtained. Cross-section surveys are most often realized with long interval between two surveys (in general from five to more than ten years). Therefore they do not allow the monitoring of behavioural evolutions, and imply the use of old data, especially when the interval between two surveys is high. On the other hand, continuous surveys allow the production of data which is always up to date, and the monitoring of the evolution. But special attention needs to be paid to the consolidation of data through several years as sample size is generally too low on a yearly basis. Furthermore, it has been observed that in some cases data quality reduces over time. A specific strategy needs to be developed in order to motivate the interviewer and survey team and guarantee the quality of continuous survey data. Panel surveys also allow the monitoring of behavioural evolution, but at the individual level. Their main limitations are related to the refreshment of the sample survey.

Travel surveys can be completed in different places. Home interviews give the possibility to gather more complete data, for example through the use of travel diaries that are left to the interviewee to record trips for longer time periods, or geographical positioning devices that survey respondents can carry with them to improve data precision. However home interviews are not useful to investigate trips in the study area that are made by people not living in it. Therefore, they can be complemented by roadside surveys, where a subset of car drivers crossing a cordon bordering the study area or a screen-line inside it are briefly interviewed; and by transit surveys, where passengers are interviewed while travelling or near transit facilities such as bus stops or stations.

Surveying modes can also be different. In face-to-face surveys the interviewer is with the respondent during the interview. In **telephone surveys**, contact is made by telephone and the interview is conducted over the telephone. In postal surveys the respondent receives the questionnaire by post; he or she then fills in the questionnaire and returns it, again by post. Lastly, in web-based surveys the questionnaire can be sent by e-mail, and the respondent returns it in the same way. A more efficient possibility is that the questionnaire is implemented on a web page that can be visited and filled in by the respondent. Postal and web-based surveys are self-administered, implying lower costs but likely self-selection biases in the sample. Furthermore, a lower trip declaration is often observed. In practice, several of the above modes may be used in the same data collection effort. But the combining of data needs careful analysis.

Surveys are more and more often performed with computers in order to enter data in real time. These surveys used software called CAPI, CATI and CAWI (computer-assisted personal, telephone or web interviews, respectively). The use of computers has clear advantages, such as the automatic building of the data set and the possibility of performing instant consistency checks of the responses, or geographically referencing trip origins and destinations through geocoding.

The actual structure of **mobility** surveys that concentrate on personal travel behaviour is now fairly well established. The survey generally begins with the collection of socio-economic characteristics on the household, and on the individual, then all the trips and activities are collected with their characteristics. Sometimes attitudinal data are then collected, generally only for a subsample. More personal data like income are collected at the end of the survey. Experience indicates that an activity-based interrogation gives better results than a trip interrogation in terms of number of declared trips. When preparing the questionnaire and the survey protocol, great attention should be paid to reducing respondent burden.

Travel surveys are being implemented in many countries of the Western Hemisphere. However it should be pointed out that in many other countries this is not the case. Unfortunately in those countries where such a data collection effort is carried out, data might not be available to the analyst. On the other hand, in some cases including the United States National Household Travel Survey, microdata are released on the World Wide Web. Whenever data from travel surveys are not available and a survey cannot be implemented, the analyst must resort to other indirect yet incomplete sources of mobility data. The most important three are perhaps censuses, that usually contain questions related to commute trips; consumer expenditure surveys, from which economic figures concerning the transport consumptions of individuals and households can be drawn; and time use surveys, where information can be obtained concerning the amount of time spent travelling.

International comparison of travel survey data is generally problematic due to methodological differences which impact upon trip declaration. Furthermore underlying definitions (for example of long-distance trips, or concerning trip purposes) limit the comparability. Some efforts are realized at regional or national level in order to harmonize the methodology, as in Nordic countries for national travel surveys or in France for household travel surveys.

Further reading

Bonnel, P. and J. Armoogum (2005). National transport surveys: what can we learn from international comparisons? COST 355 WATCH presentation, Berlin, 25 November. Available at http://cost355.inrets.fr/IMG/ppt/WG3-Berlin-251105-Patrick_Bonnel-NTS_International_Comparison.ppt.

Richardson, A.J., E.S. Ampt and A.H. Meyburg (1995). *Survey Methods for Transport Planning*. University of Melbourne: Eucalyptus Press.

Stopher, P. (2009). The travel survey toolkit: where to from here? In P. Bonnel, M. Lee-Gosselin, J. Zmud and J.-L. Madre (eds), *Transport Survey Methods: Keeping up with a Changing World*. Bingley: Emerald.

Stopher, P. and C. Stecher (2006). *Travel Survey Methods: Quality and Future Directions*. Oxford: Elsevier.

Patrick Bonnel and *Marco Diana*

travel time budget

The concept of a 'travel time budget' (TTB) was perhaps first advanced by J.C. Tanner in 1961, but it is generally associated with, and certainly given widespread exposure by, Yacov Zahavi and his co-authors in several studies produced in the late 1970s and early 1980s. A TTB refers to the idea that people have a certain amount of time that they wish to spend on travel. Proponents generally go beyond the suggestion of an individual-specific budget, however, to the observation that the actual size of that budget, as an average taken at a regional or national scale, is relatively stable across time and space. At the extreme, the TTB is viewed almost as a universal constant: 1.1 to 1.3 hours per person or traveller per day, according to various studies.

The position of the TTB concept in the transportation profession is paradoxical. On the one hand, the concept has shown a stubborn persistence, despite the fact that the more closely it is examined, the more elusive it becomes. One reason is the common observation that at the aggregate level, when travel speeds increase over time, travel distances tend to increase so as to keep travel times approximately constant. This links the TTB concept to the **induced demand** debate, with one extreme arguing that, at least from **energy** and **air quality** standpoints, it is useless or even counterproductive to make capacity or operational improvements that increase overall speeds, since people will simply take advantage of the improvement to travel more.

On the other hand, the TTB idea may initially appear to clash with one of the most fundamental tenets of travel behaviour theory: that travel time is a disutility to be minimized. Obviously, under a TTB, travel time is not minimized but is kept constant. In and of itself, however, the TTB concept does not conflict with this principle. Travelling greater distances is entirely predictable (has higher utility) when the greater attractiveness of the more distant destination outweighs the disutility of the additional travel required to reach it. Thus, if individuals use saved travel time to visit more destinations, and/or destinations that are farther away but more attractive, they are still increasing their utility and their **demand** for travel is still purely derived. The TTB concept simply adds a hypothesized behavioural constraint to the form that utility is expected to take.

The apparent paradox of the TTB concept may therefore be due simply to a failure to make the models realistic enough, rather than to a contradiction of the principles on which the models are based. Several studies have addressed ways of incorporating the TTB concept into **travel behaviour models**. More recently, researchers have used the concept to predict future **mobility** as incomes rise and slower modes are replaced by faster modes.

A variety of explanations for a stable TTB – economic, behavioural, even physiological – have been posed. Some researchers suggest that aggregate stability is the result of counteracting factors that offset increases in travel time in some cases, with decreases in others. These interactions could work at the **disaggregate** and aggregate levels. If this is the case, however, the mechanisms that ensure that counteracting factors result in outcomes that remain stable (especially with numerous changing factors over time and space) are not well understood.

One possible mechanism is the existence of an unobserved, desired travel time budget. The human being is viewed as a bio-psychological unit who seeks to maintain a reasonable fixed daily routine, including a travel time budget. If the existing travel time expenditure exceeds an ideal budget, stress will set in and ways to reduce travel time will be sought. Other researchers have explained the concept via the utility-maximizing approach, suggesting that utility is optimized at an amount of travel that for most people is greater than zero. Under this formulation, stable mean observed travel times may result from random deviations on either side of the ideal budgets consistently cancelling each other out across the population. A final view is that the apparently stable travel time expenditures may simply reflect the relatively small range of time out of a fixed 24-hour day that is left over for travel after other essential and more desired activities are accomplished.

A plethora of studies of travel time expenditures have been published. Comparisons across different data sets are problematic. For example, not all data sets include all modes of travel. Some studies report travel time per person, while others report travel time per traveller (meaning those who travelled at all during the survey period, a definition that is sensitive to the length of the period) or, in early studies (including Zahavi's), per traveller using motorized modes. It is troubling that stability sometimes appears with one basis and sometimes with another. Variations in the type and design of the data collection instrument used in the study (for example travel, activity or time use diary) also jeopardize comparisons.

What do these studies find? At the most aggregate level, travel time expenditures sometimes appear to be stable. Even at that level, however, results are often stratified by variables such as auto ownership, showing variation rather than constancy. Several recent studies that examine travel time expenditures for a given metropolitan area across several decades have documented overall increases in travel time, whereas others have found stability. However, data collection improvements over time may have led to increases in the amounts of travel measured, which are then confounded with any changes in the actual amount of travel itself.

Even researchers who argue for the stability of travel time expenditures at the aggregate level acknowledge that there is considerable variation at the disaggregate level. Travel time expenditure is found to be related to individual and household characteristics (for example income level, **gender**, employment status and car ownership), attributes of activities at the destination (for example activity group and activity duration) and land use characteristics (for example density, spatial structure and level of service).

The overall conclusion to be drawn is that the claim of the definitive existence of a constant travel time budget over time and space is not supported by the empirical evidence. However, it appears that individual travel time expenditures are behavioural phenomena that can be productively modelled as a function of numerous variables.

Further reading
Mokhtarian, P.L. and C. Chen (2004). TTB or not TTB, that is the question: a review and analysis of the empirical literature on travel time (and money) budgets. *Transportation Research A* **38**, 634–45.

Patricia L. Mokhtarian

travel time values

The value of travel time savings (VTTS) is the monetary value that is attached to the possibility to save a particular amount of travel time. When a household's or firm's behaviour is taken into account, VTTS is considered as a scarce resource that can be reallocated to other activities, both productive and unproductive. In the case of public administrations, VTTS can be one of the most important benefit categories in **benefit–cost analyses** aimed at justifying investments in a transport infrastructure that makes it possible for people to save travel time. Consequently, VTTS is a key variable both for private economic actors and for public administration choices among alternatives leading to different travel times.

In this respect, a body of methodological and empirical research on VTTS has been developed. The seminal work is by Becker, which introduces and discusses the basic formulas that were subsequently adopted to calculate VTTS both in passenger and in freight transport. Despite their different theoretical frameworks and settings, there is an analytical equivalence of VTTS for passenger and for freight transport.

For both the formulation of VTTS emerges from a maximization problem, based on microeconomic theory, which has recently focused on behavioural models of **discrete choice theory**. In particular, for freight transport, firms maximize a profit function and not a utility function as in the case of many passengers undertaking. Moreover, in the case of freight transport, there is often a methodological problem arising from the difficulty in identifying the economic actor whose profit function has to be maximized, for example in the context of own-account opearatives. Even though the decision about the mode of transport and route is generally made by the shipping firm, the VTTS might be part of the profit function of the firm which is sending the goods, which in turn is linked to the firm or consumer that is to receive them. This is particularly relevant in the case where the focus of analysis is centred on integrated logistics processes.

The analytical framework adopted to value time saving in freight transport is linked to the constrained maximization of a profit function P, that is:

$$Max\ P\ (p,\ w,\ Z,\ S). \tag{1}$$

In this objective function, P is profit, p is the price of the good which is shipped, w is a row vector of the costs related to the production factors, Z is a vector of transport-related attributes, and S is a vector of observed and unobserved company characteristics. In a situation in which a firm can choose among several alternative modes i of transport ($i = 1. . ., j, . . .I$), z_t^i and z_c^i are related to the time and cost attributes of alternative i. Consequently, the company will prefer mode i to the alternative j if:

$$P^i(p,\ w,\ z_c^i,\ z_t^i,\ S) > P^j(p,\ w,\ z_c^j,\ z_t^j,\ S). \tag{2}$$

The data obtained from transport managers are focused on the choice concerning Z. It is an open question as to the extent a manager captures, in the prices of products and inputs, all the indirect effects on profit of infrastructure or provision of the availability of factors, Further, by looking at the difference in profit between two transport alternatives i and j, it is possible to estimate dP/dZ, and, from this, to calculate VTTS:

$$VTTS = \partial P\ /\ \partial\ z_t\ /\ \partial P\ /\ \partial\ z_c. \tag{3}$$

Expression 3 states that the VTTS in the case of freight transport is equal to the marginal rate of substitution between time and money; that is, the monetary value that firms attach to the possibility of saving a certain amount of time.

As opposed to freight transport, when passengers are considered, the economic actor whose utility U is being maximized is unambiguous.

Within this framework, further economic concepts concerning the value of time include: the value of time as a resource; the value of time as a commodity; the value of saving time in a certain activity. In general, the fundamental definition of VTTS emerges from **discrete choice theory** as the 'amount the individual is willing to pay to reduce by one unit his or her travel time'. The passenger utility function U that has to be maximized is:

$$Max\ U\,(G,\,L,\,W,\,t) \tag{4}$$

subject to:

$$G + c_i = wW$$

$$L + W + t_i = \tau$$

$$L \geq \alpha\,G$$

$$i \in I,$$

where G is aggregate consumption, L is leisure time, W is working time, t is exogenous travel time, c_i is travel cost, w is wage rate, t_i time assigned to travel, τ is total time available, α is consumption time per unit G, and I is the set of available modes i ($i = 1, \ldots, I$).

The solution of this constrained maximization problem gives rise to the expression:

$$VTTS = w + \frac{\partial U / \partial W}{\partial U / \partial G - \alpha\theta} - \frac{\partial U / \partial t_i}{\partial U / \partial G - \alpha\theta}, \tag{5}$$

where θ is the Lagrange multiplier associated to the constraint τ.

In Equation 5, VTTS is calculated as the rate of substitution between time and cost for constant utility. Further, the equation shows that the ratio between travel cost and travel time gives a measure – in terms of direct utility – of the difference between the value of leisure (or value of time as a resource) and travel time (or value of time as a commodity). If people like working and dislike travelling, VTTS is larger than the corresponding wage rate. Despite the different settings in terms of the function to maximize and of the constraints to be taken into account, Equations 3 and 5, obtained for freight and passenger VTTS are analytically analogous. Accordingly, heterogeneities between the VTTS in freight and passenger transport should be linked to different sets of preferences of the economic agents whose utility has to be maximized, or to other attributes related to travel, or to both of these. Concerning the VTTS in passenger transport, it is difficult to elicit key factors that can give an exhaustive explanation of the VTTS, even though income, journey purpose and travel mode seem the most important. Finally, while passenger VTTS is often expressed in terms of money units per minute, freight VTTS is frequently more practically expressed in terms of money units per hour, given the longer average transport time in freight transport although this is less common with express services or air freight.

When data collection is taken into account in determining VTTS for freight and passenger transport, the methodologies usually adopted can be classified as either revealed preference (RP) or **stated preference** (SP). The main difference between these two types of methodologies is that RP studies take into account the actual behaviour of persons or firms, while SP studies try to investigate the preferences of economic actors among hypothetical alternatives. Consequently, when long-run VTTS is taken into account, SP is usually the methodology which can be adopted.

Concerning the use of VTTS, given its importance for passengers, firms and public administrations, studies have tried to estimate values since the mid-1960s. The first studies were related to passenger transport but, by the mid-1980s, freight transport analyses were more common. In this context, several variables might influence VTTS, such as the length of the trip, the type of transport and the area where the transport occurs, plus hidden economic, social and spatial variables, which are difficult to control for. In particular, it appears that there is no single measure of the VTTS which can be applied to all possible environments, because it is sensitive to the location where the trips are made. In addition, heterogeneity in freight transport is more evident than in passenger transport.

Further reading

Becker, G.S. (1965). A theory of the allocation of time. *Economic Journal* **75**, 494–517.
Bergkvist, E. and L. Westin (2001). Regional valuation of infrastructure and transport attributes for Swedish road freight. *Annals of Regional Science* **35**, 547–60.
Jara-Diaz, S.R. (2000). Allocation and valuation of travel-time savings. In D.A. Hensher and K.J. Button (eds), *Handbook of Transport Modelling* (2nd edn). Oxford: Elsevier.
Winston, C. (1981). A disaggregate model of the demand for intercity freight transportation. *Econometrica* **49**, 981–1005.

Aura Reggiani

trip distribution models

Trip distribution models are used to help understand and predict the expected number, $T(i, j)$, of trips from an origin i to a destination j. These origins and destinations could be zones – as in traffic analysis zones in urban areas; or points – like airports in modelling air-passenger flows. When applying trip distribution models, an estimate of the number of trips originating from i and destined for j is generally exogenously provided (in doubly constrained applications). In some cases only total trips from each origin are provided (origin-constrained application).

Trip distribution models constitute one of the four 'steps' of the **four-step urban transportation planning system** (UTPS) of models. The first step of the four-step system comprises trip generation and trip attraction models, which provide estimates of the total number of trips $T(i, +)$ from each origin i as well as the total trips $T(+, j)$ to each destination. The UTPS was for a long time the only systematic method used for transportation planning in metropolitan areas, and is still very widely used.

Trip distribution implies choice – a person choosing a shopping destination, a commuter deciding where to work, or having found a workplace, choosing where to live. Therefore, **disaggregate choice models** have been proposed and used for this purpose. But by far the most commonly used models for trip distribution are aggregate spatial interaction models.

Spatial interaction models focus on interactions between pairs of zones or points in space. Individual trips are examples of such interaction events. Other examples include flows of freight, money and messages. The Lowry family of land use models are based on recursive spatial interaction models.

The overwhelmingly most frequently used spatial interaction model is the **gravity model.** Some of the alternative models used, such as intervening opportunities models developed by **Lil**, are now seen to be special cases of general gravity model. A very general form of the gravity model is given by the following relations:

$$T(i, j) = A(i) \, B(j) \, F[\mathbf{c}(i, j)] \tag{1}$$

$$N(i, j) = T(i, j) + \varepsilon(i, j) \tag{2}$$

where $T(i, j)$ is, as before, the expectation $E[N(i, j)]$ of the number $N(i, j)$ of trips from origin i to destination j, F is a function and $\mathbf{c}(i, j)$ is a K-vector of measures of separation between i and j:

$$\mathbf{c}(i, j) = (c(1, i, j), c(2, i, j), \ldots, c(K, i, j)) \tag{3}$$

In most applications, $K = 1$, i.e., $\mathbf{c}(i, j)$ is a scalar valued function $c(i, j)$ of i and j – usually travel time (in the United States) or **generalized cost**. However, allowing vector values enhances its generality by permitting multiple measures of separation such as travel cost, travel time, distance and psychological barriers – as well as functions of these measures. This additional generality causes no significant difficulties.

For most practical purposes $A(i)$ and $B(j)$ can be treated as parameters to be estimated. They are, however, sometimes given explicit interpretations that may lead to additional useful insights. The trip numbers, $N(i, j)$, and therefore the 'error terms' $\varepsilon(i, j)$ in Equation 2, are random variables. When $N(i, j)$ is assumed to be Poisson, the model given by Equations 1 and 2 is called a Poisson **gravity model**.

For practical purposes the algebraic form of the function F needs to be specified further. The most common form is the weighted exponential function:

$$F[\mathbf{c}(i, j)] = \exp[\theta(1)c(1, i, j) + \theta(2)\, c(2, i, j) + \ldots + \theta(K)\, c(K, i, j)] \quad (4)$$

where the weights, $\theta(k)$, $k = 1, 2, \ldots K$, are parameters to be estimated. This form is general enough to include most algebraic forms for the function F in common use. For example it also includes power specifications of the form, $\alpha\,[c(i, j)]^\gamma$, as well as combined 'gamma' specifications, $\alpha\,[c(i, j)]^\gamma \exp[\beta\, c(i, j)]$, commonly recommended in the United States for the gravity model. In addition, the step functions used for F in many practical applications can be modelled by Equation 4, using appropriate definitions of the $c(k, i, j)$s.

In trip distribution applications, the parameters $\theta(k)$ are estimated using observed values of $N(i, j)$. These $\theta(k)$'s are assumed to remain constant over the period for which forecasts are needed. Using forecast-period values of the $c(k, i, j)$'s from exogenous sources, corresponding forecast-period values of $F[\mathbf{c}(i, j)]$ can be computed using (4). From these $F[\mathbf{c}(i, j)]$'s, together with future period $T(i, +)$'s and $T(+, j)$'s obtained from trip generation and trip attraction models, future-period forecasts of expected trip totals, $T(i, j)$, can then be estimated using an iterative method referred to as Furness iterations (or the DSF procedure). In statistics, this procedure is known as the iterated proportional fitting procedure, and in economics as the RAS procedure.

The exponential gravity model given by Equations 1 and 4 can be written as a logit model, and is a choice model which can be derived in terms of the utility maximizing behaviour of travellers. In doubly constrained applications it might also be viewed as two interlocking choice models: given an origin someone choosing a destination, and given a destination (for example a workplace), someone choosing an origin (for example a place to live). In addition, a theory of the **gravity model** based on individual satisficing behaviour was proposed by Tony Smith. However, it should be pointed out, that the gravity model, although a model of choice, is not a **disaggregated choice model**, since the characteristics of individual travellers are not considered. While there is nothing to prevent an analyst from building separate gravity models for separate sociodemographic segments, this is rarely done.

The gravity model concept is one of the oldest social science models, and dates back to the work of Carey. Since that time, forms of this model have been widely used in a vast array of applications including migration, retailing and even marriages.

The current theory of the gravity model has been given by Smith and is based on axiomatic foundations. These axioms provided both necessary and sufficient conditions for the model to hold. The axioms required for Model 1, with $N(i, j)$ Poisson are intuitively appealing and quite general. As more restrictions are placed on Equation 1, additional axioms are required. For example, additional axioms are needed when F is of the form in Equation 4. Smith has also provided axioms which are necessary and sufficient for gravity model parameters to remain invariant as underlying situations change. This discussion is of particular importance because gravity models are used for forecasting under the assumption that some model parameters usually the $\theta(k)$'s remain unchanged. This theoretical approach gives the gravity model a sounder basis than most social science models.

In urban transportation planning, there are frequently a very large number of origin and destination zones, with the consequence that most observed flows $N(i, j)$ are zero-valued. In such cases, parameters of the Poisson gravity model given by Equations 1 and 4 should be estimated by maximum likelihood methods. However, the large number of origins and destinations makes it difficult to use 'off-the-shelf' methods.

When there are not many zero-value $N(i, j)$'s, linear least squares methods may also be used. As in the case of maximum likelihood, large numbers of origin and destination zones make standard statistical software difficult to use. Sen and Sööt have given procedures in which the parameters $A(i)$ and $B(j)$ are removed by algebraic manipulation before applying weighted least squares.

In addition, a number of ad hoc procedures of parameter estimation have been proposed over the years. One proposed by the United States Bureau of Public Roads in the 1960s for a step function F is similar to a maximum likelihood approach.

Numerical methods exist for calculating asymptotic covariance matrices for maximum likelihood estimates of gravity model parameters. This allows the computation of confidence intervals for parameter estimates as well as the usual tests of significance. Corresponding covariance matrices for forecasts of trips $T(i, j)$ from an origin i to a destination j can also be obtained. When the numbers of origins and destination are large, however, such covariance matrices will be prohibitively large. However, approximate covariance matrices are also obtainable for simpler least squares estimates, which can provide a practical alternative in such cases.

It has been demonstrated that maximum likelihood estimates are quite robust with respect to violations of underlying assumptions including the Poisson assumption. Also, experience has shown that the standard errors of the $\theta(k)$ estimates are fairly small for even moderately large sample sizes.

Finally, goodness-of-fit of trip distribution models can be assessed using the standard Chi-square test. In most examples that this author is aware of, the **gravity model**, when constructed carefully, has yielded excellent fits.

Further Reading
Sen, A. and T.E. Smith (1995). *Gravity Models of Spatial Interaction Behavior.* Heidelberg: Springer-Verlag.

Ashish Sen

trip generation models

The purpose of passenger trip generation analysis is to estimate the number of trips from and to activities in an area, implicitly assuming that the amount of travel is functionally related to land use activities and the socio-economic features of the area (for example automobile ownership, household size, trip purpose and transportation system). Trip generation is the first step in the conventional **four-step travel forecasting procedure**, the other three being trip distribution, mode split and **network** assignment. The four-step process is the dominant modelling framework among metropolitan planning organizations (MPOs) in the United States to forecast activity and travel and evaluate alternative configurations in the transportation network.

In the trip generation step, two separate groups of models are estimated: trip production and trip attraction models. Trip production models estimate two types of trips: the number of home-based trip originations (trips that start or end at home) based on characteristics of the home end of the trip, and the number of non-home-based trip originations (trips which neither start nor end at home) based on characteristics of the origin zone. Trip attraction models estimate the number of trip ends for home- and non-home-based trips based on the characteristics of the origin zone for the former and the destination zone for the latter. Different production and attraction models are used for each trip purpose – for example, home to work, home to shop, home to other, work to shop, work to other, work to work, and non-home (work) to non-home (work).

Trip generation models may be used to estimate person trips or vehicle trips depending on a study's objectives. Person trips, for example, are needed to forecast transit demand, the impact of transportation improvements – for example **travel demand management** (TDM) measures – on vehicle occupancy. Vehicle trips may be used for **air quality** studies, subarea traffic analysis, long-range planning, and so on. Note that traditional trip generation models estimate unlinked passenger or vehicle trips. Trip linking has recently become a feature of activity-based trip generation models.

In practice trip production models are commonly linear models or cross-classification (or categorical) models. Independent variables for regression analysis used to estimate coefficients of linear models (or classification variables for cross-classification models) typically include the number of workers per household, the number of available cars per household, household size, household income, and so on). These models estimate trips at the traffic analysis zone (TAZ) level. **Disaggregate models** that estimate trip productions at the household or individual traveller level are also used, but less frequently, perhaps because not all data for the independent variables are usually available at the desirable disaggregate level.

Trip attraction models, on the other hand, are typically linear models that are estimated using regression analysis at the TAZ level. Independent variables commonly used include zonal floor space (possibly disaggregated by business type), zonal employment levels (possibly disaggregated by occupation type), and a number of workforce **accessibility** measures. Categorical models can also be estimated with respect to employment type, for example manufacturing, retail and office; and employment density, such as, number of employees per acre.

Occasionally, separate trip generation models are estimated for special generators. This is because several types of urban facilities are prominent destinations because of their large size and innate attractiveness to trip-makers. Examples of such facilities include airports, shopping centres and manufacturing plants. Regression analysis is typically used in this case using independent variables that are relevant for each special generator case; that is, population, racial or ethnic composition, household income, employment by industry and unemployment rate for airport trip generation; number of **parking** spaces, total person work trips, distance from major competition, age of shopping centre and floor space by type of use for shopping centre trip generation; population density, plant size, prime shift percentage, percentage of white-collar employees, and distance to the central business district (CBD) for manufacturing plants. Other special generators for which standard trip generation models may not produce reliable estimates include hospitals, military bases and colleges and universities.

Since trip productions and attractions are estimated from separate models, area-wide totals will usually be different. If necessary, this can be rectified using an iterative proportional fitting procedure that iteratively adjusts trip production and attraction zonal totals. Occasionally, trip production and trip attraction totals need not be the same. In such a case, the algorithm contracts to two solutions, one agreeing with the production totals and another agreeing with the attraction totals. The analyst could then choose the solution that better conforms to the case of interest. Assuming, for example, that trip production models are better and more stable predictors of trip rates than trip attraction models, the zonal attraction totals can be adjusted. Conversely, if trip attraction aggregates are constrained by the nature of the problem (for example fixed number of jobs) then zonal productions should be adjusted.

Trip generation models of regional scope require data inventories that are usually collected and maintained by the regional MPO. This is because MPOs must develop and maintain transportation models to support various transportation and land use policies in every urbanized area with a population over 50 000. Among data collection activities, household **travel surveys** are the most expensive and thus conducted infrequently (every 10 to 15 years at a minimum). Occasionally, MPOs resort to conducting only limited-scope surveys to update travel activity inventories. Data collection activities in smaller MPOs are even more problematic as they can only afford small-size household surveys. Such constraints create survey data quality issues (for example reliability and stability of trip generation rates) that need to be addressed before complicated modelling tasks, such as estimation of trip generation models, begin.

In cases where the sample size of a household travel survey available for estimation is small, three types of problems need to be addressed in a possibly simple and cost-effective manner: unusual observations, small number of observations or no observations. Notice that the concern is not so much on the overall size of the sample but rather the size of the sample in each cell of the cross-classification. Most applications of the four-step procedure are typically implemented using two-way classifications, for example number of adults in the household and number of vehicles. Improvements can be made by increasing the number of variables in the classification under consideration, but then the observations per cell would decline.

When sample sizes are large, estimates are generally not affected too much by a suspect observation. With small sample sizes, however, a bad observation, due possibly to a mistake in recording data or a respondent giving misleading information, can play havoc with the quality of estimates and have a profound effect on forecasts. Such bad estimates need be of concern only when they are influential. There are a great number of measures available in the literature for identifying outliers once the categorical model is cast as a regression problem. Additional measures for the identification of influential observations are also available. The analyst at this point needs to understand what behaviour is truly unusual and influential, or simply the result of a small-scale survey. If the former is true, one could drop such observations from further analysis because there is enough evidence that such observations do not belong in the same model. If the latter is true, then there is a need to improve the reliability of trip rates.

If a categorical trip generation table is based on limited observations, say just a few hundred, with few observations regarding each cell, then statistical reliability may be improved by combining categories. In such a case, reliability can be enhanced by combining table cells with like trip rates. A method for doing so is classification and regression tree (CART) analysis.

Finally, some cells might not receive an observation at all – or the analyst might find the observations too few or too unreliable. In that case, cell estimates might be imputed from observations in other cells using regression-type techniques, such as row–column decomposition analysis. Imputation can also be used in lieu of combining of cells using CART, random forests or other methods.

Other methods to address such problems with small survey samples include transferability and synthetic construction of household travel survey data. In addition to such design-based approaches, model-based approaches including small-area estimation methods have been applied in household travel surveys. Such methods are still new and require advanced technical capabilities, which are rather in short supply among small and medium-sized MPOs.

Once estimation of trip rates, trip productions and trip attractions has been completed, the analysis shifts into a validation stage. The validation of trip generation models is usually conducted using national sample data including (in the United States) the Census Transportation Planning Package, the American Community Survey, the Public Use Microdata Sample files, the National Household Travel Survey and the Longitudinal Employer-Household Dynamics data. Comparisons with relevant results from other areas are also common.

Further reading

Metaxatos, P., S. Sööt, A. Sen, V. Thakuriah, J. DiJohn and J. Jarzab (1999). A transportation planning process for linking welfare recipients to jobs. *Transportation Research Record* **1626**, 149–58.

Sen, A. and T.E. Smith (1995). *Gravity Models of Spatial Interaction Behavior.* Heidelberg: Springer-Verlag.

Sen, A. and M. Srivastava (1990). *Regression Analysis: Theory, Methods and Applications.* Heidelberg: Springer-Verlag.

Paul Metaxatos

trucking

In the latest data available from the United States Census Bureau, the expenditures on transportation by truck in 2006 were over $312 billion. Another way to look at it is that the nation's freight bill is over $1000 per person per year. The Census Bureau data notes that trucks moved more than 90 billion miles in 2006 – more than 80 percent of these loaded.

Trucking operations in the United States are classified as for-hire or private, with private carriers those that are owned by the company for whom they provide exclusive service. For-hire carriers are classified as common and contract motor carriers, grouped into the following three classes: Class I Carriers having annual carrier operating revenues of $10 million or more; Class II Carriers having annual carrier operating revenues of at least $3 million but less than $10 million; and Class III Carriers having annual carrier operating revenues of less than $3 million. These companies are further classified by the type of services they provide: full truckload carriers, less-than-truckload (LTL) carriers and package delivery service providers. LTL carriers are those that handle freight weighing less than 10 000 lbs while truckload carriers haul heavier freight in full truckloads. LTL carriers typically also provide truckload services. A further classification might specify what type of equipment is used by the carrier including van (sometimes called dry van), flatbed, refrigerated (known as reefers) and tanker trucks, to mention a few. Carriers are also categorized as providing local, regional or long-distance operations. The operations of these different companies and the working conditions for their drivers differ significantly. Drivers in local and regional operations tend to spend much of their time loading and unloading and waiting their turn at dock facilities – in return for such inconveniences they sleep at home every night. Long-distance drivers tend to stay on the road for three to six weeks at a time, sleeping in their cabs or occasionally in inexpensive motels. Long-haul drivers experience quite a bit of autonomy, despite the widespread adoption of technologies that keep them in continuous contact with dispatchers and managers.

The largest segment of the United States trucking industry is the truck-load sector, which moves full **containers** from shippers to their consignees. The largest long-distance truckload carriers use rail **intermodal** transportation when it is available and economically advantageous. **Intermodal** transportation is generally thought to be economically efficient for moves of more than 300 miles. The use of rail intermodal transportation became more popular during the mid- to late 1990s due to the two simultaneous factors. The first was a significant labor shortage and the second was improvements in technologies that made intermodal operations more efficient. Long-haul truckload drivers, known as over-the-road drivers, are typically paid by the loaded mile. A large portion of the local truck-load market involves drayage operations – those operations in service to intermodal facilities. Dray operators pick up and deliver loads to rail yards or ports and may move loads between such facilities. Dray operators typically move three to five loads per day and are typically paid a flat fee per move, though they could alternately be paid proportional to loaded distance travelled.

Less-than-truckload carriers must operate consolidation terminals where multiple loads can be loaded onto vehicles en route to nearby destinations. Demands are picked up in a local area, and delivered to a local terminal where they are sorted and loaded into line-haul trailers. These line-haul trailers move loads to break-bulk transfer terminals where the loads are unloaded and reloaded again. A load might be handled at several of these intermediate locations, enroute to its final destination. Rates for LTL services are based on the class of product carried and the weight of the shipment. Factors affecting the classification of goods include, at a minimum, the following: weight per cubic volume; value per pound; liability to loss, damage or theft in transit; likelihood of injury to other freight; risks due to hazard of carriage; and expense of handling. The costs of LTL services are sufficiently high that for some shipments it is less expensive to move the goods as a truckload movement. The shorter the distance, and the higher the classification of the goods, the more likely it is that a truckload move will be competitive in price with an LTL move. For companies with significant transportation needs, managing freight contracts can be quite complex. Most companies will have in-house transportation and logistics managers whose primary responsibility it is to manage their long- and short-term contracts with trucking companies and to see that they pay the lowest fees possible. Much of their time is spent identifying ways to move LTL freight to truckload, and to move express freight to LTL.

There are two distinct types of **courier and express services**: national and international package services like United Parcel Service (UPS) and Federal Express (FedEx); and local express services which handle both packages and irregular freight. Today UPS and FedEx run both ground and air operations and no longer rely as heavily on their **hub-and-spoke** systems. Their ground operations are built around local sorting facilities which serve pickup and delivery operations and which send partial or full truckloads to other sorting facilities across the country. These local operations are typically no more than five hours' driving time apart, so that the truck drivers can make a single round trip and return to their home locations within one work shift.

Every major city in the United States is served by several local express services that provide 2-, 4- and 8-hour express delivery services. The larger and more successful of these companies typically also provide **third-party logistics** services – that is, they balance out their irregular operations with contracts to make deliveries for retailers who provide same-day or next-day deliveries within a local area; for example express office supply stores.

A significant fraction of the trucking industry is made up of private fleets. These fleets are the transportation and logistics units of large manufacturing or distribution companies (large food and beverage manufacturers, large groceries, toy manufacturers, and so on). Private fleets are typically estimated to be responsible for about half of all trucking operations. Shifts back and forth in outsourcing have occurred since the late 1980s, but that estimate appears to be fairly robust. There have been many debates over the years about when companies should outsource their logistics services and when they should keep them in-house, along with periodic swings back and forth between rising and falling outsourcing. Many major shippers maintain a private fleet for their mission-critical transportation, and outsource the rest.

Combining contemporary information technology with traditional freight-handling systems, an increasing number of intermediary firms (**third-party logistics** companies) are already managing freight transportation for companies that choose not to handle their own shipping and receiving. Many of these manufacturers deal with multiple trucking, ocean, rail and air cargo providers. The complexities of booking and moving their freight are enormous. Freight transportation intermediaries provide a bridge between shippers and carriers, facilitating the flow of information and goods.

A major issue facing the industry today is the promise and expense related to technology adoption. Large companies have tended to be early adopters of technology – often reaping benefits due to economies of scale in procurement and economies of scope reaped from implementation. Smaller companies have been slower to adopt, for practical reasons and those related to lack of resources. The development of electronic commerce has impacted the trucking industry just as it has impacted other industries. Its primary impact has been in the area of contracting. In addition to the development of online spot markets, where shippers can obtain quotes and drivers can find available loads, the industry has seen the development of collaborative marketplaces, the use of combinatorial auctions and, recently, calls for the use of options contracts and other more sophisticated hedging mechanisms. Another major issue is that operational costs have continued to rise, with and without commensurate increases in prices. The cost of fuel and labor has continued to rise over time – threatening to erase the cost advantages realized through operational efficiencies introduced in the post-**deregulation** era.

The trucking industry is vibrant and active. The demands for movements of freight keep rising and, due to increasingly global manufacturing and distribution systems, they will continue to rise. Like all other industries, it is being impacted by emerging technologies and innovations in operating procedures. The two decades since the 1990s have seen enormous **productivity** increases in all markets.

Further reading
Tsai, M.-T., A.C. Regan and J-D. Saphores (2008). Freight transportation derivatives contracts: state of the art and future developments. To the 87th meeting of the Transportation Research Board, Washington, DC.
United States Census Bureau (2008). *2006 Service Annual Survey: Truck Transportation, Messenger Services and Warehousing*. Washington, DC: United States Census Bureau.

Amelia Regan

tunnels

A tunnel is an underground or underwater passageway in roughly horizontal direction. Tunnels on a larger scale were first constructed in the cities established by ancient civilizations for water supply and sewers. Among the earliest were reported from the Indus Valley, dated about 2500 BC. Probably a 900-metre-long brick passageway under the River Euphrates can be seen as the first tunnel for transporting non-liquids. The Romans completed a 5.6 km tunnel to drain Lake Fucino in AD 50. They also built a few **road** tunnels. Tunnelling techniques stagnated until drilling and blasting by gunpowder was introduced in Germany for mining at the beginning of the seventeenth century. In the late eighteenth and early nineteenth century there was increasing demand for improved transport by means of canals.

The canal systems required numerous tunnels. The first tunnel in soft ground was built in France and opened in 1810. The first **pedestrian** tunnel under the River Thames in England was completed in 1843. The invention of the steam locomotive early in the nineteenth century brought a rapid growth of railroad lines. Many **railway** tunnels were built during this period of expansion. Few of them were longer than 1.5 kilometres. The first great Alpine tunnel was the 13.7 km Mont Cenis tunnel at the French–Italian border, completed in 1872. Work was started with manual methods, but finished with a compressed air drill which was three times faster. The development of subway systems in cities started in the 1860s with the London Underground. The demand for subways for urban transportation in the twentieth century brought a new era of tunnelling. With the exception of some Roman tunnels, practically no vehicular tunnels were built until the late nineteenth and early twentieth century. One of the first was completed under the river in Chicago in 1870. The mass production of cars in the twentieth century led to the building of thousands of kilometres of road tunnels, ushering in a new era of tunnelling. Long road tunnels were built to connect points separated by water or mountains. Today the high traffic volumes in urban agglomerations lead to **noise** problems. To cover major roads is seen as a solution in many cities. The Table provides details of the largest rail and road tunnels.

There are two main possible ways to construct a tunnel: mining methods and cut-and-cover. A special method for underwater tunnels is to sink tubular sections. Mining methods include drilling and blasting in hard rock, and digging or advancing a shield in soft ground.

Due to the exhaust gases a ventilation system is needed in road tunnels in normal operation. In the case of a fire an emergency ventilation regime extracts the poisonous smoke. There are three possible ventilation systems:

Tunnel	Location	Date opened	Length (km)
Railway tunnels			
Seikan	Japan	1988	53.9
Channel	Britain–France	1994	50.5
Iwate-ichinohe	Japan	2002	25.8
Dai-shimizu	Japan	1982	22.2
Simplon 1 & 2	Switzerland–Italy	1906 & 1922	19.8
Vereina	Switzerland	1999	19.1
Shin-kanmon	Japan	1975	18.7
Apennine	Italy	1934	18.5
Qinling I-II	China	2002	18.5
Rokkô	Japan	1972	16.3
Furka Base tunnel	Switzerland	1982	15.4
Haruna	Japan	1982	15.4
Severomuyskiy	Russia	2001	15.3
Gorigamine	Japan	1997	15.2
Monte Santomarco	Italy	1987	15.0
St Gotthard	Switzerland	1882	15.0
Road tunnels			
Laerdal	Norway	2000	24.5
St Gotthard	Switzerland	1980	16.9
Arlberg	Austria	1978	14.0
Frejus	France–Italy	1980	12.9
Mont Blanc	France–Italy	1965	11.7
Kan-etsu	Japan	1985 & 1991	11.0
Gran Sasso d'Italia	Italy	1984 & 1995	10.2
Plabutsch	Austria	1987	9.9
Tokyo Aqua	Japan	1997	9.6
Seelisberg	Switzerland	1980	9.3
Enasan	Japan	1985	8.6
Somport	France–Spain	2003	8.6
Gleinalm	Austria	1978	8.3
Steigen	Norway	1978	8.1

longitudinal, transversal and semi-transversal ventilation (see Figure). Longitudinal ventilation systems are usually used in two bore tunnels. Transversal ventilation is essential for an efficient emergency ventilation in one bore tunnel.

For a long period of time few accidents involving large-scale fires occurred in public road tunnels. A series of road tunnel disasters started with the Mont Blanc tunnel fire (1999, with 39 fatalities). This was followed by huge fires in the 6.4 km Austrian Tauerntunnel (1999, with 12

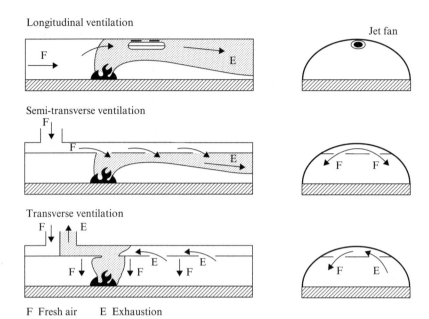

Longitudinal ventilation

Jet fan

Semi-transverse ventilation

Transverse ventilation

F Fresh air   E Exhaustion

fatalities) and the Gotthardtunnel (2001, with 11 fatalities). The worst disaster took place in a funicular railway tunnel in Kaprun, Austria which took 155 lives. Tunnel **safety** became a major public concern. Action to reduce the risk in tunnels was required. The public called for the implementation of costly measures, like the installation of sprinkler systems in all tunnels. The fact that accident and fatality rates in tunnels are in most cases not higher than on the open road was neglected in the discussion. Quantitative risk assessment (QRA) is an appropriate tool to come to rational decisions. Risk is defined by two aspects: the occurrence probability of an event and the consequences of an occurring event. Risk can never be zero. The society has to decide what is tolerable or not and how much the society is willing to pay to reduce risk. Heavy goods vehicles were involved in all road tunnel disasters. Results from QRA show that the most effective instruments are escorted convoys of heavy goods vehicles, or a minimum headway of 150 metres in front of heavy goods vehicles.

Further reading

Gobiet, W., M. Marec, G. Eberl, K. Pucher, R. Hörhan, H. Marach, O. Ludwig, T. Ciancosi and S. Elmers (2000). Brand im Tunnel. Bundesministerium für Verkehr, Innovation und Technologie, Straßenforschung Heft 500, Vienna.

Knoflacher, H. (2001). Quantitative risk analysis model: dangerous goods transport through tunnels. *Tunnel Management International* **3**, 19–23.

Organisation for Economic Co-operation and Development (2001). *Safety in Tunnels: Transport of Dangerous Goods through Road Tunnels*. Paris: OECD.

Paul C. Pfaffenbichler

U

University Transportation Centers in the United States

Mobility of freight and people has always been a critical first-order condition for socio-economic success. Any advanced society must be able to move spatially with efficiency and effectiveness. Mobility is a key element in specialization of labour, globalization of trade, urbanization and the resulting concentration of labour, networking of organizations, lean manufacturing, efficient management of procurement and inventory, and a host of other business functions critical to a developed economy. Mobility is also critical to achieving a high quality of life, the attributes of which include socialization, recreation, entertainment, worship, shopping, and more.

This importance has led to the establishment of a number of university centres concentrating on transportation. Although mobility is a key element in socio-economic success it has never had a comfortable home in academia. Academic programmes in transportation have traditionally been a subset of some other academic department (usually civil engineering). However, this appears to be changing. Several universities have developed 'Institutes' that focus on one or more aspects of transportation research and education.

Additionally, there is a growing acceptance of transportation as an interdisciplinary field by both academicians and practitioners. Interdisciplinary teaching and research seems to be a trend in university transportation programmes. There are a number of reasons for this. Firstly and most importantly, transportation has migrated from a subdiscipline of civil engineering to become an interdisciplinary field embracing economics, planning, business management, sociology, psychology and operations research, as well as engineering and a number of other disciplines. Addressing today's transportation challenges requires an appreciation and understanding of the dynamics of complex solutions. Secondly, the discipline that held the 'keys to the kingdom', namely civil engineering, is recognizing the importance of an interdisciplinary approach by the more enlightened professors and practitioners.

Another trend in university transportation centres is for them to be independent of a department or college. This is evidenced by a review of the programme characteristics of the ten national and ten regional centres. Based on programme focus areas and/or the colleges and departments involved in the centre, 13 of the 20 centres – 65 per cent – are definitely interdisciplinary or at least multidisciplinary in nature, another four appear to involve several disciplines and three focus primarily on engineering. This is directly related to the interdisciplinary nature of transportation.

A third trend is the development of strong transportation educational components at a number of universities. Education is one of six goals that a university must comply with to receive funding through the United States University Transportation Centers (UTC) Program. This has evolved in recognition for the need to train new leaders in transportation in response to the impending retirement of baby boomers. Additionally, it is also in response to the recognition that the transportation leaders and managers of tomorrow cannot just be engineers, but must also have an appreciation and understanding of the interdisciplinary nature of transportation. Thus, many new and significantly modified programmes are evolving.

The changing nature of transportation at the academic level, the need for improved knowledge, and an increase in the development of intellectual capital are validated to some degree by the increase in federal funding for university-based transportation education and research. Funding of university transportation centres by the United States Department of Transportation (USDOT) has been promulgated by Congress during the last four reauthorizations of the national surface transportation programme. The United States Congress has continually increased funding in this area through the USDOT since 1986 when it authorized $40 million for the university regional transportation centres programme for fiscal years 1987–91. Following this, Congress authorized $182 million for fiscal years 1992–97 for a variety of university education and research programmes, $248 million for financial years 1998–2003, and $624 million for the financial years 2005–2009.

Current funding for university funding transportation research and education authorized by SAFETEA-LU consists of 60 UTCs and earmarked funds for another 16 universities. Total funding for the UTC programme was increased in TEA-21, from $32.4 million per year to more than $83 million. Additionally, another $10 million per year was earmarked for specific universities. The UTC programme now consists of:

- 10 regional centres funded at $2 million per year per centre, each competitively selected within each of the ten standard federal regions;
- 10 at-large competitively selected Tier I centres funded at $1 million per year;
- 10 designated national centres each funded at $3.5 million per year;
- 22 designated Tier II centres each funded at $500 000 per year; and

- 8 designated transit centres with funding ranging from $400 000 to $2 million per year.

Further reading
http://utc.dot.gov.

Gene Griffin

urban form and transport

The relationship between urban form and transport has largely been examined from two different perspectives: studies that encompass within the definition of 'urban form' a broader concept of land use (for instance the New Urbanism), and studies that assume specific morphologic urban features. The overarching hypothesis in both strands is based on the idea that urban growth is often related to transport availability, and limited by **congestion** and adverse environmental effects due to car use (air pollution, noise, accidents). For this reason, it is often argued that specific urban transport policies can be used to tackle urban sprawl, reduce automobile dependence, increase the use of alternative transport modes, and support pedestrian **mobility**. However, the relationship between urban form and transport, and in particular travel behaviour, is complex depending on the characteristics of the urban form (average spatial aspects of the city, activity-based zoning, and so on) and the characteristics of the travel under scrutiny (travel to work, for shopping, by car, by mass transit system, and so on).

The first group of approaches consider the relationship between urban form and transport using aggregate measurements such as urban density in relation to trip frequency or average trip lengths. These analyses have shown significant links between transport and the general characterization of urban areas, and have been used to support land use policies intended to lead to different overall travel patterns in the city; in particular, to reduce car travel. Nonetheless, they do not convincingly address the problem of how specific characteristics of urban form relate to different travel patterns, and how urban form influences individual decisions. To overcome these limitations, disaggregate analyses look into these specific relationships. **Disaggregate models** consider socio-economic and travel characteristics at individual and microeconomic levels. Multivariate models yield mixed results regarding the relationships between urban form and transport, thus suggesting that modification of the urban form (for example, pre-Second

World War traditional communities and post-Second World War dispersed communities) is not always significantly correlated with changes in travel behaviour. Other models use choice methodologies to examine individual behaviour in relation to travel decisions. The urban form parameter is implicitly represented in the specification of the utility function through the use of variables such as destination attractiveness and spatial features. An application is one that examines the relationship between urban form and the 'full price' of transport by considering a simulation of the Organization of Petroleum Exporting Countries (OPEC) oil shock. The data shows no significant link between increases in the price of gasoline and urban form; that is, higher fuel cost will not induce the choice of a more compact city probably because people switch to smaller cars.

Belonging to the second group of approaches is the study of Solow and Vickrey which attempts to analyse the relationship between urban form, transport and land use using basic economic and statistical tools of variations, linear programming and control theory. In their model they analyse a rectangular urban shape with the business district distributed homogeneously in the city, and with transportation cost only in the length-ways direction. By approaching their problem in this way, they are able to isolate various sources of divergences between private and social costs that can lead to overinvestment in urban road infrastructure, especially in the centre of the city. Other studies followed, examining different urban shapes; for instance, a pie-shaped city with the central business district (CBD) located at the tip of the 'pie-slice', and a circular urban shape where transportation moves along radial and circumferential roads. These works corroborate Solow and Vickrey in that they demonstrate that cities dedicate more resources to housing at the periphery and devote more resources to transportation at the centre.

Miyao assumes a square city with a grid of horizontal and vertical roads, and defines the equilibrium traffic patterns based upon the notion that every road user selects a cost-minimizing route between the points of origin and destination. The model is noteworthy in that although he conducts the same theoretical and analytical exercise as Solow and Vickrey, his results contrast sharply with theirs. Miyao reaches the conclusion that there is a stronger tendency to build roads near the city edges than in the city centre, such that 'land-use decisions based on market rents tend to create too many roads everywhere in the city at the optimum, and the tendency toward excessive road-building is stronger near the city boundaries'.

Further reading
Boarnet, M.G. and C. Randall (eds) (2001). *Travel by Design: The Influence of Urban Form on Travel*. Oxford: Oxford University Press.

Miyao, T. (1981). *Dynamic Analysis of the Urban Economy*. New York: Academic Press.
Solow, R.M and W.S. Vickrey (1971). Land use in a long narrow city. *Journal of Economic Theory* **3**, 430–47.

Francesca Medda

urban logistics

Urban logistics, also called 'city logistics', became an interest in many European countries in the context of attempts to introduce improved inner-city freight distribution, particularly during the last decade of the twentieth century. The growth of freight transport due to changes in the economy and in the system of **logistics** provision is important for cities that represent major nodes in the **network** economy and also have large consumer markets to be served. Urban goods movement, particularly **truck** and van operations, accounts for about a tenth of daily motorized vehicle trips within cities. Truck traffic also exerts a significant negative environmental impact, contributing to air pollution (particulates, volatile organic compounds, nitrogen oxide), noise emissions and **congestion** of infrastructure.

To reduce such damage, city logistics seek to optimise logistics activities by private companies in urban areas while considering the environment, the traffic **congestion** and **energy** consumption within the framework of a market economy. Urban or city logistics is based on a common under-standing of 'problems' which include distribution costs, viewed from the perspective of private enterprises, and social or environmental costs, regarded from the perspective of the public and municipalities.

A number of measures have been considered and some introduced at the urban and the regional level. These include bundling freight flows of different carriers to increase physical **productivity**, the establishment of public logistics terminals facilitating cooperative logistics and **intermodal** activities, the setting of load limits and the establishment of underground freight transport systems. Practical experience is, however, still limited to cooperative distribution schemes, routing and scheduling improvements.

Despite ambitious plans and high expectations in the beginning of the 1990s, city logistics did not achieve most of the anticipated effects. Many projects ran over public budgets. A general barrier to implementing city logistics has been the weak participation of firms, because of the limited benefits they expect. Single firms' activity might be changed in some cases, for example by achieving productivity gains in selected **supply-chains**, yet there has been no overall effective modification of urban freight transport operations.

There are several possible reasons for this failure. First, there is a lack of precise data regarding the volume and composition of urban freight and merchandise transport. Such knowledge is a fundamental requirement for designing effective measures and identifying groups who are supposed to carry out the measures. Second, the competitive nature of the urban freight business is a constraint for implementing cooperative delivery schemes. Due to the perceived risk of market transparency, companies are not willing to cooperate with competitors. Third, public policy is characterized by generic limitations to managing or influencing private operations: transport policy originated from the provision of infrastructure, such as roads, railways and terminals, and in setting regulatory environments. Any policy that is based on demand management rather than expanding infrastructure is still an area of difficulty in public policy-making.

Since corporate behaviour primarily depends on transport prices and the quality of services offered, and, in the case of conflicts, the corporate milieux often appear to be more powerful than public policy and planning, city logistics may only work under very particular circumstances. The lack of data and knowledge limits cooperation and restricts public policy to only an influencing role in corporate decisions.

Further reading
Hesse, M. (2004). Logistics and freight transport policy in urban areas: a case study of Berlin-Brandenburg/Germany. *European Planning Studies* **12**, 1035–53.
Taniguchi, E., R. Thompson, T. Yamada and R. van Duin (eds) (2001). *City Logistics: Network Modelling and Intelligent Transport Systems*. Oxford: Pergamon.

Markus Hesse

W

Wardrop principles

The two Wardrop principles represent a milestone of **network** management theory; they are applied not only in transport, but also in other network fields such as **telecommunications** and computer network organization. In the framework of transport, they are the bases of **traffic assignment** procedures, the aim of which is to distribute users going from various origins to various destinations through routes using the links of the network, each link having a cost that is an increasing function of the number of users which pass on it. Despite their name, they are not really principles. The first one is a hypothesis on travellers' behaviour, and states that the journey times on all the routes used are equal and less than those which would be experienced by a single vehicle on any unused route; it leads to the user equilibrium (UE). The second one is a definition of the system optimum that is reached when the average journey time is a minimum; it leads to a system optimum (SO).

The first principle is akin to, but slightly different from, a Nash equilibrium that would state that no user can change their route and incur a lower cost. A lot of work has been made to explore the relations between those two concepts. It turns out that the first principle is a Nash equilibrium when the number of users goes to infinity, each of them being infinitely small (what is called the non-atomic situation). Beckmann, McGuire and Winsten have shown that in the non-atomic situation, the Wardrop equilibrium, expressed as a variational inequality problem, is equivalent to a constrained maximization programme.

Looking at the example seen in the figure of the following network, it is composed of four nodes and five oriented links, with a single origin, node 1, and a single destination, node 4; there are three routes: 1-2-4, 1-3-4 and 1-2-3-4. The cost on a link ij is: $t_{ij} = F_{ij}(T_{ij})$, where T_{ij} is the traffic on link ij. The costs and flows on the three routes are:

> Route 1-2-4: Cost: $C_{124} = F_{12}(T_{12}) + F_{24}(T_{24})$; Flow: F_{124}
> Route 1-3-4: Cost: $C_{134} = F_{13}(T_{13}) + F_{34}(T_{34})$; Flow: F_{134}
> Route 1-2-3-4: Cost: $C_{1234} = F_{12}(T_{12}) + F_{23}(T_{23}) + F_{34}(T_{34})$;
> Flow: F_{1234}

with the relationships between link flows and route flows set out in the first figure.

$$T12 = F124 + F1234$$
$$T13 = F134$$
$$T23 = F1234$$
$$T24 = F124$$
$$T34 = F134 + F1234$$

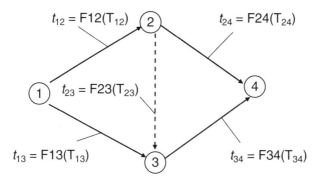

Assume the total route flow T is fixed with T = F124 + F134 + F1234 and name Cmin the minimal cost of the origin-destination (OD) pair. The first Wardrop principle (UE) says that the equilibrium values, noted by *, are such that, for any F verifying the relations between route and link flows:

$$(F^*124 – F124)\,(C^*124 – C124) \leq 0$$
$$(F^*134 – F134)(C^*134 – C134) \leq 0$$
$$(F^*1234 – F1234)(C^*1234 – C1234) \leq 0$$

These relations are the variational inequalities; they are equivalent to:

$$Min_{Tij}\left[\sum_{ij} \int_0^{Tij} Fij(uij)\,duij \right] \qquad (1)$$

subject to the constraints between links and routes flows.

This principle has known a lot of extensions. A first one is to allow for the cost of a link to depend not only on the number of users of the link, but also on characteristics of the other links (this extension allows, for instance, for the values of time to depend on the time and not to be constant). Another extension is to consider the possibility of several types of user. A third is to replace the deterministic cost by stochastic costs, and leads to the now widely quoted stochastic user equilibrium (SUE); this extension covers several situations, among which are the diversity of users, the uncertainty of links capacity and uncertainty of demand level. A more recent extension is to use the Wardrop principle for the choice of departure time – the dynamic user equilibrium.

Strangely, there are very few comparisons of the first Wardrop principle to reality. The scarce evidences on this subject come either from surveys of users or from simulation experiments. Simulations reproduce rather well the behaviours of UE such as predicted by the first Wardrop principle. But surveys of users show that in the UE the variability of route choices is not sufficiently explained by capacity restraints; the SUE model does not suffer from such a drawback but does not take into account the time lag of adaptations between, for instance, the initial changes in capacity and the subsequent changes in equilibrium. These reasons explain why recent research bears on adaptive behaviours and learning processes.

The second Wardrop principle states that the SO is reached when the total cost of transport is minimized. The important point is that the result of SO and of UE are generally different, so the natural equilibrium is not an optimum. This point is made clear through the expression of the SO programme, not similar to the UE programme (Equation 1):

$$Min_{Tij} \left[\sum_{ij} (Tij)\,(Fij) \right] \qquad (2)$$

with the same constraints as for Equation 1.

The difference between the two principles is exemplified in the Braess paradox related to the network already shown. If the cost functions of links take the specific expressions indicated in the second figure, it is easy to see that the UE is the equal split of the total traffic between the three routes 1-2-4, 1-3-4 and 1-2-3-4, while the optimum is the equal split between the two routes 1-2-4 and 1-3-4.

The paradoxical consequence is that cancelling the link 2-3 would make

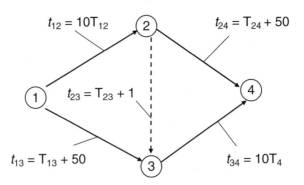

the UE identical to the SO and would then improve the situation. The way to induce to the SO is through charging each link at a level equal to the marginal cost (here $dFij/dTij$).

Further reading

Altman, E. and L. Wynter (2004). Equilibrium, games and pricing in transportation and telecommunication networks. *Networks and Spatial Economics*, **4**, 7–21.

Beckmann, M., C.B. McGuire and C.B. Winsten (1956). *Studies in the Economics of Transportation*. New Haven, CT: Yale University Press.

Braess, D. (1968). Über ein Paradoxon der Verkehrsplanung. *Unternehmensforschung* **12**, 258–68.

Wardrop, J.G. (1952). Some theoretical aspects of road traffic research. *Proceedings of the Institute of Civil Engineers, Part II*, **1**, 325–78.

Emile Quinet

warehousing

Warehouses are facilities that act as nodes in **supply-chains** for purposes such as storage, deconsolidation, accumulation and sortation. They may be required at various points in a supply-chain and therefore one may find, for example, raw materials and component warehouses, work-in-process warehouses, finished goods warehouses, distribution warehouses and centres, and local depots.

The precise roles of individual warehouses vary widely. Traditionally, warehouses have been associated with storage and this may be for 25 years or so for the storage of barrels of malt whisky as part of the maturation process, to a few days, or hours, for the buffering of components ready to be fed onto a production line. This storage role is now often associated with the concept of decoupling points, whereby inventory is held to separate efficient lean operations from the agile fulfilment of demand in volatile marketplaces. This is necessary in situations where supply lead times (for example in terms of weeks from Asia to the United States) are longer than customer lead times (for example where next-day delivery is offered), and where products need to be continually available to customers (for example as in the case of many non-fashion goods).

Other warehousing roles include deconsolidation and consolidation (for example from one manufacturer to many customers, and/or from many manufacturers to one customer); as transhipment points (for example to gain economies in the size of vehicle used for primary and secondary transport); as cross-dock centres (for example to sort goods for final customer destination); as assembly points (for example to provide final customization to individual consumer requirements); and as return centres (for example for the return of **packaging**, faulty or unwanted goods or the recovery of materials from end-of-life goods). Owing to this wide range of roles that warehouses may perform, they may be described under various names, such as **just-in-time** sequencing centres, global distribution centres, customer service centres, fulfilment centres, value-added service centres and return centres.

The internal operations of a warehouse can normally be categorized as receiving, storage, picking and dispatch. The receiving operation normally involves unloading, checking and putting away into storage. It may also include functions such as labelling and putting into appropriate unit loads (for example **containerized** goods are often received as loose cartons and then placed onto pallets for storage). The types of equipment used include counterbalance lift trucks, pallet jacks and boom conveyors, which extend into a truck or container for carton unloading.

There are many equipment types available for pallet storage, ranging from conventional racking to automated storage and retrieval systems (AS/RS) with computer-controlled cranes. Similarly for case and item storage, there is a wide range of options, including conventional shelving, flow racks, carousels and 'miniload' automated storage and retrieval systems.

The picking operation involves selecting individual pallets, cases or items to satisfy an individual customer's order. Typically, this is the most labour-intensive part of a warehouse operation. This operation may be classified as picker-to-goods (for example using man-aboard **trucks**), goods-to-picker (for example carousels and 'miniload') or automated (for example 'A-frame' dispensers). Goods are often conveyed, sometimes via an automated sorter, from picking to an order packing area, and then onto marshalling (of vehicle loads) and dispatch. The latter function typically uses similar equipment to the receiving function.

Technology plays a key part in the operation of modern warehouses. Typically, all the functions described above are directed by a warehouse management system (WMS). This receives information either directly from the main transaction systems (for example purchase order information) or from data input within the warehouse (for example from bar code scanning of goods received). The WMS may transmit data to warehouse operators by means of radio data terminals so that operations can be controlled in real time. It may also send instructions to fully automated systems (for example AS/RS). Other technology aids include pick-to-light systems, voice systems (that is, where order pickers are directed over headphones and can advise the computer via a microphone) and radio frequency identification (RFID) systems (for example where the movement of unit loads or items can be recorded automatically by means of portable or static RFID receivers).

Warehouses are vital components of many **supply-chains**, representing considerable investment and substantial annual operating costs. They also have a major impact on customer service levels, as they are often the last point in the chain before dispatch to the final customer. Modern warehouses may range from being small industrial units to facilities of over 1 million square feet, with heights extending to over 100 feet for AS/RS. Their design, implementation and operation thus require high levels of management skill. Many commentators have predicted that warehouses will decline in importance as modern **supply-chain** concepts are implemented. However, the wide range of roles that they perform and the need for decoupling points in long supply, short demand lead-time environments mean that they are vital components of many modern supply-chains.

Further reading
Baker, P. (2007). An exploratory framework of the role of inventory and warehousing in international supply-chains. *International Journal of Logistics Management* **18**, 64–80.
Christopher, M. and D. Towill (2001). An integrated model for the design of agile supply-chains. *International Journal of Physical Distribution and Logistics Management* **31**, 235–46.

Peter Baker

World Bank and transport

The World Bank is an international financial institution that provides leveraged loans to developing countries for capital programmes. The World Bank has a stated goal of reducing poverty. The World Bank differs from the World Bank Group in that the World Bank comprises only two institutions: the International Bank for Reconstruction and Development (186 member countries) and the International Development Association (168 members). It was one of two institutions created at the Bretton Woods Conference in 1944.

It sees the five key factors necessary for economic growth and the creation of an enabling business environment as:

• Build capacity: strengthening governments and educating government officials.

- Infrastructure creation: implementation of legal and judicial systems for the encouragement of business, the protection of individual and property rights and the honouring of contracts.
- Development of financial systems: the establishment of strong systems capable of supporting endeavours from microcredit to the financing of larger corporate ventures.
- Combating corruption: support for countries' efforts at eradicating corruption.
- Research, consultancy and training: the World Bank provides a platform for research on development issues, consultancy and conduct training programmes open to those who are interested from academia, students, government and non-governmental organization (NGO) officers, and so on.

Adequate transportation has been considered as a major input into the **economic development process** and the Bank has put considerable resources into the sector over the years under the five criteria. It has funded infrastructure projects and education in transportation and from the mid-1990s has fostered the **deregulation** of many transportation markets in developing countries. While the World Bank accepts that transportation can have many purposes, its focus must be on its contribution to economic development.

At the country level, effective delivery mechanisms, for both transportation infrastructure and services, are seen as facing severe constraints that the Bank seeks to tackle:

- Budget constraints limit investments, and lead to undermaintenance, hurting growth. There is a general concurrence that, for developing countries, infrastructure investments globally should be around 7–9 per cent of gross domestic product (GDP), but it is reported that only 3.5 per cent is being realized – roughly what would be needed for the transportation sector alone.
- Limited institutional capacity constrains the implementation of effective governance arrangements for private sector investments, in particular within the framework of **public–private partnerships**. Still, a combination of public and private financing will, in most cases, be required to meet expanding demand for transportation infrastructure and services.
- Weak regulatory systems often impede the implementation of adequate performance incentives in cases of limited competition or local monopolies, or they deter private sector investment when they are unable to establish a reasonably level playing field to foster

balanced competition and provide for sufficient legal comfort and contractual integrity.

In 2008 the Bank outlined its future strategy in *Safe, Clean and Affordable. . . Transport for Development*, which proposes a consolidated approach to policy aimed at:

- Safe transport. Acknowledging the importance of transport for achieving public health outcomes within its Millennium Development Goals (MDGs), the strategy stresses the need to mitigate the spread of HIV/AIDS, and to address **safety** in all transportation modes, especially road transport. Air transport, which is globally much safer, still shows a safety record significantly affecting growth and investment prospects in some regions, in particular sub-Saharan Africa. Transport and **supply-chain** security has also become a major issue in ensuring fair access of developing-country exports to developed markets, and needs to be addressed as a new global public good.
- Clean transport. Reflecting the contribution of transport to the wider environmental aims of the MDGs, the strategy encompasses the transport–**energy**–environment nexus, from energy consumption to the emissions and **climate change** impact perspectives.
- Affordable transport. Affordability concerns not only the **rural** and urban poor but also the whole freight economy, aiming at improving competitiveness to foster stronger economic growth. The Bank strategy stresses the need for better knowledge and control of transport costs, for both passengers and freight, in domestic and regional, urban and rural settings. The implementation of an effective urban transport strategy, reaching out to the growing urban poor population, is a key element of this approach. On the freight side, the cooperative work on trade and transport facilitation within its poverty reduction and economic management agenda – in particular on customs and transit issues – is to be strengthened.

The transportation sector constitutes a significant part of the World Bank's portfolio, with lending of $36.7 billion (more than 15 per cent of the International Bank for Reconstruction and Development and International Development Association commitments) since 2000. In the financial year 2009, transportation-linked lending reached $6.3 billion, more than 13 per cent of the Bank's commitments for the year, a 30 per cent increase over the previous year. While the roads and highways sector accounted for 83 per cent of transportation lending between 1997 and

2007, lending in 2008 for this sector fell by 38 per cent, accounting for 57 per cent of new commitments. At the same time, lending for railways and air transport increased to 14 per cent and 2 per cent of new commitments. Again, 2009 saw strong growth in road and highway projects, partly due to the prominence of road investments in many national economic stimulus plans. In this context, the transportation sector has been an important component of the infrastructure recovery and assets platform launched by the World Bank Group to help support infrastructure programmes in developing countries. In 2008, the Transport Sector supervised 172 projects with net commitments of $26 billion, representing 21 per cent of the Bank's portfolio. Two regions, East Asia and Pacific, and Europe and Central Asia, accounted for the largest shares of net commitments (23 and 21 per cent, respectively).

Further reading
World Bank (2007). *A Decade of Action in Transport: An Evaluation of World Bank Assistance to the Transport Sector, 1995–2005*. Washington, DC: World Bank.
World Bank (2008). Safe, Clean, and Affordable. . . Transport for Development. Washington, DC: World Bank.

Kenneth Button

World Conference on Transport Research

The World Conference on Transport Research (WCTR) is an international conference, organized jointly by the World Conference on Transport Research Society (WCTRS) and the host institution every three years. The conference is held at a different venue, with the scope to provide a forum for the interchange of ideas among transportation researchers, academics, managers, policy-makers, advisers and operators from all over the world, from a multimodal, multidisciplinary and multisector perspective. The World Conferences constitute the place where leading transportation professionals with a common interest in promoting the state of the art and state of the practice in all areas of transport research convene to learn from one another.

The primary objective of the WCTR is to identify emerging issues and opportunities of a policy-related, managerial or technical nature, which will influence transportation research, policy, management and education in the years to come. The formal actors for running a WCTR are:

- From the WCTRS: the President, the Steering Committee, the Scientific Committee of the current WCTRS and the WCTRS Secretariat.

● From the host side: the chairperson of the CDT (Conference Directorate) of the WCTR and the CDT.

The CDT deals with organizational and all non-scientific matters of the conference and assigns the handling of all scientific matters to a local programme committee. The CDT has the option, if needed, to form one or more subcommittees to provide assistance in the organizational and non-scientific matters of the conference.

The World Conference on Transportation Research has a relatively long history: Rotterdam (1978), London (1980), Hamburg (1983), Vancouver (1986), Yokohama (1989), Lyon (1992), Sydney (1995), Antwerp (1998), Seoul (2001), Istanbul (2004), Berkeley (2007) and Lisbon (2010). The series began with predecessor conferences, the International Conference on Transportation Research at Bruges (1973), and an important research conference in Paris (1975). In 1986, to provide a more stable structure, the WCTRS was established at Vancouver. The Society is now a permanent body, under Swiss law. The Secretariat is based at the Laboratoire d'Economie des Transportes, Lyon.

Special Interest Groups have been created to facilitate the exchange of ideas between researchers interested in the same topic area, approved by the WCTRS Steering Committee. The groups are divided by topics: transport and spatial development; maritime transport and ports; **safety** analysis and policy; transportation infrastructure systems; urban transport in developing countries; air transport research; **urban goods movement**; urban transport policy instruments; transport and the environment.

Further reading
http://wctrs.ish-lyon.cnrs.fr.

Dimitrios A. Tsamboulas

Y

yield management

Yield management is a form of dynamic price discrimination practised by several modes of public transport suppliers (both passenger and freight). Price discrimination involves setting prices at the levels individual consumers are willing to pay, rather than according to cost. Essentially each customer pays a different price according to their demand for the transport service. This provides the transportation undertaking with higher revenues than simply charging each user a common price. Technically, it transfers consumer surplus from user to supplier; it essentially involves 'pricing down the demand curve'.

Perfect discrimination is economically Pareto-efficient although it often meets distributional objections that the supplier of transport services is the beneficiary while the user, although not penalized, enjoys no surplus value. However, in cases where there are competitive markets and the transport supplier has fixed costs to recover, it provides a mechanism for achieving this without the need for **subsidies**. In the case of many publicly owned or regulated transport systems, price discrimination in the form of 'Ramsey Pricing' has been advocated to allow costs to be recovered. This entails varying fares or rates inversely with the elasticity of demand for the service, so as to recover costs. Unlike a private monopolist that may price-discriminate, Ramsey Pricing only extracts sufficient consumer surplus for cost recovery and does not leave the transport supplier with any economic rent.

Dynamic price discrimination (yield management) is a form of price discrimination that involves continually varying fares or rates as capacity is filled. To do this the supplier must have some degree of monopoly power to prevent potential customers simply seeking the lowest fare or rate, and having their revenues diluted. Ideally, there should also be technology that allows the supplier to know what capacity has been sold and to adjust prices fairly quickly. There are several ways in which such power can manifest itself (for example the transport supplier may be a natural or institutional monopoly), but control over information flows can be important in otherwise seemingly competitive markets.

The advent of computerized information systems has helped facilitate yield management when the transport supplier has more information than potential users. The way that prices are adjusted to extract the highest revenues from potential customers can differ; for example it may involve fares or rates rising as the time of the scheduled time of departure approaches, but rates and fares may also fluctuate up and down during this period if the capacity is filled at an uneven rate (a sudden burst of sales may lead to higher rates that may then drop if there are no sales for a period immediately following this rise).

The airline sector in particular has used this advantage in the past, initially through travel agents; and more recently, through direct online electronic booking systems, it has sought to differentiate the fares that customers pay. In maritime transport, differentiation of rates for **containers** has been observed and this again reflects the asymmetric information situation, with shipping lines having better information than shippers or forwarders. As computer information systems are becoming more sophisticated, however, the informational edge the airlines or shipping lines have enjoyed has begun to erode and the spread of fares and rates has narrowed.

Further reading

Belobaba, P.P. (2002). Airline network revenue management: recent developments and state of the practice. In D. Jenkins (ed.), *Handbook of Airline Economics*. New York: McGraw-Hill.

Brooks, M. and K.J. Button (1994). Yield management: a phenomenon of the 1980s and 1990s? *International Journal of Transport Economics* **21**, 177–96.

Kenneth Button